SUPPLEMENT II, Part 2
Robinson Jeffers to Yvor Winters

AMERICAN WRITERS
A Collection of Literary Biographies

A. WALTON LITZ
Editor in Chief

SUPPLEMENT II, Part 2
Robinson Jeffers to Yvor Winters

Charles Scribner's Sons, New York

Copyright © 1981 Charles Scribner's Sons

Library of Congress Cataloging in Publication Data   (Revised)
Main entry under title:

American writers.

The 4-vol. main set consists of 97 of the pamphlets originally published
as the University of Minnesota pamphlets on American writers;
some have been rev. and updated. The supplements cover writers
not included in the original series.
Includes bibliographies.
CONTENTS: v.1. Henry Adams to T. S. Eliot.—v.2. Ralph Waldo Emerson
to Carson McCullers.—v.3. Archibald MacLeish to George Santayana.—[etc.]
1. American literature—History and criticism.
2. American literature—Bio-bibliography. 3. Authors, American—Biography.
I. Unger, Leonard, ed.   II. Minnesota. University. Pamphlets on American writers.
PS129.A55   810′.9 [B]   73-1759
ISBN 0-684-16104-4   (Set)
ISBN 0-684-13673-2   (Vol. I)
ISBN 0-684-13674-0   (Vol. II)
ISBN 0-684-13675-9   (Vol. III)
ISBN 0-684-13676-7   (Vol. IV)
ISBN 0-684-15797-7   (Supp. I)
ISBN 0-684-16482-5   (Supp. II)

Published simultaneously in Canada
by Collier Macmillan Canada, Inc.
Copyright under the Berne Convention.

13 15 17 19   V/C   20 18 16 14 12

Printed in the United States of America

Acknowledgment is gratefully made to those publishers
and individuals who have permitted the use of the following materials in copyright.

"Robinson Jeffers"
Acknowledgment is made to Random House, Inc. for
permission to quote from the following copyrighted works
of Robinson Jeffers: *Selected Poetry of Robinson Jeffers*
and *The Beginnings and the End*, both by Robinson Jeffers. From "Hungerfield," "The Inhumanist," "Credo,"
"Mal Paso Bridge," "Dear Judas," "Tower Beyond
Tragedy." Copyright by Robinson Jeffers. Reprinted by
permission of Jeffers Literary Properties.

"Lewis Mumford"
from "To Sophy, Expectant," in *My Works and Days: A
Personal Chronicle*, by Lewis Mumford. Reprinted by
permission of Harcourt Brace Jovanovich, Inc.

"Clifford Odets"
from "Waiting for Lefty," "Till the Day I Die," "Awake
and Sing," "Paradise Lost," "Golden Boy," "Rocket to
the Moon," "Night Music," "Clash by Night." Reprinted by permission of Grove Press.

"Charles Olson"
Selection reprinted by permission of MIT Press from
Benjamin Lee Whorf, *Language, Thought and Reality*,
copyright © 1956 by The Massachusetts Institute of
Technology. From *Letters for Origin 1950–1956*, edited
by Albert Glover, by permission of the Estate of Charles
Olson and Cape Goliard Press. From *The Maximus
Poems*, copyright © 1960 by Charles Olson, published by
Corinth Books in association with Jargon Books. From
Selected Writings of Charles Olson. Copyright © 1959
by Charles Olson. Reprinted by permission of New Di-
rections. From *The Maximus Poems Volume Three*.
Copyright © 1975 by the Estate of Charles Olson and
the University of Connecticut, by permission of George
F. Butterick, Literary Executor. From Charles Olson,
The Special View of History, edited by Ann Charters.
Copyright © 1970 by the Estate of Charles Olson, by
permission of George F. Butterick, Literary Executor of
the Estate of Charles Olson. From *Maximus Poems IV,
V, VI*. Copyright © 1968 by Charles Olson; reprinted by
permission of the Estate of Charles Olson. From Charles
Olson, *Mayan letters*, edited by Robert Creeley. Copyright © 1966 by Charles Olson; reprinted by permission
of the Estate of Charles Olson. From William Carlos
Williams, *In the American Grain*. Copyright 1925 by

iv

v

SUPPLEMENT II, Part 2
Robinson Jeffers to Yvor Winters

Robinson Jeffers

1887–1962

"And west of the west / I have lived," wrote Robinson Jeffers in the epilogue to his first volume of poems. In an otherwise unremarkable book they are the most significant words, simply because at an early age and at the beginning of his literary career they point directly to where he was to make his lifelong home, body and soul. For "west of the west" was where a few years later, stone by laborious stone, he would start to build his Tor House, with its Hawk's Tower, at Carmel in California on the continent's western coast. And "west of the west" was his spirit's familiar country, as though in the wake of an immense procession winding over several thousand years he was the last frontiersman, the ultimate westerner.

> I am building a thick stone pillar upon this
>   shore, the very turn of the world, the long
>   migration's
> End; the sun goes on but we have come up to
>   an end,
> We have climbed at length to a height, to an
>   end, this end: shall we go down again to
>   Mother Asia?
> Some of us will go down, some will abide, but
>   we sought
> More than to return to a mother.

At the end of that long migration across space and through time, he seemed to stand at a precise spot, balked by the ocean, on the edge of a concluded plane, at "the very turn of the world," just before the plane reveals itself to be a revolving globe that goes down again to Asia. "Bred west of Caucasus," he seemed to stand west of a west that never quite touched east, as the Western world's final man.

Perhaps appropriately, since going west is part of the classical western experience, his childhood was spent not in California but in and around Pittsburgh, where his father, a minister, was professor of Old Testament literature at the Western Theological Seminary, and where he was born on January 10, 1887. His paternal grandfather had emigrated in 1810 from County Monaghan in Ireland, but on his mother's side he was descended from much earlier American settlers, including the McCords from Scotland; the Robinsons, who had arrived in 1730 from Ulster; and the Tuttles, who had come over as long ago as 1635 and in New Haven acquired land on which Yale University was eventually built. Seventeenth-century New England, Scottish, Northern Irish, his ancestry was deeply, vigorously Protestant; and though Jeffers was to discard Christianity and to find in its elevation of man above the rest of creation a root cause of latter-day disjunction, his mind and sensibility remained in important respects irrevocably Protestant. These ancestors were

413

outwardly of little interest to him, but some sort of affinity for them he clearly did feel, because on his rare journeys to the British Isles, it was to Scotland and especially to Ulster, lands of his forefathers, that he was drawn, rather than to England's "soft alien twilight / Worn and weak with too much humanity."

There was considerable disparity between the ages of Jeffers' parents. His father was nearly fifty at the time of his son's birth, and his mother only twenty-seven. The couple were evidently dissimilar in temperament also, for he was something of a recluse, whereas she was remembered by her daughter-in-law as being "fond of society and very gay." However, the marriage seems to have been by and large a happy one, although clearly the difference in age and personality provided models for those several occasions in Jeffers' narrative poems when lively young women are wedded, shackled, to men either much older than themselves or much more dour. "What right has a wild old man in the useless beauty of a young wife?" asks the poet on behalf of a character in "The Coast-Range Christ," able to recall from his own childhood a woman still in her thirties married to a man past sixty.

Nevertheless, of the two it was the impress of the father that was, if not the more profound, at any rate the more visible, upon the mature Jeffers. It was his father's memory that was cherished in poems, his death that was mourned, his ghost that returned in them, and his presence that Jeffers so often silently or audibly invoked. "Father, / Forgive me. I dishonored and wasted all your hopes of me, one by one; yet I loved you well." His father's most enduring gift was the laying of the foundations of a wide, traditional learning, based on an intimate knowledge of the Bible and of literature in Greek, which he began to learn at the age of five. In this cultivated and comfortable, if rather austere, home Jeffers was an only child until the age of seven, when a brother was born.

Having few companions, he passed his time in books, in daydreams, and in watchful observation of the natural world. The habit of solitariness was implanted in him early.

Between 1899 and 1902 Jeffers traveled extensively with his family in Europe, attending schools in Leipzig, Lausanne, and Geneva, and adding to his biblical and classical grounding a proficiency in French and German. In 1903 the family made their western exodus to Pasadena, and Jeffers, now sixteen, entered nearby Occidental College. He studied literature, graduated with the B.A. in 1905, and took up further study at the University of Southern California, switching to medicine in 1907, and to forestry at the University of Washington in 1910. The influence of his medical training persists in the physiological imagery and descriptions that permeate his poetry; while his studies of forestry served him daily throughout his life, as he tended the hundreds of trees that he planted around his house.

If Jeffers as a student was changeable, there was at least one constant in his life. This was his love for Una Call Kuster, two years his senior and the wife of a Los Angeles lawyer, whom he first met in 1905. Eight years of confusion, emotional storm and struggle, and parental disapproval followed for them until 1913, when Una was divorced, quite unacrimoniously. The couple were married on August 2 of that year. What had been of paramount importance to Jeffers was that their union should receive the blessing of both his parents, which it finally did a few months before their wedding.

Jeffers had been publishing poems in magazines since 1903, and in 1912 his first volume, *Flagons and Apples*, appeared, financed by himself. Writing poetry was evidently his vocation, and literature was Una's passion, so the couple's first intention, like that of such contemporaries as Robert Frost, Ezra Pound, Hilda Doolittle, and T. S. Eliot, was to go and live in England. Jeffers even confided to a friend that "probably a good deal of our future life will be spent in England or on the continent." But it was not to be. Una became pregnant; they remained in America; she gave birth in May 1914 to a daughter, who lived only one day. As Europe tumbled toward war, the Jefferses made their way up the coast to Carmel, where amid hills and trees and by the ocean they knew that they had come to their "inevitable place" that the poet was to make "Jeffers country." They were to live here for the rest of their lives, with simple tastes and modest expectations, on the basis of a modicum of inherited money, supplemented later by his literary earnings.

In December 1914, Jeffers had to endure the grief of a second death, less poignant, but more deeply disquieting to him, that of his father at the age of seventy-six. Over the next year or so his life was commemorated and his death mourned in a sonnet, "To His Father," in a lengthy elegy, "The Year of Mourning," and by an autobiographical persona in the large dramatic poem, "The Alpine Christ." Jeffers was writing poetry regularly now, descriptive and occasional pieces, odes, and especially narrative poems, which were still conventional in form and meter but which in their often startling content increasingly foreshadowed his later work. His second volume, *Californians*, was published in 1916, and in November of that year twin sons were born.

The next few months were the most critical and emotionally tumultuous of Jeffers' life. In his father, however much he had disagreed with him over mores and metaphysics, he had lost an anchor; and his consequent mental waywardness became the more pronounced as the civilization, in the name of whose highest established values, originally classical and Christian, his father had spoken, barbarized and destroyed itself on the battlefields of Europe. Now in April 1917 the United States entered the war, and Jeffers underwent an intense period of anguish over whether, when, and in what capac-

ity he should commit himself to this Armageddon. The marriage was severely strained, doubtless also by whatever circumstances inspired such luscious and passionate writing as there is in "Fauna" and "Mal Paso Bridge." But this time of trial passed, the marriage survived, and the war ended; and when in 1919 they bought land on Carmel Point, Jeffers began to heal his spirit and regulate his heart by building a permanent home, on "foundations of sea-worn granite," with "my fingers" that "had the art to make stone love stone," a steady activity that occupied him many years.

During this time of crisis and resolution Jeffers' poetry, especially its diction and measure, changed character beyond recognition. Around 1917 and 1918 this change took shapes that were obviously experimental, under the pressure of heightened emotion and events; later, with a greater sense of assurance and the effect of an achieved form, it was under the calming, stabilizing influence of stonemasonry. By about 1921, the year of his mother's death, Jeffers had finally discovered the mature voice with which he was to speak, sometimes varying the pitch, but scarcely ever the accent or phrasing, for the remainder of his life.

Coincident with this discovery, the Jefferses' lives began to take on an apparently contented, habitual, and virtually unchanging pattern. "I am as attached to this rock," he announced, "as if I were a feudal serf with an iron collar." As the boys grew older, the family did a certain amount of traveling, particularly to Una's beloved Ireland and to New Mexico, home of Mabel Dodge Luhan and Frieda Lawrence. But "to stay at home," Jeffers considered, "is more interesting"; and for the most part he did stay at home. Between 1918 and 1929, for instance, he never once visited San Francisco, little more than a hundred miles away. He spent his days nurturing his plantation; collecting and transporting boulders for the continuous building of his house; walking the hills and shores with Una and watching the birds and animals; broadly educating his sons; entertaining a few, treasured friends; and, of course, writing poetry.

Behind this outwardly tranquil life, the furies were penned in his poetry. "Imagine victims," he wrote, "Lest your own flesh be chosen the agonist ... Burn sacrifices once a year to magic/Horror away from the house." So, about once a year, starting in 1924 with *Tamar and Other Poems*, he "imagined victims," "burned sacrifices," and published a new volume, generally consisting of one or two agonizing, burning, horror-filled narrative or dramatic poems, supplemented by twenty or so shorter meditative, descriptive, or prophetic poems composed during the same period.

These volumes brought Jeffers a wide readership for a poet and a wider reputation, with enthusiasts as ardent as those who celebrated Walt Whitman. The apogee of this fame was probably reached somewhere around the early 1930's. But just as Whitman, though almost sanctified by some, was reviled by others, so also was Jeffers. For traditional moralists and rationalists, eventually for the New Criticism, Yvor Winters led the way most effectively, with a systematic demolition in 1930; while among populists and Marxists, Jeffers gradually damned himself by his historical "defeatism" and lofty impartiality. By the end of the 1930's the careless, utterly inaccurate imputation to him of incipient fascist sympathies was heard more than once. Having been famous, Jeffers became first notorious and then neglected, "a poet without critics."

Jeffers, however, was apparently unaffected either by zealous admirers or by scornful adversaries. What did affect him, though, violently disrupting his detached, even tenor of mind, as it had done over twenty years previously, was the United States' entry into another world war, the coming of which he had long predicted. Intensely isolationist, outragedly pacifist, intimat-

ing in one suppressed poem that he was every bit as capable of patriotically motivated treason as Ezra Pound, he railed against American and Allied leadership in a volume of poems, *The Double Axe*, published after the war, from whose prevailing sentiments his publishers felt bound to dissociate themselves in a prefatory note.

Nevertheless, through waxing and waning renown, the character of the Jefferses' daily life scarcely changed. The sons took careers in forestry and accountancy, and presented their parents with a succession of grandchildren. Jeffers and his wife were usually to be found at Carmel, traveling only to the eastern United States on a reading tour in 1941 and to Ireland again in 1948. Then in January 1949 Una fell ill, to linger, declining, until on September 1, 1950, she died. They had been together in their Carmel quietness for thirty-six years. He had loved her devotedly, more dependently than is disclosed in the poetry. Uneasy in company, he had become habituated to sheltering behind her. A forceful, possessive, protective woman, she had been an immeasurable source of strength to him. He worked deep into his sorrow for her in the narrative poem "Hungerfield":

September again. The gray grass, the gray
  sea,
The ink-black trees with white-bellied night-
  herons in them,
Brawling on the boughs at dusk, barking
  like dogs—
And the awful loss. It is a year. She has
  died: and I
Have lived for a long year on soft rotten
  emotions,
Vain longing and drunken pity, grief and
  gray ashes—...

His epitaph for her concludes the poem, the words of one who, believing in no personal immortality, conjures a pantheistic reunion out of barely tolerable agony.

> Here is the poem, dearest; you will never
> read it nor hear it. You were more
> beautiful
> Than a hawk flying; you were faithful and
> a lion heart like this rough hero
> Hungerfield. But the ashes have fallen
> And the flame has gone up; nothing human
> remains. You are earth and air; you
> are in the beauty of the ocean
> And the great streaming triumphs of
> sundown; you are alive and well in the
> tender young grass rejoicing
> When soft rain falls all night, and little
> rosy-fleeced clouds float on the dawn.
> —I shall be with you presently.

But it was not to be "presently." He outlived her by more than eleven years, lonely but not alone, since one of his sons and his young family had come to live at Tor House. While taking delight in his grandchildren, he returned to those "quiet and solitary ways" that had long been essential to him. In his last few years, as his bodily strength faded slowly, he wrote only short poems, some of his finest, celebrating the universe, the physical and natural worlds, from atom to galaxy; inveighing against the social world; and musing on suicide, but emphatically rejecting it, as he had always done. He died at home on January 20, 1962, ten days past his seventy-fifth birthday.

What a reader must find most noticeable about the young Jeffers is his exceptional precocity at the age of sixteen but his lack of development over the next decade. Like his similarly forward contemporary, Ezra Pound, he began, unsurprisingly, by echoing a variety of late Victorian poets, among them Dante Gabriel Rossetti, who accorded him a "passionate springtime" of appreciative "intoxication"; William Butler Yeats in his Celtic-twilight period; and the hearty Henry John Newbolt. In "Man's Pride" he rings a note of airy didacticism that probably owed something to Percy Bysshe Shelley:

> What is man that he should be proud?
> And what is the race of men
> That they should think high things?
> Behold, the deep cries aloud,
> The high mountains answer again,
> The swift wind stops and sings. . . .

Sounded there already is his conviction of human insignificance alongside natural grandeur; and elsewhere a later characteristic, imaginative vantage point is prefigured in the youthful romantic's preference for a sublime pulpit, "A Hill-Top View," from which to measure man.

In contrast with that of Pound, however, who over the next half dozen years was more than anybody else to alter the shape and scope of poetry in English, Jeffers' writing evolved by scarcely an irregular foot. In 1912, when Pound was articulating the principles of imagism and of modernist poetics in general, Jeffers produced in *Flagons and Apples* a volume, consisting chiefly of love poems, that abounded in conventional fin-de-siècle sentiments and postures, that was dyed in the bittersweet, lacklove world-weariness of a speaker either "mad and drunken" or "blind and deaf and broken," and awash with alliterative liquids and an imagery of old wine and crimson partings, wailing winds and soulless stars.

The poetry is no worse than that in many contemporaneous volumes; it is usually competent, and there are effective moments. But it is wholly, uninterruptedly derivative; and there are no intimations of what is to come. Jeffers' love for Una at this time was substantial enough, but not these literary loves of *Flagons and Apples*, the Helens, Canidia, Nyssa, Aileen-of-the-Woods, and a "pretty waitress."

When his second book appeared four years later, Jeffers had been living for some time in his "inevitable place" at Carmel. As the title, *Californians*, suggests, he at least now knew that he was not a compatriot of Rossetti's: all the eleven story-poems have Californian settings, and the "Invocation" is addressed to the lodestar of the westward historical process. The verse forms are still traditional, in particular blank verse and ottava rima, but the lines, being basically pentameter, are longer and weightier than those in *Flagons and Apples*. He is stretching toward the spaciousness of line and the gravity of pace that are to be the hallmarks of his mature poetry. The influences and affinities are more proper to him, too: chiefly John Milton, William Wordsworth, Shelley, Ralph Waldo Emerson, and Edwin Arlington Robinson, an essentially Protestant (or nonconforming) succession. Wordsworth's importance for the young Jeffers stands out precisely by the intensity with which the poet is castigated for his apostasy in becoming "apologist for kings and priest and lies."

If Jeffers has not yet found his style here, he has found several of his subjects. True to his romantic and transcendentalist heritage, toward which the names of Wordsworth and Emerson must have directed us, all good in *Californians* resides in the natural world or in the simpler forms of rural life, and in the isolated, integrated self rather than in the group or mass. Alone amid nature, a descendant of Wordsworth's leech gatherer, Stephen Brown, in the poem of that name, has become "self-stationed, self-upheld as the all-beholding sky," an exemplary figure. Conversely, the city only withers, crushes, corrupts, "rotting" its prisoners away. Lindsay, alone again "At Lindsay's Cabin," has saved himself from that "life / Alien to men though all composed of men, / Unfriendly, menacing, fearfully alive"; whereas "The Old Farmer," retiring in poor health to live with his

son in the city, breaks his homesick heart there and commits suicide. Peter Graham, narrator of "Maldrove," bewailing a "cankered world" in this "dreadfully degenerate age," and dreaming of "lovely and glorious sons, / Successors of these little and verminous ones," is a more extreme creation, drawn from that late nineteenth-century world in which the language of degeneration and regeneration became current. Graham may not speak for Jeffers, but this is the kind of large distaste that was to point him toward his "Inhumanism," the terms of which are already at hand, in the question asked rhetorically in "A Westward Beach":

> Can man wash off humanity
> And wed the unmarriageable sea?

There are also in these poems specific narrative prefigurations, notably in "The Three Avilas," with its tale of incest and double sibling murder, the tangled stuff of so many stories to come, and in this case also, seemingly, in part a device for exhuming his own earlier guilt about the original character of his relationship with Una.

Jeffers writes in this volume not only as a resident of California, but also as, imaginatively, the latest of history's westward travelers. The final coast may have been reached, but the questions remain and tantalize. "What farther west? What wanderings more sublime?" "When Alaska is peopled, will Venus lack ploughland? / I have dreamed that our children may even ascend to the stars."

Although he wandered and ascended no further himself, Jeffers was deeply imbued with a frontier mentality, and in some respects his lifework may be seen as a continuous attempt to find new ways, now that no more territory lies ahead, of putting the East, population, society, and history, behind him. Such a cast of mind must assume, in simplified outlines, that only man is ugly and that only nature or land sparsely settled is beautiful. Jeffers was always acutely responsive toward the beautiful, and indeed it is expressly the beauty of nature that first enchants him and in which value inheres.

Californians concludes with an "Ode on Human Destinies," which itself concludes as an ode to beauty, although in this instance a beauty less natural than ideal:

> I, driven ahead on undiscovered ways
> Yet predetermined, do not fail to see,
> Over the fog and dust of dream and deed,
> The holy spirit, Beauty, beckoning me.

Jeffers did not publish any more poetry in book form for another eight years, but that long period of silent struggle, painful transformation, and eventual poetic self-revelation has been brilliantly reconstituted by Jeffers' lifelong devotee and self-styled disciple, the poet William Everson (Brother Antoninus). As a consequence of Everson's painstaking literary detective work, two books now exist that represent Jeffers at this interim time of most radical change. *The Alpine Christ and Other Poems* contains poems not collected elsewhere and adjudged by Everson to have been composed mainly in 1916. *Brides of the South Wind: Poems 1917–1922* also consists of uncollected poems and fragments but in addition contains poems that were to appear in the 1924 publication of *Tamar and Other Poems.*

"The Alpine Christ," despite its many missing pages and sections, is an immense dramatic poem, indebted in part to Shelley's *Prometheus Unbound* and in part, Everson is surely right to propose, to Thomas Hardy's *The Dynasts.* It is composed predominantly in blank verse, with passages of prose and colloquial dialogue, and with choruses reminiscent of measures as different as those of Algernon Charles Swinburne's "Hymn to Man" and Emerson's "Merlin." It is the poem of a man grieving the death of a father and, more to the point here, the death of a father's religion and culture; and it is the poem of a man horror-stricken to the marrow after long, solemn, if distant, contemplation of the European war. It is no less than a total statement about the spiritual and psychological condition of the Western world after two years of carnage—a statement anguished, though not despairing, of heroically proportioned fatalism. (In 1916, it might be remembered, Mark Twain's determinist tour de force, *The Mysterious Stranger*, was posthumously published, final word from that post-Christian fatalist literary generation of Ambrose Bierce, Stephen Crane, Frank Norris, and in England of Hardy.)

In the world of "The Alpine Christ," God is dead. Only impersonal Fate rules in Eternity. Power presides, not purpose, least of all justice. The sole value that can be given to life is in terms of human love, preached here by the holy simpleton, Manuel; but this love, in its very conception and being, is inseparable from grief and agony. "The Alpine Christ" is the unachieved work of an unformed poet, whose vision is running far ahead of his poetic and dramatic capabilities. But it is also the work of a man of rare seriousness and largeness of imagination, which for all its incompleteness is a valuable relic of the war years.

The war continues to cast its shadow over many of the poems gathered by Everson for *Brides of the South Wind;* for instance, over "The Coast-Range Christ," which Jeffers liked well enough to retain for publication in *Tamar.* This is a narrative poem in rhyming couplets, whose protagonist, David Carrow, a conscientious objector and visionary Christian idealist, is erotically drawn to a married woman called Peace. He fights down her temptation, but she, scorned, has it rumored about that he has forcibly abused her, so that he is hunted out and killed for a coward and a rapist by his outraged father. Carrow is evidently a mask for Jeffers, likewise tormented at this time by problems of conscience and desire, both challenging his father's ghost and seeking chastisement from it.

The armistice and its immediate aftermath are treated in "God's Peace in November," a sonnet sequence aching with the consciousness of insoluble contradictions, between those celebrating victory and those still suffering, between rich and poor, between God and man, between public and private, and between the terrible knowledge possessed by Europe and the ignorance of California, where "we have not suffered enough / To understand."

Finally, in "The Beginning of Decadence," like Pound in *Hugh Selwyn Mauberley* and *The Cantos* although less vehemently, Jeffers gives vent to his retrospective fury against jingo poets and battle-hungry churchmen, against massacre-minded war leaders, against profiteers and liars and postwar avengers.

But war is not the chief subject of the book. That subject is Jeffers' discovery, simultaneous and intertwined, of psychological integrity and a unique poetic speaking voice. Having experienced at length his own vulnerability, his suffering sensitivity, he was slowly learning, especially while building his house, how to stiffen his backbone and strengthen his breastwork "with ribs of rock round a hot soft heart." And within that lesson he was also learning, belatedly but definitively, how to speak in accents of his own ("To the Stone-Cutters"):

Stone-cutters fighting time with marble, you
    foredefeated
Challengers of oblivion. . . .

and, in "Continent's End":

At the equinox when the earth was veiled in
    a late rain, wreathed with wet poppies,
    waiting spring,
The ocean swelled for a storm and beat its

boundary, the ground-swell shook the
beds of granite.

Here at last are the sounds of authentic Jeffers.

The style, which served him for a lifetime, was forged over a period of about three years. Until the age of thirty, in virtually all the poems of *Californians*, Jeffers had employed regular meter and rhyme. The first release was from rhyme; and it was as a release that Jeffers explicitly felt it. During his turmoil in 1917, when war and sex together shattered his ethical composure, rhyme was one of the shapes of authority that in defiant, exhilarated, nihilistic abandon he pledged himself to cast off ("Mal Paso Bridge"):

Therefore I swore to drink wine while I could,
Love where I pleased, and feed my eyes
With Santa Lucien sea-beauty, and moreover
To shear the rhyme-tassels from verse.

He went back to being a constant husband and to drinking wine in moderation; but apart from its intermittent, reassuring usage over the next year or so and its later appearance in occasional loose-limbed sonnets, rhyme had disappeared for good from his verse.

The device of alliteration, however, was retained permanently, to be employed with decreasing conspicuousness and increasing subtlety. When used to excess or harnessed for a few strides to an anapestic canter, it is obvious that Swinburne has been the tutor; but often it has a regulating function in the manner of Old English poetry, which Jeffers admired. These lines from "The Beginning and the End" will show the persistent role and the various musical parts that alliteration (and indeed assonance) play in his verse:

Meanwhile they had invented

Chlorophyll and ate sunlight, cradled in peace

On the warm waves, but certain assassins
    among them
Discovered that it was easier to eat flesh

Than feed on lean air and sunlight: thence the
    animals,

Greedy mouths and guts, life robbing life,

Grew from the plants. . . .

Shearing the rhyme from his poetry, and also the unrhymed pentameter on the grounds that blank verse had been exhausted by earlier masters, Jeffers arrived by another route at the open ground that Pound and William Carlos Williams had cleared for themselves a few years earlier. As his characteristic poetry emerged, it was often taken to be either a free verse broadly in the tradition of Whitman's *Leaves of Grass* or a prose-poetry deriving from the Authorized Version of the Bible.

Certainly, Jeffers owed much to both books. With Whitman he felt what has been called "a profound fellowship," despite their obvious great differences, some of which at least can be explained in terms of the two generations of fearful history that separated them. However, as far as form is concerned, what the poets share does not go much beyond the sheer, capacious length and adaptability of line; although this is enough to align Jeffers more closely with Whitman than with any other American antecedent.

In the case of the Bible, as the son of his father, Jeffers could not help but be saturated in the Holy Book, so that every so often one may hear an echo of the verbal texture of the Song of Solomon or a rhetorical reminiscence of Ecclesiastes or the Book of Job. But as with *Leaves of Grass*, one staple element of Jeffers' verse is missing from the poetry of the translated Bible. And that is, for all Jeffers' absolute break with the world of rhyme and traditional

meter, a notion of rhythmic regularity, of predictability, of prior aural design.

As Jeffers confessed in 1930 to Arthur Klein, a student of his work: "People talked about my 'free verse' and I never protested, but now I am quite touched to hear that someone has at last discovered the metrical intention in it." He goes on in the same letter to mention Coleridge's regularity of accent rather than syllable in "Christabel," Old English accentual verse, and, briefly, quantity.

In principle therefore (if only in principle), or in gesture or intention, Jeffers' verse is governed by a rhythmic norm, which consists of a regular number of accents to the line or pair of lines, a stress prosody that is derived from such examples as those just cited. Within the lines the weight is also distributed according to quantity, as in the classical poetry familiar to Jeffers from childhood and, in the case of Greek, translated by him throughout his life, and as in some of the experiments of Swinburne, a more celebrated and flamboyant classical scholar, so many aspects of whose poetry (alliteration, phrasing, prosody) were incorporated more or less audibly into Jeffers' mature style.

However, the primary influences on Jeffers' poetry are not literary but natural. Living within the sound of the ocean and within sight of the mountains, planting his long-lived trees, handling, transporting, and positioning his granite boulders, Jeffers in his few remarks about poetry and poetics always refers to the qualities of the natural world—to "tidal regularity" or "tidal recurrence," to "perpetual renewal"—and, for the subject matter, to the "essential element" of "permanence."

What he was after was a natural condition, neither freedom nor strict rule, but the broadly timed recurrences and variable regularity of nature. If William Carlos Williams, seeking a freedom from the old that would nevertheless be a "new order" to satisfy an inner need, discovered for himself the regularity of the variable foot, perhaps one may say that Jeffers for similar reasons discovered for himself the regularity of the variable line. His fullest statement is this:

I want it rhythmic and not rhymed, moulded more closely to the subject than older English poetry is, but as formed as alcaics if that were possible too. The event is of course a compromise but I like to avoid arbitrary form and capricious lack or disruption of form. My feeling is for the number of beats to the line. There is a quantitative element too in which the unstressed syllables have part. The rhythm comes from many sources—physics, biology, beat of blood, the tidal environments of life, desire for singing emphasis that prose does not have.

"Morro Bay," from a late volume, *Hungerfield and Other Poems*, is chosen almost at random for its shortness, so that it may be printed in full to demonstrate in its typicality the simple aural constituents of Jeffers' poetry. These are alliteration, constant but irregular; and a stress pattern, regular but not fixed, here over five pairs of lines, the first line of the pair (of five or six stresses) being visually longer than the second (of basically four stresses), but since it contains many syllables of short quantity, lighter and swifter.

Beautiful years when she was by me and we
    visited
Every rock and creek of the coast—
She gave life from her eyes. Now the bay is
    brown-stagnant
With rotting weed, and the stranded fish-
    boats
Reek in the sun; but still the great rock hangs
    like a thundercloud
Over the stale mist and still sea.

They say that it swarms with rattlesnakes—
    right—the stored lightnings
In the stone cloud. Guard it well, vipers.
That Norman rockhead Mont St. Michel may
    have been as beautiful as this one
Once, long ago, before it was built on.

This natural, elemental rhythm was a fit vessel to carry the burden of his poetry—or its message, let us unabashedly call it—since he indeed was a man with a message, a preacher's lesson, even if he purported not to be much concerned whether anyone listened to it. The main clause of this message was that man had drastically abused, distorted, or wholly emptied out his relationship with nature, that he had lost touch with the primary elements of life, and that he had extravagantly overvalued the importance of his place in the cosmos and the natural order of things, all with catastrophic consequences for himself: that this was a universal human condition but especially was it true of the Western world, that is to say, the entire Judeo-Christian pale, and even more particularly was it true, perhaps with the character of a terminal disease, of modern, industrial, secular, or materialistic society. In some shape or other this was either the meditative focus or narrative spring of nearly all that he wrote over his forty years of mature life as a poet, in some fifteen narrative poems set around Carmel, in a half dozen dramatic poems based upon Greek, biblical, or Germanic legend, and in about two hundred and fifty shorter poems.

Jeffers' first premise is not an intellectual proposition but a sensory commonplace: that the universe is beautiful, beautiful because it is beautiful, beautiful to behold as a spectacle, the eyes raised to the stars, beautiful to contemplate in its composition, the mind dwelling upon the cell and the atom. There can be few poets, and certainly there are no other modern poets, who employ the words "beauty" and "beautiful" as often as Jeffers does; and he does so without embarrassment, apology, or fanciful elaboration. He does not ask us to ponder the nature of the beautiful but merely seeks to remind us, since we are continuously forgetful, that it is always there, beside, before, and around us.

Beauty may appear in many forms; in earlier years, during aviation's romantic youth, to this high priest of antimechanism it could come even in mechanical guise. In poems from his 1925 volume, it is in "the navy's new-bought Zeppelin going by in the twilight, / Far out seaward;" or in the "bitter earnestness" of the deep-sea fishermen returning to harbor, the engines of their boats throbbing through the fog, "following the cliff for guidance" as they go about "their business among the equally / Earnest elements of nature." Beauty may be "intense and terrible" with "great seas jagging the west and on the granite / Blanching" in "Gale in April"; or it may be come upon, not in energetic, elemental drama, but in quiet meditation upon "the beauty of things," the "one beauty," the rhythm of the wheel "of life as of death and of light as of darkness."

Half a lifetime later, having come through the worst of his grief over Una's death, he knows once again that "to feel / Greatly, and understand greatly, and express greatly, the natural / Beauty, is the sole business of poetry," for "it is only a little planet / But how beautiful it is." It is altogether appropriate, therefore, that the last words of his last volume invite us to expect and enjoy, while watching the activities of the natural world, "not mercy, not mind, not goodness, but the beauty of God."

God, the final word in Jeffers' works. For Jeffers, God may be either immanent or transcendent, to be perceived within the world, or to be sought within the self. The immanent predominates: the universe is all-beautiful, a radiant manifestation of God, who is all, the all that is God. The eyes should merely have to see to believe, the lungs should merely have to breathe to inhale God's spirit.

In "The Answer" we are told, simply, that "Integrity is wholeness, the greatest beauty is / Organic wholeness, the wholeness of life and things, the divine beauty of the Universe." In the long poem "The Inhumanist," the old man, who is the figure in Jeffers' poetry most nearly approaching a guru or fount of wisdom, rejoices in "the stars, the winds and the people: one energy, / One existence, one music, one organism, one life, one God."

The American transcendentalist heritage is clearly visible here: the links with Emerson, whom he had read so thoroughly as a young man and who was also introduced to the perfect whole by his sense of beauty; and with Whitman, who heard and beheld God in every object and saw something of him each hour of the twenty-four. It is often a virtual pantheism, with God not only "the whole splendor of things and the sacred stars, but also the cruelty and greed, the treacheries / And vileness, insanities and filth and anguish." Above all, God and his beauty, the beauty that is God, are experienced in natural and elemental power, whether in the stallion, the hawk, and the eagle, or in the vast eons-long beating of the universal heart and in cosmic "faceless violence, the root of all things."

That is Jeffers, the visionary pantheist, looking out on the physical world that had always seemed to him, he told a correspondent, "immeasurably more real" than the soul. But he could own to another, more inward conception of God, one closer to that of his Protestant forebears, a transcendent or at least an exclusive God, to be awaited in the patient, mystic air of the "soul's desert" at those times when, outside, the dust storms of human fury, most likely of war, obscured the "astonishing beauty of things."

But however meditative and mystically inclined, Jeffers did not travel in spirit across the Pacific to the faiths of the Orient, like so many fellow-Californian poets, especially of the succeeding generation. He might express a considerable regard for Buddhism and Oriental religions, for their quietism and cyclical view of existence, and he might scorn the "anthropoid God" of "decaying Christianity." But he was always at the farthest point of the West rather than at the beginnings of the East. Differing from an Asian contemplative in his poem "Credo," he finds "in my blood / Bred west of Caucasus a harder mysticism." The "harder mysticism" is a philosophical materialism that attributes a prior reality to matter before mind, to the world before the soul, to the light in "the beauty of things, not men."

This materialism within an essentially religious temperament is testimony, first, simply to Jeffers' exceptional, respectful sensitivity toward the objective, tactile, physical world, his poetic comprehension of the thingness of things; and second, to the effect upon him at an impressionable age of nineteenth-century positivist modes of thought. The American literary generation immediately senior to him, whether influenced directly by science (for instance by Charles Darwin and his popularizers) or by literary-theoretical mediators like Émile Zola, must have seemed predominantly atheist and materialist, or at least cynically commonsensical: the aging Mark Twain, Stephen Crane (another minister's son), Frank Norris, Ambrose Bierce and Jack London (local lights in California), and Edgar Lee Masters (who became a personal friend).

In such an intellectual atmosphere, as he rebelled against his father's faith and undertook medical studies that required a scientific attitude and curiosity, the foundations of a lifelong materialism were laid, never to be thoroughly broken up and demolished. Thus, although Jeffers may rightly if, loosely, be described as a quietist, and then again as a pantheist, he must also be recognized as a firm materialist, convinced alike of the primacy of matter and of personal mortality—a "hard, mystical" materialist, to use his own terms of self-description.

Jeffers' is a poetic materialism that for closest analogy sends us back as far as two thousand years to one of the few figures he openly acknowledges in his poetry and to whom he pays tribute: the Roman poet Lucretius, author of the great expository poem, the epic of a joyous materialism, *De rerum natura.* Jeffers adapted Lucretius' title for his celebration of the earth and the galaxy, "De Rerum Virtute"; he gave Lucretius and Plato the heroic parts in one of his poems on historical decline, "Prescription of Painful Ends"; he deferred to Lucretius in his own powerful poem on natural origins and destiny, "The Beginning and the End"; and in general he seemed to watch and muse upon the world's aimless frenzy from a similarly cool, elevated position, "the little stone-girdled platform" of his Hawk's Tower, Lucretius' "quiet citadel, stoutly fortified by the teaching of the wise." Apart from the few English and American poets previously mentioned, the only other figure who ever came near to being as influential upon him was Friedrich Nietzsche, whose hostility to Christianity was another spur to his rebellion in those early years and whose dictum, "The poets lie too much," he was fond of repeating.

It was this sense of the marvelous "divinity" of the physical universe that Jeffers felt to be so drastically missing from the mind of modern, Western man. The basis for any sort of sanity, any sort of integrity, must be reverence for the cosmos, in which man is such a tiny item, when viewed from amid the salutary dimensions of

Carmel Point, against the background of ocean and redwood forest, beside the time spans of mountains and planets. (A tiny item, maybe, but part of that divine whole, so that, of course, "even / The poor doll humanity has a place under heaven.") Thus, the best life that can be lived by man is one that leaves as much space as possible for silent wonder at natural processes and their invisibly slow evolution, for quiet amazement at the immense splendor and all the diminutive miracles.

It should be a life lived in a simple relation to nature, such as can be found most readily in the pastoral stage of human development and in the less technologically advanced forms of cultivation. It can perhaps be discerned in an earlier American ideal, in Michel de Crèvecoeur's American farmer, surviving in California in a few inaccessible valleys at the end of unpaved roads. "The Coast-Road" presents a picture of such life and what threatens it in the 1930's:

> I too
> Believe that the life of men who ride horses,
>   herders of cattle on the mountain
>   pasture, plowers of remote
> Rock-narrowed farms in poverty and
>   freedom, is a good life. At the far end
>   of those loops of road
> Is what will come and destroy it, a rich and
>   vulgar and bewildered civilization dying
>   at the core. . . .

And the picture, repainted for his last volume, is virtually unaltered:

> What's the best life for a man? To ride
>   in the wind. To ride horses and herd
>   cattle
> In solitary places above the ocean on the
>   beautiful mountain, and come home
>   hungry in the evening
> And eat and sleep. . . .
> I will have shepherds for my
>   philosophers,

> Tall dreary men lying on the hills all
>   night
> Watching the stars, let their dogs watch
>   the sheep.

But these are disappearing ways of life, or nostalgic myths and timeless idylls, as Jeffers knew only too well. The dominant theme i human history, certainly in Western history, has been quite different. It has been a history not of man's accommodation with nature, but of his separation from it, subjection of the earth, exploitation of its gifts, and self-appointment as lord of creation. In his lifelong treatment of man's relationship with nature, Jeffers writes both within and against the Judeo-Christian heritage. He can be said to be within it insofar as he subscribes to an idiosyncratic, naturalistic version of the doctrine of original sin and of the fall, and insofar as his work continuously illustrates the consequences of that sin and the manifestations of the fall in so many facets of human behavior. He is against it, radically, insofar as he would regard that heritage, and even more so its secular succession of whatever political emphasis, as being from its very beginnings a direct expression of that original sin, in its initial presupposition of man's privileged or central place in the universe.

The sin, to put it in the most broadly traditional terms, is the sin of pride, man's arrogant promotion of himself above the level accorded him by God. And if God is identified with the cosmos, then the original sin occurred at that mythic moment when man first felt himself to be singled out as distinct from the rest of creation and superior to it, with the earth a stage for the drama of his energies and the heavens an auditorium concentrated on a God, formed in man's own image, whose attention is fixed upon the inner and outer life of his own proudest creation.

For Jeffers, then, the loss of paradise coincided with the development of an isolating self-consciousness. (In "Margrave" he even plays with the fancy of the far, speeding stars of an expanding universe "fleeing the contagion / Of consciousness that infects this corner of space.") In terms of biological evolution, this moment, he intimates in "Original Sin," must be as original as the appearance of the species *Homo sapiens*. In consequence, the human race's few heroes include those whose scientific discoveries have had the effect of eroding man's self-importance and returning him toward his rightful place in the scheme of things. Thus, the old man of "The Inhumanist" wonders to whom he should dedicate the cairn of stones he has erected:

"To whom this monument: Jesus or Caesar or
    Mother Eve?
No," he said, "to Copernicus: Nicky
    Kupernick: who first pushed man
Out of his insane self-importance and the
    world's navel, and taught him his place."
"And the next one to Darwin."

Because of this "insane self-importance" and the breaking of the umbilical connection with nature, "life's norm is lost" and "monsters possess the world," toying with atomic power. Twenty years before the invention of nuclear weapons, in a poem entitled simply and comprehensively "Science," Jeffers already envisages the potentiality of total destruction, as nature is reassembled into ever more terrifying new energies:

Man, introverted man, having crossed
In passage and but a little with the
    nature of things this latter century
Has begot giants; but being taken up
Like a maniac with self-love and inward
    conflicts cannot manage his hybrids.
Being used to deal with edgeless dreams,

Now he's bred knives on nature turns them
    also inward: they have thirsty points
    though.
His mind forebodes his own destruction; . . .

And Aphrodite concludes in the dramatic poem "The Cretan Woman," composed in the early 1950's against a background of nuclear bomb testing, the Korean War, and accelerating domestic prosperity:

In future days men will become so powerful
That they seem to control the heavens and
    the earth,
They seem to understand the stars and all
    science—
Let them beware. Something is lurking
    hidden.
There is always a knife in the flowers. There
    is always a lion just beyond the
    firelight.

But of course the threat of doom appears in the shape not only of physical destruction but also of the spiritual reduction that follows upon the heedless abuse of nature by a too clever, too prolific race. So, decades before the word "ecology" ventured far from the textbooks and before lip service to conservationist sentiments became conventional piety, Jeffers in "The Broken Balance" was

Mourning the broken balance, the hopeless
    prostration of the earth
Under men's hands and their minds,
The beautiful places killed like rabbits to
    make a city,
The spreading fungus, the slime-threads
And spores; my own coast's obscene
    future. . . .

Jeffers saw megalomania and introversion as the major, pervasive psychological expressions of this "broken balance," the species dangerously self-aggrandized and hopelessly self-centered. As he explained to James Rorty in connection with one of his narrative poems:

There is no health for the individual whose attention is taken up with his own mind and processes; equally there is no health for the society that is always introverted on its own members, as ours becomes more and more. . . . All past cultures have died of introversion at last, and so will this one, but the individual can be free of the net, in his mind. . . .

So the narratives and dramas, with their sexual heat, scorching jealousies, incestuous couplings, family murders and massacres, homestead holocausts, and crazed, towering ambitions, enact for us time and again individual catastrophes that are microcosms of the conclusive disaster overhanging our whole megalomaniac, introverted civilization.

Nearly all these poems are flawed in some quite conspicuous respect; frequently they spill into melodrama, macabre or ludicrous, and into monstrous horror shows; and one or two are undoubtedly failures as vital poetry, coherent psychology, or credible stories. It is certain that Jeffers' finest art is to be found either in his short poems or in sections of these longer poems that are in effect detachable, self-contained lyrics. Nevertheless, like few other modern writings, for powerful, extended stretches the best of these poems have something of the gravity, the awesomeness, and the grandeur of ancient tragedy. They are charged with Jeffers' dread-filled, brooding knowledge of the seriousness of his imagination's task ("Imagination, the traitor of the mind, has taken my solitude and slain it."); and they are freighted with his sense of enormity in the breaking of taboo, in the bursting of conventional limits, in the upturning of nature, and in the excavation of the psyche's

depths. As he wrote in "Apology for Bad Dreams":

> It is not good to forget over what
>   gulfs the spirit
> Of the beauty of humanity, the petal of a
>   lost flower blown seaward by the
>   night-wind, floats to its quietness.

There is in Jeffers a primordial quality, at the very least an exceedingly old-fashioned quality, that touched him on several occasions with the original imagination of tragedy.

"Tamar," the first of these narratives, was written in 1922 and derived from the story in the second Book of Samuel, where one of King David's sons, Amnon, rapes his sister, Tamar, and is later killed on the orders of his brother, Absalom. In this poem, as in several others, Jeffers makes incest central to his story, in part because within the world of the family it is the most intense, shocking form of the conflict between natural energy and customary morality, but, especially and programmatically, in his own explanation, because it is the appropriate symbol for the introverted character of the whole race. However, in contrast with the biblical Tamar, a passive victim distracted with shame, Tamar Cauldwell is the forceful, flamboyant, driving spirit behind the action of Jeffers' poem. She lives in the isolated family home, overlooking the ocean, with her widowed father, David, a Bible-reading farmer, her brother, Lee, her mother's sister, Stella, and another aunt, the idiot Jinny. The setting is specific and realistic (California at the time of World War I), but the story has an essentially mythic quality, with Tamar often as much elemental as human, a personified natural force upturning conventional morality, as when she seduces her brother in the cold mountain pool:

> Was it the wild rock coast
> Of her breeding, and the reckless wind

In the beaten trees and the gaunt
    booming crashes
Of breakers under the rocks, or rather the
    amplitude
And wing-subduing immense earth-
    ending water
That moves all the west taught her this
    freedom?

Tamar and Lee become lovers, until she finds herself with child by him. To cover herself, she takes another lover, Will Andrews, with a distaste that she did not feel for her brother, for now "the house is broken / And any thief can enter it."

But this incest is not the family's first. From her Aunt Stella, who sees visions and hears voices, she discovers that the same license had been taken more than forty years previously by her father and his long-dead sister, Helen. The House of Cauldwell is rotten to the core from the root. In this putrid atmosphere, Tamar's desire turns to loathing, of men, of life, and of the source of life, with "all the world growing hateful, both her lovers / Hateful, but the intolerably masculine sun hatefullest of all."

She dreams of the oblivion of the present human race and the beginning of a new race out of the union of her father and herself; and, to atone for the sins of her ancestors who had slaughtered the Indians or driven them from their lands, she is symbolically enjoyed in an orgy by the ghosts of a vanished tribe. She comes to wield over the hopelessly corrupted house ever greater destructive power, taunting her father, racked by his lustful body and Christian guilt, and the two young rivals for her bewildering affections. At length she maneuvers all the men into her bedroom and drives Lee and Will into a violent, maddened fight in which Will is stabbed to death. Aunt Jinny, unconscious agent of purification, sets fire to the house; and with Tamar in nihilistic delight clinging to Lee against his escape and with the father calling upon the pity of Christ, the house collapses to its infernal doom, consuming all the inhabitants. A people turned inward upon itself has suffered an ultimate punishment for its self-absorption. The human blot has been erased; the things of nature reassert their permanence.

Grass grows where the flame flowered;
A hollowed lawn strewn with a few black
    stones
And the brick of broken chimneys; all about
    there
The old trees, some of them scarred with fire,
    endure the sea wind.

"Tamar" is an impressive and memorable poem, but a puzzling one, because of the author's ambivalent feelings about Tamar herself, who is simultaneously an emblem of exhilarating freedom and a vehicle of the utmost impurity. Jeffers himself recognized this confusion of purpose, when in retrospect he admitted to the poem's "tendency to romanticize unmoral freedom."

"Roan Stallion," composed about three years later, is a more compact poem and possessed of a greater symbolic clarity. Again the central and exciting figure is a woman, of Scottish, Spanish, and Indian ancestry, whose name, California, immediately designates her as the quintessence of the West, "erect and strong as a new tower." The mother of an infant daughter, Christine, she is married to Johnny, a farmer of sorts but chiefly a drunken gambler, "burnt-out ... twisted ... shriveled with bad living." He represents contemporary humanity at its most diminished and degraded, slothful, greedy, physically debauched, spiritually null. In contrast, California is characterized by her love and care for her child, by her sense of obligation, by her pertinacity and quiet courage, and by her religious imagination and faith.

Johnny and the humanity he typifies having nothing to offer her, she begins to look away from the human for a God "not in man's shape" to awaken and stretch her ready spirit.

> Humanity is the
> start of the race; I say
> Humanity is the mould to break away from,
>   the crust to break through, the coal to
>   break into fire,
> The atom to be split.

The nonhuman shape in which this deity appears to her is that of Johnny's magnificent stallion, the embodiment of everything of which its master is a negation—beauty, power, nobility, cleanliness, aspiration.

One night under a brilliant moon California steals out of the house and down to the corral, leaps onto the horse, and in a simulacrum of resplendent sexual union rides this "savage and exultant strength of the world" to the mountain top. Dismounting "here on the calvary" with "nothing conscious / But the possible God and the cropped grass," she prostrates herself before this natural divinity.

After such communion, there can be no going back to suffering Johnny's abject humanity. The following night when, lurching and stumbling, he pursues her out of the house with his dog, she lures him into the corral, where the dog frets and snaps at the mighty stallion. Slipping out of the corral, she runs back to the house, fetches a rifle, shoots the dog, and watches from a distance in the moonlight, curious and detached, as the horse tramples Johnny to death. "Then California moved by some obscure human fidelity / Lifted the rifle." She shoots the stallion and "turned then on her little daughter the mask of a woman / Who has killed God." There will be no more degradation; there will be the dignity of loving and raising her child amid natural surroundings; but there

will be no more exaltation. At the last California has chosen humanity. The God, beautiful, powerful, elemental, but amoral and unhuman, she has killed.

The announcement of a truth that is free of any human relation is also the end of "The Tower Beyond Tragedy," which was published in the same volume as "Roan Stallion." This dramatic poem is Jeffers' version of the *Oresteia* and the *Electra* plays. In character it owes most to Aeschylus, and the events of the story loosely follow those of the *Agamemnon* and the *Choephori*. However, Jeffers' final purpose is to release Orestes from history and human concerns rather than, as in the *Eumenides*, to have him return to Argos and participation in its affairs, after judgment and the lifting of the curse. For Jeffers' Orestes, history is hopeless, and the curse is to be human. His Cassandra foresees a cyclical future of ever swifter rises to ever wider power and ever greater catastrophe. She curses in succession Athens, Rome, Spain, France, and England, yet there is still

> A mightier to be cursed and a higher for
>   malediction
> When America has eaten Europe and takes
>   tribute of Asia, when the ends of the
>   world grow aware of each other
> And are dogs in one kennel, they will tear
> The master of the hunt with the mouths of
>   the pack: new fallings, new risings, O
>   winged one
> No end of the fallings and risings?

That future, perpetually gestating another Trojan war, another Vietnam, is what Orestes, in ancient Greece, in modern California, would cast off. And his sister's offer of her body to him, to entice him to reenter history, take up power, and rule in his father's place, is again, as in "Tamar," a small, single instance of the total racial inversion. It is all a huge imbroglio in which Orestes sees men writhe

> like a full draught of fishes, all matted
> In the one mesh; when they look backward
>   they see only a man standing at the
>   beginning,
> Or forward, a man at the end; or if upward,
>   men in the shining bitter sky striding
>   and feasting,
> Whom you call Gods. . . .
> It is all turned inward, all your desires
>   incestuous, the woman the serpent, the
>   man the rose-red cavern,
> Both human, worship forever. . . .

Bearing a message of salvation by detachment from the world, he takes to anonymity and the high, wild country, as one "Who had climbed the tower beyond time, consciously, and cast humanity, entered the earlier fountain."

Jeffers' next narrative poem, *The Women at Point Sur,* published in 1927, was his longest and the only one to occupy a volume by itself. Like Tamar Cauldwell, the poem's protagonist, the Reverend Dr. Barclay, is a demonic hero, source of chaos and destruction at the same time that he is often the voice of sentiments that Jeffers elsewhere approves. However, Jeffers claimed shortly after the poem's publication that this was exactly his cautionary intention, to point out the dangers of the idea of "breaking out of humanity" being "misinterpreted in the mind of a fool or a lunatic." So Barclay's inhumanism does not release him from the burden of human involvement and turn him outward toward nature and God, but throws him inward on destructive sexuality, nihilism, self-deification, and the totalitarian domination of others. He is Jeffers' most Faustian creation, which is also to say most Ahab-like in his attempted refusal of human limits and pride in having "voyaged outside the maps, these waters not charted," to "break through to" the "power behind the appearances." His exuberant self-reliance must furthermore be ironically reminiscent of Emerson: "Nothing you can do is wicked. I have seen God. He is there in the hill, he is here in your body."

The preacher is very much a casualty of the war, in which he has lost in turn his son, his Christian faith, and his moral compass. Abandoning his church and his congregation ("I have nothing for you"), he wanders down the coast in search of more complete and pliant disciples, and finds lodging at a farmhouse. Here he begins to strip from himself the layers of traditional, Christian restraint, in the main by ever more extravagant sexual acts. First, he buys sex from the farm's Indian servant girl; then he encourages a lesbian relationship between two of the other girls there; and finally he rapes his daughter, April, who has come looking for him.

Gradually, this fiery revivalist is transformed into a diabolic messiah, exerting a lethal influence upon those he has gathered around him, in a manner that must bring to mind certain other horrifying evil geniuses of more recent years, also emanating, significantly, from California. One of his entourage murders her infant daughter to save her the pain of life and to atone for the "crime" of conceiving her; Barclay's daughter, "without brakes, without rudder" since her father's rape of her, kills herself in front of him to feel at the last "one thing done wisely / In the vast insanity of things." Ever more nihilistic ("I preserve nothing") and ever more megalomaniac ("believing himself God"), delirious with salvationist mission ("I'll save the beasts, too"), the crazed minister makes his way alone into the hills, where at the entrance to a deserted mine he collapses, dying but still self-exalting ("I am inexhaustible"), bequeathing a legacy of madness and despair.

Although *The Women at Point Sur* is not entirely successful as a narrative, it does present a disturbing, compelling study of revivalist excess and mesmeric, apocalyptic leadership, lunatic or evil forms that have cast such shadows over the forefront or corners of later history.

"Cawdor," published the following year, has less overt didactic purpose than the previous long poems. It is a tale of sexual rejection and revenge, of accidental killing and fearful self-punishment, set in California in 1909. The title, of course, sends us to *Macbeth,* but for little more common property than blood and atmospherics; it may also bring to our notice how often Jeffers' main characters have names with Scottish associations (Cauldwell, Barclay, Cawdor, and later Thurso, Fraser, Bothwell, and Ferguson), presumably to suggest from the first instant an ambience of repressed, explosive, puritanical passion.

In "Cawdor," Martial, an old farmer, just now blinded in a fire from a bursting oil drum, is led down the valley by his daughter, Fera, to Cawdor's farm, where he stays for the brief remainder of his ill-fortuned, maimed life. Cawdor, a brooding widower with three grown children, takes pride in the hard, tough life he has led and in the violent, populist hatred he feels for "the fooled and rotten faces of rich and successful men. / And the sons they have." After Martial's death, he marries Fera, who is as wild-natured as her name, a being from an earlier time easily at home in a bloody, freshly flayed puma skin. She falls for Cawdor's elder son, Hood, and having been resisted by him, tells Cawdor that he has raped her. Cawdor pursues his son up the mountain, where after a brief struggle Hood falls to his death over a precipice. There remains for Fera first to attempt suicide and then, after teasing her husband with further lies and fantasies, to reveal the truth to him of his son's innocence. Tempted to strangle her but then turning upon himself,

Cawdor, his horror and remorse overflowing, gouges out his own eyes, those offending eyes that had first desired Fera—a modern Oedipus on a farm in California.

Those are the principal events of the story; but there is yet to be mentioned the finest passage in the poem, several pages of Jeffers' greatest poetry, in which he wrote of the death by revolver shot of a caged eagle, its spirit soaring away from its body and from the physical earth in ever wider circles of space and time. Like the roan stallion, like the many hawks in his shorter poems, the eagle is the symbol of a strength, a purity, a nobility, a wisdom, and a farseeing vision beyond the scope of shortsighted, entangled, enervated humanity. Higher still and higher, it looks further still and wider upon the alternations of pride and pain, of life and death, of the yearning to be born and the yearning to be quiet, until its visionary spirit enters and encloses itself in peace at the zenith. It is a sustained piece of sublime writing.

Jeffers' Jesus, the subject of his next dramatic poem, "Dear Judas" (1929), has more than a little in common with the megalomaniac, power-hungry Barclay of *The Women at Point Sur.* This poem, the form of which was influenced by the Japanese No plays, is a treatment of the later stages of the gospel story, in particular of Judas' betrayal of Jesus. It opens with the flat statement of a materialist premise: "They have all died and their souls are extinguished."

Jesus is not metaphysical; indeed, the mainspring of his psychology is his obsession with his physical parentage. It is the shame of his probable bastardy that has driven him to discover God to be his father and to make his mark upon the world with a supposedly supernatural authority. He burns with a truly revolutionary ardor to transform the world and rule the future. His zeal, though, is purificatory and uplifting rather than humanitarian; it is inspired by his mystic confidence in his own lofty, magnificent spirit. As with Barclay, it is of Ahab stretching after the mystery of the white whale that we are reminded, as Jesus proclaims the "lightnings," "pinnacles," and "towers" of his soul and its "immeasurable height above men." "All greatness is a wrestling with time."

Recognizing that he will not be able to establish his revolutionary kingdom during his lifetime, Jesus invents heaven and hell as devices of reward and terror with which to implement his sway over the future. He goes to his death exulting in his unprecedented domination of human history.

> I go a stranger passage to a greater
>   dominion
> More tyrannous, more terrible, more true,
>   than Caesar or any subduer of the
>   earth before him has dared to dream
>   of . . . no man shall live.
> As if *I* had not lived.

In contrast with this Jesus who is all energy and leaping spirit, Judas is introspective, moral, and ethical, a decent, worried, concerned, liberal humanist. Aching with pity and bowed beneath the world's suffering ("the moaning of men and beasts torments me . . . . others' joy is not mine, / Only their pain"), he has sought in Jesus a reformist leader who would make living a little kinder and sweeter for all. But as Jesus' dream goes wild and mad, his modest hope turns to a nightmare vision of Roman suppression, with "all the roadside masted with moaning crucifixion." Sensitive and anguished, he betrays Jesus "to get the firebrand locked up, to save the city," expecting, in his softheaded benevolence, that Jesus will go to the lunatic's cell rather than the rebel's cross. He leaves the drama, pathetic, well-intentioned, self-loathing, to hang himself; in his ears ring Lazarus' terrible last words upon this good neighbor's in-

volvement with the overreaching superman who was Jesus:

> you enter his kingdom with him, as the
>   hawk's lice with the hawk
> Climb the blue towers of the sky under the
>   down of the feathers.

"Dear Judas" was coupled in its volume with "The Loving Shepherdess," a study, commented Jeffers, of "nearly pure" love, in contrast with the misdirected affections and passions of the gospel figures. It is the least eventful and the most tender of Jeffers' poems, and of lighter weight than others, although it has not wanted for admirers. Clare Walker, the shepherdess, with her little flock of sheep wanders the Californian coast along much the same paths as Barclay (who is mentioned in the poem, as are Tamar and Cawdor, all inhabitants of this Jeffers country); but, unlike Barclay's, her spirit is formed not of the will to power but of love, and her vision is a selfless one of peace and delight for all created things. Rather than being a child of the Protestant fundamentalism in which most of Jeffers' characters have been molded, she has about her a quality of the Franciscan or even, loosely, of the Hindu, in her refusal to restrain love or to interfere with the processes of nature, even at the certain cost of her own life.

Six years later, in 1935, Jeffers again made Christianity the central issue of a dramatic poem. This was in "At the Birth of an 'Age," which was derived from Germanic legend and set at the time of Europe's change from a heroic, pagan culture to the Christian one. Writing of the birth of this Christian age within sight of its end (of its faith, he considered, although not of its secularized ethics), Jeffers could charge his poem with an ominous historical significance that more than compensates for the dramatic weaknesses. For the poem is structurally broken-backed: its first part is a dramatic reenactment of the deaths of Nordic heroes, dying by their honor and their dishonor, by their courage and their treachery; and the second part is a series of spiritual and philosophical tableaux, revealing some of the components of the culture that will supersede this paganism. These include the Greek Prometheus, the Norse Hanged God, and Christ.

Masked simply as The Young Man, Christ speaks here not as the exhilarated megalomaniac of "Dear Judas," but as a disillusioned, self-confessed, false prophet, who has clamped upon mankind a "ridiculous delusion" of personal immortality in a further world. Self-tormenting ("If Judas for a single betrayal hanged himself, / What for me, that betrayed the world?"), he prays that he himself and his myth of divinity be forgotten and that only his message of human love and brotherhood be remembered. Predictably, Jeffers does not end on such an uncharacteristic note, and the most compelling and conclusive poetry is given to the Hanged God, whose privilege it is to speak the language of exalted, inhumanist indifference:

I am also the outer nothing and the wandering
    infinite night. These are my mercy and
    my goodness, these
My peace.

However extravagant and horrifying the incidents of their plots may be, Jeffers' narratives from the 1930's are all predominantly realistic in conception and characterization rather than mythic. The principal poems are "Thurso's Landing" (1932), "Give Your Heart to the Hawks" (1933), "Solstice" (1935), and "Such Counsels You Gave to Me" (1937). They are all tales of unrelieved disaster and destruction: in "Thurso's Landing" of infidelities, two suicides, an accidental crippling, and a mercy killing; in "Give Your Heart to the Hawks" of infidelity, fratricide, subsequent corrosive guilt, and two further suicides; in "Solstice" of a mother's murder of her children to keep them from their father and her flight into the mountains; in "Such Counsels You Gave to Me" of a son's patricide and attempted incestuous seduction by his mother.

In each poem the strongest personality is a woman: Helen Thurso, Fayne Fraser, Madrone Bothwell, and Mrs. Howren. And each of these women is the lively but unfulfilled and discontented wife of a dour or coarsened husband. It is the wilder, more instinctual female energy that directs the turn of events. The men, further from nature, are governed by stubborn will and the pride of possession (Reave Thurso); by whiskey and the inward torture of a Puritan conscience (Lance Fraser); by the values of the city and mechanical progress (Bothwell); by an anti-imaginative materialism (Howren); and by intellectual ambition (his son Howard).

Between sexual desire and traditional morality, between independent self and conformist society, between nature and culture, the people of these stories, of this coast and country, are bruised, cracked, and crushed. There are, it is true, positive attributes to be distinguished amid the welter of catastrophes: such qualities as courage and endurance, responsiveness to the natural world, self-reliance, and a preparedness to face the music, however discordant. And there are moments of awe (humanity's "terrible shining" against "the dark magnificence of things" in "Thurso's Landing") and of melodramatic elevation (Madrone Bothwell's barbaric "fierce unsubdued core" that is translated into the storm-wracked heights of the Rocky Mountains in "Solstice"). But the prevailing sense is of man's contemptible insignificance, of the unimportance of his self-induced suffering, and of the inconsequence and superfluity of his life.

The emphasis in these poems falls on the pettiness and ugliness of humanity rather than on the inhuman beauty and the natural divinity that Jeffers tells us elsewhere it is the poet's business to praise and in so doing restore man to his right, small, contented place. Without such constructive purpose, with few such rhapsodic notes, with little of the mythic or transcendent dimensions, these realistic narratives risk too much becoming mere dismal catalogs, newssheets of crime and cruelty, fury and folly.

These furies and follies Jeffers saw gathering over many years toward their inevitable conclusion in a second world war. Virtually all that he wrote at this time sounded with the approach of war, so that in the prefatory note to *Be Angry at the Sun* (1941) he felt bound to lament his "obsession with contemporary history."

This volume opens with "Mara," another tale of infidelity, marital hatred, and suicide, set as usual in California, but now in a world enlarged by radio to include the voice of Hitler, "wailing" like "a lost child." The situation is familiar. A heavyhearted protagonist, Bruce Ferguson, is married to a lively, spirited wife, Fawn, who is having an affair with Bruce's more vigorous younger brother, Allen; while upstairs in the same house their father lies painfully dying, despised by their misused and embittered mother. However, what differentiates Ferguson from most of the previous characters in the realistic narratives is that his pain is primarily philosophical. His thoughts and dreams run on the coming of war and its attendant horrors, on historical decline and the collapse of values ("Nobody knows the difference between right and wrong. / So the wolves will come back to Europe"), and on the crippled weakness of good in the world and the brute strength of evil. "I guess you think too much, honey," says a girl in a bar. And weighed down with thinking, he hangs himself, so as not to feel "two thousand years of instruction sag underfoot / Like a rotted floor," and "the great retreat from truth and the moral confusions / Deeper confounded." He dies a victim of mind and pessimism, leaving

to his wife and brother the gift to pursue their affair in "freedom and happiness."

Also in this volume is "The Bowl of Blood," a masque that features Hitler, who comes anonymously as The Leader to seek counsel from a medium. Jeffers' attitude toward Hitler here as elsewhere is a most ambivalent one, deriving from the poem's basic contention, which is that Hitler is no more than anyone else a master of history but its creature: "Listen: the man does not have power, / Power has the man." "Whoever thinks this man is more wicked / Than other men knows not himself." Hitler's original patriotic motives were unambiguously commendable ("Blood and soil are poetry, you can fight for them"), but now, having put on power and taken to himself a cast of disciples, like Jeffers' Barclay and Jesus before him, he is caught on the public stage and destined to "play out the tragedy," the requisite descent into "Exhaustion and shabby horrors and squalid slavery, / The Russian theme."

It is an utterly fatalistic view of history, working itself out here in Europe. Hence, while always fearfully assuming the likelihood of America's eventual involvement, Jeffers was politically an absolute isolationist, at this time of American history when isolationism had ready political meaning. For, history was "what our people came over / From stifled Europe to escape."

That last statement of unqualified, separatist Americanism, in the tradition of Emerson, Thoreau, and Whitman, was made by Hoult Gore in Jeffers' most shocking and sensational poem, "The Love and the Hate," which forms the first part of *The Double Axe,* published in 1948 with his publisher's disclaimer. The volume consists almost exclusively of poems inspired either by the war or by the still vaster theme of the collapse of the Christian era.

In "The Love and the Hate," written in 1944, the young soldier, Hoult Gore, having died in battle on a Pacific island, returns home not just as a ghost, but as a stinking, slimy, putrefying corpse. Licensed by his personal fate to speak on behalf of the slaughtered, he is the uninhibited mouthpiece of all Jeffers' horror of war, mutilation, and violent death, and all his irrepressible hatred of those who, for whatever cause, send others out to die. Through Hoult, who before his final decomposition, in this witches' broth of a story, shoots his father for supporting the war, Jeffers gives voice to sentiments of quite amazing ferocity:

I wish that every man who approved this war,
In which we had no right, reason nor justice,
Were crawling there in the fire's way with his
    back broken, . . .

Three years after this unrestrained howl of rage and vicarious pain, Jeffers attached to the poem—for relief, for balance, for transcendence—a second part entitled "The Inhumanist." This latter poem is less a narrative than a treasury of wisdom, a new book of proverbs, a seasonal round of fifty-two sections that ends with the beginning of a fresh dawn, after the utter dead end of "The Love and the Hate." The only common element is the Gore estate, which is now the home of the main character, who is called simply "the old man." After Hoult Gore's obliterating nihilism, he purifies a cursed spot with the most extended articulation of "inhumanism" that Jeffers ever composed. From mass society and mass politics, from secular humanism and from anthropocentric religion, even from the human race, the old man is unequivocally disaffected. "But still remains the endless inhuman beauty of things . . . and there is endurance, endurance, death's nobler cousin. Endurance." He counsels stoicism and self-adjustment on the personal level, with space enough between fellow men to permit steady contemplation of the whole, marvelous, sentient, natural divinity ("nothing is not alive"),

the quiet adoration of which restores and redeems man. Precisely:

    Moderate kindness
Is oil on a crying wheel: use it. Mutual
    help
Is necessary: use it when it is necessary.
And as to love: make love when need
    drives.
And as to love: love God. He is rock, earth
    and water, and the beasts and stars;
    and the night that contains them.
And as to love: whoever loves or hates man
    is fooled in a mirror.

Of his remaining longer works two were adaptations from Euripides, the Greek tragedian who lived in a time of deep-seated cultural change most like Jeffers' own. In his *Medea* (1946), the title figure, after only slight modification of her Euripidean character, takes her fit place in Jeffers country among his other wild, passionate women confronting the less instinctive world of men. (She had indeed been reincarnated previously in "Solstice" as Madrone Bothwell.) Jeffers' language thrills to her barbaric, elemental, "dark" nature, as it is thrown in deathly conflict with Jason's convenient, opportunistic, "better-lighted" reason. She begins with the wish that "from that blue sky the white wolf of lightning / Would leap, and burst my skull and brain." She goes out, revenged, inaccessible to pity, beyond humanity: "Now I go forth / Under the cold eyes of the weakness-despising stars:—not me they scorn."

The second adaptation was of *Hippolytus,* published in 1954 under the title "The Cretan Woman." The most conspicuous aspect of this poem is Jeffers' attribution to Hippolytus of an explicitly homosexual formation, which finds expression in his fastidiousness, his clean-limbed, athletic camaraderie with Alcyon and Andros, and in his fatal inability to respond to Phaedra. Over the tragedy Aphrodite presides and disposes, delivering in the closing lines a homily on hubris that seems pertinent less to the particular drama it concludes than generally to the technological civilization of the twentieth century.

In the same volume with "The Cretan Woman" is "Hungerfield," a short narrative written a year or so after Una's death, the finest passages of which are addressed to her memory. The poem had first and last a therapeutic function for Jeffers, for its subject is the coming to terms with the death of loved ones, with the pain of their dying, and with the fact of their deaths. Hawl Hungerfield's failure to do so, his refusal to let his mother die and be dead, starts a plague of death that does not complete its course until it has devoured all the animals around his farm, his brother, his wife and children, and himself. While Jeffers resigns himself:

> It is no good. Una has died, and I
> Am left waiting for death.

He waited many years and learned, doubtless with the help of "Hungerfield," how to renew purpose in his daily living and rediscover "the beauty of God."

Such beauty was a common one, the beauty that is all around us, of which we are a part; but perhaps it was a rare God, emanating from the peculiar intensity of Jeffers' response to that beauty. He responded simply and powerfully at a time when complication and subtlety were the prevailing poetic modes. It is in part owing to this direct accessibility of speech that he has been found to be "the most sui generis" of modern American poets, the most "his own man." Indeed, as a poet, he does seem to stand apart from his generation, and the literary contemporaries he calls to mind are quite miscellaneous.

In the case of the claustrophobic, doomed, self-destroying families of his narrative poems, there is surely a correspondence with Eugene O'Neill, and with William Faulkner, who would seem to have read "Tamar" closely. But neither of his major connections is American. First there is Yeats, fellow dweller in a stone tower in the west of a country, similarly patrician in temper and declamatory in style, albeit in more traditional meters, and likewise haunted by images of disastrous change. And second, there is D. H. Lawrence, for a posthumous volume of whose poems Jeffers wrote an introduction, and whose widow the Jeffers family came to know and visit. Both Lawrence and Jeffers were rebellious scions of Protestant fervor and the puritan conscience; both were resounding, vatic voices improvising on the free-verse line of Whitman; and both were in pursuit of sources of power and light beneath and beyond the human.

O'Neill, Faulkner, Yeats, and Lawrence make a most various company. But if a single category is sought in which Jeffers may be properly situated, it must be a geographical one. He is very much a western American, a Californian poet, to be read as an elder poetic kinsman of Kenneth Rexroth (for all that writer's surprisingly heated antipathy to Jeffers), and of such diverse but distinctively western poets as William Everson, Gary Snyder, Charles Bukowski, and Jack Spicer, all of whom have acknowledged, briefly or at length, Jeffers' extraordinary achievement.

Indeed, it is impossible to imagine Jeffers living and writing anywhere except in the west of the American continent, perhaps even anywhere except in a house within sight and sound of the Pacific Ocean. For he is in every respect and in all assumptions a westerner, an heir of the frontiersman of myth, a direct descendant of the westward-looking literary romantics. Behind him stand Emerson and Whitman, travelers in mind and gesture, and Henry David Thoreau, frontiersman by analogy in *Walden*. And larger still out of a further past looms James Fenimore Cooper's exemplary hero, Natty Bumppo, for whom also God disclosed himself in natural beauty, albeit in more Christian, less pantheist shape; for whom also the good life consisted of living as closely as possible in accord with nature, taking from it only what was essential in the way of food and clothing for survival; and for whom also the greatest threat to the good life (of society as well as of the individual) lay in the heedless, exploitative misuse of the natural world by a proliferating, densely packed population.

In a late poem, "Passenger Pigeons," Jeffers considers the possibility of man's self-extinction despite his present billions, just as in his death-dealing arrogance he had previously annihilated the countless numbers of the passenger pigeon. By a nice, absolutely appropriate irony, this is the species that is subjected to wholesale, black-farcical massacre, to Natty's contemptuous disgust, in the first book of the Leatherstocking Series, nearly a century and a half before, in the early years of American westward and industrial expansion. Cooper saw ahead with such alarming clarity; and it was further along the same line of sight that Jeffers gazed.

Thus, a redeemer, in the poem of that title, has to redeem a history of indiscriminate rapacity, mechanized utilitarianism, extirpation, and genocide—the history of a people who

. . . have done what never was done before.
    Not as a people takes a land to love it
    and be fed,
A little, according to need and love, and
    again a little; sparing the country
    tribes, mixing
Their blood with theirs, their minds with

all the rocks and rivers, their flesh
    with the soil: no, without hunger
Wasting the world and your own labor, without love possessing, not even your
    hands to the dirt but plows
Like blades of knives: heartless machines;
    houses of steel: using and despising
    the patient earth . . .
Oh, as a rich man eats a forest for profit
    and a field for vanity, so you came
    west and raped
The continent and brushed its people to
    death. Without need, the weak
    skirmishing hunters, and without mercy.

So, removing himself as far as possible from that continuous process of history, Jeffers found himself a place where, with hands to the dirt, he planted his trees in the patient earth and slowly built his house, not of steel, but of stone. It was a life's work, a life's dedication; but in any time span longer than the individual's, merely a moment's holding action. History (which is "what our ancestors came over / From stifled Europe to escape") advances, a progress that may be delayed but not deflected:

We have built the great cities; now
There is no escape. We have gathered vast
    populations incapable of free survival,
    insulated
From the strong earth, each person in himself helpless, on all dependent. The
    circle is closed, and the net
Is being hauled in.

There was no further to go. Centuries, millennia even, of westward yearning and outreaching were coming to an end. The globe's circle was closed. It was the moment that Whitman had awesomely imagined years before, projecting himself in space and time until, in "Facing West from California's Shores,"

"Long having wander'd since, round the earth having wander'd / Now I face home again." What then, he had wondered, what then?—and indeed he had left his poem on a question: "But where is what I started for so long ago? / And why is it yet unfound?" In that same cast of westward mind, Jeffers spent most of his life "facing west from California's shores," with no further western land before him but with the end of the West, he felt, piling up and darkening the sky behind him, as he looked outward, away from humanity.

This circular shape of westward movement around the globe was repeated for Jeffers in the shapes he discerned of the many cycles of culture. The cycles, smaller and larger, intersected one another—Judaic, Greco-Roman, Nordic—and were all contained within the vaster cycle of Western history. During his lifetime, he believed, the Christian cycle had turned, with its weight of at least fifteen centuries, heavily downward. Rising swiftly to meet its fall, to cut its descending path with terrifying, clashing possibilities, was the age of the machine:

> The first of these curves passing
>   its noon and the second orient
> All in one's little lifetime make it seem
>   pivotal.
> Truly the time is marked by insane splendors
>   and agonies.
> But watch when the two curves cross:
>   you children
> Not far away down the hawk's-nightmare
>   future: you will see monsters.

As with cultures, so with nations. In the case of his own country, Jeffers saw its history in terms of an ever steeper decline from a high point, probably in the early years of independence, as a republic of austere, self-reliant libertarians, to its present condition of a sprawling, luxury-loving, parasitic, bureaucratized empire. From his "ideally, aristocratic and republican"

position, as Una characterized his politics, he addressed a number of public poems over the years to the American nation. Already in the early 1920's he felt that a "perishing republic" was "heavily thickening to empire"; by the 1940's "Now, thoroughly compromised, we aim at world rule, like Assyria, Rome, Britain, Germany, to inherit those hordes of guilt and doom."

No, he saw little hope for the world, if by the world is meant the world of power politics and historical tendency. That story was just the one about original sin, the tale of hubris writ large, larger, and ever more destructive. As a result of his political pessimism, he has often, although much less frequently of late, been misinterpreted as nihilistic or life-denying or despairing. Such judgments are very far from the truth.

Of course, Jeffers knew that to be alive was to suffer, that pain was intrinsic to life: "The poets who sing of life without remembering its agony / Are fools and liars." But he also knew for himself that to be alive was not, very much not, to be in despair, nor, save when personal sorrow or public catastrophe prompts it, to be unhappy. As he politely replied to Dorothy Thompson in 1938: "You speak of the present isolation and spiritual despair; and I must confess that I value the isolation and don't feel the despair." He valued the isolation because it enabled him to concentrate his rapt attention upon the enormous beauty of the world; and he didn't feel the despair because, with the "bad dreams" exorcised in his stories, as he explained early on in his "Apology for Bad Dreams," from contemplation of the world's beauty his spirit drew a constant serenity.

In fact, Jeffers should be seen as finally and essentially a religious poet. His was a great, solemn, watchful, meditative spirit, concerned, as he wrote, "with permanent things and the permanent aspects of life." It is in such a spiritual context that he may be associated with the

Greek tragedians and with the Old Testament prophets. He has that kind of weight, that kind of seriousness, that kind of salutary fierceness. He is a major poet, uncomfortable, disturbing, savage at times, yet inspiriting and enhancing. We neglect him at the peril of our own seriousness.

Selected Bibliography

WORKS OF
ROBINSON JEFFERS

POEMS

Flagons and Apples. Los Angeles: Grafton, 1912.
Californians. New York: Macmillan, 1916.
Tamar and Other Poems. New York: Peter G. Boyle, 1924.
Roan Stallion, Tamar, and Other Poems. New York: Boni and Liveright, 1925.
The Women at Point Sur. New York: Boni and Liveright, 1927.
Cawdor and Other Poems. New York: Liveright, 1928.
Dear Judas and Other Poems. New York: Liveright, 1929.
Descent to the Dead. New York: Random House, 1931.
Thurso's Landing and Other Poems. New York: Liveright, 1932.
Give Your Heart to the Hawks and Other Poems. New York: Random House, 1933.
Solstice and Other Poems. New York: Random House, 1935.
Such Counsels You Gave to Me and Other Poems. New York: Random House, 1937.
The Selected Poetry of Robinson Jeffers. New York: Random House, 1938.
Be Angry at the Sun. New York: Random House, 1941.
Medea. New York: Random House, 1946.
The Double Axe and Other Poems. New York: Random House, 1948.

Poetry, Gongorism and a Thousand Years. Los Angeles: Ward Ritchie, 1949.
Hungerfield and Other Poems. New York: Random House, 1954.
The Beginning and the End and Other Poems. New York: Random House, 1963.
Selected Poems. New York: Vintage, 1965.
Not Man Apart, edited by David Ross Brower. San Francisco: Sierra Club, 1965.
Jeffers Country. San Francisco: Scrimshaw Press, 1971.
The Alpine Christ and Other Poems, with commentary and notes by William Everson. Monterey, Calif.: Cayucos Books, 1974.
Brides of the South Wind: Poems 1917–1922, with commentary and notes by William Everson. Monterey, Calif.: Cayucos Books, 1974.
The Double Axe and Other Poems, Including Eleven Suppressed Poems. New York: Liveright, 1977.

LETTERS

The Selected Letters of Robinson Jeffers, 1897–1962, edited by Ann N. Ridgeway. Baltimore: Johns Hopkins, 1968.

BIBLIOGRAPHIES

Alberts, Sydney S. *A Bibliography of the Works of Robinson Jeffers.* New York: Random House, 1933.
Nolte, William H. *The Merrill Checklist of Robinson Jeffers.* Columbus, Ohio: Charles E. Merrill, 1970.
Tate, Allen. *Sixty American Poets, 1896–1944,* rev. ed. Washington, D.C.: Library of Congress, 1954.
Vardamis, Alex A. *The Critical Reputation of Robinson Jeffers.* Hamden, Conn.: Archon, 1972.

BIOGRAPHICAL AND CRITICAL STUDIES

Alexander, John R. "Conflict in the Narrative Poetry of Robinson Jeffers." *Sewanee Review,* 80:85–99 (January–March 1972).
Bennett, Melba Berry. *The Stone Mason of Tor House: The Life and Work of Robinson Jeffers.* Los Angeles: Ward Ritchie, 1966.

Boyers, Robert. "A Sovereign Voice." *Sewanee Review,* 77:487–507 (Summer 1969).

Brophy, Robert J. *Robinson Jeffers: Myth, Ritual and Symbol in His Narrative Poems.* Cleveland: Case Western Reserve University Press, 1973.

Carpenter, Frederic I. "The Values of Robinson Jeffers." *American Literature,* 11:353–66 (January 1940).

———. *Robinson Jeffers.* New York: Twayne, 1962.

Coffin, Arthur B. *Robinson Jeffers: Poet of Inhumanism.* Madison: University of Wisconsin Press, 1971.

Cunningham, Cornelius C. "The Rhythm of Robinson Jeffers' Poetry as Revealed by Oral Reading." *Quarterly Journal of Speech,* 32:351–57 (October 1946).

Demott, Robert. "Robinson Jeffers's 'Tamar'." In *The Twenties,* edited by Warren G. French. Deland, Fla.: Everett, Edwards, 1975.

Dickey, James. "First and Last Things." *Poetry,* 103:320–21 (February 1964).

Everson, William. *Robinson Jeffers: Fragments of an Older Fury.* Berkeley, Calif.: Oyez, 1968.

———. "Archetype West." In *Regional Perspectives: An Examination of America's Literary Heritage,* edited by J. G. Burke. Chicago: American Library Association, 1973.

Flint, Frank S. "Verse Chronicle." *Criterion,* 11:276–81 (January 1932).

Gregory, Horace. *The Dying Gladiators.* New York: Grove Press, 1961.

Highet, Gilbert. *People, Places, and Books.* New York: Oxford University Press, 1953.

Kunitz, Stanley J. "Day Is a Poem." *Poetry,* 59:148–54 (December 1941).

Lutyens, David B. *The Creative Encounter.* London: Secker and Warburg, 1960.

Monjian, Mercedes C. *Robinson Jeffers: A Study in Inhumanism.* Pittsburgh: University of Pittsburgh Press, 1958.

Nolte, William H. "Robinson Jeffers as Didactic Poet." *Virginia Quarterly Review,* 42:257–71 (Spring 1966).

Powell, Lawrence Clark. *Robinson Jeffers: The Man and His Work.* Pasadena, Calif.: San Pasqual Press, 1940.

Robinson Jeffers Newsletter. Los Angeles: Robinson Jeffers Committee, Occidental College (1962–   ).

Scott, R. I. "Robinson Jeffers's Tragedies as Rediscoveries of the World." *Bulletin of Rocky Mountain Modern Language Association,* 29:147–65 (1975).

Shebl, James M. *In This Wild Water: The Suppressed Poems of Robinson Jeffers.* Pasadena, Calif.: Ward Ritchie, 1976.

Squires, James Radcliffe. *The Loyalties of Robinson Jeffers.* Ann Arbor: University of Michigan Press, 1956.

Waggoner, Hyatt H. *The Heel of Elohim: Science and Values in Modern American Poetry.* Norman: University of Oklahoma Press, 1950.

White, Kenneth. *The Coast Opposite Humanity.* Llanfynydd, Carmarthen: Unicorn Bookshop, 1975.

Wilder, Amos N. *Theology and Modern Literature.* Cambridge: Harvard University Press, 1958.

Winters, A. Yvor. "Robinson Jeffers." *Poetry,* 35:279–86 (February 1930).

—*R. W. BUTTERFIELD*

Cotton Mather

1663–1728

ALL his life, Cotton Mather worried over his importance in history. Was he only an insignificant provincial, ineffectually trying to prop a moribund Puritan tradition with a grab bag of pedantic tags? Or was he chosen to counsel and lead his people into the final new day? His questions parallel our own. Is Mather any more than a literary grotesque, a credulous witch-burning embarrassment to American history and even to the history of American Puritanism? Or is he a neglected ancestor, the first to articulate some central problems of American culture? The question of whether he was central or irrelevant will not go away, in part because it was the problem he could never settle for himself.

Mather wanted urgently to be more than just another New England minister. On one of his special days of fasting and humiliation in 1692, he pleaded characteristically with God "that Hee would accept of Service at my hands, and make a singular Use of mee, in the Awakening of my people." To be singularly used was always Mather's hope. He had been a child prodigy, entering Harvard College at the age of eleven. He came from the most distinguished family of intellectuals that had yet existed in America, and he wanted to be worthy of that heritage. He believed, in fact, that God had promised him a special role in his country's history and that an angel had been dispatched to him bearing that promise.

Mather's hopes for prominence were in a sense fulfilled. From his early twenties until his death, he was pastor of the Second Church of Boston, perhaps the most prestigious pulpit in New England. From that vantage point he was able to embroil himself all his life in the politics of the colony; he led a small revolution, served as a spokesman for the next governor, and carried on a running battle for years with another governor. While still in his middle thirties he sent off to the press his *Magnalia Christi Americana* (1702), a vast history of New England.

Over the course of his life Mather produced a staggering volume of work; his bibliography numbers 468 separate items. In his own time he was acknowledged to be New England's representative in the world of letters, through his wide correspondence and his membership in the Royal Society. Both as the historian of the Puritans and as a vivid instance of Puritanism himself, he has never disappeared from the general consciousness; many people who have never read a word of his feel that they have a distinct sense of his personality.

In the style and emotional tone of his writings and in the extent of his public reputation, Cotton Mather has stood out from the Puritan ministers of New England. Only Jonathan Edwards, two generations his junior, is comparably recognized as a representative Puritan. Of that group, some were arguably more tough-minded than he, or more impressive as theologians. His father, Increase Mather, no doubt exercised more influence. But succeeding generations have remembered the name of Cotton Mather when they have sought for an exemplar of American Puritanism.

The cost of his prominence has been ridicule and abuse, beginning in his own time. His writings on witchcraft provoked a malicious and influential personal attack that has been successful up to the present in making him look like a superstitious booby and an exploiter of mass hysteria. John Oldmixon, an English Grub Street historian who relied on Mather's work for his own account of America, sneered at the *Magnalia* as a medley of "*Puns, Anagrams, Acrosticks, Miracles, Prodigies, Witches, Speeches, Epistles,* and other Incumbrances."

When Mather initiated inoculation for smallpox in 1721, the first significant medical innovation in America, he was rewarded with savage abuse in the newspaper of James Franklin. And James's sixteen-year-old brother Benjamin satirized Mather's often prolix defenses of benevolence by naming the author of his first periodical letters Silence Dogood. Mather accepted such abuse as an inevitable part of his calling. To be "despised and rejected of men" was even evidence of a Christlike vocation, and Mather was bolder than other Puritan ministers in seeking parallels between his own life and that of Jesus Christ. Abuse was to be suffered, not returned in kind. God would at last exalt his suffering servant.

What distressed Mather far more than abuse, as his diary and letters indicate, was indifference. There could hardly be any spiritual significance in being ignored and unread. His predecessors in the Puritan clergy had enjoyed considerable political influence and even power; his own career saw that influence fade almost completely. Puritanism was in decline by the end of the seventeenth century, and by the time

Mather died the old fighting faith had evolved into a staid and comfortable weekly routine.

However much Mather may have denied the decline, he was too sensitive an observer not to have registered the change. After the mixed response to the *Magnalia,* Mather found it impossible to find a publisher for his longest and most ambitious works. To his lasting humiliation, his longest work, a massive commentary on the Bible entitled the *Biblia Americana,* went unpublished (as it remains to this day). His audience, his publishers, and his friends of importance in England had silently pronounced him and his style of writing dated and irrelevant. "I have no Expectation that any thing performed by my Mean Hand, should find any great Reception on your side of the Water," he wrote to an English correspondent in 1724. "Especially since the prodigious Depravation of Gust among you, which renders every thing unpalatable, but what shall have Qualities which I will never be reconcil'd unto." The style he adopted was in his eyes part of his New England identity. If such a style was despised, it seemed as if America itself was pronounced inconsequential.

History has freed Mather from the irrelevance he feared. Not the victory of Puritanism but its defeat has thrust him into continuing grotesque prominence. For three centuries he has been an emblem of the narrow-minded, credulous, long-winded provincial minister. His contemporary adversaries have been succeeded by generations of commentators who have scored points against the Puritans by attacking him.

Cotton Mather is the favorite author of that transplanted New Englander Ichabod Crane; long hours of reading Mather's accounts of witchcraft prepared Ichabod for his midnight ride through Sleepy Hollow. During the nineteenth century a succession of Unitarian minister historians exorcised the specter of their Puritan ancestry by denouncing Mather. William Carlos Williams includes Mather as one of the life-denying forces in his narrative of false directions, *In the American Grain*. Katherine Anne Porter planned to write a biography of Mather, of which only a few sketches were published; in them he is depicted as a hideous prig.

Even when the Puritans enjoyed a revival of scholarly reputation in the twentieth century, at the hands of Samuel Eliot Morison and Perry Miller, Cotton Mather was conspicuously excluded from favor. The scorn of a great historian endures; Perry Miller uses Mather to exemplify the intellectual and spiritual disintegration of New England. The most recent students of Mather's career have tried to rescue him from this slough of abuse, but he will not readily be restored. I suspect that so long as the country's Puritan heritage is an uncomfortable memory, Cotton Mather will have to be ritually excoriated.

Cotton Mather's importance cannot be separated from the general impact of Puritanism on American writing and culture. Few would deny the lingering aftereffects of Puritan habits of mind in America—least of all those who have seen those influences as pernicious. But Mather's own experience was, rather, of Puritanism's waning force. He survived into a time terribly foreign to him, an era dominated by shrewd, quarrelsome, and secular men. In his last years he was all alone, the last man who had dared to believe in a glorious national destiny for America as the vanguard of Reformed Christianity.

Mather's real strength came from his consciousness, never fully explored or acknowledged, that he was defending a dying tradition. It was that tradition that made him distinctive, since he could no longer enjoy that sense of membership in an ongoing movement that first-generation Puritans could feel. That consciousness brought on his extraordinary productivity.

He was determined to restore the faith of the first days, even if that restoration could be no more than his own imaginative act. "But whether *New England* may *live* any where else or no," he wrote in the introduction to the *Magnalia,* "it must *Live* in our *History!*"

Even Mather's early years would have provided much to perplex and disorient him. The New England with which he identified so strongly was gradually growing and expanding. From the small beginnings at Plymouth and Massachusetts Bay, it had become four sturdy colonies that worshiped as independent congregations. But expansion had been mixed somehow with decline—a paradox for Mather, who saw God's hand in the expansion. Persistence in belief was somehow combined with vague symptoms of a disintegration of belief. As the church historian of New England he could not readily identify a single direction that the country was taking. Much of what he saw was discouraging.

The Puritans who settled in America started off with a belief in their own historic centrality. They were to be a city upon a hill, looked on by all nations. Puritanism in those days was a mass movement possessed by a sense of its own irresistible historic mission. So strong was the desire in early Massachusetts to hear at last an awakening ministry that a limit had to be set for the number of sermons a person might attend in a week. Succeeding generations of Puritans would look back on the zeal of those founding fathers and compare it to the faith of the first-century Christian Church, the great age of saints and martyrs. Such a standard of piety, recovered now after 1,500 years, could hardly fail to be a sign of Christ's glorious return and the beginning of the millennium. It does not need to be mentioned that such a belief was inherently vulnerable.

Even at the time of Mather's birth, on February 12, 1663, Puritanism as an international movement was in retreat. Charles II had recently recovered the throne that his father had lost in the English Civil War. English Puritans, their revolution won but unfulfilled, turned away from their former public ambitions and resigned themselves to being the godly minority in a country that would not be a New Jerusalem.

American Puritans clung to the earlier sense of historic mission, but their persistence was threatened in all directions. The first generation in New England had set high standards for admission to church membership in order to preserve the purity of each congregation. The standards were intimidating to the next generation; the so-called Half-Way Covenant of 1662 had to be introduced in order to baptize the children of those believers who could not report the requisite religious experiences.

The political solidarity of the church-state in Massachusetts was based on the charter granted in 1629, which allowed the colony virtual self-government. That charter conflicted with the royal government's colonial policy. Although adroit stalling measures preserved the charter from revocation for a while, the Massachusetts Puritans were ultimately protected by little besides the government's relative indifference to them. They could remain in charge at the cost of seeming to be insignificant.

There were more signs of deterioration during Mather's youth. To the north French Canada was expanding. A handful of Quakers appeared in Massachusetts preaching and disrupting Puritan religious services; banishment and, later, executions dealt with those inroads, but the punishments stirred up controversy inside the colony and out. In 1675 King Philip's War broke out suddenly, an Indian war that left the frontier settlements in ruins and their population decimated; the Indians of New England would never again seem like a people

reaching out for conversion. By the end of the reign of Charles II, when Mather was in his early twenties, the Massachusetts charter was revoked; the elected legislature was abolished, and under James II the colony was to be governed by the Anglican Sir Edmund Andros.

In response to such discouraging developments, the Puritan clergy took to denouncing the country for its errors and spiritual inertia in sermons of which the standard formula was later to be called the jeremiad. The denunciations of the jeremiad have been taken as symptoms of growing secularization among the people and despair among the clergy. It seems more accurate to say that those reiterated warnings of God's wrath kindled against New England represent the most fervent assertion of the country's continued importance in history. The New Englanders were still God's chosen people, the jeremiads said; and those whom God loves, he chastens. Increase Mather, the father of Cotton Mather, was perhaps the most powerful and influential of these denouncers of the country.

This was the situation in New England as Cotton Mather was growing up. He could not have viewed these confusing symptoms with detachment, nor could he have failed to try finding some meaning in them. His identity was tied to New England; unless God had a special purpose in mind for America he was nothing but a ridiculous provincial. Even his name attached him to America. "Cotton" came from his grandfather, John Cotton, one of the leading first-generation ministers. His other grandfather, Richard Mather, hardly fell short of Cotton in prominence. The two had done much to formulate and defend the New England position on theology and church government. Richard Mather had married John Cotton's widow; Increase Mather, Richard's youngest son, had then married his stepsister, Maria Cotton. Cotton Mather's connection to the New

England way was biological; he could not have discarded it without defying an especially potent set of ancestors.

His father Increase had graduated in one of the earliest Harvard classes and soon after emigrated to England, where he continued his education and preached in the last years of the Commonwealth. When the restoration of Charles II closed opportunities for him in England, he returned to America and soon succeeded to a prominent Boston pulpit. On the first important public occasion after his return, he disagreed with his father on the Half-Way Covenant, though he later changed his mind and joined in the consensus position.

Increase Mather's years in England helped to give him special prestige in New England; when he returned to England in 1688 to represent Massachusetts in negotiations for a new charter, he could move familiarly in social circles that included Richard Baxter, the leading dissenting minister in England, and Robert Boyle, the scientist and theologian. From 1685 to 1701 Increase Mather was president of Harvard. He continued to serve as the teacher of the Second Church in Boston (the North Church) until his death in 1723 at the age of eighty-four.

Cotton Mather spent his entire life in the shadow of his father, whom he survived by only five years. It was a shadow he welcomed. Prominent fathers can easily be a burden, an obstacle to the development of a distinct and viable identity. Cotton Mather, however, insisted on seeing his father as his greatest advantage. He became his father's associate at the Second Church and remained at that post until his death. In his own writing he would refer to himself as "Mr. Mather the younger."

Few people would openly challenge Increase Mather; his power and presence were too imposing. Cotton Mather was more exposed to attack. The father could be described in the New England context as cosmopolitan. The son never traveled out of New England and scarcely ever left Boston. Increase Mather had differed from his own father. Cotton Mather consistently took his father's public positions, in keeping with the commandment to honor his parents. Of Cotton Mather's profoundest hopes recorded in his diary, many regard fame and prominence for Increase Mather. In later life he referred to his father as *Adoni Avi,* meaning in Hebrew "Lord my Father." Only once is there any record of Cotton Mather's directly contradicting his father. When Increase, piqued by what he considered the colony's ingratitude, threatened to stay in England in 1690, his son wrote a stern reminder of his responsibilities to New England. To remain in England would be a yielding to temptation, wrote the younger Mather, a desertion of his identity, his family, and his son.

Throughout his life Cotton Mather looked to his father for approval. He did not seek to discover or establish an independent stance; real independence from his father and his father's beliefs would have been horrifying to him, because he believed his father to be a saved man. Instead he sought acceptance, a state inevitably beyond his control. For no matter how hard he tried or how dutiful he might appear, his acceptance could be withheld by his father or by God.

This was the psychological situation of any Puritan. A strong analogy linked Mather's father, the rightly constituted powers that be, and God; scripture demanded obedience to them all. Other Puritans might rebel against the parental heads of governments by seeing rebellion as obedience to God. Cotton Mather found such a position difficult to sustain; even at those moments in his political life when he was acting as a resister of authority, he insisted on voicing his resistance through the rhetoric of submission to a superior political authority. His father was for him "our patriarch," and he could describe showing his work to his father as if he were submitting it to a spiritual arbiter.

That Mather's father was loving and fiercely protective made his attachment all the firmer. Cotton Mather came, in fact, to expect from others the sort of deference and sense of place that he rendered unhesitatingly himself. In those changing times that deference was not so readily granted.

Much was expected of a child with such a father and such ancestry. Cotton Mather responded early to those expectations. His father's journal records the evidence of his early childhood piety. At the age of eleven he was ready to enter Harvard, demonstrating like other entering students a spoken command of Latin and a reading familiarity with Greek. He had already begun to study Hebrew. During his adolescence he was troubled by stuttering, to the point of thinking himself incapable of entering the ministry. Prayer and discipline brought his speech under control, so that he was able to preach his first sermon in 1680 at the age of seventeen.

Around this time he began keeping a sort of diary that he called his "Reserved Memorials," a record primarily of his spiritual exercises through life and the evidences of divine attention to him. Later on, the diary also recorded Mather's occasional bitter reflections on the neglect and abuse he was receiving. It was also a sort of spiritual account book; Mather would record his prayers and then later note in the margins the time when they had been fulfilled.

Mather never achieves the depth of self-analysis that one can see in the journals that Jonathan Edwards kept during his college years. Edwards' account of his sinfulness reveals a capacity for psychological penetration; Mather's recorded failings seem more the spontaneous outbursts of a complex and emotionally charged personality. "Was ever man more tempted, than the miserable Mather!" he exclaims in his diary in 1703. (The wonder of it can be expressed only in a sentence artfully rich in *m*

sounds.) "Should I tell, in how many Forms the Divel has assaulted me, and with what Subtilty and Energy, his Assaults have been carried on, it would strike my Friends with Horrour."

A powerful narcissistic impulse betrays itself throughout the "Reserved Memorials," but they preserve a fuller record of his interior life than we have from any other Puritan of comparable intellectual powers. His focus is on his own inner state; there are fewer of the specific details of daily life that are so well preserved in the diary of his friend Judge Samuel Sewall. The diary is a record of attempts to see in all his worldly encounters the material for spiritual insight. He prepares a list of ejaculatory prayers that he is to utter to himself on seeing commonplace events. On seeing a man on horseback, for example, he is to pray, "*Lord,* thy *Creatures* do serve that man; help him to serve his *Maker.*"

For Mather there was no contradiction involved in anticipating or even programming pious perceptions. He was continually at work trying to set his inner life in order, not through the attainment of some ruling insight but through painstaking attention to a host of separate duties. Benjamin Franklin later tried to achieve moral perfection by a comparable procedure, but he eventually gave up the effort and adjusted to a workable but imperfect character. Mather never stopped trying to make himself worthy.

Mather's attention to his own inner state was no doubt a manifestation of deep self-absorption. As a celebrator and inviter of himself in his diary, he can make Walt Whitman (in his *Song of Myself*) seem by comparison cool and dispassionate. But the demands of Puritan belief strongly seconded a person's impulse toward a preoccupation with self. Salvation was to be achieved by faith, a particular psychological condition, and not by works, the sum of one's overt behavior. The saved person had available a state called "grace," in which God entered into the heart to console and redeem it. To attain this state of grace it was necessary to be "reborn," a metaphor intended to suggest an utter change of personal identity. This rebirth was expected to be as important an event as one's original birth; it could be as terrible and wonderful as birth. But it was not easy to be sure that one had been reborn. If one returned completely to one's former life and mental habits, the experience assuredly had not been authentic.

In his teens, after graduation from Harvard, Mather had experienced traumatic fears that he was only a *"Refined Hypocrite,"* one who behaves well overtly and believes smugly in his own spiritual well-being. On the day of the last judgment the secret hearts of all would be laid bare; he would have to face the saved citizens of Boston as one of the elect or of the reprobate. Worse still, he thought, "*How shall* I be able to Look my own Father in the Face, at the Day of Judgment?" Cotton Mather turned to his father for spiritual counsel, and his father was strongly encouraging. Soon the son came to enjoy feelings of divine acceptance. Throughout his life Increase Mather himself lived with spiritual terrors and uncertainties that his son never experienced. Remaining unsure of his salvation, he wished for his son a better inner life than his own.

The message that Cotton Mather preached, especially in his early years, was one of hope and comfort. He was only twenty when he was asked to become pastor of the Second Church; he could not pretend to the wisdom and accumulated authority of the senior ministers of Massachusetts. What qualified him in his mind to speak was a sense of his special ancestry and of his special gift of eloquence. He eagerly recorded in his diary his success in moving congregations to strong emotions, and there is every reason to believe his reports. His emphasis on hope was new in Boston. His father's char-

acteristic note had been that of somber warning; in a sermon to Harvard undergraduates about the drowning of two students while ice skating he could see the deaths as an omen of the decline of the college, of the New England churches, and of New England itself. The son, by contrast, could find even in the execution of a murderer an occasion to depict God's forgiveness.

Though there were genuine temperamental differences between the two Mathers, their differences of emphasis derive also from a difference in their roles. New England churches, where possible, were supposed to have two ministers, a teacher and a pastor. The teacher was to speak of right doctrine; the pastor was to concern himself with the care of souls. This division of labor was another American Puritan tactic to keep in balance potentially divisive forces: a cold, intellectual rigor that might disregard psychological needs and a fervent evangelical spirit that might lack theological respectability. Increase Mather was the teacher at the Second Church; Cotton Mather was its pastor.

Mather's diary records how eagerly he embraced his pastoral responsibilities, praying for particular people who were still unredeemed, tending to poor widows, organizing prayer groups and seminars. It was also more natural for the pastor to respond spontaneously in his sermons to immediate occasions—the death of a child (including his own, in several cases), the departure of troops in a campaign against Canada, an outbreak of smallpox. On one occasion Mather delivered extemporaneously a sermon on God's voice speaking through the thunder, to accompany a violent storm that broke out at meeting time. Mather took special pride in his ability at what New Englanders would call "improving" an occasion.

By far the largest number of Cotton Mather's published works were sermons. Even his other works include or adapt sermons or sermonic rhetoric. To literary people the Puritan sermon has commonly seemed to bear no relation to the products of the literary imagination. It is even widely felt that the sermon is a form inherently dreary and deadening to both preacher and hearer. This attitude would perhaps have seemed curious to the Puritans, who found sermons profoundly appealing to the imagination. So emotionally satisfying were Puritan sermons in the mid-seventeenth century that they were able, in effect, to drive their competition, the London stage, out of business. For Puritans the sermon was a highly ambitious form of expression, since it was an attempt to convey the inexpressible presence of God. It was also the most valuable mode of public expression, because its aim was to produce salvation. The Puritans trimmed away other elements of the religious service so as to make the sermon stand out.

By itself a sermon was a dramatic occasion. The minister confronted the congregation; together, both confronted God. Often there was more tangible drama on hand as well. Cotton Mather's first published sermon, *The Call of the Gospel* (1686), was addressed to a condemned murderer, James Morgan, who had repented and hoped that his change of heart might save him in his imminent future existence. Though not unusual in itself, this one instance will serve as an example of Mather at work in his natural form. Even here, when Mather is only twenty-three, a striking difference between the father and the son appears, as well as those special qualities that made Mather's sermons distinctive.

Two other sermons were preached in the days before Morgan's execution, one of them by Increase Mather. Increase's sermon is a baleful underscoring of the heinous nature of the murder, which was done in a fit of passion with an iron spit. The sermon sets forth the condemned man as a horrid example of the consequences of drunkenness and neglect of sermons, sins that Morgan had confessed to committing. Although the prisoner had repented and urgently hoped before his death for divine forgiveness, Increase felt it necessary to emphasize in the preface to the published sermon that *"Late Repentance is seldom true."*

Cotton Mather's sermon takes quite a different approach. His text, from Isaiah, is an invitation from God to look on him and be saved, and Cotton insists on applying the text to Morgan as well. "Yea, who among us all, at the reading of these *glad Tidings* unto us, can forbear joyning with the Rapturous shouts of Heaven, with that Angelical, and Evangelical Out-cry ... *Glory to God in the highest, on earth peace,* Good-will *towards men?*" The rhetoric implies a minister and a congregation unified by a common fervent belief. Where Increase's sermon is austere, precise, and analytical, Cotton's language tries to convey a note of rapture and collective solidarity that includes even the criminal in chains before him. To generate this sense of rapture, he employs metaphors that are deliberately paradoxical, forcing his hearers out of the conventional sense of things. "Verily," he says, "a man does no sooner *look* on *Jesus Christ* in a way of *Believing,* than a Sentence of *Salvation* is passed upon him, and all the *Promises* yea, and all the *Attributes* of the Eternal Jehovah are engaged for the execution of it." Morgan's condemnation provides a metaphor for assured salvation.

Both the Mathers had spoken to Morgan, who had specially requested that Cotton preach for him. Also at Morgan's request, Cotton accompanied the condemned man on his final walk to the gallows. Already elevated to the status of a symbolic figure in the drama of salvation, Morgan turned to the young minister for his cue. "I beseech you Sir," Morgan said (as Mather recalled later), "speak to me. Do me all the good you can: my time grows very short:

your discourse *fits* me for my Death more than any thing." As the two men walked along the Boston streets, they went through a final cram course in redemptive theology; Morgan acknowledged the justice of his sentence and repented of his earlier anger at being buried in a mean grave.

The execution sermons (printed after the first edition with a transcript of Morgan's last conversation with Mather) sold well; Mather's sermon was the first fulfillment of his early promise and an indication of his readiness to involve himself actively in the spiritual lives of others. This trait has commonly been described as meddlesomeness, but it seems likely that Morgan was grateful for it in his last minutes.

Cotton Mather's sermons of his twenties were sufficiently in demand to be published. A common stance in those sermons was that of the redeemed youth speaking against unregenerate age. Nearly all the members of his congregation would have been older than he, and his status as a young prodigy was already making him vulnerable. It would have been hard for any young man to dominate a settled congregation by the sheer force of personality, even if his authority had not seemed to depend in part on his father. And the young Mather was not disposed to intimidate; he wished, rather, to inspire. He could not pretend to a large experience of the world; he relied rather on a body of surrogate experience derived from his multifarious reading, in the Bible, the church fathers, and the classics. (Mather's library eventually came to be the largest in New England and perhaps in all the colonies.)

The rhetoric of Mather's sermons required a sense of common feeling with his congregation that would enable him to express their spiritual longings and to experience their spiritual trials. But the established and comfortable congregation of the North Church was two generations away from the founding of the colony. When

Mather employed the first-person plural with them, his usage did not reflect a mutual sense of kinship. He was urging a relationship that his hearers must have understood as a sermonic convention.

Mather was grateful for the opportunity to preach to a congregation that was so large and had such traditions. By contrast Jonathan Edwards, who succeeded to the pulpit of a distinguished grandfather, always treated the Northampton church as his rightful portion and maintained that post with such independence of his congregation's good feelings that at last it removed him.

We can have no sure way of gauging the effect of Mather's sermons on his audiences. Many were printed and some reprinted, so he must have been widely read. But the Puritan sermon had always called for more than pleased acceptance. It was a call to salvation. The first generation of ministers often counted sermons as the decisive spiritual stimulants in their lives. When young Samuel Sewall was joining the church and agonizing over the authenticity of his own sense of conversion, he studied old sermons as textbooks in self-questioning. Cotton Mather's sermons seem not to have been studied in the same way. His popularity was clearly connected to certain literary qualities. It was his standing as a man of letters, as much as his piety and doctrinal correctness, that ensured his good reception in Boston.

But local success was not enough. His "Reserved Memorials" indicate that he hoped for a wider field of action; he felt that he had received divine assurances that Europe would soon be moved by the Holy Spirit to cast off false belief and that he himself would be significantly involved in that spiritual transformation.

Mather had no thought of leaving New England, so Europe was an audience that could be reached only by the written word. Even his earliest preserved letters indicate his interest in contemporary European history; when he writes about it, he displays an intense excitement with the scale of events and the rapidity of change. He feels no transoceanic separation from the campaigns of William of Orange or the policies of Louis XIV. Later he even learned French and Spanish so as to write treatises in those languages urging conversion. England was the audience he addressed most directly in his early years, after his own New England. The disparity in character between his two audiences was a problem he could never resolve and, I think, never fully understood.

Mather's pastoral impulses drew him into the politics of New England beginning in the late 1680's. From the start New England had proudly called itself a theocracy, and the minister's duty was to advise the temporal authorities about the Lord's will. After the Massachusetts charter was revoked and the arbitrary government of Sir Edmund Andros was imposed by James II in 1686, Increase Mather was sent to London to plead for a restoration of the charter.

Cotton Mather represented his father's position during the three years that Increase was in England. When the news of the Glorious Revolution arrived in Boston, the citizens used the opportunity to overthrow the government and imprison Andros. Cotton Mather was involved in the insurrection and wrote a defense of it, *A Declaration of Gentlemen and Merchants and Inhabitants of Boston, and the Country Adjacent,* that was published immediately (on April 18, 1689). That brief document links the overthrow of Andros (and implicitly of James II, his master) with the overthrow of Catholicism. In other respects it is an early appearance of the rhetoric of the Declaration of Independence. At this moment, when he was twenty-six, Cotton Mather had the greatest public influence that he would ever attain. He had engineered a revolution, albeit tiny, and defended it to the world.

His father found it impossible to win back the old charter from King William, whose military campaigns on the Continent delayed the decision for some time. The best deal that Increase Mather was able to get included a royal governor and an elected colonial legislature; the king would let the elder Mather nominate the governor. Back in Massachusetts, Increase was widely criticized for not getting back the old charter. In defense of his father Cotton wrote and circulated in manuscript a set of four "Political Fables." In each of them Increase is represented by some flying, exalted character that is beyond the range of the other figures, including Cotton himself. The opponents of the Mathers and the new charter are represented as contentious and ungrateful animals. In tone the fables are debonair and good-humored; they are more an attempt to defuse the antagonism than to counterattack. By describing the confrontation as a quarrel of animals, Mather lifts the issue out of the context of moral error, where satire or denunciation would be called for. His aim is not to ridicule his opponents but to cajole them into agreeing.

But the new charter remained widely unpopular. When Mather's handpicked governor, Sir William Phips, arrived, a body of disgruntled opposition was already mustered. Phips was a Massachusetts man who grew up a poor boy in Maine and made his fortune by recovering sunken treasure in the Caribbean. In 1690 he had joined the Mathers' church.

Cotton Mather eagerly took on the task of representing Phips's position. His attachment to Phips reveals his crucial weakness as a political writer. He had no genuinely independent position; he was an apologist, not an advocate. The role of apologist forced him into asserting that the new charter was even preferable to the old from the perspective of the people. He felt he had to defend Phips at any cost, even though the bluff former sea captain showed himself to be ill-tempered, imprudent, and incompetent as a commander in a disastrous military expedition against Quebec. Even after Phips's governorship broke down, Mather began a biography of him, an urgent defense of the governor as New England's representative. Phips was recalled to London and died there. Mather brought out the biography anonymously in 1697, though his hand in it was inescapable.

One function of the *Life of Phips* was to defend the Mathers' position. The previous seven years had brought the new charter, the witchcraft trials, and the ill-fated expedition against Quebec; they were not easy years to applaud. It seemed natural to Mather to use biography as his means. The wisdom of the Mathers' policies would be vindicated by their intimate connection with the life of a redeemed and public-spirited man. The genre of the Protestant saint's life dictated a glorious ending won through difficulties; difficulties could thereby seem a portent of the happy end. Unfortunately, Phips himself was not really plausible as a saint, and the Mather policies still looked vulnerable. Cotton Mather's political stances were inconsistent, and not simply because he made considered adjustments to new circumstances. He tried both to defend his father's position and to seem to speak for the consensus position of New England as a whole.

Mather was really temperamentally unsuited to cope successfully with the political life of Massachusetts in his times. His special virtues as a writer brought on that unsuitability. His eye was too fixed on an ideal vision of New England, a mythic version of its history, for him to respond appropriately to the factional differences then current. As a writer he faced a dilemma. His ultimate concern was with history, not local but universal; he wrestled, as his ancestors had, with the question of how New England fit into the cryptic plans in the Bible for redemption of the world.

In the course of his life Mather became increasingly preoccupied by the millennium, the

grand conclusion to history. Yet his belief in the existence of such a grand preordained scheme obliged him to examine closely the local symptoms that might suggest God's intentions. He could be most sure of himself in dealing with an event like the Andros insurrection, an occasion in which dramatic actions were to be taken with some awareness of larger meanings. But in the petty politics of Massachusetts under the new charter, he could find no sense of proportion. He was not inclined to dismiss an event as trivial. Instead, since he knew that God communicates continually with his people, he seized on the trivial as evidence of God's will.

Mather's attempts at anonymity in the *Life of Phips* suggest another problem. He was like a man who believes that his voice is too loud but cannot make it softer. His early problems with stuttering must have taught him the importance of speaking out clearly. His experience and his culture would not have prepared him for anonymity or the concealment of identity; how could one conceal being a Mather? Humility was a crucial spiritual virtue that might seem counter to self-display, but humility could also entail the public confession of one's own inadequacies and imperfections. Mather's political involvements in the late 1680's and 1690's left him feeling exposed, inescapably the object of public attention. He could not conceal his own style, nor could he pretend to be someone else. And from Saint Augustine in particular, whom he quotes throughout his writings, he would have learned the dangers to one's soul of pretending to be another person.

Yet concealment of identity was a prevailing literary strategy in his times. The English Augustan writers were perfecting a prose style that brought out ironies and nuances and avoided insistent and unqualified statement. Mather at times tried to conceal his own hand or to curtail his use of the first person. When he began his autobiography, which he entitled *Paterna,* he resolved not to say who he was. The omission was awkward, because it prevented him from referring to any of his own writings and because the manuscript was specifically meant to be read by his own son and was not explicitly intended for publication. (It was finally published in 1976.) It was far more natural for Mather to proclaim his own authorship boldly, as he did in the general introduction to the *Magnalia Christi Americana.* He describes there various strategies of anonymity or concealment that he might have employed. "Whereas now I freely confess, 'tis COTTON MATHER that has written all these things."

The *Magnalia Christi Americana* (the title means "great works of Christ in America") is an immense history of New England, running to 850 closely printed folio pages in its first edition of 1702. Mather's subtitle reads "the Ecclesiastical History of New-England, from Its First Planting in the Year 1620. unto the Year of our LORD, 1698," but he was in no way limiting it by its title to a mere aspect of New England history. Other histories of New England had been written. Governor William Bradford, for example, had written *Of Plymouth Plantation,* an extensive and often eloquent history of the Pilgrims. Mather consulted Bradford's unpublished manuscript and followed it closely. But none of the earlier histories was as ambitious in scope as the *Magnalia.* It quickly superseded all other records as a source of information about New England, and even those who criticized or ridiculed Mather borrowed from him and accepted his view of events as the standard Puritan view.

Benjamin Franklin cites the *Magnalia* in the early pages of his *Autobiography* for Mather's characterization of his grandfather. Mather himself quoted the English dissenting minister Vincent Alsop, who had said of it that his colleagues should read the whole thing through twice, as he had done. In a half-mocking but appreciative mention of Mather in 1869, Harriet Beecher Stowe pointed to the work's centrality to New England's historical self-awareness. And Nathaniel Hawthorne paid Mather's literary imagination a mixed but genuine compliment in describing the *Magnalia* as a "strange, pedantic history, in which true events and real personages move before the reader with the dreamy aspect which they wore in Cotton Mather's singular mind."

The work as a whole was divided into seven books (the number seven had, of course, numerous biblical significances). The first book, "Antiquities," describes the earliest conceptions of the New World and the first process of settling. The second book is devoted to the biographies of the governors of New England, starting with William Bradford and John Winthrop and continuing to Mather's own time; he added the already published *Life of Phips* as an appendix to that book. In the third book Mather provides biographies of sixty of the founding ministers of New England. Harvard College and its most significant graduates are the subject of the fourth book. (Writing before Yale, the second college, had been founded, Mather could see this as a full account of advanced education in New England.) The fifth book records the church platforms and assorted statements of principle that assemblies of the American Puritans had arrived at, going back to the Cambridge Platform of 1648 in which Richard Mather had been instrumental. The sixth book is a loosely organized collection of strange and marvelous occurrences that manifested the presence of God's will in New England. And the seventh book presents a record of the conflicts that the church in New England had gone through—with Roger Williams, Anne Hutchinson and the Antinomians, the Quakers, the Indians in King Philip's War, and the war with the French and Indians that had been going on since 1688. The structure of the entire work is loose and flexible; individual sections could be filled out by pieces that Mather had already published separately. His biography of his younger brother Nathaniel and a sermon on Boston city improvement, for example, are included in the *Magnalia.*

The inclusion of such material has been used as evidence that the work as a whole is merely an anomalous omnium-gatherum that lacks any coherent structure or sense of movement. But Mather felt strongly that his method of organization permitted him greater scope. When Daniel Neil's history of New England, with a more conventional organization, appeared seventeen years later, Mather complained that its chronological sequence had made it merely "a dry political story."

Mather understood that a chronological order would lead to a necessary emphasis on specific events, and the real history of New England that he wished to chronicle had involved much more. When he writes the life of John Winthrop, the first governor of Massachusetts, in the second book, his title is "Nehemias Americanus," the American Nehemiah. The crucial fact that Mather wants to convey is not that Winthrop was a patient and adroit leader of the young colony but that he realized in America the biblical role of Nehemiah, the just governor who built the walls of Jerusalem. Winthrop's actions and personal qualities are implied by his relation to the Bible; "Nehemias Americanus" is the most inclusive description that can be made of him.

Much of the *Magnalia* is biography. In relying on biography to convey the growth of the American church-state, Mather was imitating the precedent of John Foxe's *Acts and Monuments of These Latter and Perillous Dayes* (1559), best known as *Foxe's Book of Martyrs.* (That work, probably the most likely book after the Bible to be owned by an English-speaking Protestant, describes the growth of the English Reformation as a story of individual martyrs,

especially under Queen Mary.) For Foxe, and in a somewhat different way for Mather, the divinely inspired character of the national church can best be dramatized by seeing the lives and deaths of its saints.

As a biographer Mather was careful about searching out facts. He does include material critical of his subjects, always including the attacks made against them in their own lives. He says of John Cotton, for example, that he was perhaps too self-denying and forbearing. There is even humor in many biographies, although characteristically it takes the form of illustrating his subjects' good natures. The names of these ministers and governors are the occasion for continual puns: Samuel Stone is "a precious *jem,*" "a *Load*-Stone and a *Flint*-Stone"; Ralph Partridge had the innocence of a dove and the loftiness of an eagle and at last "*took Wing* to become a *Bird of Paradise.*" Names were not irrelevant to Mather, whose urge was always to find meaning everywhere.

Overall, despite the individual characterizing touches, the impression that these biographies leave is not one of diversity. For one thing, there is no clear sense of difference between them and Mather; there is no acknowledgment that aspects of their lives have been uncommunicated and are not fully known and understood. There is no genuine order of priority among them. Each in turn is remarkable for goodness, but no one stands out above the others.

In the third book Mather includes a set of four longer biographies entitled *Johannes in Eremo* (John in the Wilderness) as well as *The Triumphs of the Reformed Religion in America,* a longer biography of John Eliot, the apostle to the Indians. These are out of proportion with the other lives of ministers because they had already been published separately. The other ministers treated in this book are organized in the order in which they died, rather than in any order of importance or merit. It would be hard to say, on the basis of the *Magnalia* alone, which figures had been central in the making of New England. The subjects blur together as one reads.

A main motivation for writing the *Magnalia* was to vindicate New England's existence. In the first chapter of the first book Mather alludes to a pronouncement of Pope Zacharias in the eighth century that it was heresy to believe in the existence of unsuspected and inhabited lands in the antipodes of Europe. The Church of Rome, says Mather, is not only the enemy of Protestantism; it has denied the existence of America. Even Saint Augustine denied that human beings lived anywhere besides Europe, Asia, and Africa. The American continents had been concealed by God until the right moment in history, Mather observes—until the Renaissance and the Reformation revived true learning and true religion. America has a special place in biblical prophecy, according to him; in the last days before the end of the world, the four corners of the earth will acknowledge Christ. America's place in prophecy explains its importance in history.

All historians have been restive with Mather's treatment of his material, but he was not really writing history. Though Mather seems to have been careful in his use of materials and energetic in seeking information, the *Magnalia* in essence is really an exposition of the ways in which New England's history fits a biblical pattern. The history in the Old Testament of the Jews, who had escaped from Egypt and then later from captivity in Babylon to settle in the land that the Lord had given them, was for Mather a systematic prefiguration of the story of God's people in New England. The resemblances were not fortuitous but inevitable. Bradford had been an American Moses, leading his people into an American wilderness. John Eliot, the Puritan missionary to the Indians who translated the Bible into Algonquin, is com-

pared to Enoch and Aaron. The number of references to the Hebrew patriarchs, church fathers, and leaders of the Reformation can seem baffling unless the reader recognizes that they are central to the work's interpretive scheme.

Mather's narrative procedure is based on a method of biblical interpretation called typology. According to typology the events and personages of the Old Testament are meant to be seen as a systematic foreshadowing of the life of Christ, who is the great antitype (the figure whom those types describe). Typology is thus a mode of symbolic interpretation, but the symbolic relationships are not subject to varying interpretation. Meaning is fixed and intrinsic; it is the work of God. Just as the Hebrews had come out of Egypt through the Red Sea, Christ was baptized in water by John before he began his ministry. As Moses had given laws or as David had led the people of God, Christ was lawgiver and king. In all ways Christ was greater than the types of him, but the types serve to explain more fully the significance of his life.

From the beginning the American Puritans had described their collective experience in terms of such biblical parallels. Mather's *Magnalia* realizes that rhetoric in literature, laboriously dramatizing the parallels between Israel and New England until at last his reader can no longer see the uniqueness of events or personalities. New England's history becomes, in Mather's hands, a fulfillment of biblical prophecy.

One inherent danger for a Christian in describing New England as a new Israel is that the prophecies describe doom as well as promise. Israel broke its covenant with the Lord. Mather cannot affirm the past without warning about the present, and yet his own impulse to celebrate the goodness of New England would not permit him to see episodes such as the antinomian controversy as anything but a momentary interruption in the colony's development. There had been change since the first generation, but change had to mean progress, ultimately considered, since every change brings the millennium closer. The date of that great event was already set, and Mather tried hard to guess it. At one point he had speculated on 1697; he later predicted that Roman Catholicism might collapse on schedule in 1716. His thoughts in his later years turned increasingly toward describing an apocalyptic future that would vindicate his persistence in the New England way. In this light he read the conflicting signs of the present.

The *Magnalia* insists on classical parallels along with the biblical parallels for New England's history. Winthrop is like Lycurgus of Sparta or Numa Pompilius of early Rome, lawgivers to their peoples. But Winthrop is also superior to the figures of the classical past, through his peculiar qualities of Christian self-restraint. "In fine, the *Victories* of an *Alexander,* an *Hannibal,* or a *Caesar* over *other Men,* were not so Glorious, as the *Victories* of this great Man over *himself,* which also at last prov'd *Victories* over *other Men.*" It was traditional to combine classical and biblical antecedents, especially in the most ambitious work: Dante Alighieri and John Milton, for example, systematically blend these two great sources of knowledge. The *Magnalia* is full of echoes and references to Milton and Vergil. It might be best, in fact, to consider the work as designed to be an epic.

Naturally the epic writer seeks not only to record but also to transform his material. Mather's epic intentions declare themselves from the first sentence of the general introduction. His real subject is not so much facts as wonders. "I WRITE the *Wonders* of the CHRISTIAN RELIGION, flying from the Depravations [depraved conditions] of *Europe,* to the *American Strand.*" The epic qualities of the work explain in part Mather's style, which has been much discussed and not often appreciated. Mather's sentences are long and frequently filled with quotations in Latin and Greek. Mather could not really resist such flourishes in a work so grandly conceived. Such choice flowers, he admitted, were "almost unavoidably putting themselves into the Authors Hand." Yet he also described his as "a Simple, Submiss, Humble *Style.*"

The contradictions in Mather's own descriptions of his style suggest that he was trying to do many things at the same time. His sentences labor to combine lament and encomium, history and prophecy, decline and promise, humility and exultation. "I am sure *New-England* has a *True Church* to People it," he could write in book 7, and further on in the same paragraph, "it must after all be confessed, that we have one Enemy more pernicious to us than all the rest, and that is *our own Backsliding Heart,* which has plunged the whole Country into so wonderful a *Degeneracy,* that I have sometimes been Discouraged from Writing the *Church-History* of the Country. . . ."

The discrepancies in the record do not vex Mather much. For him they are a proof that Christ's great works in America cannot be wholly fathomable. Sir Henry Vane, briefly a governor of Massachusetts and an adversary of Winthrop, is a puzzling figure for Mather. Without further effort at interpretation he quotes a contemporary criticism of Vane's term as governor and a description of Vane's heroic death.

When Mather describes the witchcraft episode in Salem, he remarks on the confessions of witchcraft that were retracted after the episode was over. "And though more than twice Twenty had made such voluntary . . . Confessions, that if they were all *Sham,* there was therein the greatest Violation made by the Efficacy of the *Invisible World,* upon the *Rules of Understand-*

ing Humane Affairs, that was ever seen since *God made Man upon the Earth,* yet they did so recede from their *Confessions,* that it was very clear, some of them had been hitherto, in a sort of a *Preternatural Dream,* wherein they had said *of them selves,* they *knew not what themselves.*" Both confessions and retractions were wonderful. At a time when such a capacity for wonderment was increasingly identified as superstition and credulity, Mather clung to the capacity, because he believed such wonders were the material of all contact between God and man.

Cotton Mather is particularly associated with the witchcraft trials in Salem in 1692. For in the midst of the public furor, he wrote a small book entitled *The Wonders of the Invisible World,* which defends the witchcraft trials and tries to show them to be a fitting stage in New England's history. All those who have been disposed to see him as ridiculous, credulous, and ultimately a menace to civilization have seized on this work as proof. Those who have disliked the Puritans anyway have been happy to agree. Those who have respected the Puritan contribution have often contemptuously dismissed the book and its author. It is certain that *The Wonders of the Invisible World* was disastrous for Mather's reputation both in his own time and afterward.

The episode at Salem has taken on a mythic significance that far exceeds its historical importance at the time. There were scarcely any measurable political, economic, or social consequences of the event for the colony at large. Yet everyone with even a smattering of knowledge of colonial American history has heard of the Salem witchcraft trials. And the meaning of the events there is supposedly also common knowledge. For one thing, it is thought, the whole occurrence was a public turmoil stirred up by the Puritan ministers, who skillfully worked their gullible congregations into a frenzy as a means of exercising control. According to this view, Cotton Mather had the foremost responsibility for stirring up the community. There was no witchcraft being practiced at Salem, the popular version goes—nothing but a few hysterical and manipulative adolescent girls. Many people assume that the American Puritans were unusual in believing in witchcraft and that such a belief is a sure sign of a twisted mind. So Mather's firm belief in the existence of witches can best be explained by dissecting his lamentable psychological state.

This version of the events at Salem is an almost unrecognizable distortion of the facts. That the myth should persist so long, despite the careful efforts of historians and literary scholars, suggests that the myth is an important cultural phenomenon in its own right. The Salem witchcraft episode is a tragedy that has been turned into a morality tale, complete with all the forces of good and evil. The Puritans themselves, who had little taste for tragedy but a vast appetite for stories of good and evil, would not have agreed with the mythic version, but they would understand its form.

Witchcraft was in fact practiced in Salem, though probably not much more than a few spells were cast to predict the future. Virtually everyone involved—accusers, accused, and the general public—believed in the existence of witches and witchcraft before anything ever happened. The Bible acknowledged and condemned the existence of witchcraft; so did many learned men of the sixteenth and seventeenth centuries, some of whom dabbled in it themselves. The tragic victims who went to the gallows protesting their innocence (witches were hanged, not burned, in America) believed in the existence of witchcraft as firmly as everyone else; they would not endanger their immortal souls by admitting to witchcraft and thereby escaping execution.

The incident in Salem was only an American

manifestation of a widespread European fascination with spirits and the occult during the Renaissance. One side of that fascination took the form of researches into magic and the occult by such philosophers and scientists as Giordano Bruno and Sir Isaac Newton. (Newton practiced alchemy, speculated on the validity of judicial astrology, and wrote a posthumously published book on the biblical prophecies.) Another side of that fascination appeared in the thousands of executions for witchcraft during the seventeenth century; 160 people were burned to death in Wurzburg in 1629, for example. Against such a background Cotton Mather's belief looks a good deal less bizarre.

Individual cases of witchcraft had appeared earlier in the century in Massachusetts, though they were hardly common occurrences. A few people were convicted of witchcraft and executed. The records about the supposed witches suggest them to have been emotionally disturbed; at least some of them probably believed that they were in league with the devil. What made the outbreak at Salem noteworthy was that there seemed to be a complex conspiracy of witches involved. Salem had a history of quarrels and bad feeling. The sense of frustration and malaise that afflicted the whole colony— the revocation of the charter, wars with the Indians, a general feeling of lost purpose—must have been a factor. Sir William Phips ordered a special court to hear the cases in June 1692. The Mathers and other ministers issued advice to the judges to beware of relying on spectral evidence but to proceed vigorously against any possible demonic conspiracy.

As the summer advanced, the court found accusations multiplying, and it sent nineteen men and women to the gallows. The public had strongly supported the initial investigations, but by the end of the summer, opinion was shifting. At an informal meeting of the judges and Cotton Mather at Samuel Sewall's house, it was decided that the younger Mather should publish an account of the court proceedings. The book was hastily written, cobbled together from odd materials that Mather had at hand; it was ready for the press in about three weeks.

It was certainly natural for Cotton Mather to write such a defense of the court. Its members were friends of his; he was in a familiar position as an apologist. The court had been convened by Increase Mather's handpicked governor, Phips, who had been on the frontier all summer fighting the Indians and was now insisting that the reasons for the court's existence be defended against possible attacks. Moreover, Cotton Mather had his own personal and ideological reasons for discussing the world of spirits.

For others the Salem witches were an urgent problem without any larger metaphysical significance. For Mather the strange behavior of the possessed girls and the reports he had obtained about unnatural events were evidence concerning one of the great philosophical questions of the century. Since René Descartes's destruction of the old edifice of Aristotelian physics, one of the great problems had been whether physical events took place through mechanical causes alone or whether spirits were engaged in some way in causation. Descartes's mechanistic philosophy was hardly satisfactory as a description of many physical phenomena; even worse, in the eyes of his critics, it seemed to deny that God and his angels were active in running the world. The view that spirits did not direct phenomena was called, by Mather and others, Sadduceeism, after the early Jewish sectarian movement that denied the existence of spirits and an afterlife.

Cotton Mather knew that angels existed, because he had seen one himself. His diary records in Latin the visit of an angel while he was alone and praying fervently in his study. The angel was a dazzlingly bright-winged creature; it promised him that his books would be published in Europe as well as America and that he would play a great part in the momentous final events shortly to come. And the angel applied to him the description in Ezekiel of a cedar in Lebanon of great beauty and stature and many branches. His diary also records at various points what he called "Particular Faiths," powerful inward assurances of some good that the Lord would do him or his family.

To affirm the existence of active angels meant affirming the existence of active devils as well. One side effect of Mather's more hopeful preaching message was a special emphasis in his sermons on the importance of angels and devils. Where his father was more likely to locate evil in the depths of the human heart, Cotton tended to see evil as something carried by devils, who are external agents.

Several years before the Salem events Mather had examined and written about the case of several Boston children, the Goodwins, who had supposedly been bewitched by an old Irish woman, Goodwife Glover. He wrote up the record of his investigation of the whole case in a pamphlet called *Memorable Providences* (1689). He clearly thought of himself as a careful empirical observer; he notes both the ambiguities in Goody Glover's confession and the uncanny behavior of the Goodwin children. When he wrote to the Salem court reporter, Stephen Sewall, for representative trial transcripts, he appealed for the most convincing cases. "I am willing," he wrote, "that when you write, you should imagine me as obstinate a Sadducee and Witch-advocate as any among us: address mee as one that Believ'd Nothing Reasonable." Mather saw *The Wonders of the Invisible World* as both a vindication of Massachusetts justice and a further demonstration of the work of spirits in the world. As the letter to Stephen Sewall indicates, he was not testing a hypothesis; he was building a case, and he seems to have been worried about convincing himself as well.

Mather's understanding of the behavior of spirits helped him to explain the sudden outbreak in Massachusetts:

The *New-Englanders* are a People of God settled in those, which were once the *Devil's* Territories; and it may easily be supposed that the *Devil* was exceedingly disturbed, when he perceived such a People here accomplishing the Promise of old made unto our Blessed Jesus, *That He should have the Utmost parts of the Earth for his Possession.*

The Salem incident was therefore a counterattack in a cosmic battle. Although Mather warns in the conventional way that witchcraft was a sign of God's wrath for the colony's degeneracy, his greatest emphasis is on the collective solidarity that he hopes this crisis will bring. If only they can all weather this crisis together, "we shall soon Enjoy *Halcyon* Days with all the *Vultures* of Hell, *Trodden under our Feet.*" He notes the dissatisfactions with the proceedings that some people have shown, and he approves of that spirit of caution just as he approves of the zeal of the prosecutors. The devil's most dangerous work, he says, is in sowing discord among good men:

The Embroiling, first, of our *Spirits,* and then of our *Affayrs,* is evidently, as considerable a Branch of the Hellish Intrigue, which now vexes us, as any one Thing whatever. The Devil has made us like a *Troubled Sea;* and the *Mire* and *Mud* begins now also to heave up apace.

As he hurried to prepare the book for publication, Mather added to it various accounts about the detection of witchcraft. He included a sermon that he had delivered two months earlier; on that occasion he had speculated enthusiastically that the witchcraft outbreak was a convincing sign of the imminent end of the world. The Bible indicates that the times just before the end will be particularly difficult; the sermon compares the predestined history of the world with the lives of the righteous, who often experience trials and despair not long before their last moments. The sermon concludes by conjecturing that on the basis of biblical prophecies as applied to the history of the Reformation it may well be that the end of the world will come in only five years, in 1697.

After filling out the book further with materials at hand, Mather added the accounts from several trials that had taken a long time to get to him. The book as a whole is a strange amalgam that shows the haste with which it was assembled. It was popular enough to be reprinted several times in Boston and London and then again in several editions in the mid-nineteenth century.

A few days before *The Wonders* appeared, Increase Mather published a treatise entitled *Cases of Conscience Concerning Evil Spirits Personating Men,* a critique of the use of spectral evidence to convict witches. The result of Increase's treatise was the collapse of the court at Salem and the eventual freeing of those who were awaiting trial or had already confessed. Once again father and son seemed to be working at cross purposes.

The difference between the two books seemed so great that the Mathers found it necessary to publish a denial that Cotton Mather had disagreed with his father. The final result of the whole controversy was that Increase Mather earned the credit for stopping the proceedings at the same time that Cotton Mather seemed to be persisting in the delusion. Cotton did feel the same scruples about spectral evidence that his father did, but he was too absorbed in justifying his friends on the court, and ultimately in justifying New England itself, to acknowledge the problem. Five years later, on the occasion of a public day of fasting and humiliation, Sewall publicly recanted his role in the proceedings. Cotton Mather never recanted officially, but in

his *Life of Phips* he describes the entire affair as too perplexing for human understanding to resolve perfectly. Sewall bravely acknowledged the evil in his own conduct. Cotton Mather saw the colony as confused by forces too subtle for it.

Mather did not have to wait long for the attitudes expressed in *The Wonders* to receive scathing criticism. In 1700 Robert Calef, a Boston merchant, published in London his *More Wonders of the Invisible World,* assembled out of his correspondence with Mather, his own descriptions of Mather's practices in diagnosing witchcraft, and textual examinations of Mather's writings on witchcraft. It depicts Mather as compounded of equal parts of gullibility, meddlesomeness, and a secret prurience, which manifested itself in fondling the bodies of possessed women. Opponents of the Mathers probably provided materials for Calef, whose writing suggests both industriousness and venom. Mather knew what Calef was up to before Calef's book went to press, but he limited himself to prayers and ineffectual denunciations. It was hard for him to accept the fact that someone in Boston could be out to get him and even harder for him to accept the possibility that God would permit such a thing to happen.

As the century turned, Mather found the Particular Faiths he was receiving increasingly baffling. They promised further important public services for his father. Instead, Increase Mather's adversaries in 1701 maneuvered him out of his post as president of Harvard. Even closer to home, Cotton's wife appeared to be dying. Particular Faiths assured him that she would recover, but her condition over a period of months gradually worsened. Mather tried intense prayers and fasting, but to no avail.

The frustration of the Particular Faiths, like the ambiguous ending of the witchcraft trials, left Mather unsure about his relationship to the invisible world. He did not question his faith, but as the eighteenth century began his practice changed subtly, becoming less declarative, more meditative. Before, a typical sermon might have been *A Midnight Cry,* which is full of exhortations in the first-person plural and calls for a general renewal of the covenant in his congregation and a more vibrant faith. His characteristic later sermon depicted the pious individual, not the saved community. Piety and good deeds became his great emphases over the last thirty years of his life.

Piety was the crucial concept in an international movement in the early eighteenth century. Its advocates in Lutheran Germany came to be called Pietists, and Pietism was the great theological issue there during this period. Cotton Mather came in contact with that movement through his reading and correspondence; Auguste Francke of the University of Halle, the leading Pietist theologian of the time, was an important correspondent and influence.

The old connection between the American Puritans and their dissenting brethren in England, which had been vital for Increase, was fading for Cotton. His correspondence in the eighteenth century indicates that he detected signs of incipient Deism in the writings of the English dissenters. Moreover, they seemed insufficiently energetic about helping to get his books published. He turned more to the Church of Scotland; in 1710 the University of Glasgow made him a Doctor of Divinity, a title of which he was particularly proud. The greatest intellectual influence, though, came from Pietists at Halle.

Piety referred to a spiritual state with certain distinctive features. In many ways akin to Puritanism and springing from the same roots in the Reformation, Pietism preached the essential importance of experiential religion. It concentrated less on matters of dogma or church polity; Lutheran and Puritan Pietists might disagree about the meaning of the Eucharist or the

organization of congregations, but they were united in their concern for the holy life. Pietism pointed to a more passive, accepting attitude toward life. Where an earlier Puritanism had more often stressed virtues of discipline, courage, and resoluteness, Pietism stressed humility, obedience, purity, patience, and a rejection of worldly vanities. This tendency to deny the world had subtle political implications. Outwardly, Mather never contradicted the belief in New England's destiny so strongly expressed in the *Magnalia* and *The Wonders of the Invisible World,* but his thought moved away from visions of a special national mission. His diary records his doubts and discouragements with the direction of events in New England; Pietism offered a way around such doubts.

Earlier American Puritanism had been especially preoccupied with the conversion experience itself—whether it could be prepared for, its relation to the efficacy of the sacraments, its role as a precondition to church membership. For the first two generations of Puritan thinkers, that first entry of the Holy Spirit into the elect person's heart was crucial; righteousness in thought and action afterward were examined as evidence of whether the experience had been genuine. For Cotton Mather and the Pietists the history of one's spiritual life after this first acceptance was more important; they thought in terms of development, renewal, and ultimately of maturity. Puritans had always honored aged righteousness, but they had speculated less on the stages that would lead to a godly old age. Much of Mather's preaching and writing in his last thirty years was designed to help lead a person through significant and recurrent elements in the pious life, like childbearing, solitary prayer, obedience to parents, instructing children, and setting an example for others. In the words of the subtitle to *The Heavenly Conversation,* one of his sermons particularly influenced, according to its preface, by Francke and the German Pietists, he was inculcating "the Methods of Conversing With a Glorious CHRIST in *Every Step* of our Life."

Deeds of pure love were Mather's preoccupation. He did not take part in the line of acute religious psychologists in American Puritanism that stretched from Thomas Shepard, Thomas Hooker, and John Cotton to the greatest of them, Jonathan Edwards. Rather, he preached righteous actions, the doing of good. There has been a tendency, therefore, even among some of the most sophisticated Puritan scholars, to see Mather as one for whom good deeds were enough for salvation, as if Mather had somehow bumbled into what any Puritan would consider heresy. Mather knew that actions considered merely as overt behavior did not save anyone; he was speaking of actions that come spontaneously from a good heart. By guiding a person to right behavior, moreover, he hoped to be guiding him to a better heart. The best-known title of one of Mather's most important works expresses his intentions directly—*Essays To Do Good.*

Its longer title, *Bonifacius. AN ESSAY Upon the GOOD, that is to be Devised and Designed, BY THOSE Who Desire to Answer the Great END of Life, and to DO GOOD While they Live,* reveals Mather's complicated intentions. The great end of life is still to glorify God; *Bonifacius* proposes to provide certain patterns by which God may be glorified in the world. First published in 1710, it was one of Mather's most popular works. It was revived early in the nineteenth century and went through nineteen editions by 1845. Part of the impetus behind the little book was the endorsement of Benjamin Franklin, who gave it credit for influencing him at an early age. In a letter to Mather's son Samuel in 1784, he wrote that the book "gave me such a turn of thinking, as to have an influence on my conduct through life; for I have always set a greater value on the character of a *doer of good,* than on any other kind of reputation; and if I have been, as you seem to think, a useful citizen, the public owes the advantage of it to that book."

Though it is instructive to see Franklin and Mather thus linked together, there were central differences in what they expected from good deeds. Franklin always believed that good deeds offered authentic satisfaction; he took the sort of pleasure in his benevolent achievements that one can take from one's own possessions. Mather, on the other hand, had insisted that good deeds were an urgent duty that could never be done sufficiently or adequately. Our times of unfruitfulness ought properly to be a source of humility and frustration, to remind us of how little we have really done. To do good, Mather prescribes the spiritual state of Puritanism—a complementary relationship between anxiety and the urge to be up and doing.

Both Mather and Franklin favored forming voluntary organizations for benevolent purposes—the prototype of the Kiwanis and the Rotary. Mather advocated societies of young men who would meet weekly, keep a helpful eye on each other, and organize their discussions around useful religious topics, "not the *disputable* and *controversial* matters, but the points of *practical piety.*" Soon after settling in Philadelphia in 1726, Franklin formed such an organization, called the Junto, organized according to rules similar to those Mather recommended except that practical piety had shifted subtly into civic benevolence. Franklin, and after him the other young men in the group, saw much to be done for Philadelphia, and by the time they were through, the city had a lending library, a system of volunteer fire companies, a college, and a modern hospital. Franklin's kind of good deeds transformed Philadelphia.

Mather had no program for Boston; he never got any group going in a sustained way, in part because he saw the minister in such a group as a spiritual coordinator rather than a member. When Mather spoke of specific improvements, he could not be content to see them as goods in themselves:

Perhaps almost every *Proposal* to be now mentioned, may be like a *Stone* falling on a *Pool; Reader,* keep thy Mind *Calm,* and see whether the Effect prove not so! That one *Circle* (and *Service*) will produce another, until they Extend, who can tell, how far? and they cannot be reckoned up.

Ralph Waldo Emerson would later use the image of the circle as a symbol of spreading influence. Like Mather he had far less relish than Franklin for the concrete and limited good of something like the Franklin stove.

In many ways *Bonifacius* looks forward to modern attitudes toward family and social relationships. In a section on home life Mather warns against making children fear their parents. A child should be hit only for vicious or insubordinate behavior; normal relations with children are to be carried on through elaborate manipulation. He is particularly vehement against the practice of schoolmasters' beating their students, a nearly universal custom that persisted long after Mather's denunciation. Education for him consisted above all in the truths of religion, but he also suggests that parents teach even a child who is to be liberally educated some useful trade or craft. Addressing himself to doctors, he writes cogently about the psychological dimensions of sickness. "I Propound then, Let the *Physician* with all possible Ingenuity of *Conversation,* find out, what matter of *Anxiety,* there may have been upon the Mind of his *Patient;* what there is, that has made his Life *Uneasy* to him." As a pastor, Mather thought of himself as a healer of troubled souls. Tolerant and forgiving by nature, he continually emphasizes his own readiness to subordinate doctrinal differences among well-meaning Protestants.

But some of Mather's own psychological weaknesses emerge in this book as well. He emphasizes repeatedly what had by this time become an obsessive theme in his writing, that the doer of good must expect to be abused in return. Mather's reiteration of this theme amounts to a subtle kind of self-pity, and the degree to which he was abused could seem in a perverse way the measure of his worth. Franklin at the beginning of his *Autobiography* recommends personal vanity as an incentive for bringing benefits to society as a whole. Mather closes *Bonifacius* by recommending humility. One should actually seek "to be *Despised and Rejected of Men;* and Patiently to bear the Contempt, and Malice, and Abuses of an *Untoward Generation. . . .* 'Tis an Excellent thing to come to *Nothing . . . Hear* it with as much of Satisfaction as they can *Hope* it. Embrace *Exinanitions;* Embrace *Annihilations.*" What Mather calls humility seems more like the despair of a man who saw his efforts and personality slighted by the community that he was called to serve.

Mather's emphasis on good deeds came as part of his disposition to accommodate with what he saw as the forward evolution of international Protestant thought. There were, to be sure, elements of current thinking of which he was suspicious, including the spreading tendency toward denying the personality of God implied by the Bible and replacing the Old Testament Father and the New Testament Son with an uncharacterized principle of order and benevolence. Writing to the prominent English dissenting minister and hymn writer Isaac Watts, Mather expressed his resistance to that tendency as part of his loyalty to "the uniting of all good men in a syncretism of piety." Wherever possible, Mather sought ways of remaining true to the old tenets of New England theology while taking part in the progressive movements of his time.

One way of being both enlightened and orthodox was through science. The Puritans in England and America had always been receptive to the investigation of nature. They shared in the traditional view that natural law would corroborate scripture, revealing a God of wisdom and order. Mather's early investigations of the symptomatology of witchcraft, however deluded they may seem to us, were carried on in a spirit of critical experimentation. He had tried to note the evidence of demonic possession as carefully as possible.

But witches were not Mather's only scientific interest. From 1712 onward he sent records of various observations of nature that he had made or collected to the Royal Society of London. In return the society named him a fellow in 1713. (He would occasionally identify the author of his shorter works simply as "a Fellow of the Royal Society," another of Mather's fumbling efforts to reveal his identity by concealing it.) The Royal Society did not print the bulk of Mather's extensive contributions. These letters, which Mather called collectively his *Curiosa Americana,* sometimes make rather strange reading. One entire letter is devoted to various cures he has heard of that have come to the afflicted by way of dreams, another proof of the efficacy of the invisible world. He concentrated on the wonderful and bizarre at a time when the best work in science was concerned with the explanation of regularities like the known movements of the moon and planets. The letters reveal him to be more a poet by disposition than a scientist; the impetus behind his scientific observations, as with much else, was his sense of wonder.

Mather's interest in science led him also to write *The Christian Philosopher* (1721), which developed the parallels between experimental science and Christian theology. Mather was quite up to date in his awareness of contemporary science; he accepted Newtonian physics, and his explanation of it was the first exploration of its implications by an American. There

is no trace of anxiety in his tone as he expands on the lessons of piety that can be derived from natural creation. Our own perspective in time would suggest that Mather's confidence was unwisely placed. As science has continued to take hold of natural phenomena, God has been a hypothesis increasingly less required. Mather, though, felt with some cause that it was he who had broken with the past by affirming the religious relevance of natural science. He could look back with approval at the overthrow of Aristotelian physics, the complexities of which he pronounced unintelligible. Scholastic philosophy, moreover, was tainted by the continued endorsement of the Church of Rome. The physics of Descartes was no more amenable to religion, since it claimed to find for every natural phenomenon a material cause. Newton, by comparison, not only explained the physical world better, his explanation was based on a mysterious nonmaterial cause—gravity. "*Gravity* is an Effect insolvable by any *philosophical Hypothesis;* it must be religiously resolv'd into the *immediate Will* of our most wise CREATOR, who, by appointing this *Law,* throughout the material World, keeps all Bodies in their proper Places and Stations, which without it would soon fall to pieces, and be utterly destroy'd."

The Christian Philosopher, as its name suggests, was intended to serve both religion and natural science (or philosophy). The religion that it propagated would be free from doctrinal disputes. "Behold, a *Religion,* which will be found *without Controversy;* a *Religion,* which will challenge all possible Regards from the *High,* as well as the *Low,* among the People; I will resume the Term, a PHILOSOPHICAL RELIGION: And yet how *Evangelical!*" The essays in the book proceed from light, the stars, and the planets to natural phenomena like rain, hail, gravity, and magnetism, and end with the animals and man—a traditional scholastic sequence of presentation. Mather relies heavily on his own library, the best in New England, to provide him with material. Preoccupied as always with curious and instructive facts, he did not fully recognize the extent to which a revolution in theory had taken place in natural science. But as he describes the progress of understanding the rainbow, he applauds Newton as "the *Perpetual Dictator* of the learned World."

The essays typically begin by presenting a synopsis of the present state of knowledge on a subject and end with an extended praise of God. Mather's tone is buoyant and enthusiastic; he is free of the bitterness about his critics that shows up so regularly in his late works. Coming at last to man, he devotes a long essay to the human anatomy. His impulse is to see everything that God has created serve some purpose. Even male teats are functional, he asserts, and he cites a report from Denmark that they can provide milk if needed. The reader of *The Christian Philosopher* waits in vain for what would seem the inevitable Puritan corollary to this praise of the body's functioning—that man's inner state is nonetheless in disarray. But if Mather's natural philosophy is evangelical, it does not lead to an Augustinian restlessness with the soul's inadequacies. This was the eighteenth century, and Mather was happy to show that he could share its confident grasp of creation.

His interest in science and his impulse to do good led Mather in 1721 to one of his greatest and most controversial achievements. He had seen epidemics of smallpox pass periodically through Boston, each leaving its toll of disfigurement and death. During the epidemic of 1721 Mather took steps to implement a procedure of inoculation, a controlled infection, that he had seen described in the *Transactions* of the Royal Society. Together with Zabdiel Boylston, a Boston physician, he began to encourage people to try the procedure.

The public was outraged; it appeared as if Mather wanted to spread the disease deliberately. He was attacked in James Franklin's *New-England Courant,* and someone even threw a handmade grenade into his bedroom window, which failed to explode when it landed. Even the fact that Mather had cited the practice as employed in Africa was held against him. The best-trained physician in Boston, Dr. William Douglass, denounced Mather's procedure as a crackpot scheme. In fact, Mather's theoretical knowledge of medicine was extraordinary for an American. His treatise on medicine, *The Angel of Bethesda* (written in 1722), finally published 250 years after it was written, shows him to have been the first significant figure in colonial medicine. Throughout the epidemic Mather tended the sick himself, even dressing their sores for them. Few people were better prepared than he to deal with abuse.

After this shaky start, the technique became established; even his old enemy Dr. Douglass adopted it a few years later. It was a risky procedure—later in the century Jonathan Edwards died of a smallpox inoculation—but it was the best protection against smallpox until Dr. Edward Jenner discovered the cowpox vaccination in 1796.

That episode offered one of the few satisfactions of Mather's later life. Throughout the first decade of the eighteenth century he was involved in a bitter feud with the governor, Joseph Dudley. Mather had relished the role of spokesman and spiritual adviser that he had played for Phips. Dudley had long been connected with the merchant class that was moving to deny the ministers their former role as the supervisory conscience of the theocracy. Mather was forced into a frustrated and often angry opposition— not a comfortable role for a man who liked to be forgiving and enjoyed advising prominent men. Gradually his view of the state was changing; in *Bonifacius* he found no important role for the magistrate in doing good beyond setting a pious example and avoiding corruption.

In his personal life Mather suffered repeated

anguish. Of his fifteen children, only two survived him. After the death of his first wife, Abigail Phillips, whom he had married in 1686, Mather married a second time, in 1703 to Mrs. Elizabeth Clark Hubbard. She died ten years later, and in the same month five of his children died. In his diary Mather admitted that he found his house more tranquil without the bustle of small children. After a two-year courtship he married Lydia Lee, who seems to have aroused his greatest amorous interest. But she turned out to be subject to paranoid frenzies. She would rummage through his "Reserved Memorials" to steal or blot them. Her violent outbreaks, which would alternate with passionate reconciliations, led Mather to fear for his children's health and safety. Mather's oldest son Increase showed no signs of continuing the family line. He quarreled, got into debt, did not go to Harvard, and was even accused of siring a prostitute's child.

Mather was an affectionate if manipulative father; his son's behavior left him helpless with sorrow and confusion. In 1724, just when Lydia's violent behavior had reached a new peak, word came that young Increase had been lost at sea. Old Increase had died the year before, leaving his son no money but several dependent relatives to look after. The last ten years of his life brought financial troubles that Mather was ill-equipped to handle. At one point he barely avoided bankruptcy. His diary of these years is a sad record of helpless floundering, with hints even of suicide. Nevertheless, he continued to preach and write.

Mather had always been closely attached to Harvard College, though his love for the school seemed to him increasingly unrequited after his father was forced out of the presidency in 1701. (He was also concerned about the new college that had been established in Connecticut and wrote to a wealthy London merchant, Elihu Yale, to persuade him to endow the school.) In 1724 a new president of Harvard had to be chosen; despite Mather's preeminent standing as the only American with any reputation in the international community of letters, the position was offered in turn to two inferior and less controversial men, Joseph Sewall and Benjamin Colman. Frustrated that he could not affect education in New England directly, he put down his thoughts in writing. His last important book, *Manuductio ad Ministerium,* a handbook describing the proper education for a minister, appeared in 1726.

Nearly thirty years had passed since he had completed the *Magnalia,* and his goals had shifted emphasis. The earlier Mather had stressed American spiritual achievements; the later Mather emphasized an ecumenical spirit of piety that sought to embrace Congregationalists, Presbyterians, Anglicans, and Lutherans in England, Scotland, and Germany. Mather had addressed a general audience before; and the boisterous display of erudition then, the wealth of quotations in Latin and Greek that he laid before his reader, were an attempt to equal in style the grandeur of his subject. In the *Manuductio* Mather addresses students for the ministry. His tone is that of an old man addressing a son who has chosen the ministry; his own son Samuel, who would eventually succeed him as minister at the Second Church, had been at Harvard not long before. The clarion note of affirmation in the *Magnalia* had been a symptom of the desperation that Mather really felt about the American church's decline. Now he sounded more intimate and comfortable; he no longer needed to raise his voice to be heard.

The *Manuductio* describes the education suitable for a minister—the mental attitude, the indispensable reading, the personal habits to be acquired. "In the FIRST Place, *My Son,* I advise you to consider yourself as a *Dying Person,* and one that must *shortly put off this Earthly Tabernacle,*" Mather instructs in the first paragraph. That attitude of disregard for the things of this world eliminates the possibility of leisure in which subjects might be studied in themselves. In that spirit Mather examines first the program of study for a liberal education and then the necessary texts. Elements of the traditional seventeenth-century Harvard education are mixed with new influences. On one hand he endorses Johann Heinrich Alsted's encyclopedic collection of late medieval and Renaissance lore; on the other hand he recommends Pierre Bayle's *Historical and Critical Dictionary,* a classic of the early Enlightenment. Natural philosophy gets an enthusiastic description, with a summary of its progress from Aristotle and the Scholastics to the time of Newton.

The *Manuductio* is not just a compromise between old education and new. Mather intends it as a model education for a kind of minister different from either the dated Harvard product or the new latitudinarian Anglicans, whose preaching seemed to him un-Christian. One significant change in the curriculum is a greatly reduced role for logic. Mather's disdain for logic is emphatic; he sees it as little more than hairsplitting. Nor does he allow much time for metaphysics and ethics. The small part assigned these subjects is symptomatic of a striking shift away from the preoccupation with intellectual rigor characteristic of the first Puritans.

The study of logic is of no real use in perfecting a person's capacity to reason, Mather asserts. "The Power and Process of *Reason* is *Natural* to the Soul of Man; And those *Masters of Reason,* who argue the most *Rationally,* and make the most *Rational Researches* into the true State of Things, and who take the most *Reasonable Measures* for their Conduct, and who in all things arrive to the most notable Discoveries, I pray, what sort of *Logicians* are they?" The minds Mather would train will trust in their own natural reason and their own pious

goodwill, not in their capacity for disciplined analysis.

For one so steeped in scholarship himself, Mather does not dwell lovingly on the delights of learning. He provides a considerable list of books for his student son, but they are to be used, not enjoyed for their own sake. For many books Mather suggests only a cursory reading. Even in the case of Saint Augustine, whom Mather cites so frequently and favorably, he cannot endorse Cornelis Jansen's instructions to read all his works ten times through. The *Manuductio* is just as much about rules of health and practical conduct as it is about studies. Mather is not concerned with a body of learning but with a certain kind of consciousness. Studies are important only as a means to achieving and preserving that consciousness.

Among the studies Mather considers is poetry. Although he admits that some are incapable of responding to poetry, he would not wish his student son to be unpoetical. He expresses a guarded approval of Homer and Vergil. Despite serious moral defects in both, the reader can also find moral virtues, as well as "abundance of Rare *Antiquities.*"

Writing poetry can be a relaxation and an aid to good style, but it must not engross the student's attention. "Be not so set upon *Poetry,* as to be always poring on the *Passionate* and *Measured* Pages. Let not what should be *Sauce* rather than *Food* for you, Engross all your Application. Beware of a *Boundless* and *Sickly* Appetite, for the Reading of the *Poems,* which now the *Rickety* Nation swarms withal." Much literature is without value; in fact much of it serves diabolical ends, including most of the modern plays and fictions.

The subject of poetry leads Mather to the question of style, which he discusses in an extensive passage. Literary style and the standards of taste in style had long been concerns of Mather's. He describes the style he prefers as one aiming at "*Vigour* sensible in every *Sentence*," with ample use of allusion. "The Writer pretends not unto *Reading,* yet he could not have writ as he does if he had not *Read* very much in his Time; and his Composures are not only a *Cloth of Gold,* but also stuck with as many *Jewels,* as the Gown of a Russian Embassador." But such a style is no longer respected, Mather observes. Instead a standard of false simplicity has elbowed the old ornateness out of its way.

Mather fervently denounces the style of his times, which he saw as no real standard at all but rather a transient fashion dictatorially imposed by insubstantial wits. The freedom to write in one's own way was lost. "After all, Every Man will have his own *Style,* which will distinguish him as much as his *Gate* [gait]." Mather does not propose to replace one standard with another, but to let everyone write in his own way.

The freedom of style that Mather hoped for was no longer available in the age of Joseph Addison, Alexander Pope, and Jonathan Swift. In the seventeenth century a multitude of varied and individual prose styles had flourished; Francis Bacon, Robert Burton, John Milton, Izaak Walton, and Sir Thomas Browne had all walked with their own gait. Mather was the last of those distinctive voices. The new style was exemplified in Addison's *Spectator,* the model that Benjamin Franklin used when he taught himself to write. It was a public style, the style of a man in society, a style that deliberately avoided the expression of powerful feeling. Above all, it was the style of a universal consensus; it could not be used by someone with an urgent and idiosyncratic insight. It is no wonder that Mather recoiled from it. He felt himself all his life to have been a voice crying in the American wilderness; he saw the defense of his own style as a defense of his countrymen's freedom of expression.

Mather took his style with him to the grave. When he died, on February 13, 1728, there were no disciples to take his place. The tradition he had spent so much effort at shoring up seemed to have expired as well. His most prominent contemporaries, whose names are known only to scholars today, were eager to fall into the gait of the eighteenth century; and a tradition of bloodless piety, against which Edwards, Emerson, and T. S. Eliot would in their turn react, took hold in the Boston pulpits.

Yet, despite the great disparity between his hopes and achievements, Mather was not a failure. He managed to keep American Puritanism alive and intellectually active at a time when it might have retreated into a sterile provincialism. If he was the originator of little, he was the perpetuator of much, and his peculiarities have been impressed on the image of Puritanism. The *Magnalia,* with its gigantic storehouse of anecdote, has served as a collective self-portrait of Puritan America. The long-standing popular association between the Puritans and the Salem witchcraft proceedings can be traced to Mather's defense of the court in *The Wonders of the Invisible World.* The so-called Puritan work ethic, that loathsome national neurosis which is always just a half-generation behind us (though we, of course, have freed ourselves from it), raised its hideous head early in Mather's *Essays To Do Good.* That book also served as the first inspiration for the American tradition of organized benevolence. Mather did not create the alliance between Puritanism and empirical science, but he energetically perpetuated it at a point where science seemed increasingly to offer illustrations for Deists; overt conflict between science and religion was postponed for 150 years. And by persisting in his own style despite the authority of English Augustan standards for prose, Mather was establishing a first essential precedent for the idiosyncratic modes of discourse that have distinguished American intellectual life. Americans before him had already started thinking in peculiar ways of their own; hereafter they would also tend to sound different as well. That American writers have walked with their own gait, even sometimes marching to a different drummer, is so in part because Mather insisted on doing so himself.

In its witness to a dying tradition, Cotton Mather's career anticipated a situation common among subsequent American writers. Much of our best writing has come from those who believed that history was burying the culture that had formed them. In "The Custom House," the essay that introduces *The Scarlet Letter*, Hawthorne testifies to his condition as a survivor from an older Salem; the sense of identity he has acquired from that connection is so insistent that it must be acknowledged before he can release the story to his readers. Life on the Mississippi had changed utterly by the time Mark Twain wrote about it, but he returned to it again and again. For Henry Adams almost all of his education was an explanation of why his own family past had unsuited him for the present. Speaking for his author, F. Scott Fitzgerald's Nick Carroway closes the life of Gatsby by talking about what his Midwest had been like, a place where families and social status and moral values were settled. Even William Faulkner, who offers a most ambiguous picture of the older South, writes during a time he believes to be dominated by Snopeses. These writers do not become sturdy defiers of change, in the model of the European conservative, and they do not see the past as timeless and unchanging. Nor are they nostalgic; the past they represent is still too alive for them to embrace its bygone quaintness.

Though he belongs in this tradition, Cotton Mather would not have admitted that Puritanism was a dying tradition, any more than he

could have conceded that God had withdrawn from the active governance of the world. He always insisted on seeing the passionate godliness of the first Puritan settlers as somehow present and recoverable. As an ongoing international movement that was continuing the Reformation, however, Puritanism was beyond Mather's powers to rescue. It would require the tough-minded intellectual rigor of Jonathan Edwards to transform the old creed into a sinewy and resilient ideology, but that effort meant the deliberate abandonment of that international consensus which Mather had believed in so much. Mather was always less concerned with theoretical cogency than with pious behavior and the doing of good. What survived him was not an ideology but a set of cultural reflexes.

If Mather failed as a prophet, he succeeded as a literary figure. He found Puritanism a collection of quirky provincial traits; out of the variety of personalities who peopled New England in the seventeenth century he fashioned in the *Magnalia* a monolithic collective identity. That identity has refused to disappear. The last American Puritan has always just died out; for 250 years we have been announcing that we have finally left our Puritan past behind. Cotton Mather can claim a good deal of credit for the tenacious survival of Puritanism in America.

Selected Bibliography

WORKS OF COTTON MATHER

A complete listing and description of Cotton Mather's 468 separate works can be found in Thomas J. Holmes's bibliography. The following works are available in editions published since the eighteenth century.

The Wonders of the Invisible World (1692). In *The Witchcraft Delusion in New England,* edited by Samuel G. Drake. 3 vols. Roxbury, Mass.: W. E. Woodward, 1866. Reprinted New York: Burt Franklin, 1970.

Magnalia Christi Americana, or The Ecclesiastical History of New England (1702). Edited with an introduction by Thomas Robbins. 2 vols. Hartford: Silas Andrus, 1853. Reprinted New York: Russell & Russell, 1967.

Magnalia Christi Americana, books 1 and 2, edited by Kenneth B. Murdock. Cambridge: Harvard University Press, 1977.

Bonifacius, An Essay upon the Good (1710). Edited with an introduction by David Levin. Cambridge: Harvard University Press, 1966.

The Christian Philosopher: A Collection of the Best Discoveries in Nature, with Religious Improvements (1721). Gainesville, Fla.: Scholars' Facsimiles & Reprints, 1968. (Contains an introduction by Josephine K. Piercy.)

The Angel of Bethesda (written 1722). Edited by Gordon W. Jones. Barre, Mass.: American Antiquarian Society and Barre Publishers, 1972.

Manuductio ad Ministerium: Directions for a Candidate of the Ministry (1726). New York: Columbia University Press (Facsimile Text Society), 1938. Reprinted New York: AMS Press, 1978.

Diary of Cotton Mather, edited by Worthington C. Ford. 2 vols. Boston: Massachusetts Historical Society Collections, 7th. ser., vol. VII (1911–1912). Reprinted New York: Ungar, 1957.

The Diary of Cotton Mather D. D., F. R. S. for the Year 1712, edited by William R. Manierre. Charlottesville: University Press of Virginia, 1964.

Selected Letters of Cotton Mather, edited by Kenneth Silverman. Baton Rouge: University of Louisiana Press, 1971.

Paterna: The Autobiography of Cotton Mather, edited by Ronald A. Bosco. Delmar, N. Y.: Scholars' Facsimiles & Reprints, 1976.

BIBLIOGRAPHIES

Holmes, Thomas J. *Cotton Mather: A Bibliography of His Works.* 3 vols. Cambridge: Harvard University Press, 1940. Reprinted Newton, Mass.: Crofton Publishing, 1974.

Nolan, Charles J. "Cotton Mather: An Essay in Bibliography." *Resources for American Literary Study,* 8:3–23 (Spring 1978).

BIOGRAPHICAL AND CRITICAL STUDIES

Beall, Otho T., Jr., and Richard H. Shyrock. *Cotton Mather: First Significant Figure in American Medicine.* Baltimore: Johns Hopkins University Press, 1954.

Benz, Ernest. "Ecumenical Relations Between Boston Puritanism and German Pietism: Cotton Mather and August Hermann Francke." *Harvard Theological Review,* 54:159–93 (1961).

Bercovitch, Sacvan. *The American Jeremiad.* Madison: University of Wisconsin Press, 1978.

———. "Cotton Mather." In *Major Writers of Early American Literature,* edited by Everett Emerson. Madison: University of Wisconsin Press, 1972. Pp. 93–150.

———. "New England Epic: Cotton Mather's *Magnalia Christi Americana.*" *Journal of English Literary History,* 33:337–50 (1966).

———. *The Puritan Origins of the American Self.* New Haven: Yale University Press, 1975.

Breitweiser, Mitchell Robert. "Cotton Mather's Crazed Wife." *Glyph,* 5:88–113 (1979).

Calef, Robert. *More Wonders of the Invisible World.* In *The Witchcraft Delusion in New England,* edited by Samuel G. Drake. 3 vols. Roxbury, Mass.: W. E. Woodward, 1866. Reprinted New York: Burt Franklin, 1970.

Elliott, Emory. *Power and the Pulpit in Puritan New England.* Princeton, N. J.: Princeton University Press, 1975.

Hansen, Chadwick. *Witchcraft at Salem.* New York: George Braziller, 1969.

Levin, David. *Cotton Mather: The Young Life of the Lord's Remembrancer, 1663–1703.* Cambridge: Harvard University Press, 1978.

———. "The Hazing of Cotton Mather: The Creation of a Biographical Personality." In *In Defense of Historical Literature: Essays on American History, Autobiography, Drama, and Fiction.* New York: Hill & Wang, 1967. Pp. 34–57.

Levy, Babette. *Cotton Mather.* Boston: Twayne, 1979.

Lowance, Mason I., Jr. "Cotton Mather's *Magnalia* and the Metaphors of Biblical History." In *Typology and Early American Literature,* edited by Sacvan Bercovitch. Amherst: University of Massachusetts Press, 1972. Pp. 139–62.

Mather, Samuel. *The Life of the Very Reverend and Learned Cotton Mather.* Boston: Samuel Gerrish, 1729.

Middlekauff, Robert. *The Mathers: Three Generations of Puritan Intellectuals, 1596–1728.* New York: Oxford University Press, 1971.

Miller, Perry. *The New England Mind: From Colony to Province.* Cambridge: Harvard University Press, 1953.

Porter, Katherine Anne. *Collected Essays and Occasional Writings.* New York: Delacorte, 1970. Pp. 313–51.

Stoeffler, F. Ernest. *The Rise of Evangelical Pietism.* Leiden: E. J. Brill, 1971.

Van Cromphout, Gustaaf. "Cotton Mather: The Puritan Historian as Renaissance Humanist." *American Literature,* 49:327–37 (1977).

Warren, Austin. "Dr. Cotton Mather's *Magnalia.*" In *Connections.* Ann Arbor: University of Michigan Press, 1970. Pp. 24–44.

Wendell, Barrett. *Cotton Mather: the Puritan Priest.* New York: Dodd, Mead, 1891. Reprinted with an introduction by Alan Heimert, New York: Harcourt, Brace and World, 1963.

—ORMOND SEAVEY

Lewis Mumford

1895–

"With the whole world of ideas in ruins [in 1918], it was plain that the day of the wreckers and excavators was over: the time had come for the architect, the plan, the organized corps of workers. Who was capable of directing those forces in America? That was a question which bore directly both upon literature and upon social life."

From "Prelude to the Present" (1931)

Lewis Charles Mumford was born in Flushing, Long Island, New York, on October 19, 1895, the only child of Lewis Charles Mumford, a lawyer, and Elvina Conradina Baron Mumford. Of the lower-middle class into which he was born Mumford was later to write that he, along with Karl Marx, did not think much of it; but nevertheless its inevitably unstable mixture of poverty and gentility was to leave a mark on his later development, if only by impelling him to revolt against it. More important than his class origins, however, seem to have been the immediate circumstances of his family. In the various accounts of his childhood and early youth—autobiographical, semiautobiographical, or semifictionalized—there is never any mention of a father. The omission is striking and significant. The absence of a father, of someone to model himself on or contrast himself with, is undoubtedly one of the factors that was to lead Mumford in early maturity to be unable to define either his own identity or the direction of his life. And it was also to lead him to seek after and eventually to reject substitute fathers like Patrick Geddes or older substitute brothers like Van Wyck Brooks. It may even have unconsciously stimulated in him a preference for the generation immediately preceding his father's, the generation that he was to write about so glowingly in *The Golden Day* (1926) and *Herman Melville* (1929).

Mumford knew this older "ideal" generation intimately in the person of his grandfather, a former headwaiter at Delmonico's and a gentle, upright man who had left Germany after 1848 in order to escape conscription. To this rather unassuming figure Mumford was to attribute, in his "Self-Portrait" of 1936, what "little real education" he had received as a boy, chiefly as a result of taking "walks around the city" with him. This grandfather, indeed, is the protagonist of Mumford's account of his childhood in the December 22, 1934, issue of the *New Yorker,* in which his mother is drawn far less distinctly and favorably. It is the grandfather who takes Mumford out into the real world, who introduces him to John L. Sullivan, to exotic saloons, exciting racetracks, and noisy German beer gardens, as well as to the wonders of the Metropolitan Museum of Art and the American Museum of Natural History. Old Grandfather Graessel is a real person, not just a figment of nostalgia or social preconceptions; and yet it is difficult to escape the impression that Mumford is puffing him up at the expense of other, less responsive figures.

Poor as the Mumfords were, they were able to afford a nanny. Many years later Mumford was to confide in Joel Spingarn that as a direct result of having had a governess as a child, his ego had become so inflated that he had assumed the entire world was subject to his whims. Be this as it may, and whatever the cause, it must soon be clear to any serious student of Mumford's work that modesty was and is not his strong point.

Despite social and economic problems, Mumford's childhood was not unhappy. Though often lonely, he did not hide behind a wall of books; he often succeeded in making friends, and as a star pupil he also gained a security in school that he lacked at home. His years at Stuyvesant High School were especially rich and rewarding in this respect. In his novella, "The Little Testament of Bernard Martin, Aet. 30" (1928), which, like James Joyce's *Portrait of the Artist as a Young Man* (1916)—to which it is so clearly indebted—is thinly fictionalized autobiography, Mumford describes his time at Stuyvesant as consisting of hours that "do not crawl: the hours are not empty: the clock says neither tick nor tock. The moments become monuments: each moment shelters a memory." Here Mumford first tasted the sweets of success and admiration as a prospective electrical engineer, as a cheerleader, as class president, and as a member of the drama society founded and advised by an enterprising teacher of English, Thomas Bates. Bates had introduced the young Mumford to the plays of George Bernard Shaw, and thereby, as a self-consciously Shavian letter of January 23, 1914, testifies, revolutionized his

life. Mumford not only read Shaw but he went a step further; he "studied his ideas. Monstrous! In one year I was changed from a weak-kneed conservative (with no philosophy and hardly any opinions) to a rather wild young man with a brick in my right hand and a red flag in my buttonhole." At about this time too Mumford discovered Samuel Butler and H. G. Wells and soon managed to transform himself into a thoroughly up-to-date young man. In fact, his first nonschool publication was a newspaper article (1914) written in response to an open invitation to take issue with Shaw.

Publicly, Mumford was beginning to show unmistakable signs of future success; privately, there were setbacks. To begin with, he was sickly: at sixteen he contracted malaria; and soon thereafter he was diagnosed as having tuberculosis, a disease for which he had to be treated until he was nearly twenty. Possibly even more disturbing to a sensitive young adolescent passing through a difficult puberty was the sense of his own physical ugliness. As he was to note in one of the published fragments of his autobiography, he felt himself at this time to be "an altogether unattractive creature, even to myself," who withdrew into an inner world of fantasy in which all his failures were miraculously compensated. This phase was to pass with his teens, but, as the adult Mumford is careful to point out, "the scars that accompanied this growth remain: the sense of being physically unattractive to girls, with its self-protective aloofness and simulated disdain, in order to avoid the possibility of rejection."

Not that the adolescent was pathologically shy. The list of his girl friends begins at age eleven and quickly lengthens. At fifteen Mumford fell in love, an experience he took seriously enough a full fifty years later to devote a chapter to the girl, Beryl Morse, in his autobiography. Looking backward, he was even inclined to think that "his almost daily letters to her during the first stage of our friendship did as much as anything else, perhaps, to turn my mind away from technology to literature. . . ."

By 1912, when Mumford graduated from high school, he no longer wanted to be an engineer. Now he hoped for a career as a reporter; he started off at the bottom as copyboy for the *New York Evening Telegram* and ended up a few months later in the same position. More lasting was his commitment to furthering his education at City College, where he attended night classes from 1912 until 1914, taking a variety of subjects but expecting eventually to specialize in philosophy. As in high school, Mumford throve in an environment of admired and admiring father figures who dispensed rewards more quickly and generously than customary among journalists. In the account of his adolescence published in the *New Yorker* on December 4, 1937, Mumford depicts his classes and teachers in almost heroic terms. "Our discussions were battles," he writes, "and though we often lived to change sides, there was nothing tentative or hesitating in our espousals." One figure especially, that of his English professor, Earle Palmer, emerges as superhuman—"a frail but ageless figure, half pixie, half demon. . . .My Harvard friends have overfilled me with tales about their famous Copey, but none of them has ever made me feel the least regretful that I missed the histrionic Harvard professor. One touch of Palmer's ruthless sincerity was at least half a college education."

The most crucial event of Mumford's education, however, took place in a biology class, where in 1914 he encountered the work of Sir Patrick Geddes, the Scottish sociologist and city planner. Geddes—the "Jovian father" or "master," as Mumford would henceforth refer to him—was to leave a deep and lasting imprint on this young student, to the point even of providing a model for the kind of life he was to lead. Of Mumford's debt to Geddes' thought

and of his difficult relations with him as a man, more will be said later; for the moment it is enough to point out that Geddes inspired Mumford to carry on where his walks with his grandfather had left off; that is, to undertake a systematic "regional survey" of New York City as a total—and not merely as a literary—organism. As a result, Mumford was to note as early as 1919 in his journal that his "present interest in life is the exploration and documentation of cities. I am as much interested in the mechanism of man's cultural ascent as Darwin was in the mechanism of his biological descent." The budding cultural historian had already struck root, deep in fertile Geddesian soil.

The outbreak of World War I in Europe did not at first have much of an effect on Mumford, though later—especially in his correspondence with Brooks and in the "Prologue to Our Time" (1962, 1974)—he was to see the pre-1914 world as the proverbial Edwardian garden bathed in sunlight, and the post-1914 world as a twilight gradually deepening into night. In actual practice, Mumford after 1914 did very little differently until he was drafted into the navy in 1918. He continued to play tennis, indulge in intellectual pastimes, take random notes, run after girls, plan a novel in 1917 called "The Soldier's Testament"—the word "testament" runs ominously through many of Mumford's creative efforts—and take on odd jobs for brief periods: in 1916 as an investigator for the Joint Dress and Waist Board in New York City and in 1917 as a laboratory helper at the Bureau of Standards Laboratory in Pittsburgh.

In the navy Mumford trained at Newport as a radio operator, carrying, as he was later to remember, "Plato or Emerson in my sailor's blouse." His sympathies, to judge by "The Little Testament," seem at this time to have been on the side of Germany, the country he had been planning to visit in 1914. "If this was a good war," so Bernard swears, "we'd be fighting the Limies." For a time Mumford was stationed in Cambridge, Massachusetts, but he never saw action; indeed, as he was later to recall in a letter to his future wife, Sophia Wittenberg, his time in the navy was singularly peaceful, even on a personal level. For the first time since puberty he was free of sexual urges.

After being discharged in late 1919, Mumford drifted into literary work of various sorts, chiefly as a reviewer for the *Dial* and later as its associate editor. From this moment might be said to date the beginning of the first phase—the literary phase—of Mumford's career. To be sure, Mumford had already been writing plays, stories, and even novels for at least three years, but he had had scant success getting any of these pieces produced or published. His job at the *Dial* was the first sign of literary appreciation, however modest.

Not that even here Mumford's career moved directly forward. There was another sidestep before he settled down to write the series of literary and cultural studies of America—what he was to call his American Gallery. This step was to take him to London. It was, of course, a step that many members of Mumford's generation were taking at this very time. The postwar American intellectual in Europe is a cliché of the period. But with Mumford the motive was different. He was not turning his back on America but heeding the call of his master, Geddes. In London he lived at LePlay House, became acting editor of the *Sociological Review,* and won the friendship of Victor Branford, Geddes' associate; but he was not to meet the master himself, with whom he had corresponded since 1915. And he was to grow increasingly aware that Britain, sociology, and perhaps even Geddes himself were not finally preferable to America. In 1920, after only six months abroad, Mumford returned to New York, rejecting appeals to stay on or to join Geddes as his assistant in Palestine or Bombay.

Mumford did not reach this decision on entirely intellectual grounds. The underlying reason for his return was a reason of the heart, a reason named Sophia Wittenberg. Over twenty-five years later, in *Green Memories* (1947), Mumford was to remember, in a vivid portrait, how he first met this "young goddess" at the *Dial* in 1919. It was to this quite non-Geddesian being that he confessed in a letter of September 1920 that he had postponed "Geddes's offer until we at least had had the *chance* to mate," and that by doing so he was preferring "that which most vitally mattered."

If this seems an awkward declaration of love, it is nonetheless characteristic of Mumford the theoretical, inexperienced, clumsy, and devoted lover. The picture he draws of himself in "The Little Testament" is even more awkward and embarrassing. The heroine of this novella, Eunice, is not simply Sophia Wittenberg, but a composite of various women in Mumford's life; even so, there is enough of Sophia Wittenberg in her to suggest that Mumford's ineptness nearly destroyed the marriage before it had a chance to get established. In the novella, the crisis is stated—and resolved—in melodramatic terms: the triumphant male rejects the suppliant female, only to yield manfully to her in the end. The bits and pieces of Mumford's published correspondence with his wife during these years, along with occasional journal entries, suggest that the real story was neither quite so simple nor so satisfying to his ego. How low the marriage had sunk, as well as part of the reason why it had sunk so low, emerges from a "random note" jotted down almost two years after his marriage. "On the whole," he writes, summing up his impressions of the marriage, "it has permitted me to do more work than I had ever been able to do before; so that, by marriage, I have gained a little and lost nothing, in the final balance."

Stability came to the marriage only with the

birth of their first child, named—in honor of the
master—Geddes. It was occasions like this that
brought out the poet in Mumford, ever a very
occasional inhabitant of his soul. The poem he
wrote "To Sophy, Expectant" on Christmas
Day, 1924, concludes with a stanza that communicates wonderfully Mumford's warm feeling for the family, for a love that includes pro-
creation as well as recreation:

> "In stalk and flower was delight:
> Yet more, my love, they are to me
> Now that the ripening seed will fall
> To make love's happy Trinity."

During the 1920's Mumford was to make a
name for himself as a journalist, critic, and cultural historian, especially of the American
scene. Under the leadership of Van Wyck
Brooks, he joined in trying to reclaim what was
best in the American cultural heritage, both literary and architectural. Though it is probably
too much to say that Mumford and his friends
succeeded in this task, they certainly did attract
new attention to hitherto neglected aspects of
the American past. This is especially true of
Sticks and Stones (1924) and *The Brown Decades* (1931), which deal with the nonliterary
arts—mostly architecture—in a way and at a
level of critical sophistication that had not been
experienced in America before. Even so, Mumford's best books of this period are *The Story of
Utopias* (1922) and that powerful piece of lyrical criticism on New England themes, *The
Golden Day* (1926). Neither, however, was as
commercially successful as his psychocritical
biography, *Herman Melville* (1929), which was
a book-club selection and which still exercises
an influence on Melville studies today.

While Mumford was establishing himself as
a critic and cultural historian, he was becoming
reluctantly but increasingly aware of his comparative failure as an artist. It was a failure to
which he was never to be reconciled. Even very

late in life he would put in claims to be taken
seriously creatively as well as critically, as in
the 1975 publication of "The Builders of the
Bridge," a long, rambling "epic" play that deals
with the building of the Brooklyn Bridge.
Mumford had originally written this play half
a century earlier, between 1925 and 1927; and
it had been preceded by another, equally long
play, still unpublished, called "Sumach and
Goldenrod: An American Idyll," covering the
years 1859–1864. In a note attached to "The
Builders of the Bridge" Mumford remarks that
the fault of the play was that it had too many
characters, something he believed may have
been caused by his reading Tolstoy at the time.
The play, however, is anything but Tolstoyan;
the echoes are rather of Ibsen (especially *The
Master Builder*) and of Eugene O'Neill. But it
is inferior Ibsen and O'Neill, full of talk, but
very dry talk, lacking in emotional intensity or
drama. The best parts are really the detailed
and impressionistic stage directions, in the manner of O'Neill and Shaw, something that suggests that Mumford's creative talent lay in the
direction of descriptive rather than dramatic
writing. Certainly his specifically architectural
writings, such as the "The Sky Line" column
(1931–1963) in the *New Yorker*, reveal great
skill in descriptive writing, as do the frequent
purple passages that highlight all of his work.
The evocations in *Green Memories* of Dutchess
County, his summer home from about 1926 and
his permanent home since the mid-1930's, are
among the best things he ever wrote.

Mumford abandoned "The Builders of the
Bridge," as he wrote in 1975, at the promptings
of his "literary conscience," though it is perhaps
characteristic of the vagaries of that conscience
that only four years later, in *My Works and
Days*, he was to remark that he had no doubts
"as to its suitability for production on film."
And although he stopped writing plays in the
1920's and—with one exception—was never to

attempt any creative work on such an ambitious scale again, he wrote confidently to Babette Deutsch in August 1930 that he was perhaps "at last ready to write novels and plays: and I can't pretend that I have ever been before." The exception was "Victor," a remarkable and remarkably curious attempt to write a novel in verse, a novel on which Mumford stopped working in 1939 and of which only two fragments have appeared. The very fact that Mumford should even have conceived such a project—especially after the damning things he had said in *Herman Melville* about the formal inappropriateness of *Clarel*—is extraordinarily puzzling. It may be, as the strong traces of his reading of T. S. Eliot indicate, that Mumford was trying to do for the novel what Eliot had done in the 1930's for the verse drama. But a more likely explanation is that Mumford may have been determined to stack the cards against himself in advance, as if he were trying to deflect anticipated criticism away from himself and toward an archaic form. Be this as it may, probably the fairest overall estimate of Mumford the creative artist comes from Mumford himself, in a letter to Brooks, after a part of "Victor" had appeared in the *New Yorker:* "There is a buried poet and playwright beneath the visible monuments of my life, whose rotting bones have perhaps made the grass greener." Certainly, if that artist manqué had not been an essential ingredient of Mumford's make-up, the two great series of cultural histories, The Renewal of Life and *The Myth of the Machine*—on which his future reputation will undoubtedly rest—would not have been the powerful and moving documents they are.

In extenuation of Mumford's failure as an artist, it should also be stated that he never devoted his full energies to success. Art was merely one of several fields that he was, as it were, cultivating simultaneously. If the results in one of these fields proved disappointing, there was still hope for a rich harvest in the others. So, as we have seen, during the 1920's and early 1930's, Mumford spent at least as much time preparing himself to be a critic as he did trying to be an artist—and not merely a critic of literature but of society and of things in general. In 1923 he helped found—and until 1933 actively participated in—the Regional Planning Association of America, which met frequently and informally to discuss what was wrong with American architects and urban planning. Besides Mumford, this small group of about twenty included such people as Clarence S. Stein, Henry Wright (the Victor of "Victor"), Stuart Chase, Benton MacKaye, and Catherine Bauer. Mumford benefited a great deal from these meetings and discussions, both personally, as with Catherine Bauer, whose lover he was later to become, and publicly, as in his editing of the famous 1925 regional planning issue of *Survey Graphic.*

This group presented a kind of counterweight to Mumford's membership in what might be called either the "American Caravan" group—after the anthology they published between 1927 and 1936—or the "Troutbeck" group—after Joel Spingarn's country house. This group (or groups), including others such as Van Wyck Brooks, Ernest Boyd, Paul Rosenfeld, and Alfred Kreymborg, was as "literary" as the regional planning group was "socioarchitectural." Indeed, under Spingarn's tutelage, Mumford spent a year reading through the great aestheticians, only to conclude that his time had been wasted. Even so, in 1924 Mumford published a dialogue, "Aesthetics," in which the critical positions of Spingarn and Brooks are pitted against each other in a way that makes them clearer and more persuasive than is the case even in their own writings. It may indeed have been Mumford's success in representing this kind of intellectual conflict that led him to believe he possessed a gift for genuinely dramatic dialogue. If so, he would have done well to examine more carefully the ambiguous praise of Brooks's letter of February 1925, in which Mumford's "happy touch" for dialogue is compared, not with someone like Shaw, but with Lowes Dickinson.

In 1925 and 1929, Mumford traveled to Europe for several months, both times to Geneva. There, at the instigation of Brooks and the invitation of Alfred Zimmern, he lectured to a variegated collection of young people from all over Europe; and out of the first set of these lectures, he fashioned a year later *The Golden Day*. From Zimmern, another father figure, he derived his enormous admiration for the achievements of the Greek city-state, a lasting admiration throughout Mumford's major work. Geneva, and especially the Calvinist traditions of the city, also left an impression, helping to confirm his theoretical preference for regional culture and government. And, of course, Geneva was the home of that archregionalist and advocate of the city-state, Jean Jacques Rousseau, whom Mumford praised many years later as the man whose style he admired above all others. Thus the Geneva of John Calvin and Rousseau, fused with that of Zimmern and the League of Nations, became a kind of incarnation of all that Mumford hoped for in a modern urban and regional community.

The end of the 1920's represents a clear break in Mumford's life. With the publication of his biography of Melville in 1929, he reached the peak of his fame as a literary critic; and for the first time he had pushed himself to the limits of his capacity as a writer. Writing about Melville became, as he himself gradually grew aware, a way of writing indirectly about his own situation; and gazing into the depths of Melville's despair, he felt as if he were probing and, as he wrote to Brooks, shaking the foundations of his own being. What had happened to Melville, however, Mumford was determined would

not happen to himself: he would not let his despair damage or destroy his vitality; he would not be content to travel the longest and the dreariest journey to the very end. He would not be bound, as he believed Melville had been tragically bound, by the sexual mores or social conventions of his day. He would break free of those bounds; he would take a lover.

He did. He took Catherine Bauer, who, as he observes naively and melodramatically in *My Works and Days,* "played the part of Hilda Wangel in Ibsen's play: the voice of the younger generation [Mumford was all of thirty-five at the time], bidding the Master Builder to quit building modest, commonplace houses and to erect instead an audacious tower, even if, when he had reached the top, he might fall to his death." The affair lasted for about four years: she was the first of "three young women, besides Sophia," who "successively played active but different parts in my maturation." From her, he learned to break "through some of the limitations in my own character and experience, and . . . release energies needed for the work I was at last ready to do." Or, as he remarks elsewhere, in connection with his weekly art column in the *New Yorker* from 1932 to 1937, this experience "played an essential part in my emotional education which complemented my experience in love."

As in the case of his earlier marital postmortem, there is in these comments a rather unfortunate sense of Mumford's using other people in order to further his work or his "education." Certainly anyone who can conclude, after devoting himself to an intense study of Melville's life, that Melville's chief problem was sexual repression and that the cure would have been for him to take a mistress seems on balance rather simplistic. And someone who can go beyond this kind of analysis to actually use it as a justification—or rationalization—for starting an affair himself seems worse than simplistic, seems, in fact, slightly monstrous. To be sure, the monster may really be the octogenarian Mumford providing an explanation for a Mumford fifty years younger, an explanation which that more youthful and spontaneous person might have rejected out of hand. Perhaps—but then again perhaps not. It is difficult to escape the impression that Mumford belongs to that category of egotist who sees life as a vast classroom, with himself as the prize pupil. One is reminded of W. H. Auden's choice of Goethe—incidentally, one of Mumford's heroes—to represent this type. Between Goethe and his Roman mistress there can never, Auden says, be any real communication, for "between those who mean by life a / *Bildungsroman* and those to whom living / Means to-be-visible-now, there yawns a gulf / Embraces cannot bridge."

It is only fitting that a man for whom loving another person was an educational experience should have begun to find his sustenance and employment increasingly within the walls of the academy. Mumford's Guernsey Center–Moore Foundation lectures at Dartmouth in 1929—later to become *The Brown Decades*—were only the beginning of a long series of university employments, which have included visiting professorships (of up to five years) at Dartmouth, Columbia, Stanford, University of Pennsylvania, Massachusetts Institute of Technology, University of California at Berkeley, Wesleyan, and Harvard. He has received honorary doctorates from the University of Edinburgh in 1965 and from the University of Rome in 1967. He was a Guggenheim Fellow in 1932, 1938, and 1956 and has been awarded numerous honors and medals from academic or related organizations. Between 1935 and 1937 he was a member of the Board of Higher Education in New York City. A dissertation has even been written, with Mumford's active cooperation, on his work as an educator.

All of these academic positions and honors

are, of course, to some extent inevitable external trappings of the successful modern American writer—or of the modern American writer "in residence"—which virtually amounts to the same thing. But with Mumford the connection is particularly intimate and particularly ironic. For he is proud that he never finished his B.A. In his books and correspondence, he repeatedly treats the university as an institution inimical to what he sees as the real values in life. In *The Brown Decades*, he praises himself while praising Frederick Law Olmsted for not finishing a degree at Yale: "This combination of wide travelling, shrewd observation, intelligent reading, and practical farming formed Olmsted's education: it was plainly a far more substantial discipline than the courses he had taken intermittently at Yale, . . ." In the second volume of *The Myth of the Machine*, he attacks "most of our larger academic institutions" for being "as thoroughly automated as a steel-rolling mill or a telephone system."

This is all very well for an independent thinker to say; and it is no doubt arguable that Mumford's attacks are fully justified. But is Mumford independent? He has actively sought and accepted associations with the very universities he denounces. This is as if Henry David Thoreau had written "Civil Disobedience" while serving as Concord police chief. There is something fundamentally amiss about a man who says one thing and does another.

This criticism of Mumford would not be worth making if it did not touch an aspect very basic to his work: that is, that this work is, on the one hand, the most learned and massive attack mounted against the institutions of modern life in America, and, on the other hand, a product of those very institutions.

With the 1930's and the coming of fame, with the withdrawal to rural Amenia, New York, with his espousal of family life—they had another child, Alison, in 1935—with the perennial writing and giving of lectures and the visits as professor, with the work on and the publication of The Renewal of Life series, Mumford's career becomes chiefly a recital of honors and book titles. With one notable exception: World War II. Mumford was to become one of the earliest and most vociferous American intellectuals to break with his pacifist-socialist principles and to advocate an active policy of preparation for war. His resounding "Call to Arms," published in the *New Republic* in May 1938, produced an initial reaction ranging from incredulity to scorn, but with the Munich crisis and the clear evidence of Hitler's expansionist aims, Mumford was perceived in hindsight to have been right. As a result, when a year later he published *Men Must Act,* a more fully argued version of the "Call to Arms," it was favorably reviewed, even in the pages of the *New Republic.*

Mumford's change of political direction at this time, though more sudden and severe than that of most of his contemporaries, is symptomatic of a larger change in the political climate of America. Up to this time Mumford had been, politically speaking, a fairly typical American literary intellectual: attacking warmongers, especially American warmongers; sympathizing with the Soviet Union; denouncing the injustices of the Versailles Treaty; praising Germany (before 1933) as the most progressive of all capitalist societies; and ascribing the Great Depression to inherent faults in the entrepreneurial system. As early as 1930, he had put forward his notion of "basic communism" in an essay entitled "What I Believe," a notion that was to gain greater currency when he developed it in *Technics and Civilization* (1934). In April 1932 he sent Brooks a draft of a "Manifesto" that represented an "effort to formulate a non-doctrinaire view of Communism, drawn up by Waldo Frank, Edmund Wilson" and himself. The manifesto was never pub-

lished, suggesting that Mumford had his doubts about it; and indeed, as he wrote to Brooks, he distrusted the Communists but was "sympathetic to their *tactics.* . . ." But of one thing he was sure; he was no patsy liberal. "I have never been a Liberal," he proclaimed in "What I Believe," "nor do I subscribe to the notion that justice and liberty are best achieved in homeopathic doses."

The change of mind Mumford underwent about Germany, about Versailles, and—after the Ribbentrop-Molotov pact—about the Soviet Union bears some of the earmarks of a religious experience. A new moral and even stridently moralistic tone enters his writing at this time, as is evident even from the titles of his books, *Men Must Act* (1939) and *Faith for Living* (1940). In the first book, Americans are warned to beware of British hypocrites. They have sold the Czechoslovakians down the river and will not hesitate to do the same to the United States. Hence no arms are to be sold either to the British or to their allies, the French. Moreover, the Soviets are really the original fascists. Mussolini and Hitler are merely the pupils of Lenin and Stalin. Americans will have to be prepared to go it alone. Only a free people armed can resist the onslaught. Hence Mumford went out, as he recalls in *Green Memories,* to buy a .30-30 hunting rifle, anticipating that he might have to use it in a guerrilla war against the German conquerors.

In *Faith for Living* Mumford treats the same subject somewhat more sedately. He reverts to a moral position, ultimately derived from Ralph Waldo Emerson, that he had first enunciated in "What I Believe," namely that "evil and good are phases in the process of educative growth; and who shall say which is the better teacher?" This hardly sounds like propaganda against fascism, since, if taken literally, it could be read to mean that following, say, the evil "teacher" Hitler might be just as "educative" as following the good teacher Churchill. But, of course, this is not a doctrine to be taken literally. It is merely an inflated and potentially highly misleading version of the parable of the prodigal son: namely, that an uncloistered or repentant virtue is preferable to a cloistered and untested one.

There are other misleading and even downright disturbing elements in the "philosophy" of *Faith for Living.* As Sidney Hook points out in his essay "Metaphysics, War, and the Intellectuals" (1940), there is a basic contradiction in Mumford's argument. On the one hand, there is his

. . . advocacy of compulsory enrollment in labor battalions, at least for one year's service, of every girl and boy in the country; his belief that the family must be cultivated as the nuclear cell of the healthy society, that it must be attached to the soil and homestead, that divorce is too easy and the birth-rate too low; . . . that women have neglected the household arts, that they have drained themselves of passionate sexuality by doing men's work, relying too much upon machines and not enough upon their own resourcefulness. . . .

Yet, on the other hand, there is the problem that none of these proposals follows from Mumford's basic tenets or from his "religious faith." And there is the even greater problem that, in a work supposedly written to combat fascism, the answers Mumford puts forward "are compatible with metaphysical doctrines which he abominates, since almost every one of his proposals is part of the totalitarian creed." In the final analysis, as Hook says, there is something frightening about "a metaphysical passion, which blinds us to the little we know, even as it lashes us for not knowing everything."

Hook was not alone in commenting on the contradictory nature of *Faith for Living.* In a long essay, "The Faith of Lewis Mumford" (1940, 1945), James T. Farrell suggests that the basic source of these contradictions lies in Mumford's adherence to a tradition of radical conservatism, a tradition based on an organic conception of society and that derives, in Mumford's case, from two nineteenth-century French reactionary political writers, Joseph Marie DeMaistre and Louis Gabriel DeBonald, via Patrick Geddes and Victor Branford. As a consequence Mumford is led to idealize the Middle Ages and to interpret history sentimentally. "He makes arbitrary judgments of good and bad," Farrell writes, "using the 'organic' as a criterion of evaluation." Moreover, he substitutes the "functional conception of society" for the "class conception":

The assumption that society is an organism removes the hypothesis of economic determinism from its central position as a primary premise in the analysis of history and of social problems. Instead of looking on society as a structure organized in terms of productive relationships and economic interests, you see society as a whole.

As a consequence, "his descriptions of, and assertions about, fascism contradict one another and are wholly confusing. He who confuses us concerning this question only helps to disarm us for the real struggle that we must make against this very real menace."

Confused and even self-contradictory though Mumford's metaphysical passion may have been, it was sincere. It permeated his whole life during this period; and it probably gave him the strength to withstand the traumatic shock of his beloved son's death in battle in the fall of 1944. This was undoubtedly the darkest moment in Mumford's life. He coped with it in perhaps the only way he knew how: he wrote about it. And the work that came out of this suffering, *Green Memories,* is—in terms of its depiction of personality and its intense sense of place—the most moving and powerful book Mumford ever wrote. Ironically, it is of all his books the one that has attracted least attention.

There was also another, if far lesser, crisis caused by the war. Because of Van Wyck Brooks's support for the award to Charles Beard of a medal by the National Institute of Arts and Letters, Mumford nearly severed a friendship of a quarter-century's standing. Although he thought well of Beard personally—and indeed had been inspired by Beard at Dartmouth to start work on what was later to become The Renewal of Life—Mumford considered Beard's later historical work the epitome of what was wrong with America's attitude toward the outside world. "When I examine Beard's doctrine and his influence," he wrote Brooks in February 1945, "I think that he probably contributed more than any other single writer to the cynicism and defeatism which was so characteristic of our young people in the thirties. . . ." Mumford's opposition to the award led him to resign from the institute in 1949, counting it a greater honor to stay out than to remain inside. And it led him, too, to speak openly to Brooks for the first and only time in their lifelong exchange of letters. The fault with Brooks's work, Mumford told him in December 1947, was that it was superficial: "the tragic choices and the tragic decisions in the lives of our great writers, all those elements that caused them to be despised and rejected by their own countrymen, not only in their own lifetimes but long after, have somehow escaped you. . . ." Mumford's attack, along with the implication that his attitude in the Beard affair had revealed the same reluctance to face the darker side of life, hurt Brooks deeply. The friendship nevertheless survived, and the letters once again resumed their accustomed litany of books published and books planned. But even so, something was gone. Mumford now knew that, despite Brooks's invariably lavish praise, he was really alone.

He was to remain alone; and the sense of that aloneness pervades the letters—and occasionally the books—of Mumford's later years. Again and again, there are complaints that no one reads him anymore, that no one even reviews him anymore, that he has lost all influence over the younger generation. As the honors and medals accumulate—including an honorary knighthood of the British Empire in 1975—as the number of dissertations grows, as he sees himself become the grand old man of regional and urban planning, he becomes increasingly dissatisfied and insecure. To overcome that insecurity, to reassure himself that he still matters, he published his letters to and from Brooks (1970) and to and from Frederic Osborn (1971). But was he right to do so? "The letters [to Brooks], when I finally saw them in Xerox," he writes Osborn in August 1969, "turned out to be disappointing; so that I am not sure that my reputation will be brightened by their publication." He has the same doubts about the Osborn letters when Osborn suggests that his publisher is interested in bringing them out; but though he voices these doubts, he goes ahead with publication anyway.

In the 1970's Mumford also published three miscellaneous collections of his work: *Interpretations and Forecasts: 1922–1972* (1973); *Findings and Keepings: Analects for an Autobiography* (1975); and *My Works and Days: A Personal Chronicle* (1979). All of these books contain interesting material, ranging from neglected essays to poems, from random notes on random subjects to excerpts from his autobiography, from self-revealing (or self-advertising) prefatory notes to letters to old friends and sections of his old books. They are all, in one way or another, substitutes for the autobiography that he refuses to publish during his own life-time. They are interesting but interesting primarily to those who already have an interest in Mumford. They are really the kind of books that ought to have been edited by someone else, preferably posthumously. As it is, they tend—like the Osborn and Brooks letters—to diminish Mumford's stature rather than increase it. The continual insertion and assertion of Mumford's ego make him seem more of a querulous old man than a great cultural historian and author of The Renewal of Life series and *The Myth of the Machine*. The republication, and in some cases the re-republication, of essays and letters inevitably grows tiresome and irritating. One is finally left with the impression that the aim of the whole enterprise is not to gain new currency for Mumford's ideas, but to keep his name in the public eye at all costs.

When the dust has cleared, the Mumford of this last retrospective phase will be mercifully forgotten, except for his autobiography. It will be the three preceding phases of his life that will matter: the opening period devoted to the criticism and revaluation of American literature, architecture, and culture; the middle period concerned with tracing the roots of the modern urban and technological crisis in the West; and the third period, more embittered and less hopeful than the second, dealing with the whole of human history and with what Mumford sees as the human compulsion to become progressively (or degressively) more inhuman.

Of these three phases, the second and third are those in which Mumford has done his most ambitious and probably his most lasting work; but from a strictly literary point of view it is principally for the books of the years 1922–1931 that he is today remembered. It was a time during which Mumford had identified himself with Van Wyck Brooks's grandiose quest to recover for America a "usable past," as Brooks put it in his famous 1918 essay. In the

introduction to the Brooks letters, Mumford recalls that "we became fellow workers in the task of reclaiming our American literary heritage, too long neglected, or apologetically depreciated," so that "between 1921 and 1931, partly under his [Brooks's] influence, I made it [this task of reclamation] my main concern." There were others too who followed Brooks's example—notably Waldo Frank, Paul Rosenfeld, and Alfred Kreymborg—and eventually the recovery of the past was to lead to a more direct attempt to salvage the present, specifically in the publication of the five volumes of *The American Caravan; A Yearbook of American Literature* (1927–1936), of which Mumford was one of the founding editors. Fundamentally this effort can be interpreted as an attempt to establish a balance against the increasing influence of the so-called lost generation, especially Eliot and Hemingway. The *American Caravan,* despite its unfortunate title (both chic and "sheik"), was resolutely American, expecting to discover new and typically American oases of hope. It consisted, as Mumford summarized its aims in 1931, of "a handful of writers who were in the act of achieving a coherent philosophical position, and who were not committed to caging experience in some narrow cell, from whose confines they could count the rest of the world well and happily lost."

As may be apparent from even this sketchy survey, the search for a usable past was ultimately also a search for a usable future. Mumford understood this very early on. In a remarkable essay, entitled "The Collapse of Tomorrow" (1921), he argued that

. . . what we call the future is in a sense always an illusion, and the greatest disillusion that Europe possibly suffers from is the loss of something that never existed outside the minds of those who moulded their activities in terms of it—the loss of a tomorrow. . . . Civilization is the magic instrument by which men live in a world of time that has three dimensions: the past, the present, and the future. When neither security of life nor continuity of works is maintained, civilization must necessarily collapse.

It is this profound sense of the interconnectedness of the past with the future that helps to explain why Mumford devoted himself, as he did, almost simultaneously to a study of utopian idealism in *The Story of Utopias* (1922) and to the specifically American past in the series of books that make up his American Gallery. What he was looking for was an ideal past—or the idea of an ideal future, which really amounted to the same thing—which we as Americans could connect ourselves with, both emotionally and intellectually, and thereby give purpose to our lives and direction to our society.

In the preface to the 1962 edition of *The Story of Utopias,* Mumford maintained that he had never been a utopian himself. "More than once," he wrote,

people have suggested to me that I should present my own utopia; and by that fact they betray that they do not in the least understand the nature of my work. One of the titles of a chapter in my book *Faith for Living* is: "Life is Better than Utopia," and that of another chapter in a later book is: "Regression to Utopia." Both these brief statements imply, if they do not fully express, my deepest convictions.

Mumford is right about people who ask such questions not really understanding his work; but he is right for the wrong reason. For either he himself does not quite appreciate the significance of his work—especially of his early work—or else he is not being quite ingenuous. For he is unquestionably a utopian idealist whose work, from its very beginnings, is based on very definite assumptions as to how man should live, both individually and communally.

Look, for instance, at these two, quite different "brief statements" from *Sticks and Stones* and judge if they are not utopian: "The just design, the careful execution, the fine style that brings all uses into harmony [in the New England community] . . . was the outcome of a common spirit, nourished by men who had divided the land fairly and who shared adversity and good fortune together"; and, a little further on, "would it be an exaggeration to say that there has never been a more complete and intelligent partnership between the earth and man than existed, for a little while, in the old New England village?" The title—and much of the substance—of Mumford's third book, *The Golden Day,* is utopian; the very idea that there was once a "golden" time is a fundamental characteristic of the utopian cast of mind. Mumford's survey of utopias in *The Story of Utopias*—fascinating exercise in intellectual history though it is—is not the work of a mere historian impartially seeking to classify and etiologize. Behind *The Story of Utopias* is another, more personal story: the story of a utopian hoping to show his readers the way to paradise.

Every utopian is of course also an antiutopian. The ideal of the good place implies the reality of the bad place. Every heaven must have its hell. Hence the golden day is matched by the gilded age, or is followed by the brown decades; hence fifth-century B.C. Athens—the ideal of *The Condition of Man* (1944) and *Art and Technics* (1952)—is followed by Rome and preceded by Egypt; hence the ideal—also Thomas Carlyle's ideal and a frequently cited ideal in Mumford's work from *The Golden Day* to *The Myth of the Machine*—of the "medieval synthesis" is broken up by the Renaissance and the Reformation; hence the integrated world of Dante—as in the essay "Dante as a Contemporary" (*Findings and Keepings*)—yields to the disintegrating, analytic world of Descartes.

Mumford's idea of the "idolum," as first put forward in *The Story of Utopias,* is important in this respect. Though actually the word means little more than the more commonly used *Weltanschauung*—and for that reason, no doubt, has failed to gain currency—"idolum" does suggest that utopia is not a state but rather a state of mind. "Whilst it holds together," Mumford writes, "this world of ideas—this idolum—is almost as sound, almost as real, almost as inescapable as the bricks of our houses or the asphalt beneath our feet." It is this concept of idolum that permits Mumford to do something unique in the criticism of utopian literature, namely to place fictions such as Plato's *Republic* or Thomas More's *Utopia* on the same level as realities such as the cities and country houses of the industrial revolution. Mumford was able to do this because ultimately for him the idea always shapes the reality, not the other way around. Consequently Coketown or Bleak House, and their real-life equivalents in Victorian England, are just as much the products of human imagination as are the philosopher king and H. G. Wells's samurai.

This basically Hegelian position, first enunciated in *The Story of Utopias,* was to remain the philosophical basis for all of Mumford's subsequent work, and, in fact, to provide the justification for that work. The primary task of the reformer is not, as Marx and his followers believed—after turning Hegel on his head—to change the class structure and to seize control of the means of production: to alter, in other words, the material conditions of man's existence. The primary task of the reformer is rather to change people's minds about what the aims of a society are and what constitutes the good life. This is why Mumford can conclude his survey of utopias, real and imaginary, by saying that "since the first step towards eutopia is the reconstruction of our idola, the foundations for eutopia can be laid, wherever we are,

without further ado." This is why we need a usable past, a confirmation that there once existed an idolum that supported the good life, so that we can, by reconstructing this idolum and adapting it to changed social and technological conditions, live the good life again. This is also why all of Mumford's books end with exhortations—even sermons—to change our ways and, to use his favorite word, to "renew" ourselves. These expressions of hope are so frequent and always so much of a piece that they sometimes strike the reader as a set of clichés to be used, and reused, as convenient uplift at the end of his books; but to believe this would be a mistake. The hope that man's way of thinking can be changed is fundamental to Mumford's whole endeavor. It is what makes him write.

Not surprisingly, Mumford's conception of the course of human history—even, in his later work, of the course of universal history—is idealistic and Hegelian. This is stated as early as *The Golden Day,* where we are told that

. . . the mission of creative thought is to gather into it all the living sources of its day, all that is vital in the practical life, all that is intelligible in science, all that is relevant in the social heritage and, recasting these things into new forms and symbols, to react upon the blind drift of convention and habit and routine. Life flourishes only in this alternating rhythm of dream and deed: when one appears without the other, we can look forward to a shrinkage, a lapse, a devitalization.

History, as for Hegel, is the progressive realization of the spirit, though, again as in Hegel, it is not a simple, straightforward process. "Every formative idea," Mumford writes in *The Condition of Man,*

in the act of prolonging its existence, tends to kill the original living spirit that brought it forth. And yet, without undergoing this transformation and extension, the idea would have remained inoperative and self-enclosed. In this perpetual tension between the life-forming impulses within the self, which are the source of creative social developments, and the fulfillment of the idea in life and practice, in the processes of community, lies the very kernel of history.

This is also why Mumford evolves, in *The Conduct of Life* (1951), the apparently paradoxical notion of God not being the prime mover but the final end of universal history. "The universe does not issue out of God," he writes,

in conformity with his fiat: it is rather God who in the long processes of time emerges from the universe, as the far-off event of creation and the ultimate realization of the person toward which creation seems to move. God exists, not at the beginning, but at the end. . . .

History is the movement toward the perfection of mankind, a movement that will never end but that, like the calculus, will forever be approaching its end.

It is this Hegelian conception of the nature of history that makes of Mumford a "vitalist" rather than a "mechanist." Mumford's vitalism, to be sure, also has other roots—in Geddes, in Samuel Butler, in Carlyle, Ruskin, and the other great Victorians—but it is ultimately founded on Hegel. It is only this vitalist position, according to Mumford, that can account for the progressive development of a complex physical and chemical universe out of an original mass consisting only of hydrogen atoms. One of his favorite demonstrations of the truth of the vitalist view is Hans Driesch's argument that "no one ever succeeded in building a house by throwing stones at random at the site: at the end of a century one would still have only a pile of stones." It is this perception that allows Mumford to see Darwin's theory of natural se-

lection not as the deathblow to religious faith but, on the contrary, as the most convincing proof of man's divine progress. Darwin had revealed "that the creative process was not over but was constantly going on, reaching back into a cosmic evolution. . . . the mode of evolution was neither random nor pre-determined, yet some basic tendency towards self-organization, unrecognizable until billions of years had passed, increasingly gave direction to the process."

Although Mumford did not fully develop this philosophical position until the final volumes of The Renewal of Life series, it already existed in embryo in *The Story of Utopias*. In that work, too, Mumford broached another concept fundamental to his outlook on life, something he called "utopian thinking" or, in another context, "simultaneous thinking." In his later preface to *The Story of Utopias,* Mumford explains what he means by this kind of thinking and why he found it so attractive:

. . . the classic utopian works had all treated society as a whole, and had, in imagination at least, done justice to the interaction of work, people, and place, and to the interrelationship of functions and institutions and human purposes. Our own society—indeed this ranks as the characteristic vice of all "higher" civilizations—had divided life into compartments: . . . Utopian thinking, as I came to regard it, then, was the opposite of one-sidedness, partisanship, partiality, provinciality, specialism.

In a 1931 letter to Catherine Bauer, Mumford elaborates on this kind of integrated vision:

Perhaps one ought to call it contrapuntal or even better symphonic thinking. One ought to coin a word which would describe its opposition to linear thinking: our present day notion of coordination . . . is that of keeping linear thinking in parallel rows at the same rate of movement, whereas simultaneous thinking involves reciprocal and [timely] modifications of the whole.

As Mumford acknowledges in this letter, he owed this concept to Patrick Geddes; and he makes the same acknowledgment in the preface to *The Story of Utopias*. "Thanks to the example set by my earliest master, Patrick Geddes," he writes, "this belief in balance and wholeness was already deeply implanted in me when I wrote the present book. I had renounced the rewards, if not the toil, of the specialist, and had consciously embarked on my career as a 'generalist.' . . ."

Geddes himself owed much of his "simultaneous thinking" to the German idealist tradition, to, for example, Friedrich Schlegel's notion of "symphilosophy" and his (failed) attempt to integrate all the arts and sciences into a single whole. Even so, it was Geddes' determined effort, in both private and public life, to make this integration work that impressed Mumford most deeply; it was this that made him Mumford's "master."

Geddes is today a forgotten literary figure. In America he is mentioned chiefly in discussions of his influence on Mumford; and there are not many such discussions. Part of the reason for this neglect is that Geddes appears to have been, according to Mumford, an "oral teacher like Socrates." Another part of the reason is, as Mumford does not point out, that he refused to play the part of Plato to Geddes' Socrates. He would agree to be his disciple, but he would not be his amanuensis; he would not, in fact, even be his biographer.

Mumford's relationship with Geddes was complex and difficult, and a full appreciation of it will have to await the publication of their correspondence. Pending that event, one can tentatively say that it bears all the earmarks of a father-son conflict. Geddes himself clearly came to consider Mumford a substitute for the son he had lost in World War I. In the memoir of Geddes that Mumford published in *Encounter* in September 1966—really an excerpt from his autobiography—Mumford quotes Geddes as saying to him in 1923, the first time they met: "'You are the image of my poor dead lad,' he said to me with tears welling in his eyes, 'and almost the same age he was when he was killed in France.'" Mumford was flattered, but he would have none of it, at least not then and certainly not so overtly. Later on, after Geddes had removed his powerful—and even overwhelming—personality from Mumford's presence, and after Geddes had stopped the oral torrent of monologue and resumed the calmer written stream, Mumford was able to reflect on what it was that connected and separated the two men. The admiration remained; his "sense of Patrick Geddes' greatness survived the whole summer I spent in his company." But there also remained the consciousness that if he wished to retain his independence and if he was to do what a true disciple of Geddes would do, he would have to refuse any collaboration. He would even have to betray, as he noted in 1935—three years after Geddes' death—the master.

But if Mumford could not be the son Geddes wanted him to be, he could try to make up for the loss in other ways. When in 1925 Mumford's son was born, he named him almost inevitably, Geddes; so that, as it were, Geddes lost a son but gained a grandson. And in his books Mumford went repeatedly out of his way to state his debt to Geddes, sometimes in terms that strike one as excessive, almost as if Mumford were trying to make good for some earlier sin of omission. So, for example, in *The Condition of Man,* Geddes is transformed into the very type of Mumford's ideal man; he is the "one figure whose life-interests fully represent the forces I have been describing." And in the introduction to Philip Boardman's biography of

Geddes (1944), Mumford delivers what is almost a paean to a superhuman Geddes who had lived a life that fused the urban and the rural, manual work and concentrated thinking, empirical surveys and profound philosophical reflection, action and contemplation. Perhaps the final and greatest compliment Mumford paid to Geddes is that he succeeded, even if only partially, where Geddes failed: he brought the message of an integrated life and an integrated community to a vast and often sympathetic public.

All of Mumford's more ambitious books are characterized by the utopian or simultaneous thinking that he ascribed to Geddes. This is true of *The Story of Utopias,* as it is of the whole of the American Gallery. There is not the space here to examine each picture in this gallery in detail, but they can be briefly surveyed and characterized. *Sticks and Stones* (1924), Mumford's second book, is, despite its breezy title, a serious social history of the United States, focusing on the growth of community life and of cities. It begins by establishing the New England town as the ideal against which the subsequent course of American history is to be measured. The ideal is partly justified by identifying the New England town with the last dying embers of the medieval order. Also, unlike New York or most other towns in the United States, the foundation of Puritan New England was primarily religious, not commercial. Hence "material good formed the basis, but not the end, of their life." Like Plato's republic, these communities of simple, white, clean, honestly crafted clapboard houses deliberately limited their size, so as to ensure the possibility of significant contact among the inhabitants.

With the breakup of the New England community in the eighteenth and nineteenth centuries, there came the triumph of the pioneer, who functions here as the archetype of modern man: eager to exploit the land—to "loot" it—and then move on to other lands and more loot. The pioneer, unlike the Puritan, is rootless and ruthless; and when he moves into the city he becomes the entrepreneur, another looter who divides up the land into "rectangular blocks" which he can "sell by the front foot and gamble with as easily as if he were playing cards. . . ." He lives, according to Mumford, not the good life but the goods life.

With the new gridiron cities, with their blood-and-iron ethic, come the slums and the skyscrapers: both of which are equally anticommunal and antihuman. The skyscraper especially becomes for Mumford the symbol of the senseless, cancerous growth of the megalopolis. As he points out, the skyscraper, wedged as it is among other skyscrapers, cannot even be seen as a whole, except in photographs; "these obdurate, overwhelming masses," he writes, "take away from the little people who walk in their shadows any semblance of dignity as human beings." They, along with our sewers, tell the real story of our civilization. They are as ugly and menacing as the old New England town was beautiful.

This is not to say that the industrial age is all bad. When extraordinary individuals—heroes like Henry Hobson Richardson or John and Washington Roebling—pit their wills against the gilded age of the pioneers and the entrepreneurs, then the results can be admirable and enduring. "The building of the Brooklyn Bridge," for example, "showed how well industrialism could handle its problems when its purposes were not limited by the necessity for sloppy workmanship and quick turnover. The story of its building is a tribute to both science and humanity." But except for the great bridge and a handful of rather atypical buildings, the industrial age was an architectural wasteland.

Sticks and Stones is a lively and challenging book, still well worth reading today. This is so, even though it tends, like most of Mumford's work, to overstate its case, to make larger claims than the evidence it adduces can support. What about the ideal New England town, for example? Was it quite so ideal in comparison with the secular towns that succeeded and replaced it? Did the Puritan towns limit their size for humane reasons of social intercourse, or was their main objective to keep close tabs on each other? Was not the old New England town, as Nathaniel Hawthorne and others have charged, a little more like hell than like heaven? Was it not, like the ideal Platonic republic, something of a prison?

These questions are not answered in *Sticks and Stones* nor even directly dealt with. Significantly, there is no detailed discussion of any particular New England town; and there is no attempt to trace the supposedly good life of any particular New England family. Instead, there are lyrical descriptions of the New England landscape and the white colonial houses. These can be moving, but they are not persuasive. In this respect, the unacknowledged model for *Sticks and Stones*—Thomas Carlyle's *Past and Present* (1843)—is more effective. Abbot Samson and Cedric the Saxon, though idealized, are at least specific individuals with whom we can identify and whose reality we can at least imagine; and for this reason we are more inclined to accept, even with reservations, Carlyle's medieval synthesis than we are Mumford's Puritan synthesis.

Mumford's next book, *The Golden Day* (1926), goes back further than its predecessor in search of the origins of the American idolum. The American is now seen primarily as a displaced European, or, as the epigrammatic opening sentence of the book puts it, "the settlement of America had its origins in the unsettlement of Europe." The Puritans are no longer the ideal town-planners of *Sticks and Stones*. In fact, Protestantism is now blamed for the condition of modern American man and even of Western man in general. It was Protestantism that demolished the Catholic medieval synthesis; and the Protestant, when he moved to America, became the pioneer. "Protestantism, science, invention, political democracy," Mumford writes,

all of these institutions denied the old values.... Thus in America the new order of Europe came quickly into being. If the 19th century found us more raw and crude, it was not because we had settled in a new territory; it was rather because our minds were not buoyed up by all those memorials of a great past that floated over the surface of Europe. The American was thus a stripped European; and the colonization of America can with justice be called the dispersion of Europe....

Amid this morass of Protestant pioneers, however, there was an oasis of cultivated men. Again the place is New England, but the time is different. "In New England," Mumford explains, but does not explain why, "the inherited medieval civilization had become a shell; but, drying up, it left behind a sweet acrid aroma, and for a brief day it had a more intense existence of the spirit." This was the golden day of American culture, lasting from 1830 to 1860. It was a day that "nourished men, as no other has done in America before or since." It was the day of Emerson, Thoreau, Whitman, Hawthorne, and Melville—the so-called golden five; and "we who think and write to-day are either continuing [their] first exploration, or we are disheartened, and relapse into stale formula, or console ourselves with empty gestures of frivolity." These outstanding men, because they had lived at a time when the old medieval order had not yet entirely vanished and the new industrial system had not yet wholly triumphed, were able to integrate life and thought with a modicum of success.

The golden day ends with the outbreak of the Civil War and the victory of the pioneer; but the fact that there had once been such a day proves that a similar day may dawn again, a great consolation for those who, like Mumford, continue to dwell in darkness.

The Golden Day is a brilliant book. Brooks told Mumford that he did not think that "there is another mind in the country with such a grasp over so many different elements and aspects of American life. You have beaten us all hollow." George Santayana complained to him in a letter that Mumford had misunderstood him completely, but that nevertheless *The Golden Day* was "the best book about America, if not the best American book, that I have ever read." The critical press in general joined in a chorus of praise: "enormously stimulating" (*Survey*); "no more thought-provoking analysis has ever been made of the progress of American culture" (*Yale Review*); "incessantly provocative" (*Saturday Review*); "written with distinction" (*Journal of Philosophy*); "brilliant and fascinating" (*American Historical Review*).

The book was brilliant and it is still brilliant. But its dazzle is of the sort that sometimes serves to illuminate more the author's personality and prejudices than the nature of his subject. As in Mumford's earlier books—for that matter, in his later books as well—there is a sharp division between heroes and villains; and there is an insistence on making a partial truth do the work of a whole truth, or an epigram the work of pedestrian fact. His incessantly provocative treatment of Edgar Allan Poe is symptomatic. Poe, Mumford maintains, is "the literary equivalent of the industrialist and the pioneer." Poe's fantastic stories "have their sources in a starved and limited humanity. . . . Terror and cruelty dominated Poe's mind; and terror and

cruelty leave a scar on almost every tale and anecdote about pioneer life." James Fenimore Cooper had dreamed about the pioneer; Poe, in realizing the dream, had turned it into nightmare. And "there is scarcely a page of reliable testimony about pioneer life which does not hint at this nightmare."

This is brilliant, but it is hardly just. Poe as pioneer? The suggestion is almost ludicrous. Poe is just as much the inheritor of the romantic movement and of the glorification of the Middle Ages as are Mumford's fabulous golden five. Poe's nightmares are imported from Germany, not from the Wild West. Mumford himself is a product and continuer of this very same tradition. And what about Mumford's "reliable" evidence? Are we really to believe that all those pages of pioneer life that do not deal with the supposed "nightmare" are, by that very reason, not reliable? This is to establish an unreliable criterion of reliability.

Herman Melville (1929) is the climax of Mumford's work as a literary critic. It originated in an offer by George Doran in July 1927 to publish a 35,000-word biography of Melville, but within a year the book had increased by nearly three times. In the end it was to become the first of Mumford's "big" books. It stands in the Brooks tradition of psychobiography, making considerable use of the literary productions of Melville as a means to understanding the man. Consequently it is always the personality of the author that is in the forefront of Mumford's book, not the works. But despite this emphasis there is much that is valuable, in a strictly literary sense, especially the chapter on *Moby Dick*.

Aside from the influence of Brooks, part of the psychologizing of the book can be explained by Mumford's need to correct the long-standing misinterpretation of Melville as a misanthropic madman. In this task he succeeded admirably.

He showed convincingly that Melville, though plunged into a state of deep despair immediately after publishing *Moby Dick* and *Pierre,* was never mad. If anything, it was his society that was mad.

As in *The Golden Day,* the importance of Melville is accounted for in terms of his having come to maturity in a period of transition, at a moment when the old culture was nearly in dissolution, when the embers flared up briefly and gloriously before going out altogether. New York City, Melville's birthplace, along with the New England states, was between 1820 and 1860 "in many respects in the same situation as Attica between the birth of Socrates and the death of Plato." The young Melville was an American Athenian, with all the poise, aplomb, and confidence of the Athenians. "I have called this quality youth," Mumford writes about the young traveller to the South Seas; "but it is what the Athenians called virtue; and as soon as we depart from it we are hoary with sin, and there is no health in us."

Unfortunately this young New York Athenian's development was hampered by the very non-Athenian morality of the Victorian age. It kept him from going straight and true; it warped and stunted him, and forced his growth—for growth was inevitable—into directions away from the light. Instead of adopting a sane attitude toward women, Melville insisted on setting them up on pedestals. When he married Elizabeth Shaw, he discovered to his dismay that it is difficult to live with a woman on a pedestal. "Some day he will learn," Mumford concludes patronizingly, "that women, like whales, are objects of natural history. . . ."

Melville is nonetheless a great writer; he and Whitman are the greatest American writers. *Moby Dick* "is one of the supreme poetic moments of the English language"; in the nineteenth century, only Dostoevsky rivals him in religious and emotional profundity. To think of him as a mere writer of romances is to mistake him completely; he is a poet and philosopher. Like Dante, he "clothed his thoughts in poetic vision."

It is only in this context that one can properly appreciate *Moby Dick.* It is a poetic epic, not a novel, even though it appears to be written in prose. The last chapter especially rises to unprecedented heights: it achieves integration at a level and at an intensity that is overwhelming. "One must go to a Beethoven," Mumford remarks, "or a Wagner for an exhibition of similar powers: one will not find it among the works of literature."

The whale itself, according to Mumford, is a symbol of the force of destruction, both within and outside man, which it has been the duty of Western culture, from the Greeks to the present, to combat. But not to destroy, for it cannot be destroyed: to destroy destruction is to become subject to the force of destruction oneself. This is Ahab's tragic mistake. It is like trying to annihilate the second law of thermodynamics: success would mean stopping the whole process of the universe. Man's aim should not be to seek power, for ultimately power is always identical with destruction; man's aim, in fighting destruction, should be to achieve himself, to grow ever more human. This is the significance of the hunting of the whale; it is the hunt itself that is the end, not the whale; for "without such a purpose, life is neither bearable nor significant. . . ."

Melville was never to reach the heights or probe the depths of *Moby Dick* again. Thereafter his life went steadily downhill, both privately and publicly. But since the peak he had scaled had been so lofty, even his slopes were higher than those of most of his contemporaries. This is true even, as it were, of the foothills, so that it is in no way inappropriate for Mumford to devote a considerable amount of attention to Melville's poetry, and especially to *Clarel.*

Mumford recognizes that *Clarel* is an artistic failure, but it is a remarkable failure, greater than others' successes. In its covert allusions to an unconsummated love affair in Italy, *Clarel* also provides a key to Melville's failure to grow beyond *Moby Dick.* He lacked—because his society lacked—the courage to go beyond the constraining sexual mores, and as a consequence he dammed up the sources of his creativity.

Herman Melville, like its predecessor, was loudly acclaimed by the critics, though for the first time there were rumblings from the academic world that all was not well. Stanley Williams pointed out in the *Yale Review* that Mumford had committed a serious blunder in his analysis of Melville's friendship with Hawthorne, by suggesting that Hawthorne's story, "Ethan Brand," depicted Melville himself. This was obviously impossible, since "Ethan Brand" had been published a year before *Moby Dick.* In *American Literature,* A. H. Starke also complained that Mumford had misrepresented completely the nature of Melville and Hawthorne's parting, an event that had been described accurately in earlier studies of Melville and Hawthorne. This misrepresentation led Starke "to suspect that he [Mumford] uses his material with the freedom of a dramatist and not with the exactness of a biographer." And in a later issue of *American Literature,* Robert Forsythe confirms Starke's suspicions by showing in detail how Mumford had repeatedly distorted the plot of *Pierre.*

These are disturbing criticisms; and they clearly disturbed Mumford. He never published a book of literary criticism—or a biography—again. This is a pity, for while there are undoubtedly errors of fact in *Herman Melville,* the interpretation of Melville's career and of most of his work is not seriously affected by these errors. Subsequent critics might question and even dismiss much of that interpretation, especially the eccentric analysis of Melville's sexual life, and they might argue, with justice, that Mumford fails to give due artistic credit to *Billy Budd;* but even so *Herman Melville* is a book that has helped to shape those very critics' understanding of Melville. It may be too much of a young man's book, too full of enthusiasm, too careless of the facts; but it is certainly anything but what Archibald MacLeish called it, "dull." It is an extraordinary achievement and a classic of Melville criticism.

In *The Brown Decades* (1931), Mumford goes over some of the same ground he had covered earlier in *Sticks and Stones* and *The Golden Day,* but here he tries to make up—in the words of his later preface—for "a failure to do justice to the creative forces in America after the Civil War." *The Brown Decades* is primarily devoted to architecture, though some attention is also paid to painters like Winslow Homer and Albert Pinkham Ryder, and there is even an occasional comment about a literary figure like Walt Whitman or Emily Dickinson.

Despite the titular admission that the decades following the Civil War were neither golden, as the decades preceding had been, nor even white, as during the period of the flowering of New England, the brown decades were nevertheless productive and important. "It is time," Mumford proclaims, "that we ceased to be dominated by the negative aspects of the Brown Decades." There were great forces and men at work in this period. There was Frederick Law Olmsted, the architect of New York's Central Park; there were John and Washington Roebling, who built the Brooklyn Bridge, which has now become for Mumford "perhaps the most completely satisfying structure of any kind that had appeared in America"; there was Henry Hobson Richardson, a mighty figure "who almost single-handed created out of a confusion which was virtually worse than a mere void the beginnings of a new architecture"; there was Louis Sullivan, "the Whitman of American architecture"; and there was—and is—Frank Lloyd Wright, the climax of the brown decades as well as their conclusion: with Wright modern architecture is finally born, and there is again gold on the horizon.

The Brown Decades is an original and valuable book. It sheds light on a period and on aspects of American culture that were still shrouded in darkness when it appeared. If it did not receive the critical accolades that some of Mumford's earlier books had garnered, the press still treated it with respect; and over the years it has continued to exercise an influence, as Mumford notes, even greater than *Sticks and Stones*. It is certainly not, as Mumford claims in *The Culture of Cities* (1938), "exasperatingly superficial." No superficial book could have established Mumford, as this book did, as one of the foremost American critics of architecture. Some reviewers might complain, to be sure, that there were too many disagreements between subjects and predicates for their liking. Mumford always wrote quickly and much—perhaps too quickly and too much. But he also wrote well. This, for example, is how he sums up and justifies the whole outlook of the post-Civil War generation: "One might as well expect a high sense of tragedy in an undertaker, as heroism in the generation that follows a war: meeting death is one thing, and disposing of the remains is another." This is just the sort of insight that hit home to a generation that was itself postwar. This is all very good. Yet it is disturbing that in *The Brown Decades* Mumford had written a book in which the late nineteenth century had been given a valuation utterly different from the one he had ascribed to it in *The Story of Utopias* and in *The Golden Day*. At first this period is treated as wholly Cimmerian, a blight of slums and country-house hypocrisy; next it turns out to be not quite so bleak, though definitely day is darkening into night; and fi-

nally, in *The Brown Decades,* it has become almost pleasant and promising: it is brown and not black, brown as in rows of comfortable brownstone houses or even as in brown, plowed, and fertile fields. What to make of this inconsistency? Maybe nothing, for after all a man, especially an Emersonian man, has a right to change his mind. But after too many changes, it is hard to put one's faith in him.

Perhaps the most perceptive appreciation of *The Brown Decades* was published only years later. It came in a letter of October 1931 from Brooks. "What bowled me over all the time I was reading," he wrote, "was the thought that all these sketches and ideas are properly fragments of the great book that has to be written and that nobody in the world but Lewis will ever be able to write. I mean, The History of American Culture, in six volumes, on the scale of Gibbon's *Rome,* also written in the grand style and from a point of view that is absolutely and everlastingly *central*." In his reply, Mumford admitted that Brooks was right in suspecting that *The Brown Decades* was merely a byproduct of a far greater and mightier work. He had been planning such a work for at least two years; and he had communicated these plans to Joel Spingarn: "I plan to do something larger, more terrible, than the ordinary novel or play, and one must use a good part of one's life in the mere absorption of nourishment before one is ready for such a task." At about the same time, in April 1929, he wrote delphically in "Dante as a Contemporary" (*Findings and Keepings*) that while another *Divine Comedy* was not to be expected, still

. . . the audacious effort itself is a challenge. The poet who would resolve our chaos will be as deliberate as Dante. He will not order experience by turning away from and renouncing it, as our academic humanists advise; but, confronting it, dominating it, he will convert it with implacable will into the materials of art. To achieve this, even decently to fail at this, he will have to be a poet, but such a poet that men will mistake him equally for a scientist, a technician, a philosopher, a statesman.

Or even, one might add, for a "generalist."

Ironically for a work conceived on such vague, if massive, lines, Mumford gave it the working title of "Form." By the end of 1930 this book was completed and Mumford sent it to Alfred Harcourt, his publisher. Harcourt sent it back, with the suggestion that Mumford "do a more thorough job; and the four volumes of the 'Renewal of Life' series followed." They followed—but slowly; the last volume did not appear until 1951.

In 1932, Mumford spent the summer in Europe gathering materials for the book; and in the winter and spring of the following year, he was already busy writing. "The book has taken charge of me," he wrote Brooks in March 1933, "and it drives me to work harder than anything I had ever attempted before." By June the book had burgeoned into three books which, Mumford said, "all my life has been a preparation for writing. . . ." His avowed aim now was to fire a "grand broadside at the mechanists and the mammonists from within their citadel, by one who knows how to use their own weapons for exactly what they are worth. . . ."

The first broadside was *Technics and Civilization* (1934). Like all the volumes in the series, and like the two volumes of *The Myth of the Machine,* it is an enormously intriguing and challenging book. But, as such, it is impossible to do justice to it in the brief space available here. Only the outlines of Mumford's achievement can be suggested.

Technics and Civilization traces the development and sociocultural impact of machinery from the Middle Ages to the present. The first and in many ways the most important machine

is the clock—a point Mumford had already made in *The Golden Day.* It was a machine that arose out of the needs of the medieval monasteries to regularize their prayers and their work. Initially religious, the time machine and the time sense soon became primarily secular: a vehicle to achieve profit rather than increased communion with God. Quantity and quantification replaced quality and spontaneity; now only numbers counted, or only those who counted the numbers. Thus came to an end the eotechnic age (1000–1750), an age based chiefly on water and wood.

Now a new age dawned, the paleotechnic age (ca. 1700–1870), founded on coal and iron. Its leaders were the capitalists, energetic city dwellers who asserted their independence from the Church and even, less consciously, from God. They were primarily Protestants; and it was they who finally destroyed the medieval synthesis. Symbolically, the quantifiers went underground, seeking their riches out of sight of God: "Mine: blast: dump: crush: extract: exhaust—there was indeed something devilish and sinister about the whole business. Life flourishes finally in an environment of the living." Armies and war were also profitable for the quantifiers, especially since "an army is a body of pure consumers." The carboniferous capitalists disemboweled the insides of the earth and infested its surface with the plagues of slums and factories.

Finally, with the perfection of the hydraulic turbine in 1832, came the neotechnic phase; now the inventor and, to a lesser degree, the entrepreneur were replaced by the scientist and the manager. Twentieth-century man is still at the beginning of this new phase, a phase in which the machine will finally be integrated into life, and in which the dominant machine values will at last be made subject to the values of life. The danger here is that this process may be impeded by the carboniferous capitalists on the one hand, and by the irrational and romantic primitivists on the other. Mumford warns that there is no turning back to an eotechnic paradise; the only way to integration is to move forward into harmonious neotechnicality. And, while the year is 1934, with economic depression at home and fascists rampant abroad, there is hope: "One can now say definitely, as one could not fifty years ago, that there is a fresh gathering of forces on the side of life."

Although generally sympathetic to this vision of neotechnic bliss, Auden was not entirely convinced, as one can see from the following stanza from his "Letter to Lord Byron" (1936):

We're entering now the Neotechnic Phase
    Thanks to the Grid and all those new
        alloys;
That is, at least, what Lewis Mumford says.
    A world of Aertex underwear for boys,
    Huge plate-glass windows, walls absorbing
        noise,
Where the smoke nuisance is utterly abated
And all the furniture is chromium-plated.

There were others who were even less sold on the glitter of neotechnicality. Writing in the *American Review,* John Gould Fletcher mocked a utopia in which

. . . the grime of our factories will vanish, thanks to electric power-houses, where everybody will live in garden villages, read the works of Mr. Frank Lloyd Wright and Mr. Waldo Frank and others of Mr. Mumford's friends, practice eugenic sex, . . . and subscribe to something Mr. Mumford calls "basic communism."

Even Frank complained in the *Saturday Review* that Mumford had fallen prey to the pragmatist wiles of John Dewey. And Stuart Chase greeted with delight in *Books* "the most lucid and persuasive exposition of the promise of technics in human terms that it has been my good fortune to read. Mr. Mumford not only accepts the machine, he glories in it." Certainly, to judge by the reviews, if Mumford had hoped to infiltrate and destroy the citadel of the enemy, he had failed dismally. To all appearances, he had become one of the enemy himself.

The next volume in the series, *The Culture of Cities* (1938), considers the development of the city as being, along with language, "man's greatest work of art." Here again we are presented with the integrated medieval city, living in social harmony and filially linked with its rural surroundings. Again this city is destroyed by rapacious capitalists. With the rise of centralized power in the fourteenth century came the baroque city, a forced and unnatural growth, artificially beautiful and without any living connection to the land. With all its faults, however, the baroque city is still preferable to its successor, the creation of the carboniferous capitalists: Coketown, the city of the dreadful night.

Adapting Patrick Geddes' scheme of the evolution of cities, Mumford identifies six stages: eopolis, the village community; polis, an association of such villages; metropolis, one city emerging as dominant over a group of villages; megalopolis, the beginning of urban elephantiasis; tyrannopolis, the parasitic slum city; and necropolis, the collapse of organized city life. Unlike biological evolution, however, urban evolution, according to Mumford, does not inevitably pass through all of these stages, nor is any one of these stages inevitable. The city is always capable of self-regeneration or renewal.

As must be clear from this scheme, the ideal city is the metropolis. The examples that Mumford cites are "Platonic Athens: Dantean Florence: Shakespearean London: Emersonian Boston." The characteristics of such cities include "long distance trading . . . large-scale development of library and university as storehouse and powerhouse of ideas." In the twentieth century virtually no such cities exist; but they are coming into existence: they are the garden cities, conceived, by Ebenezer Howard in 1898 and first built in Letchworth, England, soon thereafter. They are the proof that "the cycle of the machine is now coming to an end" and that "throughout the world, a consensus is gradually being established among men of good will and effective competence."

The Culture of Cities was the most successful and is still the best-known of The Renewal of Life series. Not surprisingly, it was to this subject and to this book that Mumford returned more than twenty years later in *The City in History* (1961), for which he was to win the National Book Award. And after the war he was proud to learn that members of the Polish underground had studied *The Culture of Cities* as a handbook for reconstructing their ruined urban centers. He had reason to be proud; it is a remarkable achievement and was immediately recognized as such. Some readers might complain that it was too long; some, like Howard Mumford Jones, that it was too learned; others, like Malcolm Cowley, that it used too much fancy Greek terminology; but most would have gone along at least partway with Alistair Cooke's verdict that it was the masterpiece of "the most remarkable social critic of our time."

The Condition of Man (1944) diverges from its two predecessors by focusing on man's inner world, rather than on the external technological or social circumstances of his existence. Like *The Story of Utopias,* it sees the "idolum" as the primary condition of man. It also conceives of Athenian culture as the closest approximation to the ideal, because this culture integrated man, society, and nature; and "out of an organic society arises an equally organic sense of the person." The chief fault of Greek culture, however, was that it failed to take sexuality seriously and, consequently, to take women seriously. This failing contributed to, but did not necessarily cause, the downfall of Greece,

which came suddenly and unexpectedly—a fate that, according to Mumford, may lie in store for our own culture.

The Roman idolum, which destroyed the Greek, represented discipline rather than spontaneity. The Romans—to use Oswald Spengler's terminology, which Mumford does not use but by which he is clearly influenced—were civilized, not cultured. Their very success, since it was external and material, was their failure. As Rome expanded, the inner supporting framework gradually decayed, until the inevitable moment came when, as William Butler Yeats put it in "The Second Coming," "the centre cannot hold" and things simply fell apart.

But before Rome fell, the outlines of a new and great building were visible within it: the Apostolic Church. From among the ruins of Rome there arose the new, Christian idolum, which, like its Greek ancestor, was based on individual rather than collective man, on the values of the spirit rather than those of the flesh, on culture rather than civilization. "The great empires of the ancient world," Mumford maintains, "Babylonia, Persia, Macedonia, Rome, had tried to build a universal state on the basis of power and law alone: Jesus tried to found a wider community on the basis of love and grace." This Christian idolum, though often perverted and even contradicted in practice, informed and inspired the Western world until the mid-fourteenth century.

The immediate cause of the collapse of the Christian synthesis was the Black Plague, which "marks a line between two ages: on one side, unity, and on the other disintegration." From then on it was downhill all the way, as capitalism and Protestantism combined to reestablish the values of discipline and material success over those of love and sacrifice. From Martin Luther one road leads downward to Kant and Hegel, and then precipitously—and inevitably—to Hitler. Another, less horrific but ultimately equally cataclysmic road leads downward from Hans Fugger and Galileo to a scientific hell dominated by the mechanistic Caliban of science, a hell in which there is no room for either the divine (Ariel) or the human (Prospero). These are the modern hells of primitivism or technological capitalism, and neither the romantics nor the Marxists will ever be able to lead us out of it. There is no easy escape, no ready ascent to heaven. The only way out is a way that appears to lead partly backward but really goes forward, a way that passes through garden cities, through a revived sense of family life and children, through a decentralization of all aspects of life. The movement must be away from mechanical organization and toward organic community.

As a number of reviewers realized, *The Condition of Man* is a religious book. To Daniel Bell in the *Atlantic Monthly* it seemed a paradoxically secular religion, and to Ordway Tead in the *Saturday Review* the "acknowledgement of religion as critical and powerful seem[ed] somehow timid and restrained," but to the *New Yorker* reviewer it was a downright revivalist "celebration of basic Christian values" which "has some of the strident fervor of a reformed sinner turned missionary...." By now Mumford had definitely become what Van Wyck Brooks was later to call him in *The Writer in America* (1953), "a prophet" of the line of Emerson, Thoreau, Ruskin, Morris, and Patrick Geddes. As such—sadly but fittingly—he came to be heeded less and less in his own country.

The Condition of Man was originally intended to be the last installment of The Renewal of Life series, as Mumford himself acknowledges in the opening pages of the book. But he soon came to realize that he had not said all he wished to say on the subject, that he needed at least another volume to deliver his message of renewal to the world. Hence he set to work on his overtly Emersonian "prophetic" book, *The Conduct of Life* (1951), which was to become the finally final volume in the series. It is by far the most subjective and moralistic book in the tetralogy, almost as if Mumford felt that his earlier mammoth surveys had obscured his essential meaning by their very size. Ironically, *The Conduct of Life* also turned out to be a massively learned book.

The central idea behind *The Conduct of Life* is that life should be conducted in a way that will improve its quality and only secondarily its quantity. This may seem truistic, but then Mumford is not afraid here—as he had been earlier in his American Gallery—to seem truistic. His revision of Nietzsche is almost trite: "Reverse Nietzsche. Not *Be Hard*! but Be *tender and sensitive*!"

This sounds very much like watered-down Christianity, but, oddly, enough, *The Conduct of Life* does not carry on the revaluation of Christianity begun by its predecessor. Indeed Mumford here attacks Arnold Toynbee specifically for suggesting that Christianity can be the vehicle for saving our civilization. Instead Mumford puts forward a curiously anarchistic view—or philosophy, as he calls it—that maintains that life is essentially unsystematic and that therefore the conduct of life must be equally unsystematic. This view, explicitly derived from Emerson but owing at least as much to Samuel Butler, contends that "no organism, no society, no personality, can be reduced to a system or be effectually governed by a system." Unlike Butler, however, the ideal unsystematic man is not a hedonist like Townely in *The Way of All Flesh* but rather the "balanced man," of whom the closest modern approximation is, according to Mumford, Albert Schweitzer. Just how such an ideal—essentially one of Christian self-sacrifice—can be reconciled with an unsystematic affirmation of life Mumford does not explain. But, in any case, the renewal of life will come with the acceptance of the ideally balanced man and with the consequent multiplication of such men, who will be rooted in region and family but will also be receptive to the larger flow of life and ideas beyond their immediate environs.

If Mumford's aim in *The Conduct of Life* was to change the conduct of modern life, it must be admitted that he failed. Life has continued to muddle along unsystematically, but this lack of system has not been visibly conducive to an affirmation of life. As Reinhold Niebuhr pointed out in the *New York Herald Tribune,* there was "little in past history to warrant the hope that the course of history can be changed as simply as he supposes, or by actions as unconcerted as he suggests." And Lionel Trilling, writing in the *New Yorker,* objected to Mumford's insistence that "we cannot possibly save civilized society unless we become perfect men and acquire every good quality men can possibly have." What Mumford wants, Trilling continued, is not a civilized society but the City of God.

Mumford's sense that The Renewal of Life series did not succeed in renewing life and that, on the contrary, life was everywhere deteriorating rather than improving, led him to another massive effort to marshal the cultural history—and now even the prehistory—of the world in order to prove that renewal was the only alternative to extinction. The first volume of *The Myth of the Machine,* subtitled *Technics and Human Development* (1967), consciously echoes the first volume of The Renewal of Life series, *Technics and Civilization.* Once again, Mumford goes over the spectacular but often tragic history of man's mechanical progeny. But unlike the earlier study, the machine is now defined much more broadly to include man's greatest mechanical inventions: language and society.

The real significance of the myth of the machine is that the machine is a myth—indeed, the greatest of all myths. The machine is, in other words, an "idolum." Language is an idolum; society is an idolum. They are the human means of conceiving of and coming to terms with external reality. As such, they are absolutely fundamental and necessary to human life and human development. But absolutely fundamental too is the realization that they are only part of that life and development.

What Mumford, however, refuses to recognize clearly in *The Myth of the Machine* is that the machine myth that generated language and large-scale society is also responsible for the perversions of language and society: for propaganda and for war. The god may be *ex machina* but so is the devil. Instead, Mumford looks for the culprit elsewhere, maintaining, for instance, that primitive human society was almost paradisiacally innocent and that "millenia passed before man would take the life of his own kind in cold blood." This seems naive, though perhaps not so naive as his assertion that cruelty originates with the transition from a hunting to a farming economy. "When the hunter goes after big game," Mumford writes,

he often risks his life to get the food: but the cultivator and his descendants risk nothing but their humanity. This killing in cold blood, this suppressing of pity toward creatures man had hitherto fed and protected, even cherished and loved, remains the ugly face of domestication, along with human sacrifice.

If Mumford were really to take seriously what he says here, he would have to abandon entirely his doctrine of a return to the small garden city and to a revitalization of rural values.

The machines of language and society are fundamentally good. These *Ur*-machines turn bad only when they grow big, when they become megamachines. This happened for the first time, according to Mumford, in Egypt, with the creation of the idolum of kingship. Kingship brings with it the megamachines of bureaucracy and army, both organized to construct and to destroy massive material abstractions such as pyramids or, in our day, space rockets. Inevitably, megamachine societies, like Egyptian society or our own "kingly" society, are self-destructive; after they destroy themselves it becomes possible for smaller and more human societies to establish themselves on their ruins. This is what happened after the fall of Rome. During the Middle Ages, social and technical machines were small and consequently life values superseded machine values. This balance might have lasted indefinitely, since "a genuine polytechnics was in the making" at this time; but the reappearance of the centralized megamachine during the Renaissance destroyed this medieval harmony.

The second volume of *The Myth of the Machine,* subtitled *The Pentagon of Power* (1970), traces in detail the reconstruction of the Egyptian megamachine since the Renaissance, culminating in the modern social megamachines of the United States and the Soviet Union. In doing so, Mumford goes over much of the same ground covered in *The Condition of Man*: what might be called the great tradition of scientific quantification, from Copernicus to Buckminster Fuller. This is the idolum on which the modern military-scientific priesthood is based. Its power is always associated with death, with mummies in Egypt or mummies in Red Square. Its motto is Ahab's: "All my means and methods are sane; my purpose is mad." This time, however, Ahab is armed with hydrogen bombs.

Opposed to pentagonal power and geometric quantification is a vague program of reform that is virtually identical with that of late Victorians like William Morris and Samuel Butler. Mumford agrees with Butler that the "central problem of technics" is to create a society in which machines are controlled by men, even if

this means deliberately suppressing new inventions. He agrees with Morris that society must be decentralized and the pentagon of power dismantled; instead man must live in small communities, close to the soil, fostering art and craftsmanship. There is not much new in this program; and for the first time it is put forward without the usual accompaniment of trumpets. The Mumford of *The Myth of the Machine,* while still hopeful, is a darker Mumford. The end of mankind is in sight: either by atomic self-immolation or else—in Mumford's view even more horrible—by a self-adaptation to technology that, as in Aldous Huxley's *Brave New World,* will remake humanity in the image of the machine.

Mumford's original aim in his two great series had been to penetrate the citadel of the quantifiers and the power worshippers by disguising himself as one of their own. Once inside, he would then blow up their fortress, using their own weapons. This undertaking is like assuming that if one wishes to cure a madman, one must first learn to think like a madman. There is something to be said for such an assumption; but there is also something to be said against it: the madman may succeed in persuading one that it is he who is sane. This is a danger that all of Mumford's work of the middle and late periods continually runs and to which it sometimes succumbs. The accumulation of facts, the recital of theories, the citation of scholars, the compilation of bibliographies all mount up to a vast and imposing pile not unlike a pyramid, within which, deeply hidden, there lies the desiccated mummy of an inspiration. We, as readers, are dazzled, even bewildered by Mumford's mighty literary construction; and we marvel at how easily he moves great masses of intellectual stone and raises them singlehandedly to enormous heights. He is a brilliant literary engineer. But are we renewed? Are we filled with a passionately new faith in life? Do we feel reborn? Alas, it must be admitted, we do not. A poem by Wordsworth or a sonata by Beethoven renews us more fully and profoundly than do the four long volumes of The Renewal of Life.

This is unfortunate. Mumford the great researcher, Mumford the great cultural and intellectual historian—and in these categories Mumford is undoubtedly great—have somehow lost track of Mumford the poet. The poet is there, or at least his remains are. But it is a shadowy presence, never realized in the flesh, never the compelling spirit that will move us as we should be moved. This is why Mumford's great rival and model, Oswald Spengler, will always remain a more powerful and appealing figure than Mumford, for he knows that the truths of the heart cannot be spoken by the brain. That is why it is symptomatic of Mumford's whole outlook that he despises Martin Heidegger and even the existentialists in general. It is symptomatic too that Mumford has no love or appreciation for music: for architects, yes; for painters, yes; for engineers, yes; even for poets, though chiefly for American poets. But as far as the thousands of pages of his books are concerned, music simply does not matter. Why not? Because music is the only art that cannot be visualized, that cannot be translated into words or organized into concepts.

What it finally amounts to is that Mumford is a religious man without the religious impulse. In 1930 he wrote to Babette Deutsch that he had spent "thirty happy years without any active commitment to any orthodox religion"; and in the introduction to The Memoirs of Waldo Frank (1973) he confessed that it was only "by wrestling with Frank's passionate metaphysical convictions, which I could never make my own, that I opened the way to another more satisfactory to me—one that, as Emerson had put it, includes the skepticism as well as the faiths of mankind." An answer that mixes doubt with faith, reason with mysticism, may be satisfying personally, but it will never serve as the basis for a renewal of life. Faith that struggles with doubt, as in the great mystics or in a poet like Gerard Manley Hopkins, may do so; but never a doubting faith. The doubting St. Thomas is the least of the apostles, though he may be a necessary one. That is why the four books of The Renewal of Life cannot be the gospels for our time; they are at best only vast and learned sketches of the modern gospels that still remain to be written.

Selected Bibliography

WORKS OF LEWIS MUMFORD

The Story of Utopias. New York: Boni and Liveright, 1922.

Sticks and Stones, A Study of American Architecture and Civilization. New York: Boni and Liveright, 1924.

The Golden Day, A Study in American Experience and Culture. New York: Boni and Liveright, 1926.

The American Caravan; A Yearbook of American Literature, edited by Lewis Mumford, Van Wyck Brooks, Alfred Kreymborg, and Paul Ronsefeld. New York: Macauley, 1927–1936.

Herman Melville. New York: Harcourt, Brace, 1929.

The Brown Decades, A Study of the Arts in America, 1865–1895. New York: Harcourt, Brace, 1931.

Technics and Civilization. New York: Harcourt, Brace, 1934. Volume 1 of The Renewal of Life series.

The Culture of Cities. New York: Harcourt, Brace, 1938. Volume 2 of The Renewal of Life series.

Men Must Act. New York: Harcourt, Brace, 1939.

Faith for Living. New York: Harcourt, Brace, 1940.

The South in Architecture. New York: Harcourt, Brace, 1941.

The Condition of Man. New York: Harcourt, Brace, 1944. Volume 3 of The Renewal of Life series.

City Development, Studies in Disintegration and Renewal. New York: Harcourt, Brace, 1945.

Values for Survival; Essays, Addresses, and Letters on Politics and Education. New York: Harcourt, Brace, 1946.

Green Memories, The Story of Geddes Mumford. New York: Harcourt, Brace, 1947.

The Conduct of Life. New York: Harcourt, Brace, 1951. Volume 4 of The Renewal of Life series.

Art and Technics. New York: Columbia University Press, 1952.

In the Name of Sanity. New York: Harcourt, Brace, 1954.

The Human Prospect, edited by Harry T. Moore and Karl W. Deutsch. Boston: Beacon Press, 1955.

From the Ground Up: Observations on Contemporary Architecture, Housing, Highway Building, and Civic Design. New York: Harcourt, Brace, 1956.

The Transformations of Man. New York: Harper, 1956.

The City in History: Its Origins, Its Transformations, and Its Prospects. New York: Harcourt, Brace, and World, 1961.

The Highway and the City. New York: Harcourt, Brace, and World, 1963.

The Myth of the Machine: Volume 1. *Technics and Human Development.* New York: Harcourt, Brace, and World, 1967.

The Urban Prospect. New York: Harcourt, Brace, and World, 1968.

The Myth of the Machine: Volume 2. *The Pentagon of Power.* New York: Harcourt Brace Jovanovich, 1970.

The Van Wyck Brooks–Lewis Mumford Letters: The Record of a Literary Friendship, 1921–1963, edited by Robert E. Spiller. New York: Dutton, 1970.

The Letters of Lewis Mumford and Frederic J. Osborn, A Transatlantic Dialogue, 1938–70, edited by Michael R. Hughes. Bath: Adams & Dart, 1971; New York: Praeger, 1972.

Interpretations and Forecasts, 1922–1972: Studies in Literature, History, Biography, Technics, and Contemporary Society. New York: Harcourt Brace Jovanovich, 1973.

Findings and Keepings: Analects for an Autobiography. New York: Harcourt Brace Jovanovich, 1975.

My Works and Days: A Personal Chronicle. New York: Harcourt Brace Jovanovich, 1979.

BIBLIOGRAPHY

Elmer S. Newman. *Lewis Mumford: A Bibliography, 1914–1970.* New York: Harcourt Brace Jovanovich, 1971.

BIOGRAPHICAL AND CRITICAL STUDIES

Abercrombie, Neil. "Mumford, Mailer and Machines: Staking a Claim for Man." Unpublished dissertation. University of Hawaii, 1974.

Ashton, Dore. "Lewis Mumford." *Boston University Journal,* 23:3–7 (1975).

Boardman, Philip. *Patrick Geddes.* Chapel Hill: University of North Carolina Press, 1944.

Brooks, Van Wyck. "Lewis Mumford: American Prophet." *Harper's,* 204:6–7, 46–53 (June 1952).

———. *The Writer in America.* New York: Dutton, 1953.

———. *Days of the Phoenix.* New York: Dutton, 1957.

———. *From the Shadow of the Mountain.* New York: Dutton, 1961.

Conrad, David R. *Education for Transformation: Implications of Lewis Mumford's Ecohumanism.* Palm Springs, Calif.: ETC Publications, 1976.

Cowley, Malcolm. *—And I Worked at the Writer's Trade.* New York: Viking, 1978.

Dow, Eddy Weber. "Lewis Mumford's First Phase: A Study of His Work as a Critic of the Arts in America." Unpublished dissertation. University of Pennsylvania, 1965.

———. "Van Wyck Brooks and Lewis Mumford: A Confluence in the 'Twenties'." *American Literature,* 45:407–22 (November 1973).

———. "Lewis Mumford's Passage to India: From the First to the Later Phase." *South Atlantic Quarterly,* 76:31–43 (Winter 1977).

Edwards, Paul E., Jr. "Lewis Mumford's Search for Values." Unpublished dissertation. American University, 1970.

Farrell, James T. *The League of Frightened Philistines, and Other Papers.* New York: Vanguard, 1945. Pp. 106–31.

Ford, Reginald Eugene, III. "Lewis Mumford: A Rhetoric of Liberal Optimism." Unpublished dissertation. University of California, Berkeley, 1976.

Glicksberg, Charles I. "Lewis Mumford and the Organic Synthesis." *Sewanee Review,* 45:55–73 (Jan.–Mar. 1937).

Hook, Sidney. "Metaphysics, War, and the Intellectuals." *Menorah Journal,* 28:326–37 (Oct.–Dec. 1940).

Kazin, Alfred. *On Native Grounds.* New York: Reynal & Hitchcock, 1942.

Lewis, Thomas S. W. "'O Thou Steeled Cognizance': The Brooklyn Bridge, Lewis Mumford and Hart Crane." *Hart Crane Newsletter,* 1:17–26 (1977).

Martin, Dennis M. "Modern American Literary Nationalism." Unpublished dissertation. University of California, Los Angeles, 1973.

Matthiesson, Francis O. *American Renaissance.* New York: Oxford University Press, 1941.

Mumford, Lewis. "An Appraisal of Lewis Mumford's 'Technics and Civilization' (1934)." *Daedalus,* 88:527–36 (Summer 1959).

Novak, Frank George, Jr. "Lewis Mumford as a Critic of American Culture." Unpublished dissertation. University of Tennessee, 1975.

Salmagundi, no. 49 (Summer 1980). Special Lewis Mumford issue. Contains essays by Joseph Duffey and Thomas S. W. Lewis.

Wasserstrom, William. *The Legacy of Van Wyck Brooks: A Study of Maladies and Motives.* Carbondale: Southern Illinois University Press, 1971.

West, Thomas Reed. *Flesh of Steel: Literature and the Machine in American Culture.* Nashville: Vanderbilt University Press, 1967.

White, Morton, and Lucia White. *The Intellectual Versus the City.* Cambridge, Mass.: Harvard University Press & MIT Press, 1962.

—PETER FIRCHOW

Joyce Carol Oates

1938 —

IT may seem odd that a writer whose work is so often associated with the violent, the grotesque, and the bizarre should have been strongly influenced early in her life and in her subsequent writings by Henry David Thoreau's *Walden*, yet both aggression and contemplative withdrawal have a place in the writings of Joyce Carol Oates. These two tendencies do not antagonize, but complement, each other: the physical violence that has offended so many readers and critics always has its counterpart in the mental or spiritual realm; and a oneness with nature, though it is only seldom portrayed explicitly, is always just beneath the surface as at least a partial solution to the disruption and fragmentation of modern life.

Oates insists, even in the bleakest moments of her writing, that there is a connection among all living things, and that the false boundaries erected by individual egos can trick us into thinking we can function in a vacuum, indifferent to the larger whole. The disturbing aspects of her writing often make a reader uncomfortable because they emphasize the hidden life that seethes in a more primitive core of our being. In this respect she is akin to D. H. Lawrence, Joseph Conrad, and even Fëdor Dostoevsky, as well as to the school of American naturalism in which she is so frequently placed.

Oates was born on June 16, 1938, in Lock-

port, New York, a small town on the Erie Canal. Her education in a one-room schoolhouse and the fact that she was not exposed to very many books as a child did not prevent her from composing stories while she was still very young. These handwritten stories with covers she designed herself became more sophisticated in appearance when, at twelve, she learned how to type.

Writing seems always to have formed a part of Oates's life, though her first story to be published, "In the Old World," did not appear until 1959, when she was a student at Syracuse University. It won the college fiction prize offered by *Mademoiselle* magazine, and her writing has been winning prizes ever since: the National Book Award (in 1970, for *them*), a Guggenheim Fellowship, the Rosenthal Foundation Award of the National Institute of Arts and Letters. So frequently did she win the O. Henry Prize Awards that a special award was created for her, for continuing achievement. Were she to write no more, her reputation would already be secured.

After receiving the B.A. from Syracuse in 1960, graduating as class valedictorian, Oates attended the University of Wisconsin, where she obtained an M.A. in 1961. It was there that she met and married Raymond J. Smith; and while the Smiths were in Beaumont, Texas, the following year, Oates began work on a Ph.D. at Rice University in Houston. Her studies were interrupted (and never resumed) by a move to the University of Detroit, where she taught English until 1967. From 1967 to 1978 she and her husband taught at the University of Windsor in Ontario, where they jointly founded *The Windsor Review*. In 1978 Oates became a member of the Creative Writing Program at Princeton University. As a critic as well as a fiction writer she has made valuable contributions to literature and literary scholarship. She has written on tragedy and comedy, visionary writers, and individual authors ranging from William Shakespeare to Norman Mailer.

Oates's first published volume, a collection of short stories titled *By the North Gate* (1963), was followed by her first novel, *With Shuddering Fall* (1964). Together these two works establish many of the themes that were to be of major concern in her later work. The setting of the novel, and of most of the stories, is Eden County, Oates's fictional rural landscape loosely based on the Erie County in which she grew up.

As with William Faulkner's Yoknapatawpha County, or Margaret Laurence's town of Manawaka, certain inhabitants and locales of Eden County turn up in different works, though sometimes they are inconsistent or out of character with previous descriptions. For instance, Oates's first published story, "In the Old World," collected in *By the North Gate*, has as its central character a young man, Swan Walpole, who tries to expiate his maiming of the eye of a black youth. Swan is a major figure in Oates's second novel, *A Garden of Earthly Delights*, where he has the last name Revere (Walpole had been his mother's maiden name). The incident recounted in the short story does not figure in the novel, but is consistent with Swan's character even though the works were pub-

lished seven years apart. The two works in no way depend on one another for meaning, but such overlapping of character and incident was to become a significant characteristic in Oates's later writing, in which stories and characters often serve as glosses on each other.

Oates's first two novels are, by her own admission, nineteenth-century in structure, by which she means that the life portrayed is complete and full of innumerable details. Her love of detailed descriptions carries into the later novels as well, creating a sense in the reader of being reminded of a person or place previously known. In Oates's most successful writing the thoughts and emotions of a character are transmitted with such force that there is a merging of consciousness between character and reader, so that the sensitive reader becomes aware of a greater life force in which he or she participates. This awareness is not always pleasant, nor is it meant to be: "A happy book," Oates maintains, "is like a happy person—there's nothing to be done to it or for it." One of the characters in the collection *The Hungry Ghosts* voices a similar sentiment when, as a poet whose wells of inspiration have run dry, he turns to plagiarism because he cannot write poems about being happy. Joy exists only indirectly in most of Oates's work.

Oates's first novel, *With Shuddering Fall*, establishes many of the directions and themes that were to continue to be important to her and to her later work. It was conceived of as a religious work with a theme of obedience and love that transcend any concept of good or evil. It is set in the northwest hills of Eden County, and the landscape leaps into life as Oates describes its farms, their people, and the bareness of their lives.

Eden County is not a paradise, and in fact often appears to be quite hellish to its inhabitants. Its name evokes not an innocent world, but a reminder of what we have lost and the resulting spiritual poverty of our lives. One focus for this contrast is Karen Herz, a young girl who is susceptible to religious experience and fascinated with the workings of destiny. Returning from Sunday Mass, she retreats to her room to kneel and feel the excitement of "the secret ecstasy of these prayers, their burning, breathless power." When her father reads from the family Bible the story of Abraham's willingness to sacrifice his son as an act of obedience, Karen meditates on the "strange dignity" of fulfilling one's destiny that way, "forever bound by the inhuman plot of a story manipulated by God Himself!"

The importance of this idea to Karen becomes the driving energy of the novel. When her father is severely beaten by Shar, a race-car driver who grew up on a nearby farm, he instructs Karen to kill Shar, and not to come home until she has done so. Thus Karen, like Abraham, sets out to fulfill her destiny in a manner that seems to remove from her actions any questions of moral good or evil, and places them solely in a context of obedience to her father's command. As Karen runs after, and then off with, Shar, he becomes increasingly drawn to her and finds himself more vulnerable than he dares to admit. In the summer races he begins to feel "a queer little force" that lures him "in to the center, to death," in a totally irrational way.

Shar functions on an intuitive level. He knows that "for auto racers death came not through surrender to the center, but through surrender to the outside—to centrifugal force, a sudden careening off the track." Though he leaves Karen to escape this force she wields on him, he is ultimately drawn back to her by that same force, and acknowledges to himself that they are hopelessly entangled, never to be free of each other. Karen kills him by rejecting him

totally when he most wants her to be with him always. Her silence when he asks what he is supposed to do provides an answer they both understand: in the Fourth of July race his car smashes into the outer wall of the track, killing him in an act of surrender to an inexplicable force.

Karen, too, has surrendered to an outside force, and fulfilled her father's command, yet she still needs to be purged of her actions. She spends the fall in a mental hospital; and even when she returns home, it is three days before her father will see her. Yet the novel ends with a moment of reconciliation as the Herz family attends Sunday Mass together. The purple vestments of penance and the plea of the *Kyrie* bind Karen to her father in the ritual of sacrifice, and the service ends with benediction, after which Karen and her father once more affirm their love for one another. Shar's sacrifice, though apparently senseless, partakes of this moment in a way that seems more real than the ritualized actions of the Herz family.

The structure of the novel parallels Karen's spiritual journey. Its three sections are named after the seasons of spring, summer, and fall. "Spring" appropriately ends as Karen runs off with Shar, marking the end of her youth, her innocence, and her conventional life with her family. "Summer" is the time of the seething emotional encounter between Karen and Shar, and culminates in the death of Shar, subsequent riots in the streets, and Karen's collapse. It is in the "Fall" that her physical and spiritual recoveries take place, yet she will never regain the relative innocence of her previous existence. The title of the novel indicates whose sacrifice is the greater. It derives from the last line of a poem by George Meredith that questions why one should fall "with shuddering" into the breast of death, since both death and life are gifts of the same spirit of nature. Shar embraces death as the inevitable solution to his love for Karen, while Karen embraces what she imagines to be her necessary destiny in an act of obedience that appears sterile next to Shar's sacrifice.

Oates's concern with the power of redemptive love is at work here, though it does not reach its fullest statement until the later novel *Do with Me What You Will*. It is less interesting in this first novel because ultimately we find we do not care very much what happens to Karen. She is interesting and curious, but does not engage our sympathies. This may be partly because neither she nor Shar is entirely credible: they sometimes appear to be exaggerations or surreal figures who are allegories rather than flesh and blood. Yet both triumph in their own way: Shar through death, and Karen by surviving the battering of her body, her mind, and her spirit. Yet her obedience to her father's command does not mean she will necessarily obtain any reward.

Oates once stated that in working herself out of her religious phase in this novel, she tried to show that having faith may often leave someone nowhere after all. Karen is home at the novel's end, but she has acted on the basis of the faith of her family while she remains outside of it: "They could not but love her, who had strengthened their faith in the vague beliefs they mouthed and heard mouthed to them in the ceremony of the Mass." Her own faith has been twisted by the experiences of that summer: the death of Shar, her miscarriage, and her mental breakdown. When she finally returns home, the land that shaped her seems unreal and a betrayal to her. She is forced to the realization that "No ground is holy, no land divine, but that we make it so by an exhausting, a deadly straining of our hearts."

With Shuddering Fall is important to an understanding of much of Oates's later work. It announces the important themes of homecoming and return to one's origins, and the essential need for compassion. Her characters do not necessarily show compassion to one another, but it is invariably present in Oates herself and in her attitude to those who populate her novels. There is no condemnation, and often a quiet admiration, for those who, however unlovable they may appear, manage to survive. This in itself is seen to be a triumph.

From this first novel it can also be discerned that Oates's concern is not for those who are "happy," though a number of her later characters do appear to be relatively content with their lot. But neither is her concern solely for the tragic or the grotesque for their own sakes. Like Flannery O'Connor, on whom she has written several illuminating essays, Oates uses the grotesque to accomplish something that reaches far beyond mere shock. O'Connor uses it to reach the holy, the divine element that permeates our daily lives. Oates uses it to reach through to the natural world and to illumine it in such a way that we are able to see ourselves as we really are, however unflattering such a view may turn out to be.

Another major concept that the first novel introduces is the impact of ancestry and upbringing on a character. Both heredity and environment play crucial roles in the formation of Oates's characters. While modern psychology has revealed that such influences are critical in determining personality, they are rarely portrayed in fiction, and even more rarely are they portrayed with the accuracy and believability Oates provides. One can never be certain, and in fact it would most likely be incorrect to assume, that the character who greets us in the first chapter of one of Oates's novels is going to remain in the spotlight for very long. More likely, that character will be the ancestor of one who will come to occupy the major role in the novel. Characters are never given to us out of context, out of their families and the environment in which their growth occurred.

This is one advantage that Oates's novels have over her short stories, where the form demands compression and generally presents us with only a short span in a character's life. In the novels Oates indulges her preoccupation with sources and formative incidents. One of the clearest memories of Karen's childhood is an event that occurred when she was three years old. Running through the grass, she was scooped into the air by Shar and handed over to her father. The incident is alluded to on several occasions by those who were involved in it, and especially by Karen on the day of Shar's death. She has a dream of running home to her father to announce that everything has been finished, and in her dream becomes once again the small child lifted up by Shar and, after a moment's fear, given over to her father's arms. With Shar's death she begins her journey home, and in this sense Shar has for the second time returned her to her father.

The effects of ancestry are even more clearly seen in Oates's second novel, *A Garden of Earthly Delights* (1967). There are three parts to the novel, each belonging to and named for one of the men who is crucial in the formation of the character of Clara Walpole. Not surprisingly, these are her father, her lover, and her son. For in terms of Clara's affections, the man she eventually marries has no stature at all compared with them. For Clara it is a marriage of convenience, enabling her to provide a home for her son.

The novel begins on the day of Clara's birth, and the activity and life of the migrant workers among whom she will grow up are seen through the eyes of her father, Carleton. Through him we see once again the theme of returning home: Carleton is preoccupied with "going back" to Kentucky. He tries to keep the memory of home alive, for the memory is equivalent to the reality for him; and if he loses it, he fears, he will never be able to get home again. Yet he secretly

knows he will not return, as do the other workers who also talk about giving up their migratory lives. Nevertheless, Carleton always carries within him a graphic image of freedom, imagining it as a horse running alongside the pickers' bus, keeping time with it while completely independent of it. This is also the way he fantasizes himself: "free, able to glide along inches above the ground, easily outdistancing this old bus. A young Carleton, running along, letting his arms swing—."

Clara inherits her father's spirit, for she too balks at their bridled life. There is no temporary solace to be found in religion, as there was for Karen. Clara's one visit to a local church leaves her unable to fathom why God should be watching her when there are surely other people who are more interesting to look at. Certain that God will never bother with her, she feels relieved when she literally runs away from the service. On that same day Clara meets Lowry, attracted to him because his blond hair reminds her of her father. In his face she thinks she can see the presence of the God of whom the minister had spoken, present as a force like that of hunger. This hunger drives her after Lowry, with whom she runs off that same night. Unlike Karen's running after Shar, Clara's action is one that liberates rather than binds her. She feels as if she has been carried away by a great cooling breeze that has finally caught up with her. Karen's act was one of obedience; Clara's is one of defiance.

Her father tries to follow her to reclaim her. Carleton's brief journey after Clara ultimately is also his journey to freedom. He suffers a breakdown, and in his confusion imagines he sees his people patiently waiting for him to come home. Entering a church to await his death, he does not die, but lingers for another two months in a strange hospital bed as his mind empties and cleanses itself of memory and desire. It is a purgatorial state we are not allowed to enter, for Oates carries us along with Clara into her new life. Yet much of Oates's writing partakes of just such a purgatory, in which people are kept waiting and suffering but are ultimately certain that they will triumph. The vision of paradise is postponed rather than denied as her characters move through the natural world, hungry and yearning to be full.

In fact, such hunger becomes a major image of Oates's later fiction as the affluent stuff themselves with food yet are unsatisfied. The concept appears as early as the story "First Views of the Enemy" (1964), which ends with a mother and her son glutting themselves as a way of holding on to their possessions and shutting out the disturbing image of the less fortunate Mexican children encountered earlier that day.

But for Lowry and Clara security is not so easy to obtain. When they finally achieve a physical union, it is beside the Eden River, from which Clara has just emerged. This Eden has its resident serpent in the form of the bloodsucker, attached to Clara's foot, that leads directly to Clara's first sexual encounter. But it is not a fall from innocence, for Oates seems to be concerned chiefly with the ironies of the situation and the way in which Clara's eyes become opened, so that she can now calculate coldly how she will take control of her life.

This is very different from the previous novel's concern with working out one's destiny and fulfilling the duties of obedience. Clara, unlike Karen, brings all the "accidents" of her life into control. Pregnant by Lowry, who will not yield to marriage and a family, she keeps her pregnancy a secret from him and chooses Curt Revere, a wealthy businessman, to care for her by feigning love for him and leading him to believe the child she bears is his. Such deliberate planning is done out of her wish to provide her son with all the trappings of a secure life, that

which she never had but believes is necessary for genuine freedom.

So great is her desire that even when Lowry returns years later, willing to take Clara and her son with him, she refuses, solely because of the future she fears for her son. This son, though, seems quite able to look out for himself. He is called Swan because swans look cold and hard, and are fearless and potentially dangerous. In the end, what Clara has denied him proves more significant than what she has been able to provide for him. Swan's rebellion against the falseness of his position is kindled into life when he and Clara move into the Revere home. Lowry had predicted that the boy would grow up to kill things, and his sense of Swan was accurate. In a hunting adventure one of Revere's sons is accidentally shot in Swan's presence. The event jolts Swan, who had moments earlier been disgusted with the shooting of a chicken hawk, but now feels that there is within himself a bird fluttering about, desperately trying to get out. Like his grandfather Carleton's visions of liberation, Swan's, too, represent a struggle to rid himself of his uneasiness and his limitations.

Oates warns against over-allegorizing Swan or, by extension, any of her characters. Swan tells his girl friend that he does not want "to be a character in a story, in a book. I don't want to be like someone in a movie. I don't want to be born and die and have everyone watching— reading along. Everything decided ahead of time—." But of course he *is* a character in a book, and everyone *is* watching his birth and his death.

Implied here is the belief that in literature, as in life, although everything is not predestined irrevocably, there is a sense in which, like Karen in the earlier novel, we have a destiny to fulfill. This destiny involves our ability to mesh with the natural rhythms of the universe, to accept death as well as life, and not to fall with shuddering into the mysteries of life. Just as Eden County and the Eden River surround episodes that are far from paradisiacal, so the "garden" of the novel's title is akin to the *Garden of Earthly Delights* painted by Hieronymus Bosch, a garden in which, even in its prelapsarian state, cats catch mice and animals devour each other as part of the natural cycle of life.

Swan acts out the destructive aspect of the destiny foreseen by Lowry in the murder–suicide in which he shoots first Revere and then himself. Clara, who has witnessed the horror, passes her remaining days in a nursing home, passively watching violent television shows. She is in the same situation as her father was for the last months of his life, unable to care for herself and suffering the sudden loss of a child who has gone his own way. From such correspondences it seems that for Oates the sins of the fathers are frequently visited upon the children, not distinguishing between personalities but transcending them. Just as we cannot escape our childhood, so we perpetuate the forces of that childhood onto the next generation of children. Eventually the cycle will be exploded and result in destruction, but that destruction will often herald a new and higher consciousness.

Such a concept is at work in Oates's third novel, *Expensive People* (1968), the narrative of a young man that culminates in his shooting of his mother. The self-conscious first-person narration includes comments on the creative process as well as addresses to the reader and attempts at analyzing the motives and actions of characters.

Richard Everett's parents are filtered to us through his eyes with an uncannily adult understanding of their character and behavior. Although the work is obviously not condoning murder, it is attempting to lay bare many of the pretenses and falsities of an affluent society.

Oates does not deal with the rural poor, as in her two previous novels: her concern here is with those who live in luxury amid beautiful things. The influence of this environment is felt just as strongly as that of the world of migrant workers or "white trash," and it is just as pernicious in its ability to destroy. Richard's mother, Nada (shortened from Natashya), is sumptuously elegant but inhabits a world in which moral values are as foreign as her name. It is no accident that the name she uses means "nothing," and all pretensions are dissipated with finality when Richard discovers at her funeral that her original name had been the less exotic Nancy. The aura of Nada had been fabricated to conceal a common woman who is an ironic version of the American dream of the self-made success. She has achieved wealth and status, but at the expense of family and moral values.

Richard's response to his surroundings is understandably one of distrust: he often believes he is not living with his true parents but with "cruel step-parents," that his true ancestors would be "foreign and exotic and not quite speaking my language," but that he would be able to "tame" them into closeness with him.

The novel is unique to Oates's work in several ways: we remain in the world of the child-adolescent, who is not followed into maturity and parenthood. Richard's narration suggests that at the end of his memoir he will terminate his life. It is also Oates's only novel that deals so self-consciously with its own literary techniques and tries to assess itself as it progresses. For instance, there is a section entitled "How to Write a Memoir Like This," and shortly afterward a section that purports to be reviews of *Expensive People* that appeared in, among other places, *Time* magazine, the *New York Times Book Review*, and *New Republic*. A story supposedly written by Nada is one that Oates herself had previously published in the *Quarterly Review of Literature*, but in the novel it is followed by a critique. Some of these techniques are in the same tradition as James Joyce's "Oxen of the Sun" chapter of *Ulysses*, experimenting with different prose styles and voices. But here the connection is between the events of the novel and how the objective viewer will judge those events; it is not solely an artistic preoccupation with language.

The merging of the real and fictive worlds extends into Oates's poetry as well as her prose. One poem, "From the Dark Side of the Earth," contains the striking instance of the persona of the poem casually addressing the person to whom he is speaking as "Joyce." Generally the poetry is more transparent than the prose in revealing Oates's own attitudes and emotions. But the ability to synthesize living persons and turn them into characters helps to make Oates's fiction plausible and energetic. She does this especially well in her collection of stories *All the Good People I've Left Behind*, and in her academic satires *The Hungry Ghosts*. In *Expensive People* it is obvious that Oates found the first-person narrative an exciting voice to use.

The events of the novel merge with an awareness of the work in progress. Fact and fiction blend in the novel itself, for it is from one of Nada's notebook entries that Richard gets the idea to become a sniper. The entry contains an idea for a short novel, *The Sniper*, about a young man who leads two lives, one public and the other secret. He frightens people by becoming a sniper but initially does not hurt anyone. After several shooting episodes he finally kills someone, and Nada's entry is uncertain as to whether the young man should know he has planned this all along or not. Richard, too, knows, and yet does not know, that his destiny is sketched out before him when he discovers the notebook. He is aware that his heart "began

to pound as if it knew something already that I myself did not know." Once again we are given a character who must fulfill his destiny. The notebook entry outlines Richard's future: he buys a gun, goes out on three sniping missions without harming anyone, and on the fourth commits murder by killing his beloved Nada when she is about to desert her family.

In these first three novels each of the dominant male characters searches for freedom from the limitations of his existence. Shar finds his liberation only through death. Carleton seeks to return home; Lowry is restlessly on the move; Swan and Richard both attempt to cope with their romantic feelings toward their mothers by killing either their mother or their "rival."

Another parallel development in these novels lies in the quest to fulfill one's destiny. Karen never takes charge of her life, but pours her energies into obedience to her father's command. She is the least interesting of Oates's female protagonists, largely because she is absorbed by her sense of duty and never emerges as an independent being. Clara, in contrast, takes control of her life the day she organizes Swan's and her future, and the rest of her actions are devoted to bringing that future into the present. She achieves her goal at a price, for Swan is denied the freedom Clara so eagerly sought for herself. Richard comes into his own the first night he goes out as a sniper. He tells us that he slept well that night, for he had at last "discovered" himself. What he fails to realize is that he has not really discovered himself at all, but has merely assumed the role of a potential character in one of his mother's stories. Nada thus creates her son twice, by physically bringing him into the world and providing him with his new self-image and status as a child-murderer. Thus, after Richard pulls the trigger to kill Nada, he tells us that he did not "come alive" as he had done previously; rather, "the world cracked in pieces around me." He has not discovered his true self after all, but only destroyed what he loved.

These first three novels, then, while obviously quite different from one another in their surface details, have an underlying unity and are often considered a trilogy. In each is a basic concern with how character reflects one's background and becomes one's future or destiny. Although all of Oates's characters have freedom of choice, they submit to what seems to them a predetermined or unavoidable course of action. At the conclusion of the third novel, Richard seriously doubts the consolation of his free will. He is left stuffing himself with bananas, cookies, bread, candy, lettuce, sauces, and jams, "carried along on the wave of a most prodigious hunger." He is seeking an answer to the emptiness inside him and wants to stuff it into silence once and for all. If he does intend to commit suicide, as he has indicated he would throughout his memoir, it will most likely be done by gorging himself, as a relative of Nada's had supposedly done.

The final image of fatness stuffing itself to satiate its spiritual hunger tells us as much about Richard as he has told us about himself in his entire narrative. He has shunned descriptions of lovely spring days because writers are better equipped to write of the inferno and purgatory than of paradise. Oates's novels do the same, avoiding the bliss of Eden and focusing on the sufferings of the world. Whether or not paradise is to be gained through such suffering is beyond her concern. In her writing there is, by her own admission, "only the natural world," a distinction that sets her apart from writers such as Flannery O'Connor, with whom she is often compared and whose stories are permeated with a constant awareness of the supernatural. Oates argues that the problem of living in this world is sufficient concern for a writer, without having

to bring in "an extra dimension." The infernal and purgatorial aspects of life provide her writing with all it needs; paradise is left for the contemplations of others.

Richard's hunger is symptomatic of a spiritually depleted society. Fatness is an illness for Oates, and Richard is only the first in a string of characters who are or become fat as a manifestation of their inner poverty. The most grotesque of these is the Pedersen family in *Wonderland*, whose family dinners have been likened to the Mad Hatter's tea party. But preceding this novel was Oates's novel *them* (1969), which won the National Book Award in 1970. It expands the implications of "fatness" at a critical point in the life of its main female character, Maureen Wendall. When Maureen undergoes a mental breakdown, she withdraws into silence and sweets, becoming grotesquely obese, sullen, dirty, and drab. In contrast, her recovery is marked by a revulsion for food and a regaining of her former, thinner body. Like Lewis Carroll's Alice in her dream world, Maureen expands and shrinks as a physical reflection of her psychological state. But this is only one aspect of *them*, and not the most important one.

In *them* Oates is once again concerned in part with the effects of literature on life and the question of which is more "real." It purports to be a work of historical fiction based on the life of a student Oates taught at the University of Detroit, though Oates has since indicated that Maureen is not a "real" person and that her letters are also a fiction. Maureen's questioning is therefore a self-accusation of Oates and what she represents. One of the letters asks, "Why did you think that book about Madame Bovary was so important? All those books? Why did you tell us they were more important than life? They are not more important than my life." These questions demand to be answered by both the readers and the writers of fiction. Maureen asks, "You write books. What do you know? . . . Oh, we women know things you don't know, you teachers, you readers and writers of books. . . ."

But the existence of *them* would seem to be proof that Maureen is wrong at least about certain writers of books. Oates is able to use the lives of unintellectual people as the material for her fiction and to give their actions meaning and significance on a more universal level. We can learn from their mistakes and can achieve through their emotions and experiences a growth that we might not otherwise undergo in our own lives. In writing *them*, Oates indicates that she is concerned with this role and responsibility of the artist in handling the "real" world so that we can see its most awful potentialities and, by seeing and understanding them, can learn how to deal with them. Although the central characters in *them* suffer and often appear to be leading lives of quiet desperation, Oates has pointed out that the crucial thing about their lives is that they all survive. And not just by muddling through: they manage to obtain what to them are major achievements, even though to outsiders the characters seem to be social failures.

Oates quite rightly has called attention to the essential cheerfulness of these characters, a happiness that is retained amid viciousness, pettiness, even criminal acts. There is a self-sufficiency to them, a cool-headed independence, and thus freedom from middle-class values. In their humble ways they achieve the realization of the American dream that Nada had only parodied: they forge their destinies completely on their own, and create for themselves a life that is, for them at least, a success, attained solely through their own contrivances. They are willing to make enormous sacrifices to reach their goals, which, however petty they may seem to us, are magnificent triumphs for them.

This in part explains the apparent grotesqueness of much of Oates's work. What is distorted may often be restored by being seen through corrective lenses. The shocking effect is aimed at making us sit up and take notice of something that has become perverted in our accepted daily lives. Oates is aware that she is addressing a society that has accepted violence as a way of life. By portraying abhorrent actions in vivid detail, she tries to reawaken in us a sense of horror at what is really at stake. This is mostly true of *Wonderland* and *The Assassins*, but her other novels also contain a good dose of destruction that can be used to reconstruct a kind of victory.

In *them* the narrative begins with Loretta Botsford's lover being shot to death by her brother Brock. Loretta marries the policeman who helped her move the body and protected her brother, and these two apparent losers become the parents of the two main characters of the novel, Jules and Maureen Wendall. There is a strong suspicion that Jules was fathered by Loretta's lover, but whether he was or not, his life is branded from its very conception with violence and unlucky love. Yet Jules is clever and calculating. Like Clara, Lowry, or Swan, he is an adult even while he is young. As a child his sister Maureen sees him as a magician, able to create things in the air.

Jules is able to "create" his life by knowing what he wants and overcoming any obstacles to obtaining it. He pursues Nadine, the girl of his dreams, who comes from a wealthy family well beyond Jules's social reach. He very nearly gets her, for she runs away with him, but deserts him when he falls ill with the flu. When they meet again and try to be lovers, Nadine is unable to reach a climax, and shortly thereafter shoots Jules—though not fatally. Jules's spirit, temporarily lost, is rekindled when he becomes an activist in the Detroit race riots of 1967, and learns that "the old Jules had not truly died but had only been slumbering." In the end, after fatally shooting a policeman, he bids good-bye to Maureen, heads west to a new life, and thus triumphs in his overcoming of destiny, heredity, and environment. Jules is the furthest remove possible from Karen Herz. He sees no limitations imposed on him by familial obligations or class structures. He fulfills no destiny but, rather, creates his own life, a magician in the most practical aspects of living.

Maureen tries to do the same thing. Like Jules, she thinks of herself as spirit struggling to break free from the burdens of the flesh. Like Carleton in *A Garden of Earthly Delights*, she often imagines her real self detaching itself from the body that is engaged in mundane activities. Carleton had seen this other self as a wild horse outdistancing the bus in which he rode. Maureen feels it as "the terrible pressure of water wanting to burst free." She yearns to join that other self, her real self, which is able to free itself and escape, and even turns to look back at her.

The struggle between body and spirit is of course not new in literature, but Oates has a fine talent for presenting it in a way that keeps her writing very much in the realm of the natural world, and she resists lengthy indulgence in metaphysical speculations or theories. There is in her writing no glaring dichotomy between the body and the spirit. Both are aspects of a unified whole, and function together. When a character's body becomes grotesque, obese, or maimed, it has a direct counterpart in the soul. Like Dorian Gray's portrait, much of the physical violence in Oates's stories is actually a graphic picture of what is happening to a person's inner being.

In Oates's art, though, there is always the awareness that even realistic fiction is not the same as lived experiences. In an epigraph to one of her critical essays, Oates cites Paul Klee's statement that "Art does not reproduce what we see. It makes us see." This is an answer to Maureen's infuriation with the world of literature that she reveals in her letters to Oates as teacher. On the one hand, Maureen can read the novels of Jane Austen and feel excited to know that in comparison with her own life, the world of these novels seems more real. The events of her life seem less convincing and permanent to her than what she has discovered in her reading. But when she accuses Oates of just writing books and not knowing anything about life, she cannot know that she is a character in one of those books, thereby making her life both more and less real at the same time.

Just as the play-within-the-play of sixteenth-century drama has been revived in much modern drama, so Oates has extended the concept to literature, so that in a Joycean sense *them* is a book containing the makings of the book called *them*. Oates is, indirectly, a character in her own novel. When Maureen "wakes up" from her bout of depression, breakdown, and obesity, she writes to Oates precisely because she senses that they are alike in many ways. Thus her angry letters are also an externalization of the dilemma that any sensitive writer must face.

The closing section of *them* is titled "Come, My Soul, That Hath Long Languished...." The title exposes the languishing hunger that has been both Maureen's and Jules's all along, the desire to escape the confines and limitations of the body and to satisfy the soul's longing to be free and unencumbered. Later characters of Oates's are actually able to accomplish this, but Maureen must express the yearning by stuffing herself with sweets. At the conclusion of the book, she has succeeded in winning the love of her married professor, marrying, becoming pregnant, and repudiating her past and her family. When Jules visits to bid her good-bye as he prepares to go west, she announces that she does not intend to see "them," any of her family, any more. Yet because of her new status as a married woman about to become a mother, Jules indicates that she has in fact become one of "them."

Once again a character finds she cannot escape what she is. Attempts to repudiate or ignore one's family or childhood will only cause those influences to surface elsewhere in someone's life. Yet *them* is also a novel of triumph, of two people who triumph in their limited ways over circumstances that had weighted them down, and of the triumph of the spirit over the flesh in achieving its will despite the obstacles along the way.

Wonderland (1971) extends these concepts, but is in some ways less successful than *them*. Some of its characters are so extreme that they become oppressive; one ceases to care what becomes of them. The novel is best read as a surrealistic account in the manner of Lewis Carroll's *Alice in Wonderland*, from which its title is taken. Exaggerations, abrupt transitions, and questions of identity abound. Carroll's work had a profound effect on Oates when she was very young, and many of its qualities find their way into her writing. Oates herself has cited what are for her the most significant aspects of Alice's stories: that the child within us will triumph, that we will all eventually find salvation, that the complexities of life must be recognized in perspective for what they are, and that we are all participants in the game of life. It is not especially easy to recognize all these points in *Wonderland*, which remains a dark novel and does little to suggest any final "triumph." Oates rewrote the ending two years after its publication, in an attempt to change the negative feeling of the conclusion; but the revision, slightly more optimistic, still does not alter the tone of all that precedes it.

Jesse Vogel had as a child escaped the murder–suicide of his family by his father and been adopted by Dr. Karl Pedersen, whose unusual family of obese geniuses nearly stifles Jesse. Like Carleton and Maureen, Jesse likes horses when he is a child, but not because they are a symbol of freedom. The attraction is drawn from their being big, heavy animals that are "like life that had run down into pure flesh, enormous muscular mounds of flesh, perfectly obedient and indifferent." *Wonderland* likewise weights down the spirit by the encumbrance of a suffocating body. Attempts at transcendence are aborted, unfulfilled, or led astray by drugs and violence. The hunger of the spirit is sharply etched in the overstuffing of the body. Jesse joins both Richard Everett and Maureen Wendall when he experiences a ravenous hunger in the center of his body. It leads him to the home of Dr. Pedersen, where bodies are stuffed with food as spirits go unnourished. Ironically, it is Dr. Pedersen who advocates the doctrine that the spirit is stronger than the body, even as his daughter Hilda moves from cheerful prettiness to become "a beetle-browed girl with a woman's body shapeless as a tub." Jesse is able to free himself from the oppressiveness of the Pedersen household only when he is disowned for helping Mrs. Pedersen run away. She is dragged back, unable to escape, but Jesse finds himself free.

But the homes he has escaped are a part of him. Even when he is in medical school, he feels he is "in disguise" as a normal young man. Food is now unbearable to him, much as Maureen finds herself repulsed by it once she is "cured." When Jesse sees a fat man, he cannot help staring in disgust and thinking that fat people are sick. Even later, as a doctor, Jesse "hated fat people. Hated crazy people," finding such fat a "spiritual obscenity." Jesse's changes of his name accompany his inner growth: he is born Jesse Harte but abandons the name to become a Pedersen. Jesse's "heart," his core and his ancestral roots, are removed from him and sublimated. When he can no longer be a son to Pedersen, he adopts his grandfather's name, Vogel. The word means "bird," and marks Jesse's attempt to restore the spirit that has been suffocating within him.

Jesse, like Maureen, tries to assume a normal life and repudiate his background. But once again the sins of the fathers seem to be visited on the children. When his daughter Shelley runs away from home, trying to free herself of her father, Jesse goes after her. Oates revised this ending to underline the return home and the ambiguity of Jesse's role as protector or as an angel of death. Jesse's wife Helene has likewise had to free herself from her past life as the daughter of a brilliant surgeon who found his research with cats unsatisfying because of their lack of personality. Only Jesse appears to be locked into his role at the end of the novel.

The work is a low point in Oates's career, and she has stated that it "is probably an immoral novel" in its depressing and dark atmosphere. Jesse's emotions often seem to have been recorded from the author's immediate experience, and his ideas about a "story" indicate that this may well have been the case: "He had the idea that what people thought were stories were fragments from shattered wholes, the patterns, the brain waves, of a certain man at a certain time in his life, the record of his controlled and uncontrolled inner life: therefore all writing was autobiography, wasn't it?"

If this is true, then *Wonderland* represents what must have been a difficult and perhaps depressing stage in its author's life. Yet like its predecessors it is concerned with the return home, the completion of a cycle in someone's life, and the acceptance by him of his childhood and the events that formed him. Oates's characters seem trapped by their families as frequently as they seek to escape them. It is perhaps a flaw in *Wonderland* that it is never

clearly shown how Jesse's early life—the murder of his family and his involvement with the Pedersens—creates the situation that leads his daughter Shelley to run away from home. Jesse escaped the early homes of his life, but does not seem in the end really to have escaped at all.

In Oates's sixth novel, *Do with Me What You Will* (1973), the central character does manage to escape. Elena is perhaps the most liberated and affirmative of Oates's protagonists thus far. She surmounts obstacles with a detachedness often bordering on oblivion. She alone is able, at the end, finally and literally to walk away from the home and situation that were gradually snuffing out her life, and to seize the makings of what she believes will lead to a better life. Until that moment she has been the victim the title of the novel describes, shuttled back and forth by the pushiness of her mother and, later, by the rigidity of her husband. It is through her lover that she begins to loosen these bonds and discover her inner spirit. The narrative is a form of flashback as she and Jack, her lover, survey the incredible string of events that brought them together. And it is no accident that her lover is an antagonist of her husband's, representing all that her husband found demeaning in the legal profession they share.

Once again Oates begins her narrative when the main character is still a child. Elena is seven years old when her father "kidnaps" her from a schoolyard in Pittsburgh and drives her to California. Elena, like Jesse, experiences a childhood trauma that colors her character, but the difference is that her kidnapping was an act of love, an attempt to rescue her from the domination of her mother, Ardis. Despite her father's obvious instability, Elena realizes how deeply she loved him: he alone tried to free her rather than to program her life. Ironically, his desire to do so caused him to imprison her physically in their rented room to protect her.

Fathers pursue their daughters in Oates's novels, if not literally (as do Carleton and Jesse), then through their mental holds on them (as Herz has on Karen, and Jesse on Shelley). Their pursuits represent the internal pull of family, which frequently has done its lasting work long before the character realizes he or she is firmly locked in its grip. This pull is not represented as being either good or ill in itself. It is shown as one of the facts of life, often responsible for later griefs and troubles, but also credited with stimulating personal awareness and eventual liberation.

Elena is also pursued by her mother, a vague presence throughout the novel who is metamorphosed into different names and personalities but is always in the background of Elena's life. When she is undergoing a mental crisis, Elena's first instinct is to telephone Ardis—now called Marya—and say that she wants to come home for a while. But the connection is broken and her call is not returned for a month. Looking back on the incident, Elena recalls that "Staying alive is not so complicated as dialing a telephone number."

This might be the theme for much of Oates's fiction: the fact of existence is something always with and around us, but it is the details of daily routine that mire us and complicate our lives so that we lose an awareness of the larger world we inhabit. Nagging in the background is the constant sense that there is a grander scale on which life is balanced; but this perspective is forever being overshadowed, seen through a glass darkly, making its presence felt in moments of mental crisis or breakdown or in times of recollection, when past is assumed into present and a unity is perceived. Such moments are never sustained indefinitely; they may cease with a person's "cure" or rehabilitation into society and the resumption of a functional life. This is what happens to Maureen Wendall and,

to a lesser degree, to Jesse Vogel. It occurs too for Karen Herz, while Clara Revere remains in a never-never land of mental vacuity. Richard Everett shatters his world when he kills Nada, whose name ("nothing") indicates the emptiness of the social world he resists. It is only in *Do with Me What You Will* that Oates first has a character break away in an act of faith and step out into uncertainty, accompanied only by love and by the pain that she has suffered and that has taught her.

Elena's life acts out the book's epigraph, Henry James's statement that "the world as it stands is no illusion, no phantasm, no evil dream of a night; we wake up to it again forever and ever; we can neither forget it nor deny it nor dispense with it." The nightmarish wonderland of the previous novel has been left behind for the waking world Elena discovers. By using the real world, Elena finds herself able to reach out to an acceptance of life's greatest gifts: love, faith, and an awareness of the eternal present. The means by which she does so violate our standards of social propriety. She not only leaves her husband but also causes her lover to abandon his wife and child. She is acting not on precepts or mores but on intuition, the same intuition that had made her, years earlier, leave the schoolyard with a stranger who turned out to be her father.

The earlier incident was an obvious act of blind trust, and it was only after yielding to such faith that its purpose was revealed to her. Similarly, Elena's departure with Jack at the end of the novel has to be an act of blind trust between the lovers. The future is withheld from them, just as it is from the reader, who is left not knowing where they go or how they live thereafter, knowing only that they *are* together, looking back over their lives. Any further knowledge would defeat the significance of Elena's act. She does not know, and she does not worry, where her future with Jack will lead. She only knows that she must seize that future in order to attain peace.

When the lovers finally meet, they are able to smile at each other, "as if seeing each other for the first time, a look between them of pure kinship, of triumph." In one sense they actually are seeing each other for the first time as they really are, free of encumbrances and able to focus on their bond, their kinship in having escaped their suffocating lives with people who tried to force them into roles they refused. Their escape, then, is indeed a triumph, even though the final admission of the novel is that they are not entirely able to forget everything else. But this, too, is kept under control. Although the past can never be totally eradicated, it can be subordinated to present circumstances and become paler as time passes.

The shock of present and past melting together is felt by Elena when she sees a photograph of the child Jack is going to adopt. The particular child fades from her sight and resurfaces as another, perhaps Elena herself, as she becomes aware of the cyclic completion created by the patterns of birth and death, and the possibility of freezing time into an eternal present. The instant recalled by a photograph is an artificial attempt to locate the universe in time, to compress its vastness to a particular small occasion. It is the antithesis of the experience Elena has while visiting Jack's client, Meredith Dawe, in the hospital. A radical whose lectures and beliefs are directed toward "the obliteration of matter," Dawe transmits to Elena a deep, restful peace that she is to remember all her life. Yet at the end he is left an inmate of Michigan State Prison, writing lengthy letters to the judge who sentenced him, the power of his life reduced to the penning of words that go unheeded. Dawe sees the continent as "a despoiled and vandalized Garden of North America,

which begs us to purify it and restore it to its original innocence."

Oates has returned to one of her earliest and most durable themes, the corruption of our world and the plea that we open our eyes to what we are destroying. But Dawe's plea is unanswered, and he is reduced to a sense of futility and intimidated into silence. In a similar way his lawyer, Elena's lover, gives himself over to the power of words when he loses Dawe's case. Jack responds by turning on his "Self-Starting Self-Stopping Word Machine," the part of his mind that is programmed to give him orders and make him say the right things. It directs him to a conventionally respectable life while blotting out his emotions and intuitions. His decision to leave with Elena is a negating of that life and an affirmation once again of the freedom of the human spirit.

In *The Assassins* (1975) Oates returns to a bleaker view of the human spirit, as if the ghosts of *Wonderland* needed further exorcising. The narrative is at times oppressive and dark, but at the same time there are several new aspects introduced into her work. Each of the three sections bears the name of one of the central characters, all members of the Petrie family. Together they narrate three strands of parallel events seen from their own perspective. These events are centered on the apparent assassination of Andrew Petrie. His two brothers, Hugh and Stephen, and his wife, Yvonne, are the three persons who provide a composite view of events for the reader.

Because there is no consistent point of view, the plot of the novel becomes less significant than the emotional development of its three central characters. Hugh, a political cartoonist, is given a first-person narrative that enables Oates to record accurately his gradual mental breakdown. His sense of humor never deserts him, even in his attempted murder–suicide, intended to be a protest against "the vulgarity of modern life." His murder "victim" is a brook trout on his plate in a restaurant; in his "suicide" attempt he shoots himself in the head rather than in the mouth, lest his Freudian psychoanalyst misunderstand his action. Hugh's black-comedy sense of humor overcomes him at his brother's funeral, when he collapses trying to restrain his laughter as he imagines himself projecting his ventriloquist's voice into the dead man's coffin. Hugh had thought his idea was a way of transcending the mournful situation and raising it from the level of tragedy to high comedy.

The Assassins is by no means a comic novel, but there are indications that Oates sees comedy as a way of facing the unknown and horrible aspects of death and overcoming them. The epigraph from Friedrich Nietzsche reflects this: "Everybody considers dying important; but as yet death is no festival." Nor is death a festival here. It is sudden, bloody, and shocking. Hugh's attempt at suicide fails miserably, leaving him blind and paralyzed. But at the very outset of his narrative, from his hospital bed, he assures us that he still makes jokes, that the comedy of life goes on and will outlive us all.

Oates presents characters who are caught in life, unable to explain its quirks of fate yet forced to go on living. In this sense Hugh and Stephen succeed. Yvonne, the widow, does not. She tries to avoid mourning by throwing herself into the outside world and by trying to organize her husband's writings. Men become impotent in her presence, for she suppresses creative forces. She had been dominated by her husband's brilliance, and the lover she takes after his death is bound to her solely because they had both loved Andrew.

Stephen, the youngest brother, represents the other side of the artistic personality, and is surely a literary ancestor of Nathanael Vickery

in Oates's *Son of the Morning*. Touched by God at age twelve, Stephen is able to leave his body; but even when he is "in" his own body, he feels he is only living within his "host," Stephen Petrie. His awareness of being an aspect of God in a human form appears to be a spiritual pride that must be humbled. This is a new type of character for Oates: the prophet who eventually feels God depart from him and is left in a spiritual vacuum, awaiting God's return.

Although each of the three central characters is intriguing, the novel as a whole is not entirely satisfactory. The identities of the "assassins" are presented too subtly for the average reader to grasp. Andrew was not really assassinated at all; he committed suicide, disguising his deed as an assassination to assure his reputation and the authority of his writings. Similarly, the graphic account of his widow Yvonne's murder and dismemberment is only a projection of Yvonne's imagination, a symbol of her spiritual death and willingness to join her husband in abandoning life. It is a weakness of the novel that such important events are not clarified for the reader.

Unless Oates intended to pose a puzzle that only the most astute and imaginative reader could solve, she has cheated her readers of one of the major insights the novel offers. For each of the four Petries is his or her own assassin, although only one of them, Andrew, actually dies. The mystical Stephen is left at the end a wanderer, deprived of his God and homeless, a spiritual assassination having left him destitute. We are left at the end of the novel with the feeling that things are unfinished; it may be argued that this is one aspect of realistic fiction, but there is still a desire for just a little more help in filling in the blanks.

Together, *Wonderland* and *The Assassins* plunge into the darker depths of Oates's talent. They were necessary aspects of her development as a writer; but, having served their purpose—exploring the lowest despair possible, and ultimately surviving it—such aspects are no longer essential in her writing.

In *Childwold* (1976) and *Son of the Morning* (1978) Oates's talent rises from the depths and soars to new and dizzying heights. The rural landscapes and their inhabitants are vividly depicted. Her descriptive technique, with its richness of line and eye for the small but essential detail, makes one feel merely reminded of a world already known. In *Childwold*, Oates deals with the concept of the artist who "creates" his beloved. The creator here is Fitz John Kasch, an intellectual with a Harvard Ph.D. whose passion for the adolescent Laney Bartlett leads him to think, "I will transform her: I will invent her." In the tradition of Pygmalion, and later of Vladimir Nabokov's, Humbert Humbert in *Lolita* (1955), Kasch quite self-consciously uses his intellect to seek a rebirth and a redemption through loving a young girl. His thoughts and his speech quite deliberately echo and paraphrase the many writers and thinkers he has read. Thus he alludes to *Walden* when he announces that he returned to the scene of his birth "because I wished to live deliberately, to retreat from history, both personal and collective."

Yet Thoreau went to Walden not to escape but "to front only the essential facts of life." Kasch is ultimately forced to reduce his life to those essentials as well. He meditates on the name of Laney's family's farm, Childwold, and tries to find in it a formula that will release its enchantment on him. Most of his mentors have been enchanters of one sort or another: Meister Eckhart, Blaise Pascal, William Shakespeare, Jakob Boehme, St. Augustine, Soren Kierkegaard, Nietzsche, Rainer Maria Rilke, G. F. W. Hegel, George Santayana, and William Butler Yeats. Paraphrases of their writings are widely scattered among and absorbed into

Kasch's own thoughts, which themselves are preoccupied with the power and utility of words.

Oates's recording of his thoughts infuses new life into a term that has become a cliché, the "stream of consciousness" technique. The mind flow she transcribes is not a dull and pedantic connecting of sundry details, but a lively process that awakens new meanings in language and finds poetry in the banal. To cite only one instance from a multitude: thinking of Laney as his "lily of the snowfields," Kasch later transforms the idea into "My Lilith of the fields, the snowfields of Childwold. Unmanner of men. Must let her go: she can't make me other than I am now and must be forever, forevermore, forevermortal...."

It is through Kasch's eyes that Laney comes to life for the reader. He is her co-creator with Oates (who has of course created him). The incarnational force of words is the link, the ability to make the word become flesh. Kasch's permutations on the single word "Childwold" make the connection explicit: "In the beginning is the Word. No things but in words, through words!—no-thing, nothing, that is not first breathed." Oates as poet is most clearly seen in this novel, which embodies not only the poet's delight in words but also a sense of awe at their power to create and to destroy.

Childwold is also a return to one of the themes of Oates's first novel, the concept of coming home, of undertaking a pilgrimage through this world. Kasch describes himself at the start as a voyager and a pilgrim who returns to the place of his physical birth. The remainder of the novel charts his attempt to achieve his spiritual rebirth. He knows he cannot deny or transcend his ancestry, that he *is* his ancestors. This is a knowledge that many of Oates's earlier characters lack, and they suffer for that ignorance. (One thinks especially of Clara and

Maureen.) Kasch is able to attain a sense of spiritual rapture not through his love for Laney but by loving her mother, Arlene, a figure of abundance, fertility, fullness, and joy. Her life is given over entirely to the creative force: having borne nine children, she is happiest when she is pregnant and mothering. Kasch feels that his pilgrimage has ended when he returns to Arlene. But his ecstatic joy ends suddenly when he has a fight with Arlene's former lover and kills him.

It is almost as if Oates were warning her readers that the vision of paradise is too great to bear in this life, and that it is perhaps foolish to overreach human limits to try to perpetuate it. Kasch's final retreat is away from all action, into permanent seclusion. It is a bitter result of his failure fully to integrate the spirit and the flesh. Kasch's soaring intellect is plummeted to earth when his body takes over in the fatal fight. In contrast, Arlene's world is that of nature and the body, yet it is she who acknowledges that "everything worked out as it should. . . . If only people could know it at the time. . . ." Her earthy approach really is not very different from Kasch's more mystic attempts at understanding life, for both of them accept the "real" world and also the pulse that quickens it, and seek to integrate the two. Arlene has in some ways succeeded at doing so where Kasch has failed, yet with each we sense that the other half of the picture is left out.

A number of Oates's earlier short stories deal with a similar situation, in which emotional life is inhibited by intellectualizing or withdrawing from human relationships. One of her best-known stories, "In the Region of Ice," presents the conflict in Sister Irene, a nun teaching English at a university, when a student demands a relationship that threatens her inner isolation. She rationalizes her refusal to respond at his moment of greatest need, thereby encasing herself in emotional "ice." Similarly, Pauline, in "Bodies," is a sculptress who can work only heads; and the central characters in the stories "Stigmata" and "Shame" are, like Sister Irene, apparently religious but also have shut themselves off from emotional warmth and selfless giving. Such people deny the interconnectedness of all living things, accepting their isolation, which is contrary to the natural patterns of the world.

Oates has obvious affinities with D. H. Lawrence and also with Walt Whitman, for all three writers embrace the whole of nature as we find it, serpents in the garden and all, and are undogmatic in presenting their view as art. Oates never preaches: through her writing she offers theories of reality. In her essay "The Myth of the Isolated Artist" she writes: "The greatness of a work of art usually blinds us to the fact that it is a hypothetical statement about reality—a kind of massive, joyful experiment done with words, and submitted to one's peers for judgment."

This is certainly true of *Childwold* and also of her subsequent novel, *Son of the Morning*. In the latter Oates is overtly concerned with religion for the first time since her first novel, although, as previously noted, Stephen in *The Assassins* seems to have been a forerunner of this novel's protagonist. His descendant here is Nathanael Vickery, a preacher touched by God when he was five who becomes a modern-day prophet, witnessing to thousands until the day he feels God's power withdrawn from him. Nathan is an ambiguous character. The very title of the novel reinforces his ambivalence for it is not God but Lucifer, the fallen angel, who is known as the Son of the Morning. Nathan is overtly a witness for God, but his popularity and following grow until his disciples nearly deify him. Even after his "fall" rumors circulate promising his return. Yet in all the thoughts and prayers of Nathan's that the reader is permitted to overhear, there is a genuine note of belief and self-effacement and a total dedication to the will of God.

Perhaps the novel's dedication provides a clue to Nathan's situation. This is the first work of Oates's that is not dedicated to a specific person or persons, but to "One Whose absence is palpable as any presence." In asserting the reality of an Other that does not depend on physical proof or knowledge, Oates has us enter a state where faith in anything must, by its very nature, imply an absence of knowledge. In Nathan's final darkened condition he is nevertheless able to assert, "So I wait for You, and will wait the rest of my life." Whether he is in the midst of the mystic's dark night of the soul, or in a permanent state of solitude, is never answered. When he sees a stained glass window, it almost leads him into meditation, but it quickly becomes "merely colored glass again, fitted cleverly together." Transcendence appears to be denied him, yet Nathan continues his "lifetime's habit of addressing [God]," speaking to Him out of the depths as if He were still quite near.

It is as if Nathan himself has dedicated this book and then recounted his own spiritual success and demise. At the outset of the novel we learn that his spiritual darkness has already lasted for three years. It is accompanied by his partial physical blindness, a result of a self-blinding that was an attempt to cast out the eye that had offended him by allowing fleshly temptation to enter his body. Yet after this stabbing, Nathan feels he is finally "above sin," thereby inviting a spiritual pride that necessitates a fall. His followers begin to address him as "Master," and he is able to survive physical attacks totally unharmed. But with the sudden awareness of God's withdrawal from him, Nathan senses the loss of all his props, of all that gave his life its meaning. As he "limps" from church to church, seeking what he once knew so intimately, his doubts become more concrete and less emotional. Observing a celebration of the Mass, he thinks: "You were not coaxed down into the priest's magical instruments—You did not enliven the wine, or slip into the stamped-out bits of bread." This is a long way from the responses of Karen Herz to the mystical element of the Mass that inspires and finally pardons her.

Oates's concern for the spiritual life has left the realm of ritual and formal dogmas, and entered a condition in which only the self is ultimately able to discover truth, and must be independent of all teachers and masters other than itself. This is a very Eastern concept, one that sees all truth and knowledge as residing within each person and waiting to be called forth through observation and meditation. Such is the final condition of Nathanael Vickery, who is at last stripped of all his beliefs and supports, and left, apparently, bereft of all hope, yet in his darkness is able to assert that he is still waiting and, if need be, will wait for the rest of his life.

Son of the Morning is rich in symbolism and allegory, more than any of Oates's previous novels. Oates relies on the easily accessible metaphors of the Christian faith to raise obvious parallels between Nathan's life and the life of Christ. Even the section titles of the novel indicate this: "The Incarnation," "The Witness," "Last Things," and "The Sepulcher." These parallels are not meant to discredit the validity of Christ's earthly life but, rather, to use that life as a convenient vehicle for an extended metaphor, the tenor of which is the individual's own spiritual state of mind over its broadest range of experience. For at both ends of Nathan's religious progress there is one constant: at the height of his missionary career and in the depths of his anguished sense of loss, Nathan never ceases to be aware of the higher order of the universe. There is no despair in his final waiting, just a constant and intense observation of the world about him. Nathan appears to have transcended emotion as well as desire and attachment, and even in his broken state there is no bitterness, only resignation and acceptance.

The workings of an exceptional mind are a genuine concern in these last two novels of Oates's as well as in a novella she wrote at about the same time, *The Triumph of the Spider Monkey* (1976). Its hero, Bobby Gotteson (the surname alone, "God's son," links him thematically to Nathanael Vickery), is described as a "maniac" who is on trial for hacking nine women to death. Yet because it is recounted in the first person, Bobby's story arouses sympathy and some measure of understanding of why he behaves as he does. The sanity of the apparently mad and the madness of those who seem rational is a traditional theme of literature, but it is rare that we have the opportunity to listen in on the "madman's" thoughts and discover the depths of his character for ourselves. Through him we receive an overt statement of the tension between body and spirit that has raged through Oates's novels: "He scorned the body. Gotteson made love to the spirit, he sang his melancholy-cheerful ballads to the spirit."

The actual murders are a confusion of body and spirit in which Gotteson feels that the body has taken over completely, yet also argues that the acts were spiritual ones in which "the great moment was the one in which I felt my opponent's ego collapse." Gotteson's "redemption" occurs with his last murder, when instead of feeling his usual pity for females as their egos crumble, he becomes aware that his victim is looking into the heart of a mystery. He stays with her as she dies, hoping to share something of her experience, and realizes that at that moment she was not "trapped" in being truly female, but shared an essence of existence with Gotteson himself.

These last three works show an increased awareness that the barriers separating people from each other are artificial, and that all are truly one family, even one self, under the skin. *Night-Side* (1977) is a collection of short stories particularly concerned with this aspect of existence. In examining the darker regions of consciousness, these tales deal with dreams, telepathy, madness, and other forms of psychic awareness. Oates's subsequent collection, *All the Good People I've Left Behind* (1979), contains certain characters who appear in more than one story, and all the stories examine highly sensitive and intimate personal relationships.

Together these two volumes assert the connections people have with the cosmic Self, the universal Other, and other persons they encounter. The realization that everything is connected is worked out in both vertical and horizontal dimensions. As one character in the story "Sentimental Journey" says, "There are mystical connections between people sometimes . . . between people who are, you know, sympathetic with each other." He adds that he has experienced coincidental situations that are in fact "certain small miracles." Small miracles make up the essence of many of the stories in these collections, and although it is tempting to differentiate between the two works by labeling one "supernatural" and the other "social" or "human," from Oates's point of view it appears that both are equally "natural," and that the natural world includes mysteries, perceptions, intuitions, and miracles.

A rather simplistic explanation of these stories is found in "Further Confessions," one of the last stories in *Night-Side*. The central character utters a truth he has felt since he was a child: "The world is a fathomless mystery." As he faces apparitions of death from the "night-side" of earth, he is better able to accept his life itself as an immediate answer to those fathomless mysteries and to rid his world of all apparitions.

Similarly, the central character of the title

story, "Night-Side," affirms the reality and value of this world while confronted with the attractions of the darker spirit world. Jarvis, an investigator for a psychic research society, witnesses the "conversion" of an unbelieving colleague, Perry Moore, when a séance puts him in contact with a dead friend. Moore fanatically pursues this contact, becoming unbearably intolerant of skeptics, or "heretics," until he dies suddenly of a stroke. Jarvis is faced with the choice of responding to Moore's visitation in a dream, with its plea to salvage his secret journals, or to resurface into the world of the living, to reassert the exuberant joys of life in the flesh. Jarvis' decision to come ashore from his morning swim represents his affirmation of the present and solid world over the floating, dreamlike state of the world of spirits and shadows. Without denying the existence of this other realm, he makes the only choice possible in the light of his knowledge: to emerge from the water to his proper medium, to carry out the work he must do in the "day-side" of the world he inhabits.

This theme runs through the stories of *Night-Side* in an eerie and portentous pattern, presenting less-explored areas of consciousness and integrating them into the present world. Natural and supernatural become interchangeable as the distinction between them blurs to show them as one world with many facets. The characters may be apparent social misfits, as in "The Giant Woman" and "Exile"; professional people, as in "The Snowstorm" and "The Sacrifice"; or loosely based on "real" people, as in the moving tale "Daisy," which is modeled on the poignant and painful relationship between James Joyce and his mad daughter Lucia. All are disturbing but enlightening explorations into the darker mysteries of human existence. The characters remain separate individuals, but at the same time assume the role of an Everyman as they probe regions that are a part of the consciousness of all human beings.

One of the most striking aspects of Oates's fiction—novels, short stories, novellas, plays, and poems—is its high degree of organization. The novels especially, perhaps because the form demands it, experiment with different points of view and chronological disruptions, but are always tightly woven. The structure does not self-consciously impose itself on plot or character, as it does in, for instance, Joyce's *Ulysses*, but functions as an organizing principle. In the same way, the short stories and poems in the collections are placed in a careful sequence, so that one benefits most by reading an entire collection in its published order, so as to understand the separate items it contains.

This is perhaps most necessary for Oates's collection of stories *All the Good People I've Left Behind*, a series in which particular characters reappear in several stories that recount the varying relationships within a group of loosely affiliated people. Oates's interests appear to be focused on the connections that unite and also transcend her individual characters, and not solely on the personalities as being of interest in themselves. No one character emerges as central; all exist only in relationships. More than any of her previous works, these ten stories insist that we do not, and cannot, live detached from others, and that we can transcend the commonplace only insofar as we realize that there are invisible threads connecting us to one another and to the universe itself. Even though good people are frequently left behind, their effect remains, and is assimilated into one's being. Some characters appear in only one of the ten stories, yet the collection would suffer from their omission.

In the story "Sentimental Journey," Annie Quirt (who appears in more stories than any of the other characters) literally recalls into her life one of the people she had left behind a decade earlier, but the meeting becomes a nightmarish situation when she discovers he is not the person she had imagined from the past, but a frightening and disturbed being. Annie must once more leave him behind as she escapes to Quebec City. Her life there, recounted in the story "Walled City," leads her to the thought that "the world must have been perfect always . . . . It must have been my perception of it that was sick."

The different perceptions of the world over a period of time are illustrated in the title story, which presents the shifting relationships between two married couples. It spans sixteen years, and at the end of that time it is obvious that the characters as they were initially presented have been "left behind." The changes they undergo are not presented judgmentally, even though one of them meets a tragic and bitter end. They are seen to be almost inevitable changes, part of an evolutionary cycle in which all things change, yet the greater whole in which they move remains constant; the world remains, as Annie had said, "perfect always."

Joyce Carol Oates is undoubtedly one of the most prolific writers of today, but all she has written so far may well be just a prelude to the full blossoming of her talents. Her most recent works—the last two novels, collections of stories, and the novella—indicate that her writing may be moving in new directions that will ultimately prove of considerable importance to contemporary thought and literature. These latest works have a more metaphysical or visionary thrust to them than her previous volumes. Their characters function on a more universal level and point to dimensions other than the literal. Yet any generalities about Oates's work so far are risky, since we can expect many more volumes of writing from her and must withhold any definitive judgments about directions or trends in her work.

Many of these "early" (for so the future will regard them) works record a restlessness and even an impatience with the limitations of perception that, as William Blake stated, prevent us from seeing the universe as it really is, as a whole. At times this restlessness is perceived by the reader only as an uncertainty as to how a particular work ought to be read, leaving the reader unable to rise very far above the literal level of the text. He or she may be helped considerably by Oates's essays and critical works, which clarify many of her intentions and beliefs about fiction. Although these ideals are not always conveyed in her stories, when she does succeed in making her beliefs known, as she does so stunningly in her most recent work, the results are like her description of the first ripe pear of the season in her poem "That": "costly beyond estimation / a prize, a riddle / a feast." The thought of many feasts yet to be held for her readers is sufficient to whet the appetite for what is still to come.

Selected Bibliography

WORKS OF JOYCE CAROL OATES

NOVELS AND NOVELLAS

With Shuddering Fall. New York: Vanguard, 1964.

A Garden of Earthly Delights. New York: Vanguard, 1967.

Expensive People. New York: Vanguard, 1968.

them. New York: Vanguard, 1969.

Wonderland. New York: Vanguard, 1971; Greenwich, Conn.: Fawcett, 1973 (revised ending).

Do with Me What You Will. New York: Vanguard, 1973.

The Assassins. New York: Vanguard, 1975.

Childwold. New York: Vanguard, 1976.

The Triumph of the Spider Monkey. Santa Barbara, Calif.: Black Sparrow Press, 1976.

Son of the Morning. New York: Vanguard, 1978.

Unholy Loves. New York: Vanguard, 1979.

Bellefleur. New York: E. P. Dutton, 1980.

Angel of Light. New York: E. P. Dutton, 1981.

A Bloodsmoor Romance. New York: E. P. Dutton, 1982.

Mysteries of Winterthurn. New York: E. P. Dutton, 1983.

Solstice. New York: E. P. Dutton, 1985.

COLLECTED SHORT STORIES

By the North Gate. New York: Vanguard, 1963.

Upon the Sweeping Flood. New York: Vanguard, 1966.

The Wheel of Love. New York: Vanguard, 1970.

Marriages and Infidelities. New York: Vanguard, 1972.

The Goddess and Other Women. New York: Vanguard, 1974.

The Hungry Ghosts: Seven Allusive Comedies. Los Angeles: Black Sparrow Press, 1974.

The Poisoned Kiss and Other Stories from the Portuguese. New York: Vanguard, 1975.

The Seduction and Other Stories. Los Angeles: Black Sparrow Press, 1975.

Crossing the Border. New York: Vanguard, 1976.

Night-Side. New York: Vanguard, 1977.

All the Good People I've Left Behind. Santa Barbara, Calif.: Black Sparrow Press, 1979.

A Sentimental Education. New York: E. P. Dutton, 1981.

Last Days. New York: E. P. Dutton, 1984.

POETRY

Women in Love and Other Poems. New York: Albondacani Press, 1968.

Anonymous Sins and Other Poems. Baton Rouge: Louisiana State University Press, 1969.

Love and Its Derangements. Baton Rouge: Louisiana State University Press, 1970.

In Case of Accidental Death. Cambridge, Mass.: Pomegranate Press, 1972.

Wooded Forms. New York: Albondacani Press, 1972. Single poem.

Angel Fire. Baton Rouge: Louisiana State University Press, 1973.

Dreaming America and Other Poems. n.p.: Aloe Editions, 1973.

A Posthumous Sketch. Los Angeles: Black Sparrow Press, 1973.

The Fabulous Beasts. Baton Rouge: Louisiana State University Press, 1975.

Women Whose Lives Are Food, Men Whose Lives Are Money. Baton Rouge: Louisiana State University Press, 1978.

OTHER FICTION

Scenes from American Life: Contemporary Short Fiction, edited by Oates. New York: Random House, 1973.

Miracle Play. Los Angeles: Black Sparrow Press, 1974.

CRITICAL BOOKS

The Edge of Impossibility: Tragic Forms in Literature. New York: Vanguard, 1972.

The Hostile Sun: The Poetry of D. H. Lawrence. Los Angeles: Black Sparrow Press, 1973.

New Heaven, New Earth: The Visionary Experience in Literature. New York: Vanguard, 1974.

The Profane Art. New York: E. P. Dutton, 1983.

CRITICAL ARTICLES

"Melville and the Manichean Illusion." *Texas Studies in Literature and Language,* 4:117–29 (Spring 1962).

"The 'Fifth Act' and the Chorus in the English and Scottish Ballads." *Dalhousie Review,* 42:119–29 (Autumn 1962).

"The Comedy of Metamorphosis in the *Revenger's Tragedy.*" *Bucknell Review,* 11:38–52 (December 1962).

"The Existential Comedy of Conrad's 'Youth.'" *Renascence,* 26:22–28 (Fall 1963).

"The Alchemy of *Antony and Cleopatra.*" *Bucknell Review,* 12:37–50 (Spring 1964).

"Porter's 'Noon Wine': A Stifled Tragedy." *Renascence,* 27:157–62 (Spring 1965).

"Ionesco's Dances of Death." *Thought,* 40:415–31 (Autumn 1965).

"Masquerade and Marriage: Fielding's Comedies of Identity." *Ball State University Forum,* 6:10–21 (Autumn 1965).

"The Ambiguity of *Troilus and Cressida.*" *Shakespeare Quarterly,* 17:141–50 (Spring 1966).

"Building Tension in the Short Story." *Writer,* 79:11–12, 44 (June 1966).

"Chekhov and the Theater of the Absurd." *Bucknell Review,* 14:44–58 (Winter 1966).

"Ritual and Violence in Flannery O'Connor." *Thought,* 41:545–60 (Winter 1966).

"Essence and Existence in Shakespeare's *Troilus and Cressida.*" *Philological Quarterly,* 46:167–85 (April 1967).

"Background and Foreground in Fiction." *Writer,* 80:11–13 (August 1967).

"Man Under the Sentence of Death: The Novels of James M. Cain." In *Tough Guy Writers of the Thirties,* edited by D. Madden. Carbondale: Southern Illinois University Press, 1968. Pp. 110–28.

"The Double Vision of *The Brothers Karamazov.*" *Journal of Aesthetics and Art Criticism,* 27:203–13 (Winter 1968).

"The Art of Eudora Welty." *Shenandoah,* 20:54–57 (1969).

"Art at the Edge of Impossibility: Mann's Dr. Faustus." *Southern Review,* 5:375–97 (April 1969).

"Yeats: Violence, Tragedy, Mutability." *Bucknell Review,* 17:1–17 (December 1969).

"Tragic Rites in Yeats' *A Full Moon in March.*" *Antioch Review,* 29:547–60 (Winter 1969–70).

"With Norman Mailer at the Sex Circus: Out of the Machine." *Atlantic,* 228:42–45 (July 1971).

"The Short Story." *Southern Humanities Review,* 5:213–14 (Summer 1971).

"New Heaven and New Earth." *Saturday Review,* 55C:51–54 (November 4, 1972).

"A Personal View of Nabokov." *Saturday Review,* 1:36–37 (January 1973).

"The Myth of the Isolated Artist." *Psychology Today,* 6:74–75 (May 1973).

"Art: Therapy and Magic." *American Journal,* 1:17–20 (July 3, 1973).

"The Death Throes of Romanticism: The Poems of Sylvia Plath." *Southern Review,* 9:501–22 (July 1973).

"The Visionary Art of Flannery O'Connor." *Southern Humanities Review,* 7:235–46 (Summer 1973).

"A Visit with Doris Lessing." *Southern Review,* 9:873–82 (October 1973).

"The Teleology of the Unconscious: The Art of Norman Mailer." *Critic,* 32:25–35 (November–December 1973).

"The Unique/Universal in Fiction." *Writer,* 86:9–12 (January 1974).

"Disguised Fiction." *PMLA,* 89:580–81 (May 1974).

"Other Celebrity Voices: How Art Has Touched Our Lives." *Today's Health,* 52:31 (May 1974).

"Is This the Promised End?: The Tragedy of *King Lear.*" *Journal of Aesthetics and Art Criticism,* 33:19–32 (Fall 1974).

"'The Immense Indifference of Things': The Tragedy of Conrad's *Nostromo.*" *Novel,* 9:5–22 (Fall 1975).

"Updike's American Comedies." *Modern Fiction Studies,* 21:459–72 (1975).

"Many Are Called . . ." In *American Poets in 1976,* edited by William Heyen. Indianapolis: Bobbs-Merrill, 1976. Pp. 202–11.

"Jocoserious Joyce." *Critical Inquiry,* 2:677–88 (Summer 1976).

"Lawrence's *Götterdämmerung:* The Tragic Vision of *Women in Love.*" *Critical Inquiry,* 4:559–78 (Spring 1978).

BIBLIOGRAPHIES

Catron, Douglas M. "A Contribution to a Bibliography of Works by and About Joyce Carol Oates." *American Literature,* 49:399–414 (November 1977).

McCormick, Lucienne P. "A Bibliography of Works by and About Joyce Carol Oates." *American Literature,* 43:124–32 (March 1971).

CRITICAL STUDIES

Adams, R. M. "Joyce Carol Oates at Home." *New York Times Book Review,* September 28, 1969, pp. 4–5, 48.

Allen, Bruce. "Intrusions of Consciousness," *Hudson Review,* 28:611–15 (Winter 1975–76).

Allen, Mary I. "The Terrified Women of Joyce Carol Oates." In *The Necessary Blankness: Women in Major American Fiction of the Sixties.* Urbana: University of Illinois Press, 1976. Pp. 133–59.

Avant, John Alfred. "An Interview with Joyce Carol Oates." *Library Journal,* 97D:3711–12 (November 15, 1972).

Batterberry, Michael and Ariane. "Focus on Joyce Carol Oates." *Harper's Bazaar,* 106:159, 174, 176 (September 1973).

Bellamy, Joe David. "The Dark Lady of American Letters: An Interview with Joyce Carol Oates." *Atlantic,* 229:63–67 (February 1972).

Bender, Eileen T. "Autonomy and Influence: Joyce Carol Oates' *Marriages and Infidelities.*" *Soundings,* 58:390–406 (Fall 1975).

Boesky, Dale. "Correspondence with Miss Joyce Carol Oates." *International Review of Psychoanalysis,* 2:481–86 (1975).

Bower, Warren. "Bliss in the First Person." *Saturday Review,* 51:34–35 (October 26, 1968).

Burwell, Rose Marie. "The Process of Individuation as Narrative Structure: Joyce Carol Oates' *Do with Me What You Will.*" *Critique,* 17, no. 2:93–106 (December 1975).

————"Joyce Carol Oates' First Novel." *Canadian Literature,* 73:54–67 (Summer 1977).

Clemons, Walter. "Joyce Carol Oates: Love and Violence." *Newsweek,* 80:72–74, 77 (December 11, 1972).

Creighton, Joanne V. "Unliberated Women in Joyce Carol Oates' Fiction." *World Literature Written in English,* 17:165–75 (April 1978).

————. "Joyce Carol Oates' Craftsmanship in *The Wheel of Love.*" *Studies in Short Fiction,* 15:375–84 (Fall 1978).

————. *Joyce Carol Oates.* Boston: G. K. Hall (Twayne), 1979.

Dike, Donald A. "The Aggressive Victim in the Fiction of Joyce Carol Oates." *Greyfriar,* 15:13–29 (1974).

Duus, Louise. "'The Population of Eden': Joyce Carol Oates' *By the North Gate.*" *Critique,* 7:176–77 (Winter 1964).

Fossum, Robert H. "Only Control: The Novels of Joyce Carol Oates." *Studies in the Novel,* 7:285–97 (Summer 1975).

Giles, James R. "Suffering, Transcendence, and Artistic 'Form': Joyce Carol Oates' *them.*" *Arkansas Quarterly,* 32:213–26 (Autumn 1976).

Goodman, Charlotte. "Women and Madness in the Fiction of Joyce Carol Oates." *Women and Literature,* 5:17–28 (1977).

Grant, Mary Kathryn, R.S.M. *The Tragic Vision of Joyce Carol Oates.* Durham, N.C.: Duke University Press, 1978.

Harter, Carol. "America as 'Consumer Garden': The Nightmare Vision of Joyce Carol Oates." *Revue des langues vivantes,* Bicentennial Issue:171–87 (1976).

Kazin, Alfred. "Oates." *Harper's,* 243:78–82 (August 1971).

Key, James A. "Joyce Carol Oates' *Wonderland* and the Idea of Control." *Publications of the Arkansas Philological Association,* 2:15–21 (1976).

Kuehl, Linda. "An Interview with Joyce Carol Oates." *Commonweal,* 91:307–10 (December 5, 1969).

Liston, William T. "Her Brother's Keeper." *Southern Humanities Review,* 11:195–203 (Spring 1977).

Park, Sue Simpson. "A Study in Counterpoint: Joyce Carol Oates' 'How I Contemplated the World from the Detroit House of Correction and Began My Life over Again.'" *Modern Fiction Studies,* 22:213–24 (Summer 1976).

Petite, Joseph. "'Out of the Machine': Joyce Carol Oates and the Liberation of Women." *Kansas Quarterly,* 9:75–79 (Spring 1977).

Pickering, Samuel F., Jr. "The Short Stories of Joyce Carol Oates." *Georgia Review,* 28:218–26 (Summer 1974).

Sullivan, Walter. "Where Have All the Flowers Gone?: The Short Story in Search of Itself." *Sewanee Review,* 78:531–42 (Summer 1970).

"Transformations of Self: An Interview with Joyce Carol Oates." *Ohio Review,* 15:50–61 (1973).

Waller, Gary F. *Dreaming America: Obsession and Transcendence in the Fiction of Joyce Carol Oates.* Baton Rouge: Louisiana State University Press, 1978.

Wegs, Joyce M. "'Don't You Know Who I Am?': The Grotesque in Oates' 'Where Are You Going, Where Have You Been?'" *Journal of Narrative Technique,* 5:66–72 (January 1975).

—DIANE TOLOMEO

Clifford Odets

1906–1963

*F*LORRIE cries to Sid in *Waiting for Lefty,* "But something wants us to be lonely like that—crawling alone in the dark." As a youth, Clifford Odets was apparently as stricken as his young lovers with a sense of alienation from the bleak America of the Great Depression. "I've always *felt* homeless," he told Michael Mendelsohn late in his life, even though he had been born in Philadelphia, on July 18, 1906, into a family of Lithuanian Jewish immigrants that had gained financial security before Odets was out of his boyhood. The eldest child and only son of Louis and Pearl Geisinger Odets, Clifford Odets was brought up in the lower-middle-class milieu of the Bronx in New York City, and was educated at P.S. 52 and at Morris High School. At the age of seventeen, failing many of his subjects, he dropped out of school. According to legends that Odets apparently built up around himself after his rise to fame in 1935, his enraged father smashed the youth's typewriter upon learning that his son wished to become a writer rather than an advertising copywriter. Young Odets supported himself by acting jobs in radio and with Harry Kemp's Poets' Theatre and Mae Desmond's Stock Company. It is difficult to extract fact from fancy concerning much of Odets' early experience, including his oft-proclaimed feelings of suicidal depression and homelessness, for he

tended after 1935 to tell his story often, to a great many interviewers, frequently altering the facts to suit the circumstances.

Perhaps, like many of his contemporaries, Odets tended to locate the source of his unrest in the social inequities he saw while growing up; perhaps, too, his awareness of social injustices led to his brief association with the Communist party in 1934. Probably he found some release from his feeling of isolation, as well as a sympathetic community, through joining a junior acting company of the Theatre Guild in 1929, after having understudied Spencer Tracy in the brief run of *Conflict* earlier that year. In 1931 three leading Guild directors—Cheryl Crawford, Harold Clurman, and Lee Strasberg— broke away from the organization and, with Odets as one of the founding members, established perhaps the most distinguished theater company in the annals of American drama, the Group Theatre.

It is difficult to imagine a more integrative atmosphere for a troubled young actor and aspiring dramatist. In his splendid history of the Group Theatre (1931–1941), *The Fervent Years,* Harold Clurman remembers closing-night curtain calls in 1931:

. . . a man in the balcony shouted: "Long live the Soviet Union!" Franchot Tone, on the stage, shouted back, "Hurrah for America!" Both outcries might be described as irrelevant, but evidently there was something in the air beyond theatrical appreciation.

If the political spirit of the times was often quite leftward, the Group Theatre was not doctrinaire; indeed, Clurman recalls that its goals were to exploit the Stanislavski method and the Moscow Art Theater tradition of ensemble acting, with the view that their theater should stand as a metaphor for society as a more cohesive, collective entity. The only "philosophy" was to be a generally optimistic socialism, and such playwrights as Sidney Kingsley, Maxwell Anderson, Paul Green, and William Saroyan provided some of the best dramas of the 1930's in support of that concern. The Group further served as a model for such "workers' theaters" as the Theatre Union and for the much more broad-ranging Federal Theatre Project (1935–1939), the first government-sponsored theater in America. The Group fostered the distinguished careers of such directors as Harold Clurman, Lee Strasberg, Elia Kazan, and Stella Adler (who was also an actress), and of stage designers Boris Aronson and Mordecai Gorelik. Quite possibly no finer group of actors and actresses has existed in American theater history than the Group contingent, which included such luminaries as Morris Carnovsky, Luther and Stella Adler, John (then Jules) Garfield, Frances Farmer, Howard DaSilva, and the young Karl Malden. The Group Theatre, wrote Clurman, was important "because it organized its actors as a permanent company and trained them in a common craftsmanship which . . . became emblematic for the era [and made] the stage an instrument of social enlightenment."

Odets' association with such an organization contributed significantly to his development as a dramatist. "I don't think I would ever have written a play," he observed in 1936, "if it hadn't been for the Group. . . . They helped me to assert my values." Odets' great strength as a creator of lively, developed characters stemmed at least in part from the Group's ensemble system: the composition of the troupe substantially influenced the form of Odets' plays. After writing for them an unsuccessful draft of *Awake and Sing!* (then entitled *I Got the Blues*), Odets, according to Clurman in *The Fervent Years,* locked himself in a hotel room early in 1935, in an attempt to produce a work that would win a prize for one-act plays, and emerged three days later with *Waiting for Lefty.* Upon its enthusiastic reception, Odets revised *Awake and Sing!* and it soon opened to both popular and critical acclaim.

The year 1935 became Odets' annus mirabilis as two more plays, *Till the Day I Die* and *Paradise Lost,* appeared by December. The young playwright was the new sensation of the New York theater, but his acclaim was not merely the result of the social themes in these plays. Commenting on the force of his dialogue, Clurman recalls: ". . . but it is not precisely naturalistic speech, for Odets' writing is a personal creation, essentially lyric, in which vulgarity, tenderness, energy, humor, and a headlong idealism are commingled." Unfortunately, Clurman's appraisal was not heeded, as critics and public alike crowned Odets as a Great Depression playwright limited to social themes. That stereotype was to plague him for the remainder of his life, and has continued to diminish his reputation as a serious artist.

Waiting for Lefty was first staged on January 6, 1935, at the Civic Repertory Theatre, with such Group stalwarts as Russell Collins (Harry Fatt), Elia Kazan (Agate Keller), Odets himself as Dr. Benjamin, and Lee J. Cobb as an extra. Sanford Meisner and Odets directed what is still doubtless Odets' most famous and most widely anthologized play. It has permanently labeled him as the archetypal "prophet of the proletariat"; indeed, its simple action of the coming to awareness of a group of urban taxi drivers that mass action is needed to defeat the machinations of a corrupt union is reminiscent of other agitprop works of the period by such playwrights as John Wexley, Marc Blitzstein, and Albert Malta. Yet even in this early play, Odets' themes and form show promise of richer things to come than were achieved by any of the social dramatists of the period. In *Waiting for Lefty,* Odets articulates the themes and motifs of individual loneliness in the modern world, the historical dislocations that made this loneliness almost inevitable, and the saving energy and dynamism of ordinary people that allow the suffering individual's existential decision to struggle toward dignity and moral value in the face of both political oppression and the hopelessness and alienation that seem to be metaphysical forces of the modern age.

Waiting for Lefty is composed of two framing scenes and five "episodes" (six in the original version). As the play begins, Harry Fatt, a "well fed and confident" union boss, backed by a hired gunman, is trying to persuade the drivers to delay a strike. The crowd he addresses, planted among the audience, calls out for Lefty Costello, their elected leader, to speak; but since he is nowhere to be found, Fatt allows the crowd to be addressed by their committee, "this bunch of cowboys you elected." Fatt is so confident of the weakness of these six men that he waves away the gunman, allowing the committee members to speak. The heart of the play lies in the stories told by the committeemen in their "episodes," which reveal their degrading financial impoverishment, gradually inciting the men to social solidarity by the end of the play, in the famous "STRIKE, STRIKE, STRIKE!!!" at the curtain.

The first and third "episodes" concern the disastrous effects of the cabdrivers' inability to earn a living wage. Joe Mitchell, the first to speak, admits that "my wife made up my mind" that they need a strike; after a slow fade we see a lighted circle, in which Joe and his wife Edna play their story. In perhaps the most powerful scene of the play, Edna scornfully forces Joe to take responsibility for their lives, ultimately implying that she will leave him unless he takes action by trying to urge the other drivers to strike. At first, Joe echoes the myriad weak men in Odets' plays (Myron Berger in *Awake and Sing!,* Leo Gordon in *Paradise Lost,* Jerry Wilenski in *Clash by Night*), as he whines, "Jeez, I wish I was a kid again and didn't have to think about the next minute." Edna retorts acidly, "But you're not a kid and you do have to think about the next minute. You got two blondie kids sleeping in the next room. They need food and clothes." Their furniture gone, Edna bitterly accuses her husband and "any other hackie that won't fight" of moral cowardice. She forces Joe's evasiveness into action as she cries:

I know this—your boss is making suckers outa you boys every minute. Yes, and suckers out of all the wives and the poor innocent kids who'll grow up with crooked spines and sick bones. Sure, I see it in the papers, how good orange juice is for kids. But dammit our kids get colds one on top of the other. They look like little ghosts. Betty never saw a grapefruit. I took her to the store last week and she pointed to a stack of grapefruits. "What's that!" she said. My God, Joe—the world is supposed to be for all of us.

Spurred by Edna's disgust and anger, Joe leaves in search of Lefty and strike plans. Less optimistic is the resolution of "The Young Hack and His Girl," the third episode. Florrie, her life a drudgery of counter work and caring for her aged mother and brother Irv, screams at Irv, "Don't you see I want something else out of life. Sure, I want romance, love, babies. I want everything in life I can get." Her desire centers on her fiancé of three years, Sid Stein, an impoverished driver, despite Irv's warnings that she must stay away from him because he lacks the money to make a good husband. ("Nowadays is no time to be soft. You gotta be hard as a rock or go under," Irv warns her.) Odets' persistent theme of homelessness echoes in Sid's lament to Florrie, "You and me—we never even had a room to sit in somewhere." In the most poignant scene of the play, the two lovers pathetically try to escape despair through a Hollywood fantasy, accompanied by a doleful dance that ends with Sid's burying his head in Florrie's lap, defeated by "the 1935 blues."

Less powerfully moving than these two domestic scenes are the two "professional" episodes in which Miller, a former lab assistant, and Dr. Benjamin, a former charity ward intern, tell the stories of their disavowal of systems they have found corrupt. Miller, another man from the urban lower classes who reads "nothing but Andy Gump" in the newspapers, may not have Dr. Benjamin's middle-class awareness of radical issues, but his intuition leads him to punch Fayette, the reactionary industrialist, in the mouth after refusing to spy on a chemist with whom he has been assigned to make poison gas. Dr. Benjamin, displaced from his position by a less qualified physician who is Gentile and better connected politically, manages to elicit from his superior, Dr. Barnes, some radical sympathies as Barnes admits, "In a rich man's country your true self's buried deep." Another "professional" episode (originally the fifth), "The Young Actor," which Odets chose to drop from the final version, features Philips, first seen "isolated clear on the stage," desperate for a part and expecting to become a father in a few weeks, not knowing "what buttons to push," beseeching the producer, Grady, "I'm an artist! I can—." Grady's reply echoes the indifference of Fatt and the modern world to the spiritual and the aesthetic:

That's your headache. Nobody interested in artists here. Get a big bunch for a nickel on any corner. Two flops in a row on this lousy street nobody loves you—only God, and He don't count. We protect investments: we cast to type. Your face and height we want, not your soul, son.

This scene ends with Grady's stenographer having sympathy for the youth and handing him a dollar and a copy of the *Communist Manifesto*. Perhaps Odets ultimately eliminated this scene not so much because of its agitprop obviousness as because Philips was one middle-class character too many in a play in which dramatic power derives, ironically enough, from the self-oppression of the lower class.

In the final version the "Interne Episode" is preceded by the "Labor Spy Episode." Though very well positioned structurally, it is not at all effective dramatically, since after the first two men have spoken, Fatt feels he must introduce Clayton, a labor spy, in order to dupe the cab-drivers out of a strike. Most improbably, Clayton is unmasked by one of the crowd as his brother. Odets is on much surer ground in the final scene, with Agate Keller, minus an eye lost at age eleven from working in poor factory conditions, who wears his glass eye "like a medal 'cause it tells the world where I belong—deep down in the working class!" With heavy irony Keller sums up the previous speakers' anger, presenting a strongly Marxist line as he incites the men to band together for an immediate strike.

The news that Lefty Costello has been murdered by Fatt's goons is anticlimactic, for the men are ready to act as a group for the first time, as Odets makes clear by the blocking and the choral speeches near the conclusion. Though Keller's final speeches are clearly Marxist, Odets universalizes the "storm-birds of the working-class" atmosphere by Keller's oft-forgotten last lines, "And when we die they'll know what we did to make a new world! Christ, cut us up to little pieces. . . . put fruit trees where our ashes are!" Keller's final image, the most arresting in the play and prefiguring Odets' final work, *The Flowering Peach,* universalizes the political content of the play: though these men suffer from intolerable working conditions, they finally become organic, lifelike, as they learn to make decisions for themselves, to grow, and to become—in Martin Buber's terms, to risk a response.

Throughout his career Odets would use the political and social struggles of the 1930's as a vehicle for man's universal struggle to avoid moral solipsism by connecting to values beyond the self, by becoming responsible. The stage imagery in *Waiting for Lefty* shows this clearly. In the stage directions introducing episode 1 ("Joe and Edna"), the members of the committee are seated "very dimly visible" outside the spotlight, at the edge of which Fatt sits complacently blowing smoke into the lighted circle where Joe and Edna struggle. In contrast, at the end Agate Keller is in the middle of the stage, surrounded by a human wall of committeemen and other cabdrivers, joined in human solidarity for a better and more dignified life. Odets' existential theme is doubly underscored as Keller says, "Don't wait for Lefty! He might never come," for in the chaos of Florence's "crawling alone in the dark," only men who take direction of their own lives can have any chance against Harry Fatt and his gunman.

Though in parts crudely written, *Waiting for Lefty* is a better work of dramatic art than is commonly acknowledged. Odets shows his ability to create a living, feeling (though not always thinking) character in few words and in restricted compass. This trait is particularly clear in the presentation of Edna Mitchell, whose clipped, angry responses toward her weak husband barely conceal a powerful attachment to him, and in Florence and Sid, whose jokes, posturing, crying, and meaningful silences strive to

mask their growing awareness and horror of the trap of diminishing social expectations from which they probably will never escape.

Part of the tension in the play is that Odets arouses expectations of only a social melodrama but gives us more universal concerns to empathize with, as an undercurrent of less obvious action begins to surface as early as "Joe and Edna." Odets' potential for tragedy is evident even in this unrefined early drama. Neither the characters nor the form of the play is static, as several characters develop (Joe, Miller, Barnes) and Odets imparts an intelligible unity and coherence to the action. What is most interesting (and unusual in so young a writer) is that the suspense is generated not merely by causal, sequential development of action and character, but also by a contextual, comparative progression of event and character that allows the audience that sympathy so peculiar to Odets, given the rudimentary form of his early work. As Odets shows us different people confronted by threatened or actual loss of financial security, and we see them react with similar anger and disillusion, he elicits not only the expected feelings of political anger, but also the unexpected, deeper ones of social binding against the chaos of experience and the metaphysical injustices of modern life. Further, *Waiting for Lefty* fuses O'Neillian expressionism with naturalism as the barren stage (three years before Thornton Wilder used the device in *Our Town*), disconnected scenes, and flashbacks both bring the audience into the play and show modern man's isolation and alienation. Thus *Waiting for Lefty* emerges beyond social melodrama, as a significant representation of the human condition.

In his careful study of the formal aspects of Odets' plays, Edward Murray chooses not to devote analytical chapters to *Waiting for Lefty* or *Till the Day I Die,* feeling that these early efforts do not support a high estimate of Odets' craft. *Till the Day I Die* is probably the least regarded of his dramas: one early critic, Percy

Hammond, dismissed it as mere "brutal senti-mentality." Produced as the curtain raiser of a double bill with *Waiting for Lefty,* Odets' "anti-Nazi play" is considerably more than that: it is a powerful condemnation of all dehumanizing systems that would enslave the individual. Comprising seven scenes, *Till the Day I Die* recounts the story of Ernst Tausig, a Berlin Communist who is imprisoned by the Nazis for printing antifascist leaflets and is gradually destroyed, brutally by his Nazi captors and more subtly by his comrades, who are duped by the Nazis' lies that Tausig has become a collaborator and lose their trust in his loyalty. Odets broadens the thematic thrust of other antifascist plays of the period, such as Elmer Rice's *Judgment Day,* by depicting a protagonist manipulated and destroyed by two systems, both equally dismissive of his individuality and humanity.

Much of the dramatic power of this underrated play comes from Odets' farcical mode, particularly in scenes 3 and 4, where the source of the evil of fascism is revealed to be its profound ignorance. Marx Brothers antics frame the senselessly degrading violence of the trooper, Thunderbolt, who on a simple bet casually knocks men unconscious with gun butt or fist. His evil is banal, unpremeditated, and so horribly natural to the storm troopers that the audience is induced to hate not only Nazis but any form of unthinking brutality or inhumanity. This prepares us for scene 6, one of the most moving in Odets' entire canon, in which Tausig is tried in absentia, on charges of being an informant, by a jury of a dozen Communist party members and is blacklisted, even by the woman who bears his child. The "Groupthink" (the term was actually coined years later by George Orwell in *1984*) is summed up by one comrade: "Every unit paper in the country must carry his name and description. For our purposes he is deadly, dangerous." The tension of the scene is heightened when Tilly Westermann, Tausig's lover, reads a note from him, smuggled through the underground, proclaiming his loyalty to the cause. By this device Odets plays to the audience's wish that the party will keep its trust in Tausig, as befits their social ideals.

But Odets' power lies partly in defeating our sentimental expectations. Stieglitz, a leading theoretician just released from detention camp, is asked to speak. As he reveals a mind sundered by the horrors of his incarceration, the will of the party is fixed; and as the door slams locked behind the retreating Stieglitz, all hands rise in confirmation of the guilty verdict—even those of Tausig's brother Carl and Tilly. Tausig is thus cut off from party, home, friends, and the social community for which he has sacrificed so much. He is the archetypal scapegoat figure in his own community.

Odets' skill in minor characterizations enhances this crucial scene. Lest we end in complete lack of sympathy with the party members, Julius, who cannot be seated for the discussion because "I left my shoe in the corner. My foot is cold," gives us in one superb stroke the sufferings of an individual and of an entire social group. He is seen later, but not heard, as he comes over to Tilly when she reads the pathetic note from the tortured Tausig. To heighten the ambiguity of the scene at the end, when Tilly's hand slowly rises to condemn her lover, a nameless man is heard eating nuts loudly, oblivious to the symbolic damnation that is taking place for the perceived needs of the group.

Other characters are nicely delineated with a minimum of details. Here is another of Odets' sometimes neglected dramatic skills—his ability to allow individuals to emerge from recognizable type characters, thus satisfying both the average and the more discriminating theatergoer. This accounts in part for the surprising density of texture in many of Odets' plays— even in such overtly simple and comparatively crude early efforts as *Till the Day I Die* and *Waiting for Lefty.*

While the early newspaper critics were correct in condemning the often clumsy dialogue of *Till the Day I Die,* the improbability of Duhring's "good Nazi" stereotype, and the sentimentality of the conclusion, the density of texture allows even Odets' apparently simple plays to contain a surprising amount of emotional power. For example, Tilly is at once a dedicated, driving party worker, who teases Tausig about his "male chauvinism," and his sympathetic lover. In the moving fifth scene Tausig, momentarily released by the Nazis in the hope that he will lead them to other party members because he is mortally ill, staggers to Tilly's dimly lit room, where she has avoided capture by pretending to be a prostitute. "It is true our work comes before our personal happiness. But we must try to wrest some joy from life," she admits realistically. In the final scene they are framed in the light from their cigarettes, as they were in the first scene by the light of the burning documents they momentarily touched together just before they were captured by the storm troopers. The lovers discuss their unborn child, the hope not only of their movement but also of the world. Tilly speaks memorably of what once was:

I had a nice coat once. I had a mother. I had a father. I was a little girl with pigtails and her face scrubbed every morning. I was a good child. I believed in God. In summer I ate mulberries from our own tree. In late summer the ground was rotten where they fell.

She speaks these lines also to Carl, Tausig's younger brother, a rabid radical whose demise we are led to expect because of his hotheadedness early in the play. Ironically, it is Ernst Tausig who will die, in large part because of the ignorant intemperance of what Carl represents. Perhaps Carl is the other side of Schlegel, the brutal Nazi captain who, fearing his orderly Adolph's "expressive hands," viciously smashes Tausig's with a rifle butt. Carl allows his love for his brother to be dissipated by his zeal for what he perceives is a valid cause; like Schlegel, he sacrifices his humanity for an abstraction. In the trial scene Carl is a fine blend of polarized emotions, first speaking sentimentally of the music he and Ernst once shared, then ironically hardening into the argument that fascists have always used to sacrifice man to the state: "We must expose this one brother wherever he is met. Whosoever looks in his face is to point the finger. Children will jeer him in the darkest streets of his life!" Odets skillfully shows Carl's repression of the injustice he knows he has done in casting out his brother, in failing to acknowledge him, as Tilly forces Carl to take refuge at first in unreason to safeguard his need to kill Ernst. But Carl ultimately refuses to kill his brother, and even learns from Ernst's sacrifice: "Who am I to sit in judgment?" And after Ernst's suicide he provides the play's benediction, "Let him live. . . ."

Ernst goads Carl to the realization that man's common humanity is greater than any social cause. Throughout the play he echoes Odets' frequent theme that "A man must have some place." His place is in the faces of the children he saw in Moscow: "When I saw them I understood most deeply what the revolution meant." At the end, a completely broken man, Ernst has been reduced to wandering the streets, buying perfumed soap because it reminds him of the smell of tulips he and old Baum discussed months before, at the start of the play. Though Ernst's final "Day must follow the night" speech is strained agitprop, he is nonetheless a pathetic figure. Listlessly holding the Nazi "wooden money" Baum had warned him against, he is condemned by its unwanted presence to his comrades' censure, an early victim of the power of a massive, organized media campaign to manipulate the opinion of a credulous people.

None of Odets' plays is richer in character, comic incident, depiction of ethnic identity, and memorable language than *Awake and Sing!*, considered by most critics to be his most distinguished play in a comic mode. The first of four Odets dramas to be staged on Broadway in 1935 (opening on February 19), *Awake and Sing!* continues his preoccupation with themes of risk and commitment, at both a deeper and a broader level. Young Ralph Berger's desire to transcend his Bronx beginnings is the dramatic pivot here; and the battle over his destiny is joined by Bessie, the archetypal Jewish mother whom Odets makes somewhat sympathetic despite her possessive, restrictive preoccupation with respectability. Her father, Jacob, is a faded Marxist who urges the boy to "Go out and fight so life shouldn't be printed on dollar bills." Ralph dreams of faraway, romantic sounds of trains at night and the evening mail plane bound for Boston ("I get a kick the way it cuts across the Bronx every night."), yet he indecisively allows his domineering mother to control both his paycheck and his love interest with Blanche throughout much of the play.

Gerald Weales's comprehensive historical-critical volume on Odets correctly identifies Bessie as the antagonist against whose values Jacob must struggle to teach Ralph (and by extension Ralph's sister, Hennie) to rebel. The most vital character in *Awake and Sing!*, Bessie is a tense amalgam of insecurity and pride who can repress her father's socialist wisdom with "Never mind, Pop! Pass me the salt," and yet badger Schlosser the janitor and justify her success ethic to Morty: "He didn't have skates! But when he got sick, a twelve-year-old boy, who called a big specialist for the last $25 in the house? Skates!" Confronted by Ralph with her guilt in marrying off the pregnant Hennie to ineffectual Sam Feinschreiber (for whom "life is

a high chill wind weaving itself around his head"), Bessie is capable of driving her father to suicide by smashing his cherished opera records, the aesthetic and spiritual focus of his life; yet Odets preserves great stature for her in her last long speech:

Ralphie, I worked too hard all my years to be treated like dirt. It's no law we should be stuck together like Siamese twins. Summer shoes you didn't have, skates you never had, but I bought a new dress every week. A lover I kept—Mr. Gigolo! . . . Or was Bessie Berger's children always the cleanest on the block?! . . . If I didn't worry about the family who would? . . . here without a dollar you don't look the world in the eye. Talk from now to next year—this is life in America.

To Ralph's reply that "If life made you this way, then it's wrong! . . . it can't stay like this," Bessie wearily replies before she goes off to bed:

"Mom, what does she know? She's old-fashioned!" But I'll tell you a big secret: My whole life I wanted to go away too, but with children a woman stays home. A fire burned in *my* heart too, but now it's too late. I'm no spring chicken. The clock goes and Bessie goes. Only my machinery can't be fixed.

Jacob throws himself with all his strength and principle against Bessie's materialism. From his first line, in which he reminds Ralph that his name in the paper is but a certain kind of success, the old man opposes his daughter: "But Ralph you don't make like you. Before you do it, I'll die first. . . . This is a house? Marx said it—abolish such families." Jacob's son Morty hears from the old barber, "To each face a different haircut. Custom built, no ready made." He worries that Ralph "dreams all night of fortunes. Why not? Don't it say in the movies he should have a personal steamship, pyjamas for fifty dollars a pair and a toilet like a monument?" Jacob sees Ralph slipping into the same arid values that have corrupted and made ineffectual the boy's father, Myron, whom he charges:

The present smiles on you, yes? It promises you the future something? Did you found a piece of earth where you could live like a human being and die with the sun on your face? ... on these questions, on this theme—the struggle for existence—you can't make an answer.

Odets' uncompromising honesty in *Awake and Sing!* extends even to Jacob's risking to see himself in a less favorable light. Shortly before Bessie smashes his records, he admits to Ralph that he has not acted often enough as he had advised the boy, that too often he has had "a glass tea" like Myron, acquiescing in Bessie's dominance. But he ultimately decides, with the prophet Isaiah, to "Awake and sing, ye that dwell in dust, and the earth shall cast out the dead," and slips off the roof on a winter night, leaving Ralph his insurance policy so that the youth may escape the moral decay of Bessie's house.

It is the tenderest of the many ironies in the play that Ralph decides not to take Jacob's money, partly because of his grandfather's sacrifice and partly because of Hennie's decision to leave Sam and go off with her real love, the bitter yet life-affirming war veteran, Moe Axelrod (who wins her with "Nobody knows, but you do it and find out. When you're scared the answer's zero."). Ralph comes to maturity, realizing that his mother has suffered and sacrificed just as Jacob has, that society has strongly influenced her success ethic, and that Jacob didn't die "for us to fight about nickels." So he will stay in Bessie's house but no longer be Bessie's boy, as Moe recognizes with his penultimate line, "I wouldn't trade you for two pitchers and an outfielder."

Perhaps no Odets play is as rich in urban eth-

nic humor as *Awake and Sing!* In his 1978 critical volume on Odets, Harold Cantor has exhaustively analyzed Odets' linguistic devices, including Yiddish humor, wisecracks, epigrams, and other verbal strategies. Since the play represents such specifically Jewish-American themes as the fragmented, incongruous nature of experience, the uncertainties of modern urban life, and the middle-class yearning for security, it is suitable that Odets should bring his most famous family to brilliant life with such lines as Bessie's praise of actress Polly Moran, "a woman with a nose from here to Hunt's Point, but a fine player," or her encomium to Wallace Beery, "He acts like life, very good." Odets' famed ear for dialect shows in Sam's fear at Hennie's disengagement from him, "It don't satisfy me more, such remarks, when Hennie could kill in the bed," or Bessie's early angry shot at her father, "He opens his mouth and the whole Bronx could fall in."

Frequently, Odets' Chekhovian strain will reveal itself in ambiguous subject references, like Jacob's defense of his book collection, "It needs a new world," or janitor Schlosser's skewed syntax as he and Bessie squabble over the respectability quotient of Bessie's household: "In a decent house dogs are not running to make dirty the hallway." S. J. Perelman has parodied Odets' more clumsy lines amusingly—one need only read Sid's words to Florrie in *Waiting for Lefty*, "But that sort of life ain't for the dogs which is us. Christ, Baby! I get like thunder in my chest when we're together," to understand the source of Perelman's barbs—but at his best Odets is a superb stage poet.

Odets' handling of the comic form is perhaps the finest aesthetic quality of *Awake and Sing!* Bessie's household, as utilitarian as it may be, upholds the celebration by comedy of man's social nature; and perhaps no American play except Eugene O'Neill's *Ah, Wilderness!* comments more generously on the benefits of family life. The healing, renewing force of the comic vision that celebrates man's ability to endure even after Jacob's suicide also manages to lift Ralph's spirit and make him capable of a more responsible act than would previously have been possible for him. The tolerance of comedy for even the weak and the foolish renders amusing the passive Myron's disordered ramblings about Valentino, as Odets reveals man's innate capacity for ludicrousness and self-delusion. The automatism of Myron and Bessie nicely supports Henri Bergson's theories of one of the main sources of laughter in comedy, while Moe's defensive sarcasm toward Hennie and his oral fixation on fruit reveal the power inherent in the derisive and the incongruous as two other staples of laughter in Odets' capable hands.

The comic fact that, because of the narrowness of his vision, man seldom sees the changing conditions that make him ludicrous before he has a chance to adjust to them also provides tragedy, often just the other side of comedy. Bessie's actions are indeed despicable throughout much of the play. Having struggled for a decent material life for more than twenty years, she has raised a family that is opposed to her values because she does not see that Ralph and Hennie have different goals, that her middle-class aspirations have made her sacrifice honesty and integrity. In holding her family together, Bessie has derogated her father and treated her daughter as a thing to be manipulated, presumably (by Bessie's standards) for her own good. Seemingly at the surface level the most organic character in the drama, Bessie is really an automaton who confuses the validity of motive and act. Again the audience's expectations are derailed, for Odets writes more than another "Marxist play": Jacob is often weak, by his own admission, and after his death Moe and Ralph discover he has never read some of his cherished books. The meaning of *Awake and Sing!* extends beyond the limits of social drama, to universal dimensions.

Bessie's fears that families will be thrown out of their homes, "all the furniture on the sidewalk," are realized for the more prosperous Gordon family at the end of *Paradise Lost* (1935), the first of three further "family" plays in which the mood, both socially and humanistically, is darkened considerably beyond that of *Awake and Sing!* Most critics and audiences have been confused by its dark ambiguities and disappointed in Leo Gordon's ringing speech at the end, given the catastrophes that have befallen his sons and the betrayal of his friendship by his friend and partner, Sam Katz. Edward Murray's volume dismisses the play completely, and even Michael J. Mendelsohn's discriminating, balanced critical study regards *Paradise Lost* as an unquestioned failure. Odets, often an unreliable critic of his own work, is correct in considering it his best early play. Perhaps only in *Golden Boy* and in the much misunderstood *Clash by Night* would Odets manage the excellent fusion of formal and thematic effects that he achieves here.

Paradise Lost is an allegory of the loss of a romantic dream to the carnage of modernism. Over the two and a half years covered by the drama, we observe the downfall of all that Leo Gordon has believed in: the promise of capitalism; the devotion of Sam Katz; the decline and fall of his beloved elder son, Ben, to a dimly understood success myth; and the physical erosion of his son Julie to a paralysis emblematic of the rot of the present century. "You can't read a paper nowadays," Leo muses. "The world has a profound dislocation." As he realizes Julie is dying, he beseeches his wife, Clara, ". . . what is happening here? Once we were all together and life was good." One of Odets' great comic creations, Gus Michaels, like Gaev in Anton Chekhov's *The Cherry Orchard,* mutters, "The whole world's fallin' to pieces, right under our eyes." Pike, the engaging Marxist furnace man, transcends Agate Keller's purely political concerns as he says sadly, "No one talks about the depression of the modern man's spirit, of his inability to live a full and human life." Leo and Gus strive to think and talk of these things, and Gus finally accomplishes a positive act by selling his precious stamp collection for a paltry sum, to try to help Leo and Clara after Sam Katz is found to have embezzled most of the money from the company he and Leo founded more than twenty years before.

But Leo's ultimate tragedy—and the power of *Paradise Lost* lies in its tragic ending—is that for all of his effort to think liberally and wisely, he finally takes little decisive action, allowing himself to be trapped by a falsely romantic dream similar to the "faraway places" fantasies of Moe Axelrod and young Ralph Berger in *Awake and Sing!* Clara, practical yet kinder than Bessie Berger, tells us at the start that she has married "a fool, but I love him." Leo is trusting and honest, but will not look at the pictures of starving men that Pike tries to show him and fails to vote because "one side is as bad as the other." Deluding himself that happiness can never be found in material things, he promises to "face certain facts" tomorrow, but rarely does. He comforts himself with such mystical beliefs as "Maybe each hour is for some profound purpose ... ," forgets where he puts his checks, and relegates to Sam all care of the "practical" sides of the business—and most of the worries that in their turn help drive Sam into mental, and thus moral, decline. Leo is the essentially passive man whom Dietrich Bonhoeffer would criticize for doing nothing, perhaps in hopes of avoiding taint, but ironically failing in the dream of service to others by his inaction. "Who are we, Mr. Gordon?" Pike reminds him. "Who then are we with our silence?"

Leo recognizes, but does not act. His realization, "We cancel our experience. This is an American habit," is Odets' most powerful denunciation of the American dream before

Golden Boy. Its power comes not only from a Marxist but also from a more universally humanistic perspective. In the play's most mordant irony, Leo finally tries to act in the real world of affairs when he attempts to give the two homeless men Gus's stamp money. Though moral in his concern for others, he is naive, as the homeless Williams reminds him, in his assertion that he alone is responsible for their condition. Williams tells him he lives in a democratic dreamworld. "This kind of dream paralyzes the will—confuses the mind," says the homeless Paul, just before Leo's final, long "The world is beautiful" speech. Odets has thoroughly prepared his audience for this passage by Leo's passivity and dreaminess, and we ought not to find it surprising, since it bespeaks an illusion in which Leo has been ensconced throughout the drama.

Though Odets' stage directions tell us that all are "deeply moved by this vision of the future," the last sound as the curtain slowly descends is Foley's fanfare for his "prosperity block party," held on the street where the Gordons' possessions have been deposited; the juxtaposition with Leo's final speech invests the resolution with a somber tragic irony. Leo Gordon has lost more than he knows, for his paradise was an illusion, yet one that might have been a reality had he had the vision and the courage to act upon its premises of honor, and a commitment to a value outside the self. Odets' wistful problem drama is his subtlest play in both structure and characterization, and perhaps the finest American example of this genre. Only Odets' frequent consignment to the role of social dramatist has kept *Paradise Lost* from the wide audience it deserves.

Between late 1936 and mid-1939, Odets worked on what Harold Clurman called his last class-conscious play, *The Silent Partner,* which the Group Theatre never staged (though the Actors Studio presented twelve performances of it in May 1972). Strong thematically but weak in any credible objective correlative, this more stridently radical version of *Waiting for Lefty* was unsuccessful because, according to Clurman, Odets' "political awareness was more a matter of sentiment than the outcome of any studied ideology or concrete experience." If *The Silent Partner* lacked Odets' developing skills of symbol and characterization, in *Golden Boy* (1937) he further refined talents shown in *Paradise Lost* for subtle dramatic foreshadowing, music imagery and symbolism, and character development. Kewpie, the ruthless urban hoodlum in *Paradise Lost* (" . . . when you're in a jungle you look out for the wild life. . . . I'm out to get mine."), anticipates Odets' most memorable character, the musician-boxer Joe Bonaparte, in his searing self-revelation, "I'm sore on my whole damn life." Ben's self-destructive pursuit of success in *Paradise Lost* is only an important minor theme in that play, but Joe Bonaparte's transformation from musician to callous challenger for "Monarch of the Masses" is Odets' most dramatically powerful (if also his most theatrically and thematically obvious) embodiment of the essential hollowness of the modern version of the American dream.

Odets' early plays, as well as O'Neill's, frequently gain dramatic density from the tension between romantic and modern attitudes and from the conflict of values created in a protagonist who is often confused and divided by psychic tremors. Joe Bonaparte is caught between the organic, life-renewing values of his father, his brother Frank, and Tokio, his trainer, and the mendacity, even brutality, of such men as Roxy Gottlieb and Eddie Fuseli.

Some of the most brilliant and moving scenes in the play involve Mr. Bonaparte, first seen seated beneath plaster busts of Mozart and Beethoven, talking with his old friend Carp about the violin he has bought Joe for his approaching twenty-first birthday. The issue is joined, gently and abstractly at first, as Carp uses Arthur Schopenhauer to support his fears concerning the increasing mechanization of society, while Bonaparte affirms his faith in Joe's love for music. "Music is the great cheer-up in the language of all countries," he says. Rooted in the encompassing affirmative rhythms of natural forces, he assumes that men cannot go wrong if they abide by their nature. So bound up is he in his love for his son that he introduces himself to the fight manager thus: "My name is Joe Bonaparte's father." Fearful of the boxing business, he nevertheless remains flexible, realizing that Joe must freely decide what he wants. "Help Joe find truthful success" is all he asks. But when he realizes that Joe has completely rejected music, yet still wants his father's approving word before departing for his second bout, Bonaparte hastily embraces his son but also cries out his opposition to this "unnatural" aspect of Joe's character: "*No! No word! You gonna fight? All right! Okay! But I don't gonna give no word! No!*"

Joe's downfall is most skillfully presented by Odets through the father's eyes. In Joe's dressing room before a big fight that, if won, will next match him against the other leading contender for the championship, Mr. Bonaparte recognizes sadly that "he gotta wild wolf inside—eat him up!"—that his son's zeal to fight has passed the stage of competition and become, in his terms, unnatural. "Now I see whatta you are . . . I give-a you every word to fight . . . I sorry for you," he mourns. After his son has left for the ring, the old man examines an older fighter's gnarled knuckles and thinks, "So strong . . . so useless. . . ." All that remains as the tragic events inexorably unfold is for the father to welcome his son's corpse "home . . . where he belong. . . ."

The forces arrayed against Mr. Bonaparte are too strong for any sense of dynamic organicism to survive. Even Lorna Moon, the least of Joe's nemeses, admits at the beginning of the play, "It's the Twentieth Century— ... no more miracles." Carp warns, "Fortunes! I used to hear it in my youth—the streets of America is paved with gold." Roxy Gottlieb, who has a "piece" of Joe early on, screams at Mr. Bonaparte, "We offer him *magnitudes! ...* for the money that's involved I'd make Niagara Falls turn around...," making the obsessive modern error of applying quantitative measurement to qualities that do not readily admit of such evaluation. Joe's ultimate fall comes when he meets the Satanic figure of Eddie Fuseli. A mobster who takes control of most of Joe's contract, he is driven by sadistic compulsions that he does not understand to remake Joe into his own image, wanting him not just to win, but to kill in the ring. One of Odets' most repellent characters, Fuseli emerges from the gangster-type character of, for example, Maxwell Anderson's *Winterset,* to become the antithesis of all human values, his face depicted as gray, "dead," "inarticulate," first observed in the arena "above, unseen," representative of mechanized force that will destroy Joe long before his Duesenberg crashes in Babylon, Long Island.

Karl Jaspers has said that tragic protagonists often exist in boundary situations where their control and knowledge—especially of themselves—are tenuous. Joe is especially vulnerable to Fuseli because he knows himself so little. Confused, having felt rejected all his life because of his small stature and bookish habits, needing to avenge himself for dimly comprehended feelings of humiliation, Joe fights in a travesty of the mythic initiation to maturity indicated by the approach of his twenty-first birthday. "Tomorrow's my birthday! I change my life!" he cries to his father at the start of his boxing career. But the goals are the possessions and status that Jacob warned Ralph against in *Awake and Sing!*—these and the ever present vengeance: "People have hurt my feelings for

years. I never forget. You can't get even with people by playing the fiddle. If music shot bullets I'd like it better...." He gets his wish in the most horrifying scene of the play as, his hand broken after the Lombardo bout, he screams out to Eddie Fuseli ("the only one here who understands me"), "Hallelujah!! It's the beginning of the world!" Even after he has accidentally killed in the ring, he is still so in the grip of forces within himself that he does not understand that he seeks escape with Lorna in his Duesenberg: "We'll drive through the night. When you mow down the night with headlights, nobody gets you! You're on top of the world then—nobody laughs! That's it—speed. We're off the earth—unconnected!"

Important here is not only Joe's hostility to natural forces, but also the similarity of these feelings to his musical motivation: "If music shot bullets I'd like it better...." Fuseli corrupts Joe spiritually, because Joe's music is at least in part a compensation for his feelings of humiliation, a way to seal himself off from engagement with the world. Thus it is not improbable that Joe could give up his music so easily when he found something equally "unconnected" and more tangibly remunerative, nor that Joe could take the final self-destructive ride. Odets' tragic vision integrates the manner of Joe's dying with the manner of his living. *Golden Boy* is his finest tragic play, and ranks with the best of those American tragedies in which the actions spring from the conventions of melodrama: Eugene O'Neill's *Desire Under the Elms,* Tennessee Williams' *Orpheus Descending,* Arthur Miller's *All My Sons,* Maxwell Anderson's *Winterset,* and Edward Albee's *Who's Afraid of Virginia Woolf?*

Odets termed his next two plays romances, but *Rocket to the Moon* (1938) strains the conventional limits of the genre far more than does *Night Music.* About *Rocket to the Moon* there hovers an air of hopes eternally disappointed, possibilities forever unrealized. Approaching midlife, the dentist Ben Stark attempts to break away from his thin-spirited wife, Belle, to go to the moon—represented for him by his young secretary, Cleo Singer—in a play structured symbolically from afternoon to night and from June to the end of August. Odets turns this whimsical comedy into yet another meditation on the failure of indecisive modern man to connect to subjects outside himself, to risk a human response even with those he thinks he loves. Ben Stark discovers girl, wins girl, and then loses girl forever—ironically, due to self-determined inaction.

For Ben, a dreamer, thought is ever the father of the wish. His father-in-law, Mr. Prince, the self-styled "American King Lear" and one of Odets' happiest creations, has offered Ben sufficient money to start up a more lucrative practice, but Ben cannot muster the inner conviction needed to oppose his wife's fear of taking chances. Often staring at the rear of the Hotel Algiers, where he fancies liaisons take place, as he muses upon his beloved William Shakespeare, he settles for "a life where every day is Monday," as Prince acidly describes it, trying to wake him up. "Never look away from a problem, Benny. . . . When you look away from the problem, it don't disappear. But maybe *you* might disappear!" warns his father-in-law. Ben recognizes Belle as a major part of the problem, but lacks the will to translate his perception into action until he senses that Cleo is just as insecure, lonely, and unfulfilled as he. He almost stands up to his wife over his feelings for Cleo, but Belle knows too well just how to manipulate his fear and guilt. When, at the end of the play, Ben receives Cleo's declaration of love, he crumbles into old habit and mumbles to Cleo only about his "second-hand life, dedicated to trifles and troubles. . . ." Cleo sensibly decides to risk going off on her own so that she may live more fully, for "Ben isn't free. He's a citizen of another country"—and, she might well add, the man is dead.

Like Leo at the end of *Paradise Lost*, Ben tries emotionally to insist that the experience has made him feel something new, that "this is a beginning" for him; but the wiser Prince wearily tells him simply to go home. "Almost laughing," Ben repeats the same line he had said earlier, almost in self-congratulatory relief: "Sonofagun! . . . What I don't know would fill a book!" Odets' closing stage direction makes clear the thematic point: "The room is dark, except for red neon lights of the Hotel Algiers. . . ." There is no security, only opportunity; but Ben is relieved not to have to face this truth, and instead will probably face a series of eternal Mondays for the duration of what will pass as his life.

The sadness of this slight moral tale is considerably enlivened by some of Odets' finest characterizations. Cleo is frightened, sentimental, and ignorant (to a point that drove George Jean Nathan, ever an Odets nemesis, to sum up the thematic content of the play in part as "Modern conditions are hostile to the perpetuation of true love. . . . Emotional and sexual experience broadens one . . ."); yet she possesses a winsome charm, courage, and purposefulness that belie her years and scant education. Finding that she has absolutely no opinions on anything, as Prince has told her earlier, she does her best by malapropisms or opinions borrowed from others (usually Prince) to set her intellectual disarray in order. She is genuinely loving and kind, and not immature psychologically, realizing that Willy Wax, the producer, regards her merely as a bonbon and that debonair and experienced though he is, Prince (who has proposed to her) is at the end of his life, while she is just beginning hers. There is a quite genuine transformation in her character, for the pretty confection of Act I would hardly have been capable of her completely earned resolution (as opposed to Ben's final self-delusion):

I'll go up all those roads till I find what I want. I want a love that uses me, that needs me. . . . It's getting late to play at life; I want to *live* it. Something has to feel real for me. . . . None of you can give me what I'm looking for: a whole full world, with all the trimmings!

Her impish "You see? I don't ask for much . . ." hints at least at a glimmer of ironic self-awareness that is completely absent when she and Ben first fall in need with each other.

Ben's confidants, Frenchy, Phil Cooper, and Prince, provide an ironic counterpoint to the wistfulness of the "romance." "Who's got time to think about women! I'm trying to make a living!" wails Cooper. Wise, lascivious Frenchy labors mightily to rescue Ben from his emotional dormancy with such remarks about Belle as "Every generous impulse on your part brings her closer to insecurity." He justifies his frequent naps by "Why not? Just had my lunch. A snake eats a rabbit and falls asleep, don't it? Why should I be better than a snake?" And he tries to separate for Ben false dreams from true ones: "Love is no solution of life! Au contraire. . . . You have to bring a whole balanced normal life to love if you want it to go!" Prince cries to Ben, "Your nose is just the right shape to fit your wife's hand!" and proffers Cleo to him with another line that only Clifford Odets could conceive: "Look at her, Benny! Isn't she beautiful? Womanhood is fermenting through her veins. . . ." Though realizing that Ben's case is hopeless, the audience is nonetheless grateful that this gallery of loonies exists in the cause of a cautionary tale. *Rocket to the Moon* is no romance, but it is a sprightly, lively, and thoughtful comic performance.

Odets' final play for the Group Theatre,

Night Music (1940), is less formally coherent than *Rocket to the Moon,* though it is whimsical and elfin in spirit and Detective A. L. Rosenberger is one of Odets' most delightful characterizations. "I am in love with the possibilities, the human possibilities," he tells the angry Steve Takis, who represents for the dying Rosenberger not only the youth of the country but his spiritual son as well. In several of his plays, Odets uses the archetypes of the wise father and the errant son toward a tragic resolution, as in *Golden Boy* and *Clash by Night.* Here, though, Steve learns to listen to the wisdom of the experienced father, and *Night Music* ends in celebration rather than in horror and human waste.

Steve Takis' bitter anger against the external world is healed by Rosenberger's profound awareness of the healing power, the revitalizing principle, of love. He realizes the truth of Blackmur's observation (in another context) that the young rebel needs "the delicate submission of the arrogance of thought to the movements of life." Steve has been badly hurt by the deaths of his parents (his mother to cancer, which prompts Rosenberger to quip of his own cancer, "These higher class diseases are international, like music."). Further, he has landed in New York out of a job and his anger is all-encompassing, even extending to Fay Tucker, a warm, bright, young woman whose only sins are that she too is jobless and that she comes to love Steve, thereby threatening his defenses. Both young waifs end up at the shabby Hotel Algiers, hardly the symbol of dreams that it is in *Rocket to the Moon.* Rosenberger tries to protect them from the evils of the city (particularly the hurrying man's stolen fur piece: "It's got eyes? Look in the eyes—if it winks, it's stolen goods."), sees to it that they have something to eat, and says to Takis, "It's a Saturday night. You got a weekend here, in New York, the greatest city in the world. You are ready for a crisp adventure, like a toasted sandwich. Go and enjoy yourself." He follows them through the park, where they meet young Brown, also a homeless youth and "prime spitter" who is ready to join the army for a bed and food. Always Rosenberger counsels them against despair. He helps Fay to achieve independence from her grasping philistine of a father: "To fall, Miss Tucker, is permitted. But to get up is commanded."

In a pivotal scene at the World's Fair, beneath a statue of George Washington symbolically so huge that only its legs and a sword are visible, Rosenberger completes Steve's and Fay's educations and supervises their launching into the world. To the "night music" of the crickets, Rosenberger counsels Steve:

There are two ways to look, Mr. Takis—to the past or the future. . . . You are feeling mad. Why shouldn't you feel mad? In your whole life you never had a pretzel. You think you have to tell me it's a classified world? . . . But your anger must bear children or it's hopeless. . . . You have the materials to make a good man. But stop breaking things with your fists. . . . God gave you a fine head—use it, dear boy.

Rosenberger, never maudlin, adds, "Sincerely yours, A. L. Rosenberger, your old Dutch uncle." This moving declaration begins to break down Steve's defenses; and in a beautiful expressionistic scene he plays a love song to Fay on the clarinet, his own night music communicating what his incoherent, often blustering words cannot. Fay's lovely admonition to Steve against joining the army with Brown is the highlight of her own spiritual development (abetted by Rosenberger, who has become her spiritual father as well as Takis'): "It's war to make a living, to keep respect, to be in love!"

In the old detective's parting reminder that Washington declared, "You are the people," he symbolically sends Steve toward the energy of the city, away from the stasis of the past and toward personal authenticity. But in the gossamer world of *Night Music*, Odets allows little sentimentality; Steve's rejoinder to his mentor's ringing speech is an ironic, "Thanks, Fatso." He has learned that his former rigidity has made him ineffectual and ludicrous to boot, that, as Rosenberger says, "Everything remains to be seen." Though Odets' most misunderstood and most lyrical drama has never been commercially successful, it remains one of his three or four best works and stands with Thornton Wilder's *The Skin of Our Teeth* in the highest rank of American expressionistic comedy.

Odets' personal life darkened as the end of the 1930's approached. His three-year marriage to Luise Rainer, the Viennese actress who had won an Academy Award in *The Great Ziegfeld* in 1936, had not been happy (Clurman recalls in *The Fervent Years* that she had urged Odets to end *Rocket to the Moon* by having Cleo marry Mr. Prince), and they were divorced in 1940. (Odets' second marriage, to Bette Grayson in 1943, ended in divorce in 1951.) Neither *Rocket to the Moon* nor *Night Music* had been well received by critics or audiences, and the demise of the Group Theatre was imminent. The final disappointment that would send Odets to Hollywood for the second of three screenwriting stints was the overwhelmingly poor reception of *Clash by Night* (1941), perhaps caused in part by the miscasting of Tallulah Bankhead as Mae. It is a powerful psychological drama, but one whose unremitting pessimism caught both audiences and critics unprepared.

This somber story of the moral downfall of decent but passive Jerry Wilenski, through his wife's adultery with his best friend, is saved from triteness by Odets' superior characterizations of the three principals and two supporting characters, Jerry's elderly father and his uncle, Kress, perhaps Odets' most venal characterization. Kress's understanding of his victim helps him to destroy him more easily: "No manhood in the boy!" he comments early in the play; and this is an apt, if at the moment unintended, analysis of Wilenski, played memorably in the six-week run of the play by Lee J. Cobb. Wilenski is a thirty-seven-year-old child-man, emotionally dependent upon his wife, Mae, a restive spirit who has married him more out of need than love. Rooted in concrete things, his work, his physical strength, and his wife and infant child, this "Polish Apollo" neither thinks of his wife's needs nor considers a friend's wisdom that "Whatever happens in marriage you must think about. . . . Marriage is not a convent. It's not a harbor—it's the open world. . . . It's being out at sea in a boat." Instead, Wilenski dreams of childhood: "But you sit around an' no one tells you what to do—that's the worst thing!"

Wilenski's discovery of Mae's adultery stops history for him; his simple world now seems absurd, unendurable. Instead of fighting for her, recognizing her needs for a more mature intimacy, he regresses to his childhood, fantasizing to his father:

We had those Christmas cards when I was a boy—a little warm house in the snow, yellow lights in the windows . . . remember? It was wonnerful . . . a place where they told you what to do, like in school. . . . (Beginning to cry) I wished it was like on the Christmas cards again, so nice and warm, a wonnerful home. . . . No, I wished I never grew up now.

Despite this need for dependency, Wilenski is not the only member of the ignorant armies of the play. The lovers, Mae and Earl Pfeiffer, trapped by lower-class origins, self-disgust, and lack of education and opportunity, come to each other out of loneliness and lack of self-understanding similar to that which will ultimately destroy Wilenski. Earl feels himself "floating down the river like a barge," but for the few days before his murder by Wilenski he will find in Mae an answer to the frequently asked question in Odets' plays: "Where is home?" (The scene in which the lovers grope toward an understanding of each other's needs is one of the great psychological episodes in American drama.) Bitter, cynical, yet decent, Earl has been drawn, ironically, into the Wilenskis' lives by Jerry himself, through Wilenski's need to identify with a stronger, more self-possessed, and possibly authoritarian figure. It is Kress who will ironically satisfy Wilenski's need for dependency as he goads him into killing Earl. While the motives for Kress's action are not made sufficiently clear, he too is implicated in the world of unconsidered passion and ignorance that brings either moral or emotional destruction to the members of the triangle. Joe Doyle, the overly explicit conscience of the play, warns that "Paradise begins in Responsibility." As in *Golden Boy*, Odets ascribes men's horrors to their lack of vision and self-knowledge.

Few Odets dramas establish atmosphere congruent to theme as brilliantly as *Clash by Night*. The first scene is particularly effective as Wilenski and his wife while away a June evening on the porch in the heat. Music predominates, as it so often does in Odets, but as a warning symbol foreboding destruction. Wilenski listens to his father's old Polish song about "the little old house, where you wanna go back, but you can't find out where it is no more, the house. . . ." Mae, bored and listless, sings "The Shiek of Araby," symbolizing her discontent with her marriage. After she has gone inside, Jerry can only repeat the lyric mindlessly, vainly attempting to reach toward a connection with her as he follows her into the living room, trying to control his pitiful environment, his little dream. John Gassner has praised Odets as a "scenewright"; nowhere is the dramatist's power in construction of the expository and foreshadowing scene more evident.

In Mae's final awareness that she must suffer for another, not just herself, that she and the incoherently praying Wilenski have unwittingly established a kinship of mutual loss, Odets achieves a first-rate tragic drama, sharing with O'Neill a capacity for the remorseless working out of the inevitable process from unawareness to carnage. His unrelenting drama possesses too many formal flaws to achieve the grandeur of O'Neill's great tragedies, but *Clash by Night* is nonetheless a play of deep psychoanalytic insight and great dramatic power. Even though its action in other hands could be mawkish or banal, Odets' play holds us as O'Neill's do, because in times of crisis life tends to imitate melodrama and Odets skillfully communicates the immediacy and tension of such situations.

That Odets' remunerative Hollywood screenwriting provoked considerable ambivalence in him from the earliest of his three periods there (1936–1938, 1943–1947, 1955–1961) is evident from details in several of his plays. In *Clash by Night* the sound of "fraudulent" movie dialogue is heard as Wilenski stalks his prey in the projection booth, symbolically locked from the inside; the ineffectual Myron Berger in *Awake and Sing!* naively places his faith in the restorative powers of the "Marvel Cosmetic Girl of Hollywood"; and Willy Wax in *Rocket to the Moon* and Steve Takis throughout much of *Night Music* are seduced by the blandishments of Hollywood. Harold Clurman remembers that after his initial period in Hollywood, "Odets began to worry about himself; he was his own greatest problem." (Frank Nugent had greeted Odets' 1936 potboiler about the Chinese Revolution, *The General Died at Dawn*, with the legendary thrust,

"Odets, Where Is Thy Sting?") As early as 1935 the playwright voiced his ambivalence and guilt over his desire for material success and fame during an interview with A. J. Liebling, by worrying about his new status as a celebrity who "receives fantastic offers from Hollywood, invitations to address ladies' clubs, one hundred and fifty telephone calls a day and a lot of solemn consideration from guys who write pieces for the dramatic page."

Because of the practice of collaborative scriptwriting in the film industry, it is difficult to determine exactly how many screenplays Odets was responsible for, though it is clear that he had nothing whatever to do with his own plays that reached the screen (*Golden Boy, Clash by Night, The Country Girl,* and *The Big Knife*). A reading of three screenplays in typescript at the Library of Congress film archive for which he receives sole credit reveals that, despite occasionally incisive psychological moments, they add nothing to his artistic reputation. In *Deadline at Dawn* (1946), a philosophically inclined taxi driver (well played by Paul Lukas) pronounces of a murder suspect such lines as "The divine being made many loathsome creatures—but none so low as a woman with a cold heart." Things get worse in *The Story on Page One* (1960) and especially in *Wild in the Country* (1961), in which an aspiring young writer (played by Elvis Presley) weeps over his deceased mother, "Death, he's a quick one, ain't he?" Of a much higher order is Odets' poignant rendering of Richard Llewellyn's novel *None but the Lonely Heart* (1944), Cary Grant's one "serious" film, which Odets also directed. Young Cockney Ernie Mott— "tramp of the universe . . . like some homeless breath of wind . . ."—grows beyond self-preoccupation and learns to commit himself to other people as he undertakes an archetypal quest for "a human animal which don't look for a master." Odets again deals nicely with the father-son motif, and despite some sentimentality the script is quite moving both in its themes of self-victimization and brotherhood and as a social document of wartime London.

While it may be possible that film writing honed his playwriting technique, it is uncomfortably true that in the twenty-two years left to him after the production of *Clash by Night,* Odets completed only three plays—*The Big Knife* (1949), *The Country Girl* (1950), and *The Flowering Peach* (1954)—none of which stands with his finest achievements. In an essay written in 1972, Harold Clurman bluntly pointed to the beginnings of a personal deterioration as early as *Golden Boy,* which "foreshadows his inability to resolve the conflict which led to his own final destruction." Clurman's biographical approach may oversimplify the complex case of a man eager for both fame and artistic integrity; as Gerald Weales points out, it was for the body of his plays that Odets received the Award of Merit Medal for drama in 1961 from the American Academy of Arts and Letters. What seems clear is that Odets perceived himself as having compromised his art to some degree by devoting so many years of his life to work that did not test his full potential. His close friend, playwright William Gibson, speaks judiciously in an interview with Michael Mendelsohn about screenwriting and the artist's integrity:

He sells time, and that is the only thing which cannot be replenished. Whether there is any kind of damage to one's standards by working in movies I do not know. I think that we too glibly assume that there is. . . . But you cannot write a movie and a play at the same time.

There has been speculation that Odets testified before the House Committee on Un-American Activities (HUAC) in May 1952 out of fear that *The Country Girl* would not be filmed without his cooperation. Perhaps he perceived this act also as a compromise of his ideals and of his loyalties to his former friends and associates in the Group Theatre. It is certain that the testimony of Odets and Elia Kazan prompted Morris Carnovsky's bitterness toward Odets for many years, Carnovsky and Stella and Luther Adler feeling that Odets was partly to blame for Carnovsky's being blacklisted from the entertainment industry for several years in the 1950's because he had elected not to testify.

Odets' testimony was his first public admission of his association with the Communist party for eight months in 1934–1935. Most members of the Group Theatre had been interested in the Moscow Art Theater, and this doubtless led some to an interest in Marxism. Odets informed HUAC of his comic-opera journey to Cuba in 1935 with a group of writers and union officials, ostensibly investigating the plight of labor and students under the Batista-Mendieta regime, more probably publicizing the activities of the Cuban dictatorship. The group was arrested unceremoniously upon arrival in Havana harbor and shipped back to New York the following day. That event, together with increasing pressure to write agit-prop plays, prompted Odets to abandon the Communist party shortly thereafter, as he explained to the committee:

I didn't respect any person or any party or any group of people who would say to a young creative writer: "Go outside of your experience and write outside of your experience a play." I knew that as fumbling as my beginnings were, and they certainly were, that I could only write out of my own experience, out of my own incentive. I couldn't be given a theme and handle it. It was not my business. It meant to me, if I may say it this way, a loss of integrity. And so I persisted in going along on my own line and saying and writing what did come out of my true center. And whenever this happened, I got this violent opposition in that press and I became further disgusted and estranged from them.

Odets' guilt at having betrayed the trust of his former Group Theatre associates and at having survived the witchhunt without being blacklisted may well have been intensified by the death of John Garfield a year after his own rather more heroic testimony before HUAC. (Edward Murray relates that Odets sobbed uncontrollably at Garfield's graveside.) Certainly, Odets' noble words about artistic integrity before HUAC must not have squared with his perception, revealed so clearly in *The Big Knife*, that an artist courts spiritual depletion by devoting years of his career to less than his best efforts.

In *The Big Knife*, Charlie Castle (years ago Charlie Cass, a struggling actor on the legitimate stage) has fallen victim to a Hollywood machine ostensibly so vicious that having corrupted his soul, it must take his life as well. After years of playing stereotyped parts in return for huge financial rewards from his studio, he no longer cares for the liberal politics that once sustained him; and he humiliates both his wife, Marion, and himself through a series of tawdry sexual liaisons. He has even allowed the studio to pressure him into evading responsibility for killing a man years ago in a hit-and-run accident, while drunk, by forcing his best friend to go to jail for him. Now the studio boss, Marcus Hoff, threatens Charlie with exposure and prison if he will not sign another lucrative long-term contract. The strained improbability of the action is heightened when Hoff suggests to Charlie that he be an accomplice in the murder of a starlet who, unknown to Marion, was in the car the night of the accident and who now threatens to go to the police with her story in order to avenge herself against Hoff for manipulating her career. Feeling that Hollywood destroys all it touches ("Don't they murder the highest dreams and hopes of a whole great people with the movies they make?"), Charlie commits suicide as final vengeance against Hoff for having corrupted him.

The incredible series of events and coincidences almost obscures the fact that Charlie is at least as much to blame for his corruption and his problems as the evil system. Despite Odets' protestations that *The Big Knife* was intended as a universal statement about the average man's difficulty in maintaining his dignity in a corrupt world, it is difficult to avoid the inadequate objective correlative of the play and Clurman's reminder that Charlie's self-destruction is a slim, transparent allegory of an "Odets lacerated by self-accusation" for betraying his talent. While the contrived action makes clear that Charlie is obsessively attracted to the Hollywood that is destroying him, the thematic thrust denies that obvious fact. The play falls apart under its author's psychic discomfort with his materials. The final suicide is more punishment for guilt than affirmative triumph, since nothing is affirmed.

While *The Big Knife* contains some vital characterizations (particularly Marion and Smiley Coy, Hoff's hatchet man) and occasionally trenchant dialogue, including Charlie's famous lines from Victor Hugo, the romantic source of his youthful inspiration and idealism ("Love people, do good, help the lost and fallen, make the world happy, if you can!"), it is Odets' first play that does not unsparingly reveal the major role played by weakness of character in human misery. It is that striking avoidance of his previous toughness and sincerity—and not the widely alleged absence of social concern—that may account for the curious lack of thematic density and resonance in Odets' late plays.

If *The Country Girl* also rather obviously dramatizes Odets' continuing conflict over desire for material success and for artistic growth, it is a stronger performance than *The Big Knife* and, with Odets directing, proved to be both critically accepted and his first commercial success since *Golden Boy* thirteen years earlier. Frank Elgin, once a distinguished stage actor but presently a disintegrating alcoholic, gets one last chance at a good part on the faith of a young director, Bernie Dodd. But Elgin has become so terribly dependent upon his long-suffering wife, Georgie, that his own sense of inadequacy threatens throughout rehearsals to send him back to the bottle and oblivion. Elgin has convinced Dodd that it is Georgie who is alcoholic and resentful of his successes, playing upon Dodd's own failed marriage and resultant insecurity and misogyny. The central action involves the working out of the conflict between Georgie and Dodd for Elgin's career and soul. Improbably, Elgin scores a great success on opening night and Georgie, tempted to leave him for Dodd, finally decides to stay with the man-child to whom she is so symbiotically attached.

Once again Odets shows his awareness of the passively dependent male's psychology: Elgin is the last in a generally distinguished line of such characters as Myron Berger, Ben Stark, Jerry Wilenski, Charlie Castle—and Bernie Dodd, as well. Elgin's manic-depressive swings are made more theatrically than dramatically credible, but Dodd is more interesting as he becomes increasingly hostile to Georgie for "ruining" her husband. Projecting his own dependency needs for a strong, maternal woman onto Elgin, he unconsciously wishes to win Georgie from him, even though he dimly realizes that such an eventuality would destroy both his play and, probably, Elgin's tenuous hold on reality. Like Jerry Wilenski, both Elgin and Dodd fear rejection and unconsciously seek to return to the security of childhood, and can resort to destructive behavior when this illusion fails to be realized. Yet Dodd is mature in several ways, at least at the conscious level, assuming responsibility for Elgin's comeback and employing all his considerable theatrical knowledge to accomplish this.

It is perhaps hanging one more gun on the wall than will be fired (Anton Chekhov's warning to playwrights) for Odets to make Dodd attracted to Elgin as a father figure, for the playwright strains Georgie's characterization by inserting this motive in her persona as well. The need of this supposedly strong woman for Elgin "as a father" is dubious, seeming to contradict her knowledge of his long-term drinking problem, which itself suggests an element of masochism in her having stayed with him for so many years. It is difficult to believe Georgie when she says to her husband, "I married you for happiness. . . ." The source of her psychological weakness and her exact status as a "country girl" are insufficiently resolved by Odets; as a result the theatrically exciting effects of the play are not all dramatically earned, and texture is sacrificed to structure. These flaws account for the rather hermetically sealed quality of *The Country Girl:* it seems to refer to little outside its own narrow world except, perhaps, to excessive wish fulfillment on the part of its author.

Happily, Odets' final play is more fully dimensional than *The Country Cirl.* Never published in complete form, *The Flowering Peach* came close to capturing for Odets his sole Pulitzer Prize, the trustees overruling the Columbia Faculty Committee and awarding the prize for 1955 to Tennessee Williams' *Cat on a Hot Tin Roof.* If *The Flowering Peach* does not show Odets at the peak of his powers, there are present in his retelling of the Noah legend considerable dramatic inventiveness, rounded characters, wry humor, and a return to the thematic vigor of the early family plays.

"All men are Jews," Bernard Malamud has said, to indicate that Jewish suffering can stand as a metaphor for universal human misery. Throughout his career Odets anticipated many of the ideas and motifs of such Jewish American writers as Malamud and Edward Lewis Wallant, particularly themes of the need for a sense of community and the human aptitude for rising beyond suffering to attain moral harmony and dignity. Odets' Noah, a frequently drunk authoritarian, is one of his most appealing characters, as he tries both to obey to the letter God's injunction to build an ark in order to save at least a remnant of the human family, and to persuade his radical son, Japheth, to compromise his ideals and accede to the family's standards and traditions. Once again Odets employs the generational conflict: Noah vigorously opposes Japheth's wish to equip the ark with a rudder, staunch in his view that if God had wanted Noah to build a rudder, he would have made that clear at the start. Odets amusingly dramatizes the intimate antagonism between the father and the son, as Japheth argues, "And God didn't tell you to invent the hoe and the rake and yet you did!" to which Noah can only reply, "I was a youngster then—what did I know? If you'll ast me today, I'm sorry I done it! . . . It made work too easy an' people for loafers!"

The Flowering Peach gains much of its power and charm through Noah's character transformation. Realizing that Japheth's humanism is ultimately closer to godliness than his own procrustean morality, Noah learns to grow toward a more moderate anthropocentricism:

I'm thinkin' back a good many years. My father's father, Methusaleh . . . he knew I was born for something special—what you call a BIG JOB! "Go out, Noah, go out an' preach repentance to the world!" Yeh, that was the story! (Sighing) What should I tell you? Evil is a stone wall. . . . I hurt my head a lotta times!

Though the several subplots in *The Flowering Peach* rarely cohere with the main theme of Noah's growing self-awareness, the old man's coming to maturity is one of Odets' most moving dramatic passages. At the end of the play as the ark pulls in to a new shore, Noah accepts from Japheth a branch of flowering peach and murmurs, "From the new earth." Mute for a moment with the recognition that aboard the ark they have faced themselves as well as external dangers, and have conquered both (the dying Esther had whispered to Noah, "I'll tell you a mystery."), Japheth realizes that he too has learned: "Maybe God changes when men change." As his children go off to found their families, Noah prudently chooses to live with Shem, his materialistic son, whose thriving manure briquette business means fuel for the new age, for "It's more comfortable. . . . Write sometimes. . . ." Odets refuses to sentimentalize the resolution, and this realism nicely balances Noah's last great speech, as he beseeches God for proof that he will not destroy the world again, and receives only the rainbow in answer:

But what I learned on the trip, dear God, you can't take it away from me. To walk in humility, I learned. And listen, even to *myself* . . . and to speak softly, with the voices of consolation. Yes, I hear You, God—Now it's in man's hands to make or destroy the world. . . . I'll tell you a mystery.

As in *Awake and Sing!* and *Paradise Lost*, the base of Jewish family comedy undergirds the dramatic structure. The fruit imagery of Japheth's final gift of love and forgiveness to his father resonates with Odets' frequent use of such images in earlier plays: Wilenski's old father in *Clash by Night* mumbling "have eat orange"; Moe Axelrod's obsession with fruit as a replacement for Hennie's love in *Awake and Sing!*; and Clara Gordon's repeated offerings of fruit to the members of her suffering family in *Paradise Lost* are all used symbolically by Odets to indicate the possibilities for regeneration in the cohesive family unit. Odets' superior ear for terse, ironic Jewish dialect also gives the play buoyancy. Esther nags Noah at his news of the coming flood, "Noah, Noah, tell the truth—when they gave out the brains, you weren't hiding behind the house? ... Answer me a question, a *realism*—why should *we* be saved?" Noah's attempts to evade God's having chosen him to save life are also amusing: "You are All and Everything an' I'm unworthy.... All I do is cough an' spit. Pass me by, pass me by. Please...." God's refusal to do so and Noah's reluctant acceptance of the challenge to transcend his former self make *The Flowering Peach* the best of Odets' late plays.

Though by his own account Odets was to begin several plays after 1954, none was completed. Whether or not a guilty conscience over his comfortable life in Hollywood caused an artistic decline will remain debatable until the appearance of Margaret Brenman Gibson's authorized biography. On July 23, 1963, Odets entered Cedars of Lebanon Hospital in Los Angeles for treatment of stomach problems; the condition was soon diagnosed as inoperable cancer, and Odets died on August 14, 1963. Harold Clurman recalls that Odets was troubled by his ambivalence between material and artistic success until the day he died, and remembers Odets on his deathbed in Hollywood: "I saw him turn to the wall and cry out, with a lofty dramatic gesture (he was always an 'actor'), 'Clifford Odets, there is so much more work to be done!' But he knew it was too late for him. That was his (American) tragedy."

"I admired O'Neill," Odets recalled late in his life. "I am influenced by O'Neill in terms of becoming a big American dramatist." If it is certainly fair that Odets' critical reputation today is less substantial than O'Neill's, it is indeed unfortunate that his position lags far behind that of other prominent dramatists in whose company he rightfully belongs. Despite weaknesses also typical of O'Neill, such as sometimes straining an incident beyond its dramatic effectiveness, and his penchant for the overblown line—speeches like Charlie Castle's praise of his wife, "She's the iron hoop that holds my staves together," remind us of John Mason Brown's quip that at his worst Odets sounded as if he were writing with pen held in clenched fist—it must be remembered that Odets compiled a record of first-rate plays superior to that of Maxwell Anderson, William Saroyan, Elmer Rice, Thornton Wilder, or Edward Albee. Perhaps the tendency of critical reputations to rise and fall in Spenglerian cycles may someday remove the "Clifford One-Note" stigma that has clung to Odets since the end of the 1930's because of the facile categorizing of his dramas as social tracts.

In any event, Odets' achievement compares well even with O'Neill's in his great themes of the individual's search for self-fulfillment and self-transcendence, the importance of the family to one's sense of "belonging," the American ambivalence between material goals and spiritual ideals, and the necessity of individual responsibility amid the chaos and unreason of the modern world. In *Golden Boy* and *Clash by Night* Odets produced fine tragedies in a country not renowned for its tragic drama. In American dramatic literature, only O'Neill and Tennessee Williams are superior in the tragic form, and only they are Odets' masters in the psychological delineation of character. Whereas Williams' and Arthur Miller's characters frequently seem determined by their environments, in Odets we sometimes sense the possibility of growth and change. Ralph Berger and Mae Wilenski establish with those who love them at least some sense of the kinship of victimhood, learning to share suffering, choosing to accept the limitations of life and to assume responsibilities willingly, not resentfully—in Malamud's terms, to become assistants for subjects beyond the self.

Only O'Neill outstrips Odets in the variety of dramatic genres in which he achieved first-rate plays; besides tragedy, Odets did fine work in comedy, the problem play, and the quasi romance. Odets also excels in his capacity to suggest much through compressed, concentrated detail, a skill that can be seen even in his least esteemed play, *Till the Day I Die:* at the end of scene 5, in little more than a page of dialogue Odets moves rapidly from the pathos of Tausig's shattered readiness for sleep to his brother's entrance, thence to the immediate need for Carl's escape and Tilly's lightning ruse to effect his safe departure. If a writer can be evaluated at least partly in terms of his influence, Arthur Miller and William Gibson have stated their indebtedness to Odets, and Tennessee Williams' and Paddy Chayefsky's plays show resemblances to Odets' hard-edged poetic dialogue among common urban people. Clearly, Odets' lyrical presentation of ordinary people poised in constricted spaces metaphoric of the modern condition, his fusion of the spirit of the Great Depression with more universal themes, his sense of the growing urbanization of American life, and what Clurman has termed his "radical humanism" qualify him as a serious artist. In his best plays—*Awake and Sing!, Paradise Lost, Golden Boy, Night Music,* and *Clash by Night*—Odets belongs with Williams and Miller, high in the second rank of American dramatists.

Selected Bibliography

WORKS OF CLIFFORD ODETS

PLAYS

"*The Silent Partner*" [Act II, scene 2]. *New Theatre and Film,* 4:5–9 (March 1937).

Six Plays of Clifford Odets. New York: Modern Library, 1939. (Contains the shorter version of *Waiting for Lefty, Till the Day I Die, Awake and Sing!, Paradise Lost, Golden Boy,* and *Rocket to the Moon,* as well as a preface by Odets and three introductions by Harold Clurman.)

Night Music. New York: Random House, 1940.

Clash by Night. New York: Random House, 1942.

The Big Knife. New York: Random House, 1949.

The Country Girl. New York: Viking, 1951.

Waiting for Lefty (complete version). In *Representative Modern Plays: American,* edited by Robert Warnock. Chicago: Scott, Foresman, 1952.

The Flowering Peach. (Never published in complete form, this play is in typescript at the Theater Collection, New York Public Library.) An abridged version was published in *The Best Plays of 1954–1955,* edited by Louis Kronenberger. New York: Dodd, Mead, 1955.

SCREENPLAYS

Deadline at Dawn (1946), *The Story on Page One* (1960), and *Wild in the Country* (1961). (Unpublished continuity scripts in the Library of Congress.)

None but the Lonely Heart. In *Best Film Plays, 1945,* edited by John Gassner and Dudley Nichols. New York: Crown, 1946; repr. New York: Garland, 1978.

MISCELLANEOUS WRITINGS

Beals, Carleton, and Clifford Odets. *Rifle Rule in Cuba.* New York: Provisional Committee for Cuba, 1935.

"Some Problems of the Modern Dramatist." *New York Times* (December 15, 1935), sec. 11, p. 3.

"I Can't Sleep" (monologue). *New Theatre,* 3:8–9 (February 1936).

Introduction to Nikolai Gogol, *Dead Souls,* translated by Constance Garnett. New York: Modern Library, 1936.

"Democratic Vistas in Drama." *New York Times* (November 21, 1937), sec. 11, pp. 1–2.

"Genesis of a Play." *New York Times* (February 1, 1942), sec. 9, p. 3.

The Russian People, in *Seven Soviet Plays,* edited by Henry W. L. Dana. New York: Macmillan, 1946. (American acting version of Konstantin Simonov's *The Russian Question.*)

"Two Approaches to the Writing of a Play." *New York Times* (April 22, 1951), sec. 2, pp. 1–2.

"How a Playwright Triumphs" (discussion with Arthur Wagner, September 1961). *Harper's,* 233: 64–74 (September 1966).

BIOGRAPHICAL AND CRITICAL STUDIES

For relatively complete listings, see the bibliography in Cantor (below), pp. 214–229.

BOOKS

Aaron, Daniel. *Writers on the Left.* New York: Harcourt, Brace and World, 1961.

Brooks, Cleanth, R. W. B. Lewis, and Robert Penn Warren. "Clifford Odets." In *American Literature: The Makers and the Making,* vol. 2. New York: St. Martin's, 1973.

Brown, John Mason. *As They Appear.* New York: McGraw-Hill, 1952.

Cantor, Harold. *Clifford Odets: Playwright-Poet.* Metuchen, N. J.–London: Scarecrow Press, 1978.

Clurman, Harold. *The Fervent Years.* New York: Hill and Wang, 1957.

————, ed. *Famous American Plays of the 1930s.* New York: Dell, 1959.

Downer, Alan S. *Fifty Years of American Drama.* Chicago: Regnery, 1951.

Dusenbury, Winifred L. *The Theme of Loneliness in Modern American Drama.* Gainesville: University of Florida Press, 1960.

Freedman, Morris. *American Drama in Social Context.* Carbondale: Southern Illinois University Press, 1971.

Gassner, John. *The Theatre in Our Times.* New York: Crown, 1954.

Gibson, William. Introduction to *Golden Boy* (musical version). New York: Atheneum, 1965.

Goldstein, Malcolm. "Clifford Odets and the Found Generation." In *American Drama and Its Critics,* edited by Alan S. Downer. Chicago: University of Chicago Press, 1965.

————. *The Political Stage: American Drama and Theater of the Great Depression.* New York: Oxford University Press, 1974.

Gorelik, Mordecai. *New Theatres for Old.* New York: Samuel French, 1940.

Griffin, Robert J. "On the Love Songs of Clifford Odets." In *The Thirties,* edited by Warren French. DeLand, Fla.: Everett-Edwards, 1967.

Krutch, Joseph Wood. *The American Drama Since 1918.* New York: George Braziller, 1957.

Mendelsohn, Michael J. *Clifford Odets: Humane Dramatist.* DeLand, Fla.: Everett-Edwards, 1969.

Murray, Edward. *Clifford Odets: The Thirties and After.* New York: Ungar, 1968.

Nathan, George Jean. *Encyclopaedia of the Theatre.* New York: Knopf, 1940.

Shuman, Robert Baird. *Clifford Odets.* New York: Twayne, 1962.

Sievers, Wieder David. *Freud on Broadway.* New York: Hermitage House, 1955.

Warshow, Robert. *The Immediate Experience.* Garden City, N.Y.: Doubleday, 1962.

Weales, Gerald. "The Group Theatre and Its Plays." In *American Theatre* (Stratford-upon-Avon Studies 10), edited by John Russell Brown and Bernard Harris. New York: St. Martin's, 1967.

————. *Clifford Odets: Playwright.* New York: Pegasus, 1971.

ARTICLES

Clurman, Harold. "Found: A 'Lost' Play by Odets." *New York Times* (April 30, 1972), sec. 2, pp. 1, 21.

Cowley, Malcolm. "While They Waited for Lefty." *Saturday Review,* 47:16–19, 61 (June 6, 1964).

Fagin, N. Bryllion. "In Search of an American Cherry Orchard." *Texas Quarterly,* 1:132–41 (Summer–Autumn 1958).

Fiedler, Leslie A. "The Breakthrough: The American Jewish Novelist and the Fictional Image of the Jew." *Midstream,* 4:15–35 (Winter 1958).

Hayes, Richard. "The Flowering Peach." *Commonweal,* 61:502–03 (February 11, 1955).

Hyams, Barry. "Twenty Years on a Tightrope." *Theatre Arts,* 39:68–70, 86 (April 1955).

McCarthy, Mary. "Realism in the American Theatre." *Harper's*, 223:45–52 (July 1961).

Mendelsohn, Michael J. "Odets at Center Stage: A Talk with Michael J. Mendelsohn." *Theatre Arts*, 47:16–19, 74–76 (May 1963); 28–30, 78–80 (June 1963).

Miller, Arthur. "The Family in Modern Drama." *Atlantic*, 197:35–41 (April 1956).

Nathan, George Jean. "The White Hope Gets Paler." *Newsweek*, 15:42 (March 4, 1940).

O'Hara, John. "Desire Under the Rose." *Newsweek*, 19:46 (January 12, 1942).

Willett, Ralph. "Clifford Odets and Popular Culture." *South Atlantic Quarterly*, 69:68–78 (1970).

Young, Stark. "Awake and Whistle at Least." *New Republic*, 82:134 (March 13, 1935).

—*FRANK R. CUNNINGHAM*

Charles Olson

1910–1970

SCATTERED poets on the fringes of American literature might have found in Charles Olson a new Moses to lead them home from literary exile. His 1950 essay "Projective Verse" proclaimed the need to participate in local reality unimpeded by ego, and for each to feel the rhythms of his breath and to hear the syllables of his native speech. Early sections of *The Maximus Poems* (1960), his major poetic sequence, demonstrate and fulfill these demands. They insist on long, breath-related lines and marginless pages while a metamorphic, expansive figure called Maximus weaves through, liberating and liberated, a local inhabitant of the Cape Ann town of Gloucester, Massachusetts.

Yet, despite Olson's gradually increasing influence on his readers and despite the growing numbers of poets among them, the dispersion of poets continues. And, similarly, as the sequence grew to three volumes (*The Maximus Poems, Maximus Poems IV, V, VI,* and *The Maximus Poems Volume Three*), Maximus the citizen disappeared and the Gloucester locale was gradually abandoned until both returned in the posthumously published *Volume Three*. Nevertheless, even when Olson was searching for a cosmic locus for his sequence, he claimed Gloucester as his adoptive mother and place of origin, and the sea itself as spiritual father.

In actual fact, Olson was born inland in Worcester, Massachusetts, on December 27, 1910. He was the son of Karl Joseph Olson, a Swedish letter carrier father, and Mary Hines, an Irish mother who was "only the most beautiful woman in Southern Worcester." At points in the Maximus sequence he effectively scrutinizes his family history and even refers to the Worcester trolley tracks as his "inland waters." Yet, for the poet it was Gloucester, not Worcester, "where fishing continues / and my heart lies."

Before finally renting his own house in the Fort Point section of Gloucester in 1957, Olson spent memorable boyhood summers there with his family and thereafter adopted Gloucester as his "home." In 1929, the summer after he entered Wesleyan University, Olson acted and took dance classes at the Gloucester School of the Little Theater, experiences that figure in two early Maximus poems and inform the six-foot, eight-inch poet's notion of "stance" or posture in the essay "Projective Verse." In 1932, after graduating Phi Beta Kappa from Wesleyan, he returned for the summer to Gloucester and the theater.

Olson continued to be "uneducated," as he put it, at Wesleyan, where he earned a master's degree in 1933; at Yale, where he took further graduate courses on a fellowship; and at Harvard, where he was a doctoral candidate in American Studies and studied under F. O. Matthiessen. He left Harvard in 1939 without submitting a dissertation, but he had won a Guggenheim fellowship to continue research on Herman Melville begun at Wesleyan. Olson's Melville studies were the basis for his master's thesis, for the paper "Lear and Moby-Dick" (1938), and eventually for his maverick 1947 critical study, *Call Me Ishmael.*

In 1940, Olson moved to New York, where he worked briefly for the American Civil Liberties Union and for the Common Council for American Unity until 1942. He then took a post in Washington, D. C., as assistant chief of the Foreign Language Section in the Office of War Information. But by 1945 Olson had ended his political career. Apparently disenchanted, he resigned from the Office of War Information and refused U. S. Post Office and Treasury Department appointments. According to Paul Christensen's informative *Charles Olson: Call Him Ishmael* (1979), Olson discovered during this brief excursion into liberal politics that the American government and economic system "dissolved communal life in a deliberate leveling of the population into competitive individuals."

There followed a period of exploration during which Olson traveled to Florida, then returned to Washington. During this time he wrote the final revisions of *Call Me Ishmael* and regularly visited Ezra Pound, then confined to St. Elizabeth's Hospital in Washington. In 1948 he received another Guggenheim fellowship for a study of racial interaction in the settling of the American West and saw the publication of a pamphlet of his poems, *Y & X.* That same year he began what was to become a long and fruitful association with Black Mountain College, the pioneering, innovative, experimental college

in North Carolina that has since become known as a point of origin for the most avant-garde movements in dance, painting, music, and poetry in the 1950's.

Olson was first a visiting lecturer, then director of a summer theater program in 1949, and finally a faculty member and rector of Black Mountain College from 1951 until its closing in 1956. It was not until the college was sold that Olson returned to Gloucester. His stay at Black Mountain College coincided with the presence there of such diverse talents as artists Josef Albers and Robert Motherwell, choreographer Merce Cunningham, composer John Cage, and poets Robert Creeley, Robert Duncan, John Wieners, and Ed Dorn. A loose-knit community of artists, students, and teachers, Black Mountain College formed the actual basis for Olson's poetic conception of "polis," the civic ideal ascribed to Gloucester in *The Maximus Poems.*

Ideas of such visitors to Black Mountain College as mathematician Hans Rademacher, with whom Olson studied topology, and architect R. Buckminster Fuller, whose geodesic dome graced the campus one summer, left impressions on Olson, just as modern scientific thought had left imprints on the works of James Joyce, T. S. Eliot, Ezra Pound, and William Carlos Williams. Like these earlier contemporary writers, he tried to accommodate a modern view of the ever-changing physical universe to man's timeless need for language and form. But, unlike Joyce and Eliot, Olson depended more upon mapping than memory to locate man in the universe. His concern with the aesthetic and philosophical significance of projective geometry and topology suggests that the new mathematics provided a major thematic and aesthetic focus, as well as a motive for much of Olson's poetry and for his famous essay "Projective Verse." By 1950 and the publication of that essay, the new geometries had become no less than a "redefinition of the real" for Olson, a view of reality that sees space as inseparable from matter.

The result is that Olson's poetry does not lend itself readily to summary or evaluation. Throughout his work he attempted to "stay in the condition of things"; but as much as he admired John Keats's "negative capability," the ability "to remain in uncertainties . . . without any irritable reaching after fact and reason," his own vision and poetry were shaped more by the discontinuities of a universe in flux than by an organic view of the world. Keats's dramatistic suspension of personality did not suit Olson's purposes. Olson preferred an intellectual form of self-abnegation more typical of philosophers, mathematicians, and historians. His greatest achievement was that he transformed this apparent handicap into poetic effects that included a "new stance toward reality"; the metamorphic, metaphoric figure of Maximus; *The Maximus Poems,* an open-ended poetic sequence that is less time-bound than Pound's *Cantos* and less local than Williams' *Paterson;* and a vocabulary from every available modern discipline of thought.

Perhaps Olson's major contribution is that he represents what his poem "The Kingfishers" refers to as "the will to change." Olson, more than such modern American poets as Pound, Wallace Stevens, Williams, or Robert Lowell, gives the impression of being a sign of the times. Only a few recent novelists leave the reader with the same feeling of being propelled into the future. Even Olson's most admiring fellow poets do not approach his prosodic breadth, thematic inclusiveness, and perpetual motion.

The sensibilities of contemporary American novelists—Kurt Vonnegut, Thomas Pynchon, and Ishmael Reed, for example—provide clues to the nature of Olson's poetic achievement. His poems reject the limitations of a poetic speaker's perspective for the relative omniscience of a more inclusive focus. In consequence, all sorts of references, allusions, and sources impinge upon and enter into his poetry. In addition, Olson frequently relies upon random coincidences, even in his own creations.

Most of Olson's early poetry is in *Archaeologist of Morning* (1970), which includes all of his poetry authorized for publication during his lifetime, except the Maximus sequence. His 1950 essay "Projective Verse" expresses the position implicit in poems written between 1945 and 1951 more precisely than it does that of his later work. The essay, as the title and opening paragraphs show, is as much a dismissive characterization of most contemporary poetry in 1950 as it is a prescription for future poets:

Verse now, 1950, if it is to go ahead, if it is to be of essential use, must, I take it, catch up and put into itself certain laws and possibilities of the breath, of the breathing of the man who writes as well as of his listenings. (The revolution of the ear, 1910, the trochee's heave, asks it of the younger poets.)

Citing Pound, Williams, and Keats as forerunners, Olson does not at all claim to be the inventor of "open" verse. Nevertheless, the energy of his essay and its use of terminology borrowed from mathematics and physics made a powerful impression on his contemporaries. Part I of the essay refers to "closed" verse as "inherited line, stanza, over-all form, what is the 'old' base of the non-projective." "Open" poetry is "projective, percussive, prospective." The poet working in "open" learns how to transfer poetic energy, "the *kinetics* of the thing." The next thing he discovers is a kind of poetic materialism, the law that "FORM IS NEVER MORE THAN AN EXTENSION OF CONTENT." Finally, he discovers the essence of the poetic process. Olson puts it dog-

matically: "ONE PERCEPTION MUST IM-
MEDIATELY AND DIRECTLY LEAD TO
A FURTHER PERCEPTION." A related for-
mula comes in the guise of an incantation:

THE HEAD, by way of the EAR, to the
      SYLLABLE
the HEART, by way of the BREATH, to the
      LINE.

This formula is born of Olson's belief that the
syllables of language are rooted in human intelligence, while its rhythms are physiologically
inspired.

The second, shorter part of his essay is more
relevant to Olson's total work. His insistence
that projective verse requires a "new stance toward reality outside a poem as well as a new
stance toward the reality of a poem itself" suggests the exploratory nature of all phases of his
poetry. Noting that Pound and Williams were
each involved in a movement called "objectiv-
ism," Olson proposes "objectism" instead. The
term, he says, implies "getting rid of the lyrical
interference of the individual as ego, of the subject and his 'soul' . . . by which western man has
interposed himself between what he is as a creature of nature . . . and those other creations of
nature which we may . . . call objects." That
poet and poem are also "objects" was always a
presupposition of Olson's poetry. Guarding
against lyricism, ego, and "soul," he sought new
forms to express the reality shared by man and
"those other creations of nature." But when
subjectivity and "soul" demanded inclusion in
Olson's later work, projective verse had not
evolved along lines adequate to the task.

Olson's essay tries to "scientificize" poetics
by arguing that the typewriter has given the
modern poet "the stave and bar a musician has
had." He often used the typewriter to great effect in his poems, as a method of denoting sound
relationships. Yet, his early poetry does not always suggest its open structure by such visual

representation as spacing and placement of
phrases, and the visual aspects of his later
poems are related more to topology and topography, and to abstractions and mapping, than
to breath or sound.

No single exemplary Olson poem reveals a
pattern typical of his entire development; but a
double movement pervades the early years of
his poetry, with poems such as "The Praises,"
"The K," and "There was a Youth whose
Name was Thomas Granger" achieving formal
and tonal self-transcendence, and poems such
as "The Kingfishers" and "In Cold Hell, in
Thicket" demanding continuation instead of
resolution. As early examples of "open" verse,
these poems present patterns of discovery that
are sometimes repeated in Olson's later poetry.

"The Praises" is a celebration of "process" as
it modulates from inquiry to revealed truth and
sings the praises of the secret processes common
to history, thought, nature, and poetry. "There
was a Youth whose Name was Thomas Granger" exemplifies "humilitas," the "realization
that a man is himself an object" that Olson
thought essential to all men as well as to pro-
jectivist poets. "The K," in its transformation of
rhetorical observations into perceptions, is a
very early example of the "new stance toward
reality" required of the poet. Olson's most famous poem, "The Kingfishers," is a desperate
search for form and order that tests the uses
and limits of "the lyrical interference of the
ego" by using an Olson "persona." "In Cold
Hell, in Thicket" anticipates characteristics of
the long Maximus sequence and comes as close
as Olson ever does to a dejection ode.

Olson's best-known poem, "The Kingfishers" is, paradoxically, both a good example
of projective verse technique and atypical of
Olson's poetry. Although written before the
essay "Projective Verse," examples of Olson's
energy principle abound in it, including magnificent use of "the advantage of the type-

writer." Yet "The Kingfishers" also employs a poetic voice and meditative mode that is usually associated with lyric poetry and disavowed by Olson. Nevertheless, it is among the strengths of this poem that it depends upon a speaking voice so distinct that it is almost Olson's "persona." In it Olson assumes the voice of primitive, unaccommodated man, the stripped-down ego that has always been the true subject of meditative poetry, a mode that he soon abandoned for a less introspective stance.

"The Kingfishers" is both a projective sequence and a meditation on endless change, with a theme-and-variations structure that reinforces both open-endedness and repetition. The opening statement ("What does not change / is the will to change") immediately emphasizes human willfulness in a changing universe. It also implies that at least one element recurs in this state of constant change. The word "change" is stressed twice, underlining the simultaneously progressive and futile nature of human thought. The repetition of words and syllables later becomes a basic structural technique, while variations on the theme of change inevitably include recurrent ideas and motifs.

Variations on the theme of change do not necessarily correspond to numerically ordered sections. For example, part I constitutes more than half the poem and is subdivided into four sections. In it there are modulations from a party scene to deeper thoughts comparing the life cycle of kingfishers with the revolutionary process expressed by Mao. Further meditations on war and peace in the history of Mexico build up to a desperate recapitulation of a universal law of change that includes the inevitability of death and the fragility of "a state between / the origin and / the end."

The shorter part II compresses several motifs from part I into a meditation on baptism and burial rituals of the Aztecs. The poet's stance shifts from philosophical perspective to bitter anguish at man's violent nature. Part III is his attempt to transform bitterness into resignation, to regain perspective, and to control his own outrage. In the context of the poem the conclusion is inadequate. The question "shall you uncover honey / where maggots are?" remains, and the answer is nowhere in the poem. Yet such a "downbeat" conclusion is not typical of Olson.

Part I, section 2, contains Olson's most quoted lines. In itself it is a marvelously self-enclosed, complete poem. In the larger context it seems a non sequitur. Yet its beautifully balanced double movement appropriately contrasts the single-minded repetitiveness of the preceding section.

I thought of the E on the stone, and of what
    Mao said
la lumiere"
        but the kingfisher
de l'aurore"
        but the kingfisher flew west
est devant nous!
        he got the color of his breast
        from the heat of the setting sun!

As images of "la lumiere de l'aurore" and "the heat of the setting sun" are woven together, only brief reiteration of "but the kingfisher" recalls the more prosaic first section. The interweaving technique is not new with Olson, nor is the image of kingfishers that "catch fire" as they fly, but the juxtaposition of the "E on the stone" and Mao's poetry of revolution with the kingfisher symbol of decline is uniquely Olson's, a combined vision of the simultaneous processes of history and life as recurrent change. There is ideological justification for concluding section 2 with continued quotation from Mao, simultaneously revealed as a part of the cycle of rise and fall, inevitable as the kingfisher's nest, but also merely another swing of Time's pendulum.

As it helps to know about mathematical allusions in "The Praises" and about Olson's uses of William Bradford's *Plymouth Plantation* as a source for "Thomas Granger," so it is important to read "The Kingfishers" in light of its borrowing from William Hickling Prescott's *Mexico, and the Life of the Conqueror Fernando Cortés* (1898) and William Carlos Williams' essay "The Destruction of Tenochtitlán" (*In the American Grain* [1925]. Williams' imaginative reconstruction of Mexican history explains several otherwise mysterious associations that appear in part I, section 3, of "The Kingfishers," and it may well have been a major source for the poem.

In section 3 "the jungle / leaps in" and there is neither recollection nor disciplined synthesis. These lines are not like T. S. Eliot's "heap of broken images" but are, rather, a tumult of unspecified references and disparate quotations. They represent change as chaos in a flood of thoughts about primitive impulses of men throughout history, specifically Mexican history. Interpreted history or history-as-poetry constitutes the remainder of section 3. Olson "borrows" almost verbatim from Prescott. He only changes "All was now confusion, tumult, and warlike menace, where so lately had been peace and the sweet brotherhood of nations" to a more laconic form:

In this instance, the priests
(in dark cotton robes, and dirty,
    their dishevelled hair matted with blood, and
        flowing wildly
over their shoulders)
rush in among the people, calling on them
to protect their gods

And all now is war
where so lately there was peace,
and the sweet brotherhood, the use
of tilled fields.

Undoubtedly some readers will view such borrowing as questionable poetic practice. Yet the context of Prescott's words in *Mexico, and the Life of the Conqueror*, compared with their context in "The Kingfishers," makes it clear that the historian necessarily reduced his sentiments to sentimentality and his facts to footnotes. Montezuma's gifts assume new connotations in the poem, and one of many battles between Spaniards and Aztec priests takes on generalized moral significance. Apparently both Williams and Olson read Prescott and, like D. H. Lawrence, both were intensely interested in "what was slain in the sun." Yet, despite their similarities, Olson does not accept the "religious practices" of the Aztecs with Williams' detachment, nor does he characterize Montezuma and the priests as "such a surface lifted above the isolate blackness of such profound savagery." Rather, he tries desperately to understand the relationships of Montezuma and his priests, feather and stone, Aztec and conquistador, civilization and anarchy.

In contrast, Williams described the Aztec hecatombs with the relative equanimity of an anthropologist:

Here it was that the tribe's deep feeling for a reality that stems back into the permanence of remote origins had its firm hold. It was the earthward thrust of their logic; blood and earth; the realization of their primal and continuous identity with the ground itself where everything is fixed in darkness.

He went on to describe the idols:

. . . of extra-human size and composed, significantly, of a paste of seeds and leguminous plants . . . together with human blood, the whole then being consecrated with a bath of blood from the heart of a living victim.

Williams noticeably betrays some anguish at man's inhumanity in the opening of his next essay, "The Fountain of Eternal Youth," where he comments:

History begins for us with murder and enslavement, not with discovery. No, we are not Indians but we are men of their world. The blood means nothing; the spirit, the ghost of the land moves in the blood, moves the blood.

In "The Kingfishers," Olson seems to be trying to answer Williams' indictment, and in section 4 he restates the law of change, a new humanism to counter the violence of section 3. The theme originally stated so concisely is all but dissipated in restatement. By the end, though, the conventional wisdom of tired cliché is revitalized through insistent echoes of ancient Mexico and modern technological culture:

> . . . the message. And what is the message?
>   The message is
> a discrete or continuous sequence of
>   measurable events distributed in time
>
> is the birth of air, is
> the birth of water, is
> a state between
> the origin and
> the end, between
> birth and the beginning of
> another fetid nest
>
> is change, presents
> no more than itself
>
> And the too strong grasping of it,
>   when it is pressed together and condensed,
>   loses it

This very thing you are

From the labored reiteration of phrases comes an incantation to the law of change. From exhausted dejection arises a dispassionate but forceful conclusion, a restatement of "the law" in different terms. Indian lore and Alfred North Whitehead, Mexican gods and technological terminology are juxtaposed to relay this

"message." Section 2 used the method of interweaving motifs; section 4 interweaves whole philosophies. To contain the horror of section 3, the fourth brings into relief the unifying force of change as a universal principle.

Were the poem to end at this point, it might have conveyed the theme adequately. Yet, it is crucial to the poetic realization of Olson's message that poet and poetry are part of the unending process of change. Accordingly, part II returns to the psychological heart of the poem, "the heart of darkness" that Olson refuses to deny, "the new 'double-axis' of primitive-abstract" cited in his "Letter to Elaine Feinstein."

In part II the poet's interest in anthropology translates into an immediacy and urgency found nowhere else in the poem. Associations with Prescott's history of Mexico and Williams' essay are clear, as is the allusion to Mao, yet the intensity of Olson's reaction is entirely his own. Carefully rendered dichotomies of East and West, birth and death, culture and genocide serve only to enrage the poet who knows how inseparable these poles are. Intellectual perspective fails as he extrapolates from scholarly citations to a condemnation of all culture. From brief references to Aztec rites, the section builds to a crescendo of personal outrage at the violent basis of civilization. It is a recognition that Olson repeats with reference to the Mayans in a letter to Robert Creeley written at the beginning of his six months on the Yucatán Peninsula before he joined the Black Mountain College faculty. It is dated February 24, 1951:

. . . don't let even Lawrence fool you (there is nothing in this Mexican deal, so far as "time in the sun" goes: . . . but this is a culture in arrestment, which is no culture at all . . . when I say that, however, I give these people much more head, than their recent slobberers for the

    arrestment, surely, was due to the stunning (by the Spanish) of the Indian, 400 yrs ago . . .
culture is confidence, & surely, Mao makes

Mexico certain . . . (this whole Peninsula . . . is
a muzzle rammed for firing)

The point is, the arrestment, is deceptive: it is
not what fancy outsiders have seen it as, seeking, as they were, I guess, some alternative for
themselves (like DHL & his Ladybird). . . .

Point (2) above, was VIOLENCE—killing, the
heart, out, etc: those sons of bitches, those
"scholars"—how they've cut that story out, to
make the Mayan palatable to their fucking
selves, foundations, & tourists!

Recollection and repetition, synthesis and in-
terwoven lines are forcefully brought together
in part II of "The Kingfishers" to point out the
paradox of any philosophy and to call into question the original theme in the light of the violence of human history. Three fragments of Indian lore are cited, including an excerpt from
one of Prescott's notes on the Aztec naming ceremony. The fragmentation of thought continues
until it is abruptly cut short by associations of
the temples of Tenochtitlán with "human gore"
and "dry blood." By the end of part II, the
theme of change is submerged in an outcry of
revulsion worthy of a Jacobean playwright:

> with what violence benevolence is bought
> what cost in gesture justice brings
> what wrongs domestic rights involve
> what stalks
> this silence
>
> what pudor pejorocracy affronts
> how awe, night-rest and neighborhood can rot
> what breeds where dirtiness is law
> what crawls
> below

There is a loss of expansiveness in invective.
The bitterness of part II calcifies into the stac-
cato assertions of a sputtering old man. In fact,
William Shakespeare's *Timon of Athens* is the
source of the line "how awe, night-rest and
neighborhood can rot."

With part III the poet shifts ground
completely:

> I am no Greek, hath not th' advantage.
> And of course, no Roman:
> he can take no risk that matters,
> the risk of beauty least of all.
>
> But I have my kin, if for no other reason than
> (as he said, next of kin) I commit myself, and,
> given my freedom, I'd be a cad
> if I didn't. Which is most true.
>
> It works out this way, despite the
>   disadvantage.
> I offer, in explanation, a quote:
> si j'ai du gout, ce n'est guères
> que pour la terre et les pierres.
>
> Despite the discrepancy (an ocean courage
>   age)
> this is also true: if I have any taste
> it is only because I have interested myself
> in what was slain in the sun
>
>   I pose you your question:
>
> shall you uncover honey/where maggots are?
>
>   I hunt among stones

There are no suspensions of syllables or jux-
tapositions of phrases typical of open verse until
the last three lines. Instead, there are fairly regular four-foot lines organized into four stanzas
of four lines each. They give the impression of
uniformity, consecutiveness, and control, not
exploration or fragmentation. The sense of a
"closed" formal structure is further reinforced
by the patterning of sounds and repetitions of
words.

The Olson "persona" reverts to apologia, suggesting that preceding attempts at philosophy
and satire were inadequate in the face of the
poet's discoveries. He admits the "disadvan-
tage" in claims of kinship over those of literature and philosophy, yet accepts Arthur Rimbaud's bitter formulation for himself. The logic

of associating kinship with Rimbaud's "la terre et les pierres" and "what was slain in the sun" is peculiar to Olson, for he never loses sight of history as "the confidence of limit as man is caught in the assumption and power of change." Yet, in the context of this poem, the discovered "limit" of brutal blood lust is not acceptable. Thus the poem ends on a note of decided dejection:

shall you uncover honey / where maggots are?

I hunt among stones

In "The K," his meditation on human volition, Olson discovers both the circular movement of the poem and the secret of his own attention as an act of will. The double process of "There was a Youth whose Name was Thomas Granger" yields both a folk-tale and a moral vision from an examination of historical source material. The secret of "The Praises" is that all knowledge is important primarily in its use. Paradoxically, the only revelation of "The Kingfishers" is that neither theme nor form develops further when the poet confronts the impulse to violence. When the object of attention is man's inhumanity, then Olson's shapes necessarily waver between fragments and imitations of past forms, for exploration ends in revulsion and disgust impedes discovery as limits of art and life mix.

Olson's search for order took a different form in "In Cold Hell, in Thicket," a short, open sequence that begins in desolation but ends with a belief in human action. In many respects this 1953 poem resembles "Asides on the Oboe," another humanistic poem of doubt and belief written by Wallace Stevens ten years earlier. Each poem represents a crucial stage in the poetic development of its author. As "Asides on the Oboe" anticipated Stevens' "Notes Toward a Supreme Fiction," "In Cold Hell, in Thicket" seems to have been a major impetus for the sustained sequence of *The Maximus Poems.* It

may be that poetic progress for both men depended upon their articulating images of an ideal man.

The two poems are remarkably similar in subject, tone, even expressions, despite differing poetic techniques. Nevertheless, Olson called Stevens "a profound misleader." In a letter of June 13, 1952, to *Origin* editor Cid Corman, Olson wrote:

... i do not include Morse on Stevens, and the reason ... is not any difference from Stevens— it is never that easy—but the degree of apprehension of the reality contemporary to us.... Stevens is a profound misleader simply that he is in a deeply important area (what I have yet no better word for than *ornamentation*: ... I would still say none of us are that far along that we can say (((we might *do*))) what it is
IN COLD HELL, was my try

It is that deep, that is a wholly different disposal of attention to *anything.*

It is what all the cry of myth & rite is falsely about

It is how men take life (collectivism is another of its signs)

Yet it shall come to be in its own guise—and modern man is altogether too literate yet (in his thinking, in his trying to push it into existence, like as tho he were capable of couvade!

You see, the problem is to clear ourselves of the negatives—all Greek myth as we distribute our attention to it *after* Herodotus, as well as such men of decoration as Stevens....

Although Olson may have been "misleading" in citing Stevens as one of "the negatives," he never doubted the seriousness of Stevens' approach to the same problem he attacks in "In Cold Hell, in Thicket." It is the problem of a loss of faith that is for the poet a loss of voice and a loss of meaning. In many of Stevens' major works there is a search for a "supreme fiction." In Olson's poetry the search is more often for space, orientation, size, and a flexible relationship between man and the universe established "by fixes only."

"In Cold Hell, in Thicket" says that man is "in hell or in happiness, merely / something to be wrought, to be shaped, to be carved, for use ..." but that nevertheless, by nature

> He shall step, he
> will shape, he
> is already also
> moving off

In "The Praises" Olson asserts that " ... for a man to act after he has taken thought, this! / is the most difficult thing of all"; but he never seeks, as Stevens did, "the time to think enough." Where Stevens' quest included timelessness, Olson's passion is for space and motion. This basic difference is inherent in the two poets' attempts to resolve the doubt and end the dejection so prevalent in modern poetry.

A finished projective poem, "In Cold Hell, in Thicket" exemplifies the maxim from "Projective Verse" that "FORM IS NEVER MORE THAN AN EXTENSION OF CONTENT." Like "The K" and parts of "The Kingfishers," it is a poetic realization of self-transcendence. But, unlike these earlier examples, it is also an open-ended sequence that anticipates characteristics of the long Maximus sequence. A metamorphic speaker, a search for space, and a fusion of speaker and place make "In Cold Hell, in Thicket" seem very much a prototype of *The Maximus Poems.* It is also a point of departure from early, more self-contained projective verse to the more continuous affirmations of the sequence. As it reveals the "secret" of man-as-object in the "shape" of an open sequence, it prepares the way for Maximus to merge with his Gloucester locale and emerge as a principle of history.

The further development of projective verse into an open, changing, yet continuous sequence depended, as "The Kingfishers" did, upon repeating certain elements while remaining exploratory and open-ended. A cumulative progress characterizes *The Maximus Poems,* but this forward movement cannot easily be understood without closely reading the entire sequence as it moves from poem to poem and from discovery to discovery.

The figure of Maximus, the town of Gloucester, and Olson's search for what he called a "new discourse" create a structural unity, however temporary, within the progressive continuity of these poems. Eventually, even these three principles diffused into little more than echoes in the fragmented discontinuity of the end of the sequence. In the first twenty-two Maximus poems, though, they appear often enough to structure the sequence before "documentation" and a new conception of poetic process enters in the twenty-third poem.

The discovery of poetic space in "In Cold Hell, in Thicket" lay in the transition from "thicket" to "field." In *The Maximus Poems,* space is initially represented by Gloucester, geographically bounded, yet omnipresent in past, present, and future. This structural freedom is achieved primarily through the invention of Maximus, who is like a Vonnegut hero on a "time warp," never limited in time, often absent, yet nevertheless specifically earthbound. A protean figure like the speakers in several modern sequences such as Williams' *Paterson* and Pound's *Cantos,* Maximus shares in the "metamorphic tradition" identified by Bernetta Quinn. He even resembles the "trickster" figure of Indian legend, although Maximus' "shapechanging" is rarely mischievous or malicious. He can be subject or object, person or place, and, like Gloucester itself, he is limited only in terms of geography and spatial relations.

Olson's focus on the city is part of his desire for "alternative discourse" appropriate to a "human universe." In Williams' *Paterson* the search for a language "to make them vocal" slowly moves out from the city. In *The Maximus Poems* the replacement for the old discourse develops only where a vital culture and human perception interpenetrate in Gloucester. Williams' quest increasingly relies upon symbolic metaphor. In *The Maximus Poems*, Olson's ideal language presumably resembles topology, which is defined as geometry that describes relations invariant under distortion. For the writer, as Olson said in a speech at Black Mountain College in 1956 (published in Ann Charters' *Olson/Melville: A Study in Affinity*):

It comes down to fact and form. A writer, I dare say, goes by words. That is, they are facts. And forms. Simultaneously. And a writer may be such simply that he takes an attitude towards this double power of word: he believes it is enough to unlock anything. Words occur to him as substances—as entities, in fact as actual entities. My words were space, myth, fact, object. . . .

More key words in the essay "Projective Verse" suggest that such "entities" as "process," "humilitas," and "attention" inform *The Maximus Poems* even when the sequence is sometimes less "projective" than meditative or less exploratory than didactic.

The open, continuous sequence often seems at variance with the temporary resolutions of its components. Its "kinetics" is not always as apparent as lyrical moments or didactic repetitions in specific poems or groups of poems. Yet the exchange and reinforcement of energy between the long poem and its parts reflect the simultaneously continuous and discrete universe that Olson felt an artist had to reenact. Previous poems were inquiries into the nature of man and the modern universe. *The Maximus Poems* establish interpenetration of man and universe in the very specific terms of Maximus and Gloucester.

The first twenty-two poems generally fall into groups more or less unified according to their uses of Maximus, historical documentation, and the time and space of present-day Gloucester. The first four establish Maximus and bring in the themes of the invasion of Gloucester by the lies of "pejorocracy" (like Pound's *usura*, it is the ascendancy of lies and diminution of meaning in language) and the dissonant "mu-sick" of ownership. Poems 5, 6, and 7 remind the citizens of Gloucester that their only hope of "polis," the essential heterogeneous community, lies in their own use of their eyes, since the life of the community depends upon individuals' perceptions and awareness. In the eighth and ninth poems the problem of definition and discovery identified in the essay "Human Universe" appears in poetic form.

In poems 10 through 17, Maximus becomes more and more merged with the history of Gloucester, dissolving altogether in some poems as the "facts" of history come to the fore. The only return to the Maximus of preceding poems is in the brilliant twelfth poem, "Maximus, to himself," where the price of being a poet is not alienation but a slow and painful self-realization. Poems 13 through 16 echo the tone of "Maximus, to himself" as they confront the dejection and disillusionment that seem to be the inevitable concomitants of human exploration and discovery. However, with the seventeenth poem, "On first Looking Out through Juan de la Cosa's Eyes," the poet's faith in human attention returns as the world is rediscovered through the eyes of the cartographer de la Cosa and a new "mappemunde" is created.

Poems 18 through 22 return temporarily to Maximus. They also introduce some concerns "relating to the care of souls," including questions of morality, honor, and a new nobility. In letter 22 nobility and honor consist in being the writer who stops the "battle" to celebrate a moment of beauty.

Letters 12, 17, and 23 culminate larger

curves of movement within the formal progression of the first twenty-three poems. At first the Maximus figure, *logopoeia* or "PLAY of the mind," and documentation of Gloucester's origins are central poetic postures in the quest for a new use of language. But with the twelfth poem the emphasis changes, as Maximus confronts a deep disillusionment almost as paralyzing as that revealed in "The Kingfishers." Techniques of self-assertion, Pound's *logopoeia* ("the dance of the intellect among words"), and documentation, as they were used in early poems, are still basic to the first eleven Maximus poems; but after "Maximus, to himself" they are often exchanged for more free-associative explorations and fragmented forms.

After the twelfth Maximus poem, the organizational principle of Olson's "epic" lies somewhere between the immediacy of a rhapsodic oral tradition and symphonic timelessness. In letter 15, Olson characterizes his new emphasis as "Rhapsodia," the "songs stitched together" technique of epic poetry. Linda Wagner has defined modern epic in her work on Williams through a more complex musical analogy, with "the symphonic" a "reflection of modern man's consciousness" that conveys "a sense of time-lessness—or rather of the unity of all time." The seventeenth poem, "On first Looking Out through Juan de la Cosa's Eyes," restores energy to the open sequence and typifies the combination of rhapsodic and symphonic in a single poem. Thereafter, poems 18 through 22 return to Maximus' perspective, the play of ideas, and the memories and histories of Maximus and Gloucester; but they return with an increasing reliance on dreams and meditations.

Letters 15 through 22 were written at Black Mountain College in only nineteen days of May 1953, in what Daniel Hise in *boundary 2* described as "an unusual burst of creativity" preceding a "crisis of direction" that left Olson "backing and filling before he was able to get

the sequence moving again." Perhaps, as Thomas Whitaker has remarked about Williams' *Paterson,* the formal progression of an open sequence is necessarily "one of descent and emergent order—one of repeated release from blockage and renewal of alertness."

A new conception of the poetic process was at work when the second "run" of Maximus poems was written in Gloucester four years later. Beginning with letter 23, Olson's preoccupation was with history as a structuring principle. That part of the sequence will be examined later, with special emphasis on Olson's use of concepts presented in *The Special View of History* (1970) and the documents, heroes, and villains of Gloucester's past.

The opening three Maximus poems are both a thematic introduction and a poetic model of the process of the sequence. As in "In Cold Hell, in Thicket," their motive for motion and their impulse to overcome dejection, as well as their aversion to stasis, are manifest in movement. Like most poems in an open sequence, they function doubly, as individually complete poetic structures and as links in a sequence that is itself an opening to further poetry.

Approximately contemporaneous with "The Praises" and "The Kingfishers," these three poems were written during 1949–1951. Yet in sequence they seem products of a single impulse. They preface the Maximus sequence by introducing the motifs of Maximus, the city, and the outcry against "pejorocracy" and ownership. They also form a symphonic development. Separately they project three voices of Maximus, but together they seem more like musical movements, related in their continuity and recapitulation of themes, rhythmic breaks, and resolutions.

From the "offshore" ode of letter 1 through the history-as-poetry of letter 2 and the diatribe against ownership of letter 3, the overall symphonic movement begins with a presentation of themes and motifs, then shifts to a slow section, and ends with a recapitulation and resolution of themes. Letter 1 builds to a crescendo; letter 2 slows the pace as it elaborates the themes; letter 3 resolves the movement with rhetorical recapitulation of the "wondership stolen by / ownership."

The curve of movement of these three poems is often repeated with degrees of variation throughout the sequence. The lyrical celebration of possibility that characterizes letter 1 is a touchstone and dominant tone that returns at those points when dejection and disillusionment have been strongest. The "hidden city" revealed in letter 2 is another point of reference visited over and over again to document the viability of "polis." The fusion of lyric and personal history in letter 3 is a model of persuasive rhetoric in an epic voice that becomes prevalent whenever Maximus tries to convince Gloucester of its unique value.

The sequence begins again with the fourth poem, "The Songs of Maximus," a mini-sequence or "song cycle" that introduces a new sort of lyricism at the same time that it incorporates the praise, parable, and exhortation that characterized the first three poems. It anticipates the more personal tone of poems like "Maximus, to himself" (letter 12) and "Maximus to Gloucester, Letter 19 (A Pastoral Letter," and even such a dream poem as letter 22.

At first glance the form of "The Songs of Maximus" echoes the songs and snatches of a wandering minstrel. On closer reading, the six songs are bound together in an open structure paradigmatic of the entire extended open sequence. Throughout the sequence, and emphatically in the invitation of song 6 to "sing" at the end ("you sing, you / who also / wants"), Olson requires participation in the form, whether it is a lyric, a meditation, an exhortation, a story, a parable, or even a document. The fragmented sentences of Maximus appear everywhere in the

sequence, yet in "The Songs of Maximus" they contribute to an effect of lyrical buoyancy that contrasts with the more prevalent hesitancies, fragmentations, and indirections of later poems. It is as if the rhapsodic technique alluded to in letter 15 were accomplished here in miniature, "the songs stitched together" just adequately covering one who usually prefers being "out at the elbows."

"Rhapsodia" is again exchanged for "the symphonic" and preoccupation with Gloucester's past, present, and future in the next three poems. In contrast with letters 1 through 3, letters 5 through 7 are less "literary" examinations of Gloucester, polis, and poetry. As they work out the roles of artist and history, they recombine rhetoric, documentation, and subjective expression in a letter writer's focus on specifics that gives a new perspective on "polis." These were among the poems written by Olson in the spring of 1953, at Black Mountain College, which may account for their tone of catharsis. In any case they contribute to a sense of the sequence as an exchange of letters with Gloucester, a felt need for unity and continuity rather than for poetic form or theory.

The implication of these three poems is that the "hidden city" will not tolerate the perversions of its truth that Olson found in the platitudes about the common man expressed in the new literary magazine *Four Winds,* which was edited by his friend Vincent Ferrini and published locally in Gloucester. Letters 5, 6, and 7 represent a poet's recovery of "polis." And they demand that he revitalize the language of this "human universe" with at least the same care that Gloucester's men gave to fishing.

In "Tyrian Businesses" and letter 9, Olson begins to explore the necessary relationship between definition and discovery later marked in the essay "Human Universe." These two poems also predict the modulations in letters 10, 11, and 12 from inquiry to assertion, with a great deal of exploration in between. Despite obscurities, they take stock, extol realism and "measure," and finally rely upon an absolute relation of language to experience in order to discover and define Maximus and Gloucester.

Despite its assertive tone, "Tyrian Businesses" tries to prove empirically that the "names" and "verbs" of its second section correspond to the hypothetical "objects" and "actions" of the first. Letter 9 is less complicated, relying on memory and associations, but it also compares two kinds of knowledge. Its contrasts between "men's affairs" and the poet's work, between deeds and words, and between history and poetry lead to the discovery of the inseparability of each as a measure of the other. The eighth and ninth poems also provide an important turning point in the sequence because they reestablish the faith in "alternative discourse" that allows Maximus to document the founding of Gloucester in the next two poems.

A new sort of "truth" begins with letters 10 and 11. The care, attention, and "measure" of preceding poems are taken for granted and the sequence regains momentum. The newfound method for achieving dynamic stability is, as in letter 9, both poetic and historical, a reintegration of definition and discovery in the context of inquiry into Gloucester's origin.

At this point in the sequence, historic materials are still primarily evidence of the rhetorical truths of earlier poems. Yet, paradoxically, a recovery of denotative language, an absolute faith in "fact," is the major revelation of these two poems. The story of Gloucester's origin does not wholly sustain the belief in exploration and discovery that seems to motivate the sequence. Historical facts transform poetic joy into confrontation with the dogma, parochialism, and persecution that was concomitant to Gloucester's founding by the Dorchester Company and Captain John Smith. Yet, despite the self-limiting nature of Maximus' inquiry, these poems insist upon a physical connection with the germinative energy of the past.

They return to Gloucester's geographic reality. Stage Fort and Tablet Rock, the fishing stage that was the original site of the first house and the thirty-foot-high rock commemorating the fight for Cape Ann's fishing rights, are concrete evidence that "the sacred & profane" were once vital in Gloucester. Stage Fort and "the rock" are sources of daimonic energy for Maximus. They are physical connections between past and present that infuse historical documentation with poetic life, add human value to the language of "fact," and point toward a solution to the problem set forth at the beginning of letter 10:

on founding: was it puritanism,
or was it fish?

And how, now, to found, with the sacred &
    profane—both of them—
wore out

Poetic solutions lie in renewed emphasis on *humilitas,* the recognition and respect for man-as-object that is strangely exemplified in John Smith's projection of the settlers as objects of his attention:

"they (the settlers) have been my wife,
        my hawks, my hounds,
my cards, my dice, in totall my best content"

For Olson, John Smith is yet another source of energy, like the rock. He is a heroic image of possibility, in contrast with the "shrinkers":

The Capteyne
he was, the eye he had
for what New England offered,
what we are other than
    theocratic. . . .

The rediscovery of a hero, a "sacred" place, and the *humilitas* appropriate for "founding" renews possibilities for continuing the sequence. Nevertheless, the tendency toward constriction remains. Even as Maximus seeks new methods "for forwarding" in letters 10 and 11, a corresponding recalcitrance follows in the brilliant "dying fall" of letter 12.

The inevitable dejection of "Maximus, to himself" echoes the loss of motion in the beginning of letter 10. What remains poetically fresh, despite Maximus' doubts, are the facts of founding and the words of the documents recording them, a combination of poetic and historical method that begins to be systematic only after it is more fully expressed in *The Special View of History* (1970).

The twelfth poem is among Maximus' last assertions, and a strange kind of minimal self-assertion it is. By itself the poem is an excellent modern meditation on failure. In the context of the sequence it acquires even more significance from contrasts between its opening line, "I have had to learn the simplest things / last," the tribute to John Smith that precedes it at the end of letter 11, and the exploration of values in the four poems that follow.

The dominant tone of "Maximus, to himself" is one of quiet desperation, yet Olson's despair is almost always tinged with optimism:

> I know the quarters
> of the weather, where it comes from,
> where it goes. But the stem of me,
> this I took from their welcome,
> or their rejection, of me
>
> > And my arrogance
> > was neither diminished
> > nor increased,
> > by the communication

The key word in these lines is "arrogance." A gloss on the word appears in *The Special View of History,* in the context of a transcribed lecture about objective knowledge as both experiential and methodological, both knowable and usable.

. . . what you do will stay inside what you know. This is one of the reasons, for example, for two things: (1) the constant despair for any man, therefore his need for courage; and (2) the immediate rejoining of the struggle . . . both of these two results of discrimination hold for any of us: despair, and faith. For there is a counter which includes them both, and the Latins called it "humilitas," but the word is an old Indo-European root meaning arrogance, actually (from rogo, to ask a question to or of something, to make a demand which has to be answered.) And because the demand is made of yourself (that with which you are most familiar) it turned over and became that horror and practice of western man, humility.

Indirectly, then, there is resemblance between John Smith's "femininities" and Maximus' "arrogance." The two-part structure of the poem itself is ambiguous and ironic when self-questioning and self-assertion are inseparable. The important shift in the last five lines of part II is not so much a shift from words to reality (as it is, for example, in "The K" or "Tyrian Businesses") as a shift from past tense to present.

> > It is undone business
> > I speak of, this morning,
> > with the sea
> > stretching out
> > from my feet

Again the sea and Olson's unique sense of the ecology of poetry transform a stopping point in the sequence into a point of departure.

Success and failure are expressed in personal, self-analytic, emotional terms in this poem. Yet lengthy self-questioning and briefer self-assertion also establish the extent and limits of Maximus' consciousness for the rest of the sequence.

In the next four poems Maximus' self-conscious exploration of personal values is subordinate to more intellectual, historical, and aesthetic considerations of economics. "Undone business" turns into confrontation with the terrors and failure attending the discovery of the New World. Maximus disappears from the poems and reappears again only after a consolidation of energy represented by "On first Looking Out through Juan de la Cosa's Eyes."

After the twelfth poem, Olson partially relinquishes the symphonic, rhapsodic, and epistolary methods developed as formal elements in the first nine poems. Instead, he tries to combine the faith in fact discovered in letters 10 and 11 with the "arrogance" revealed in letter 12, "Maximus, to himself," in order to reassess the "economics and poetics" of being Maximus of Gloucester. The painful self-realization of the twelfth poem echoes in the agonizing confrontation with Gloucester that characterizes the next four poems. In the seventeenth poem the pendulum swings back to reaffirm a faith in fact. As a result, a newly heroic image of Maximus reappears in the remaining five poems (18–22) written in May 1953.

With the admission of dreams into the sequence in letter 12, Olson's commitment to history and poetry takes on a new dimension, a level of meaning complementary but opposite to the faith in fact that characterizes letters 10, 11, and parts of 13 and 14. The refusal to countenance illusion and mythicize history in letter 13 is somewhat attenuated by the dream and the nightmare vision of the skeletal radiator in letter 14. There are no dreams in letters 15 through 17; but "The Twist" and letter 22 both begin with dreams, and the five poems following "The Twist" depend heavily upon dream material. Even the reference in letter 15 to poet Paul Blackburn's view of "the poem as a sleeping car" and Olson's rejoinder, "I sd, 'Rhapsodia'," recognize the need for a less constrained level of associations, a level never fully exploited because Olson found that dreams lack the continuity required for a sequence.

"Attention," like the eyes of Gloucester's fishermen and artists, continues to underlie the sequence; but, from letter 17 on, noteworthy details include maps as well as records of the past. The map central to this poem is de la Cosa's map of the world, the first "mappemunde" based on explorations of the New World:

> . . . before La Cosa, nobody
> could have
> a mappemunde

Letter 17 represents both a culmination of historical and poetic developments in the sequence and an anticipation of the "mapping" techniques more frequently used in later poems. As the poem "maps" the founding of Massachusetts syllabically, it also fuses Maximus and Gloucester in newfound geographic terms.

Inspiration, commitment, and a sense of renewal in letter 17 were necessarily preceded by dreamlessness, despair, and the deterioration noted in preceding poems. It is in the nature of the sequence to subsume and incorporate discoveries of each new poem into those that follow. Accordingly, the next five poems also rely upon the "maps" of Juan de la Cosa as they intertwine Maximus' dreams and personal history with the history and topography of Gloucester.

The tension between motion and motionlessness, facts and dreams, "la vérité" and "rhapsodia" begins to slacken in the last five poems written in May 1953, before, as Olson said, *The Maximus Poems* "got off its proper track." By the time the sequence reaches letter 22, Olson's reliance upon the dream level of associations is at its limit, and documentation of the founding of Gloucester all but ceases. Olson paraphrases Voltaire at the end of "Juan de la Cosa":

> On ne doit aux morts nothing
> else than
> la vérité

The implication is that the poem's truth will be a memorial to Gloucester's fishermen. But rigorous attempts to find proper terms of commemoration are necessarily at odds with the seductive demands of the dream landscape.

Relying on a Celtic concept of the poet as measurer of valor, Olson transposes a passage from Robert Graves's *White Goddess* in letter 22:

And what I write
is stopping the battle,

To get down, right in the midst of
the deeds, to tell
what this one did, how,
in the fray, he made this play, did grapple
with that one, how his eye flashed

to celebrate

(beauty will not wait)

men,

and girls

Olson the poet succeeds in "stopping the battle" here temporarily through frequent pauses, line breaks, and rhyme. But this concept of the poet counters Olson's original insistence on the inseparability of poetry and history, words and actions. A four-year hiatus between letters 22 and 23 resulted from the contradiction in terms. Yet, "stopping the battle" at this point also cleared the way for Olson's new conception of poetic process, the recombination of "Muthos" (myth) and "Logos" (fact) that motivates the remainder of the sequence.

Letter 22 ends with an allusion to a dream about car trouble:

(I swung the car to the left, confronted
as I was by the whole hill-front
a loading platform, the lip of it
staring at me, grinning,
you might say,
five feet off
the ground

And made it. It was only after
that the car gave me
trouble.

For there is a limit
to what a car
will do.

At this point the emphasis on limits also applies to the writer. Olson's dream of "(Trouble / with the car" is analogous to the temporary mechanical breakdown of the sequence's discovery process and to the end of a continuity based upon Maximus and "polis."

Although *The Maximus Poems* was at a standstill after the spring of 1953, the four years before Olson was "back at the MONSTER" were not uneventful. In addition to writing several non-Maximus poems, Olson published *In Cold Hell, in Thicket* (1953), *The Maximus Poems 1–10* (1953), and *Mayan Letters* (1954). At the same time, while rector of Black Mountain College and attending to its development as an arts center, and to its subsequent fiscal demise and eventual closing, he continued to work on the essays of *Human Universe* (1965). He also was divorced, remarried, and became a father for the second time during this hectic period.

In a letter to *Origin* editor Cid Corman, dated June 6, 1954, Olson wrote:

I am back at the MONSTER. Or so it became over the past year. Simply that I had to reattack. It got lost, somewhere in the '40s. And I had to find my way back on my own path. As well as its path.

feel now I have: a spate of new ones done. But also—and this was the breakthrough—altogether non-Maximus poems. Crazy.

Whether this was the wanted breakthrough remains to be seen. Poems like "Love," "The Motion," and "The Pavement" resemble Robert Creeley's work more than they do *The Maxi-*

mus Poems, and the sequence remained at an impasse until Olson's new view of the poet as historian demanded different formal constraints and principles of selection.

In the 1957–1958 version of letter 23, the new role of the poet is stated concisely: "I would be an historian as Herodotus was, looking for oneself for the evidence of what is said. . . ." By virtue of its tentative position between the dreams of May 1953 at Black Mountain College and "grey water" realities of the winter of 1957 in Gloucester, letter 23 attains poetic significance. It is a major turning point in the sequence, comparable in impact with "In Cold Hell, in Thicket" and "Maximus, to himself," despite its prosaic quality and antipoetic structure. The poems that followed it in the winter of 1957–1958 show how Olson did, in fact, come to terms with history-as-poetry and his new role as Gloucester's resident poet-historian, terms more clearly spelled out in *The Special View of History,* an invaluable gloss for clarifying and indicating thought processes that are often reduced to shorthand in the rest of *The Maximus Poems.*

These remarks were made in the course of lectures, readings, and discussions while Olson was still at Black Mountain College in 1956, but they are a guide to complex changes in poetic process that shaped the sequence from then on:

We inherit an either-or, from the split of science and fiction. It dates back at least to Plato, who used the word "mouth" as an insult, to say it lies, and called poets muthologist. . . . Story was once all *logos.* . . . "The normal characteristic function of the ancient Story Teller," says J. A. K. Thomson . . . "was not to invent. It was to repeat. . . ." to those who listened to the Stories a Muthos was a Logos, and a Logos was a Muthos. They were two names for the same thing. . . . Herodotus may have been conscious

of a difference he was making when he did add the word "history" . . . *'istorin* in him appears to mean "finding out for oneself," instead of depending on hearsay. . . .

It is Miss Harrison's analysis which I offer, from *Themis:*

. . . The tenses . . . of the mythological are never past but present and future . . . and history, like religion, myth, and poetry, share the common property that the thing done is not simply done but is re-done or pre-done. It is at once commemorative, magical, and prospective. . . . says Aristotle in the Poetics,
        'by myth I mean the arrangement of the incidents.'

Although *The Special View of History* survives as a compilation of notes and tapes from lectures, readings, and seminars, it includes significant attempts to expand Olson's earlier poetic theory by translating and elaborating the open field concept in cultural terms. Examinations of language, myth, and ritual add a collective dimension to the earlier theory as the poet's "objects" necessarily become the "facts" of history. The new process still demands *humilitas* but adds the demand of "finding out for oneself instead of depending on hearsay." Now the poet must also appropriate recorded history as part of the creative process. Hence, Olson's concern with redefining history. The following excerpt from *The Special View of History* is perhaps his most useful definition of history for the purposes of his poetry:

. . . History is the confidence of limit as man is caught in the assumption and power of change.

History is story, it means nothing else as a noun. Herodotus was the first to use the word (sign enough of the 5th century change) and he used it as a verb: to find out for yourself. . . . The evidence is there, for you did find out. It is in this sense, the prospective sense, that history in this century has re-presented itself.

If "History is story" and myth is no more than "the arrangement of the incidents," then the cultural and aesthetic dimensions of history, myth, and poetry are linked by an underlying syntax, a sequence of consecutive events and possibilities that depends upon man's participation to give form and value to human experience. By the time Olson had fully expressed his "special view," the shaping power of the sequence as a poetic form and its processive nature as "unfinished business" were felt to be congruent with history and life.

While Olson saw history, poetry, and life as less and less separate, his search for a new use of language originally articulated in the essay "Human Universe" became more important in his work. Correspondingly, he began to emphasize notions of "context" and "syntax" more than ideas of field, line, and syllable in his poetic theory. He put greater emphasis than before on location in the intrinsic relationship between "things spoken" and "things done." By 1957, Olson's poems began to look as if charting and mapping this relationship on the page were more important than finding ways to transfer poetic energy.

His earlier preoccupation with the destruction of energy became subordinate to faith in the genetic principle that "life is the chance success of a play of creative accidents" and in the space-time continuum. The absolutes of this new cosmology, as described in "The Topological" in *The Special View of History,* are "autoclytic multiplication" (the principle of randomness in creation) and space-time coincidence and proximity, physical observations that are analogous to considerations of context and syntax in poetry.

Coincidence and *proximity* . . . become the determinants of *chance* and *accident* and make possible *creative success.* . . . Suddenly what used to be aesthetic in the old cosmology—secondary, because purpose was and had to be primary, is seen to be the nature of the stain of form across all reality. And man's order—his powers of order—are no longer separable from either those of nature or of God. . . . purpose is seen to be contingent, not primordial: it follows from the chance success of the play of creative accidents, it does not precede them. The motive, then, of reality, is process not goal. Only in the relative of the coincident and the proximate can . . . the ideal (which is the possible) emerge.

Significantly, in *The Special View of History* Olson relies on an aesthetic concept to reinterpret history and humanism, and to redefine man. He also points out how the particular must be absolute in a truly relativistic theory of history. One of the many poetic implications of identifying the particular as absolute is that a poet no longer needs to assert his presence, voice, or persona as if he alone were the prime energy source. Although Olson had previously implied that the poet was part of the "field," not until the twenty-fourth poem, "a Plantation, a beginning," does he merge documentation of Gloucester's origins with personal references in a poem free of rhetoric and self-consciousness.

Olson's stress on "context" expanded his previous notion of poetic field to include all knowable history, both personal and public. Paradoxically, in *The Maximus Poems* its effect was to limit the poetic subject. In poems 24 through 30, Olson began a series of experiments with syntax, but he did not yet continue to explore new areas of knowledge and modes of discovery. Instead, these poems hark back, seeking to repossess Gloucester by reintegrating *muthos* and *logos* ("things spoken" and "things done") in a local context.

One more variation on the story of Gloucester is letter 24, "a Plantation a beginning." Yet, because nothing in the poem is subordinate to anything else, it refocuses on "the facts" in a pattern that includes information past and present, mythic and personal. The twenty-fifth poem, "Maximus, to Gloucester," begins with long verse paragraphs that lead through a leisurely flow of introductory phrases to an important point about Gloucester's topography. The "turning" of Gloucester is further reflected in short lines that weave across the page. This transition to shorter accented lines makes the timeless presence of "fisherman's field" emphatic:

> The point is not that Beverly
> turned out to be their home,
> that Conant Norman Allen Knight
> Balch Palfrey Woodbury Tilly Gray
> are Babsons Parsons there
>
>> But that as I sit
>> in a rented house
>> on Fort Point,
>> the Cape Ann Fisheries
>
>> out one window,
>> Stage Head looking me
>> out of the other
>> in my right eye
>
>> (like backwards
>> of a scene
>> I saw the other way
>> for thirty years)
>
>> Gloucester can view
>> those men
>> who saw her
>> first

The poem's last lines incorporate a reciprocal relationship between Gloucester's origin and geography in an image of balance that becomes increasingly important later in Olson's work. Stage Head is still "where fishing continues / and my heart lies." The brief lyrical dissolution of time is justified by Olson's actual location in the house on Fort Point and the topographical reality of fisherman's field, "the first place" and "the turning" that started Gloucester. In the next poem, though, radical innocence disappears as the story of Gloucester is revealed again.

"So Sassafras" achieves a uniquely experimental exploration of Gloucester's story. The compression and dispersal of energy that peaked with the "fish rush" are expressed directly here through rhythmic and syntactic shifts. The accident of events is congruent with the stream of words to the extent that poetry, history, and life are interchangeable examples of the random order of creation. Arhythmic, nonaccentual lines about the slave trade, forced labor, and other, more subtle forms of economic servitude follow, representing a deep sense of loss that contrasts with the earlier enthusiasm of "the fish rush." The loss is pervasive. Drained by money interests, just as "Europe just then was being drained swept by pox," Gloucester remains tainted.

In the next poem, "History is the Memory of Time," even the poet's "finding out for oneself" seems as dependent upon speculation as upon facts. Alternations between events and speculation about them create a "memory" effect. But, in the last four lines Olson ends with explicit assertion, forsaking the memory process for a memorial:

>> They should raise a monument
>> to a fisherman crouched down
>> behind a hogshead, protecting
>> his dried fish

These lines are one more attempt to commemorate Gloucester's fishermen. Yet, as they lead into the next three poems, they also mark the decline of fishing and the need for hard evidence to counterbalance speculation.

"The Picture," "The Record," and "14 Men Stage Head Winter 1624/25" provide evidence to answer previous speculation. They chart the poet's progress toward repossessing Gloucester by shifting emphasis from experiments with syntax to documented details of the town's history. They are both prospective and commemorative, pointing to the inevitable decline of fishing at the same time that they commemorate the nation's coastal origins.

The search for polis, faith in fact, sense of discovery, and even the quest for *mutbologos* that have characterized the sequence to this point fall off in the face of Gloucester's loss. The premature frustration of its early development reveals again the painful cost of discovery. Except for a few reflex actions in the rest of *The Maximus Poems,* the remaining efforts to repossess Gloucester are tempered by dejection. Yet poems 31, 32, and 33 continue to search for coherence as they recapitulate tensions between possibility and disillusionment, discovery and colonization, outwardness and inwardness, and documentation and exhortation. Where poems 24 through 30 tried to repossess Gloucester through prosodic experiments and documentation, these three poems temporarily abandon the search for new forms and relinquish the town to "the second comers." They turn instead to quasi-mythical figures who are less flesh and blood than directional signs mapping the new land. Despite retreat from painful documentation, they continue a last-ditch effort to salvage a mythology that is "at once commemorative, magical, and prospective," as they portray John Smith, John Winthrop, and Christopher Levett.

Olson uses Smith and Levett as signs of movement in sharp contrast with Winthrop's anachronistic colonial "stiffening." But by projecting these men as measures instead of as heroes and villains, he restores a sense of openness to the sequence and converts the despair hereafter associated with Gloucester's founding into a new hope.

Ironically, Olson's denial of a folkloric impulse often comes very close to the Puritan imaginative process that relates historic events to a providential God. He even gives his own version of the fall from grace, with Cape Ann the earthly paradise, René Descartes and Winthrop twin serpents in the garden, and Levett's settlement in Maine a possible sanctuary. Yet, although *The Maximus Poems* often resemble Puritan jeremiads, the voyage literature typified by John Smith's writing is a more likely model for Olson's effort.

In "Some Good News," John Smith, always a central figure in the sequence, takes on added significance. These references to Smith build further upon previous ones, but his importance to Olson here is more a matter of his writings. Now John Smith, not the Dorchester Company, is the "demarcation":

> Smith
> changed
> everything: he pointed
> out
> Cape Ann,
>
> named her
> so it's stuck,
> and Englishmen,
> who were the ones
> who wanted to,
>
> sat down, planted
> fisheries
> so they've stayed put,
> on this coast, from Pemaquid
> to Cape Cod.

Winthrop's distortions inevitably follow Smith's true perceptions but finally lead to the outward movement of Levett's descriptions. The legacy of Winthrop's prose was "knots where instance / hides order," not the doctrine of experience inherited from Smith and Levett. Although Olson's style sometimes partakes of "knotty" conceits and the difficult tone of Puritan elegies, his view of history cannot accommodate an incomprehensible "plan" initiated by a prime mover. For the will of God and willfulness of frustrated man, Olson substitutes "creative accidents" and "housekeeping":

"the stain of form across all reality. And man's ... powers of order ... no longer separable from either those of nature or of God."

Anne Hutchinson's trial revealed the dangerous implications of Winthrop's theocratic commonwealth. Olson was less concerned with her religious conviction than with her right

> to rouse up women
> on Thursdays
> at her house
> talking grace
> versus works, when housekeeping
>
> Dealing with reality's
> affairs. . . .

Levett is also a directional sign and measure because he wrote about building a house in Portland harbor in *Voyage into New England:*

> so we,
> who live at this poor end
> of goods, & things, & men,
>
> when materials, of each,
> are such a man can't eat
> sleep walk move go
> apart from his own dwelling,
> the dirtiness of goodness
>
> cheapness shit is
> upon the world. We'll turn
> to keep our house. . . .

Even Smith's discoveries are referred to as

> a housekeeping
>
> which old mother Smith
> started. . . .

Olson portrays Smith, Hutchinson, and Levett as natural participants in an abundant, pervasive reality. Winthrop, on the other hand, is alien, a willful, phallic patriarch.

"Capt Christopher Levett (of York)" completes the pattern of discovery, "stiffening," and renewed desire for innocence that began with the first three Maximus poems and continued with variations up to this point. The possibilities of Smith's "Good News" constricted when Winthrop's commonwealth converted outward movement to "inward act" by ignoring that

> American space
>
> was 1630 still sailors'
> apprehension not Boston's
> leaders'. . . .

Levett's House Island in Maine represents a sort of way station between Smith's discoveries and the continuing westward motion, but further possibilities of inland discovery are not even suggested until the very end of *The Maximus Poems.*

In its search for innocence, the poem on Levett marks the end of the discovery process because it finds the lesson of Smith, Levett, and the Dorchester men to be this "single truth":

> the newness
> the first men knew was almost
> from the start dirtied
> by second comers. About seven years
> and you can carry cinders
> in your hand for what
>
> America was worth. May she be damned
> for what she did so soon
> to what was such a newing. . . .

Early signs of the fragmentation that characterize the remaining volumes of the sequence appear here. The effort to incorporate discursiveness, hesitations, and digressions of logical discourse into a cumulative flow of processive discovery is necessarily unsuccessful as Olson strives to contain the inherent historical contradictions and coincidences that the poem explores.

"Capt Christopher Levett (of York)" gives up the quest for *muthologos* in order to move outward. A sort of exorcism takes place in the process, even in the face of bitter disillusionment. In this poem's last lines the word "out," used with various connotations throughout these three poems, purges the sequence of despair. "Some Good News" relayed the message that

> Out of these waters
> inland, it went.

In the poem on Winthrop, "throwing people out" was "spiritual matter," but the poem on Levett insists that

> we, who out of the side
> of her come (have cut ourselves
>
> Out of her drugstore flattened-hillside gut
> like Wash-Ching-Geka cut
> the Winnebago nation out
> of elephant . . . Out,
> is the cry of a coat of wonder. . . .

The final wondrous cry of "out" acquires great complexity, coming as it does after so many repetitions, after the harsh rhyme of "gut" and "cut," and the dental and guttural sounds of "drugstore flattened-hillside" and "Wash-Ching-Geka cut / the Winnebago nation out / of elephant." The word "out" takes on connotations of rebirth and amazement, as well as of religious expulsion and the westward, inland movement. By the end of "Capt Christopher Levett (of York)," the outward push is not only an excommunication, but also the birth trauma of a new nation. With "Out, / is the cry

of a coat of wonder" the sequence again renews itself.

The remaining poems in the volume are more a memorial to the original Gloucester than a celebration of rebirth, as they mourn the dead and confront change. There is a sea change nevertheless in these last of *The Maximus Poems.* Like every other poem in the open sequence, they function doubly. And as a group they are both a coda and a new beginning in which the relationships within the long series gradually alter, along with the ever-changing relationships of "NW shifting / man," the land itself, and the sea.

After Levett's outward movement, the sequence retreats to Gloucester, as it retreated to dreams and "inland waters" following Juan de la Cosa's "mappemunde." But these poems are not "off the track" as poems 18 through 22 were. Instead, they face the need to "step off onto the nation" and the intolerable truth that the facts of Gloucester are facts of loss. Yet, as in much of Olson's poetry, the stopping point is also a starting point, and moments of despair contain new sources of strength and energy.

The first letter on Georges Bank follows the poem on Levett but moves in the opposite direction, away from westward, inland discovery and back to the sea. The simple eloquence of the account (taken from *The Fisherman's Memorial and Record Book*) is one more memorial to the fishermen as it moves the sequence forward. It foreshadows the increasingly antiaesthetic tone of the last two Maximus volumes, while harking back to parts of letters 2 and 15. Like the inscription on Tablet Rock, Columbus' descriptions of the New World, Juan de la Cosa's map, and Smith's poem and journals, it is the sort of factual evidence that the poet-historian now depends on to maintain the momentum of the sequence.

The offshore shoals in the next poem, "1st

Letter on Georges," are controlling forces in Gloucester's life as well as one more unifying element in the sequence. These references to the shoals echo earlier ones, but now they show how illusory and dangerous a sense of stasis is when even land and sea shift. The ever-changing universe is a constant theme in Olson. In this letter it is precisely located in the treacherous geography that takes its toll in human lives. The shifting shoals also anticipate allusions to the theory of continental drift, a leitmotif of the last volumes. With this letter on Georges Bank, there is no doubt that the fact of loss is still the main fact of the sequence. The sea leads neither inland nor outward, but to a dead end, a burial ground. Yet a faint note of emotion recollected in tranquillity warns the reader that, as always, Olson resists the epic impulse in order to return to poetry that is both commemorative and prospective.

An article on a city council meeting in the *Gloucester Daily Times,* January 3, 1958, was auspicious for *The Maximus Poems.* It gave Olson a "prospective" subject that was as close as he could get to a present-day hero. If *Four Winds* editor Vincent Ferrini was the villain in the fifth poem, then councilman Burke is the hero in the thirty-fifth. Although Olson faulted Ferrini for lack of attention to the city, he shows Burke immobilized by such an effort of attention. Burke's conflict, like the poet's at this point in the sequence, was that he was "caught in the assumption and power of change." He is a throwback, an anachronism,

Against the greased ways
of the city now (of the nation) this politician
himself a twisted animal. . . .

The poem "John Burke" resolves nothing. But "A FOOTNOTE TO THE ABOVE," appended by way of apologia, points to a new direction for the sequence.

As "John Burke" marks a surviving resistance to Gloucester's decline, so "A FOOT-NOTE TO THE ABOVE" revives Gloucester in different terms. It is no longer a matter of "polis is eyes," or that the fishing stage fight was a fight "against all sliding statism," or that Smith discovered and named Cape Ann "so it's stuck." The footnote states that in *The Maximus Poems* "local / relations are nominalized" and subject and object, person and place are one:

To speak in Yana-Hopi about these matters with which I, as Maximus, am concerned (which is Gloucester, and myself as here-a-bouts, in other words in *Maximus* local relations are nominalized) one would talk, Yana being a North California tongue, & Hopi is a language peculiarly adjusted to the topological as a prime and libidinal character of a man, and therefore of all of his proximities: metric then is mapping, and so, to speak modern cant, congruent means of making a statement), I, as Mr. Foster, went to Gloucester, thus:

> "And past-I-go
> Gloucester-insides
> being Fosterwise of
> Charley-once-boy
> insides"

From here on, Gloucester exists primarily as it is incorporated in Olson / Maximus. As Maximus reappears, he merges with the city as the locus of both the local and the universal. Loss, death, and burial are still the main facts of Gloucester, but a "new" discourse transforms the city into "Gloucester-insides" and the poet into "Charley-once-boy / insides," and frees them both from the past.

The language that Olson refers to as "Yana-Hopi" is in effect a linguistic fantasy in which, as linguist Edward Sapir says of Yana, "The noun and verb are well distinct, though there are certain features that they hold in common which tend to draw them nearer to each other than we feel to be possible. But there are, strictly speaking, no other parts of speech." "Yana-Hopi" also encompasses the world view that Benjamin Lee Whorf ascribes to the Hopi in "An American Indian Model of the Universe." As Whorf notes,

The Hopi do not need to use terms that refer to space or time as such. Such terms in our language are recast into expressions of extension, operation and cyclic process provided they refer to the solid objective realm. They are recast into expressions of subjectivity if they refer to the subjective realm—the future, the psychic-mental, the mythical period, and the invisibly distant and conjectural generally. Thus, the Hopi language gets along perfectly without tenses for its verbs.

Whorf describes the grammar of the Hopi in terms of "manifested" (or objective) and "manifesting" (or subjective), instead of in terms of static, three-dimensional space and flowing time divided into past, present, and future. The "manifested" and "manifesting" are different but inseparable realms that exist in dynamic relation to each other. Whorf describes their continuousness as follows:

As the objective realm . . . stretches away from the observer . . . there comes a point where extension in detail ceases to be knowable and is lost in the vast distance, and where the subjective, creeping behind the scenes as it were, merges into the objective, so that at this inconceivable distance from the observer—from all observers—there is an all-encircling end and beginning of things where it might be said that existence, itself, swallows up the objective and subjective. The borderland of this realm is as much subjective as objective. It is the abysm of antiquity, the time and place told about in the myths. . . .

Whorf's essay acknowledges that "the relativity viewpoint" also provides an alternative to the naïve Western view of time and space. In the footnote to "John Burke," Olson tries to suggest the possibility of a new sort of language, like the Hopi or topology, where subject and object are closer than we feel they can be ("local relations are nominalized") and past, present, and future tenses are unnecessary ("metric then is mapping").

The change of emphasis at this point in the sequence is not from history to geography, or from time to space, as much as it is from the "manifested" context of historical Gloucester to a "manifesting" context of perpetual motion and change, perhaps because Gloucester's revealed history is too painful. Olson finally experiments with almost an entire poem of "alternative discourse" free of time / space and subject / object distinctions in "Letter, May 2, 1959." The difficulties of this poem result in part from the conclusions drawn in the footnote to "John Burke."

Burke, "solid in refusal," is a paradigm of the substitution of intellect for sensibility that frequently plagues the sequence from here on. When Olson's intellect is negative "in refusal," as in parts of this poem and the remaining volumes, the continuity of the sequence and its lyric moments become fragmented.

Although "Letter, May 2, 1959" signals a loss of momentum and returns to the fragmented style that characterized letter 13, it is nevertheless the first poem that views Gloucester in a context of perpetual change. The verbal mapping technique originally used in "On first Looking Out through Juan de la Cosa's Eyes" has a different purpose here. The effort now is to chart specific points in the ever-changing relationships of land, sea, and migratory man. It is no longer a matter of mapping the discovery of the New World. These "maps" are more like star charts than "mappemundes." They are "fixes" on positions in a universe in motion more than visual (or verbal) equivalents of geographic sites or the channel's depths.

Like "In Cold Hell, in Thicket," this poem finds an answer to isolation and despair in motion:

> step off
> onto the nation   The sea
> will rush over   The ice
> will drag boulders   Commerce
> was changed the fathometer
> was invented here the present
> is worse give nothing now your credence
> start all over step off the
> Orontes onto land . . .

As in "In Cold Hell, in Thicket," the poet's own motion is imbued with cosmic reference, but this time it is the earth that is in the evolutionary process of change. "The sea will rush over" and "sentimental / drifty dirty / lazy man" will continue to migrate according to "lines of force" and changing commerce.

The peripatetic exercise yields little more than conjectures about the movements of other men, the earth, and the sea in terms that almost redeem Burke's immobility. Yet, by the poem's end there is reaffirmation of these changes. Tidal rivers, the "depths of the channel," and the idea of a new start far from "this stuck-out /10 miles Europe-pointing / cape" replace the ice, the sludge, the mud, and "the rubbish / of creation" that bog down Maximus. Although principles of motion and change have been there throughout Olson's poetry, it is not until the footnote to "John Burke" and "Letter, May 2, 1959" that they are accommodated in the language and embraced in cosmic terms. By the end of *The Maximus Poems,* even Gloucester as a reference point becomes subject to continual change. The touchstone of "polis" is abandoned; the sea is a dead end; the original Gloucester is an anachronism. But Olson redis-

covers the inseparability of land, sea, and man, together with the belief that "metric then is mapping."

Before Olson refuses "Maximus song" entirely in *Maximus Poems, IV, V, VI,* he pays a final tribute to Gloucester. An annual memorial procession "when not one life was lost" is the occasion of "Maximus to Gloucester, Sunday July 19," but the poem is not a memorial. For example, in the following passage Olson transforms an elegiac subject into a marriage of earth and sea:

> When a man's coffin is the sea
> the whole of creation shall come to his
>   funeral,
>
> It turns out; the globe
> is below, all lapis
>
> and its blue surface golded
> by what happened

The poem's lyric power comes from the context of change established in the footnote to "John Burke" and "Letter, May 2, 1959" more than from Gloucester's history of loss. It is a meditation, but not an elegy. It deals more with the cosmic interdependence of life and death, and land and sea, than with the specific geography and history of loss. As this antimemorial poem continues to map changes that were alluded to in the preceding poem, it effects the final, major reversal of the sequence.

The original offshore stance of Maximus, the sailor's periplus, turns around and becomes a view of the sea from the shore. Instead of observing Gloucester from offshore islands, Maximus remains onshore, observing the parade to the Cut. The flower ceremony is an image of transformation:

> the flowers
> turn
> the character of the sea   The sea jumps

the fate of the flower   The drowned men
               are undrowned
in the eddies

          of the eyes
          of the flowers
          opening
          the sea's eyes

The disaster
is undone

Olson's refusal to mourn is consistent with his new sense of language described in the footnote to "John Burke." Without death and loss as subjects, the poet is free to explore the realm where "night and day are one." From this point in the sequence, the flowing continuity of the objective, historical, painful world of Gloucester gradually becomes the more subjective, discontinuous area that Whorf describes as "the realm of HOPE or HOPING" in the Hopi grammar.

In "April Today Main Street" the poet carefully avoids the wind from the harbor and turns his attention away from the original Gloucester. As he walks the streets of "the Gloucester / which came late enough, April, 1642, to stick," Olson/Maximus takes his first hesitant steps beyond the self-imposed, self-enclosed boundaries of the objective realm of history manifested in the city.

A one-word paraphrase of Smith's poem, "The Sea Marke,"

       . . . "Slow,"
       Smith cried

       Upon you
       as he died,

reverberates throughout the poem and even colors the question that ends the volume:

       . . . Biskie Island?

       to this hour sitting
       as the mainland hinge

of the 128 bridge
now brings in

what,
to Main Street?

Main Street is sheltered from the "mean easterly . . . coming up each cross street" but has no protection against inland influences. Even "the Gloucester which held" is subject to change. With this final recognition and acceptance of his growing distance from the original Gloucester, Olson ends his study of the "manifested" city and the more historic, objective aspect of the sequence.

In the next two volumes the sequence eventually moves away from Gloucester and then finally back again by way of outlying Dogtown, describing a larger, more distant, "manifesting" world. As the context of the poem expands, the syntax changes too. In an extreme reduction of *muthologos,* words are as often topographical place holders as verbal references. And the speed and immediacy of each poem gradually begins to take precedence over the continuity of the sequence. Like Whorf's translation of the Hopi verb for "hoping," Olson's later poetry often "refers to the state of the subjective, unmanifest, vital and causal aspect of the Cosmos, and the fermenting activity toward fruition and manifestation with which it seethes."

During his last ten years, Olson wrote poems that both culminated and fragmented his incremental, continuous earlier work. They may be a "truer" poetry than *The Maximus Poems* or early *Archaeologist of Morning* poems, but they are no longer poems of discovery or exploration. Olson's poetry is usually characterized by the effort to stay "open," but volumes 2 and 3 of the Maximus sequence raise several questions about the process and limits of open form. From projective verse, through a cumulative series of discoveries, to *muthologos* (or poetry-as-history), Olson maintains a sense of positive syntax, context, and continuity. But in *Maximus Poems IV, V, VI* (1968) and *The Maximus Poems Volume Three* (1974), he often sacrifices the continuity of the sequence and its self-transcendent moments to illustrate principles. As he implied in "for Robt Duncan, who understands what's going on . . . ," his purpose by then was to show that "the world / is an eternal event."

In the Gravelly Hill poem the poet who had included himself so successfully in a universe of perpetual motion says "leave things alone" and, as Gravelly Hill:

leave me be, I am contingent, the end of the
                    world
is the borders
of my being

This sentiment is comparable with Wallace Stevens' "desire to be at the end of distances" in the second poem of "The Rock" sequence. Yet, whereas Stevens wrote a late poem entitled "The Poem That Took the Place of a Mountain," Olson's later poetry often gives the impression that mountains, rocks, or hills will replace poems.

Fragmentation and calcification may be in the nature of the "unmanifest" universe, but after 1959 the sequence seems increasingly disoriented. Instead of the earlier double movement of "succession and simultaneity" or alternations between manic affirmation and depressive transcendence, there is "stiffening" and a breakdown. The substitution of intellect for sensibility takes its toll. Dogma is an essential aspect of the new discourse. Both the second and third volumes of the sequence often allude to earlier work, demanding knowledge of the whole to a greater degree than the first volume did. They shed light on preceding parts of the sequence, but in turn they require a sense of Olson's overall cosmology, a systemless system that slowly evolved as he tried to create lan-

guage compatible with modern conceptions of the universe.

Nevertheless, as these poems alternate between echoes of the "manifest" world and speculations on the "subjective" realm of myth, there are occasional triumphs like this brief mapping:

                            by the way into the woods
Indian   otter
                                         orient
"Lake"   ponds

         show me
                        (exhibit
      myself)

Ambiguous verbal reference and the rigidly fixed spacing of each word explore a poetic ecology of self and surroundings that is finally Olson's central concern. An elegant sound pattern reinforces the relationship, with repetition of long *a* in "way" and "Lake" and similarity between syllabic appearances of "orient" and "exhibit" leading the reader into the poem just as the poet was led into the woods. "The way" leads to the end parenthesis of "myself)," a word in which the first syllable is as unique in the poem as the human figure in the Cape Ann landscape.

Most of the other poems in *IV, V, VI* and *Volume Three* do not "orient" the reader but have an opposite, disorienting effect. Nevertheless, the poetry-in-motion compels us by its sheer momentum. Its language, speed, and immediacy effectively communicate the principle of endless change originally established in "The Kingfishers." The ebb and flow of change are mirrored in movement from land to sea and back again, with Dogtown the place of origin where sea-father and mother-city meet. Back-and-forth motion between Dogtown or Portland and Gloucester's coast provides both a topographic and a mythic ground for the end of the sequence.

In the winter 1957–1958 poems, Olson discovered how painful it was to confront history through poetry. Thereafter he seemed more determined to discover "alternative discourse." Geologic references to earth and stone throughout the 1959 and 1960 poems paved the way for later allusions to Eleusinian mysteries, Gnostic wisdom figures, and prehistoric mother goddesses. A corresponding emphasis on cyclical time also led to the use of more experimental syntax, nonreferential words, and symbols.

Olson became a *muthologos,* a poet-historian combining myth and fact, when he no longer felt the two were separate. *Rhapsodia,* the "sewing" together of episodes and perceptions, became less relevant the more he assumed that all fragments automatically cohere. *Humilitas,* the sense of self-as-object, was subsumed in the integration of subject and object. And there was less need for attention to syllable and line as formal principles.

What stayed poetically valuable was Olson's attempt to find a new use of language and a cosmology consistent with the true nature of the universe. He said in *Poetry and Truth,* subtitled "The Dogmatic Nature of Experience," in the 1968 Beloit Lectures:

One must ask that any act of yours or my life or anyone else's, be not actually that life but its act or production. And that that is something which is essentially our language. I don't care in what form it occurs, and I'm not speaking aesthetically. And that that act be—or that production—is something that one can even specifically call something that neither realism or idealism even covers, that both bend your attention away from, the transcendent.

As dogmatic and unpoetic as Olson's delayed efforts at "the transcendent" often were, they were nonetheless heroic attempts to go beyond realism and idealism through acts of language. When, occasionally, there is a glimpse of a new direction among his late poems, even the failures seem a valuable legacy.

At the end of *Maximus Poems IV, V, VI,* the expanding energy of the sequence reverses to implosive inclusiveness. At first the "outward push," the need to "get it all further," resulted in the growth of projective verse into the long sequence. Then alternations between symphonic and rhapsodic forms developed. Poetic mappings followed. Eventually the sequence was transformed into "alternative discourse." But when symbolism and synchronicity became myth in book 5, Olson brought the outer universe into his poems more than he projected his poems outward. He still refused to distinguish poet and poem from environment, believing all to be in one field, but after book 5 the field's forces were more centripetal than centrifugal.

The consolidation that began in book 5 continued in book 6, with a difference. Book 6 depends upon more localized sounds and subjects, echoes that introduce earth as a familiar part of the human universe. Its repetitions of themes and phrases convey a passive relaxation that rarely appears earlier in the sequence. Appropriately, the opening fragment returns to the city under the protective aegis of an earth goddess:

> The earth with a city in her hair
> entangled of trees

The poems that follow review previous symbols, now safe and familiar. Despite an occasionally oracular tone, discontinuities are presented without tension, as if they were connected. Hereafter the sequence is a magnetic, all-inclusive force attracting anything in its field; it no longer strives for coherence.

The "Fort Point Section" returns from Dogtown to the geographic and historic fortification that was Olson's home. It seems to resolve the sequence at last. Yet, despite the way these last fourteen poems tie up loose ends in phrases like "spread the iron net" and "*the River Map* and we're done," they are also poised for new explorations. The closing poem of *Maximus Poems IV, V, VI* incorporates both a transformation and a return to origins:

> I set out now
>
> in a box upon the sea

As it recalls the ancient myth of the Night Sea-Crossing, this fragmentary poem presents the possibility that the sequence's end, like Gravelly Hill's, is a new beginning.

In *Volume Three,* published posthumously in 1974, several scattered poems point in a new direction at the same time that they reflect upon an earlier, more human universe. The difference between these poems, written after Olson left Gloucester to teach at the State University of New York at Buffalo in 1963, and the poems written five and ten years earlier (primarily at Black Mountain College in 1953 and at Gloucester in 1958) is that Olson's interest in "man-as-object" changed at last to include subjective man. In the more successful of these poems, intellectual rigor is often mitigated by a dramatic, centered focus. The sequence becomes less important than its parts. Although Olson did not live to oversee its publication, *Volume Three* frequently replaces the efforts of *IV,V,VI* at universality with a renewed emphasis on individual human possibility. Nevertheless, by the end of *Volume Three* there is an overriding sense of dejection. Lines like these abound:

> Nasturtium
> is still my flower but I am a poet
> who now more thinks than writes, my
> nose-gay

and

> I live underneath
> the light of day
> . . .
> My life is buried

or the final poem:

> My wife my car my color and
>   myself

The death of Olson's second wife in a car accident in March 1964 was a turning point in his later poetry. With "Maximus to himself June 1964," the pathos, anguish, and "memorial words" of earlier poems give way to numb pain:

> no more,
> where the tidal river rushes
>
> no more
> the golden cloak (beloved
> World)
>
> no more dogs
> to tear anything
> apart—the fabric
>
> nothing like
> the boat (no more Vessel
> in the Virgin's
> arms
>
> no more dog-rocks
> for the tide
> to rush over not any time again
> for wonder
>
> the ownership
> solely
> mine

Echoing the phrase "wondership stolen by ownership" from letter 2 of *The Maximus Poems,* the poet makes an apologia of his elegy, taking upon himself the responsibility for negating "wonder" as he mourns his loss. Thereafter, the poetic pace changes. Yet Olson remained faithful to such earlier concerns as "the divine" and an "actual earth of value," even though "the bright body of sex and love" was gone.

It may be that Olson's poetry would have taken a different direction had his wife survived and had he himself lived longer. There is at least one more incipient "stage" of development apparent in poems like "The Festival Aspect," "*Maximus of Gloucester,*" the sonnetlike sixtyninth and seventieth poems, and the anguished poem in praise of his father. In them he had begun to unite his inner, subjective state with his perceptions of the cosmos in local images that were neither mystical nor symbolic.

When Olson gave form and direction to the ever-present tension between thought and feeling in his early projective poems and in the beginning of the sequence, every impasse presented the possibility for new discoveries. By the time subjective states had been intellectualized and diverted into a poetic cosmology, the sequence required an elaborate, extrapoetic superstructure to maintain its momentum. With the final volume and its recurring theme of personal death, the poet's original motivations of joy, fear, and anger came bubbling to the surface again.

The fragmentation of *Volume Three* is more personal than philosophical. The poet questions his own necessities as he tries to map one more section of Dogtown in the poem dated "Tuesday April 25th 1966":

> shall I
> lay out those lots as well or
>
> fall now in sleep
> on this grass and
>
> do that work for you
> tomorrow?

Olson did not often question his purposes; but here, having returned once more to Cape Ann, he tried to convey a relaxation never before admitted. Unfortunately, the sequence had carried the weight of too many other changes to be open to this one. Consequently, *Volume Three,* with some outstanding exceptions, is mainly anticlimactic. Had Olson survived its publication, he might have strengthened it, but that speculation remains purely conjectural.

Olson became ill with cancer of the liver while teaching at the University of Connecticut. He died in New York City on January 10, 1970. His friend and fellow poet Robert Duncan had visited him there a week earlier and wrote:

> . . .tremendous change in the look of the man . . . only the minimum flesh remaining. . . . It was not grievous or sorrowful; he was fiercely concerned about the stage he is in . . . I see him always ahead along a way (the way or quest of what those of us who set out in 1950 with a mission in poetry were promised to). . . . He was concerned to tell me he had done his work.

Selected Bibliography

WORKS OF CHARLES OLSON

Call Me Ishmael. New York: Reynal and Hitchcock, 1947.

Maximus Poems 1–10. Stuttgart: Jonathan Williams, 1953.

Mayan Letters, edited by Robert Creeley. Mallorca: Divers Press, 1954.

Maximus Poems 11–22. Stuttgart: Jonathan Williams, 1956.

The Maximus Poems. New York: Jargon/Corinth, 1960.

A Bibliography on America for Ed Dorn. Writing 1. San Francisco: Four Seasons Foundation, 1964.

Human Universe and Other Essays, edited by Donald Allen. San Francisco: Averhahn Society, 1965.

Proprioception. Writing 6. San Francisco: Four Seasons Foundation, 1965.

Charles Olson Reading at Berkeley, transcribed by Zoe Brown. San Francisco: Coyote, 1966.

Selected Writings, edited by Robert Creeley. New York: New Directions, 1966.

Maximus Poems IV, V, VI. London and New York: Cape Goliard/Grossman, 1968.

Pleistocene Man. A Curriculum for the Study of the Soul, I. Buffalo: Institute of Further Studies, 1968.

Causal Mythology. Writing 16. San Francisco: Four Seasons Foundation, 1969.

Letters for Origin 1950–1956, edited by Albert Glover. London: Cape Goliard Press, 1969; New York: Grossman, 1970.

The Special View of History, edited by Ann Charters. Berkeley: Oyez, 1970. (Compilation and transcription of tapes, lectures, and notes.)

Archaeologist of Morning. London: Cape Goliard Press, 1970; New York: Grossman, 1971.

Poetry and Truth. The Beloit Lectures and Poems, transcribed and edited by George F. Butterick. Writing 27. San Francisco: Four Seasons Foundation, 1971.

Additional Prose: A Bibliography on America, Proprioception, & Other Notes & Essays, edited by George F. Butterick. Bolinas: Four Seasons Foundation, 1974.

The Maximus Poems Volume Three. New York: Grossman, 1974.

Charles Olson and Ezra Pound: An Encounter at St. Elizabeth's, edited by Catherine Seelye. New York: Grossman, 1975.

CRITICAL STUDIES

Butterick, George F. *A Guide to the Maximus Poems of Charles Olson.* Berkeley: University of California Press, 1978.

Charters, Ann. *Olson/Melville: A Study in Affinity.* Berkeley: Oyez, 1968.

Christensen, Paul. *Charles Olson: Call Him Ishmael.* Austin: University of Texas Press, 1979.

Dembo, L. S. *Conceptions of Reality in Modern American Poetry.* Berkeley and Los Angeles: University of California Press, 1966.

Duncan, Robert. "Notes on Poetics, Regarding Olson's 'Maximus.'" *the Review,* no. 10: 36–42 (January 1964).

Goodwin, K. L. *The Influence of Ezra Pound.* New York: Oxford University Press, 1966.

Kenner, Hugh. *A Homemade World.* New York: Knopf, 1974.

Paul, Sherman. *Olson's Push: Origin, Black Mountain and Recent Poetry.* Baton Rouge: Louisiana State University Press, 1978.

Rosenthal, M. L. *The Modern Poets.* New York: Oxford University Press, 1960.

———. *The New Poets.* New York: Oxford University Press, 1967.

Stepanchev, Stephen. *American Poetry Since 1945.* New York: Harper and Row, 1965.

Von Hallberg, Robert. *Charles Olson: The Scholar's Art.* Cambridge, Mass.: Harvard University Press, 1978.

Weatherhead, A. Kingsley. *The Edge of the Image: Marianne Moore, William Carlos Williams, and Some Other Poets.* Seattle: University of Washington Press, 1967.

RELATED WORKS

Bradford, William. *History of Plymouth Plantation 1620–1647,* edited by W. C. Ford. 2 vols. Boston: Houghton Mifflin, 1912. (Source for "There was a Youth whose Name was Thomas Granger.")

Duberman, Martin. *Black Mountain: An Exploration in Community.* New York: E. P. Dutton, 1972. (A nontraditional "history" of Black Mountain College.)

Herodotus. *The Histories,* translated by Aubrey de Selincourt. Baltimore: Penguin Books, 1954. (Basis for Olson's idea of the poet as historian.)

Hesiod. *Theogony,* translated by Richard Lattimore. Ann Arbor: University of Michigan Press, 1959. (Source for several mythological poems in *IV, V, VI* and *Volume Three.*)

Kramer, Samuel Noah, ed. *Mythologies of the Ancient World.* New York: Doubleday, 1961. (Useful guide to mythological allusions.)

Marks, Robert W. *The New Mathematics Dictionary and Handbook.* New York: Bantam Books, 1964. (Useful guide to mathematical allusions.)

Miller, Perry, ed. *The American Puritans, Their Prose and Poetry.* Garden City, N. Y.: Anchor, 1956. (Some precedents for Olson's poems on the founding of Gloucester.)

Neumann, Erich. *The Great Mother: An Analysis of the Archetype,* translated by Ralph Manheim. Princeton: Bollingen, 1972. (Essential source of *Maximus IV, V, VI.*)

Prescott, William H. *Mexico, and the Life of the Conqueror Fernando Cortés.* 2 vols. New York: Peter Fenelon Collier and Son, 1898. (Source for "The Kingfishers.")

Quinn, Sister M. Bernetta, *The Metamorphic Tradition in Modern Poetry.* New York: Gordian Press, 1966. (Analyzes the metamorphic perspectives in modern poetic sequences.)

Wagner, Linda W. *The Poems of William Carlos Williams: A Critical Study.* Middletown, Conn.: Wesleyan University Press, 1964. (Seminal study of the development of a poetic sequence.)

Whitaker, Thomas R. *William Carlos Williams.* New York: Twayne, 1968. (Analyzes Williams' creative process.)

Whitehead, Alfred North. *An Anthology,* edited by F. C. Northrop and Mason W. Gross. New York: Macmillan, 1961. (Sampling of ideas influential in Olson's later work.)

Whorf, Benjamin Lee. *Language, Thought & Reality.* Cambridge, Mass.: M.I.T. Press, 1956. (Crucial in footnote to "John Burke" and thereafter.)

Williams, William Carlos. *In the American Grain.* New York: New Directions, 1956. (Source for "The Kingfishers.")

———. *Paterson.* New York: New Directions, 1963. (Major contemporary American poetic sequence.)

SPECIAL ISSUES OF MAGAZINES

boundary 2, 2, nos. 1 and 2 (Fall 1973/Winter 1974). (Contains articles by Charles Altieri, Maxine Apsel, Matthew Corrigan, Cory Greenspan, Daniel Hise, John Seoggan, Catherine Stimpson.)

Massachusetts Review, 12, no. 1 (Winter 1970). (Contains "A Gathering for Charles Olson," with contributions by William Aiken, John Finch, M. L. Rosenthal.)

OLSON: The Journal of the Charles Olson Archives, nos. 1–10 (1974–1978). (Contains previously unpublished poems and prose, notes, transcriptions, and notes on lectures by Olson, as well as a list of Olson's reading compiled by George Butterick.)

—*MAXINE OLIAN APSEL*

Francis Parkman

1823–1893

FRANCIS PARKMAN was born in Boston on September 16, 1823, when the western frontier stretched down the Mississippi River and two-thirds of the nation was yet unbounded and unsettled. Seventy years later, on his birthday, almost two months before his death on November 8, the last major land rush took place in the Indian territory of Oklahoma, and all but four of the contiguous states had joined the Union. To many events of the American nineteenth century, Parkman was an unwilling witness: the displacement of the Indians, the slaughter of the buffalo, the Civil War, and the gradual retreat and disappearance of a line of demarcation between civilization and savagery. Each was in its way unwelcome testimony to the national commitment to physical expansion and material growth. Parkman belonged to a different age, one that cherished the values of culture as interpreted in Boston. At the same time, quite unlike his fellow Brahmins, he was devoted to the wilderness and all it signified. In the summer of 1846, when travel beyond the Mississippi was still uncommon, he rode out on the Oregon Trail in search of the primitive romance of the wild; but his true frontier lay among the Adirondacks, along the Penobscot and St. Lawrence rivers, and on the shores of the Great Lakes, a frontier that had closed sixty years before his birth.

Parkman inherited a rich legacy of social and cultural traditions, properly centered on Beacon Hill in the "three-hilled city of the Puritans." Like many of the patrician clans of Boston, his family had achieved a graceful harmony of solid commercial prosperity and intellectual distinction. On the paternal side, his great-grandfather, Ebenezer Parkman, had graduated from Harvard in 1721 and served for most of his life as the minister in Westboro, Massachusetts. Parkman's grandfather, Samuel Parkman, built a fortune in the China trade that made possible much of his grandson's scholarship. Through his mother's family, Parkman was allied to one of Boston's most eminent families, the line descended from the great Puritan, John Cotton (whom he later accused of writing "long-winded sermons"). The clerical tradition so strong on both sides of his family was carried on by his father, the Reverend Francis Parkman, pastor of the New North Church (which another Parkman had helped to found). He had studied with William Ellery Channing, the guiding spirit of American Unitarianism, played an active role at Harvard as his forefathers had, and was remembered by Richard Henry Dana, Jr., as a "strange, minute, whymsical man, with a good deal of quiet wit," a "thin piping voice," and a drawl. In appearance and temperament Francis, Jr., resembled his mother, a reserved woman from whom he drew his strong but carefully hidden emotions.

"Causes antedating my birth," Parkman wrote later in life, "gave me constitutional liabilities to which I largely ascribe the mischief that ensued." His father suffered a nervous collapse in 1845, and throughout his life seems to have manifested an extreme excitability. Parkman inherited his father's nervous constitution. His indifferent health soon gave way under the tremendous pressures to which he subjected his system, and by the age of twenty-four he was an invalid, incapacitated by mental pain of a neurotic character that has never been adequately diagnosed. One great benefit that shaped the rest of his life derived from his poor health as a child: at the age of eight, his parents sent him to live with his maternal grandfather, Nathaniel Hall, outside Medford, Massachusetts, where he had retired from business.

Though his stay did not have the intended effect on his physical condition—he remained, as he said, "sensitive and restless, rarely ill, but never robust"—its consequences for his mental development were enormous. The school he attended was nearly a mile distant in Medford, but the Middlesex Fells lay just across the boundary of Nathaniel Hall's land. An average student at the time, Parkman received his real childhood education in the woods. Barren of any sign of humanity, the Middlesex Fells offered wildlife and a sense of primitive remoteness in which he could create the illusion of exploring a pristine land. After four years of "collecting eggs, insects, and reptiles, trapping squirrels and woodchucks, and making persistent though rarely fortunate attempts to kill birds with arrows," his blissful exile came to an end and he returned to Boston permanently.

The natural literary consequence of Parkman's young life in the woods was a taste for the works of James Fenimore Cooper and Sir Walter Scott. Their novels and the realization that he would never be healthy enough to lead a fully active life turned his interests toward literature. In the fall of 1840, after three or four years of preparatory schooling during which he was distinguished for his efforts in "the rhetorical department," he entered Harvard, as had nearly all the men in his family before him. His career there was unusual, for he determined during his sophomore year to write the history of the "Old French War," or, as he more aptly called it, "the history of the forest." This goal endured throughout his life, and though the shape of his project changed gradually over the years, his original enthusiasm for his subject is as visible in the last of his works as in the first.

Even more impressive than the firmness of his plan is the maturity with which Parkman sought the means to fulfill it. With characteristic foresight and energy, he took from Harvard exactly what he needed, carefully balancing the requirements of the college with his own. The history of the forest was to be based on a combination of scholarly research exacting to a degree not common in the early nineteenth century, thorough experience of forest life, and personal inspection of historical sites scattered across the eastern United States and Canada.

Fortunately, Parkman found at Harvard one of the few men in the country who could teach him about historical writing as a profession: Jared Sparks, who held the recently created McLean professorship of ancient and modern history, the first professorship of history in America. He offered the young undergraduate valuable bibliographical aid; in return Parkman dedicated his first historical work, *The Conspiracy of Pontiac,* to Sparks. Writing to his former professor in 1851, he even proposed an "elaborate life of La Salle, your name as well as my own to appear on the title page."

Though he was a popular and social undergraduate, Parkman lived alone after his freshman year in order to accommodate the intensity of his preparatory reading. At the same time he began to convert himself into a consummate woodsman. He worked out in the new Harvard gymnasium, hired a former circus rider to refine his horseback skills, and, with "Injuns on the brain," roamed the local marshes endlessly, rifle in hand, sometimes venturing over to Medford and the woods of his childhood. From the letters of this period a brief self-portrait of a hunter, poised man of leisure, and penitential rogue emerges: "One great amusement of mine has been to sit in a grove of pine or hemlock, a cigar in my mouth, and rifle across my knee, and take off the heads of the chick-a-dees with the bullet. But I have come to the conclusion that the sport is too barbarous."

Coupled with his extensive extracurricular reading in history, Parkman's physical regimen proved too strenuous; it gave him the skills of a backwoodsman but broke his frail health. Afire "to paint the forest and its tenants in true and vivid colors" and "to realize a certain ideal of manhood, a little mediaeval, but nevertheless good," he applied "heroic remedies" to his sensitive system. The result was severe heart strain and nervous fatigue in his junior year; to recover his health, he left Harvard and sailed for Europe in November 1843.

Although he had often expressed his resentment toward American cultural dependence on Europe, Parkman found many things abroad suited to his taste, particularly the lack of onrushing transformation and self-conscious national progress. "Here in this old world," he wrote in his journal, "I seem, thank heaven, to be carried about half a century backwards in time." He climbed Vesuvius with Theodore Parker, entered a Passionist monastery in order to understand more fully the psychological workings of Roman Catholicism (he read Cooper's *The Pioneers* instead of devotional literature), visited a reprobate uncle in Paris, saw Charles Dickens' London (where he immedi-

ately visited George Catlin's gallery of portraits of American Indians), and toured Scotland, discovering that "Sir Walter Scott is everywhere." In truth, he did not leave America far behind.

Parkman's European tour was merely the longest of numerous excursions that had punctuated his years at Harvard. Each summer vacation the young historian packed his rifle, notebook, and other essentials, recruited a usually hesitant companion, and headed for the wilderness. Traveling to his favorite White Mountains and Maine in 1841, Lake George, Lake Champlain, and the Green Mountains in 1842, Montreal and Quebec in 1843, and Concord and the Berkshires in 1844, he crisscrossed New England in search of forest hardships and historical lore. Parkman's motto for these summer trips, which made no small contribution to his ill health, might have been taken from an entry written among the White Mountains in 1841: "There was a path, but I did not avail myself of it." His friends Dan Slade and Henry White complained bitterly of this propensity in him, for together they learned the stumbling, blind, pathless nature of exploration in the woods. The journals of these trips (and later rewritings like "Exploring the Magalloway" in *Harper's* magazine for November 1864) vividly record confusion in the forest, repeated drenchings, cold nights, and Parkman's ceaseless attempts to lead his friends farther from the path and the "dwellings of men."

A clear literary purpose is evident even in the earliest of Parkman's backwoods notebooks. He underwent the tortures of breaking trail in order to write from experience about exploration and forest warfare, and he learned to narrate the trials of French and English soldiers by recounting his own. At first, details of landscape, incident, and personality are sometimes lost in the folds of his prose, but it is remarkable how quickly he attained his true strength as a writer.

All his life Parkman was a much better narrative than descriptive artist. The actions of men had for him a cleanness and intent that his prose could imitate; when he turned to the face of nature in his early writings, he frequently became embroiled in his own emotions and in descriptions recollected from romantic literature. Reading his first journal, written at seventeen, one can envision him weighing his phrases as he stared out over the White Mountains in 1841:

On each side, thousands of feet below, stretched a wide valley, girt with an amphitheatre of mountains rising peak after peak like the black waves of the sea, the clouds now sinking over their summits, now rising and breaking, disclosing yet more distant ranges, and then settling thick and heavy so that nothing was visible but the savage rocks and avalanche slides of the neighboring mountains looming dimly through the mist.

Mannered though this is, it reveals the core of a descriptive style that Parkman would simplify and strengthen as he grew older.

Parkman spent 1845 and 1846 fulfilling his father's wish that he enter a regular profession by studying law at Harvard; he took the LL.B. in 1846. There were no illusions about his true purpose, though: he continued his historical reading and published in the *Knickerbocker* magazine prose sketches based on historical fact and his own nearly calamitous experiences in the White Mountains.

Most important, Parkman also began preparations for his first major historical project by touring the Old Northwest Territory in search of information and scenic background relating to the conspiracy of Pontiac, whose confederacy of Indian tribes attempted to repel the English from the frontier after 1763. Only one preparatory exercise remained: to attain a deeper understanding of the Indian character. "I have also read almost all the works on the Indians," he wrote in a letter of 1843, "and have arrived at least to one certain result—that their character will always remain more or less of a mystery to one who does not add practical observation to his closest studies."

Once again strenuous labor had overstrained Parkman's faculties, this time affecting his eyes, and vacation seemed in order. On April 1, 1846, he left New York for St. Louis, there to meet his cousin Quincy Shaw (who had proposed the trip) and set off on what he glibly called "a tour of curiosity and amusement to the Rocky Mountains," the most important "summer's journey out of bounds" in his life.

In 1846, from St. Louis to San Francisco, the whole West was in ferment. That year more than 2,500 emigrants, seeds of a new empire, rolled alongside the Platte River, crossed the Rockies, Sierras, and Cascades, and settled in Oregon and California. An entire spiritual tribe was on the march, for the Mormons, goaded by persecution, had fled from Nauvoo, Illinois, toward the basin of the Great Salt Lake. Following Lansford Hastings' *Emigrants' Guide to Oregon and California,* the Donner party probed a new cutoff through the Wasatch Mountains, missed the season for crossing the Sierras, and found themselves buried in snow just short of the Central Valley. Southward, down the Santa Fe Trail, rolled a steady stream of traders' wagons and, behind them, Colonel Stephen Kearny and his troops, headed for Mexico and the conflict that would bring California into the Union and Zachary Taylor into the White House. Out of this migration a prodigious literature grew, and Parkman's *The Oregon Trail* is an acknowledged classic of its genre.

At Westport, Missouri, Parkman found emigrant trains waiting to "jump off," a ragged crowd of Indians and vagabonds, and a few men capable of assisting him in his grand design. Among the latter were Pierre Chouteau, who could describe Pontiac from life, and Henry

Chatillon, Parkman's guide and hunter, in whom he saw signs of "that race of restless and intrepid pioneers whose axes and rifles have opened a path from the Alleghenies to the western prairies."

Parkman came to the West as a sportsman and ethnologist, not to witness the great movement of a people but to observe the race that would inevitably be destroyed by it. A Federalist and a Brahmin, he was partially cut off from the emigrants by his social background and wealth; he shared their miseries and met most of the notable parties on the trail, but failed to understand the spirit that moved them: "I have often perplexed myself to divine the various motives that give impulse to this migration; but whatever they may be, whether an insane hope of a better condition in life, or a desire of shaking off restraints of law and society, or mere restlessness, certain it is that multitudes bitterly repent the journey, and, after they have reached the land of promise, are happy enough to escape from it." The emigrants understood him no better.

A month after leaving Fort Leavenworth, Kansas, where he met Colonel Stephen Kearny, Parkman and his small band, including Chatillon and the Canadian muleteer Deslauriers, rode into Fort Laramie, Wyoming. The opening stages of the journey did not savor of pure adventure. Joining a rather ridiculous set of English sportsmen, the travelers were lost within hours of their departure. By the time they reached the main trail near the Big Blue River, Parkman had become thoroughly disgusted with the Englishmen, who welcomed the prospect of traveling in company with a wagon train. After days of chasing stray stock and enduring the slow progress of heavily laden wagons on muddy trails, the small party from Boston took "French leave" of the Englishmen and emigrants in order to travel at their own pace.

They soon encountered a band of Oglala Sioux Indians whose chief was Old Smoke, a friend of Henry Chatillon. There, on the western plains, Parkman made his first true contact with the race he had dreamed about for years and had met only in a degenerate state in the Old Northwest and New England.

Warriors, women, and children swarmed like bees; hundreds of dogs, of all sizes and colors, ran restlessly about; and, close at hand, the wide shallow stream was alive with boys, girls, and young squaws, splashing, screaming, and laughing in the water. At the same time a long train of emigrants with their heavy wagons was crossing the creek, and dragging on in slow procession by the encampment of the people whom they and their descendants, in the space of a century, are to sweep from the face of the earth.

Among Old Smoke's people Parkman was offered an Indian bride.

Because of the dysentery and eye fatigue that plagued Parkman throughout his trip, the landscape of what is now Nebraska and Wyoming took on a darker meaning, but its charm was stronger than any other he had seen.

I used to lie languid and dreamy before our tent, musing on the past and the future, and when most overcome with lassitude, my eyes turned always towards the distant Black Hills. There is a spirit of energy in mountains, and they impart it to all who approach them. At that time I did not know how many dark superstitions and gloomy legends are associated with the Black Hills in the minds of the Indians, but I felt an eager desire to penetrate their hidden recesses, and explore the chasms and precipices, black torrents and silent forests, that I fancied were concealed there.

For Parkman the wilderness was always the final proving ground of a man; it was so for Robert Cavelier de La Salle and it would be so for the young Brahmin. He was occasionally foolhardy, but displayed remarkable stamina and courage during the middle portion of his western trip. After waiting nearly a month for a rendezvous with the Indians, he set out through extremely dangerous country, accompanied only by a newly hired Canadian named Raymond, in search of the Oglala, hoping to join them as they moved toward a tribal meeting that he assumed would be the final preliminary to war with the Snakes. Coming through a gap near the Medicine Bow range in Wyoming after a painful ride, Parkman could see the plains through which Laramie Creek flows and, spread out there, "the tall lodges of the Ogillallah. Never did the heart of wanderer more gladden at the sight of home than did mine at the sight of that Indian camp."

From July 15 until August 2, 1846, he followed this village, living in the lodge of its principal chief, Kongra Tonga, or Big Crow. Without exaggeration, those eighteen days formed the central episode of Parkman's life, an oasis of savagery to which he mentally returned when he wished to escape the nineteenth century, and to which he owed the peculiar force and insight of much of his later writing.

Restrained only by the course of his illness, Parkman entered without hesitation into the life of the village: he provided a feast of "dog, tea, and bread"; joined the buffalo hunters in the kill and in devouring the raw liver of their prey; earned great esteem for his "fire-medicine" by making fireworks from the pages of John C. Frémont's *Expedition;* and provoked his own social conscience by informing the Indians, in their own rhetoric, that where he came from, "The squaws were far more beautiful than any they had ever seen, and all the men were brave warriors." The tribe moved from the plains, where it performed several "surrounds" to obtain buffalo meat and hides, up into the Black Hills (really a part of the Laramie Mountains), where they gathered lodgepoles in the forest. A war party was discussed by a brave named White Shield, but to Parkman's disgust it was called off because of White Shield's "inflammation of the throat." (Accounting for his desire to see the Indians at war, Parkman sagely observed, "No man is a philanthropist on the prairie.")

On the eve of his departure, he rode up above camp for a final look about him before returning to Fort Laramie. In spite of his disillusionment with the Indians, his disgust at their unromantic nature, Parkman felt a strong regret at what he knew must be a final parting from a disappearing race.

Evening approached at last; the crests of the mountains were still bright in sunshine, while our deep glen was completely shadowed. I left the camp, and climbed a neighboring hill. The sun was still glaring through the stiff pines on the ridge of the western mountain. In a moment he was gone, and, as the landscape darkened, I turned again towards the village. As I descended, the howling of wolves and the barking of foxes came up out of the dim woods from far and near. The camp was glowing with a multitude of fires, and alive with dusky naked figures, whose tall shadows flitted, weird and ghost-like, among the surrounding crags.

Parkman rejoined Shaw and Chatillon, and the men traveled down to Bent's Fort, Colorado, and caught the northern section of the Santa Fe Trail, where they met scattered soldiers from the military units that had passed up and down it during the summer. By the middle of September they had ridden onto "the prairies of the poet and novelist," amazed at their fertile beauty. On September 26, after having traversed the eastern half of the Oregon Trail and the northern half of the Santa Fe, they reentered Westport, savages in appearance. After a shave and change of clothes, the two cousins bid farewell to the man of whom Parkman said, "I have never, in the city or in the wilderness, met a better man than my truehearted friend, Henry Chatillon."

The Oregon Trail was written under the worst of circumstances. Back in Boston, Parkman's dysentery cleared up; but with the need for absolute mastery of his ills removed, the long-delayed collapse soon followed. In a third-person autobiographical letter written in 1868, he later described his state: "To the maladies of the prairie succeeded a suite of exhausting disorders, so reducing him that circulation at the extremities ceased, the light of the sun became insupportable, and a wild whirl possessed his brain. . . . All collapsed, in short, but the tenacious strength of muscles hardened by long activity." Along with arthritis, which crippled him in 1851, this was the "enemy" he would battle for the rest of his life. As always, he compensated as best he could, and learned to write by dictation. Installments of *The Oregon Trail* began to appear in the *Knickerbocker* magazine in February 1847, and in 1849 it was published in book form.

The Oregon Trail has been a consistent favorite of Western literature ever since its publication. Historians have lamented that it does not provide an adequate analysis of the emigration of 1846—Bernard DeVoto's "year of decision"—and critical readers, often writing with tense social piety, have complained again and again that Parkman misunderstood the West, the Indians, the pioneers, that he was in fact unfitted for his experience by the very nature of his Brahmin background. *The Oregon Trail* is autobiography, a trial of the spirit judged not in terms of inwardness but in the language of the wilderness, of external warfare, of survival. One need not expect from Parkman the self-analytical suppleness of Henry Adams or the metaphysical voyaging of Herman Melville. His autobiographical impulses seem crude in comparison, but they are nonetheless vital.

History and autobiography are closely linked in Parkman's mind: each measures conflict. *The Oregon Trail* assesses the degree of his adaptation to the wilderness and its native inhabitants, and his conflict with an ideal of heroism threatened by assault from within. For Parkman history and autobiography record man's efforts to prevail against a harsh external world; his enduring metaphor for the conditions of reality against which all men struggle is the wilderness. His insistence on evaluating himself and his historical heroes against a primitive and alien terrain accounts for the inevitable bleeding of autobiographical impulses into his historical works (as in *La Salle and the Discovery of the Great West),* and it explains the utter failure of his autobiographical work of fiction, *Vassall Morton,* in which the hero's final triumph is a foregone conclusion.

The West, the mountains, the village of Kongra Tonga are the places where Parkman met his values face to face. That he was nearly delirious with illness much of the time is not merely an incidental matter of fact, but a metaphorical validation of the experience through which he was passing. It was his equivalent of the initiatory fasts and dream visions undergone by Indian boys on the verge of manhood, a dark unveiling of impossible romance and inevitable disillusionment. *The Oregon Trail* begins and ends exactly where it should, on the borders of civilization—and, for Parkman, on the edge of achievement.

While *The Oregon Trail* appeared at intervals (its publication caused even his father to understand the intensity of his purpose) Parkman began mentally to recast the notes, manuscripts, and books he had gathered over the past five years in preparation for writing *The Conspiracy of Pontiac.* Like his fellow historian W. H. Prescott, he learned to use a ruled grid for writing. His sisters, cousins, and eventually his wife, Catherine Scollay Bigelow, whom he married on May 13, 1850, did his reading for him. He felt that the awkward process of composing in his head, dictating, and having his words read back to him strengthened his work. The effort of writing also buoyed Parkman's spirits. "His health improved under the process," he later wrote, "and the remainder of the volume—in other words, nearly the whole of it—was composed in Boston, while pacing in the twilight of a large garret." Beginning with the episode he knew best, the siege of Detroit, he discovered that his book progressed more quickly than he had anticipated. The opening chapters of *Pontiac,* those that describe the Indians and the preliminary history of the struggle between New France and New England, were written last.

Published in 1851, *The Conspiracy of Pontiac* is at once prologue and epilogue to Parkman's vast history, *France and England in North America.* The seven volumes that appeared between 1865 and 1892 narrate the exploration and settlement of New France, or Canada, between the first voyage of John Cabot in 1497 and the final negotiations in 1763 that followed the collapse of Canada. *Pontiac* straddles these volumes; it begins with an account of the eastern Indian nations, the race for whom "the black and withering future must have stood revealed in all its desolation," and closes with their defeat and the death of Pontiac. As a result it is a curiously divided work. Before beginning his tale of the multitribal onslaught led by the Ottawa war chief Pontiac in a desperate attempt to ward off English possession of the territory they had won from the French by the Treaty of Paris, Parkman recapitulates the development of New France and New England and the history of their wilderness wars. In three chapters he surveys the terrain it would later take him seven volumes to explore in detail.

The heroes of his full-scale history appear here in miniature: the Jesuit martyrs Jean de Brébeuf, Gabriel Lalemant, and Isaac Jogues;

the explorer La Salle, Louis Frontenac, George Washington, and Major Robert Rogers; and the two doomed warriors Louis de Montcalm and James Wolfe. Chronologically, the main section of *The Conspiracy of Pontiac* comes last in Parkman's works, for the story it tells about the years 1763–1769 follows the fall of New France, the event that closes *Montcalm and Wolfe.*

As Parkman had originally conceived the history of the forest, it had more affinities with the novels of Cooper or Scott than with traditional historical literature. He did not envision the full scope of his later work until after *Pontiac* was well under way; and in a certain sense the historicity of this book was incidental to its original design. Parkman wrote in the preface:

The history of that epoch, crowded as it is with scenes of tragic interest, with marvels of suffering and vicissitude, of heroism and endurance, has been, as yet, unwritten, buried in the archives of governments, or among the obscurer records of private adventure. To rescue it from oblivion is the object of the following work. It aims to portray the American forest and the American Indian at the period when both received their final doom.

In 1854, when his historical goals had become more defined, he confided to Charles Scribner that *Pontiac* "was designed as a tableau of forest life and Indian character. The subject was chosen with this view, and not on account of any peculiar historic importance attaching to it. Great pains were however taken to secure fullness and accuracy of historic detail."

One cannot escape the conclusion that Parkman's depiction of the Indians is harsh and unsympathetic. He was praised for rejecting the romantic notion of the "noble savage," but the frequent severity of his comments on the Indians did not pass unnoticed. Herman Melville attacked Parkman's uncharitable characterization of the Sioux in his review of *The Oregon*

Trail (published in *Literary World,* 1849) and Theodore Parker faulted *Pontiac* for the same offense in a letter to Parkman of December 22, 1851.

Parker, though, also observed the ambivalence of Parkman's feelings about the Indians: "You evidently have a fondness for the Indians—not a romantic fondness, but one that has been tempered by the sight of the fact." The structure of *Pontiac* fully reflects this ambivalence. The opening chapter presents in summary form Parkman's "objective" conclusions about Indian society and psychology; with extensive revisions and a somewhat broader range of subject it appeared in the *North American Review* for July 1865 and July 1866 and as the introduction to *The Jesuits in North America* (1867), the second volume of his series. Parkman casts his thoughts in neutral prose appropriate to the ethnological task he sets himself. "Among all savages," he reasons, "the powers of perception preponderate over those of reason and analysis; but this is more especially the case with the Indian."

Within the narrative of his histories, though, the Indians appear in a different guise. They become romantic figures—not Fenimore Cooper's noble savages to be sure, but actors in a primitive romance, the kind closest to Parkman's heart. Describing life in an Indian village, he adapts his own experiences; and his prose reflects emotional qualities that lie beneath the surface, qualities that have nothing to do with ethnology or objectivity:

Night has now closed in; and the rough clearing is illumined by the blaze of fires and burning pine-knots, casting their deep red glare upon the dusky boughs of the surrounding forest, and upon the wild multitude who, fluttering with feathers and bedaubed with paint, have gathered for the celebration of the war-dance.

Quite simply, the Indians are more mysteriously evocative (an appropriate literary virtue

in a tale "more worthy the pen of the dramatist than that of the historian") when perceived as "weird and ghost-like figures" than when brought into a historical foreground of detached analysis. To Parkman, Pontiac and his confederates seemed to lend an additional romance to the forest, for Pontiac was the hero of a distant drama of high proportions: "His faults were the faults of his race; and they cannot eclipse his nobler qualities."

The remission from pain brought by the writing of *Pontiac* came to an end shortly after its publication in 1851. Severe arthritis confined Parkman to a wheelchair or to walking with canes; and his mental "enemy" returned in full force in 1853. During the next few years writing was usually prohibited by his doctors, so, with the same enthusiasm he brought to his historical research, he turned for relief to the culture of roses. (This hobby culminated in *The Book of Roses* [1866], which for years remained one of the standard books on the subject.)

In his few painfree moments Parkman also worked on a minor project, a loosely autobiographical novel that was published in 1856. *Vassall Morton* was the only book that Parkman repudiated in later life. The plot concerns the trials that young Vassall Morton, a duplicate of Parkman with the added gift of strong health, undergoes in his effort to win Miss Edith Leslie and to defeat his archenemy, an anemic and diabolical villain. Like Parkman, Morton is interested in history and ethnology, and he spends fully as much time in the White Mountains persuading his hesitant friends of the virtues of outdoor life as Parkman did. A major section of the book concerns his imprisonment in Europe (engineered, of course, by his enemy) and his eventual escape.

A patchwork of autobiographical fragments drawn from his journals, the only merit of *Vassall Morton* is an infrequent glimpse of Parkman's reactions to Boston society. The emotional situations are so vapid, the narrative line so abruptly maneuvered, that it is hard to perceive any resemblance between this work and Parkman's historical writings. Wilbur Schramm has stated that *Vassall Morton* "expresses the personal philosophy which its author rigidly excluded from his other published work." But this personal philosophy rides like flotsam on the surface of the novel; it has not been given the artistically valid shape that distinguishes Parkman's historical works. *Vassall Morton* is completely static, an autobiographical parable of Parkman's illness, which was told more truthfully and with far greater power in *The Oregon Trail* and *La Salle and the Discovery of the Great West*.

In spite of his unrelenting physical torment and its mental reflection, which he described as "an iron band, secured around the head and contracting with an extreme force," Parkman enjoyed a domestic happiness during the mid-1850's that did much to assuage the evils of his condition. His wife bore him a son, Francis, and two daughters, Grace and Katherine. After the death of Parkman's father in 1852, the family divided the year between Boston and a summer home in Jamaica Plain, Massachusetts, which Parkman called his "box in the suburbs." There, when he could, he rowed and fished on Jamaica Pond, tended his proliferating gardens and greenhouses, and kept the cottage filled with flowers.

Preparations for the work that would fill the rest of his life had begun as soon as *Pontiac* was sent to the publisher, and by the autumn of 1856 Parkman was well enough to make a brief excursion to Quebec and Montreal. The peaceful domestic interlude of these years was soon ruptured, though; in 1856 he discovered that Benjamin Perley Poore, whom he had employed as a copyist for almost seven years, had relied on his blindness to defraud him by charging him for the copying of useless manuscripts. A far more serious crisis occurred when his son

died of scarlet fever in 1857; and when his wife died the following year, the tragedy was complete. His health collapsed entirely. Leaving his daughters in the care of his sister-in-law, he went to Paris to seek the treatment of specialists.

It seems to have taken nothing less than the Civil War to pull Parkman out of this slump. For a man as obsessed with action as he was, it was a bitter blow to be forcibly withdrawn by illness, in the prime of his life, from a struggle in which friends and kinsmen were dying. After visiting the Forty-Fourth Massachusetts Infantry in September 1862, he wrote to his most trusted correspondent, Mary Dwight Parkman: "When I left them, I was sick of life." In his fine biography of Parkman, Mason Wade observed that the "Civil War brought out the best qualities of the Brahmin type; the emergency and the principles at stake enabled them to forget their fastidiousness and play public roles." With his pen Parkman did what little he could: between 1861 and 1864 he wrote eleven letters to the *Boston Daily Advertiser* on various aspects of the war. With three articles written between 1878 and 1880 on the "Woman Question" and the issue of universal suffrage, they represent the core of his political philosophy.

Parkman's Civil War letters are primarily the rhetorically turgid cries of a class forcibly removed by Populist politics—the triumph of Jacksonian democracy—from the leading role it had occupied during the early years of the republic. No word occurs in these letters so often as "culture." The idea of culture takes many analogical forms in Parkman's political, intellectual, and botanical works; it is an all-encompassing theory for him, perhaps most simply expressed in *The Book of Roses,* completed just after the war: "That [culture] which is founded in the laws of Nature, and aims at a universal development, produces for its results not only increased beauty, but increased symmetry, strength, and vitality." In *La Salle and the Discovery of the Great West* he stated the corollary: "The culture that enervates instead of strengthening is always a false or partial one." This was the principle that led Parkman to the woods from Harvard, a belief in the balance of mind and body acquired through discipline and conflict. In a letter to the *Daily Advertiser* dated September 4, 1861, he developed the political form of this idea and applied it to the Union:

There is close analogy between the life of nations and of individuals. Conflict and endurance are necessary to both, and without them both become emasculate. . . . A too exclusive pursuit of material success has notoriously cramped and vitiated our growth. In the absence of a high interest or ruling idea, a superficial though widespread culture has found expression and aliment in a popular literature commonly frivolous and often corrupt. In the absence of any exigency to urge or any great reward to tempt it, the best character and culture of the nation has remained for the most part in privacy, while a scum of reckless politicians has choked all the avenues of power.

Though Parkman believed that "the vigorous life of the nation springs from the deep rich soil at the bottom of society" (as he wrote in his extremely important review of Cooper's works in 1852), he also felt that only the leadership of a cultured oligarchy could draw forth from that soil the fruit it was capable of bearing: "No expansion of territory, no accumulation of wealth, no growth of population, can compensate for the decline of individual greatness."

Parkman perceived the Civil War as a struggle for ascendancy between two forms of society: the North, in which "our material growth so greatly exceeds our other growth that the body politic suffers from diseases of repletion," and the South, the culture of which "has long been the heart and focus of its political life,

while that of the North has been rather an excrescence upon the vital system than a part of it." The Civil War came down to this: "A head full of fire, a body ill-jointed, starved, attenuated, is matched against a muscular colossus, a Titan in energy and force—full of blood, full of courage, prompt for fight, and confident of victory. Strong head and weak body [the South] against strong body and weak head [the North]; oligarchy against democracy." Though Parkman despised the South for its "treacherous" secession, his were the principles of oligarchy and culture, the active role of the most cultured men in the country, versus uncultured democracy and mediocrity, the triumph of the marketplace, and "the reign of shopkeepers."

The true reward of Parkman's early training and the preliminary survey of his subject in *Pontiac* was the engendering of a coherent vision of an entire historical period, stretching from the first landfall of the French in the New World to their irrevocable cession of New France to the English in 1763. In a time of grandiose historical projects, when history by its very nature seemed to imply monumental scope and, in Henry Adams' phrase, "nothing but mass tells," Parkman's theme was one of the best.

Recalling his first cursory glance at *The Conspiracy of Pontiac,* the philosopher and historian John Fiske remarked on his own typical ignorance of its subject: "Had that conspiracy been an event in Merovingian Gaul or in Borgia's Italy, I should have felt a twinge of conscience at not knowing about it; but the deeds of feathered and painted red men on the Great Lakes and the Alleghenies, only a century old, seemed remote and trivial."

The historical epoch closed by Pontiac's conspiracy soon seemed neither remote nor trivial. Over a span of twenty-seven years, between the appearance of *Pioneers of France in the New*

World in 1865 and *A Half-Century of Conflict* in 1892, Parkman brought before an increasingly appreciative public his vivid interpretation of a largely forgotten but overwhelmingly significant period in American history. He gave shape to an era and, as Frederick Jackson Turner observed, even more remarkably turned the "raw product" of unwritten history into a "great work of art."

When *Pioneers of France in the New World* was published in 1865, Parkman had already begun writing the next two volumes of his history and had collected many of the documents and manuscripts for still later volumes. His theme had acquired substance, and in the introduction to *Pioneers* he brought it forth in conceptual form. This introduction is not only a record of intent but also an index to his historical motivations. "The subject," Parkman wrote, "to which the proposed series will be devoted is that of 'France in the New World,'— the attempt of Feudalism, Monarchy, and Rome to master a continent where, at this hour, half a million of bayonets are vindicating the ascendancy of a regulated freedom."

Parkman's conception of the dynamic principle behind the battle for North America is a simple one, and one we have seen before:

New France was all head. Under king, noble, and Jesuit, the lank, lean body would not thrive. Even commerce wore the sword, decked itself with badges of nobility, aspired to forest seigniories and hordes of savage retainers. Along the borders of the sea an adverse power was strengthening and widening, with slow but steadfast growth, full of blood and muscle,—a body without a head. Each had its strength, each its weakness, each its own modes of vigorous life: but the one was fruitful, the other barren; the one instinct with hope, the other darkening with shadows of despair.

Here again, in Parkman's analysis, are the principles at stake in the Civil War. His persistent metaphor of conflict between head and body is remarkable because, in his scheme of things, the conflict cannot be resolved satisfactorily. To develop the obvious analogy, the implication of "culture" in Parkman's sense is compromise, a reconciliation of competing claims. In roses one can graft together beauty and strength; between nations, though, the reconciliation of the metaphorical antagonism between head (the absolutism of New France) and body (New England's potential democracy) is harder still, for it results in war and the eventual triumph of one principle over another. Parkman's desire for balance between autocracy and democracy, between head and body, is thwarted by the inevitable tendency of a political system to drift toward one extreme or the other.

It is thus a commonly repeated error to see in Parkman simply the conventional views of "Whig" historians who discover in the process of history the gradual triumph of the cause of liberty and who regard the past as a spiral moving steadily upward toward the present. This would be a naive reading of Parkman's pessimism. Neither absolutism nor democracy is a satisfactory solution, and any compromise between them is uneasy. "Extremes meet," Parkman wrote in *The Old Régime,* "and Autocracy and Democracy often touch hands, at least in their vices." Between New France and New England (and their political systems) his sympathies are clearly divided, as the terms of his metaphor for their conflict suggest they must be. This division of sympathies, as much as his desire for historical precision, makes *France and England in North America* as vivid and accurate a work as it is.

One of the peculiar virtues of Parkman's subject was the fact that the "springs of American civilization, unlike those of the elder world, lie revealed in the clear light of History." The trials of Europeans exposed to the wilderness held the most intense interest, for "the wilderness," he wrote in *La Salle,* "is a rude touchstone, which often reveals traits that would have lain buried and unsuspected in civilized life." Primitive America and its primitive inhabitants evoked two entirely different reactions from the people who settled on its eastern coast and those who settled along the St. Lawrence River.

In spite of his strongly Puritan heritage, Parkman approved the more vigorous response of the French: "While New England was a solitude, and the settlers of Virginia scarcely dared venture inland beyond the sound of a cannon-shot, Champlain was planting on shores and islands the emblems of his faith." The economic forces that impelled the French to penetrate the forests led New England to "material progress" within its established confines. "Assiduity in pursuit of gain was promoted to the rank of a duty, and thrift and godliness were linked in equivocal wedlock." English relations with the Indians were contemptuous and fearful; a recurring error in policy that had disastrous effects. "As a whole," Parkman concluded, "[New England] grew upon the gaze of the world, a signal example of expansive energy; but she has not been fruitful in those salient and striking forms of character which often give a dramatic life to the annals of nations far less prosperous." He would have applied the same analysis to the North during the Civil War.

But New France was utterly different. Few families had settled there; rather, mainly priests, soldiers, and fur traders, none of them likely to foster the growth necessary to shore up the new colony. Yet these "banded powers, pushing into the wilderness their indomitable soldiers and devoted priests, unveiled the secrets of the barbarous continent, pierced the forests, traced and mapped out the streams, planted their emblems, built their forts, and claimed all as their own."

However different in political and religious attitudes from Parkman, these were the men who embodied most fully his somewhat medieval ideal of manhood pitted against an unyielding country. Furthermore, theirs was not a policy of destruction. The French infiltrated the forests, learned to live easily in the wilds, and sought to convert the Indians, not through force and an austere religion but through brotherhood and a sensual creed that they could wonder at if they could not understand. Moreover, the "scheme of English colonization made no account of the Indian tribes. In the scheme of French colonization they were all in all."

In the abstract struggle between Liberty and Absolutism, Parkman defers to the "destined" victory of the former, but this overarching conceit is partially an accretion to his basic decision to write the history of the forest. It provides cultural and ethical validation for a history of the French explorers, missionaries, and coureurs de bois whom Parkman understood with deep sympathy, and whom he brought back to life in the early volumes of *France and England in North America.*

His historical method and his theory of history, such as they are, receive their fullest expression in the introduction to *Pioneers.*

Faithfulness to the truth of history involves far more than a research, however patient and scrupulous, into special facts. Such facts may be detailed with the most minute exactness, and yet the narrative, taken as a whole, may be unmeaning or untrue. The narrator must seek to imbue himself with the life and spirit of the time. He must study events in their bearings near and remote; in the character, habits, and manners of those who took part in them. He must himself be, as it were, a sharer or spectator of the action he describes.

This may be taken as a credo of what was called the "literary" school of historical writing, exemplified at its best by Parkman and by W. H. Prescott and John Lothrop Motley, whose major works appeared at midcentury. To this "literary" desire Parkman also brought exacting research characteristic of the later "scientific" school of history. As in *Pontiac,* though, his first priority was narrative, not the marshaling of evidence or the analysis of historical forces, or, as Jared Sparks expected, the indignation of a moral historian. What he gives us in place of these things, which have dated so rapidly in the works of his peers, is a superb reading and retelling of the past.

In the second part of *Pioneers of France in the New World,* where his proper theme truly opens, Parkman's historical method is brilliantly displayed in an overt manner. At one point his source, Samuel de Champlain's journal, reveals a world that is filled in by Parkman's practiced eye for natural detail. The historian and explorer seem to meet in an unchanging landscape.

As we turn the ancient, worm-eaten page which preserves the simple record of his fortunes, a wild and dreary scene rises before the mind,— a chill November air, a murky sky, a cold lake, bare and shivering forests, the earth strewn with crisp brown leaves, and, by the water-side, the bark sheds and smoking camp-fires of a band of Indian hunters.

Parkman is no less capable of interpolating action from the sketchy details of his sources. To be a "sharer or spectator of the action he describes" meant placing his subjects in a fully realized setting. In *Pontiac,* where he had first attempted this, the descriptive passages frequently had no apparent connection to the narrative; they often were merely indulgent excursions based on Parkman's own experiences. But in *Pioneers* the relationship between description and narration is much closer: for Champlain the wilderness was a mysterious, all-pervasive element, and Parkman's abundant use of scenic description becomes an extension of his theme, the exploratory penetration of the forest.

Describing Champlain's progress up the Richelieu River toward the lake to which he gave his name, Parkman achieved a synthesis of narrative action and natural description that is typical of him at his best in these early volumes.

Walls of verdure stretched on left and right. Now, aloft in the lonely air rose the cliffs of Beloeil, and now, before them, framed in circling forests, the Basin of Chambly spread its tranquil mirror, glittering in the sun. The shallop outsailed the canoes. Champlain, leaving his allies behind, crossed the basin and tried to pursue his course; but, as he listened in the stillness, the unwelcome noise of rapids reached his ear, and, by glimpses through the dark foliage of the Islets of St. John he could see the gleam of snowy foam and the flash of hurrying waters. Leaving the boat by the shore in charge of four men, he went with Marais, La Routte, and five others, to explore the wild before him. They pushed their way through the damps and shadows of the wood, through thickets and tangled vines, over mossy rocks and mouldering logs. Still the hoarse surging of the rapids followed them; and when, parting the screen of foliage, they looked out upon the river, they saw it thick set with rocks where, plunging over ledges, gurgling under drift-logs, darting along clefts, and boiling in chasms, the angry waters filled the solitude with monotonous ravings.

If we have any doubts about the accuracy of Parkman's perceptions or the tangibility of his narrative, he satisfies us with an apt footnote: "In spite of the changes of civilization, the tourist, with Champlain's journal in his hand, can easily trace each stage of his progress." The extraordinary balance of Parkman's use of historical sources and his own firsthand observation of the sites in question improves throughout *France and England in North America.* He was a master of the amalgamation of personal impressions with what James Russell Lowell called "the rights of facts, however disconcerting, as at least sleeping-partners in the business of history." Quite simply, it is the basis of his literary reputation.

Champlain is the first of Parkman's heroic explorers and the most attractive. Following Jacques Cartier, who first sailed up the St. Lawrence River, in 1608 Champlain founded a settlement at Quebec, which he then used as a base to explore the upper reaches of the Ottawa River, Lake Champlain, and Lake Huron. It was he who began the Canadian policy of supporting the Huron Indians in their warfare against the Iroquois. Describing Champlain's progress toward the future site of Quebec, Parkman clearly adumbrates his importance in the history of New France.

A lonely ship sailed up the St. Lawrence. The white whales floundering in the Bay of Tadoussac, and the wild duck diving as the foaming prow drew near,—there was no life but these in all that watery solitude, twenty miles from shore to shore. The ship was from Honfleur, and was commanded by Samuel de Champlain. He was the Aeneas of a destined people, and in her womb lay the embryo life of Canada.

Like Aeneas (and like Parkman), Champlain was caught between two traditions. According to the historian, he belonged "rather to the Middle Age than to the seventeenth century," yet the spirit of discovery was strong within him, a sure sign for Parkman that modernity was stirring. Champlain belonged to a type of epic different from that of Aeneas. When he wandered into the forest in pursuit of a bird, he did not discover, as Aeneas did, that it was the dove of Venus; and, instead of gaining access to his forefathers in the underworld, Champlain was simply lost on a virgin continent: "He had found paths in the wilderness, but they were not made by human feet."

Champlain had not planned to found a new empire; like most of the early explorers, he was searching for a northwestern route to the Indies. Yet his character was formed for the paternal role the new colony required; he administered a firm justice and at the same time displayed considerable patience with the men who surrounded him; and he won Parkman's further praise for his interest in horticulture. The heroes of Parkman's later works are almost all flawed in various ways; and of all the explorers who appear in *France and England in North America,* only Champlain resembles his medieval ideal of piety and manliness, what he once called "Religion towards God, devotion towards women." He was the "faithful soldier," the *"preux chevalier,* the crusader, the romance-loving explorer," who died in 1635 in the village of Quebec.

Jesuit influence predominated in Quebec when Champlain died. *The Jesuits in North America in the Seventeenth Century* (1867) examines the fragile web of missions they established across hundreds of miles of wilderness. Parkman's interest in this religious order pervades his works, for he perceived it as a particularly insidious force in Canadian history. Yet, whatever he makes of their failings in other volumes, the Jesuits of this book are Christian heroes. Even in *Pioneers* his enchantment with their missionary activities bursts forth: "Who can define the Jesuits? The story of their missions is marvellous as a tale of chivalry, or legends of the lives of saints." Romance, as much as historical importance, was the basis of his interest.

But Parkman was a connoisseur of the romantic, and he distinguished carefully between a tale of chivalry and the lives of saints, for he felt the latter were in large part the results of credulous and overwrought imaginations. For the corporeal warfare of the Jesuits he had just and ample praise; but he wrote, as he often said, as a heretic, and he viewed their spiritual fantasies with a scorn exceeded only by his contempt for Indian mythology and religion. His brief stay with the Passionists in Rome in 1844 had not gone far toward revealing the inner motions of the Catholic spirit; and for the Jesuits, who, he claimed, "had revived in Europe the mediaeval type of Christianity, with all its attendant superstitions," he felt little spiritual sympathy.

Parkman's attitudes toward the Jesuits are part of a larger feeling of anticlericalism and reflect the coolness of his own religious beliefs. His Unitarian upbringing resulted in a poorly concealed dislike for the Puritans and the strictures of New England orthodoxy, a dislike conceived, no doubt, when Sundays came and he was brought home from his grandfather's farm to attend church. In one respect the Jesuits were distinctly preferable to the clergy of Parkman's New England: though they employed an "equivocal system of morality," and though their spiritual exercises did "horrible violence to the noblest qualities of manhood," yet "action is the end of [their] existence." In contrast, the "pope" of nineteenth-century Unitarianism seemed pale: "I remember to have had a special aversion for the Rev. Dr. Channing, not for his heresies, but for his meager proportions, sedentary habits, environment of close air and female parishioners. . . ." For Parkman the clergy of New England, seventeenth-century and nineteenth-century alike, were too often emasculate, though there were remarkable exceptions, his great-grandfather among them. Against this background the Jesuit missions, built among the Huron tribes and torn apart by the Iroquois, seemed an amazing work of unlikely heroism.

Parkman's primary objection to the Jesuits was their effect on the young colony of New France.

Quebec wore an aspect half military, half monastic. At sunrise and sunset, a squad of soldiers in the pay of the Company paraded in the fort; and, as in Champlain's time, the bells of the church rang morning, noon, and night. Confessions, masses, and penances were punctiliously observed; and, from the governor to the meanest laborer, the Jesuit watched and guided all. The social atmosphere of New England itself was not more suffocating.

To Canada's secular heroes—explorers, soldiers, and woodsmen—the Jesuit presence was a deterrent and an unconscionable (for Parkman) violation of intellectual independence. In the following volume he described La Salle's reason for leaving the Society of Jesus, surely an extension of his own reaction to its principles: to find himself "the passive instrument of another's will, taught to walk in prescribed paths, to renounce his individuality and become a component atom of a vast whole,—would have been intolerable to him."

Yet the same creed made heroes out of the strangest raw material. At one point in *The Jesuits,* Parkman supposes a Lenten meeting of the missionaries still alive in 1649.

Here was Bressani, scarred with firebrand and knife; Chabanel, once a professor of rhetoric in France, now a missionary, bound by a self-imposed vow to a life from which his nature recoiled; the fanatical Chaumonot, whose character savored of his peasant birth,—for the grossest fungus of superstition that ever grew under the shadow of Rome was not too much for his omnivorous credulity, and miracles and mysteries were his daily food; yet, such as his faith was, he was ready to die for it. Garnier, beardless like a woman, was of a far finer nature. His religion was of the affections and the sentiments; and his imagination, warmed with the ardor of his faith, shaped the ideal forms of his worship into visible realities. Brébeuf sat conspicuous among his brethren, portly and tall, his short moustache and beard grizzled with time,—for he was fifty-six years old. If he seemed impassive, it was because one overmastering principle had merged and absorbed all the impulses of his nature and all the faculties of his mind.

From this account one man, Isaac Jogues, is conspicuously absent. His story is typical of the heroism displayed by all these men. Captured by the Iroquois in 1642, he endured their incredibly brutal tortures, and baptized and instructed their children during intervals of peace. Two years after his capture he escaped, and after a long and difficult journey, returned to France, where he was summoned before the queen. She "kissed his mutilated hands, while the ladies of the Court thronged around to do him homage." Almost immediately he sailed again for the mission in Canada, where he was murdered by the Iroquois in 1646. The Iroquois warriors made martyrs of most of these men (and the Catholic Church has sanctified them), but before they died, the Jesuit missionaries had demonstrated their effect on the Hurons: an Indian from one of the mission tribes was "a savage still, but not so often a devil."

In spite of the perpetual terror caused by hostile Indians and in spite of the somber influence of the Jesuits, the spiritual atmosphere of New France had about it a picturesqueness and charm that could not be discovered in iron-clad New England. The founding of Montreal in 1642 by Paul de Maisonneuve and his associates (mainly from the Sulpitian order) is a fine example of these qualities, and Parkman's account deserves to be quoted at length, for it is one of the most admirably conceived passages in the early volumes of *France and England in North America*. Sailing upriver from the comparative safety of Quebec, Maisonneuve and his companions came in sight of the shoreline that had first been considered for settlement by Champlain.

Maisonneuve sprang ashore, and fell on his knees. His followers imitated his example; and all joined their voices in enthusiastic songs of thanksgiving. Tents, baggage, arms, and stores were landed. An altar was raised on a pleasant spot near at hand; and Mademoiselle Mance, with Madame de la Peltrie, aided by her servant, Charlotte Barré, decorated it with a taste which was the admiration of the beholders. Now all the company gathered before the shrine. Here stood Vimont, in the rich vestments of his office. Here were the two ladies, with their servant; Montmagny, no very willing spectator; and Maisonneuve, a warlike figure, erect and tall, his men clustering around him,— soldiers, sailors, artisans, and laborers,—all alike soldiers at need. They kneeled in reverent silence as the Host was raised aloft; and when the rite was over, the priest turned and addressed them:—

"You are a grain of mustard-seed, that shall rise and grow till its branches overshadow the earth. You are few, but your work is the work of God. His smile is on you, and your children shall fill the land."

The afternoon waned; the sun sank behind the western forest, and twilight came on. Fireflies were twinkling over the darkened meadow. They caught them, tied them with threads into shining festoons, and hung them before the altar, where the Host remained exposed. Then they pitched their tents, lighted their bivouac fires, stationed their guards, and lay down to rest. Such was the birth-night of Montreal.

Is this true history, or a romance of Christian chivalry? It is both.

From this Parkman turned to a darker romance of secular errantry. Long one of his most popular books, *La Salle and the Discovery of the Great West* (originally published in 1869 as *The Discovery of the Great West*), is also one of the most flawed historically. A strong, dramatic narrative of the discovery of the Ohio and Illinois rivers and the navigation of the Mississippi, the effectiveness of *La Salle* depends on the telescopic isolation of its hero, who, in his determined way, holds center stage in the wilderness. Recent scholarship on La Salle and the documentary sources for his life, though biased in its own ways, has shown that the great body of material assembled by Pierre Margry, which Parkman used in the revision of *La Salle,* was presented by its editor in a manner betraying his extreme prejudice on behalf of the explorer. The effect of Margry's editorial bias is easily overemphasized, for Parkman's revision of *La Salle* in 1879 only makes more evident the fact that he, too, had something at stake in bringing La Salle forward as the greatest explorer of New France.

In portraying his hero, Parkman permitted himself an unaccustomed latitude in the use of obviously questionable documents and in the interpretation of evidence. The reader of *La Salle* finds it impossible to escape the conclusion that he also put more of himself into this characterization than into any other. *La Salle* is an oblique reflection of *The Oregon Trail* and the subsequent course of Parkman's life, the historian and the explorer protagonists in a valiant struggle against all odds.

"The wild and mournful story of the explorers of the Mississippi" begins in the mid-1660's with La Salle's rejection of the Jesuits, with whom he had been associated in youth. For Parkman this had dual significance, and it forms the basis for two predominant strains in his portrait of La Salle: the explorer's battle against an unseen host of enemies (mainly Jesuits and government officials) and his spiritual kinship with the modern world.

Claims for the latter are somewhat exaggerated. Virtually by fiat Parkman declares the modernity of La Salle's temperament in comparison with that of other explorers. He portrays Jacques Marquette, who with Louis Jolliet discovered the Mississippi in 1673, as a spiritual brother to the Jesuit missionaries, enshrouded by romance, led on by his devotion to the Virgin Mary. On the other hand "stands the masculine form of Cavelier de la Salle. Prodigious was the contrast between the two discoverers: the one, with clasped hands and upturned eyes, seems a figure evoked from some dim legend of mediaevel saintship; the other, with feet firm planted on the hard earth, breathes the self-relying energies of modern practical enterprise."

Needless to say, this comparison begs any number of questions. Marquette did not seem so ethereal in Parkman's account of his adventures on the Mississippi. Nor does Champlain come off well in comparison.

The enthusiasm of the disinterested and chivalrous Champlain was not the enthusiasm of La Salle. . . . He belonged not to the age of the knight-errant and the saint, but to the modern world of practical study and practical action. He was the hero not of a principle nor of a faith, but simply of a fixed idea and a determined purpose.

In his fine article on *La Salle,* William R. Taylor has pointed out the depth of Parkman's interest in the motivation of his hero. It seems clear that what Parkman heralds as the dawning of the modern sensibility is the emergence of individual will (and, one might add, of neurosis). It is less important for him that La Salle discovered the Illinois and Ohio rivers and explored the Mississippi to its mouth, crossing back and forth to Canada to perform each of these feats, than that he did so against almost insuperable obstacles. In comparison with the blind determination of La Salle, the deeds of Champlain, Marquette, and the Jesuits seemingly have less value because they were performed with some dedication to a higher cause.

This interpretation indicates the central flaw that runs throughout *La Salle.* Without entering into the substantial claims of his enemies (and, what is worse, allowing La Salle to defend himself in his letters), Parkman presents the explorer as a beleaguered hero beset by hostility. Again and again La Salle emerges unscathed from a thicket of persecution and is typified as a man in whom "an unconquerable mind held at its service a frame of iron, and tasked it to the utmost of its endurance." In the face of "disasters, sorrows, and deferred hopes; time, strength, and wealth spent in vain; a ruinous past and a doubtful future; slander, obloquy, and hate," La Salle becomes "the patient voyager" with "unmoved heart," breathing the calm spirit of heroism.

La Salle is the dark hero, and his story the dark heart of Parkman's entire historical work. One searches for irony or a sense of balance in his portrait, but there is little of either. The weakness of the rhetoric he uses to characterize the explorer signifies the intensity of his desire to create a hero of heroes, a "pioneer of Western pioneers." Unquestionably, La Salle was a great explorer; just as certainly, though, the grandiose nature of his plans was more than a mere "chimera." His final work of exploration on the desolate coast of Texas, four hundred miles from the mouth of the Mississippi, where he wished to be, ended in dismal failure, his assassination, and the death of almost all his fellow settlers.

Overshadowing Parkman's portrait of La Salle is his personal myth of masculine heroism. The reflections of the historian in his image of La Salle have often been commented upon, and for good reason. With the same determination he attributes to the explorer, Parkman struggled against his infirmities, completing against all odds the work he undertook at the age of eighteen. The myth of masculine heroism, which was fully embodied in his own life, unfortunately warped his estimate of La Salle. Although it sustained him in the worst of his painful circumstances, his romantic reverence for masculinity, determination, and unyielding perseverance in the pursuit of a "fixed idea" led

Parkman in *La Salle and the Discovery of the Great West* into an unintended parody of his most cherished ideals.

The first three volumes of *France and England in North America* primarily concern the periphery of Canadian society. The exploits of Champlain, the Jesuit missionaries, and La Salle unfold in the interior of the continent, removed by weeks and months of travel from the lower St. Lawrence; behind them only a fragmentary image of the settlements at Quebec and Montreal emerges. In the next two volumes, *The Old Régime in Canada* (1874) and *Count Frontenac and New France Under Louis XIV* (1877), Parkman reverses the proportions. The political and religious turmoil in Montreal and Quebec, the economic life of Canada, and the character of its people and institutions are all brought forward, while the explorers move about on a very remote stage. The plan for both *The Old Régime* and *Frontenac* is laid out in the preface to the earlier of these works: "In the present book we examine the political and social machine; in the next volume of the series we shall see this machine in action."

The organization and subject of *The Old Régime* necessitated a loss of dramatic effectiveness. The book is divided into three parts: "The Feudal Chiefs of Acadia" (added in the revised edition of 1893), "Canada a Mission" (in which Parkman's account of François de Laval and the Jesuits provoked a considerable controversy among Canadian readers), and, most important by far, "The Colony and the King." As in *A Half-Century of Conflict,* completed almost twenty years later, Parkman tries to compensate for the miscellaneous nature of his subject matter by resorting to an unusual number of overt, manipulative rhetorical devices. He replaces strong narrative with a strong narrator; indeed, the overriding structure of the work is highly artificial. The necessary flatness of much of his subject also leads him to compensate with excessive descriptive detail.

In the previous volumes Parkman occasionally tried to draw the past forward by commenting on the present appearance of many historical sites. In *The Old Régime* one is continually led back and forth from past to present to past, with very little subtlety: "Above all," Parkman recommends, "do not fail to make your pilgrimage to the shrine of St. Anne." Even when his topographical detail is confined to one tense, his prose grows florid in a way it had not done since *Pontiac:* "October had begun, and the romantic wilds breathed the buoyant life of the most inspiring of American seasons." One could describe this volume as he describes the annual fair at Montreal: "not always edifying, but always picturesque."

In an attempt to reveal the organic flaw of New France, the cause of its defeat by the British, Parkman describes in "The Colony and the King" various components of Canadian society—"Paternal Government," "Canadian Feudalism," "Trade and Industry," and "Morals and Manners." The purpose that links this episodic, anecdotal history of New France between 1661 and 1763 surfaces most visibly in the final chapter, "Canadian Absolutism." Here, Parkman presents in barest form his explanation of the failure of France to create a vital, proliferating colony in the New World. In spite of his love for the martial vigor of New France, it is largely a one-sided account, argued with the best imperative tone of New England. In his opinion three things contributed to the fall of French Canada: the character of its institutions, the "historical antecedents" of its people, and the racial temperament of the French. The people of Canada were pinioned between oppressive "paternal" and "maternal" authorities (state and church) on the one hand, and the unrestrained freedom of the forest on the other. They were, he argues, neither historically nor

racially equipped to create the conditions necessary for growth and cultural development.

In contrast, New England appears to offer all that New France lacked. Parkman seldom yields to the moralizing tendencies so prevalent in the historical writing of his time, and he is usually pessimistic in the extreme about the actual political conditions of any government; but in his account of "Canadian Absolutism" he hesitates neither to moralize nor to present the political systems of the New England colonies (usually described in highly critical terms) in a generalized and extremely favorable light. "In the building up of colonies," Parkman says, "England succeeded and France failed. The cause lies chiefly in the vast advantage drawn by England from the historical training of her people in habits of reflection, forecast, industry, and self-reliance."

A similar strain of argument occurs when he turns to the problem of race:

The Germanic race, and especially the Anglo-Saxon branch of it, is peculiarly masculine, and, therefore, peculiarly fitted for self-government. It submits its action habitually to the guidance of reason, and has the judicial faculty of seeing both sides of a question. The French Celt is cast in a different mould. . . . He delights in abstractions and generalizations, cuts loose from unpleasing facts, and roams through an ocean of desires and theories.

Parkman concludes that a "man, to be a man, must feel that he holds his fate, in some good measure, in his own hands," and that "freedom is for those who are fit for it." Whatever else one may say about the truth of these arguments and conclusions, they do not conform to modern notions of historical argument or of historical causation. These arguments and conclusions have dated more than any other element of Parkman's work.

Near the end of *The Old Régime*, Parkman

writes this farewell: "And now we, too, will leave Canada. . . . The ship sails in the morning; and before the old towers of Rochelle rise in sight there will be time to smoke many a pipe, and ponder what we have seen on the banks of the St. Lawrence." This is not merely an audacious rhetorical gesture and a feat of historical imagination; it is, in a sense, a literal leave-taking of part of his subject. Turning away from the exploration of North America, in which the French played an obviously superior role, he prepares us for a struggle between political systems in which English liberty, adapted to the conditions of the New World, eventually triumphs. *The Old Régime* marks the transition from an exploratory to a military phase of Parkman's history, and it inaugurates the shift in perspective from the French to the English that takes place in the rest of the series.

Between 1672 and 1682, and again from 1689 to 1698, Canada was governed by Count Louis de Frontenac, a domineering figure, a soldier, and a courtier. Having come to New France partly to repair his fortunes and partly to escape his wife, he became a friend and supporter of La Salle. "There was between them," Parkman wrote, "the sympathetic attraction of two bold and energetic spirits; and though Cavelier de la Salle had neither the irritable vanity of the Count nor his Gallic vivacity of passion, he had in full measure the same unconquerable pride and hardy resolution." Though there are similarities in his portraits of the two men— Frontenac's "whole career was one of conflict"—Parkman's account of the governor is far more balanced and temperate. Frontenac was a civil leader with military prowess, capable of exacting duty, if not affection, from the Canadians and admiration from the Indians.

Parkman has often been accused of writing a "great man" version of history, but his narrative of Frontenac's administration belies that charge. If, as he asserts, Frontenac is a "re-markable figure" characterized by "bold and salient individuality and sharply marked light and shadow," he nevertheless concludes that "greatness must be denied him." Frontenac was simply the most compelling governor of seventeenth-century Canada, possessing the truest vision of its needs. "His policy was to protect the Indian allies at all risks; to repel by force, if necessary, every attempt of the English to encroach on the territory in dispute; and to occupy it by forts which should be at once posts of war and commerce and places of rendezvous for traders and *voyageurs.*"

Frontenac was published thirty years after *The Oregon Trail* first appeared. In the intervening time Parkman's style had strengthened considerably. Among American historians he is without question the greatest prose artist; but his abilities, though entirely evident from the first, grew slowly. Each volume of *France and England in North America* represents a stylistic advance over its predecessors; and in *Frontenac,* Parkman for the first time achieves a consistently mature prose style. As a product of the rhetorical academic training common in early nineteenth-century American colleges, he displayed at first a natural love for cumulative periods and a rolling syntax that occasionally seems more structurally dependent on rhetorical splendor than on any inner logic. With time, though, he learned to economize. Excepting those passages that concern the Old World, about which Parkman never writes without excess, *Frontenac* contains some of his most effective writing.

The improvements in style in *France and England in North America* are not merely the result of shortening sentences, using less obvious rhetorical constructions, and moving toward an increased dependence on the simple strength of noun clusters. Parkman's greatest gain, not complete until *Montcalm and Wolfe,* is a remarkably heightened awareness of the relationship between the natural tensions of his story and the available tensions of his prose. His talent for description is a powerful tool, the resources as well as the limitations of which he did not always recognize. His enchantment with his subject occasionally calls forth reveries of descriptive writing that are not always in sequence with the demands of his narrative. This leads to a strange oscillation. When the emotional crescendo of his tale would seem to require the emphasis of a descriptive excursion, it is not always forthcoming; similarly, in obedience to the demands of his personal enthusiasm, Parkman occasionally wanders away from the immediate concerns of his narrative in pursuit of some scenic reward. In *Frontenac* this discrepancy between the two emotional rhythms of his work—one called up by the story, the other called up by his own experiences—begins to disappear; and as the rhythms begin to coincide, his writing and the overall shape of his work improve dramatically.

In the preface to *Frontenac*, Parkman commented on the extent of his preparations for the final two books of his series: "The accumulation is now rather formidable; and, if it is to be used at all, it had better be used at once." Fearing for his health, he abandoned the chronological order of his history, skipped "an intervening period of less decisive importance," and wrote *Montcalm and Wolfe*, published in 1884. The postponed volume, *A Half-Century of Conflict*, appeared in 1892. It is a relatively inconsequential work that attempts, not quite successfully, to integrate events in the years between Frontenac's death, in 1698, and 1748. Though it recounts some important occurrences—Queen Anne's War, the massacre at Deerfield, and the siege of Louisbourg chief among them—*A Half-Century of Conflict* adds little to the design of Parkman's larger work; it merely extends the portrayal of the antagonism between the French and the English begun in *Frontenac* and concluded in *Montcalm and Wolfe*.

The years during which he wrote his last two volumes were full of recognition for Parkman's extraordinary achievement as a historian. He served as an overseer of Harvard, became a fellow of the Harvard Corporation, and received honorary doctorates from Williams College, McGill, and his alma mater; he also became a member of the Royal Historical Society in London and an honorary member of the London Society of Antiquarians. The habits of a scholar did not impede his love of society, though; he helped to organize the St. Botolph Club in Boston, becoming its first president, and was active in many other social organizations. But for the most part his family and his work occupied the center of his attention.

Parkman's life during this time was quiet, spent largely on research and his extensive correspondence. He had always withdrawn from Boston in the summer, and he gradually began to seek a more distant retirement than Jamaica Plain. Beginning in 1888 he spent the summers with his daughter and son-in-law at Portsmouth, New Hampshire. There, his neighbor Barrett Wendell, a professor at Harvard, knew him, and he recalled the impression Parkman made as an old man.

When one met Mr. Parkman thus taking his ease, one grew aware of a certain boyish freshness of feeling and nature in him . . . the vigor with which he would send his boat through the water, paying scant respect to the swift tidal currents of the Piscataqua, won the instant, lasting admiration of athletic boys. You felt instinctively that the man was enjoying this simple open-air pleasure as keenly as if he were a child of ten.

Wendell seized on the vital element of Parkman's work in portraying him thus, for it is exactly that boyish enthusiasm, that love discovered in youth for the historical atmosphere of New England, that transforms the matter of history into the matter of high literary art.

Years after his doctors had predicted his death, and after completing a work that few thought he would live to begin, Parkman died on November 8, 1893. One may say of him what he said of James Wolfe: "An immense moral force bore up his own frail body and forced it to its work."

Montcalm and Wolfe survives as Parkman's supreme achievement, the greatest monument of American historical writing in the nineteenth century. With the authority of more than forty years of study, he sets forth the inevitable drift toward a final conflict between the two colonies. In Louis Joseph de Montcalm and the "gallant invalid" James Wolfe he found the heroic warriors whose concluding battle on the Plains of Abraham in 1759 provided an appropriately epic summation to the work of a lifetime.

Though it covers fewer years than other volumes, the scope of *Montcalm and Wolfe* is the broadest of any of Parkman's works: in America it ranges from Virginia and the Pennsylvania border settlements to Acadia and the St. Lawrence Valley; in Europe, Parkman follows the progress of the Seven Years' War and observes in some detail the administrative shifts in the English government between 1748 and 1763. Finally, he presents in action a remarkable succession of heroes and near-heroes: Wolfe, Montcalm, George Washington, Louis de Bougainville, François de Lévis, Jeffrey Amherst, Lord William Howe, Robert Rogers, John Forbes, and Sir William Johnson, as well as a lesser host of villains and scoundrels.

The Old French War, as it was once called, was waged along the axes of two great waterways, the junction of which was Lac St. Pierre, roughly equidistant from Quebec and Montreal. Lake Ontario and the St. Lawrence River formed one axis, running roughly east and west; the Richelieu River, Lake Champlain, Lake George, and the Hudson River formed the other, running north and south. The extreme

flanks of action were Louisbourg, in what is now Nova Scotia and was then Acadia, and Fort Niagara, at the falls between Lake Erie and Lake Ontario, as well as Fort Duquesne (now Pittsburgh), south and west of Niagara. Because the Lake George–Lake Champlain waterway was the only convenient means of communication between the two colonies, it formed the central corridor of military action. Forts William Henry, Ticonderoga, and Crown Point all lay on its shores, and each was the site of at least one important battle. While the French maintained an almost exclusively defensive war (excepting, of course, the continual harassment of the borders by Canadians and Indians), the English tried to push up Lake George and Lake Champlain and toward Quebec from both flanks along the St. Lawrence. The dénouement—Wolfe's successful assault on Quebec itself—was a surprise to everyone, for he was outmanned by an enemy ensconced in one of the greatest natural fortresses in the world.

In *Montcalm and Wolfe,* Parkman's shift in perspective from the French to the English is completed. He maintains a consistent parallel between the opposing camps and colonies, but the emotional weight of the book falls squarely on the English side. A change of character had come over both colonies and their parent countries. Louis XIV and his strong colonial ministers had given way to Louis XV and the marquise de Pompadour, whose "fatuity" "made the conquest of Canada possible." Always plagued by abuses of power, New France had become "the prey of official jackals" who vitiated the economy and demoralized the people. Moreover, Canada was at this time governed by the vainglorious Pierre de Vaudreuil, who hampered Montcalm's efforts to wage an effective campaign. What Parkman had once said of New England was now true of its foe: "She has not been fruitful ... in salient and striking forms of character."

But it was not merely the decay of New France that led Parkman to focus on the English side of the war. It was the change that had taken place within the British colonies, particularly New England. Though Parkman respected the foundation upon which the colonies were established—the search for religious liberty—he detested the actual political form they assumed. In *The Old Régime* he bitterly attacked the assumption that the early settlers had cherished a broader freedom: "Their mission was to build up a western Canaan, ruled by the law of God; to keep it pure from error, and, if need were, purge it of heresy by persecution,—to which ends they set up one of the most detestable theocracies on record." This fact, and the timidity with which the English colonists faced the wilderness at their borders, rendered them highly repugnant to Parkman.

By the middle of the eighteenth century, though, the Puritan ardor of New England had abated, a new secularism was visible in many of the colonies, and the only sectaries still repellent in Parkman's eyes were the Quakers of Philadelphia, whose passivity during Indian raids on the Pennsylvania border prolonged the agony of the settlers. A new energy animated the populace; traders, backwoodsmen, and eventually families began to penetrate the forest; and Massachusetts, New York, and Virginia produced a generation of heroes that had no contemporary counterpart in New France. The history of the forest is first and foremost a history of forest heroes. While New France had been bold and active in the wilderness, Parkman told its story; but now that the British colonies had taken the lead, he would tell theirs.

To the episodic richness of the Old French War, Parkman brings a depth of emotion that is unsurpassed in any of his other works. He quietly weights his account of the war by subtly intensifying his picture of the English forces while he undermines our sympathies with the French. Early in *Montcalm and Wolfe,* Montcalm and Vaudreuil emerge as principal spokesmen for the French; both are represented by their abundant personal and official correspondence. The use of their letters was inevitable, for Vaudreuil held the highest civil position, and Montcalm the highest military command, in New France, yet it has important implications for Parkman's characterization of the plight of Canada. Writing to his family and to his superiors in France, Montcalm appears in a flattering light. As befits the Canadian heroic counterpart to Wolfe, he is described more fully than any other French officer, and we feel a natural sympathy for a man capable of such evident affection and courage. With Vaudreuil, it is quite another matter. Boastful and ineffective, he is revealed in his letters as an agent of the moral degradation at the heart of French colonial bureaucracy.

Different as these two men are, they both represent the same echelon of Canadian society; and in this work Parkman's perspective on the Canadian social structure descends only slightly lower. Literacy did not extend very far through the ranks of the Canadian people and French soldiers: below the highest level of society, first-hand accounts of the war, in the form of letters and diaries, simply were not available. Thus, we see Canada almost entirely from a perspective (in Vaudreuil's letters) that emphasizes corruption and personal vanity or from one (in Montcalm's letters) that provides a reflection of social and official excesses and an ironic commentary on them. In *Montcalm and Wolfe* the only man in New France with whom we fully sympathize also serves as one of the harshest critics of that country.

The picture that emerges of New England and the English forces in general is created in an entirely different manner. There is no single English or colonial source that prevails throughout the book; instead, Parkman draws on the correspondence and diaries of nearly all the important officers and government officials. Furthermore, he employs in a brilliant manner the records left by humbler members of the army and the provincial populace. On the whole, literacy was more prevalent in the English and American force than in its French and Canadian counterpart. Parkman makes effective use of this difference, for he portrays a far broader range of society. By quoting numerous sermons, letters, diaries, and reported conversations, he bestows on the men and women of New England a visible life that he denies the people of New France. The fullness of his delineation carries with it a strong emotional impact. Against the narrow, corrupt world of Quebec and Montreal, New England seems fertile and resilient.

The depth of Parkman's feeling for New England and its people, as well as the breadth of his social vision in this work, nowhere appears more forcefully than in this passage, which describes the men of Sir William Johnson's army:

The soldiers were no soldiers, but farmers and farmers' sons who had volunteered for the summer campaign. One of the corps had a blue uniform faced with red. The rest wore their daily clothing. Blankets had been served out to them by the several provinces, but the greater part brought their own guns. . . . They had no bayonets, but carried hatchets in their belts as a sort of substitute. At their sides were slung powder-horns, on which, in the leisure of the camp, they carved quaint devices with the points of their jack-knives. They came chiefly from plain New England homesteads,—rustic abodes, unpainted and dingy, with long well-sweeps, capacious barns, rough fields of pumpkins and corn, and vast kitchen chimneys, above which in winter hung squashes to keep them from frost, and guns to keep them from rust.

Simple as these nouns and their cadences are, they resonate with emotional intensity. In similar passages throughout *Montcalm and Wolfe,* Parkman quietly vindicates the goodness and strength of the American heritage.

This emotional vindication has a moral dimension as well, one that is directly linked to Parkman's purpose in writing history. Though the history of the forest was initially conceived in his mind largely without ethical connotations, it was written in a spirit of moral exemplification. Like the rest of *France and England in North America, Montcalm and Wolfe* balances two contrasting historical motions. The one most commonly recognized is the familiar nineteenth-century conception of the transition from the medieval mind to the modern, from "barren absolutism" to "a liberty, crude, incoherent, and chaotic, yet full of prolific vitality." This view of history is inherently optimistic, for it implies a belief in progress, in the improvement of the human condition.

But *France and England in North America* also asserts a deeply pessimistic conclusion about historical development. Parkman's conservative history provides a series of moral exempla against which we may measure the extent of our decay. Placed against the grander dimensions of the past, Parkman concludes, the vaunted aggregate advance of the American people appears as individual decline. America, he writes,

. . . has tamed the savage continent, peopled the solitude, gathered wealth untold, waxed potent, imposing, redoubtable; and now it remains for her to prove, if she can, that the rule of the masses is consistent with the highest growth of the individual; that democracy can give the world a civilization as mature and pregnant, ideas as energetic and vitalizing, and types of manhood as lofty and strong, as any of the systems which it boasts to supplant.

The millennial language in the first clause of this sentence ironically echoes the claims of a booming nation; but Parkman's true conclusion to *Montcalm and Wolfe* and to his work as a whole is the hesitant, doubtful challenge that follows. America's history is somehow larger and nobler than its destiny, he suggests; only by studying its history well can we correct this imbalance between past and future, between promise and fulfillment.

Selected Bibliography

WORKS OF FRANCIS PARKMAN

BOOKS

The California and Oregon Trail. New York: Putnam, 1849. First published serially in *Knickerbocker* magazine (1847–49) as *The Oregon Trail*.

History of the Conspiracy of Pontiac. . . . Boston: Little, Brown, 1851. Published after 1870 as *The Conspiracy of Pontiac. . . .*

Vassall Morton: A Novel. Boston: Phillips, Sampson, 1856.

Pioneers of France in the New World. Boston: Little, Brown, 1865.

The Book of Roses. Boston: J. E. Tilton, 1866.

The Jesuits in North America in the Seventeenth Century. Boston: Little, Brown, 1867.

The Discovery of the Great West. Boston: Little, Brown, 1869. Extensively revised in the eleventh edition (1879) and subsequently published as *La Salle and the Discovery of the Great West*.

The Old Régime in Canada. Boston: Little, Brown, 1874.

Count Frontenac and New France Under Louis XIV. Boston: Little, Brown, 1877.

Some of the Reasons Against Woman Suffrage. N.p., n.d. (1883).

Montcalm and Wolfe. Boston: Little, Brown, 1884.

An Open Letter to a Temperance Friend. N.p., n.d. (ca. 1885).

Our Common Schools. . . . N.p., n.d. (1890).

A Half-Century of Conflict. Boston: Little, Brown, 1892.

The Journals of Francis Parkman, edited by Mason Wade. New York: Harper, 1947.

Letters of Francis Parkman, edited by Wilbur R. Jacobs. Norman: University of Oklahoma Press, 1960.

ARTICLES

"The New Hampshire Ranger." *Knickerbocker Magazine*, 26:146–48 (August 1845).

"Satan and Dr. Carver." *Knickerbocker Magazine*, 26:515–25 (December 1845).

"The Works of James Fenimore Cooper." *North American Review*, 74:147–61 (January 1852).

"Exploring the Magalloway." *Harper's Magazine*, 29:735–41 (November 1864).

"Manners and Customs of Primitive Indian Tribes." *North American Review*, 101:28–64 (July 1865).

"Indian Superstitions." *North American Review*, 103:1–18 (July 1866).

"The Tale of the Ripe Scholar." *Nation*, 9:558–60 (December 23, 1869).

"The Failure of Universal Suffrage." *North American Review*, 127:1–20 (July–August 1878).

"Mr. Parkman and His Canadian Critics." *Nation*, 27:66–67 (August 1, 1878).

"The Woman Question." *North American Review*, 129:303–21 (October 1879).

"The Woman Question Again." *North American Review*, 130:16–30 (January 1880).

"Francis Parkman on the Indians." *The Critic*, n.s. 5:248 (May 1886).

"A Convent at Rome." *Harper's Magazine*, 81:448–54 (August 1890).

COLLECTED AND SELECTED EDITIONS

Francis Parkman's Works. 12 (later 13) vols. Boston: Little, Brown, 1898. New Library edition.

Francis Parkman: Representative Selections, edited by Wilbur L. Schramm. New York: American Book Co., 1938.

The Parkman Reader, edited by Samuel Eliot Morison. Boston: Little, Brown, 1955.

MODERN REPRINTS

Montcalm and Wolfe. Introduction by Samuel Eliot Morison. New York: Collier, 1962.

The Oregon Trail, edited by E. N. Feltskog. Madison: University of Wisconsin Press, 1969.

BIBLIOGRAPHIES

Blanck, Jacob. "Francis Parkman." In *Bibliography of American Literature,* vol. VI. New Haven: Yale University Press, 1973. Pp. 541–56.

Spiller, Robert, et al. *Literary History of the United States of America.* 2 vols. 4th ed. New York: Macmillan, 1974.

See also bibliographies in Schramm, *Francis Parkman: Representative Selections* (1938), and Wade, *Francis Parkman: Heroic Historian* (1942), above.

BIOGRAPHICAL AND CRITICAL STUDIES

Adams, Henry. "Review of *The Old Régime.*" *North American Review,* 120:175–79 (1875).

Alvord, Clarence W. "Francis Parkman." *Nation,* 117:394–96 (1923).

Bassett, J. S., ed. "Letters of Francis Parkman to Pierre Margry." *Smith College Studies in History,* 8:123–208 (1923).

Brooks, Van Wyck. *New England: Indian Summer.* New York: Dutton, 1940.

DeVoto, Bernard. *The Year of Decision 1846.* Boston: Little, Brown, 1943.

Doughty, Howard. *Francis Parkman.* New York: Macmillan, 1962.

Eccles, W. J. "The History of New France According to Francis Parkman." *William and Mary Quarterly,* 18:163–75 (1961).

Farnham, Charles Haight. *A Life of Francis Parkman.* Boston: Little, Brown, 1900.

Fiske, John. *A Century of Science and Other Essays.* Boston: Houghton, Mifflin, 1899.

Frothingham, O. B. "Memoir of Francis Parkman, LL.D." *Proceedings of the Massachusetts Historical Society,* 2nd ser., 8:520–62 (1894).

Gale, Robert L. *Francis Parkman.* New York: Twayne, 1973.

Jacobs, Wilbur R. "Some Social Ideas of Francis Parkman." *American Quarterly,* 9:387–97 (1957).

————. "Highlights of Parkman's Formative Period." *Pacific Historical Review,* 27:149–58 (1958).

————. "Francis Parkman's Oration 'Romance in America.'" *American Historical Review,* 68:692–97 (1963).

Jennings, F. P. "A Vanishing Indian: Francis Parkman Versus His Sources." *Pennsylvania Magazine of History and Biography,* 87:306–23 (1963).

Jordy, William. "Henry Adams and Francis Parkman." *American Quarterly,* 3:52–68 (1951).

Levin, David. *History as Romantic Art: Bancroft, Prescott, Motley, and Parkman.* Stanford, Calif.: Stanford University Press, 1959.

Lewis, R. W. B. *The American Adam: Innocence, Tragedy, and Tradition in the Nineteenth Century.* Chicago: University of Chicago Press, 1955.

Nevins, Allan. "Prescott, Motley, Parkman." In *American Writers on American Literature,* edited by John Macy. New York: Dutton, 1931. Pp. 226–42.

Nye, Russell B. "Parkman, Red Fate, and White Civilization." In *Essays on American Literature in Honor of Jay B. Hubbell,* edited by Clarence Gohdes. Durham, N.C.: Duke University Press, 1967. Pp. 152–63.

Pease, Otis A. *Parkman's History: The Historian as Literary Artist.* New Haven: Yale University Press, 1953.

Peckham, Howard H. "The Sources and Revisions of Parkman's *Pontiac.*" *Publications of the Bibliographical Society of America,* 37:293–307 (1943).

Schramm, Wilbur L. "Parkman's Novel." *American Literature,* 9:218–27 (1937).

Sedgwick, Henry Dwight. *Francis Parkman.* Boston: Houghton, Mifflin, 1904.

Sullivan, James. "Sectionalism in Writing History." *Journal of the New York State Historical Association,* 2:73–88 (1921).

Taylor, William R. "That Way Madness Lies: Nature and Human Nature in Parkman's *La Salle.*" In *In Defense of Reading,* edited by Reuben A. Brower and Richard Poirier. New York: Dutton, 1962. Pp. 256–81.

Thompson, Richard A. "Francis Parkman on the Nature of Man." *Mid-America,* 42:3–17 (1960).

Vitzthum, Richard C. "The Historian as Editor: Francis Parkman's Reconstruction of Sources in *Montcalm and Wolfe.*" *Journal of American History,* 53:471–86 (1966).

————. *The American Compromise: Theme and Method in the Histories of Bancroft, Parkman, and Adams.* Norman: University of Oklahoma Press, 1974.

Wade, Mason. *Francis Parkman: Heroic Historian.* New York: Viking, 1942.

Walsh, James E. *"The California and Oregon Trail: A Bibliographical Study." New Colophon,* 3:279–85 (1950).

Wendell, Barrett. "Francis Parkman." *Proceedings of the American Academy of Arts and Sciences,* 29:435–47 (1893–1894).

Wheelwright, Edward. "Memoir of Francis Parkman." *Publications of the Colonial Society of Massachusetts,* 1:304–50 (1894).

Wrong, George M. "Francis Parkman." *Canadian Historical Review,* 4:289–303 (1923).

—VERLYN KLINKENBORG

Thomas Pynchon

1937–

For Henry Adams at the turn of the twentieth century, history was like a cannonball coming directly toward him, and he could trace its five-thousand-year curve. Its momentum increased just before Constantine set up the cross; it swerved as Johann Gutenberg printed the Bible and Christopher Columbus discovered a new world; it was given a new curve by Galileo and Francis Bacon. But in 1900 "the continuity snapped." And Adams conveyed the dislocation, in *The Education of Henry Adams* (1918), not only in his metaphors but also by picturing himself in the third person:

Power leaped from every atom, and enough of it to supply the stellar universe showed itself running to waste at every pore of matter. Man could no longer hold it off. Forces grasped his wrists and flung him about as though he had hold of a live wire or a runaway automobile; which was very nearly the exact truth for the purposes of an elderly and timid single gentleman in Paris, who never drove down the Champs Élysées without expecting an accident, and commonly witnessing one; or found himself in the neighborhood of an official without calculating the chances of a bomb. So long as the rates of progress held good, these bombs would double in force and number every ten years.

Thomas Pynchon opens *Gravity's Rainbow* (1973) with the experience of a rocket-bomb that goes beyond Adams' prediction. "A screaming comes across the sky. It has happened before, but there is nothing to compare it to now." For Pirate Prentice "It is too late. . . . No light anywhere. . . . He's afraid of the way the glass will fall—soon—it will be a spectacle: the fall of a crystal palace." But Pirate Prentice is only dreaming; and when he wakes up, we enter a nightmare that makes his dream and Adams' vision nostalgic interludes. For the V-2 rocket that appears as a brilliant point of light in the pink morning sky does not scream. "It travels faster than the speed of sound. The first news you get of it is the blast. Then, if you're still around, you hear the sound of it coming in. . . . You couldn't adjust to the bastards. No way." Worse than the nightmare experience of an ordinary air raid is anticipating the new rocket—which travels with unprecedented speed, confuses direction through time and space, and denies the logic of common sense. It not only snaps continuity, it explodes virtually before it arrives. It indeed signals that fall of a crystal palace—the rational, orderly world that had been the dream of nineteenth-century science and that, Henry Adams notwithstanding, had continued into the middle of the twentieth century as an ideal of progress in America.

The experience culminating in Pynchon's third novel is of more than the terror that pervaded England toward the end of World War

II. It is of the acceleration of unprecedented events that followed, especially as they affected the American psyche: the explosion of an atomic bomb that threatened a holocaust, a "cold war" that created worldwide tension and paranoia, a Korean war few people could understand, and then the Vietnam war—which showed that what Walt Whitman once heralded as "Nature without check," the "original energy" of America, had been channeled into forms of exploitation and imperialism, giving rise to riots in the ghettos, factionalism in major institutions, and a revolution in taste and manners. The acceleration also gathered its impetus from new forms of electronic communication, computerization, space exploration, and the growth of multinational industries; it would continue to gain momentum in the experience of Watergate and the energy crisis.

On the one hand, we are living with the results of unchecked energy—and Whitman's metaphor has become frighteningly literal. On the other hand, we are living with the results of a gathering rationalism that has sped up communications and made more information available as it has overloaded our circuits and subjected us to the possibility of total if undefinable control. Henry Adams had also foreseen this paradox:

The child born in 1900 would . . . be born into a new world which would not be a unity but a multiple. Adams tried to imagine it, and an education that would fit it. He found himself in a land where no one had ever penetrated before; where order was an accidental relation obnoxious to nature; artificial compulsion imposed on motion; against which every free energy of the universe revolted; and which, being merely occasional, resolved itself back into anarchy at last. He could not deny that the law of the new multiverse explained much that had been most obscure, especially the persistently fiendish treatment of man by man; the perpetual effort of society to establish law, and the perpetual revolt of society against the law it had established; the perpetual building up of authority by force, and the perpetual appeal to force to overthrow it; the perpetual symbolism of a higher law, and the perpetual relapse to a lower one; the perpetual victory of the principles of freedom, and the perpetual conversion into principles of power; but the staggering problem was the outlook ahead into the despotism of artificial order which nature abhorred.

Pynchon gives palpable shape to the "new world" Adams tried to imagine—in his fictional landscapes and the very form of his novels, which are at once multiple and monolithic, anarchic and ominously patterned. The landscape of *V.* (1963) is vast and inanimate. Called "Baedeker Land" by William Plater, it is populated by tourists (explorers, agents, hedonists, pursuers, sailors, wanderers, refugees, outcasts) and governed by an inescapable illusion of reality. If we find it difficult to keep track of the characters in *V.* (of Benny Profane as he aimlessly yo-yos, Herbert Stencil as he ceaselessly searches for V., V. as she continually transforms herself into new guises, and a host of cartoon characters who are always on the move), we also sense that they are moving in obedience to some universal but unnatural law. In *The Crying of Lot 49* (1966) the "new world" is a megalopolis, sprawling incoherently but likened to a printed circuit. It is either an accidental conglomeration or a network of freeways, motels, used-car lots, suburban lounges, television stations, corporate industries, and communications systems. The novel develops through a series of similar and intricate plots that may be real or imagined, connected or disconnected, actually or apparently related to a series of events originating in the early days of modern history and involving the official mail service and its revolutionary counterpart.

In *Gravity's Rainbow* the "new world" becomes "the Zone" through which Tyrone Slothrop travels, trying to escape pursuers of both the allies and axis, who may all be knowing or unknowing agents of the multinational synthetics industry that burgeoned as a result of World War II. Now the very life force of the universe is also the force of death, manifesting itself in the shape of both Slothrop's erection and the V-2 rocket. But, though Slothrop draws us into "the Zone," he disappears two-thirds of the way through a formless novel that is populated by hundreds of major and minor characters, that shifts its locus from one country to another, leaps from scientific formulas to the comics, from myth to Tin Pan Alley, from terror to slapstick—and yet ends where it began, with the nightmare of an approaching rocket. In the dark Orpheus movie theater we are addressed in the second person—it is *our* senseless nightmare and inescapable reality. And we are enjoined to sing along as the rocket "reaches its last unmeasurable gap above the roof.... Now everybody—"

History, for both Adams and Pynchon, is accelerating out of control and yet is governed by an impersonal force. And both are obsessed with history at least partly because of their personal stake in it. Like Adams', Pynchon's ancestors played a distinguished, if not central, role in American history. William Pynchon, who becomes William Slothrop in *Gravity's Rainbow,* was a patent holder and treasurer of the Massachusetts Bay Colony, helped found both Roxbury and Springfield, and served as a magistrate at the witchcraft trials of Hugh and Mary Parsons. But he also wrote *The Meritorious Price of Our Redemption* (1650), a heretic tract correcting the "common Errors" of the New England Puritans, who condemned the book to be burned in the Boston marketplace. His descendants included Joseph Pynchon, who was in line for the governorship of Connecticut until he supported the British in the Revolution; the Reverend Thomas Ruggles Pynchon, president

of Trinity College, who corresponded with Nathaniel Hawthorne to protest his characterization of the Pynchon family in *The House of Seven Gables* (1851); a surgeon, Dr. Edwin Pynchon, who invented the kind of instruments that Dr. Schoenmaker would use for Esther's nose job in *V.*; and a stockbroker, George M. Pynchon, who contributed to the military-industrial complex prior to World War II.

But while Pynchon has a personal stake in American history, he does not view the past from a personal, let alone official, perspective—indeed, in "Entropy" and *V.* he parodies Adams' speaking of himself in the third person. Quite on the contrary, Pynchon strives for anonymity, as if he were trying to become one of the dropouts of *The Crying of Lot 49* or the preterite of *Gravity's Rainbow*; and searching for clues to his life is like entering one of his novels. Matthew Winston (to whose "Quest for Pynchon" I am indebted for the biographical information I have found) discovered that there is no picture of him on his book jackets or in the freshman register of his class at Cornell, that his transcript mysteriously vanished from the university, and that his service record was burned after an explosion at the navy office in St. Louis.

The only facts Winston could uncover are the following. Pynchon was born in Glen Cove, New York, in 1937. In 1953 he accepted a scholarship to Cornell University. He entered in the Engineering Physics division of the College of Engineering, transferred to the College of Arts and Sciences as an English major, dropped out for two years to serve in the navy, and then returned to Cornell in 1957. During his last two years he was remembered as "the type to read books on mathematics for fun ... one who started the day at 1 P.M. with spaghetti and a soft drink ... and ... read and worked on until 3 the next morning." He was a member of the editorial staff of the *Cornell Writer*. And it was during 1957–1959 that he wrote "The Small

Rain," "Morality and Mercy in Vienna," "Low-Lands," "Entropy," and "Under the Rose" (later revised as a chapter in *V.*). When he graduated in 1959, he turned down several fellowships, including a Woodrow Wilson, as well as the chance to teach creative writing at Cornell. Pynchon considered becoming a disk jockey (like Mucho Maas, in *The Crying of Lot 49*) and was a candidate for the position of film critic at *Esquire,* but decided to work on *V.* while living with friends in Manhattan. Within a few months he accepted a job as a technical writer with Boeing in Seattle. Two years later he left to complete *V.,* which was published in 1963 and received the William Faulkner Award for the best first novel of the year. And that is all we know of Pynchon's personal life.

Indeed, Winston—whose search is more interesting than the facts he uncovered—ends "not with a revelation of Thomas Pynchon, but with a fresh sense of my own preterite spirit." Nor is Pynchon's publisher any more privileged. On March 30, 1973, Viking Press took out a full-page ad in the *New York Times* with a picture of *Gravity's Rainbow* between excerpts from ten reviews. Across the top, in felt-pen script, is the message: "Dear Thomas Pynchon, we thought you'd like to see the first reviews for your book."

Like Adams, Pynchon studied science. But Adams grasped only the outlines of what he read—admitting that he "greedily devoured" Henri Poincaré "without understanding a single consecutive page," and insisting that a student of history has no need to understand the scientific ideas of great men. Moreover, if he was stirred by the revolutionary impact of modern science, he could not fully accept the loss of unity or break the hold of mechanistic explanation. The law of acceleration, by which he explained the dynamic of history, is classically mechanistic: it allows for neither discontinuity nor a change in the material properties of the

moving object. In contrast, Pynchon studied engineering science and worked at Boeing. Moreover, he was born well into the century that astonished Adams, and seems to see nothing but discontinuity. That is, he not only understands but also has fully assimilated the concepts of modern science—where unity gives way to multiplicity, order to disorder, progress to entropy, continuity to discontinuity, the law of cause-effect to the rule of probability, the ideal of certainty to the necessity of uncertainty. And, as I will try to show, Pynchon confronts the paradox that Adams only began to glimpse: of a "new world" that is absolutely anarchic and yet totally governed by an impersonal order. But first let me outline some fundamental concepts that underlie Pynchon's imaginative construction of the "new land."

According to the classical Newtonian view, the physical universe was like a machine; its movement was continuous, and it could be completely explained in terms of matter and force. That is, through systematic investigation it would be possible to know all of its parts, formulate its laws with certainty, and harness its power for the benefit of man. At the end of the eighteenth century, Pierre Laplace postulated the ideal:

An intellect which at a given instant knew all the forces acting in nature, and the position of all things of which the world consists . . . would embrace in the same formula the motions of the greatest bodies in the universe and those of the slightest atoms; nothing would be uncertain for it, and the future, like the past, would be present to its eyes.

And the novel developed toward the same end—as the omniscient narrator, knowing the situation of all his characters and the laws of human motivation, embraced his world in a formula called the plot.

By the end of the nineteenth century, developments in thermodynamics were beginning to undermine the classical view. And Adams was no more ambivalent about the challenge than were some of the scientists who contributed to it. The first challenge arose from changing the model for the physical universe from a machine to a cylinder of gas. Alan Friedman, who is both a physicist and an illuminating reader of Pynchon, elucidates the consequences of this change in his useful "Science and Technology in *Gravity's Rainbow.*" He points out that a cylinder no bigger than a can of hair spray contains a trillion atoms bouncing off one another trillions of trillions of times a second. And since it would be impossible to apply Sir Isaac Newton's laws directly to all of them, the scientist applies statistical law, computes the typical path of an atom, and predicts the total pressure with extreme accuracy. Sacrificed in this approach, though, is the ability and even the attempt to predict the behavior of any particular atom. Indeed, a particular atom may behave unpredictably—subject only to chance or accident. As a result, the scientist no longer thinks in terms of certainty but only of probability, which, however high, can never reach 100 percent.

And while statistics are applied within the framework of Newton's laws, the framework is threatened by the shift in strategy and the acceptance of chance even as a practical convenience. Pynchon plays with the image of the unpredictable atom in *The Crying of Lot 49* when Oedipa, preparing for a game of Strip Botticelli, accidentally knocks over a can of hair spray and cowers on the bathroom floor as it caroms off the walls. Still thinking in conventional terms, though, she imagines that God or a "digital machine" might have computed its path. Indeed, her search for order throughout the novel reflects her refusal to accept the law of the "new world." In *Gravity's Rainbow,* Pynchon works with the image more seriously: Roger Mexico

can predict the striking pattern of the V-2 rockets with extreme accuracy, but never where a single rocket will land; and in this novel the antagonist Pointsman, rather than the protagonist, refuses to accept the limits of probability. Moreover, as Pynchon develops his singular form—or formlessness—from *V.* to *The Crying of Lot 49* to *Gravity's Rainbow*—the paths of his characters become less easy to plot.

Alan Friedman also points out that the model of thermodynamics does not in itself challenge classical physics; it only leads to the application of statistics and probability. In fact, the first law of thermodynamics is a statement of classical unity, for it asserts the conservation of energy— that energy cannot be created or lost, but only transformed. But the second law, as Adams recognized, threatened the ideal of a perfect machine, the power of which could be harnessed for the benefit of man. It states that systems tend to run down in time, for processes tend toward disorder. "Entropy," the measure of disorder, is the title of an early Pynchon story that schematizes a theme developed imaginatively in all of his novels. Indeed, he recognizes that entropy is a measure not only of energy but also of information.

According to Norbert Weiner, whose ideas were still being hotly discussed when Pynchon was in college, information is order; but, like energy, it is subject to disorganization in transit. Moreover, the very gathering of information (which, it was thought, enabled Maxwell's hypothetical demon to maintain order and to counter entropy) takes energy out of the system and contributes to the disorder. Anne Mangel argues that this is the ironic consequence of Oedipa's heroic quest: the more meanings and connections she finds, the more she contributes to the disorder of her world.

But Pynchon also seems to have recognized that information may be defined as disorder rather than as order. In information theory, the more uncertain a message, the more information it can convey. And entropy, being a measure of increasing information, becomes a positive tendency. In this light, as Thomas Schaub points out, Oedipa's search offers the possibility of hope—although the more she, and the reader, learn about the Tristero, the more we are overwhelmed by the amount of information and its uncertainty. Indeed, in each of his novels Pynchon draws us into a search for order, where the information and uncertainty become overwhelming, and where the search itself, while necessary and even ennobling, tends toward disorder.

But a key word in the second law of thermodynamics is "tends." A system *tends* to run down. We are back to probability. There is always a small chance of a system not running down—or of a force that counteracts thermodynamic entropy. The possibility of such a force is embodied in Pynchon's characters who search for order—Herbert Stencil in *V.,* Oedipa Maas in *The Crying of Lot 49,* Slothrop in *Gravity's Rainbow*—as well as in the reader, whom Pynchon compels to join in the search. As I have pointed out, the search may contribute to the disorder. Moreover, the very intimation of order may be a form of paranoia—and in each of his novels Pynchon taps the power of this pervasive modern phenomenon. But he may be discovering a positive as well as a negative source in paranoia, for it leads not only to solipsism but also to genuine community. And if it becomes a form of modern religion, it is also shown to be a fundamental religious impulse throughout Western history.

While thermodynamics threatened the classical view that scientists share with historians and artists, quantum mechanics demolished it. The science of elementary particles was just being formulated as Adams wrote *The Education of Henry Adams* (1918); in fact, the breakthrough was made by a man who anticipated

Adams' mentor, Josiah Gibbs, in recognizing the importance of thermodynamics. In 1900, Max Planck solved what had been an unsolvable problem by upsetting a fundamental assumption of classical physics: the continuity of nature. Although he struggled against having to accept it, he finally proved that light energy does not flow in a continuous stream but in bursts, jumps, discontinuous portions, or quanta. And in 1913, Niels Bohr used Planck's formula to show that electrons—considered one of the elementary particles of nature—jumped discontinuously from one orbit or level of energy to another.

Werner Heisenberg went even further than Planck, establishing the principle of indeterminacy. Since elementary particles are extremely small and travel at extremely high speeds, to observe one with accuracy would be to disturb it. Moreover, the more certain one becomes of its location, the less certain the velocity; and the more certain the velocity, the less certain the location. And the indeterminacy can be measured by Planck's minute but absolutely constant proportion. The very act of observation causes uncertainty—as Pynchon shows in the failures of Herbert Stencil and Oedipa Maas. But Heisenberg—and Pynchon—go further, and show that indeterminacy inheres in nature itself. (Heisenberg's theory is borne out by a phenomenon well known to physicists and described by Milič Čapek. When radioactive alpha particles with sufficient velocity are directed at an electrical barrier, they should mount it; with insufficient velocity they should be deflected. But if we are almost certain of their velocity, their position becomes uncertain. And there is a small probability—determined by Planck's constant—that some fast particles will be deflected and some slow particles will mount the wall. Which is exactly what happens.)

If *V.* and *The Crying of Lot 49* dramatize the uncertainty produced by a central character in the act of observation and investigation, *Gravity's Rainbow* shows that indeterminacy is inherent in Pynchon's world. For it lacks a central or unified observer even in the role of narrator. That is, the narrative voice and vantage shift so often, so discontinuously, and so disconcertingly that the narrator is never more than another indeterminate element in the field of the novel.

The "new world" that Adams tried to imagine and that Pynchon invokes is like the world of modern physics. It is discontinuous and uncertain, acting not like a machine but like a cylinder of gas, and governed not by the laws of cause-effect but by the rule of probability. Since it consists of elements in continual motion and individually unpredictable, and since the motion tends toward disorder, the "new world" appears anarchic. But since probability rules, it is also governed by an impersonal and despotic order that may result from either accident or design. Still, uncertainty is both a threat and a promise. Indeed, an unofficial axiom—known paradoxically as "the totalitarian law of physics"—states that "anything not forbidden is compulsory." It is this principle that led imaginative scientists to predict the existence of such improbable objects as quarks and neutrinos. And it can also explain the imaginative possibilities Pynchon discovers even as he pictures the modern condition in its darkest light.

I have attempted to explain the conceptual basis of what Pynchon turns into the landscape and form of his fiction—which is not to say that Pynchon's fiction is abstract. For it is loaded, indeed overloaded, with precisely rendered physical detail and accurate facts. As a result, his most fantastic scenes are palpably credible. If they do not mirror, they magnify social, psychological, and historical reality. As Esther submits to a nose job in *V.*, Pynchon not only provides a clinical account of the entire procedure: he also reveals the psychosexual needs of a young Jewish woman brought up on movies and advertisements, the affluence of American society in the 1950's, the deftness and power of a surgeon, the technological terror barely suppressed by ordinary appearances, the Faustian drive culminating in the displacement of nature by plastics, and the alignment of the human with the inanimate.

In *The Crying of Lot 49,* Pynchon draws us into the plastic megalopolis of the West Coast. When Oedipa prepares for a game of Strip Botticelli with Pierce Inverarity's agent in the Echo Courts Motel, she puts on enough of a wardrobe to satisfy a latter-day anthropologist:

six pairs of panties in assorted colors, girdle, three pairs of nylons, three brassieres, two pairs stretch slacks, four half-slips, one black sheath, two summer dresses, half dozen A-line skirts, three sweaters, two blouses, quilted wrapper, baby blue peignoir and old Orlon muu-muu. Bracelets then, scatterpins, earrings, a pendant.

When Oedipa thinks about how Metzger discovered her in the motel she chose at random, when Metzger appears as Baby Igor on the television show they are watching, and when the commercials advertise the products of Inverarity's interlocking corporations, she begins to wonder "if it's all part of a plot." Thus Pynchon infects us with the paranoia of the 1960's.

And in *Gravity's Rainbow* we are made to feel the cloying atmosphere of an English rooming house and the desperation of a hard-up American soldier as Slothrop enters the sitting room of Darlene's landlady and is compelled not only to stifle his desire but also to sample her prewar wine jellies: the safe-looking ribbed licorice drop that tastes like mayonnaise and orange peels, the stylized raspberry filled with what must be pure nitric acid, the miniature hand grenade with its tamarind glaze and center of cubeb berries and camphor gum, the sour gooseberry shell yielding to glutinous chunks saturated with powdered cloves. But, with the

V-2 rocket on its way, this episode also reveals the ambiguous fortitude of the English middle class. Moreover, it parodically reflects the sensuous taste of death that General Pudding developed in the World War I trenches and relishes in his masochistic rituals, and it foreshadows the dark playfulness of Captain Blicero's fairy-tale sadism as he oversees the development of the ultimate rocket. Indeed, Pynchon overwhelms us with concrete details, which critics continue to verify, not only of London during the rocket raids but also of the English intelligence operation, a general's memories of the Great War, the events leading to the development of the V-2, the Herero wars in South-West Africa, the reformation of the Turkic alphabet, American popular culture, the German film industry, the discovery of synthetics, the multinational corporations that thrived and burgeoned during World War II.

The physicality of Pynchon's world and the concrete facts that, as Edward Mendelson says, place him in the tradition of encyclopedic novelists, make his improbable stories frighteningly credible, and magnify social and psychological reality. But, presented with such incongruity, they are also the source of his comedy and, hence, of his affirmation. Pynchon may reveal the modern world as a wasteland but, unlike T. S. Eliot, he revels in the waste and disorder. In an early story called "Low-Lands," Dennis Flange leaves his home overlooking Long Island Sound for a garbage dump—where he can drink muscatel with his buddies and follow a beautiful gypsy through an old refrigerator, into a grotto of delight. This becomes the sewer in *V.,* where Benny Profane hunts blind, albino alligators; the night world of *Lot 49,* where Oedipa discovers hundreds of people who have dropped out of the Republic and communicate by depositing letters in containers marked W.A.S.T.E.; and the underground of the Zone, where Tyrone Slothrop escapes by disappearing from *Gravity's Rainbow.*

Which is to say that while Pynchon, more than any other modern novelist, makes us feel the tangible threat of disorder, disorder also excites his imagination. In the short story "The Secret Integration," written after *V.* and before *The Crying of Lot 49,* he focuses on a gang of children led by a boy genius. Grover Snodd's inventions do not always work, and his plans always go awry, creating problems that require new plans. But "it tickled Grover any time he could interfere with the scheming of grown-ups." And the elaborate, though continually unsuccessful, schemes of the boys shed light on the Tristero of *Lot 49* and the preterite of *Gravity's Rainbow.* Pynchon, like Grover Snodd (who must be the nascent novelist, unless it was Grover Snodd who invented him) sees that the only way to fight the adult world—or the forces of waste, disorder, and death—is through a more creative mode of disordering.

Pynchon's creativity, then, has its own demonic dimension. His impulse, like that of the devils in the medieval sotie plays, is to excite us—or bring us to life—through acts of sheer annihilation. And, if dangerous, this impulse is also moral. While still an undergraduate at Cornell, Pynchon wrote "Morality and Mercy in Vienna." The story centers on Cleanth Siegel, who finds himself becoming a confessor to the wild crew he meets at a party in Washington, D. C. He is exhilarated by the "still small Jesuit voice" inside him, which had inspired him once to set five hundred freshmen in motion, advancing on the women's dorms. Now it inspired him to make use of what he had learned in an anthropology course about Ojibwa lore—and goad a lonely Indian into massacring the guests. It would be a "moment of truth," a "miracle." And then the other, "gentle part of him" would sing *kaddish* for the dead and mourn "over the Jesuit's happiness, realizing however that this kind of penance was as good as any other." Pynchon has come a long way from his early short story. Still, Josephine

Hendin concludes that he "is the genius of his generation . . . the Antichrist who offered up his own destructiveness to illuminate yours . . . the one man who realized that the moralist of our time would have to be the devil."

Let us examine Pynchon's novels as they lead to the vision of *Gravity's Rainbow,* first, to see how he gives shape to the destructive power that governs his "new world"—whether by chance or by design—and, second, to grasp the singular morality of his demonic impulse. I will begin by placing Pynchon in the line of American writers who, like Adams, were aroused by the experience of acceleration, unchecked energy, or, as I will call it, senseless and ungovernable motion.

Walt Whitman, sounding his "barbaric yawp over the roofs of the world," invokes his persona, his subject, and the form of his poem as "Nature without check with original energy." Pynchon, whose *Gravity's Rainbow* opens with "a screaming" that "comes across the sky," sounds a yawp that makes Whitman seem like the corresponding secretary of a 4-H club. And he invokes the world of his novel with an epigraph by Wernher von Braun: "Nature does not know extinction; all it knows is transformation. . . ." In the century between "Song of Myself" (1855) and *Gravity's Rainbow,* a signal feature of American literature had been "Nature without check with original energy"—in works that strain at the seams, that defy critical description and judgment, that succeed out of their sheer bravado and power. The barbaric yawp issues from such brilliant failures as Hart Crane's *The Bridge* (1930) and William Carlos Williams' *Paterson* (1946–1958), from the monumental exuberance of Thomas Wolfe, from the kaleidoscope of John Dos Passos' *U.S.A.* (1937), from the page-long sentences of William Faulkner's narrators as they try to grasp the ungraspable, from the "grun-tu-mo-lani" of Saul Bellow's *Henderson the Rain King* (1959), from the lyric obscenity of Norman

Mailer's "disk jockey" evoking the myths and misdirected energy that brought America to Vietnam.

The barbaric yawp gets louder and more dissonant. The unchecked energy becomes more potent and more destructive. And the writers deal with this energy in a much more ambivalent fashion. But our experience of this energy, or its dynamic, also undergoes a change that is reflected in the difference between Whitman's view of "Nature without check" and Pynchon's view of nature that knows only transformation. I will try to describe this change and develop an approach to *Gravity's Rainbow,* first, by distinguishing two forms that have given expression to the unchecked energy of America—the novel of movement and the novel of motion—and, then, by describing Pynchon's encounters with unchecked energy in his three novels.

Let me begin by trying to define my key terms. Energy is the capacity to do work and the power to move. When energy is harnessed, controlled, purposeful, I will call it movement. When it is actualized toward no particular end, I will call it motion. Literary energy is the power to move a reader to laughter, pity, and fear. It is also the power to move language, images, characters, and action toward a climax, a conclusion, and a meaning. All good literature, of course, is endowed with energy. But it is interesting that we become aware of the energy, or speak of the energy, when the power of a literary work begins to exceed its form. Doesn't the fastidious critic commend the energy just before deriding the style of, say, Theodore Dreiser's *American Tragedy* (1925), or Eugene O'Neill's *Long Day's Journey into Night* (1956)? We begin to sense the energy of Whitman's "Song of Myself" in the gaps between its discontinuous sections, stanzas, lines, or phrases, and in the discontinuities of its grammar. His typical stanza is an incomplete sentence—a series of subjects with no predicate, noun phrases with no verb. We may even describe it as a series of substantives with the potency of verbs, in which, as the substantives accumulate, the potency increases. It is in this sense that we recognize the energy of a work as it exceeds its form. And it is in this sense that the poem is "Nature without check with original energy."

When we speak of movement in a literary work, we refer to a controlled energy and therefore can be more precise. For we can focus on what is going, as well as on the direction and pattern of its progress—and plot the movement of characters through time and space.

F. Scott Fitzgerald's *The Great Gatsby* (1925) and Nathanael West's *The Day of the Locust* (1939) both deal with the energy that Whitman glorified and that, undirected or misdirected, has become destructive. Both writers show the destructive energy just barely suppressed, and masked by the shimmering surfaces and tasteless facades. Both writers connect this energy with their particular visions of the American wasteland. Nevertheless, their visions are different in ways that go beyond the details of locale or history. And we can describe this difference in terms of movement or, specifically, in terms of goals, vehicles, motive power, and ends.

The goal in *The Great Gatsby* is "the green light at the end of Daisy's dock," which Fitzgerald compares to the "green breast of the new world" that "flowered once for Dutch sailors' eyes." The goal of West's characters is Hollywood, with its "Mexican ranch houses, Samoan huts, Mediterranean villas, Egyptian and Japanese temples, Swiss chalets, Tudor cottages, and every possible combination of these styles that lined the slopes of the canyon"—and, of course, Faye Greener. The vehicle for Fitzgerald is Gatsby, with his "heightened sensitivity to the promises of life," as seen through the eyes of Nick Carraway, a sensitive outsider rooted in the topsoil of American society. West's novel

contains a similar observer in Tod Hackett, but it is important to note that there is no sharply defined vehicle upon which he is focusing. The motive power for Gatsby, and for Nick, is a romantic striving; the motive power for West's characters is a vague but powerful momentum, sometimes described as the need to escape, sometimes as the drive to succeed. The end of *The Great Gatsby* is the destruction of the vehicle, the romantic protagonist, and the recognition of lost values—but the world remains intact. The end of *The Day of the Locust* is apocalypse, the destruction of the characters and the world of the novel.

Fitzgerald, whose vision of life conformed to the conventions of historical evolution and the mechanics of cause-effect, makes the dynamics of movement in the traditional novel graphically clear, for he so clearly defines the goal, the vehicle, the motive power, and the end. Fitzgerald's 1920's may be symbolized in Gatsby's yellow roadster speeding toward Daisy's home under the eyes of T. J. Eckleburg. The vehicle progresses and accelerates along a straight line until it goes out of control and causes destruction.

West's 1930's may be symbolized in the riot that concludes *The Day of the Locust*—the characters swirling irrationally, with increasing violence. West has experienced the loss of control and the destruction evoked by Fitzgerald, and has at least sensed that history does not progress and that effect does not so simply follow from cause. As a result, he creates a pattern of movement that is less easy to define. There is no vehicle. And while the novel is ostensibly linear (in that we follow the development of Tod Hackett from day to day), there is no direction, no meaningful pattern from point to point in the space and time of the novel. To put it another way, the apocalyptic ending is not caused by any choice or event in the novel.

The Day of the Locust focuses on the motive

energy rather than on a vehicle and its pattern of movement toward a goal; to describe the novel, therefore, we should speak not of movement but of motion. Motion is the process of movement without regard to what is moving. Its dynamic structure cannot be plotted in a linear, purposeful, or causal pattern; it can only be described as a process of transformations. When the transformations are irrational, when linking gives way to discontinuity and direction to aimlessness, we encounter the experience of "Nature without check with original energy."

Whitman's "Song of Myself" is designed to give the illusion of motion rather than of movement. Although the movement of the poem lacks any apparent direction, the poem does have a coherence; indeed, it is about relationship. It does have a center, the mind of the poet. And it does have an associative, if not logical, pattern of motion. Whitman could glorify "Nature without check with original energy" because he was incapable of imagining nature without check, because he believed in an ultimate coherence. Fitzgerald could see and even plot the effects of nature without check or misdirected energy, but he could not focus on the energy itself. West could focus on the energy lyrically or symbolically, but he knew of no other way to handle it than within the framework of a linear novel. As Pynchon approaches *Gravity's Rainbow,* he realizes all the implications of "the original energy" that early writers either could not accept or could not reflect in a literary form. He finally evolves a novel of motion rather than of movement—a novel that abrogates direction, that focuses on the senseless pattern of transformations that governs contemporary life.

"'Where we going,' Profane said. 'The way we're heading,' said Pig. 'Move your ass.'" Benny Profane, Pig Bodine, Pappy Hod, Herbert Stencil, Sidney Stencil, Evan Godolphin,

Hugh Godolphin, Paola Maijstral, Victoria Wren, Vera Meroving, and Veronica Manganese move their asses all over the place in Pynchon's first novel—continually going, or seeming to go, in no other direction than the way they're heading. Indeed, *V.* is about three kinds of movement that, when interconnected—or intercut—come together as unfocused, undirected, and ungovernable motion.

Benny Profane—a schlemiel but not a coward, capable of feeling but not of attachment, disturbed by the inanimate but not prepared to act against it—rejects modern society by becoming a "yo-yo." He rides the shuttle back and forth, accepting whatever comes his way— a job, a drink, a woman, a fight, a trip to Malta. But he is always ready to cut loose when the connection becomes too secure. In a threatening world he maintains his equilibrium and a minimal identity by being constantly and aimlessly on the move. That the pattern of his movement is like a yo-yo suggests its psychological, if not its geographical, limits.

Opposed to Benny is Herbert Stencil, whose movement since 1945 has been constant but purposeful. "His random movements before the war had given way to a great single movement from inertness to—if not vitality, then at least activity. Work, the chase—for it was V. he hunted . . . for no other reason than that V. was there to track down." The chase after V., with its ever-changing direction and elusive goal, allows Herbert Stencil to maintain his equilibrium in a world of space and time that reaches far beyond Benny's, and to maintain a minimal identity—as a stencil.

The third kind of movement in *V.* is manifest in the elder generation. Hugh Godolphin is an explorer. Sidney Stencil is a foreign agent, who goes wherever Whitehall tells him, and who "with no element to be out of" is "at home everywhere"—except, finally, in Malta. Victoria Wren, Vera Meroving, Veronica Manganese—

or V.—ends up as an agent for Mussolini. Even more than Stencil, she has no element to be out of and is at home everywhere. Her movement comes to be defined as "tourism":

V. at the age of thirty-three (Stencil's calculation) had found love at last in her peregrinations through (let us be honest) a world if not created then at least described to its fullest by Karl Baedeker of Leipzig. This is a curious country, populated only by a breed called "tourists." Its landscape is one of inanimate monuments and buildings; near-inanimate barmen, taxi-drivers, bellhops, guides. . . . More than this it is two-dimensional, as is the Street, as are the pages and maps of those little red handbooks. As long as the Cook's, Travellers' Clubs and banks are open, the Distribution of Time section followed scrupulously,. . . the tourist may wander anywhere in this coordinate system without fear. . . . Tourism thus is supranational, like the Catholic Church, and perhaps the most absolute communion we know on earth: for be its members American, German, Italian, whatever, the Tour Eiffel, Pyramids, and Campanile all evoke identical responses from them; their Bible is clearly written and does not admit of private interpretation; they share the same landscapes, suffer the same inconveniences; live by the same pellucid time-scale. They are the Street's own.

"Tourism," as we find it implicitly amplified in *V.,* is a constant movement with constantly changing direction. But it differs from Profane's yo-yoism and from young Stencil's chase of or search for V. in that it is not volitional, in that the motive energy does not come from within. Tourism is not a choice to escape or to pursue, but to abdicate choice. It is an acknowledged or unacknowledged obedience—or following of some authoritative and unquestionable set of directions. Such obedience may be judged harmless, if mindless, when the tourist follows

a Baedeker. It may be judged benign if the agent as tourist follows the instructions of a "friendly" government. But it becomes suspect when we begin to recognize the colonialist objectives of the "friendly" government. And it becomes fully malign when the agent's instructions come from Mussolini. The destructive potential, indeed proclivity, of tourism is implied by the identification of Karl Baedeker with his fellow Leipziger, Kurt Mondaugen. For Mondaugen, who obediently travels to South-West Africa in pursuit of atmospheric radio disturbances, is associated with the most explicit colonialism and the most frightening impulses of fascism.

Abdication of choice and of control lead to the loss of direction: we don't know where the characters are going, we can't tell the past from the present, we can't judge the political right from the political left, good from bad, comic from tragic. How are we, indeed, to judge the climax of the novel, in which Sidney Stencil (serving a government that will soon become an ally of Britain in the fight for freedom) and his former lover Veronica Manganese (serving an Italian faction not yet prepared to open a second front in the fight for total control) are both plotting to keep Malta free? And in which they join forces to compel the double agent Fausto Maijstral to leave their respective services and rejoin his pregnant wife? And how are we to judge the ending of the novel, in which Fausto's daughter Paola decides to rejoin her husband, Pappy Hod? For we can never understand the motivation of V., or of Paola, who continues to wear V.'s ivory comb. That is, we can never understand what moves them or where they are moving.

By the end of *V.* there is a total confusion, or merging, of all moral directions, and we come to sense that the three different kinds of movement are one motion: the motion of unchecked energy. There is no difference among the choice of escape, the choice of pursuit, and the choice of giving up choices. To become a human yo-yo is as mindless as to pursue an elusive goal or to become a tourist, or to become an agent. Each choice is as mechanical or aimless or menacing as that of SHROUD or SHOCK, or Esther as she submits to a nose job, or V. as she displays her glass eye with the clock iris—or the children who leave their games to undress the wounded priest and discover V., dig the star sapphire from her bleeding navel with a rusty bayonet, and run off with the clock iris.

Yet while *V.* is about motion, it is not in motion. It follows the capricious string of Benny's yo-yo and the trail of a woman whose name and shape are constantly transformed. We never know where we're going, except that it's the way we're heading, and we're heading from place to place and time to time in ways that are often bewildering. Nonetheless, the novel is not without check; and in the end we know where we have been. For *V.* is governed by an omniscient narrator, who tells the story by intercutting one strand of the complex plot with another—but all along he holds the story together in his mind and can tie up the loose ends in an epilogue. The first intercutting, of Rachel Owlglass and her MG into the story of Benny and Paola, is soon recognized to be a simple, associative flashback: "the sinister vision of Pig and that Harley Davidson alone in an alley at three in the morning" reminds Benny of Rachel and her MG. And by the epilogue we discover that all the disturbing jumps in the multistranded narratives have been simple flashbacks, or intercutting from one plot line to another. The intercutting has been the narrator's way of reinforcing the enigma of V. and the confusion of moral direction. It has also been a technique designed to maintain suspense throughout the chase, or to keep the story moving.

It is important to recognize that the narrative crosscutting employed by Pynchon in *V.* creates the illusion of discontinuity while holding the novel in check, or together. Indeed, it is like the crosscutting of the early movie chase scenes, which undoubtedly influenced Pynchon. Crosscutting is what effected the experience of the chase. Suspense is created as D.W.Griffith cuts back and forth between the helpless victim and her rescuer, but in the scene of the last-minute rescue, the two lines of action are drawn together. And while planning the crosscutting of four very different stories in *Intolerance,* each of which culminates in a last-minute rescue, he declared the

. . .stories will begin like four currents looked at from a hilltop. At first the four currents will flow apart, slowly and quietly. But as they flow, they grow nearer and nearer together, and faster and faster, until in the end . . . they mingle in one mighty river of expressed emotion.

Narrative crosscutting, therefore, derives from a sense of purpose, from a goal, and, in the novel, from the stable perspective of the narrator. At the end of Pynchon's first novel, V. remains an enigma; but what happens in the life of Herbert Stencil as he pursues her becomes clear, and the pattern of his movement secures the pattern of Benny Profane's. Moreover, the goal—where the crosscut plot lines are drawn together—and the sense of purpose implied in the narrator's design give coherence to the purposeless motion of the characters and constrain the runaway energy. The main characters have been going in no other direction than the way they've been heading, but their paths culminate in a pattern that the reader can finally plot.

In Pynchon's second novel, he abandons the stable, omniscient perspective to focus on Oedipa Maas's developing consciousness; the narrator knows only what Oedipa knows at each step in her quest. And the narrative proceeds not by the intercutting of plot lines but by the addition—indeed overloading—of information into a simple linear plot line. Oedipa's quest, her movement and goal throughout the novel, is purposeful—as she tries to piece together and comprehend the limits of Pierce Inverarity's estate. But as the information accumulates, it undermines the purposeful movement of the plot line and evokes an experience closer to the dynamic of motion that Pynchon will achieve in *Gravity's Rainbow*.

The steps in Oedipa's quest can be laid out in a chronological, continuous pattern. One day she receives a letter naming her executor of Pierce Inverarity's estate. She drives from her home to the Echo Courts in San Narciso, where she unexpectedly meets Pierce's lawyer. Then she goes to The Scope, a bar near Yoyodyne (Pierce's aerospace empire), where she learns about the Tristero; to the Fangoso Lagoons, where she learns about Pierce's investment in bone charcoal; to a performance of *The Courier's Tragedy,* where she discovers the fictional or historical connections or parallels with the Tristero and the uses of bone charcoal; to Yoyodyne, where she learns about the Tristero's current operations; through the city to discover a large but inconspicuous community that communicates through the Tristero's system of W.A.S.T.E. containers; to the home of Emory Bortz to learn about the Tristero's ancient struggle against Thurn and Taxis; and finally to Ghengis Cohen's stamp auction to await the crying of lot 49—and what she hopes will be the ultimate piece in the wild jigsaw puzzle of Pierce's estate, Western civilization, and her own identity.

More important than the linearity of action is the linear development of Oedipa Maas from a flat caricature to a sympathetic and heroic character, and the development of her mechanical responses to a series of choices involving feeling and thought. She begins as a stereotype housewife returning from a Tupperware party where the hostess had put too much kirsch in the fondue, develops into a businesswoman bent on executing Pierce's estate, then into a woman driven by the need to know and, finally, by the need to connect. At the climax of her search, having discovered countless pieces of information, she comes upon a derelict sailor and is "overcome all at once by the need to touch him.... Exhausted, hardly knowing what she was doing, she came the last three steps and sat, took the man in her arms, actually held him, gazing out of her smudged eyes down the stairs, back into the morning." The crying she awaits at the end of the novel, as critics have noted, reflects her compassion as well as her need to understand.

But the linear development of the plot—of the action of the novel and of the protagonist—is only one dimension of *The Crying of Lot 49,* for as Oedipa discovers more information in her quest, she encounters kinds of plotting that are neither continuous nor progressive, and that defy the plotting of epistemological, ideological, or moral direction. Arriving in San Narciso and choosing a motel at random, she is surprised by the entrance of Pierce's lawyer, Metzger, who claims to have found her by scouring the motels all day. Her television set is showing *Baby Igor,* an old film that Metzger claims to have starred in as a child. "Either he made up the whole thing, Oedipa thought suddenly, or he bribed the engineer over at the local station to run this, it's all part of a plot, an elaborate, seduction, *plot.*"

And the commercials involve a plot with far wider scope than Metzger's seduction of Oedipa. Fangoso Lagoons and Beaconsfield Cigarettes are two of Pierce's interests. Beaconsfield Cigarettes use a filter made from bone charcoal. Much of the bone charcoal, we later learn, came via the Cosa Nostra from a lake in Italy, where a company of American troops had lost a battle of attrition to the Nazis in 1943. We also learn that a group of Wells Fargo riders had been massacred at one of the Fangoso lakes; the charcoal from their bones was used to blacken the faces of the killers in subsequent raids. Moreover, the bones of the ambushed battalion in *The Courier's Tragedy* had been fished up and turned into charcoal, which the duke used for his perfidious correspondence.

At this point we might reflect on two kinds of plotting that are ingeniously confused in *The Crying of Lot 49*. First is the simple plotting of the action and the protagonist's development—the rational plan, chronological sequence, progressive development of Oedipa's quest—to which is added the more rational but incredibly complicated plot of *The Courier's Tragedy*. Second is the plotting for salacious, commercial, and political ends—the rational planning and steps calculated to seduce Oedipa, sell products, secure markets, and establish empires. To these we might add a third kind of plotting, which is historical. As Oedipa picks up fragments of information that lead from her present to the past, she is driven by a stronger and stronger compulsion to connect the fragments into a rational order—to plot a causal sequence of events that would explain the present in terms of the past. But the more Oedipa learns, the more difficult it is for her, and for us, to make connections. The main reasons for this difficulty are the increasing amount of data and their increasing similarity. If we could only discriminate and define the opposing forces, we could discover what led to what. But the central problem for Oedipa, and for the reader who is limited to her perspective, is in defining—or plotting—direction. And we come to discover that historical or causal direction depends upon our ability to define values—or to plot ideological direction.

Throughout Western history, Oedipa learns, consolidation and system have given rise to individualistic rebellion, but we can never determine whether the rebellion is to the right or the left. The Peter Pinguid Society, which is so conservative that it considers the John Birch Society left-wing, was founded by a man who opposed industrial capitalism—because it led to Marxism and was, therefore, part of the same "creeping horror." Moreover, the struggle for freedom requires consolidation and system, but we can never tell whether the ultimate goal is liberty or tyranny.

The novel focuses on what is central to both liberty and tyranny: the history of communication, or courier systems. The Tristero was a rebellious underground courier system that opposed the Thurn and Taxis (the established European mail service from 1300 to 1867); when it appeared in America, it fought the established Pony Express and Wells Fargo disguised as blackfaced outlaws or Indians. But in the middle of the seventeenth century, the Tristero faced a major decision. The conservatives wanted to keep the Tristero radical, as the opposition to the established central mail service. The militant radicals wanted to join the Thurn and Taxis, to make all of Europe dependent on them: "We, who have so long been disinherited, could be the heirs of Europe." From this point on, we cannot tell who is plotting against whom. Nor can we plot the ideological direction of the plotters. As a result, we can make no causal links—nor fix the fragments of information into a graspable pattern.

When Oedipa encounters the community of silent dropouts, who communicate secretly and independently by subverting the interoffice delivery system of Yoyodyne, we are led to wonder if this is a comic triumph of the underground, or if W.A.S.T.E. is not finally the product of the giant aerospace corporation itself. While one view leads us to a utopia of political, psychological, and sexual anarchism, the other leads us to a frighteningly successful totalitarianism. When we remember that the unpredictable Pierce Inverarity held a large block of shares in Yoyodyne, we are led to see the whole affair as a hoax on the part of a man rich enough to buy a cast of thousands—and the threat becomes diabolical.

Pierce Inverarity is like V., except that he is not the goal of the chase, nor do we ever even see him. All we know of him is the disembodied voice that Oedipa recalls having awakened her at three in the morning a year before the action begins:

... a voice beginning in heavy Slavic tones as second secretary at the Transylvanian Consulate, looking for an escaped bat; modulated to comic-Negro, then on into hostile Pachuco dialect, full of chingas and maricones; then a Gestapo officer asking her in shrieks did she have any relatives in Germany and finally his Lamont Cranston voice, the one he'd talked in all the way down to Mazatlán.

Lamont Cranston was the "Shadow" of radio fame, an invisible agent capable of appearing anywhere, anytime. Pierce Inverarity is introduced as a shadow undergoing continual transformation. Throughout the rest of the novel he is identified only with San Narciso—the place to which Oedipa drives to begin her quest. San Narciso "had been Pierce's domicile, and headquarters: the place he'd begun his land speculating in ten years ago, and so put down the plinth course of capital on which everything afterward had been built, however rickety or grotesque, toward the sky...." It was "less an identifiable city than a grouping of concepts—census tracts, special purpose bond-issue districts, shopping nuclei, all overlaid with access roads to its own freeway." And, as the novel develops, Oedipa learns that San Narciso has "no boundaries" in space or time.

Pierce Inverarity is shadowy and gratuitously protean; San Narciso is not only the locus of the action but also the bewildering field of its plot-less plotting. It is also the shifting ground of the developing figure of the novel—the simple linear plot line that identifies Oedipa Maas. As Oedipa pursues her quest—to comprehend San Narciso—and gathers more information, an agon develops between the figure and ground of the novel. The figure is continually threatened by the ground: the plot line is continually in danger of being absorbed by the plotless plotting. And Oedipa herself is in continual danger of giving in. If she could only give in: "She had only to drift tonight, at random, and watch nothing happen, to be convinced it was purely nervous, a little something for her shrink to fix." But if she did give in and drift at random—like Mucho with his drugs, Hilarius with his paranoia, Metzger with his opportunism, Jesús Arrabal with his political persistence, or dropouts who rebel against the system that may be coopting them—if she did give up her purposeful pursuit, she would become part of the cast of aimless caricatures that form the ground of the novel.

Oedipa continues her pursuit: her mechanical response has developed into curiosity, and then into the humanistic need to know and connect; we follow the evolution of a self, or a self-consciousness that ultimately needs others to find the limits of its identity. In the end, Oedipa's purposeful movement remains distinguished from the senseless motion of society and history. The figure of the plot stands out against the plotless plotting of its ground. But the overall experience is not so simple or hopeful.

Stanley Koteks has introduced Oedipa to the concept of Maxwell's Demon, who by sorting molecules was supposed to sustain order and maintain the purposeful movement of the system. The Demon, that is, was supposed to counteract entropy, the inevitable development of disorder and exhaustion of energy. But Maxwell's successors discovered that the new energy added to the system—the mental energy required for gathering, sorting, and piecing together information—would only contribute to the mounting disorder, and thus to the entropy. And, as Anne Mangel points out in her instructive discussion of Maxwell's Demon in the novel, Oedipa, in pursuing information and order, only contributes to the disorder and entropy of her world. By the end of the novel, Mucho has turned from Oedipa's disk jockey husband into a solipsistic drug addict, Dr. Hilarius from her psychoanalyst into a madman, and Oedipa herself from a suburban housewife into an isolated fanatic driven by her vision of disconnection. In the end, that is, Oedipa stands out clearly against Pierce's formless San Narciso, as does the path of her movement from the senseless motion that threatens to absorb it. But as the figure stands out against the ground, it is also disconnected from it. And the system as a whole is composed of disconnected fragments moving at different speeds in different directions—like the "anarchist miracle" of the deaf mutes dancing.

The story line of *Gravity's Rainbow,* unlike that in *V.* and *The Crying of Lot 49,* is unplottable, for it lacks a central subject (vehicle) or even a hierarchy of subjects, and it moves from place to place without any apparent reason or purpose. First we center on Pirate Prentice, then shift to Roger Mexico, then to Tyrone Slothrop, whose love affairs take place in a pattern identical to that of the V-2 explosions.

Now we think we have the protagonist, and we watch him being pursued by the agents of Pointsman in the name of the war effort. But, as Slothrop's pursuers multiply and he escapes them (or thinks he does) in a white zoot suit, our frame of reference begins to shift. It shifts completely when he changes to a Wagnerian costume—a helmet with horns, a pair of buckskin trousers, a green cape emblazoned with a red R—to become Rocketman, and when he later disguises himself in a pig costume. Rocketman—pursued by agents of the right and of the left, and pursuing not only what will become the ultimate rocket of the future but also the genesis of his own past—becomes the center of our attention for most of the novel.

Then he disappears from sight, and our attention is centered now on the Russian Tchitcherine; now on the Nazi Captain Blicero (code name for Lieutenant Weissmann), who controls the ultimate rocket; now on the African Enzian, half brother of Tchitcherine and former lover of Weissmann. And, as if this is not sufficiently confusing, we attend at one time or another to a cast of characters that takes up four double-columned pages in Scott Simmon's useful index.

Moreover, we are taken suddenly and erratically from London to Holland, back to London, to France, to Switzerland, and to "the Zone" of occupied Germany—which, despite the enormous number and authenticity of details, loses its geographical locus and becomes as abstract as its designation. Now we are in Germany, then back to London, and suddenly in a California movie theater. This does not take into account the innumerable dislocations as we are shuttled into the pasts of hundreds of characters—or to Africa, where black history seems to be developing to mirror the white history of northern Europe. Nor does it take into account the dislocations in style—which shifts without signal, reason, or pattern, from involved to detached, from scientific to slang, from suspenseful narrative to popular song, from scrupulous realism to antic cartooning. Dislocation, discontinuity, and confusion characterize our large impressions of the plot, characterization, and style. But so do speed, directionless motion, and transformation. Let me develop this point by focusing on the deceptively simple opening of the novel.

Gravity's Rainbow begins with a serious, realistic description of an evacuation.

A screaming comes across the sky. It has happened before, but there is nothing to compare it to now.

. . . No light anywhere. . . . He's afraid of the way the glass will fall—soon—it will be a spectacle: the fall of a crystal palace.

The "he" who has been afraid of the way the glass will fall is absorbed into a "they" who travel by train through a dark countryside and stop at an unnamed city. They are taken up in a building filled with "thousands of . . . hushed rooms without light." There is nothing to do but lie and wait, listening to the screaming of missiles that have already exploded, wondering whether one of them will come in the darkness or bring its own light. Soon the "he" is again in focus and given a name, Captain Geoffrey ("Pirate") Prentice. And we witness a scene where Teddy Bloat, hooked onto an ebony baluster by an empty champagne split in his hip pocket, begins to fall; and where Pirate "leaps off of the cot and kicks it rolling on its casters" so that "Bloat, plummeting, hits square amidships with a great strum of bedsprings."

Before we follow Pirate to his rooftop banana garden, we may turn back to see how we got from "they" to "he" and from the hushed room, waiting in terror, to Pirate's antic maisonette. We must have missed something. But there's the link; it is italicized for us. The anonymous "they" are wondering and waiting for the light. And the next paragraph begins: "*But it is already light.*" As we sit looking at the italicized link, though, we discover that the transition is only syntactical—that the daylight came offstage, or offpage; that without our realizing it, we have been transported in time and space. That, indeed, we have made what the physicist might call a quantum jump.

A quantum jump is the discontinuous movement of an electron from one ring of an atom to another, or the discontinuous transformation of an electron from one level of energy to another. And the model of the quantum jump illuminates three important features of the opening pages, which Pynchon elaborates with even more imagination and daring in the course of his novel. First is the discontinuity: a quantum jump is a discontinuous motion or a discontinuous development. The novel, as we have seen, is discontinuous in terms of character focus, plot movement, and stylistic development. Second is the abrogation of direction: just as the rocket explodes before it arrives, defying the directions of time and space, so the novel moves from one place to another and from one time to another in all possible directions. Third, and perhaps most important, is transformation. Whether we describe the electron as circling on a new ring at a new speed or as endowed with a new amount of energy, the electron—which is nothing but speed and energy—has been transformed. And our primary experience in the novel is of subjects and subject matter that can be defined only in terms of speed and energy, undergoing constant and inexplicable transformation.

Gravity's Rainbow is about speed and energy, which Pynchon, like the modern physicist, sees as the basic reality. Like the modern physicist, Pynchon forces us to discard those categories of thought that have mentally secured us, and accept a world where there are no links, no directions, but only continual transformation. Where Pynchon differs from the physicist is that he brings into his world the reality of politics and human values. He denies us the security of traditional forms, categories, directions, links—but forces us to sympathize, judge, and choose.

There seem to be no direction, no links, just random events. As Roger Mexico would have it, the world obeys only the law of probability. But, following the most disturbing transformation, lines come together, everything seems interconnected and to follow Pointsman's laws of cause and effect:

Slothrop swings the long keychain of his zoot, in some agitation. A few things are immediately obvious. There is even more being zeroed in on him from out there than he'd thought, even in his most paranoid spells. Imipolex G shows up on a mysterious "insulation device" on a rocket being fired with the help of a transmitter on the roof of the headquarters of Dutch Shell, who is co-licensee for marketing the Imipolex—a rocket whose propulsion system bears an uncanny resemblance to that developed by British Shell at around the same time . . . and oh, oh boy, it just occurs to Slothrop now where all the rocket information is being *gathered*—into the office of who but Mr. Duncan Sandys, Churchill's own son-in-law, who works out of the Ministry of Supply located where but at Shell Mex *House, for Christ's sake.* . . .

But if so much is being zeroed in, who is zeroing in on whom? What is the ultimate source? Where does it all come together? Who's on what side? What's the ultimate goal? Where are they at, where are they going?

Escaping, perhaps, in Switzerland, Slothrop asks, "Why are all you folks helping me like this? For free and all?" "Who knows?" comes the answer. "We have to play patterns. There must be a pattern you're in, right now." *Gravity's Rainbow* draws us into a world of symmetrical, repetitive, but undefinable and unnavigable dynamic patterns. There is always a pattern that we are in, but the patterns are transformed, even when they seem to repeat themselves, and we never know how to evaluate the pattern we are in or how we have gotten from one to the other. The major pattern, of course, is the V-2 rocket, which, when it loses its thrust, goes "pure ballistic" and becomes

that "purified shape latent in the sky." The shape is like the distribution curve of the explosions, and throughout the novel we sense the threat of death and ultimate destruction, of inevitability, but also of random distribution or pure chance.

On the other hand, the dominant pattern is also the shape of the rainbow, the shape of Rocketman's helmet and horns, of Slothrop's erection; and we also sense throughout the novel the promise of sexual potency. The promise is sometimes perverted; most of the sexual force is associated with sadism, masochism, and destructive escalation. But the perverted sex is countered by the love of Roger Mexico and Jessica Swanlake, however ephemeral that may be. It is also countered by the vitality of Tyrone Slothrop, not only in the joys and frustrations of his sexual encounters but also in his pursuit of freedom and justice—just as the darkness and despair of the novel are countered by its fecundity and comic spirit.

We have become accustomed to ambiguity in literature. Why, then, are we so disoriented by the ambiguity of *Gravity's Rainbow*? Perhaps because the novel is not ambiguous, or because we must reexamine the experience of ambiguity. Ambiguous derives from *ambi*, meaning "both," and *agere*, meaning "to drive." The root meaning forms an illuminating metaphor: to drive in both directions. Jay Gatsby is ambiguous because his energy has been misdirected; in that sense we see him driving in both directions. Ambiguity, then, belongs to the novel of movement, where the choices, actions, and destinies of characters can be plotted; where the subject, or vehicle, is clearly delineated; and where it moves from point to point in a continuous direction. But in the novel of motion there is no fixed subject, continuity, or direction. The patterns are all there are: now absolutely random, now exercising total control, now threatening, now promising; ultimately undefinable, unmeasurable, discontinuous, and unnavigable. And we have to learn to play the patterns.

The subject of *Gravity's Rainbow,* like that of *The Great Gatsby* and *The Day of the Locust,* is the "original energy"—unchecked, directionless, and accelerating. Fitzgerald plots the effects of this energy in terms of classical movement. West evokes an experience of motion, but he contains the energy of the novel in the form of the traditional novel of movement. With Pynchon we can say the energy exceeds the form—that is, if we consider form as a container. But Pynchon has finally developed a form, the characteristic of which is not to contain. In *V.* he generated the experience of unchecked energy in the mindless movement of his characters. In *The Crying of Lot 49* he thwarted the purposeful movement of his developing heroine by overloading information onto a simple plot line, or by undermining the plot line with a senselessly shifting ground. In *Gravity's Rainbow* he has composed a novel in terms of energy and motion and patterns undergoing constant, alogical transformation.

Slothrop learns that the

... War has been reconfiguring time and space into its own image. The track runs in different networks now. What appears to be destruction is really the shaping of railroad spaces to other purposes, intentions he can only, riding through it for the first time, begin to feel the leading edges of....

In the 1970's we learned the same lesson. We may also have learned that the conventional ways of grasping history—including that of Henry Adams—are inadequate and false, because history cannot be grasped, or contained. The experience of reading *Gravity's Rainbow* is like riding through modern history for the first time, without maps and seat belts that have given us a false sense of direction and security. And we can begin to feel the leading edges. Pynchon has subjected us to the experience of unchecked energy, of history moving without sense or direction. And, with a kind of demonic glee, he seems to have reveled in the destruction of factitious order. Having undermined our security, he leaves us precarious but free, as well as responsible for our judgments and choices of direction.

Selected Bibliography

WORKS OF THOMAS PYNCHON

BOOKS

V. Philadelphia: Lippincott, 1963.
The Crying of Lot 49. Philadelphia: Lippincott, 1966.
Gravity's Rainbow. New York: Viking Press, 1973.
Slow Learner. Boston: Little, Brown and Company, 1984.

STORIES AND ARTICLES

"Morality and Mercy in Vienna." *Epoch,* 9:195–213 (Spring 1959).
"The Small Rain." *Cornell Writer,* 6:14–32 (March 1959).
"Entropy." *Kenyon Review,* 22:277–92 (1960).
"Low-Lands." *New World Writing,* 16:85–108 (1960).
"Under the Rose." *Noble Savage,* 3:223–51 (1961).
"The Secret Integration." *Saturday Evening Post,* 237:36–37, 39, 42–44, 46–49, 51 (December 19, 1964).
"The World (This One), the Flesh (Mrs. Oedipa Maas) and the Testament of Pierce Inverarity." *Esquire,* 64:170–73, 296, 298–303 (December 1965).
"The Shrink Flips." *Cavalier,* 16:32–33, 88–92 (March 1966).
"A Journey into the Mind of Watts." *New York Times Magazine,* June 12, 1966, pp. 34–35, 78, 80–82, 84.

"Pros and Cohns." *New York Times Book Review,* July 17, 1966, pp. 22, 24. (Letter to the editor on the origin of the name Genghis Cohen.)

BIOGRAPHICAL AND CRITICAL STUDIES

(Many of the essays published in the three collections listed below were first published elsewhere.)

Fowler, Douglas. *Reader's Guide to "Gravity's Rainbow."* Ann Arbor, Mich.: Ardis, 1979.

Friedman, Alan J. "Science and Technology in *Gravity's Rainbow.*" (To be published.)

Kolodny, Annette, and Daniel James Peters. "Pynchon's *The Crying of Lot 49:* The Novel as Subversive Experience." *Modern Fiction Studies,* 19:79–87 (Spring 1973).

Levine, George, and David Leverenz, eds. *Mindful Pleasures: Essays on Thomas Pynchon.* Boston: Little, Brown, 1976. (Contains Richard Poirier, "The Importance of Thomas Pynchon"; Catharine R. Stimpson, "Pre-Apocalyptic Atavism: Thomas Pynchon's Early Fiction"; Tony Tanner, "Caries and Cabals"; W. T. Lhamon, Jr., "Pentecost, Promiscuity, and Pynchon's *V.*: From the Scaffold to the Impulsive"; Anne Mangel, "Maxwell's Demon, Entropy, Information: *The Crying of Lot 49*"; William Vesterman, "Pynchon's Poetry"; George Levine, "Risking the Moment: Anarchy and Possibility in Pynchon's Fiction"; Scott Sanders, "Pynchon's Paranoid History"; Edward Mendelson, "Gravity's Encyclopedia"; Marjorie Kaufman, "Brünnhilde and the Chemists: Women in *Gravity's Rainbow*"; David Leverenz, "On Trying to Read *Gravity's Rainbow*"; Mathew Winston, "The Quest for Pynchon.")

Mendelson, Edward, ed. *Pynchon: A Collection of Critical Essays.* Englewood Cliffs, N. J.: Prentice-Hall, 1978. (Contains Tony Tanner, "V. and V-2"; F. S. Schwarzbach, "A Matter of Gravity," and a reply by Joseph Rosenbaum; Joseph W. Slade, "'Entropy' and Other Calamities"; Robert Sklar, "An Anarchist Miracle: The Novels of Thomas Pynchon"; Roger B. Henkle, "Pynchon's Tapestries on the Western Wall"; Edward Mendelson, "The Sacred, the Profane, and *The Crying of Lot 49*"; James Nohrnberg, "Pynchon's Paraclete"; Frank Kermode, "Decoding the Trystero"; Richard Poirier, "Rocket Power"; George Levine,

"V-2"; Philip Morrison, review for *Scientific American*; Michael Seidel, "The Satiric Plots of *Gravity's Rainbow*"; Paul Fussell, "The Brigadier Remembers.")

McConnell, Frank. "Thomas Pynchon and the Abreaction of the Lord of Night." *Four Postwar American Novelists.* Chicago: University of Chicago Press, 1977. Pp. 159–97.

Ozier, Lance W. "The Calculus of Transformation: More Mathematical Imagery in *Gravity's Rainbow.*" *Twentieth Century Literature,* 21:193–210 (May 1975).

Pearce, Richard, ed. *Critical Essays on Thomas Pynchon.* Boston: G. K. Hall, 1980. (Contains Richard Wasson, "Notes on a New Sensibility: Pynchon's *V.*"; Richard Patteson, "What Stencil Knew: Structure and Certitude in Pynchon's *V.*"; John Hunt, "Comic Escape and Antivision: *V.* and *The Crying of Lot 49*"; Josephine Hendin, "What Is Thomas Pynchon Telling Us?"; Thomas Schaub, "A Gentle Chill, an Ambiguity: *The Crying of Lot 49*"; Speer Morgan, "*Gravity's Rainbow:* What's the Big Idea?"; Lawrence C. Wolfley, "Repression's Rainbow: The Presence of Norman O. Brown"; Steven Weisenburger, "The End of History? Thomas Pynchon and the Uses of the Past"; Scott Simmon, "Beyond the Theater of War: *Gravity's Rainbow* as Film"; Alan J. Friedman and Manfred Puetz, "Science as Metaphor in *Gravity's Rainbow*"; Elaine B. Safer, "The Allusive Mode and Black Humor in Pynchon's *Gravity's Rainbow*"; Marcus Smith and Khachig Tololyan, "The New Jeremiad: *Gravity's Rainbow*"; Maureen Quilligan, "Thomas Pynchon and the Language of Allegory"; Richard Pearce, "Where're They Going, Where're They at? Thomas Pynchon and the American Novel in Motion"; Beverly Clark and Caryn Fuoroli, "A Review of Major Pynchon Criticism.")

Plater, William M. *The Grim Phoenix: Reconstructing Thomas Pynchon.* Bloomington: Indiana University Press, 1978.

Puetz, Manfred. "Thomas Pynchon's *The Crying of Lot 49:* 'The World Is a Tristero System.'" *Mosaic,* 7:125–37 (1974).

Redfield, Robert, and Peter L. Hays. "Fugue as a Structure in Pynchon's 'Entropy.'" *Pacific Coast Philology,* 12:50–55 (October 1977).

Richardson, Robert O. "The Absurd Animate in

Thomas Pynchon's *V.: A Novel.*" *Studies in the Twentieth Century,* 9:35–58 (1972).

Schaub, Thomas. *Pynchon: The Voice of Ambiguity.* Champaign: University of Illinois Press. (To be published.)

Siegel, Mark Richard. *Pynchon: Creative Paranoia in "Gravity's Rainbow."* Port Washington, N. Y.: Kennikat, 1978.

Simmon, Scott. "A Character Index: *Gravity's Rainbow.*" *Critique,* 16:54–67 (December 1974).

Slade, Joseph W. *Thomas Pynchon.* New York: Warner, 1974.

———. "Escaping Rationalization: Options for the Self in *Gravity's Rainbow.*" *Critique,* 18:27–38 (1977).

Stark, John. "The Arts and Sciences of Thomas Pynchon." *Hollins Critic,* 12:1–13 (1975).

Young, James Dean. "The Enigma Variations of Thomas Pynchon." *Critique,* 10:69–77 (1968).

SCIENTIFIC BACKGROUND

Čapek, Milič. *The Philosophical Impact of Contemporary Physics.* New York: Van Nostrand, 1961.

Cline, Barbara Lovett. *Men Who Made a New Physics.* New York: New American Library, 1965.

Ostriker, Jeremiah P. "The Nature of Pulsars." *Scientific American,* 224:49 (January 1971). (For "totalitarian principle of physics.")

Wiener, Norbert. *The Human Use of Human Beings: Cybernetics and Society.* Garden City, N. Y.: Doubleday, 1956.

—RICHARD PEARCE

Delmore Schwartz

1913—1966

At present, Delmore Schwartz is probably better known through Saul Bellow's fictional portrait in *Humboldt's Gift* than through his own writing. Many who have not read Schwartz know of him as the brilliant poet acclaimed as a genius in his early twenties, but doomed to decline into madness and early death. He is remembered more for his life than for his writing. Nonetheless, during the 1970's there was a modest increase of interest in Schwartz's work. In 1974, Richard McDougall published a short critical study of Schwartz in Twayne's United States Authors series. The excellent biography by James Atlas came out in 1977; since then we have had a selection of the stories, edited by Atlas, and a selection of "last and late poems," edited by Robert Phillips.

There have been a number of articles, most of them by friends and contemporaries: William Barrett, Dwight Macdonald, Philip Rahv, Sidney Hook, Alfred Kazin, and Irving Howe. These essays contain some sharp insights that are informed by vivid firsthand memories of the man and the milieu behind the work. As the memory of Schwartz recedes into the past, his work will have to stand or fall on its own. Its revaluation, by a generation to whom he is "Schwartz" and not "Delmore," has barely begun. In tracing the course of his career, this essay will also attempt to contribute to such a revaluation.

One cannot discuss Schwartz's work without also discussing his life, for he was an obsessively autobiographical writer. When one recalls that he came to prominence in the 1930's and 1940's, and that some of his most ardent admirers were New Critics such as Allen Tate and John Crowe Ransom, this autobiographical emphasis seems a little surprising. It was fashionable at the time, among the poets Schwartz most valued, to insist on the impersonality of poetry. Although Ransom, Tate, and T. S. Eliot were sometimes more personal than they cared to admit, one must look ahead to the work of Robert Lowell, John Berryman, and Sylvia Plath in the 1960's to find poems that are personal to the same degree and in the same sense as many of Schwartz's. Whatever our conclusions about the artistic value of his poetry, Schwartz has a historical importance as the first confessional poet. In his autobiographical fiction he had the precedent of James Joyce and Marcel Proust.

It is significant that Lowell, in his famous *Paris Review* interview of 1961, credited Schwartz with some influence on his change of style. Like Schwartz, Lowell had come to value "experience" more than "polish," and he wanted to reclaim for poetry the narrative complexity it had ceded to the novel. One might say that Lowell's *Life Studies* (1959) accomplishes what Schwartz had attempted, less successfully, in *Genesis: Book One* (1943): an autobiographical poetry that revisits childhood, not to rekindle a Wordsworthian capacity for joy but to inquire into the historical and personal origins of present unhappiness.

Schwartz's unhappiness began, in a sense, even before he was born on December 8, 1913. His parents both came from Rumania in the great wave of Jewish emigration from Eastern Europe. His father, Harry Schwartz, met Rose Nathanson on the Lower East Side of New York City in 1909, and married her after a brief and stormy courtship. Harry had prospered in real estate, so the couple was able to move to a more fashionable neighborhood in Brooklyn. For a few years they were childless, for Rose Schwartz had a congenital condition that prevented her from conceiving. When Harry began to take up with other women, she thought that perhaps the arrival of a child would restore his sense of domestic responsibility. While he was away on business, she sold a bond given to her by an uncle and had the operation needed to correct her infertility. Even in the circumstances of his conception, Schwartz was a pawn in the struggle between his parents.

Then there was the matter of his first name, about which Schwartz was so sensitive that he devoted an entire play, *Shenandoah* (1941), to a family's quarrel over the naming of a son. The name they finally choose, Shenandoah Fish, is obviously analogous to Delmore Schwartz; it was also assigned to the protagonists of the autobiographical stories "America! America!," "New Year's Eve," and "A Bitter Farce." Schwartz thought of his name as a telling reminder that he was caught between two cultures. He had a traditional Jewish middle name—David. But his first name, which his parents apparently thought of as something sophisticated and "American," was an outlandish concoction, anomalous in both the Jewish context and the American.

The marriage of Schwartz's parents continued to deteriorate. A second child, Kenneth, was born in 1916, but the Schwartzes were legally separated in 1923 and divorced in 1927. Despite his unhappy childhood, Schwartz at least had the consolation of looking ahead to a large inheritance. This hope was disappointed. Harry Schwartz was able to salvage much of his fortune during the crash of 1929, but he died less than a year later. An unscrupulous executor drained away most of the estate, and what remained was tied up in litigation for years. Schwartz later thought of his father's death and the stock market crash as fatally linked, the private and public manifestations of some complex, inscrutable force. Indeed, he thought of his life in general as the product of dark determinisms: the persecution that drove the Jews of Eastern Europe to the New World; the economic collapse that made the loss of his inheritance even more bitter; the unconscious compulsions that set his parents against each other. In his fiction and poetry he usually viewed his story as a representative tragedy. He scarcely dared to desire freedom from suffering, but sought instead the tragic hero's understanding of his own suffering.

The turmoil of his family may explain Schwartz's erratic performance in school; he did well in English and other classes that engaged his imagination, but very poorly in everything else. Nonetheless, he showed early signs of literary ambition, and some of his teachers recognized his brilliance. Some of his juvenilia is preserved in *The Poet's Pack of George Washington High School* (1932). These poems are awkward and overdone in the usual way of adolescent verse, but they show a complexity of language and an awareness of modern styles (especially those of T. S. Eliot and Hart Crane) that set them apart from the neighboring contributions.

Schwartz spent the academic year 1931–

1932 at the University of Wisconsin. A temporary lack of money kept him out of school for the first half of the following academic year, but he was able to enroll at New York University in February 1933. By the time he graduated in June 1935, Schwartz was a published poet; a month later he wrote the short story "In Dreams Begin Responsibilities," which remains among his finest work. When it was published in December 1937, as the lead item in the first issue of the newly revived *Partisan Review,* it made his reputation. "In Dreams" gave him the title for his first book, and it touched upon themes, symbols, and techniques that were to become characteristic of his writing. Both for its own excellence and for its prophecy of things to come, the story deserves close attention.

Although "In Dreams Begin Responsibilities" takes its title from one of the two epigraphs to William Butler Yeats's *Responsibilities,* Schwartz's "dream" is no Yeatsian vision of a spiritual world, but a reenactment of the date on which his father proposed to his mother, shown as a silent movie in a theater. The metaphor of the movie eloquently expresses Schwartz's fatalism: what we see in a movie seems to be happening in the present, but it is in fact the record of actions already completed and, therefore, unalterable. The actions in the film are described in the present tense, and although the movie is silent, the narrator can infer his parents' feelings at every moment. The present tense and omniscient narration tend to shift our attention from the narrator to the parents; we experience the action as present, except when the narrator disrupts the events with his responses. One therefore begins to apply the metaphor of the movie not only to the past as the narrator reconstructs it in his mind, but also to the courtship itself at the time it actually occurred. The parents are not free; the marriage will be a disaster, but they cannot help choosing each other.

The handling of detail reinforces our sense that the present is a repetition of the past, that the pattern of life is futile recurrence. We follow the father's walk to the mother's house; then both parents "walk down the same quiet streets once more." During this sequence the movie is interrupted, and when it resumes, "the film has been returned to a portion just shown." In another scene the parents ride on a merry-go-round. To the narrator, "it seems that they will never get off the merry-go-round because it will never stop." If the present is a repetition of the past, it is also, by the same logic, an adumbration of the future. Toward the end of the story, the couple visits a portrait photographer and a fortune-teller. In these scenes the outcome of the marriage reveals itself as already contained in its beginning, for the portrait will not come out right; and the mother's insistence on a consultation with the fortune-teller provokes a violent quarrel, itself an ominous prediction of the strife to come.

At first the narrator manages to lose himself in the action of the movie. But as his parents stroll by the sea at Coney Island, with the inevitable proposal of marriage drawing uncomfortably close, he becomes uneasy and leaves the theater for a moment. He has been disturbed by "the terrible sun which breaks up sight, and the fatal, merciless, passionate ocean." His parents also look upon the sunlit water, but remain blind to its frightening symbolic implications. In this section the language of the story has shifted from deliberately flat, matter-of-fact narrative to lyrical evocation. The image of his parents, poised at the beginning of their lives, looking uncomprehendingly at the dazzling blankness of the sea, belongs to a class of images that recurs throughout Schwartz's work. It is, for that matter, parallel to the image of the narrator, at the end of the story, looking out at the snow on his twenty-first birthday.

The sea and the snow both stand in opposition to the darkness of the theater, and to the corresponding darkness of the photographer's studio and the fortune-teller's booth, theaters in which the parents try to look at themselves. The dark theater is regressive and womblike. Within it, one can only be the spectator of one's own dreams and memories. To some extent it simply represents the state of dreaming, but there are others watching the movie besides the narrator. To them the events are interesting but not charged with personal significance. This situation represents the plight of the autobiographical artist: What happens when one shows home movies in a public theater? It also represents the plight of anyone with a burdensome past: One can't possibly expect others to share one's own obsession with it; and in order to live in a world with others, one must win some measure of detachment from it.

The moment his mother accepts his father's proposal, the narrator loses all detachment, forgetting that the past is past. He stands up and cries to the figures on the screen: "Don't do it. It's not too late to change your minds, both of you. Nothing good will come of it, only remorse, hatred, scandal, and two children whose characters are monstrous." He is moved, at this point, by several motives: a real sympathy for his parents' suffering, but also the child's irrational, guilty sense that this suffering is all his fault, and with that guilt, the suicidal wish never to have been born. This outburst angers the rest of the audience, and the usher, a sort of superego figure, arrives, "flashing his searchlight" and threatening to evict the narrator.

When, upon witnessing his parents' quarrel, the narrator bursts forth again, the usher makes good his threat and drags him "through the lobby of the theatre into the cold light," where he wakes up "into the bleak winter morning of [his] 21st birthday, the windowsill shining with its lip of snow, and the morning already begun."

While dragging him outside, the usher has warned him: "You can't act like this even if other people aren't around!"

Coming out of the dark theater into the lobby means waking from the dream, but also the coming of age traditionally associated with twenty-first birthdays. At the end of the story, the narrator must turn aside from his origins and begin his own life. The bright blankness of the snow, the morning with its prospect of unused time, and the inviting world glimpsed through the window are appropriate emblems of beginning. In later years, as he sank gradually into despair, Schwartz used his imagery of beginning more and more mechanically, with an increasingly strident and unconvincing optimism.

But what a beginning he made! Three and a half years after his graduation from NYU Schwartz was famous. In the fall of 1935, he began graduate study in philosophy at Harvard. As a first-year student he placed work in *Poetry* and *New Caravan*, and won the Bowdoin Prize for the best essay by a graduate student in the humanities. When, in his second year of study, his mother declared herself unable to support him further, he returned to New York. Turning his full attention to his writing, Schwartz quickly made a name for himself, publishing poems, essays, verse plays, and fiction in prestigious literary quarterlies. By the spring of 1938 he felt sufficiently established to marry Gertrude Buckman, an old high school acquaintance who caught his attention when she turned up as a fellow student at NYU. At the end of the year, just after his twenty-fifth birthday, New Directions published *In Dreams Begin Responsibilities*.

Even as a young man, Schwartz was fond of the scheming and plotting that would degenerate into paranoid manipulation toward the end of his life. He lined up influential friends to secure praise for his book, working himself into acute anxiety over its reception. But his fears proved totally unfounded. *In Dreams Begin Responsibilities* succeeded beyond his fondest hopes. Allen Tate called its style "the first real innovation that we've had since Eliot and Pound"; Mark Van Doren, writing in *Kenyon Review,* found it "as good as any poetry has been for a long while, say at least a literary generation." Other high compliments arrived from Wallace Stevens, F. W. Dupee, R. P. Blackmur, and John Crowe Ransom; W. H. Auden, though more restrained in his praise, admired the book also. In November 1939, Schwartz received a letter from T. S. Eliot, who was "much impressed by *In Dreams Begin Responsibilities.*"

The praise both thrilled and terrified Schwartz. When fame was a vague and distant goal, it had seemed wholly desirable, but no sooner was it achieved than he began to wonder whether he deserved it. To some extent we may attribute this reaction to his insecurity, but it also demonstrates an instinctive honesty in judging his own accomplishment. To be sure, *In Dreams Begin Responsibilities* is a remarkable book for a man of twenty-five, and a distinguished book by all but the most Olympian standards. But fine as it is, many of Schwartz's contemporaries overpraised it. None of its poems belongs in a class with the best of Eliot, Ezra Pound, Hart Crane, or Auden, the poets with whom Schwartz was most frequently compared.

Doubtless the extravagant acclaim for *In Dreams Begin Responsibilities* reflected the critical vogue of "the tragic view of life" and the bleak look of the world on the brink of war. In retrospect, Schwartz's unremitting gloom can seem monotonous, and some of his pronouncements on history and fate belong in a speech by Polonius. Nonetheless, in the title story, in parts of "Coriolanus and His Mother," and in perhaps seven or eight of the lyrics, he

added something permanent to modern literature—no small accomplishment for any writer, young or old.

Schwartz's reputation must rest primarily on this book and the collection of stories, *The World Is a Wedding* (1948). These, with the best of the essays and a handful of later poems and stories, should secure him a place in American letters. His range was limited, and his early promise was never fulfilled, but he managed to produce a small body of minor masterworks— poems, stories, and essays that, despite their limitations, have a distinctive character of their own, not replaceable by the work of his greater contemporaries.

In Dreams Begin Responsibilities opens with the title story, which has already been discussed. The second part is a long narrative poem "Coriolanus and His Mother." As in the story, Schwartz employs the metaphor of spectatorship, although the relationship of the spectacle to the observer's own circumstances is in this case more oblique. The narrator is watching a performance of *Coriolanus;* in a blank verse that by turns imitates and parodies William Shakespeare's, he summarizes the action as it unfolds before him, interpreting the story as he retells it. He shares his theater box with four great men who aid him in his interpretations: Aristotle, Ludwig van Beethoven, Karl Marx, and Sigmund Freud (Freud, although still alive when the poem was published, ascends in Schwartz's treatment to the lofty remoteness of his dead colleagues). There is also a fifth ghost, masked and unnamed, who remains ominously silent throughout. Between the acts the narrator is transported to the stage, where he delivers prose monologues that meditate, half seriously and half ironically, on such themes as pleasure, justice, choice, and identity, with oblique reference to the play.

In deciding to recount the whole story of Coriolanus, Schwartz was exercising the narrative poet's prerogative of treating a traditional story in his own manner, just as Shakespeare had followed Plutarch. On the whole, Schwartz's account is fast-paced, and it achieves interesting effects at times by juxtaposing modern and Renaissance styles:

"Noli me tangere! How large they shout,
Each would partake of my world's
    championship,
Each thinks himself myself and I am fucked
By every craven knight vicarious there.
—Yet what a sweetness is that roaring kiss
Spreading in waves throughout the whorish
    air."

In this passage the Latin injunction recalls Sir Thomas Wyatt's "Whoso List to Hunt"; the inversions of word order in the fourth and fifth lines sound archaic. But these pentameters also find room for the psychiatrist's "vicarious," the baseball fan's "world's championship," and the physicist's "Spreading in waves." The word "fucked," planted emphatically at the end of a line, belongs to both the old idiom and the new.

In his essay "Ezra Pound's Very Useful Labors" (1938), Schwartz criticized the lack of narrative continuity in the *Cantos,* and in "The Isolation of Modern Poetry" (1941) he remarked on the absence of good narrative verse in the twentieth century, despite great accomplishment in lyric forms. "Coriolanus and His Mother" has many fine moments, but it finally confirms Schwartz's diagnosis of the problem: "Dramatic and narrative poetry require a grasp of the lives of other men, and it is precisely these lives . . . that are outside the orbit of poetic style and poetic sensibility." To the extent that Schwartz's Coriolanus remains one of those "other men," we find him dull, for his story has been better told in Plutarch and Shakespeare. To the extent that he becomes an autobiographical persona, we find him interesting, but for this we do not require the narrative

structure. Allusions to the well-known incidents of his story would suffice, woven into a much shorter, primarily meditative poem.

It is not hard to see why Schwartz found the life of Coriolanus suggestive for his own art. To begin with, his inclusion of the hero's mother in the title hints at the autobiographical connection. William Barrett remarks on Schwartz's "constant closeness to his mother, who did everything she could to prolong his narcissism, exaggerate his ego with praise, and yet in her clever and poisonous way insinuate in the child, then the boy, and then the young man, that the love and trust of anybody was not to be believed." Every word of this description applies to Coriolanus as Schwartz interprets him. One can also see in Coriolanus' aristocratic contempt for his fellow Romans a parallel to the contempt of Eliot, Pound, and other writers for modern democratic culture, a contempt Schwartz partly shared and partly repudiated. The story also raises the question of whether one can reject one's origins and still retain one's identity. Schwartz encountered this question in several ways: as an "alienated" artist on the margin of society, as a second-generation American Jew on the brink of assimilation, and as a young man who owed his existence to a marriage that he could only regard as a terrible mistake.

To some extent Schwartz reinterprets the story of Coriolanus in the way he retells it. He places Marxist rhetoric in the mouths of Brutus and the other spokesmen for the plebeians; he repeatedly compares Coriolanus with Narcissus and gives a Freudian turn to his contempt for the people by seizing on such details as his dislike of their "smell":

"You stink!" he cries. "You scum!" he shouts,
    shocked by
Their protest, offended by their being,
Nursing in mind, older than any thought,
A hatred of all who issue sweat, urine,

Or excrement, the child's profound distaste
Once for all smitten, never, alas! outworn.

Schwartz also draws out the psychoanalytic
implications of the hero's extreme need for his
mother's approval. But most of the interpretation comes in the form of commentary by the
four great men in the audience. Beethoven is
present mainly to lend his *Coriolan* overture as
background music. Aristotle speaks frequently,
but too much of what he has to say sounds like
a lecture to undergraduates on *The Poetics.* The
most interesting part of the commentary comes
from Marx and Freud, who engage in a running
debate about the nature and causes of the hero's
tragic flaw.

To Marx, the hero's mother, Volumnia, is
nothing but a living metaphor for the state. The
real mother of Coriolanus is Rome and, more
particularly, the patrician class. Coriolanus
commits his fatal mistake in believing that he,
or anyone else, exists completely as an individual. And yet the class pride that makes him
"noble" contains, dialectically, the seed of this
error; individual pride is but class pride carried
to the extreme. Freud interprets the problem as
personal rather than social, stemming from a
regressive desire to return to the womb, or to
the primary narcissism of the infant:

> "His mother's breast," intrudes the
>   Viennese,
> "Delighted him too much, fixed his disease.
> The child misunderstood, blind animal:
> Dark Id rules all, and though impersonal,
> Fixed to the womb this individual:
> 'O Mutter, Mutter, it is cold outside':
> So speaks his wish to die, such is his pride."

Coriolanus finds the entire world wanting because nowhere within it can he regain the absolute gratification he enjoyed in infancy.

It is curious that Coriolanus should be presented as an embodiment of the untamed id, for
in his hatred of pleasure and of the body, he
seems, on the contrary, a victim of a tyrannical
superego. One recalls Freud's observation, in
The Ego and the Id, that the moral demands of
a harsh superego have the same unconscious,
compelled quality as the libidinal demands of
the id. Schwartz seems uncertain whether the
denial of instinct is neurosis or nobility. More
generally, he seems unable to decide whether
his hero is reducible to Freudian and Marxist
explanations, or whether there is an irreducible
part that transcends explanation. He sometimes
entertains the possibility that something—call
it the soul, or what you will—can escape the
determinisms that trouble him so deeply.

Schwartz was finally more interested in interpreting the story of Coriolanus than in telling
it. Although his anxious sense of unseen forces
working behind outward events is typical of a
good deal of modern literature, he drove the
passion for explanation to extremes, as if the
explanation could somehow undo the events or
drain them of their power to harm. "Coriolanus
and His Mother" struggles ponderously toward
a kind of knowledge that is by its nature unat-
tainable, since explanations must stop somewhere or lose themselves in infinite regress.

Caught in his Sisyphean conception of his
art, Schwartz produced poems more notable for
their ambition, brilliance, and moral passion
than for technical assurance or formal unity.
Though he could produce felicitous lines,
Schwartz was endowed but modestly with the
auditory imagination. When he later turned
away from the intellectualism of his early poetry to an art of lyrical celebration, he could not
work the magic of a Dylan Thomas or a Theodore Roethke in that mode. But some of the
short poems of *In Dreams Begin Responsibilities* show him at his best; only infrequently
would he match their achievement afterward.

Schwartz divided the lyrics of *In Dreams
Begin Responsibilities* into two groups, the first
(and less impressive) of which he called "The
Repetitive Heart: Eleven Poems in Imitation of

the Fugue Form." With a sobriety unusual in proponents of "musical form," he added in a note: "This suite of poems might perhaps be more exactly called poems in a form suggested by the fugue, since the contrapuntal effect is of course impossible in language." Schwartz's method of suggesting counterpoint depends mainly on the repetition of key words and phrases several times during each poem; these "fugues" might uncharitably be described as sestinas or villanelles, though the pattern of repetition is less regular. Sometimes a rhythmic pattern is repeated in several consecutive phrases, and sometimes the predominantly tetrameter lines are broken with a strong medial caesura, so that one hears an "entrance," an implied lineation within the line. Schwartz does not exploit self-interruption and fragmentation, as the German poet Paul Celan was to do in his famous "Todesfuge." There is, in short, no great technical innovation here. Nor is there, except in a few of the poems, very much substance with which the form can engage.

The one poem of real distinction in "The Repetitive Heart" is the frequently anthologized "The Heavy Bear Who Goes with Me," a meditation on the dualism of body and soul. In "The Heavy Bear . . ." Schwartz's Freudian and Marxist explanations give way to a rhetoric of Platonic idealism. What looks in "Coriolanus and His Mother" like neurotic rejection of pleasure becomes a noble exaltation of the spirit over the senses. The "bear" of the title is the body itself, perceived not as the habitation of the soul but as an oafish doppelgänger who mimics the soul's gestures, coarsening them even as he makes them manifest. He is "A caricature, a swollen shadow, / A stupid clown of the spirit's motive. . . ."

Although he is an encumbrance, the bear can be pitied in his vulnerability. Enslaved to his desires and fears, he "Howls in his sleep for a world of sugar, / A sweetness intimate as the water's clasp." He has "followed" the soul "since the black womb held," and remains perpetually dissatisfied (like Coriolanus) in the less obliging world outside, where he "Boxes his brother in the hate-ridden city" and competes in "The scrimmage of appetite everywhere." He fears death and "Trembles to think that his quivering meat / Must finally wince to nothing at all."

Even in lovemaking, where one might suppose him welcome, the bear can do nothing right; instead, he

Stretches to embrace the very dear
With whom I would walk without him near,
Touches her grossly, although a word
Would bare my heart and make me clear. . . .

In refusing to be ruled by spiritual love, the body frustrates its own desires, for the spirit's "word" would gain the woman's assent, whereas the bear, touching her "grossly," drives her away. Finally, the body is the enemy of all true selfhood. The speaker complains that the bear is "Dragging me with him in his mouthing care, / Amid the hundred million of his kind. . . ." Souls are unique; bodies are interchangeable.

We encounter the Platonic Schwartz again in one of the best of the "Twenty-Four Poems" that follow "The Repetitive Heart." Its title, "In the Naked Bed, in Plato's Cave," refers to the famous parable in book 7 of Plato's *Republic,* in which prisoners, chained facing the rear wall of a cave, mistake their own shadows, and those of objects at the mouth of the cave, for the primary substance of reality. The poem reveals well the tension between Schwartz's interest in social causation and his desire to dismiss the entire time-bound world as inherently hopeless. The cave metaphor has been given a thisworldly twist, for, as Richard McDougall points out, "the world outside is the actual world and not a simile for a reality beyond it. According to this substitution of the literal for the symbolic, Schwartz's meaning seems to be the exact opposite of Plato's: the world in time (and of being in time) *is* reality itself." Yet the metaphor leads back toward its original significance as the poem progresses.

McDougall's remark applies quite well to the opening lines:

In the naked bed, in Plato's cave,
Reflected headlights slowly slid the wall,
Carpenters hammered under the shaded
    window,
Wind troubled the window curtains all night
    long,
A fleet of trucks strained uphill, grinding,
Their freights covered, as usual.
The ceiling lightened again, the slanting
    diagram
Slid slowly forth.
    Hearing the milkman's chop,
His striving up the stair, the bottle's chink,
I rose from bed, lit a cigarette,
And walked to the window.

As the narrator of "In Dreams Begin Responsibilities" must leave the darkened theater to face the world outside his bedroom window, so here the speaker must move from isolated selfhood to relation with the world. The noises he hears just before dawn suggest the difficulties of that world: the trucks "strained uphill," the milkman was "striving up the stair."

Like the unchained prisoner in Plato's allegory, the speaker turns to look at the world outside the cave. Imagery of change yields to imagery of stasis, though the objects remain very much of this world:

        . . . The stony street
Displayed the stillness in which buildings
    stand,
The street-lamp's vigil and the horse's
    patience.

This passage is followed by two remarkable lines, in which the speaker does glimpse something beyond what McDougall calls "the world in time":

The winter sky's pure capital
Turned me back to bed with exhausted eyes.

Just as Schwartz adapts Plato's idealist allegory to express a materialist idea, so in these lines he takes Marx's "capital" and makes it stand for an ideal transcendence. Like Plato's newly emancipated cave dweller, the speaker is blinded by the light, and returns to the "cave" of his bedroom. The sky is "pure capital" in the sense that its pure spirit has not been invested in any particular embodiment; it has not descended into the world in time.

After the speaker's return from the window, the stillness is broken and the day begins. Although the world has not taken on the absolute purity of the sky, it has become more intelligible and substantial than it was in the opening lines:

        . . . Morning, softly
Melting the air, lifted the half-covered chair
From underseas, kindled the looking-glass,
Distinguished the dresser and the white
    wall.

The poem broadens at its close toward a general statement about the human condition:

    . . . So, so,
O son of man, the ignorant night, the
    travail
Of early morning, the mystery of beginning
Again and again,
    while History is unforgiven.

Despite this overblown ending, "In the Naked Bed, in Plato's Cave" is unforgettable. If one had to pick Schwartz's best poem, it would be among the three or four possibilities.

"The Ballad of the Children of the Czar" also belongs on this short list. The poem begins with an image of sheltered innocence: "The children of the Czar / Played with a bouncing ball" one "May morning" in the palace gardens. But they lost control of the ball: "It fell among the flowerbeds / Or fled to the north gate."

As Schwartz develops this metaphor, it comes to stand for the precariousness of life: sooner or later, someone is bound to make the fatal throwing error. In the second section the poet presents himself at the moment when the aristocratic game of catch was played:

> While I ate a baked potato,
> Six thousand miles apart,
>
> In Brooklyn, in 1916,
> Aged two, irrational.

Although the focus has shifted to the poet, the year 1916 revises our understanding of the first section. It is the year before the Russian Revolution, and the children of the czar will soon perish with their father. The presence of the poet in Brooklyn has something to do with the czar also: the oppression of the Jews under Nicholas II resulted in his grandfather's immigration to America.

The poet can hardly sympathize with Nicholas II, but he can pity the fate of the czar's children. The third section is a meditation on the transmission of guilt from generation to generation. As Aeneas carried his father from the ruins of Troy, so each child must carry the guilt of his parents in his own psyche. The poet, though he will not be killed for his father's crimes, will be burdened, perhaps even destroyed, by the suspicion and guilt his parents have inculcated in him. We can repudiate our parents, or revolt against the czar, but one's parents were once victims of their parents, and the czar was once a child playing in the palace garden. In some final sense the guilty may be innocent; revenge, therefore, only increases

guilt. Seeing "that history has no ruth / For the individual," the poet declares, "Let anger be general: / I hate an abstract thing." The problem lies in defining this "abstract thing" and representing it in a poem.

Schwartz returns to the ball metaphor in the fourth section and generalizes it, in the fifth, to include the earth itself: "The ground on which the ball bounces / Is another bouncing ball." The world "makes no will glad"; it is "A pitiless, purposeless Thing. . . ." The section ends in a curiously obsessive, flat string of declarations:

> The innocent are overtaken,
> They are not innocent.
>
> They are their father's fathers,
> The past is inevitable.

This state of affairs, perhaps, is the "abstract thing" the poet hates.

From this lofty plane of generality, the sixth and final section returns to the poet in his second year:

> I eat my baked potato.
>
> It is my buttered world,
> But, poked by my unlearned
>   hand,
>
> It falls from the highchair down
> And I begin to howl.

The infant, vulnerable and totally absorbed in the act of eating the potato (his "buttered world"), is in the same plight as the adult, absorbed in maintaining his fragile existence amid hostile forces. The poem closes with another string of defiantly flat assertions, as grim and heavy as the fate they announce:

> Even a bouncing ball
> Is uncontrollable,
>
> And is under the garden wall.
> I am overtaken by terror

Thinking of my father's fathers
And of my own will.

The succession of rhymes and near rhymes reinforces the bluntness: "terror" and "fathers"; "ball," "-ble," "wall," and "will." It is possible that Schwartz has belabored the significance of his materials unduly. But here, for once, his search for grand historical themes within his own experience justifies itself. He locates himself within history, rather than appropriating history as a backdrop for a private melodrama.

There are several more modest successes among the "Twenty-Four Poems." "Far Rockaway," in language reminiscent of Hart Crane's "Voyages" and the seaside passage of "In Dreams Begin Responsibilities," evokes the seductive brilliance of the ocean:

The radiant soda of the seashore fashions
Fun, foam, and freedom. The sea laves
The shaven sand. And the light sways forward
On the self-destroying waves.

Vacationers lie "with the passionate sun," escaping "the rigor of the weekday," but here too the note of doom intrudes. "Time unheard moves," and a novelist, like a "nervous conscience amid the concessions," regards the scene distrustfully, reconstructing the private histories the sunbathers must carry within them.

"Tired and Unhappy, You Think of Houses" presents a similar dichotomy of seductive comfort and harsh reality. The thought of "houses /Soft-carpeted and warm," where "servants bring the coffee" entices the "Tired and unhappy" speaker. There is even a young girl singing—but what is the piece? "That song of Gluck where Orpheus pleads with Death." Even in this "banal dream," mortality will out. Better to face the harshness of urban reality, with its "anger exact as a machine!"

A more ambitious poem that similarly plays illusion against disillusionment is the "Prothalamion" Schwartz wrote to celebrate, if that is the word, his engagement to Gertrude Buckman. "Now I must betray myself," the poem begins; marriage is a "unity" but also a "bondage." Marriage means betrayal in a number of ways. The husband must not "wear masks or enigmatic clothes" before his wife; he must "betray" or reveal to her his "shocking nakedness." He must also at times "betray" or be disloyal to his own impulses in order to accommodate his wife. And his conduct in marriage will "betray" or reveal to himself the essence of his own character.

As we have already seen, Schwartz feared that his character had been irrevocably ruined in his childhood. As if to arm himself against the danger that his past will undo his marriage, Schwartz invites Marx and Freud to the wedding; they can "mark out the masks that face us there" and free the lovers from "self-deception." In a flourish of extravagance, he invites "all / Who are our friends somehow," representatives of the various arts and professions, and, for good measure, Wolfgang Amadeus Mozart, Athena, Robinson Crusoe, and Charlie Chaplin. Then suddenly, in a poignant reversal, he says:

But this is fantastic and pitiful,
And no one comes, none will, we are alone,
And what is possible is my own voice,
Speaking its wish, despite its lasting fear. . . .

To marry is to take on the care of another's body and mysterious soul. "You are heavy," he tells his bride; "when I carry you / I lift upon my back time like a fate. . . ." One remembers the "heavy bear" of the body, or the child carrying the father in "The Ballad of the Children of the Czar." The poem ends on a forced note of optimism, but not before running a diapason of misgivings. Gertrude Buckman was to leave Schwartz after four years of marriage; no one can say she hadn't been warned.

At least three other poems from *In Dreams Begin Responsibilities* deserve mention. "Father and Son," though flagrantly derivative of Yeats and occasionally marred by clumsy prosody, is nonetheless an interesting confrontation between the irresponsibility of a youth who "would be sudden now and rash in joy," and his father's intimations of guilt and mortality. The father sounds much more like the twenty-five-year-old poet than the son does.

"A Young Child and His Pregnant Mother" might be considered a companion piece for "Father and Son," but it keeps the usual philosophizing in abeyance, aiming primarily at an evocation of the child's feelings:

And now this newest of the mysteries,
Confronts his honest and his studious eyes—

His mother much too fat and absentminded,
Gazing far past his face, careless of him,

His fume, his charm, his bedtime, and warm
    milk,
As soon the night will be too dark, the spring

Too late, desire strange, and time too fast,
This first estrangement is a gradual thing

(His mother once so svelte, so often sick!
Towering father did this: what a trick!)

It is significant that Louise Bogan, one of the few reviewers with strong reservations about *In Dreams Begin Responsibilities,* admired this poem as more direct, less attitudinizing, than most of the others. One might also have expected her to like "The Ballet of the Fifth Year," which, despite momentary poaching from Crane's "To Brooklyn Bridge," is similarly straightforward. This poem also moves more deftly than any other in the volume. It contains only two sentences, the second of

which sweeps, without losing momentum, through fifteen lines. The closing image has a definite, externalized clarity unusual in Schwartz:

. . . I skated, afraid of policemen, five years
    old,
In the winter sunset, sorrowful and cold,
Hardly attained to thought, but old enough to
    know
Such grace, so self-contained, was the best
    escape to know.

"The Ballet of the Fifth Year" is not an ambitious poem, but it has a "grace, so self-contained" that most of the weightier pieces lack.

In Dreams Begin Responsibilities ends with "Dr. Bergen's Belief," a play in prose and verse that need not detain us long; even Schwartz's most admiring reviewers ignored it. Dr. Bergen has become the leader of a religious cult. He believes that the sky is the eye of God, and that problems may be solved "intuitively" by staring at the sky until illumination comes. His daughter, Eleanor, has recently committed suicide. Dr. Bergen has obtained "intuitive" assurance that the suicide was done in obedience to divine guidance; Eleanor is thus the first martyr to his cause. But Eleanor's psychiatrist produces a letter showing the cause to have been less ethereal: Eleanor killed herself because she was in love with a married man. Overcome with doubt, Dr. Bergen throws himself from the second-story balcony of his house, seeking in death the revelation that has eluded him in life. Written in Schwartz's worst grandiloquent manner, the play is interesting only for its theme: who has the truth, the psychiatrist who reduces all to mundane causes or the mystic who seeks transcendence in a world beyond this one?

The success Schwartz achieved with his first book brought him other kinds of success as well. He became poetry editor of *Partisan Review* in 1939 and, in the fall of 1940, Briggs-Copeland instructor at Harvard. He won a Guggenheim fellowship for the academic year 1940–1941, which was renewed for the following year. During these years, he turned out a number of excellent articles and book reviews for *Partisan Review, Poetry, Kenyon Review,* and other literary magazines. As Philip Rahv observed, "While it is well-known that many poets have produced their best work in their early twenties, it is only very rarely that a critic has contributed anything memorable at that age." Schwartz's career appeared to be as solidly established as a man of his age could wish. And yet, his next ventures in poetry—a translation of Arthur Rimbaud's *Une saison en enfer* (1939) and *Shenandoah* (1941)—do not show him at his best; and the ambitious *Genesis: Book One* (1943), envisioned as the first part of a major autobiographical epic in verse and prose, shows him struggling with difficulties he could not resolve.

The Rimbaud translation was badly received because of its numerous errors; Schwartz revised it for a second edition in 1940, but the damage had been done. Wallace Stevens defended it in a letter to Leonard C. van Geyzel, saying that "It might be sophomoric from the point of view of translating from one language into another and yet contain things that matter." But this defense requires us to regard the poem as a Lowellian "imitation" rather than a translation. Writing for the *New York Review of Books* in 1967, Roger Shattuck preferred Schwartz's version to those of Louise Varèse and Wallace Fowlie, though he added: "Is it sheer perverseness that makes me find Schwartz's out-of-print version best?" Maybe it was "perverseness," or the sentiments aroused by Schwartz's death the year before; one might also add that neither the Varèse nor the Fowlie is a really distinguished translation. Considered as an English poem, Schwartz's *A Season in Hell* is the liveliest of the three, but it does not

have the memorable felicity that makes one forgive the liberties in Pound's translations.

Shenandoah appeared as the eighth offering in the New Directions "Poet of the Month" series for 1941. James Atlas describes the reviews as "mixed"; but F. O Matthiessen, in his sympathetic review of *Genesis,* remarks that when Schwartz's "short verse play, *Shenandoah,* seemed slight, it became the fashion to declare that he had been overpraised and had not deserved his reputation in the first place." *Shenandoah* was not a disaster like the Rimbaud translation, but it did not do Schwartz's reputation any good. It belongs among neither the best nor the worst of his writings.

As noted earlier, *Shenandoah* deals with the naming of the protagonist, Shenandoah Fish. The adult Shenandoah witnesses and interprets the commotion occurring around his eight-day-old self on the stage. The autobiographical source of the material, if it were not already obvious, would be given away when Shenandoah's mother slips "Delmore" into a list of names for consideration. Once again Schwartz has depicted himself as a spectator watching his own origins reenacted before him. Such drama as the play can muster is provided by the conflict between Shenandoah's father, Walter Fish, and his uncle, Nathan Harris. Nathan has just finished medical school and has acquired enough sophistication to recognize the name "Shenandoah" as inappropriate. The rabbi, present for the circumcision ceremony, refuses to intervene, saying to himself: "Forbearance and humility are best: what good will it do me to become angry? The modern world is what it is." Finally, Walter Fish telephones his Gentile attorney, Mr. Kelly, to confirm his decision. *"After all,"* says Walter, *"this child is going to live in a world of Kellys!"* At the end of the play, the circumcision is performed offstage, and *"There is an appalling screech, as of an infant in the greatest pain."*

As one of his epigraphs to the play, Schwartz quotes the *Encyclopaedia Britannica:* "It is the historic nature of all particulars to try to prove that they are universal by nature. . . ." But he apparently could not trust the particulars to do so on their own. In his commentaries the adult Shenandoah extracts the last drop of significance from the proceedings. Ruminating on the argument between Walter and Nathan, he declares:

This is hardly the last time, little boy,
That conflict will engage the consciousness
Of those who might admire Nature, pray to
   God,
Make love, make friends, make works of art,
   make peace—
O no! hardly the last time: in the end
All men may seem essential boxers, hate
May seem the energy which drives the stars
(L'amor che move il sole e l'altre stelle!)
And war as human as the beating heart:
So Hegel and Empedocles have taught.

After going on to list the "world-wide causes" that have conspired to choose his name; Shenandoah embarks on a catalog of the great alienated modern writers who will "obsess this child when he can read," and perorates by saying:

This child will learn of life from these great
   men,
He will participate in their solitude,
And maybe in the end, on such a night
As this, return to the starting-point, his name,
Showing himself as such among his friends.

The speech that closes the play is similarly overwrought, rehearsing the sufferings worse than circumcision that will follow when "the horrors of modern life are your sole place," and "the dying West performs unspeakable disgrace /Against the honor of man, before God's utter gaze. . . ."

The problem with *Shenandoah* is not that it makes abstract or general statements in verse, but that the abstractions are several sizes too large for the particulars concerned. The effort to ensure that the audience understands the significance of Shenandoah's name—which is to say, of Schwartz's own—is so hysterically frenzied that one infers behind it a fear that perhaps the name is nothing but an accident, not very significant to anyone but the man who must bear it. A similar criticism can be made of Schwartz's next volume, *Genesis: Book One.*

Genesis grew out of drafts for an autobiographical poem that go back as far as 1931, when the poem was to have been entitled "Having Snow." Later, Schwartz tried writing the piece as prose, settling finally on alternating passages of prose and verse. The stylized prose, set up typographically like biblical verses, is used for narration. The poetry, for the most part blank verse but sometimes freely rhymed or metrically irregular, is reserved for analysis and commentary. Schwartz appears under the name Hershey Green. One winter night, as Hershey is trying to sleep, he thinks he sees snow falling outside the window. Going to the window, he finds that the moonlight and his imagination have tricked him. But although there is no literal snow, the illusion is a portent: the ghosts of the dead appear to Hershey and ask him to tell the "endless story" of his life. The story, which might indeed have proved "endless" if continued at the same pace, takes us from the young adulthood of Schwartz's grandparents in the old country to the incident, earlier recounted in "Prothalamion," when his mother found her husband in a roadhouse, dining with another woman. This incident occurred in 1921, when Schwartz was seven. For Hershey Green, his persona in *Genesis,* it marks the loss of innocence: "Childhood was ended here!"

We wait sixty-six pages for Hershey Green to be born; sixty-nine pages after that, he enters first grade. This exhaustive (and, for the reader, exhausting) reconstruction of early childhood reflects Schwartz's Freudianism. Though it would be difficult under the best circumstances to make a two-hundred-page book from the memories of early childhood, stranger projects have succeeded. But Schwartz's language does not, for the most part, recreate the child's experience with much vividness or exactness. It tells us what happened, and gives the names of the emotions that the child experienced, but it does little more. Hershey does not tell his story in the first person; instead Schwartz tells it in the third person, a technical decision that contributes to the lack of immediacy.

One possible explanation for the inert language of *Genesis* is suggested in a long letter to Schwartz from W. H. Auden, whom New Directions had consulted as a reader for the manuscript. In this letter (quoted extensively in the Atlas biography), Auden criticizes the assumptions outlined in Schwartz's preface. In an age when "their beliefs and values are embodied in great institutions and in the way of life of many human beings," Schwartz tells the reader, authors "do not have to bring in their beliefs and values from the outside; they have only to examine their experience with love in order to find particular beings and actions which are significant of their beliefs and values." The most fortunate of all were the authors of the Gospels, "who, as authors, perhaps had only to look up or remember." Schwartz does not consider his own situation to be so fortunate; he is defending his own need to "bring in . . . beliefs and values from outside." Nonetheless, Auden tells him: "The central fault in your poem is . . . just this false hope that if you only look up and remember enough, significance and value and belief will appear of themselves." Indeed, one might easily conclude that the "significance and value" of the incidents in *Genesis* were so overwhelmingly present for Schwartz that he forgot

how much art is needed to re-create that overwhelming presence for someone else.

All the same, Schwartz belabors the "significance and value" of each incident, great and small. The explanations are not explanations at all, but astonishingly pointless reifications of every emotion and institution into a "divinity" or cosmic force. When Mrs. Green sells a bond to finance the operation that enables her to conceive Hershey, it proves that "Capitalismus penetrates each heart." When Hershey, watching the funeral of a young woman, wishes to see the corpse naked, it means that "Love and Death have lain by each other in his mind, Eros and Thanatos, the beginning and the end, Romeo and Juliet forever composed!"

Does Hershey Green go to school? No; say, rather, that

> "The school divinity exerts its power,
> Much like the big city on a farm boy—"
> "Against the parenthood, against the life
> Made by the family divinity. . . ."

"Elucidate, go on, make lucid all, / For it will do him good!" interrupts still another ghost, but it is hard to see how such pseudo insights could do anyone any good. When an analysand indulges in such explanations, the analyst is professionally obliged to set him straight.

However sincerely Schwartz may have intended *Genesis* as a cathartic self-exploration, part of him seems to have resisted that intention. The result is a work of autobiography that evades rather than engages the hard questions that its content raises: What, as a morally responsible adult, can one do to surmount a destructive heritage? What, as a poet, can one do to make art of such intractable materials as infantile sexuality and the perils of kindergarten? Schwartz explains himself away, telling his story with a curious suppression of affect, veiling his motives in grandiose universals. The problem, then, may not be quite what Auden said it was. Schwartz may have believed that his life would interpret itself if he recorded it faithfully enough, but he shrank from the pain of reexperiencing it as well as from the pain of understanding it.

Genesis: Book One must be accounted a failure, and the excerpts from the manuscript of the unpublished *Book Two* that Atlas reprints in *New Directions 35* do not suggest that the sequel would have been much better. Nonetheless, as one might expect from a writer of Schwartz's gifts, there are interesting passages scattered through it. Not all the narration is flat; not all the insight is bogus. Details like the unexpected snowfall on Christmas Eve, and Hershey's delight at receiving a bicycle the following morning, are evocatively presented. More somber scenes also stick in the memory: Hershey, on vacation with his father, looking at his phosphorescent watch in the darkness, waiting for his father to return from one of his amours; Hershey witnessing his father's shame during the roadhouse confrontation. Even the tedious ghosts get a witty line now and then:

Forgive strange God, maker of Heaven and
    Earth,
Who made the spring and fall with a slight
    tilt
Such as vain *beaux* will give their Sunday
    hats!

Above all, one can respect what Schwartz was trying to do in *Genesis*. He was trying, in a time that favored tightly controlled lyric poetry, to write a huge, sprawling work that would triumph by its sheer intensity, sincerity, and inclusiveness. He wanted to crowd everything from his first day in kindergarten to World War I, from the right fielder's throw home in a Giants game to the stock market crash, into a single work of art.

The reception given *Genesis* was not as harsh as it might have been. The book drew praise not only from R. P. Blackmur and F. O. Matthiessen, whom Schwartz knew personally, but also from Richard Eberhart, Dudley Fitts, and Northrop Frye. But Schwartz wanted to be told that he had produced a masterpiece on the order of William Wordsworth's *Prelude,* and no one was prepared to go that far. There were also dismissive reviews from William Rose Benét and Horace Gregory, among others; nor did Schwartz's friend Dwight Macdonald care for *Genesis,* though he refrained from saying so in print.

It was a difficult time for Schwartz personally as well. His marriage was breaking up. Also, although he had risen to the rank of associate professor at Harvard, he felt burdened by his increased teaching load and ill at ease with his colleagues. In these circumstances his thirtieth birthday seemed little cause for celebration. He missed New York, and it was to New York that he returned when he left Harvard, without giving notice, in the spring of 1947.

Despite his unhappiness, Schwartz continued to produce excellent critical essays and stories, though it was a lean time for his poetry. Indeed, his next book, *The World Is a Wedding* (1948), almost equals the achievement of his first. It contains six previously uncollected stories, along with a reprinting of "In Dreams Begin Responsibilities."

In some ways the six later stories resemble "In Dreams Begin Responsibilities." They continue to use autobiographical material, and they employ the same deliberately flat style. But "In Dreams" occasionally modulates from the flat style into a more poetic language, and it supplements autobiography with the surrealistic device of the dream theater. The later work is more insistently flat, but it has a wider range of observation and a more complex treatment of relations among the characters. The exception to this generalization is "The Statues," which adopts the conventions of parable rather than those of realism.

The title story, the longest in the volume, concerns a circle of young intellectuals gathered around the unpublished writer Rudyard Bell, whom they revere as a genius. Episodic rather than tightly plotted, the story examines each of several characters in turn, with Rudyard's overbearing presence always in the background. We perceive the characters through the eye of Jacob Cohen, "the conscience of the group," its most compassionate and imaginative member. To a lesser extent Rudyard's embittered sister Laura also serves as a surrogate author. Like Jacob, she sees through the pretensions of Rudyard and his admirers, although she judges more harshly.

On the most universal level, "The World Is a Wedding" is about the difficulties of friendship, but the atmosphere of the Great Depression permeates the lives of the characters. After brilliant careers in college, Rudyard and his friends find only dull jobs or no jobs at all. The circle provides the only release for their intellectual energies. This claustral mutual dependence and the lack of prospects for advancement intensify the brittle egocentricity common in ambitious young persons even under more favorable circumstances. The meetings of the circle are full of one-upmanship, of conscious and unconscious cruelty. Even Laura, detached and lucid as her sarcasms often are, has a personal motive: She had hoped to find a husband among her brother's friends, but none of them is interested. The Depression may contribute indirectly to their indifference to her, for "their lower middle class poverty kept them from seeking out girls and entertaining the idea of marriage."

Atlas has identified Rudyard Bell as Paul Goodman, who indeed had a circle of admirers about him in the mid-1930's. Schwartz himself is Jacob Cohen. But if we read the story as autobiography, we must also find part of Schwartz

in Rudyard Bell. Rudyard has, like Schwartz, an unlikely given name yoked to a common, one-syllable surname. One of his plays centers on a poet who, like Schwartz at the time the story was written, is obsessed with his own decline from early brilliance. His conversation with his former teacher, Percival Davis, is taken from an actual exchange between Schwartz and David Prall of Harvard. We might interpret Rudyard and Jacob as "bad" and "good" versions of Schwartz's character. But to read "The World Is a Wedding" purely as autobiography is to slight its universality, its insights into the life of the 1930's and the problems of late adolescence.

The theme of the Great Depression is intertwined with those of generational conflict and coming of age. The parents of the young men in the circle, who have struggled toward assimilation and economic security, cannot understand their sons' rejection of conventional social manners and of moneymaking. Upon meeting Israel Brown, an idealistic young teacher admired by the circle, Edmund Kish's mother can only ask: "How much money does he make?" This question becomes an ironic leitmotiv in the discussions of the group.

Rudyard and his friends carry their refusal of convention and compromise to noble but self-destructive extremes. Francis French, the only member of the group to secure a teaching job in a university, is dismissed when he refuses to make a nominal denial of an accusation of homosexuality. As a result, he is reduced to "the drudgery of teaching in a high school"; he no longer has time for his intellectual interests, and spends his evenings solely in pursuit of sexual pleasure. Rudyard himself, when visited by a producer who admires his plays, feigns contempt for success so convincingly that the opportunity is lost. Among the members of the circle, *contemptus mundi* is an honorific name for sour grapes. Their social habits have been formed around the need to make failure bearable; when a chance to escape from failure presents itself, they cannot respond appropriately.

Toward the end of the story, Rudyard's group has begun to drift apart. Relations have been strained by the rivalry between Marcus Gross and Ferdinand Harrap for the affections of a girl identified only as "Irene" (as the lack of a second name suggests, Irene hardly matters in herself). Jealous of Ferdinand's victory in love, Marcus threatens to reveal Irene's previous affair with Algernon Nathan, whom Ferdinand detests. Jacob restrains him; but Laura, jealous of the attention lavished on Irene, blurts out the secret when Ferdinand arrives. Quite apart from the rancor produced by this incident (which, we surmise, is typical), the Great Depression is ending. Some members of the circle have found jobs and drifted away from the neighborhood. Rudyard, the central figure in the group, has accepted a teaching job in Cleveland, so the others must decide whether to disband or to continue without him.

At this point Jacob launches into a long eulogy for the circle. In his readings he has found the words "the world is a wedding" (which Schwartz got from the Talmud). Meditating on this oracular statement, Jacob thinks of Pieter Brueghel's *The Peasant Wedding* as an illustration of it. The wedding ceremony includes many guests who can have little portion in the joy of the bride and groom: the celibate nuns, an "unkempt and middle-aged" musician whose abstracted gaze suggests that he is "thinking of his faded hopes." Even "the suitor whom the bride refused" must be present, "perhaps among the crush that crowds the door." The parents of the couple are old: "Their time is passed and they have had their day." And yet, Jacob continues, "this too is a pleasure and a part for them to play."

Like the members of the circle, most of the wedding guests do not have what they want; only the bride and groom have happiness, and they perhaps only for a little while. But participation in the ceremony releases and transforms everyone present. In this sense "the world is a wedding," "the most important kind of party, full of joy, fear, hope, and ignorance. And at this party there are enough places and parts for everyone." The circle, for all its bickering, has been "a circle of friendship," the kind one must have "to be present at the wedding of this world."

Laura, though she speaks more briefly, speaks last. During all the self-important philosophical discussions, she has been in the kitchen cooking for her brother's friends, who repay her kindness with indifference or condescension. It is the income from her job that has supported Rudyard for so many years. She replies to Jacob: "You can't fool me . . . the world is a funeral."

As Richard McDougall remarks, "Jacob and Laura . . . define the familiar polarities of Schwartz's mind," though his definition of these polarities as "loving communion" and "analytical reason" is misleading: Jacob is at least as analytical as Laura, and far more self-conscious. Manic and depressive would be closer to the truth: an untenably complete affirmation and an insupportably dreary despair.

"New Year's Eve," the next story in the collection, treats the discontents of friendship on a smaller scale. Again the plot is slight: A group of intellectuals, including Shenandoah Fish, his girl friend Wilhelmina Gold, and his friend Nicholas O'Neil, attend a New Year's Eve party at the home of Grant Landis, an editor and co-owner of "Centaur Editions, a small publishing house" that has just printed Shenandoah's first book. Like the characters of "The World Is a Wedding," the guests at the party seek each other out in order to mitigate or forget their own unhappiness. But for the most part they spend the evening hurting each other's feelings, motivated by an insecurity that finds malice in the remarks of others and replies in kind. Although, as intellectuals and writers, they are committed to a high calling, they are at least as petty as other people.

The representative man at this gathering is Oliver Jones, a talented writer who has compromised himself by courting popularity in his fiction and flattering the powerful in his reviews. "And all this behavior," Schwartz observes, "would have been unnecessary to Oliver, had he only known that he was really a gifted author!" Unsure of his gifts, Oliver belittles all pretensions to an integrity greater than his own. He spoils the party's one brief "period of good feeling" by reading and then mocking Edmund Wilson's admiration, in *Axel's Castle,* for Marcel Proust's affirmation of "laws which we have obeyed because we have carried their precepts within us without knowing who inscribed them there...." Shenandoah leaves the party thinking, with Proust, that such laws must come from "some other world," since they certainly cannot derive from the pettiness of ours, in which writers are implicated as much as everyone else.

Schwartz left in his notes a key identifying the characters of "New Year's Eve": Shenandoah Fish is of course Schwartz himself, Wilhelmina Gold is Gertrude Buckman, and Nicholas O'Neil is William Barrett. The host, Grant Landis, is Dwight Macdonald, and Oliver Jones is an unflattering rendition of F. W. Dupee. Barrett's complaint about "The World Is a Wedding"—that it is "dull, unless you happen to know the people"—applies with more justice to "New Year's Eve." Whereas the longer story develops fictionalized characters enough so that we need not refer to their originals, "New Year's Eve" reduces character to caricature, and caricature loses its point if one doesn't "happen to know the people."

"A Bitter Farce," which follows "New Year's Eve," is more sharply focused. It tells of the young Shenandoah's encounters with anti-Semitism in his wartime summer classes. Shenandoah teaches two sections of composition, one for navy students and one for women. Discouraged by the heat of the summer and the bad prose of the navy students, Shenandoah often wanders "from discussions of spelling and grammar to ... matters which are sometimes referred to as topics of the day." On one such occasion, Shenandoah's navy class draws him into a discussion of "the Negro problem." Asked if he would marry a Negro woman, Shenandoah decides not to "lose face with his students" by answering yes. "I would not marry a Negro woman," he replies, "but there are many white women I would not marry for the same reasons...." Most of the students interpret this answer to mean "that Mr. Fish would not marry many white women as well as Negro women because he was a Jew," although this inference is incorrect.

Not long after this incident, one of the young ladies brings in a journal entry on the question: "If you had to marry one of them, which of these three would you choose, a Chinaman, a Jew, or a Negro?" A Jew would seem to be the closest racially, but, as the girl's friends point out, "there is something about Jews that other races can't stand." The student concludes with a halfhearted attempt at liberality; if "placed in that horrible position," she would "choose the one who was fairest and most honest, the kindest, and he whose ideas most nearly coincided with mine." Shenandoah declines to discuss the content of the passage. By commenting only on the style, he once more avoids confrontation.

But when provoked a third time, by a Mr. Murphy in the navy class, he can be silent no longer. He launches into a passionate defense, most of which is lost on his students. "My ancestors," he declares, "in whom I take pride, but not personal pride, were scholars, poets, prophets and students of God when most of Europe worshipped sticks and stones...." After the bell rings, Murphy stays to talk to him. "I have nothing against you," says Murphy; "you always give me a square deal." Shenandoah considers reporting Murphy to his commanding officer, for such "extraordinary lack of tact and discretion" ill becomes "an officer-to-be." But although he can find no reason for his decision, he lets the incident drop. We are left to wonder whether he does so from generosity or from cowardice. Unfortunately, James Atlas did not reprint this story in his selection.

In the next story, "America! America!," Schwartz for once succeeded in portraying a character much different from himself. The central figure, Mr. Baumann, is neither artist nor intellectual, but a modestly successful insurance salesman. Shenandoah listens to his mother's recollections of Mr. Baumann at a time when he has been feeling "a loss or lapse of identity." On this occasion "His mother's monologue began to interest him more and more, much more than ever before, although she spoke of human beings who, being of her own generation, did not really interest Shenandoah in themselves."

As he listens, he fidgets with a silver spoon, engraved with his initials, that the Baumanns gave him when he was born. This detail clearly foreshadows his climactic recognition of

... how closely bound he was to these people. His separation was actual enough, but there existed also an unbreakable unity. As the air was full of the radio's unseen voices, so the life he breathed in was full of these lives and the age in which they had acted and suffered.

He comes to understand that "the contemptuous mood which had governed him as he listened was really self-contempt and ignorance."

It is certainly the "separation" between Shenandoah and Mr. Baumann that strikes us first. Shenandoah has assumed the role of cosmopolitan and alienated young poet; he has just come back from a trip to Paris. (This detail, by the way, is not autobiographical.) Mr. Baumann is not cosmopolitan, alienated, or poetic; his success as an insurance man stems from his geniality. To succeed at insurance, " it was necessary to become friendly with a great many people," and to "join the lodges, societies, and associations of your own class and people. This had been no hardship to Mr. Baumann who enjoyed groups, gatherings, and meetings of all kinds."

Mr. Baumann values moneymaking and the good opinion of the community above all else, though the second goal often gets in the way of the first. He lacks the ruthless business instinct of Shenandoah's father, who does not allow bonhomie to interfere with profits. In a moment of weakness, Shenandoah's father takes Mr. Baumann and young Dick Baumann into his business; but upon discovering their amiable inefficiency he abruptly dissolves the partnership, the long friendship between the two families notwithstanding.

Dick Baumann inherits his father's geniality, but is unable to make a living from it. For that matter, after the stock market crash, Mr. Baumann himself has a hard time of it. His reduced circumstances are partly a result of the Great Depression, but also partly the result of his obsolete methods. As his other son, Sidney, cruelly tells him, "the old oil" no longer works in the increasingly assimilated and impersonal ambience of the community. Sidney, for his part, seems incapable of work; the daughter, Martha, makes a good marriage but becomes "more impatient with her family year by year," and eventually wishes to sever all ties with them, though her husband prevents her from doing so.

The old ways, which served well enough for Mr. Baumann, will not do for his children. They must choose between failure and a radical break with the previous generation. In either case the result is bitterness: "The lower middle-class of the generation of Shenandoah's parents had engendered perversions of its own nature, children full of contempt for every thing important to their parents."

Despite the "gulf" between Shenandoah and his mother's old friend, the two have some things in common. We learn that Mr. Baumann, like Shenandoah, enjoys sleeping late in the morning. He is "pleasure-loving," and thus an object of suspicion in the eyes of Shenandoah's father. Within his provincial world he is considered an intellectual, a more traveled and cultured man than his neighbors. And he doesn't just "sell" insurance policies, he "writes" them. Mr. Baumann's frustrated desire for high culture is typical of his generation; it finds fulfillment in the next generation, when Shenandoah and others like him become writers and scholars. But if Shenandoah completes Mr. Baumann, he has also cut his ties to family and community, and so becomes incomplete in another sense. In his isolation he has cause to envy Mr. Baumann's secure bond to a community.

"All I ever wanted," laments Shenandoah in "New Year's Eve," "was to have friends and go to parties." But by this criterion he is a failure and Mr. Baumann is a success. Thinking of his generation's "contempt" for its parents, Shenandoah

... began to feel that he was wrong to suppose that the separation, the contempt, and the gulf had nothing to do with his work; perhaps, on the contrary, it was the center; or perhaps it was the starting-point and compelled the innermost motion of the work to be flight, or criticism, or denial, or rejection.

Shenandoah finds his complementary relationship to Mr. Baumann difficult to acknowledge, but the acknowledgment is necessary for self-understanding.

"The Statues" stands apart from the other stories in *The World Is a Wedding.* Whereas the others deal with friendships and families in a quotidian social setting, "The Statues" is a parable, taking as its premise a miraculous event. One winter, at five o'clock on December 8 (Schwartz's birthday, as it just so happens), an unusual snow begins to fall in New York. It forms "curious and unquestionable designs, some of which were very human"; it also has "the hardness of rocks," so that it "could not be removed from the pavement." At first the mayor vows to get rid of the snow "as quickly as possible," but the citizens protest. There is a lull in all everyday activities—work and crime slow almost to a halt. Attendance drops at art galleries and movie theaters, for no art form, elite or popular, can compete with the astonishing snow sculptures.

The modern rational temper cannot account for this miracle. Scientists attempt to explain it by the laws of statistical probability, and even the clergy carefully avoids ascribing it to any supernatural power. Understood or not, the snowfall brings about a temporary utopia. It brings the central character, Faber Gottschalk, to discover in himself a passion for the good, the true, and the beautiful, scarcely apparent hitherto in his prosaic career as a dentist. But suddenly "a tireless and foul rain descended and to everyone's surprise utterly destroyed the fine statues." Everything immediately returns to normal, as if nothing unusual had ever happened. This story, like "A Bitter Farce," remains out of print; again, one wishes room had been found for it in Atlas' selection.

The last of the stories in *The World Is a Wedding,* aside from "In Dreams Begin Responsibilities," is "The Child Is the Meaning of This Life." It draws its characters from the household of Schwartz's maternal grandmother, Hannah Nathanson, whose fictional name is Ruth Hart. Schwartz appears under the name Jasper, but his story is subordinated to that of his mother's family. As in "America! America!" the second generation has lost the tough adaptability of the first. Ruth Hart has a generous, loving disposition and is dearly loved by all her friends. One might think that, despite the early death of her husband, she would succeed in raising capable, affectionate children. But her daughter Sarah (Jasper's mother) becomes sharp-tongued and resentful after her marriage to the rich but philandering Michael; her son Seymour is too lazy to hold a job, and gambles away what little money he has. Rebecca, the one loyal child, has helped to spoil Seymour; she even rescues him when he takes money belonging to his employer and bets it on a baseball game. She manages to make a respectable marriage to a dentist, but it is not a great success. Sarah's husband, a far better catch, repeatedly abandons his family to chase other women.

The characters are interesting, but the story lacks the power of "America! America!," in which the confrontation between Shenandoah's values and those of the Baumanns provides a much needed dramatic tension. Though only half the length of "The Child Is the Meaning of This Life," "America! America!" has more richness of implication.

If Atlas disappoints us by omitting "A Bitter Farce" and "The Statues" from his selection of Schwartz's stories, he makes up for it by restoring two noteworthy pieces that Schwartz for some reason never included in any of his books. "Screeno" was not published in any form until *Partisan Review* printed it in 1977, more than a decade after Schwartz's death. It concerns a young writer, Cornelius Schmidt, who goes to the movies and wins a game of "Screeno," apparently a variation of bingo played in theaters during the 1930's. The master of ceremonies, attempting to make conversation, asks Cornelius: "What do you do?" Cornelius replies that he is a poet. When the master of ceremonies and the audience find this amusing, Cornelius increases their hostility by reciting a passage

from Eliot's "Gerontion." Just as everyone has become suspicious of Cornelius, an old man calls out from the balcony, claiming that he also holds a winning card. The master of ceremonies tries to avoid paying the old man his prize money, although the card is indeed complete. Cornelius denounces the management as dishonest and miserly, and, in a sudden burst of generosity, gives his own prize money to the old man, though he had planned to invest it in books.

Less completely successful but also interesting is "The Commencement Day Address," which was published in the *New Directions* annual for 1937. It provides a minimal fictional scaffolding for the undecorously passionate speech of the historian Isaac Duspenser, who upbraids his audience for its frivolous indifference to history and mortality. The rhetoric of the speech is melodramatic but often powerful; perhaps the best passages of all come in Schwartz's descriptions of the ambience of the event:

An airplane gnawed overhead, bare, abstract and geometrical in the cloud-flowered sky; and its tone accented the passage of the afternoon. One listener had a firm sense of the narrow metropolitan city, its ribs bound by deep, narrow rivers, narrow on all sides, narrow in its tall towers, full of thousands of drugstores and apartment houses, full of thousands of narrow avenues, all of which stood in back of the idyllic campus scene and showed its falsity.

"The Commencement Day Address" is an odd combination of short story, essay, and prose poem; indeed, Dr. Duspenser's talk includes a prose rearrangement of "In the Naked Bed, in Plato's Cave."

After the publication of *The World Is a Wedding,* we approach the years in Schwartz's life that Saul Bellow used as material for *Humboldt's Gift:* the second marriage, to Elizabeth

Pollett, in 1949; the purchase of the rural New Jersey farmhouse in 1951; the ill-fated appointment at Princeton in 1952; the deterioration of the marriage; and, finally, the psychotic outburst against Hilton Kramer that ended with Schwartz's commitment to Bellevue Hospital for a week in 1957. During this period Schwartz alienated most of his old friends and began to lose his sense of membership in the literary community. His last book appeared in 1961, and he stopped publishing work in magazines after 1962. He taught at Syracuse University from 1962 to January 1965; despite his erratic teaching, he attracted a loyal following among the students. He might have stayed at Syracuse for the rest of his life, but instead left abruptly to spend his last months in cheap hotels in midtown Manhattan. When he died, on July 11, 1966, he was so isolated that the literary world knew nothing of his death for two days. Eventually a reporter, checking the morgue lists, recognized his name.

Received opinion has it that as Schwartz deteriorated, so did his work. "I'd bleed to say his lovely work improved / but it is not so," wrote John Berryman in one of his commemorative Dream Songs. Recently some critics have begun to question this judgment. Robert Phillips, in his foreword to *Last and Lost Poems of Delmore Schwartz,* takes issue with James Atlas' description of the opening stanza of "Darkling Summer, Ominous Dusk, Rumorous Rain" (1958) as composed of "haphazard, euphonious, virtually incomprehensible effusions." To dismiss such poetry because of its euphony, replies Phillips, "would be to dismiss Gerard Manley Hopkins, Dame Edith Sitwell, and Dylan Thomas, to name three."

But Atlas does not mean to dismiss the late poems because of their euphony. The problem is, rather, that they lack the meaning and emotional depth that would make the euphony amount to more than a technical effect. Here is

the stanza, so that the reader may judge:

A tattering of rain and then the reign
Of pour and pouring-down and down,
Where in the westward gathered the filming
  gown
Of grey and clouding weakness, and, in the
  mane
Of the light's glory and the day's splendor,
  gold and vain,
Vivid, more and more vivid, scarlet, lucid and
  more luminous,
Then came a splatter, a prattle, a blowing
  rain!
And soon the hour was musical and rumorous:
A softness of a dripping lipped the isolated
  houses,
A gaunt grey somber softness licked the glass
  of hours.

These lines, it should be added, are better than most in the later poems of this type.

A critic should not be afraid to overturn a received opinion; but sometimes a received opinion happens also to be just, and in such cases one has the dull duty of confirming it. Although the late poetry is not a total loss, it contains only two or three poems that will stand comparison with the best eight or ten of *In Dreams Begin Responsibilities.* The late fiction in *Successful Love and Other Stories* (1961) is also clearly inferior to the stories in *The World Is a Wedding.*

The nadir of Schwartz's career came in 1950, with the publication of *Vaudeville for a Princess.* This collection of poems, alternating with prose sketches in the first of its three sections, is a virtually unmitigated disaster. Schwartz tells us in a note that the title was "suggested by Princess Elizabeth's admiration of Danny Kaye." The poems aim at wit and playfulness, but the wit is leaden, the playfulness grim and willful. As noted earlier in connection with *Genesis,* Schwartz's style could become lazy, in a way that suggests an inertia born of despair. In

Vaudeville for a Princess, this despair is sometimes expressed as technical negligence. Metrical and syntactic clumsiness abounds, and in one of the sonnets, Schwartz simply doesn't bother to rhyme the last line of the sestet:

Churchill nudged Roosevelt. With handsome
    glee
Roosevelt winked! Upon life's peak they
    played
(Power is pleasure, though anxious. Power is
    free!)
Mah-jong or pat-a-cake with history:
They swayed like elephants in the gaiety
And the enormity of their success!

These lines exemplify the carelessness of the poems in other respects as well. The parenthetical sentences in the third line are awkward; the superfluous "Power is free!" looks like metrical padding; and one might have difficulty transporting the "elephants" of the fifth line to the "peaks" of the second. The tone of *Vaudeville for a Princess* was well described, in a savage but perceptive review by Hugh Kenner, as "frenetic embarrassment." The irony is too ponderous to be funny, too flippant to be profound. Rolfe Humphries, though he found the poems "solemn, owlish, abstract, and . . . entirely earless," liked the prose interludes of the first section, which struck him as witty, though "at times a bit glib." But these pieces have not worn well, and it is mostly the glibness that remains. Ranging from a discussion of automobiles to deliberately banal retellings of *Hamlet* and *Othello,* these sketches have the ephemeral quality of stand-up comedy, albeit a stand-up comedy for intellectuals.

The one good poem in *Vaudeville for a Princess* is "Starlight Like Intuition Pierced the Twelve," in which Christ's disciples, far from rejoicing in their master's completed mission, are overcome with guilt for their own inability

to match his "Unspeakable unnatural goodness." Instead of providing comfort and hope, Christ's life has exhausted the possibilities of goodness: "No one will ever fit / His measure's heights, all is inadequate: / No matter what I do, what good is it?" Christ's perfection "stares" accusingly at human imperfection, like Rainer Maria Rilke's archaic torso of Apollo. The poem makes a sad contrast with Schwartz's earlier remark, in the preface to *Genesis,* that the makers of the Gospels "had only to look up or remember" in order to find a sustaining faith.

The style of *Vaudeville for a Princess* is not yet the euphonious, rhapsodic manner that Phillips identifies as Schwartz's late style. For this we must turn to the previously uncollected work that Schwartz included in *Summer Knowledge,* the selection of his poems that he published in 1959. In this poetry, vague imagery of light and morning, and an exclamatory, occasionless affirmation, run rampant. Some of the poems continue using formal stanzas; others use a long free-verse line like that of Walt Whitman, or of Theodore Roethke in "The Lost Son" or "North American Sequence."

Without any prejudice against free verse or poetry of lyrical celebration, one must object when free verse is handled so ponderously or when celebration becomes so disembodied, so divorced from experience. The following example, which is far from the most damning that might have been chosen, will have to suffice. Here is the opening of "A Little Morning Music":

The birds in the first light twitter and whistle,
Chirp and seek, sipping and chortling—
    weakly, meekly, they speak and bubble,
As cheerful as the cherry would, if it could
    speak when it is cherry ripe or cherry
    ripening.
And all of them are melodious, erratic, and
    gratuitous,

Singing solely to heighten the sense of
    morning's beginning.
How soon the heart's cup overflows, how it is
    excited to delight and elation!

And in the first light, the cock's chant,
    roaring,
Bursts like rockets, rising and breaking into
    brief brilliance;
As the fields arise, cock after cock catches on
    fire,
And the pastures loom out of vague blue
    shadow,
The red barn and the red sheds rise and
    redden, blocks and boxes of slowly
    blooming wet redness;
Then the great awe and splendor of the sun
    comes nearer,
Kindling all things, consuming the forest of
    blackness, lifting and lighting up
All the darkling ones who slept and grew
Beneath the petals, the frost, the mystery and
    the mockery of the stars.

Some of the phrases are pleasing and evocative, taken in isolation. But as one can already sense in this passage, which is only the first half of the poem, there is no movement, only a proliferation of grandiose variations on the single image of morning. A little of this sort of description, wedded to an emotional occasion, set into motion and developed, could make a whole poem. But the rest of "A Little Morning Music" continues in the same vein. By the end of the poem, one questions the sincerity of all this joy: it seems rhetorical and manic, unmotivated by any adequate occasion, less concerned with the delights of morning than with the desperate assertion that all is well.

A few of the late poems *are* anchored in a specific occasion, and on the whole they prove to be the best ones. "'I Am Cherry Alive,' the Little Girl Sang" is spoken, as its title suggests,

by a child. It has the breathless, run-on rhythms of a child's speech:

"I am cherry alive," the little girl sang,
"Each morning I am something new:
I am apple, I am plum, I am just as excited
As the boys who made the Hallowe'en bang:
I am tree, I am cat, I am blossom too:
When I like, if I like, I can be someone new,
Someone very old, a witch in a zoo:
I can be someone else whenever I think
    who. . . . ["]

The language may strike us as slightly too precious, but it is still effective, as are the insistent rhymes.

The poems that James Atlas and Richard McDougall single out for praise are also dramatic monologues. Atlas admires the biblical group: "Abraham," "Sarah," and "Jacob"; McDougall prefers the monologues spoken by writers: "Sterne," "Swift," and "Baudelaire." All of these poems have their moments, especially "Jacob," but at times they seem too slackly written. They borrow too passively from their sources and are content with presenting a static attitude. A good dramatic monologue must progress and unfold as one moves from beginning to end.

Schwartz's borrowing is anything but passive in the wonderful "Seurat's Sunday Afternoon Along the Seine," a long free-verse meditation on Georges Seurat's *Un dimanche à la Grande-Jatte.* The source for this poem would seem to be not only the painting itself, but also Meyer Schapiro's article, "New Light on Seurat," published in the April 1958 issue of *Art News.* (The poem is dedicated "To Meyer and Lillian Schapiro.") Schwartz appears to have drawn upon Schapiro's commentary, even to the extent of adapting its language. Schapiro wrote:

With all its air of simplicity and stylization, Seurat's art is extremely complex. He painted large canvases not to assert himself nor to insist on the power of a single idea, but to develop an image emulating the fullness of nature. One can enjoy in the *Grande Jatte* many pictures each of which is a world in itself. . . .

Schwartz's words echo Schapiro's in these lines:

His vision is simple: yet it is also ample,
    complex, vexed, and profound
In emulation of the fullness of Nature. . . .

    . . .

Within this Sunday afternoon upon the Seine
Many pictures exist inside the Sunday scene:
Each of them is a world itself, a world in
    itself. . . .

More generally, Schwartz appears to have elaborated on Schapiro's description of the figures in the painting as "a secular congregation, grave and ceremonious, in their holiday communion with the summer light and air."

Schwartz's poem, though indebted to Schapiro's essay, is not a merely passive appropriation of it. Schwartz finds a pathos in the scene that Schapiro does not. The painting becomes a symbol of precarious reconciliation, in which

The Sunday summer sun shines equally and
    voluptuously
Upon the rich and the free, the comfortable,
    the *rentier,* the poor, and those who are
    paralyzed by poverty.
Seurat is at once painter, poet, architect, and
    alchemist:
The alchemist points his magical wand to
    describe and hold the Sunday's gold,
Mixing his small alloys for long and long
Because he wants to hold the warm leisure
    and pleasure of the holiday
Within the fiery blaze and passionate patience
    of his gaze and mind
Now and forever: O happy, happy throng,
It is forever Sunday, summer, free. . . .

The "happy, happy throng" should recall the "happy, happy boughs" of John Keats's "Ode on a Grecian Urn," for here, as in Keats, the permanence of art reminds us of the impermanence of life. Outside the painting, time presses on. Seurat died young, and in his brief span had little Sunday leisure. To create the apparent spontaneity of the painting,

. . . it requires the labors of Hercules,
    Sisyphus, Flaubert, Roebling:
The brilliance and spontaneity of Mozart, the
    patience of a pyramid,
And requires all these of the painter who at
    twenty-five
Hardly suspects that in six years he will no
    longer be alive!

Although the transient pleasures that the artist celebrates are not for him, the world within the painting is in a sense more "real" than his. In it people can sometimes lose their self-consciousness and fear of death in ordinary happiness. They find a summer's day by the river sufficient in itself, without any need to "describe and hold" it. The artist can pay homage to this simplicity, but he has no share in it. The poem ends wistfully:

    . . . Far and near, close and far away,
Can we not hear, if we but listen to what
    Flaubert tried to say,
Beholding a husband, wife and child on just
    such a day:
Ils sont dans le vrai! They are with the truth,
    they have found the way
The kingdom of heaven on earth on Sunday
    summer day.
Is it not clear and clearer? Can we not also
    hear
The voice of Kafka, forever sad, in despair's
    sickness trying to say:
"Flaubert was right: *Ils sont dans le vrai!*

Without forbears, without marriage, without
    heirs,
Yet with a wild longing for forbears,
    marriage, and heirs:
They all stretch out their hands to me: but
    they are too far away!"

We hear not only Gustave Flaubert and Franz
Kafka, but also Schwartz in these closing lines.
In them he has made clear, for once, his true
relation to the celebratory rhetoric in the late
poetry.

None of the poems that Robert Phillips recovered for his selection *Last and Lost Poems
of Delmore Schwartz* (1979) approaches the
power of "Seurat's Sunday Afternoon Along
the Seine," but a few of them are better than
most of the late work in *Summer Knowledge*.
One might recommend "America, America!"
(which has no connection with the story
"America! America!"), "Poem; Remember
Midsummer: The Fragrance of Box," "Spi-
ders," and the somber "All Night, All Night,"
with its bleak cry:

*O your life, your lonely life
What have you ever done with it,
And done with the great gift of consciousness?*

There are occasional striking images, of a
sensuous intensity rare in Schwartz's work.
Here, for instance, is the third of the "Phoenix
Lyrics":

Purple black cloud at sunset: it is late August
and the light begins to look cold, and as we
    look,
listen and look, we hear the first drums of
    autumn.

On the whole, though, the examples in Phillips'
book will hardly support a higher estimation of
Schwartz's late poetry. By turning away from
the personal and historic determinisms that had

burdened him for so long, he sometimes attained a measure of spontaneity and sensuous
immediacy missing in most of the early poetry.
But it is freedom in a vacuum, the volatilized
fantasy of a man who has nearly withdrawn
from all relation to the world. Only in those
poems in which some source in externality kept
him from severing that relation did he continue
to produce work of any substance.

Schwartz's last book, *Successful Love*
(1961), finds his prose style in tolerable repair,
but the stories lack the emotional force and social detail of the earlier work. The characters
are not drawn from autobiographical sources;
they are neither Jewish immigrants like Mr.
Baumann nor Jewish intellectuals like Shenandoah Fish. Schwartz's style always tended toward abstractness, and when he tried to depict
a milieu he did not know intimately, the texture
became too thin. "A Colossal Fortune" and
"The Hartford Innocents" are amusingly plotted but too long for their slight content. "An
American Fairy Tale" wittily reverses the
cliché of the philistine father and the idealistic
son: an aspiring young composer sells out and
writes advertising jingles, while the father re-
tires from his business and becomes a noted abstract expressionist painter. It's a good joke, but
little more than that.

James Atlas' selection contains only one story
from *Successful Love,* and it is unquestionably
the right one. "The Track Meet," with its savage irony and disturbing symbolism, stands
apart from—and above—the other late stories.
The narrator, Frank Lawrence, is awakened at
dawn by an unexpected English visitor, Reginald Law. Law takes Lawrence to a track meet,
at which Law is surprised to find his mother
among the spectators and his brothers among
the participants. The competition becomes a
symbolic commentary on the cruelty of human
nature, especially of human nature as influenced by a capitalist, mass-culture-dominated

society. One of the athletes kisses the lips of a girl on a billboard as if she were real; the runners punch and kick each other to gain position in the race, while the audience eggs them on. The brothers, who at first cooperated against the other athletes, begin to fight among themselves. When the race ends, an official shoots the winner, and five cheerleaders shoot the narrator's five brothers.

During these alarming events, Lawrence protests to his English companion that such tactics are "against the rules of the game." But if, as his name suggests, the Englishman represents "law," he does not stand for old-fashioned British propriety. The "law" he represents is post-Darwinian: "'Nature is unfair,' said Law, 'and existence is also unfair.'" "Law" is also the first part of "Lawrence," as we understand at the end of the story.

The narrator wants to escape from his nightmare by waking to "the little things and small actions of early morning" (the language echoes the celebratory rhetoric of *Summer Knowledge*). But waking is no escape, as Law brutally explains:

You don't escape from nightmare by waking up, you know. And if what occurred on the field were merely imaginary and unreal and merely your own private hallucination, then the evil that has terrified you is rooted in your own mind and heart. Like the rest of us . . . you not only know more than you think you know but more than you are willing to admit.

The other stories in *Successful Love* seem negligible in comparison with this one.

Schwartz's essays, although they cannot be said to have improved, remained lucid and at least intermittently interesting until he stopped writing them altogether in 1962. As a critic, Schwartz was preoccupied with the same issues as most of his contemporaries: the relationship between poetic statement and literal belief, and the tension between the need to connect poetry with a social context and the need to defend its autonomy and transcendence. His formulations of these problems usually derive from other critics, and his essays do not quite add up to a coherent and original view of literature.

Schwartz's special gift was his ability to analyze, define, and qualify the assertions of more imperious critics like T. S. Eliot, Yvor Winters, and Allen Tate. His "Poetry and Belief in Thomas Hardy" (1940), for instance, derives its central idea from the discussion of poetry and belief in T. S. Eliot's essay on Dante. But Schwartz defines more exactly than Eliot had done the ways in which a poet's beliefs do and do not affect the artistic success of a poem.

The assessments Schwartz makes of other critics, such as R. P. Blackmur and Winters, and of major writers such as Yeats, Wallace Stevens, Ernest Hemingway, and William Faulkner, show a fine ability to go straight to the essentials in a body of work, and to balance generosity with the impersonal severity that necessarily accompanies high standards. Even in a late essay, "The Present State of Poetry" (1958), he writes with a penetration and sanity untouched by the chaos of his personal life.

Selected Essays of Delmore Schwartz, edited by Donald A. Dike and David H. Zucker (1970), preserves Schwartz's best critical writings. If anything, one might wish the selection had been a little narrower, whereas in Atlas' edition of the stories, one would like a longer book. But if one adds to these two volumes *Summer Knowledge* and Atlas' biography, one gets a fairly complete sense of Schwartz's career. In England, Carcanet New Press issued Douglas Dunn's selection of the poems, *What Is to Be Given* (1976). Dunn weeded out the later poetry, perhaps too ruthlessly, although he retained "'I Am Cherry Alive,' the Little Girl Sang" and the Seurat poem. He also omitted "Coriolanus and His Mother." But for those who would rather have slightly too little than slightly too much, this volume makes a good alternative to Schwartz's own selection. McDougall's study, though uneven, is often quite perceptive; it deserves more attention than it has apparently received. A paperback selection of the best short pieces on Schwartz would also be welcome.

Schwartz deserves to be rescued from the oblivion for which he seemed destined at the end of the 1960's, but he cannot be regarded as a major poet or writer of fiction. Whether he ever possessed, as his friends believed, the potential to become a major poet, we cannot say, but it seems extremely doubtful. He had intelligence, emotional intensity, and devotion to the art, but lacked a subtle ear. Nor is Schwartz's poetry notable for visual suggestiveness. The wit that dazzled everyone in his conversation rarely informs his writing, especially his most ambitious writing. A great poet can do without a first-rate ear, without vivid evocation of the physical world, or without exceptional grace or wit. One thinks of Thomas Hardy, Alexander Pope, and Wordsworth, respectively. But can a great poet dispense with all three of these gifts?

Rather than lament Schwartz's failure to become a major poet, we may be glad that he overcame his limitations, both personal and artistic, to the extent that he did. Not to the extent that we might have hoped, but enough to make us grateful for what he has left us.

Selected Bibliography

WORKS OF DELMORE SCHWARTZ

In Dreams Begin Responsibilities. Norfolk, Conn.: New Directions, 1938.

A Season in Hell. Norfolk, Conn.: New Directions, 1939; 2nd ed., 1940.

Shenandoah. Norfolk, Conn.: New Directions, 1941. Reprinted in *New Directions 32,* edited by James Laughlin, Peter Glassgold, and Frederick R. Martin. New York: New Directions, 1976. Pp. 24–45.

Genesis: Book One. New York: New Directions, 1943. Selections from the manuscript of *Book Two,* introduced by James Atlas, appear in *New Directions 35,* edited by James Laughlin, Peter Glassgold, and Frederick R. Martin. New York: New Directions, 1977. Pp. 34–47.

The World Is a Wedding. Norfolk, Conn.: New Directions, 1948.

Vaudeville for a Princess and Other Poems. New York: New Directions, 1950.

Summer Knowledge: New and Selected Poems, 1938–1958. Garden City, N.Y.: Doubleday, 1959. Reprinted as *Selected Poems (1938–1958): Summer Knowledge.* New York: New Directions, 1967.

Successful Love and Other Stories. New York: Corinth Books, 1961.

Selected Essays of Delmore Schwartz, edited and with an introduction by Donald A. Dike and David H. Zucker and an appreciation by Dwight Macdonald. Chicago: University of Chicago Press, 1970.

What Is to Be Given: Selected Poems, edited and with an introduction by Douglas Dunn. Manchester, England: Carcanet New Press, 1976.

In Dreams Begin Responsibilities and Other Stories, edited and with an introduction by James Atlas; foreword by Irving Howe. New York: New Directions, 1978.

"Selections from the Verse Journals," with an introduction by James Atlas. *New Directions 36,* edited by James Laughlin, Peter Glassgold, and Frederick R. Martin. New York: New Directions, 1978. Pp. 40–48.

Last and Lost Poems of Delmore Schwartz, edited and with an introduction by Robert Phillips. New York: Vanguard Press, 1979.

BIOGRAPHICAL AND CRITICAL STUDIES

BOOKS

Atlas, James. *Delmore Schwartz: The Life of an American Poet.* New York: Farrar, Straus and Giroux, 1977; paperback edition, New York: Avon Books, 1978.

McDougall, Richard. *Delmore Schwartz.* New York: Twayne Publishers, 1974.

ARTICLES, MEMOIRS, AND REVIEWS

Barrett, William. "Delmore: A 30's Friendship and Beyond." *Commentary,* 58, no. 3:41–54 (September 1974).

Bogan, Louise. "Young Modern." *Nation,* 148:353–54 (March 25, 1939). (Review of *In Dreams Begin Responsibilities.*)

Bonham, Sister M. Hilda. "Delmore Schwartz: An Idea of the World." *Renascence,* 13:132–35 (1961).

Deutsch, R. H. "Poetry and Belief in Delmore Schwartz." *Sewanee Review,* 74:915–24 (1966).

———. "Delmore Schwartz: Middle Poems." *Concerning Poetry,* 2, no. 2:19–28 (1969).

Dike, Donald A. "A Case for Judgment: The Literary Criticism of Delmore Schwartz." *Twentieth Century Literature,* 24:492–509 (1978).

Flint, Robert W. "The Stories of Delmore Schwartz." *Commentary,* 33:336–39 (April 1962).

Halio, Jay L. "Delmore Schwartz's Felt Abstractions." *Southern Review,* 1:802–19 (1965).

Hook, Sidney. "Imaginary Enemies, Real Terror." *American Scholar,* 47:406–12 (1978).

Howe, Irving. "Delmore Schwartz—a Personal Appreciation." *New Republic,* 146:25–27 (March 19, 1962).

———. "Purity and Craftiness." *Times Literary Supplement,* 28:458–59 (April 1978).

Humphries, Rolfe. "A Verse Chronicle." *Nation,* 171:490 (November 25, 1950). (Review of *Vaudeville for a Princess.*)

Kazin, Alfred. "Delmore Schwartz, 1913–1966." *World Journal Tribune Book Week,* 1:17–18 (October 9, 1966).

Kenner, Hugh. "Bearded Ladies and the Abundant Goat." *Poetry,* 79:50–53 (October 1951). (Review of *Vaudeville for a Princess.*)

Kloss, Robert J. "An Ancient and Famous Capital: Delmore Schwartz's Dream." *Psychoanalytic Review,* 65:475–90 (1978).

Knapp, James F. "Delmore Schwartz: Poet of the Orphic Journey." *Sewanee Review,* 78:506–16 (1970).

Lyons, Bonnie. "Delmore Schwartz and the Whole Truth." *Studies in Short Fiction,* 14:259–64 (1977).

Macdonald, Dwight. "Delmore Schwartz (1913–1966)." *New York Review of Books,* 7, no. 3:14–16 (September 8, 1966).

Matthiessen, F. O. "A New York Childhood." *Partisan Review,* 10:292–94 (1943). (Review of *Genesis.*)

Novak, Michael Paul. "The Dream as Film: Delmore Schwartz's 'In Dreams Begin Responsibilities.'" *Kansas Quarterly,* 9, no. 2:87–91 (1977).

Politzer, Heinz. "The Two Worlds of Delmore Schwartz: Lucifer in Brooklyn." Translated by Martin Greenberg. *Commentary,* 10:561–68 (December 1950).

Rahv, Philip. "Delmore Schwartz: The Paradox of Precocity." *New York Review of Books,* 17, no. 9:19–22 (May 20, 1971).

Zucker, David. "Self and History in Delmore Schwartz's Poetry and Criticism." *Iowa Review,* 8, no. 4:95–103 (1977).

—*PAUL BRESLIN*

Anne Sexton

1928-1974

*I*N part because she wrote confessional poetry and in part because she became a sort of media event—"the mad suicide poet, the live Sylvia Plath," as she put it—it has become nearly impossible for Anne Sexton's readers to separate the poet from the poetry she wrote. Most of her readers focus on her work either as a personal case history or as a social document. Those with an interest in psychology often value Sexton's poetic efforts to recreate her repeated nervous breakdowns, her stays in mental hospitals, and her exploration of her memories, dreams, and fantasies.

Some find in Sexton's life and her poetry verification of British psychologist R. D. Laing's popularized theories that madness may be a sane response to an insane world and that insanity breeds special perceptions. Others are drawn to Sexton because they see in her suicide what A. A. Alvarez saw in Plath's death, evidence that an anguished life, and even suicide, may be the price of artistic genius.

Feminists also claim Sexton, reading her poetry as an expression of oppressed womanhood. Some feminist readers especially applaud the boldness of her confessionalism, valuing it as a rejection of literary conventions that they define as masculine. But whatever their bias, such readers tend to be generous in their praise, celebrating the poetry primarily because it so fully and openly reveals Sexton's personal pain.

In contrast, those who read Sexton's poetry in more traditional ways, evaluating it in strictly aesthetic terms, have tended to be harsh in their judgments. The persistent refrain in their responses is that Sexton indulged in an uninhibited confessionalism that she had not sufficiently crafted.

Such criticism is to a large extent warranted, particularly in terms of the later poetry, for as Sexton gained recognition, she all too often abandoned the commitment to form that characterized the best of her earlier writing. Whereas the earlier volumes contain some remarkable poems of insight, beauty, and craft, many of her later efforts are awkward, uncontrolled, sometimes sentimental, sometimes boring.

It may well be that as her notoriety grew, Sexton became unable to separate her life and her art. Although in letters and interviews she continued to affirm her determination to write poetry that had formal integrity, that contained meaning beyond the autobiographical, and that was of lasting value, she seemed to fall victim to the misconception that anything she wrote either was valid as art or was of interest because she had written it. She increasingly published poems that she had not revised at all.

In the several years preceding her suicide in 1974, Sexton began writing almost frantically about her personal torments and her needs. Because she initially had been rewarded with success for the honesty of her confessions, she now seemed impelled to confess even more honestly. But in doing so, she lost control of the poetry, worrying all the while that her success was damaging to her art. The paradox is a devastating one. Sexton became a success as a poet primarily because of her ability to disclose her private failures publicly, but that success ultimately contributed to failures in both her poetry and her life. Those failures in turn became the subject of her progressively deteriorating poetry.

The conflicting critical reactions to Sexton's poetry, coupled with the fact that she and her editors so often failed to differentiate between the memorable and the mediocre in her work, raise the unsettling question of whether Sexton was being acclaimed as a poet or as a cultural phenomenon. For example, had she lived in a different time and in a different way, would her poetry have been so easily published, so widely recognized, and often so uncritically read? Had she not, along with Plath, taken a poetry workshop directed by Robert Lowell, had she not attempted suicide and been institutionalized repeatedly for her breakdowns, had she not written quite so fully and frequently about her despairs and death wishes—indeed, had Plath not killed herself—would Sexton's poetry have been so compelling?

To do justice to both Sexton and her art, it is necessary to read and assess her poetry and her life in conjunction with each other. To do otherwise undervalues her strengths and either glosses over or glorifies her weaknesses. A year before her death Sexton wrote to her agent, Claire S. Degener, "I want to be an important poet more than a popular one." She may have been perceptive about herself when she added, "God only knows if the two go together."

Anne Sexton was born Anne Gray Harvey on November 9, 1928, in Newton, Massachusetts.

Her parents, Ralph Churchill Harvey and Mary Gray Staples Harvey, were from old, established New England families. Her father's woolen firm was successful, and Sexton's childhood was spent in a mansionlike home in Weston, Massachusetts. But by her own account her childhood was an unhappy one. Her poetry is filled with descriptions of her father's alcoholism and her mother's indifference. The third daughter, Sexton described herself in "Those Times . . ." (*Live or Die,* 1966) as

> the unwanted, the mistake
> that Mother used to keep Father
> from his divorce.

Only her great-aunt, Anna Ladd Dingley (known variously in the poetry as Anna, Nana, and Elizabeth), was a figure of love and stability for Sexton. Dingley's eventual deafness, senility, and confinement to a nursing home brought Sexton a good deal of pain.

There were early if slight hints of future psychological problems. Sexton's elementary school teachers and administrators recommended psychiatric treatment, advice her parents did not take. Later, judging her a rebellious high school student, the Harveys sent her to Rogers Hall, a boarding school in Lowell, Massachusetts. There Sexton was popular, particularly with males, and photographs from this period show her to have been an extraordinarily beautiful young girl. Although not a serious student, she did write poetry, abandoning it when her mother mistakenly accused her of plagiarism.

After graduating from Rogers Hall, Sexton spent a year at what she called a "finishing school," Garland Junior College in Boston. In the summer of 1948 she met, and a month later eloped with, Alfred Muller Sexton II, known as Kayo. The couple soon abandoned their hope that Kayo, a premedical student at Colgate University, would finish his schooling. Instead, unhappy about needing his family's financial support, he left college and went to work for a woolen firm. Sexton's letters to her parents suggest that she was enthusiastically embracing the stereotypical role of the happy young bride, concerned with clothes, cooking, and her new husband. In one letter she revealed that her "heart's desire" was an electric Mixmaster.

In 1950, at the outbreak of the Korean War, Kayo joined the naval reserve. When he was aboard ship or in Korea, Sexton lived with his family. It was during this period that the senior Sextons became concerned about her manic-depressive states. After the birth of her first child, Linda Gray Sexton, in 1953, Sexton was repeatedly hospitalized for severe bouts of depression and a suicide attempt. Kayo had completed his tour of duty and joined his father-in-law's woolen firm.

Anna Ladd Dingley's death in 1954, at the age of eighty-six, caused Sexton new emotional difficulties. The following year a second daughter, Joyce Ladd Sexton, was born. Although Sexton recalls in "The Double Image" that "we named you Joyce / so we could call you Joy," she suffered another breakdown. After months of hospitalization, she returned home, able to care only for Linda. Joy remained with her paternal grandparents for the next three years and did not think of Sexton as her mother.

In an interview with Barbara Kevles in 1968, Sexton recounted those years:

Until I was twenty-eight I had a kind of buried self who didn't know she could do anything but make white sauce and diaper babies. I didn't know I had any creative depths. I was a victim of the American Dream, the bourgeois, middle-class dream. All I wanted was a little piece of life, to be married, to have children. I thought the nightmares, the visions, the demons would go away if there was enough love to put them down. I tried my damnedest to lead a conventional life, for that was how I was brought up,

and it was what my husband wanted of me. But one can't build little white picket fences to keep nightmares out. The surface cracked when I was about twenty-eight. I had a psychotic break and tried to kill myself.

After her psychiatrist told her she "had a perfectly good mind" and "creative talent," Sexton began to watch the Boston educational television station. When she heard I. A. Richards read a sonnet and explain its form, she began writing. Her doctor encouraged her by saying, "Don't kill yourself. Your poems might mean something to someone else some day." In 1957 Sexton enrolled in John Holmes's poetry seminar at the Boston Center for Adult Education, where she met and became friends with Maxine Kumin.

Sexton repeatedly insisted that it was W. D. Snodgrass' "Heart's Needle" that actually gave her the impetus and the courage to write confessional poetry. Her admiration for Snodgrass led her to the 1958 Antioch Summer Writers' Conference so that she could work with him, an experience that began a friendship and an intense correspondence that lasted for years. On Snodgrass' advice Sexton sought admission to Robert Lowell's graduate poetry seminar at Boston University. Accounts of that seminar and of Sexton's friendship with coparticipants Sylvia Plath and George Starbuck have become part of contemporary literary history. After the class the three habitually spent the rest of the afternoon drinking martinis at the Ritz bar, talking of poetry and of death. In "Sylvia's Death" Sexton described those conversations:

the death we said we both outgrew
the one we wore on our skinny breasts

the one we talked of so often each time
we downed three extra martinis in Boston

the death that talked of analysts and cures,
the death that talked like brides with plots,

the death we drank to,
the motives and then the quiet deed

By 1959, Sexton's poems had been accepted by such major literary publications as the *Hudson Review,* the *Antioch Review,* and the *New Yorker.* With Lowell's advice about what to include (he urged her to discard about half of it and write approximately fifteen new poems), she put together the collection *To Bedlam and Part Way Back.* She signed a contract for its publication with Houghton Mifflin in April 1959.

The poetic progress of these years was marred by personal tragedy. Although both children were now living at home, Sexton continued to suffer emotional problems. Early in 1957 her mother learned that she had breast cancer and her father suffered a major stroke. In March 1959 her mother died of cancer. The following June her father suffered a fatal cerebral hemorrhage.

To Bedlam and Part Way Back (1960) is Sexton's poetic account of her excursions into insanity and of her ambivalent, often guilt-ridden relationship with her parents and her children. Several poems flirt with popular psychology, suggesting her desire to illuminate the psychological motivation behind behavior and to explore the nature of repressed emotion. Other poems focus on her concern with death, particularly her attempts to come to terms with the passage of time and with the impact that death has on the living.

The most successful poems demonstrate Sexton's early commitment to finding the rhyme, the rhythm, the image, or the voice that would best communicate and, at times, best evaluate the experience being presented. As she explained in 1965 to Patricia Marx, a rigid attention to formal concerns allowed her to be more "truthful." Comparing form to the superego, she elaborated:

. . . if you used form, it was like letting a lot of wild animals out in the arena, but enclosing them in a cage, and you could let some extraordinary animals out if you had the right cage, and that cage would be form.

She also insisted that form and content were inseparable, and emphasized her efforts to find the right form:

Content dominates, but style is the master. I think that's what makes a poet. The form is always important. . . . The poems that aren't in form have a shape, just the same. . . .

"Ringing the Bells" exemplifies what Sexton meant. The nursery-rhyme quality of the poem reinforces the motif of the childlike helplessness of those confined to mental hospitals. The poet's identification with the bell she holds during music therapy, the E flat, further suggests that being in "Bedlam" dehumanizes the patients by negating their individual personalities:

and this is always my bell responding
to my hand that responds to the lady
who points at me, E flat;
and although we are no better for it,
they tell you to go. And you do.

Significantly, as the volume progresses, the poet's voice evolves. In the early poems the stance and voice frequently are of a child who is lost, fearful, and dependent on a male authority figure. The poet assumes a more active voice as she deliberately attempts to reconcile herself to time, death, and her own psychological impulses. She also begins to explore her relationships with the women in her life. Several of the poems assume a fictional voice, but in them, too, the speaker generally is confronting the realities of life, death, and loss.

Finally, in the concluding section (part II), the poet directly asserts her adulthood. With a sure voice she takes responsibility first for her poetry and then for her relationships with her mother and daughter. In the last two poems she also acknowledges some of her needs, her failures, and her guilt.

The first poem in *To Bedlam and Part Way Back,* "You, Doctor Martin," is one of several set in a mental hospital. Addressing her psychiatrist, the poet at first ironically identifies herself as "queen of this summer hotel." By the second stanza she has likened herself and the other patients to schoolchildren:

> We chew in rows, our plates
> scratch and whine like chalk
>
> in school.

Later she says, "What large children we are / here."

Nevertheless, what the poet feels toward the doctor is anger. In the opening stanza she contrasts his freedom to "walk / from breakfast to madness," and presumably all the way back, with her own lack of control:

> I speed through the antiseptic tunnel
>   where the moving dead still talk
> of pushing their bones against the
>   thrust
> of cure.

She notes that the patients are denied knives that might be used, she seems to be telling Martin, "for cutting your throat." Still, she bitterly recognizes her dependence on him:

> Of course, I love you;
> you lean above the plastic sky,
> god of our block, prince of all the foxes.

The poem is one of the bleakest in the collection, for it depicts the institution as a deathlike place that offers little hope for a genuine cure. Even as the poet learns to mend moccasins, she is aware that another finger will break them tomorrow. Wondering "Am I still lost?" she decides that she, who once was beautiful, is now herself as she acquiesces to the meaningless talk at hand:

> counting this row and that row of moccasins
> waiting on the silent shelf.

The second poem, "Kind Sir: These Woods," is more affirmative, embodying the Laingian view that insanity may merely be a label attached to those who have "this inward look that society scorns." The poem's epigraph, a statement of Thoreau's that "Not til we are lost . . . do we begin to find ourselves," and the concluding lines of the poem further suggest that insanity may lead to a fuller and better self-understanding. By being "lost," by facing the "strange happenings, untold and unreal" that her night mind conjures up, the poet discovers that she will "find nothing worse / than myself, caught between the grapes and the thorns."

Significantly, the "Kind Sir" to whom the poem is addressed may be Snodgrass rather than Thoreau. In a letter written during this period, Sexton referred to Snodgrass as "Kind Sir." The poem may well reflect her attempts to take Snodgrass' advice that she try to find her own voice and abandon poetic "masks."

In "Music Swims Back to Me" the poet again assumes a child's voice and asks an unidentified "Mister" for help in a world that seems to provide none. A later poem in this volume, "Noon Walk on the Asylum Lawn," vividly illustrates the range of her fears. Believing that even the sun, the grass, and the sky are harmful, she concludes the poem:

> The world is full of enemies.
> There is no safe place.

"The Bells" may explain why the poet at times is drawn into a state of childlike dependency. Addressing her father, she reminisces about a childhood visit to a circus. Despite her sense of potential danger ("the bells / trembled for the flying man," the circus had "three rings of danger," and she felt small in comparison with the "rough legs of strangers"), she felt secure in her father's love:

> love love
> love grew rings around me.

Sexton's learning how to cope on her own characterizes the better poems in *To Bedlam and Part Way Back.* For instance, "Elizabeth Gone" centers on her attempt to accept her great-aunt's death. (Sexton apparently chose the name "Elizabeth" for its rhyme with "death.") The first three stanzas are structured around her inability to honor her great-aunt's plea that she be released from the "beds" that mark her dying, her funeral, and her cremation. Each stanza ends with the older woman's refrain: *let me go let me go.*

In the first stanza the poet feels helpless in the face of her knowledge that the dying woman also is helpless. Elizabeth has become childlike, her breath "grown baby short," but the poet cannot release her from "the nest of your real death," from "the human bed." In the second stanza Elizabeth has died. Hers is now an "inhuman bed," a coffin. Again the poet grieves, mourning that the body in the coffin bears no likeness to the person Elizabeth was. Even after Elizabeth's cremation, her bed now "the cardboard urn," the poet cannot accept the death:

I waited you in the cathedral of spells
And I waited you in the country of the living.

Only in the last stanza is she able to heed Elizabeth's cries, throwing out her "last bony shells." Still not fully in control, the poet screams involuntarily. Only then can she accept the death and act on it:

> Then I sorted your clothes
> And the loves you had left, Elizabeth,
> Elizabeth, until you were gone.

Sexton's control of rhyme in this poem is particularly effective. All four stanzas are constructed with an *a b a d c e* rhyme scheme, but

the power of the final stanza comes with its breaking away from the *let me go let me go* refrain of the first three stanzas. The finality of the poet's acceptance of the death is revealed not only in her actions but also in the last line of the poem, "Elizabeth, until you were gone."

The next poem, "Some Foreign Letters," is both another gentle, loving reminiscence of her great-aunt and an effort by Sexton to reconcile herself to the toll that time takes. The strength of the poem comes from the poet's dual consciousness. She is aware simultaneously of the happiness of her great-aunt's girlhood trip to Europe and of the pain that the future had brought her. As she reads her great-aunt's letters, written when Dingley was "a young girl in a good world still," the poet is aware that "life is a trick, life is a kitten in a sack." The opening lines of the poem make it clear that the great-aunt's future is the context in which the letters are being read:

I knew you forever and you were always old,
soft white lady of my heart.

Throughout the poem Sexton juxtaposes images of the great-aunt's happy love affair with a married count with her own awareness that eventually her great-aunt would lose her hearing, become senile, and be sent to a nursing home. "When you were mine," Sexton writes as she attempts to "breathe" life into the letters, "You wore an earphone." And later:

When you were mine they wrapped you out of
   here
with your best hat over your face. I cried
because I was seventeen. I am older now.

The poem, which Lowell praises as one of Sexton's "finer and quieter poems," is carefully crafted. In each stanza a rhymed couplet frames three interior quatrains. The contrasting images of past and present further intensify the sense of the devastation that time brings. Thus, the idyllic love affair is implicitly contrasted with the count's eventual death and the great-aunt's prim life. Peaceful, even dull moments in London will be lost to ensuing world wars. Skating to a Strauss waltz with the count will be replaced, as the great-aunt goes deaf, with music that has a "sour sound." The agility of their climbing the Alps will ultimately become physical helplessness.

The final stanza is the most poignant. As the poet reads of her great-aunt's youthful adventures, she has the illusory sense that she can "tell" her great-aunt of the future. Yet she is aware that she is as helpless to alter that history-to-be as her great-aunt actually had been. The final image of the poem is one of the great-aunt, long out of place in a changing world, become even more disoriented. Her once-happy affair has become her albatross, and her love, a guilty love:

Tonight I will speak up and interrupt
your letters, warning you that wars are
    coming,
that the Count will die, that you will accept
your America back to live like a prim thing
on the farm in Maine. I tell you, you will come
here, to the suburbs of Boston, to see the blue-
    nose
world go drunk each night, to see the
    handsome
children jitterbug, to feel your left ear close
one Friday at Symphony. And I tell you,
you will tip your boot feet out of that hall,
rocking from its sour sound, out onto
the crowded street, letting your spectacles fall
and your hair net tangle as you stop passers-by
to mumble your guilty love while your ears die.

"Funnel," which uses a similar juxtaposition of past and present, focuses on Sexton's sense, as the title suggests, that time has diminished the grandeur that her family's past contained. Visiting her great-grandfather's grave, she reminisces about the grand scale of his life, with its "one dozen grand pianos," "seven arking

houses," and "eight genius children" who "honored their separate arts." In contrast, the poet is engaged in more banal pursuits:

I sort his odd books and wonder his once alive
words and scratch out my short marginal
    notes
and finger my accounts.

Then she returns home to her own life:

    to question this diminishing and feed a
        minimum
    of children their careful slice of
        suburban cake.

Perhaps it was self-consciousness over the intimacy of poems such as these, but at times Sexton herself was ambivalent about the fullness with which she embraced the confessional mode. In 1960, for instance, she wrote to Louis Simpson, "I have written a new longish poem called 'The Operation' which is (damn it as I really don't *want* to write any more of them) a personal narration about my experiences this fall." Two years later she echoed that uneasiness, concluding a biographical sketch for her British editor, Jon Stallworthy, by observing, "Isn't too much of it in the poems, an almost shameful display and listing of one's LIFE STORY."

Thus, she also experimented with fictional personae. But in these poems her concerns are much like those of the confessional poems. For example, "For Johnny Pole on the Forgotten Beach" explores the impact of time by juxtaposing nostalgic memories of a happier, more innocent past with descriptions of a harsh, present reality. Once again contrasting images are carefully balanced. The first stanza describes the almost ten-year-old Johnny riding the waves:

He rode on the lip that buoyed him there
and buckled him under. The beach was strung
with children paddling their ages in,

under the glare of noon chipping
its light out. He stood up, anonymous
and straight among them, between
their sand pails and nursery crates.

The second half of the poem, with its description of Johnny's death in battle during a beach assault, is set in counterpoint to the first. Bodies are "strung out" at a noon that chips its light. Johnny again is anonymous. But the childhood game has been replaced with the grotesqueness and finality of death, and his youthfully "perfect skin" will soon decay.

Ironically, the details of this poem and another nonconfessional poem, "Unknown Girl in the Maternity Ward," were so convincing that most readers assumed them to be autobiographical. But Sexton had no brother, nor did she give up for adoption an illegitimate child, the subject of "Unknown Girl." This poem was, in fact, a deliberate effort to "disguise" the details of her life. As Sexton explained in interviews, she was attempting to communicate through the fictional situation the pain she had experienced during her three-year separation from Joy.

Two other nonconfessional poems, "The Farmer's Wife" and "The Moss of His Skin," are particularly interesting in that they explore deep, often repressed, taboo emotions. The farmer's wife, alienated from her husband despite the pleasure of "their country lust," desires more excitement or meaning than their "local life in Illinois" and their lovemaking provide. Thus, in her fantasies

> she wishes him cripple, or poet,
> or even lonely, or sometimes,
> better, my lover, dead.

The speaker in "The Moss of His Skin" is a young Arab girl who, according to the custom of her tribe, is being buried alive beside her dead father. Rather than being afraid, the child is concerned only with hiding from her mother and sisters, and from Allah, the incestuous pleasure she feels as she holds her father and "falls out" of herself.

In part II of *To Bedlam,* Sexton returns to the confessional mode. "For John, Who Begs Me not to Enquire Further" is her justification to her first poetry teacher, John Holmes, of the unconventional, unlovely, and private content of her poetry. The title refers to the volume's epigraph, a "letter of Schopenhauer to Goethe," which in itself suggests Sexton's desire to ally her poetry to a larger tradition:

It is the courage to make a clean breast of it in the face of every question that makes the philosopher. He must be like Sophocles's Oedipus, who, seeking enlightenment concerning his terrible fate, pursues his indefatigable enquiry, even when he divines that appalling horror awaits him in the answer. But most of us carry in our heart the Jocasta who begs Oedipus for God's sake not to inquire further.

The poem begins with the poet's explanation that writing about the details of her own life did have value:

> Not that it was beautiful
> but that, in the end, there was
> a certain sense of order there;
> something worth learning
> in that narrow diary of my mind,
> in the commonplaces of the asylum
> where the cracked mirror
> or my own selfish death
> outstared me.

Sexton then reveals why she rejected writing about "something outside of myself," believing that had she done so:

> you would not know
> that the worst of anyone
> can be, finally,
> an accident of hope.

But, most of all, she is certain that within her "own head," her "own bowl," some universality is to be found after all:

> At first it was private.
> Then it was more than myself;
> it was you, or your house
> or your kitchen.

"The Double Image" succeeds in the ways Sexton had hoped. It certainly is one of the most carefully crafted of her poems. She alluded often in letters to the number of years she had worked on it, the number of revisions it had undergone. She also pointed out to Barbara Kevles that she had taken some poetic liberties with the truth:

Many of my poems are true, line by line, altering a few facts to get the story at its heart. In "The Double Image," the poem about my mother's death from cancer and the loss of my daughter, I don't mention that I had another child. Each poem has its own truth. Furthermore, in that poem I only say that I was hospitalized twice, when, in fact, I was hospitalized five times in that span of time.

The title initially refers to the portraits that Sexton and her mother had painted of themselves when Sexton lived with her mother in 1955, while she was recovering from a breakdown. Linda was with Kayo and Joy was with Kayo's parents. Sexton's mother was battling cancer. The portraits were painted as a way of allowing mother and daughter to distance themselves from their very painful realities:

I cannot forgive your suicide, my mother said.
And she never could. She had my portrait
done instead.

The motif of having "a portrait done instead" serves as a refrain to each of the four stanzas of the second section. Later, the finished portraits will "hang on opposite walls" of the mother's house, facing one another as mother and daughter themselves found difficult to do.

The double image refers not merely to the literal portraits but also to the ways in which mothers and daughters reflect each other. Thus, the poem opens with the poet, at thirty, reunited with Joy after a three-year separation. The two of them stand together, looking out a window at the dying of the leaves and the seasons. The poet now understands that self-hatred led her to abandon her child, and so she has come to value belief in the self. When the child asks where fallen leaves go, the poet explains, "I say today believed / in itself, or else it fell." She urges the girl to "love your self's self where it lives." Still, she is overwhelmed by guilt for having left Joy, even as she recognizes that the child brings her a sense of renewal:

> The time I did not love
> myself, I visited your shoveled walks; you
>   held my glove.
> There was new snow after this.

In stanza 4 the poet explicitly applies the double image to Joy and herself. Despite their separation, she tells the child:

And you resembled me; unacquainted
with my face, you wore it. But you were mine
after all.

Tragically, as the poet assumes the role of mother, she grieves for her own mother:

> You call me *mother*, and I remember my
>   mother, again,
> somewhere in greater Boston, dying.

But because the poet's mother holds the poet responsible for her cancer, the poet carries a "double image" of guilt. Not only did she leave her daughter because she "would rather / die than love," but her own mother believes that that same suicide attempt was the cause of her dying:

She turned from me, as if death were
       catching,
as if death transferred,

as if my dying had eaten inside of her.
That August you were two, but I timed my
   days with doubt.
On the first of September she looked at me
And said I gave her cancer.
They carved her sweet hills out
and still I couldn't answer.

The poem offers both hope and despair. The hope comes from the poet's attempts to understand why she sought to die. She no longer will be unreflective. Yet her honesty brings with it the tormenting realization that despite her awareness of how much she was damaged by being an image through which her mother defined herself, she may be placing the same burden on Joy:

I, who was never quite sure
about being a girl, needed another
life, another image to remind me.
And this was my worst guilt; you could not
   cure
nor soothe it. I made you to find me.

The final poem in the volume, "The Division of Parts," is an attempt by Sexton to understand her relationship with her mother, so that she can go on with her own life. Unable to grieve, she instead attempts to come to terms with the death.

In many ways the process is one of rejection. She first recognizes that she has a need for religious belief, but abandons it as false. Since she can only "imitate / a memory of belief / that I do not own," she decides instead to "convert to love":

. . . And Lent will keep its hurt
for someone else. Christ knows enough
staunch guys have hitched on him in trouble,
thinking his sticks were badges to wear.

She also rejects her desire to "remain still, a mixed child / heavy with cloths" of her mother.

But she is ambivalent here. Even though she tells herself "What was, is gone," she still wears her mother's Bonwit Teller nightgown to bed. Then, dreaming of her mother, she attempts to exorcise her:

There in my jabbering dream
I heard my own angry cries
and I cursed you, *Dame*
Keep out of my slumber.
My good Dame, you are dead.

By noon the next day she realizes that she both "would still curse" her mother "with my rhyming words" and attempt to bring her "flapping back" with a litany of endearments.

In the final stanza the poet chooses to celebrate love and to accept both her mother's death and the fact that Mary Gray will always be a part of her, that she has become, in spiritual as well as literal ways, her mother's "inheritor."

As Sexton was writing the poems for *All My Pretty Ones* (1962), she began an intense correspondence with a wide range of poets, including Snodgrass, Louis Simpson, and Anthony Hecht. She sent them new poems, asking them for critiques, and invited them to do the same. She also "workshopped" her poems frequently with Kumin. In the summer of 1960, she began studying literature, enrolling in seminars at Brandeis University taught by Philip Rahv, editor of the *Partisan Review,* and by Irving Howe. She wrote to her friend Nolan Miller:

What I have been doing is reading. And that is good. I've been forming . . . Kafka, Mann, Dostoyevsky, Rilke, Faulkner, Gide—etc. A mixed bunch, picking and delighting. I wasn't kidding when I told you once that I had never read anything. I hadn't. So I'm forming, eating books, words, thinking and now and then worrying about all this intake and no output.

She also continued, along with Kumin and Starbuck, to participate in Holmes's poetry workshop. In the spring of 1961, the Radcliffe Institute for Independent Study named Sexton and Kumin their first scholars in poetry.

Despite such activities and successes, these years were punctuated with more personal tragedies and with emotional distress. Only a month after her mother's death, Sexton's father announced his plans to remarry. Sexton unsuccessfully attempted to convince him to change his mind; but before the marriage could take place, Ralph Harvey had suffered a fatal cerebral hemorrhage. The following year Sexton's father-in-law was killed in a car accident. Clearly affected by so many deaths, she wrote Snodgrass in October 1960:

There is no one new who is dead, at any rate. And that is something for me as I seem to specialize in dead people. Guilt. Guilt. etc. I guess I told you that Kayo's father was killed this March. The girl across the street died of cancer this August (. . . *I* said that she ought to die.) . . . why don't I keep my big mouth shut! [The second ellipsis is Sexton's, a device for punctuation.]

During this period, according to Linda Sexton and Lois Ames, editors of Sexton's letters, Sexton placed such exorbitant demands on Snodgrass and others "for critiques and reassurances" that she began to drive people away. She also began to worry about negative reviews, in particular James Dickey's response to *To Bedlam and Part Way Back.* In fact, Dickey was the first to recognize a problem that would plague many of Sexton's readers—that the very personal nature of her writing made a critical assessment seem inappropriate. He wrote:

Anne Sexton's poems so obviously come out of deep, painful sections of the author's life that one's literary opinions scarcely seem to matter;

one feels tempted to drop them furtively into the nearest ashcan, rather than be caught with them in the presence of so much naked suffering.

Despite such reservations, Dickey criticized the poems for lacking "the concentration, and above all the profound, individual linguistic suggestibility and accuracy that poems must have to be good." Nevertheless, he urged his readers to buy the volume because "Mrs. Sexton's candor, her courage, and her story are worth anyone's three dollars."

In *All My Pretty Ones* Sexton continues to tell her story with courage and candor, writing fully about her parents' deaths and again explaining the causes of her breakdowns. On the other hand, more fully than before, she affirms the value of love and life. This collection also is more experimental than *To Bedlam and Part Way Back,* but not always successfully so. For instance, some of Sexton's efforts at free verse seem to be more prose statements than poetry. Her images are more mixed, often chosen only for their private, associative value. Her exploration in her nonconfessional poems of psychological motivation at times seems simplistic. But most of all, some potentially fine poems are marred by moments that are awkward, by images that jar, by an uncontrolled voice.

"The Operation," a poem about exploratory surgery Sexton underwent when it was feared that she, like her mother, might have cancer, exemplifies the problems. The poem gains most of its effectiveness because of the power of a series of related images that present the womb as the source of both life and death. The poet writes of her mother's cancer:

It grew in her
as simply as a child would grow,
as simply as she housed me once, fat and
    female.

Always my most gentle house before that
    embryo
of evil spread in her shelter and she grew frail.

Later she is even more direct: "Fact, death too is in the egg."

Strikingly, despite the poet's fear in the face of the operation, she is now in control of herself. Her voice is sure, adult:

After the sweet promise,
the summer's mild retreat
from mother's cancer, the winter months of
    her death,
I come to this white office. . . .

The concluding lines of the poem are both unexpected and disappointing. The poet assumes the child's voice. Even more problematically, she abandons the image of the womb, and of the egg specifically, as a source of life and death. Instead her stomach has become like a football, and she herself, like Humpty Dumpty:

Time now to pack this humpty-dumpty
back the frightened way she came
and run along, Anne, and run along
    now,
my stomach laced up like a football
for the game.

"With Mercy for the Greedy" is also uneven. Written after her friend Ruth Soter had sent her a crucifix, the poem begins with a detailed description of the cross. But despite her need the poet decides once again that she cannot embrace Christ because "Need is not quite belief." She then reasserts the meaning poetry holds for her. The difficulty is that the initial seriousness and precision are replaced by inflated and, in some moments, meaningless language:

My friend, my friend, I was born
doing reference work in sin, and born
confessing it. This is what poems are:
with mercy

for the greedy,
they are the tongue's wrangle,
the world's pottage, the rat's star.

All My Pretty Ones contains several unrevised poems that Kumin has graciously termed "given" poems. But such poems as "Young" and "I Remember" are merely prose statements broken up into what look like poetic lines. Although the memories are pleasant, the images are often clichéd or imprecise, as in the opening lines of "I Remember":

By the first of August
the invisible beetles began
to snore and the grass was
as tough as hemp and was
no color—no more than
the sand was a color and
we had worn our bare feet
bare since the twentieth
of June and there were times
we forgot to wind up your
alarm clock. . . .

In her continued experimentation with fictional personae, Sexton chooses such diverse voices as Christ in the tomb, the father of a retarded child, an old man, an elderly seamstress, and a young girl involved in a love affair. All these poems explore psychological motivation, but with varying degrees of sophistication. Perhaps the most convincing is "The Hangman," in which the father admits his "guilty wish" that his retarded son had been allowed to die. He identifies with a Scandinavian folktale in which a king kills "nine sons in turn." The father's desire not to sacrifice his own life for the child is juxtaposed with his awareness that his wife has embraced the martyr's role:

At first your mother said . . . why me! why
    me!
But she got over that. Now she enjoys
her dull daily care and her hectic bravery.

You do not love anyone. She is not
    growing a boy;
she is enlarging a stone to wear around her
    neck.

In contrast, the motives in "Doors, Doors, Doors" seem either clichéd or exaggerated. A young man enters the priesthood, despite the prediction of neighbors that he will marry well, because "As a youngster his private parts were undersize." Two young lovers enter into their affair because the woman's husband is given to "insane abuse," because her father died, and because the man's "wild-haired wife has fled."

The better poems in *All My Pretty Ones,* as in *To Bedlam and Part Way Back,* reveal Sexton in control, both formally and thematically. For example, she told an interviewer she had rewritten "The Truth the Dead Know" three hundred times. The poem is notable because of the strength of the poet's voice and her determination, even in the face of the deaths of her parents, to continue to live and love. She has learned the importance of accepting death and of acting on that acceptance. The opening lines echo the conclusion of "Elizabeth Gone":

Gone, I say and walk from church,
refusing the stiff procession to the grave,
letting the dead ride alone in the hearse.
It is June. I am tired of being brave.

(The phrase "stiff procession" seems a disconcerting bit of gallows humor in this context.)

In the second stanza the poet chooses life. With her lover she now is willing to drive, and they go to "the Cape." "I cultivate myself," she explains, and she and her lover touch. Whereas in "Elizabeth Gone" she had waited for her great-aunt "in the country of the living," she now accepts the separateness of the worlds of the living and the dead, emphasizing "In another country people die."

The third stanza further celebrates life and love:

and when we touch
we enter touch entirely. No one's alone.

The irony, of course, is her realization that such touching is so precious that "Men kill for this, or for as much." The conclusion of the poem further mutes the affirmation. The poet is unable after all to forget the dead, thinking again of the truth that they know:

They are more like stone
than the sea would be if it stopped.

She recognizes that the dead are unreachable. By virtue of being stone, they refuse her blessing.

"The Starry Night" presents a very different view of death. By dying the poet hopes she will become part of the energy evident in Vincent Van Gogh's painting. The stars "are all alive," and death, in this poem, paradoxically has a vitality to it:

O starry starry night! this is how
I want to die:

into that rushing beast of the night,
sucked up by that great dragon, to split
from my life with no flag,
no belly,
no cry.

Kumin recalls that Sexton rewrote the title poem, "All My Pretty Ones," many times in order to "force it into the exigency of an *a b a b, c d c d, e e* stanza." She notes that Sexton was particularly proud of some of her multisyllabic rhymes: "slumber" and "disencumber," "navigator" and "look at later" and what Kumin calls "the *tour de force* final couple," "I outlive you" and "and forgive you."

The poem is Sexton's first attempt to confront her ambivalences about her father. She again uses her discovery of memorabilia as the occasion for the poem. Sorting through her father's "boxes of pictures of people I do not know" and the scrapbook he began the year she was born, she attempts to reconstruct key moments in his life. As in earlier poems, time is the central character. Holding a picture of her father as a small boy waiting "for someone to come," the poet realizes:

> My father, time meanwhile
> has made it unimportant who you are looking
>   for.

The poem depicts Ralph Harvey's weaknesses (his alcoholism and his extravagance) but also the poet's guilt at opposing his wish to remarry, his "second chance":

> This year, solvent but sick, you meant
> to marry that pretty widow in a one-month
>   rush.
> But before you had that second chance, I
>   cried
> on your fat shoulder. Three days later you
>   died.

Ultimately this poem too is about the poet's freeing herself from the past. She decides that most of the photographs and the scrapbook must go. She will keep her mother's diary for others to discover. And in the end, she will attempt to forgive:

> Whether you are pretty or not, I outlive you,
> bend down my strange face to yours and
>   forgive you.

It is interesting that Sexton referred to this particular poem as an example of how her poetry did not always reflect the truths of her life. She told William Packard:

Any poem is therapy. The art of writing is therapy. You don't solve problems in writing. They're still there. I've heard psychiatrists say, "See, you've forgiven your father. There it is in your poem." But I haven't forgiven my father. I just wrote that I did.

As she is attempting to accept her unhappy relationships with her parents, Sexton begins to write affirmatively about the value of love. In "The Fortress" she promises Linda that despite her inability to control the tragedies that time may bring, they can "laugh and touch" and share love. "Time," she says as she ends the poem, "will not take away that." In contrast, in "The Abortion" what she mourns is the death of a child "*who should have been born*" because it was conceived in the fullness of love.

Sexton also is beginning to struggle with sexual roles. "Housewife" is a bitter poem about how "Some women marry houses," while "The Black Art" embodies the fairly conventional belief that women operate primarily on the level of feeling ("A woman who writes feels too much") and men on the level of thought ("A man who writes knows too much"). Moreover, a woman writes

> As if cycles and children and islands
> weren't enough; as if mourners and gossips
> and vegetables were never enough.
> She thinks she can warn the stars.

A man, on the other hand, writes

> As if erections and congresses and products
> weren't enough; as if machines and galleons
> and wars were never enough.
> With used furniture he makes a tree.

Nor does the conclusion offer hope of a healthy relationship between people with creative energy, whatever the different motivations for it. In the poet's mind those whose "eyes are full of terrible confessions" would create between them such a "weird abundance" that even their children would "leave in disgust."

Two of the more appealing poems in this volume are ones in which Sexton gives way to whimsical fantasy. Her tribute to Snodgrass, "To a Friend Whose Work Has Come to Triumph," is Sexton's retelling of the Icarus–Daedalus story. The pleasure of the poem comes not only from her celebration of Icarus' ability to take risks and sail over the ocean, but also from the new and easy wit she displays as she contrasts the adventuresome son with his more prudent father:

> Admire his wings!
> Feel the fire at his neck and see how
>   casually
> he glances up and is caught, wondrously
>   tunneling
> into that hot eye. Who cares that he fell
>   back to the sea?
> See him acclaiming the sun and come
>   plunging down
> .while his sensible daddy goes straight
>   into town.

"Letters Written on a Ferry While Crossing Long Island Sound" has the same ease. The poet, saddened by the end of a love affair, is given new hope by her fantasy that the four nuns she sees on the ferry will suddenly fly. As they "rise / on black wings," she imagines:

> They call back to us
> from the gauzy edge of paradise,
> *good news, good news.*

Early in 1962, Houghton Mifflin accepted *All My Pretty Ones* for publication. Sexton's career was growing in other ways as well. She gave frequent readings on the college circuit, was collaborating with Kumin on two children's books, and was writing the poems for *Live or Die* (1966). Nevertheless she was hospitalized again in June of that year, an experience that led to "Flee on Your Donkey." In the fall of 1963, with Kayo's encouragement, she accepted an unsolicited travel grant from the American Academy of Arts and Letters.

Leaving the children with Kayo and her mother-in-law, Sexton and a woman companion, Sandy Robart, embarked for what she intended to be a year of travel abroad. But, as her letters indicate, the trip was almost immediately disastrous. Fearing another breakdown, she returned home within a few months, despondent, believing herself a failure. Her depressions deepened when her psychiatrist of several years, "Doctor Martin," moved away from the Boston area. Although Sexton experimented with various therapists over the next several years, she had periodic stays in the psychiatric ward of Massachusetts General Hospital and at the private Westwood Lodge.

In 1963 the Ford Foundation gave Sexton a grant to work on a play, *Tell Me Your Answer True* (later to become *Mercy Street*). But the poetry was coming slowly, and it was not until 1966 that she had *Live or Die* ready for publication. During these years she began to worry, as she would throughout the rest of her life, that her success was detrimental to her poetry. She wrote to "Doctor Martin" in 1963, "I think I have been getting to be an almost cheap artist since the first Radcliffe grant. Perhaps success is not good for me."

The same year she similarly confided to Snodgrass: "I keep thinking I'm losing myself in some mad welter of publicity." She reminisced nostalgically about the days when she was "doing the desperate and lonely and even heart breaking work of trying to write and rewrite and rewrite, 'The Double Image.' I was 'true' then." She even wondered if "Poems, maybe, should be published anonymously. You wouldn't get any readings but you wouldn't have to get so nervous."

Sexton's mode in *Live or Die* is fully confessional as she addresses the old themes: her impulses to commit suicide and her breakdowns, which are contrasted with her desire to live; her ambivalences about her parents; her wish to give love to her daughters; and her need for a religious belief, which still is not belief. But as many reviewers noted, *Live or Die* has a new lack of control. Although such poems as "Somewhere in Africa," "Sylvia's Death," "To Lose the Earth," and much of "Wanting to Die" can be ranked with Sexton's better poetry, other poems are far from successful.

To begin with, awkwardness, imprecision, and mixed images permeate the collection, as in "Those Times . . . ," when the poet describes hiding in her closet as a child:

I grew into it like a root
and yet I planned such plans of flight,
believing I would take my body into the sky,
dragging it with me like a large bed.
And although I was unskilled
I was sure to get there or at least
to move up like an elevator.

In "And One for My Dame," the demands of the rhyme scheme lead to an embarrassing couplet about her father's salesmanship:

At home each sentence he would utter
had first pleased the buyer who'd paid him off
in butter.

Sexton also increasingly turns to shocking language and grotesque images for effect. Although such efforts work on occasion, all too often they merely call attention to themselves. In "Imitations of Drowning," for instance, she writes:

I was shut up in that closet, until, biting the
door,
they dragged me out, dribbling urine on the
gritty shore.

In the otherwise remarkable "Wanting to Die," she describes her body after a suicide attempt:

I did not think of my body at needle point.
Even the cornea and the leftover urine
were gone.

There is a new violence as well. For instance, the eventually affirmative final poem, "Live," begins with an upsettingly graphic image:

The chief ingredient
is mutilation.
And mud, day after day,
mud like a ritual,
and the baby on the platter,
cooked but still human,
cooked also with little maggots,
sewn onto it maybe by somebody's mother,
the damn bitch!

And when Sexton returns to the child's voice, which often functioned so effectively in the first volumes, the effect is cloying, as in "Protestant Easter," when the eight-year-old speaker reveals:

Once I thought the Bunny Rabbit was special
and I hunted for eggs.
That's when I was seven.
I'm grownup now. Now it's really Jesus.
I just have to get Him straight.
And right now.

Once again it is when Sexton most adheres to form that she is at her best. Her elegy to John Holmes, "Somewhere in Africa," for instance, contains powerful imagery and a sure, strong tone:

Let there be this God who is a woman who
will place you
upon her shallow boat, who is a woman
naked to the waist,
moist with palm oil and sweat, a woman of
some virtue
and wild breasts, her limbs excellent,
unbruised and chaste.

Let her take you. She will put twelve
strong men at the oars
for you are stronger than mahogany and
your bones fill

the boat high as with fruit and bark from
    the interior.
She will have you now, you whom the
    funeral cannot kill.

John Holmes, cut from a single tree, lie
    heavy in her hold
and go down that river with the ivory, the
    copra and the gold.

As the title of the book suggests, *Live or Die* is organized around Sexton's poetic confrontation with her suicidal impulses. Sexton told Kevles that a letter from Saul Bellow inspired the ultimate thematic plan of the book. Writing on the back of a page from his manuscript of *Herzog,* Bellow told Sexton he had a message for her from *Herzog.* He circled the lines on the manuscript page that became the book's epigraph:

With one long breath, caught and held in his chest, he fought his sadness over his solitary life. Don't cry, you idiot! Live or die, but don't poison everything. . . .

Such poems as "Wanting to Die" glorify death. In it Sexton explains the thrill of the suicide attempt:

Suicides have already betrayed the body.

Still-born, they don't always die,
but dazzled, they can't forget a drug so sweet
that even children would look on and smile.

To thrust all that life under your tongue!—
that, all by itself, becomes a passion.

In her elegy to Sylvia Plath, "Sylvia's Death," she even calls Plath a thief for crawling "down alone / into the death I wanted so badly and for so long." Death becomes desirable, and Sexton romanticizes it in the refrain:

that ride home
with *our* boy.

"To Lose the Earth," a poem inspired by a lithograph done by Sexton's friend and illustrator, Barbara Swan, similarly presents the experience of dying as positive. Although the poem suggests that there may be initial terror, in the end there will be beauty. The music of the androgynous flutist will be better than "the music that you waited for in the great concert halls," and people who come "out of simple curiosity / remain for generations." As the poet explains it:

And you, having heard,
you will never leave.
At the moment of entry
you were fed—
—and then you knew.

The stronger thrust in this volume is toward life and love. In "Flee on Your Donkey" Sexton specifically rejects the child's stance. She no longer wants to be her doctor's "third-grader / with a blue star on my forehead." She now is adamant about facing reality:

for this is a mental hospital
not a child's game.

She embraces her poetry, believing that even when others have abandoned her, she still has her muse, "*that good nurse.*" But the real progress is evident in her new resentment of the time lost in breakdowns:

I could have gone around the world twice
or had new children—all boys.

Nor is she romanticizing insanity, for though she has "come back," she now understands:

but disorder is not what it was.
I have lost the trick of it!
the innocence of it!

Further aware that brains and hearts deteriorate in mental hospitals, she admonishes herself, "For once make a deliberate decision." The decision is to flee not only the "sad hotel" but also "the fool's disease":

> Anne, Anne,
> flee on your donkey,
> flee this sad hotel,
> ride out on some hairy beast,
> gallop backward pressing
> your buttocks to his withers,
> sit to his clumsy gait somehow.
> Ride out
> any old way you please!

"Imitations of Drowning" demystifies suicide. The poet has decided that "real drowning is for someone else." In contrast with "Wanting to Die," this poem argues that there is no pleasure to be had in "thrusting all that life under your tongue" in order to die. Rather, the act of suicide is presented as a dreadful experience:

> ... It's too big
> to put in your mouth on purpose, it puts hot
>   stingers
> in your tongue and vomit in your nose as
>   your lungs break.
> Tossed like a wet dog by that juggler, you
>   die awake.

In "Mother and Jack and the Rain" the poet explicitly chooses both art and to "endure / somehow to endure." She decides that from both the pleasures and pains of her past, "let the poem be made."

The decision to reject death is particularly strong in Sexton's poem to her daughter Linda, "Little Girl, My Stringbean, My Lovely Woman." As she watches Linda reach adolescence, she celebrates the changes in her daughter's body, allying those changes to the fullness of nature, to globe-size lemons, to "mushrooms / and garlic buds all engorged," and to ripened berries and swelling apples. She urges Linda to accept herself and to live:

> What I want to say, Lindà
> is that there is nothing in your body that lies.

All that is new is telling the truth.
I'm here, that somebody else,
an old tree in the background.

> Darling,
> stand still at your door,
> sure of yourself, a white stone, a good stone—
> as exceptional as laughter
> you will strike fire,
> that new thing!

On the other hand, there are moments in this volume that also contain some troubling psychological undercurrents. In the poem to Linda, the poet takes pleasure in the knowledge that her hands formed Linda before the "strange hands" of lovers had touched her. She admits to feelings of jealousy toward her children in "Your Face on the Dog's Neck," saying that "Love twists me." She even expresses a need to possess the fantasy son, David, who is the subject of "Menstruation at Forty." She writes that "David" would make her "wild," fulfill her, and be her support as she aged. With him she sees herself as

> never growing old,
> waiting always for you on the porch ...
> year after year,
> my carrot, my cabbage,
> I would have possessed you before all women,
> calling your name,
> calling you mine.

In their notes to the letters, Linda Sexton and Lois Ames reveal that Sexton had difficulty ending the volume because "She needed a capstone, a positive statement with which to end it. Finally, in February 1966 it came: the poem 'Live.'" The poet begins by describing how much death has been with her. A change occurs when she discovers the sun inside of her and thus is able to reject death. Instead of drowning some newborn puppies, she lets them live, a decision she universalizes. Even more important, she decides that if she cannot kill others, then she also is able to choose life for herself:

> I promise to love more if they come,
> because in spite of cruelty
> and the stuffed railroad cars for the ovens,
> I am not what I expected. Not an
>   Eichmann.
> The poison just didn't take.
> So I won't hang around in my hospital
>   shift,
> repeating The Black Mass and all of it.
> I say *Live, Live,* because of the sun,
> the dream, the excitable gift.

Although Sexton tried to kill herself the summer after she wrote this poem, the determination to live soon became more than a poetic stance. For the next few years she appeared "stable and secure" and, according to Linda and Ames, "To the joy of her friends and family, suicide ceased to be a daily threat between 1967 and 1970." She gave a great many public readings and her books were selling well. Although the critical reaction to *Live or Die* was mixed, in May 1967 she received the Pulitzer Prize for it. The following year both Harvard and Radcliffe made her an honorary member of Phi Beta Kappa.

During these years Sexton also became increasingly interested in teaching. In 1967–1968 she and a friend, Robert Clawson, taught an experimental high school literature class in Wayland, Massachusetts, funded by the National Endowment for the Humanities. When one of the students set "Ringing the Bells" to music, Sexton was intrigued. With Clawson as her manager, she formed a chamber rock group called Anne Sexton and Her Kind (a reference to the early poem "Her Kind"). The group's first public performance was at a benefit for Eugene McCarthy's presidential campaign. Sexton also began collaborating with Kumin on another children's book.

Her involvement in teaching grew. In the fall of 1968 she taught a poetry class to patients at a private mental hospital in Belmont, Massachusetts. The following winter she conducted a poetry workshop for Oberlin College students in her home, a project she repeated the next year. And she completed *Love Poems*, which was published in February 1969.

It is this volume that most belies the view of Sexton as a feminist. Many of its poems celebrate women in submissive roles. Although Sexton abandons the child's voice, the speaker of many of the poems receives her identity and her happiness from the love of a man. In "The Touch," for instance, the poet is vulnerable and unhappy until her lover gives her life:

> Then all this became history.
> Your hand found mine.
> Life rushed to my fingers like a blood clot.
> Oh my carpenter,
> The fingers are rebuilt.

In "The Kiss" her entire body is useless, a boat "no more / than a group of boards," until her lover "hoisted her, rigged her." In "The Breast" the lover's hands find her "like an architect," while she believes that it is only through young men that she can learn the truth. Moreover, only when she is defined in relationship to men—as mother, daughter, or lover—does she come alive:

> Now I am your mother, your daughter,
> your brand new thing—a snail, a nest.
> I am alive when your fingers are.

Even deception is acceptable if it will bring her sexual pleasure:

> So tell me anything but track me like a
>   climber
> for here is the eye, here is the jewel,
> here is the excitement the nipple learns.

Sexton happily assumes the role of slave in "Us," standing only when her lover calls her "princess." Only then does she become active so that the lovers together can "harvest." She is particularly self-deprecating about her role as the "other woman." In "You All Know the Story of the Other Woman," after the affair is over, she is placed "like a phone, back on the hook."

A more extended working out of the adulterous relationship is the subject of "For My Lover, Returning to His Wife," one of Sexton's best poems. The poem operates on the contrast between the wife and the poet. The wife is a monument, a sculpture, something permanent, harmonious, "in fact, exquisite." The poet sees herself as "momentary," an "experiment," a "luxury" like "Littleneck clams out of season."

But despite the wife's extraordinary qualities (she takes care of the oars and oarlocks for the family dinghy; she is an artist in her own right; she places "wild flowers at the window at breakfast"; and she nurtures her three children), she too is defined mainly as an extension of her husband. She is his "have to have." Moreover, as Sexton tells her lover:

> She is all there.
> She was melted carefully down for you
> and cast up from your childhood,
>   cast up from your one hundred favorite
>   aggies.

Thus, the wife too is victimized. Out of the poet's awareness of the wife's complexity and of her anger she gives her lover "permission" to return to his wife:

> for the fuse inside her, throbbing
> angrily in the dirt, for the bitch in her
> and the burying of her wound—
> for the burying of her small red wound
>   alive—

The poem ends with the poet again contrasting the wife and herself in a wonderful culmination of the imagery that has characterized each of them:

> She is so naked and singular.
> She is the sum of yourself and your dream.

> Climb her like a monument, step after step.
> She is solid.

> As for me, I am a watercolor.
> I wash off.

In addition to poems about love, *Love Poems* introduces a new motif that will reappear increasingly in the poetry—the relationship between sexuality and violence. The poem "Loving the Killer" is one of the first that is directly about her marriage. The context of the poem is a safari the Sextons went on in 1966, just a month after one of Anne's suicide attempts. Although she dreaded the trip, she ignored her psychiatrist's advice and went, in order, she told friends, to give Kayo his lifelong dream. The poem specifically echoes Plath's "Daddy," in which Plath wrote:

> Every woman adores a Fascist,
> The boot in the face, the brute
> Brute heart of a brute like you.

Sexton, in her turn, writes:

> Oh my Nazi,
> with your S.S. sky-blue eye—
> I am no different from Emily Goering.

and

> I will eat you slowly with kisses
> even though the killer in you
> has gotten out.

"The Papa and Mama Dance" also associates sexuality and death. It is a bizarre, non-autobiographical poem in which the speaker attempts to convince her brother to burn his draft card rather than go to war. In doing so, she reminds him of the sexual games they had played as children:

> I tell you the dances we had were really
>   enough,
> Your hands on my breasts and all that
>   sort of stuff.

But the brother prefers killing. He has become "Mr. Gunman," and denies the childhood games. Yet these games had intimations of death in them; the children playing the "Mama and Papa Dance" wore black wedding clothes.

But despite its thematic interest, on the whole *Love Poems* is disappointing. Again there are too many awkward moments. The Whitman-esque catalogs in "In Celebration of My Uterus" in particular are without grace. Other moments are more private than interesting. "The Break" is filled with details chosen, apparently, because they are literal rather than because they function to forward meaning. For instance, Sexton describes her first moments in the emergency room:

I cried, "Oh Jesus, help me! Oh Jesus Christ!"
and the nurse replied, "Wrong name. My
   name
is Barbara," and hung me in an odd device,
a buck's extension and a Balkan overhead
   frame.

There are increased references to excrement that, because they seem so unnecessary, are unsettling. In "The Break" she describes the hospital:

Across the hall is the bedpan station.
The urine and stools pass hourly by my head
in silver bowls. They flush in unison
in the autoclave.

Shortly after the publication of *Love Poems*, Sexton won a Guggenheim Fellowship (1969) that allowed her to complete her play *Mercy Street*. During the next four months she and Lois Ames spent a great deal of time in New York readying the play for production. It opened in October at the off-Broadway American Place Theater to negative reviews. Sexton eventually decided that she did not want the play ever to be published.

The following year she characterized her new book, *Transformations* (1971), as being "as far away from *Mercy Street*, that confessional melodrama, as possible." She also wrote to Claire Degener, "I'm not even sure these are poems. I think they are artifacts." Houghton Mifflin shared her doubts that the retelling of the Grimms's fairy tales in modern terms was poetry. It balked at publishing *Transformations* because the contents were not "typical" Sexton. She immediately waged a countercampaign, insisting to Houghton Mifflin editor Paul Brooks:

It would further be a lie to say that they weren't about me, because they are just as much about me as my other poetry.

I look at my work in stages, and each new book is a kind of growth and reaching outward and as always backward. . . .

Now that I've almost finished *Transformations* I see it as part of my life's work . . . a kind of dalliance on the way.

She wrote to others with equal enthusiasm. When she asked novelist Kurt Vonnegut to write an introduction to the collection, she described the poems with obvious pleasure:

They are small, funny and horrifying. Without quite meaning to I have joined the black humorists. I don't know if you know my other work, but humor was never a very prominent feature . . . terror, deformity, madness and torture were my bag. But this little universe of Grimm is not that far away. I think they end up being as wholly personal as my most intimate poems, in a different language, a different rhythm, but coming strangely, for all their story sound, from as deep a place.

Houghton Mifflin eventually published the book, which brought Sexton some of the most positive reviews of her career. Christopher Lehmann-Haupt, of the *New York Times*, for instance, praised it as being "a funny, mad, witty, frightening, charming, haunting book." He, like other reviewers, believed Sexton had found a balance in it between confessionalism and craft, and he noted with pleasure her technique of turning "the fairy tales into comic strips and other pop-art artifacts." Indeed, the contemporaneity of the language and the images, coupled with a breezy sort of pop psychology, give the book its freshness and its charm.

"Rumpelstiltskin" exemplifies Sexton's method. To begin with, the dwarf is given a motive for stealing the child, his awareness that "no child will ever call me Papa." By alluding to Truman Capote, Sexton literally fleshes out the image:

> He speaks up as tiny as an earphone
> with Truman's asexual voice.

Sexton begins the poem by saying that Rumpelstiltskin represents the inner self:

> Inside many of us
> is a small old man
> who wants to get out.

He is not the superego, not "the law in your mind," but the more dangerous id, J. Edgar Hoover's "the enemy within." He is sexuality:

> . . . the law of your members,
> the kindred of blackness and impulse.
>   . . .
> It is your Doppelgänger

Sexton does not judge this inner self harshly. Rumpelstiltskin's desire for a child is understandable:

> . . . he wanted only this—
> a living thing
> to call his own.
> And being mortal
> who can blame him?

The miller's daughter also is given psychological validity. She initially is the victim of her fa-

ther's bragging and a sheltered childhood:

> Luscious and round and sleek.
> Poor thing.
> To die and never see Brooklyn.

Because of her naiveté she easily promises the dwarf her unborn child, but after the baby's birth she "thought him a pearl" and desperately wants to keep him.

The denouement of the poem comes with the recognition that Rumpelstiltskin too has a split self. Thwarted in his desire for a child, he tears himself in two, revealing one side of himself as a nurturing parent, "soft as a woman" and "part papa," and the other side "a barbed hook," the doppelgänger.

The blending of the Grimms's fairy tales and pop culture permeates the book. The associations often are surprising and as often illuminating. Thus, the evil fairy in "Briar Rose (Sleeping Beauty)" is explained by the fact that "her uterus [is] an empty teacup." The queen in "Rumpelstiltskin" is "as persistent / as a Jehovah's Witness." Little Red Riding Hood's cape becomes "her Linus blanket," and Snow White "opened her eyes as wide as Orphan Annie." Cinderella, sooty before the ball, "walked around looking like Al Jolson." Other poems benefit from Sexton's sardonic use of contemporary slang. Snow White, in her foolish habit of opening the door to the wicked stepmother, is "the dumb bunny" and the dwarfs become "those little hot dogs." After she has been tied up so tightly that she swoons, Snow White is revived and is "as full of life as soda pop."

Transformations also seriously explores the nature of relationships by examining the deeper psychological motives people have for their actions. For instance, Snow White's stepmother is unable to cope with her aging. The wife and the parson in "The Little Peasant" similarly are concerned with growing old, hoping that their lovemaking will make them young. The mother in "One-Eye, Two-Eyes, Three-Eyes" favors her deformed children because, like the mother in "The Hangman," her martyrdom brings her pleasure. The king in "The Maiden Without Hands" marries the crippled woman because her deformity seems a talisman that might keep him whole. And despite the apparent pleasures of lesbianism in "Rapunzel" ("A woman / who loves a woman / is forever young"), Rapunzel outgrows "mother-me-do" because

> The world, some say,
> is made up of couples.
> A rose must have a stem.

Marriage comes in for its share of criticism in the transformations. In both "The White Snake" and "Cinderella," the conventional happy endings are perceived as sterile. In "The White Snake":

> They played house, little charmers,
> exceptionally well.
> So, of course,
> they were placed in a box
> and painted identically blue
> and thus passed their days
> living happily ever after—
> a kind of coffin,
> a kind of blue funk.
> Is it not?

Cinderella and the prince have an equally uninteresting fate:

> like two dolls in a museum case
> never bothered by diapers or dust,
> never arguing over the timing of an egg,
> never telling the same story twice,
> never getting a middle-aged spread,
> their darling smiles pasted on for eternity.
> Regular Bobbsey Twins.
> That story.

"Iron Hans" more seriously dramatizes one of Sexton's usual concerns. The poem begins with a preamble that documents how those who are different make others "move off." In a reference to herself, Sexton writes:

> Take a woman talking,
> purging herself with rhymes,
> drumming words out like a typewriter,
> planting words in you like grass seed.
> You'll move off.

Hans, of course, only "appeared . . . to be a lunatic." In reality he is more gentle, more just, and more powerful than anyone else. He was just under a spell, which the boy he helps has broken, and so:

> Without Thorazine
> or benefit of psychotherapy
> Iron Hans was transformed.
> No need for Master Medical;
> no need for electroshock—
> merely bewitched all along.

Sexton was appointed lecturer in English at Boston University in 1969, as she was writing *Transformations* and planning her next two volumes: *The Book of Folly* (1972) and *The Death Notebooks* (1974). She wrote to Degener:

I think I would like to do a book of very surreal, unconscious poems called *The Book of Folly.* After that I would like to do a very Sexton, intense, personal, perhaps religious in places book called *The Death Notebooks.* . . .

This period also brought new psychological torments. Her sister-in-law, Joan Sexton, was killed in a car accident only six days after being married for the second time. Sexton became newly plagued by thoughts of suicide, writing to Philip Legler, "I think I'm so busy fighting the suicide demons that I have little time for love. . . . I hope to hell my present shrink can help me work this out before it's too late." She began to write to friends about her desire for some sort of religious belief.

The major importance of *The Book of Folly* lies in what it reveals about Sexton's mental state. Although at times it suggests her return to more intricate rhyme schemes (as in the sonnet sequence "Angels of the Love Affair"), formally the book is deeply flawed. It may be that in her effort to write "surreal, unconscious poems," she had decided that simply simulating the life of her mind was enough. Thus, her streams of consciousness evidence what seems to be almost purely free association. The result often is an overabundance of mixed, private, and unappealing images.

Such poems as "The Doctor of the Heart" reassert her desire to live. In others the old guilt is present. In "Dreaming the Breasts" she again feels responsible for her mother's death:

> I ate you up.
> All my need took
> you down like a meal.

She even implicitly assumes the burden for her great-aunt's senility, asking in "Anna Who Was Mad," "Did I make you go insane?"

But there are two new notes in such poems: tenderness and a new accusatory stance. Thus Sexton writes in "Dreaming the Breasts" that after her mother's mastectomy, she plants her breasts:

> so that your great bells,
> those dear white ponies,
> can go galloping, galloping,
> wherever you are.

On the other hand "The Hoarder" insists that her mother's attitude about toilet training led the poet to be "a hoarder of words":

> it was the diaper I wore
> and the dirt thereof and my
> mother hating me for it and me

loving me for it but the hate
won didn't it yes the distaste
won the disgust won and because
of this I am a hoarder of words

Two of the prose pieces, "Dancing the Jig" and "The Letting Down of the Hair," portray speakers who were victims of psychologically destructive families. "Dancing the Jig" and the poem "The Other" further suggest that such victimization led to an "other," a doppelgänger responsible for the poet's inability to be in control.

A particularly revealing sequence is "The Death of the Fathers," a series of poems that both describe the Electra complex of the poet toward her father and suggest that Ralph Harvey may not have been her natural father. The sequence is dominated by the poet's dual sense that her father had been cuckolded and that she had, in some ways, assumed her mother's role in relationship to him.

The opening poem, "Oysters," describes the poet's rite of passage at fifteen from childhood into womanhood as she eats oysters, "this father-food," during a luncheon with her father. As J. D. McClatchy notes, the "father-food" has sexual implications:

> It was a soft medicine
> that came from the sea into my mouth,
> moist and plump.
> I swallowed.
> It went down like large pudding.

At nineteen, in "How We Danced," the poet "orbited" with her father while her mother danced "with twenty men." The poem has sexual implications as the poet tells her father "the serpent spoke as you held me close / The serpent, that mocker, woke up and pressed against me." In "The Boat" the father steers the family's Chris-Craft containing his wife and his daughter "out past Cuckold's Light" and through a dangerous wave. The unity the three momentarily feel doesn't exist in the next poem, "Santa." The poem begins nostalgically, with the poet watching her mother, who is "that tall," kiss her father as he masquerades as Santa Claus. When the poet realizes that Santa has "Daddy's cocktail smell," his voice "slithery like soap," she is disillusioned. Her father is relieved that the charade is over. Years later they reenact the scene, but with a difference. The daughter, now "tall enough," kisses the father.

In "Friends," perhaps Sexton's most terrifying poem of childhood memories, she remembers a stranger who took liberties with her, putting his tongue in her mouth when he kissed her and beating her "on the buttocks with a jump rope" when her father was "gone on a trip." "An oily creature," he "knew Mother too well." The poem ends with the poet again assuming a child's voice, pleading with her father to assert his paternity as she asks:

> He was a stranger, Father.
> Oh God,
> he was a stranger,
> was he not?

"Begat," the final poem in the sequence, supplies an answer from the stranger himself, who, years after the father's death, calls to announce, "I am your real father." The poet denies the connection and, despite her father's flaws, reclaims him because "He is my history."

The sexual violence of the stranger reappears in other poems in *The Book of Folly*. The husband in "The Wifebeater" kisses "With a tongue like a razor." The assassin in the poem of that name finds the thought of the impending murder sexually exciting. In "Santa" the poet describes her husband "with a crowbar breaking things up." The prose fable "The Ballet of the Buffoon" also is extremely violent. A perverse tale about a Mr. Ha-Ha who cons other men into murdering their wives, its moral is

"Every man kills his wife. It's a matter of history." Even young girls know that violence, with its sexual implications, will come to them, and they sing, "When will the gun come to me."

The Book of Folly also indicates Sexton's desire to continue working in the mode of *Transformations*. "The Jesus Papers" transforms biblical tales with the goal of humanizing, as they modernize, Christ. Sexton justifies the tone by the epigraph "God is not mocked except by believers." But the effort often seems strained. For instance, in "Jesus Cooks," when Jesus wants to feed the multitudes, he asks God to "send down a short-order cook." God later advises, "Work on the sly / opening boxes of sardine cans."

Sexton also reveals her usual psychological preoccupations. Jesus, in "Jesus Asleep," has incestuous desires for Mary:

> Jesus slept as still as a toy
> and in His dream
> He desired Mary.
> His penis sang like a dog.

But instead of giving in to the taboo, Jesus sublimates his desire into art:

> He made a statue out of His need.
> With His penis like a chisel
> He carved the Pietà.

Mary Magdalene displays some of Sexton's traits. In "Jesus Raises up the Harlot" she is so grateful for Christ's attention that she "followed Jesus around like a puppy" and "became His pet." She even forsakes her fornications because

> His raising her up made her feel
> like a little girl again when she had a father
> who brushed the dirt from her eye.

Perhaps the most successful poem of the volume is its opening one, "The Ambition Bird." Confronting her insomnia ("the business of words keeps me awake"), the poet acknowledges that she "would like a simple life." Still, she writes poetry because it is her "immortality box," her "lay-away plan," her "coffin." She acknowledges her various motives for writing: a desire for suicide, a wish to be a Michelangelo, a hope of creating God or man, a wish to "unlock the Magi," a need to affect others, an urge to be like Icarus. But the poem ends poignantly, quietly, with the question:

> Dear God, wouldn't it be
> good enough to just drink cocoa?

and with a determination to

> get a new bird
> and a new immortality box.
> There is folly enough inside this one.

But the folly was to increase. In the two years after the publication of *The Book of Folly* in the fall of 1972, Sexton's life seemed to accelerate, sometimes out of control. Writing to a friend, she worried that her life was "becoming like the Perils of Pauline. It is exaggerating itself." She intensified her campaign to convince Boston University to pay her on the same scale as they paid their male writers, particularly John Barth. In February 1973 she asked Kayo for a divorce. The time was difficult for Sexton, her family, and her friends. Linda Sexton and Lois Ames describe her as asking friends "to care for her like a child" and, in the end, alienating those close to her because of her exhausting demands. She regretted her decision to leave Kayo, who had attempted to convince her to stay in the marriage. She began to turn more to religion for solace. But most of all, she began to write frantically.

Thus, between June 1972 and her death a year and a half later, Sexton wrote poetry for four collections: *The Death Notebooks, The Awful Rowing Toward God* (1975), *45 Mercy Street* (1976), and the final section of *Words for Dr. Y* (1978). She seldom revised, noting that she had written the first draft of *The Awful Rowing Toward God* in twenty days with "two days out for despair, and three days out in a mental hospital." Although she deemed the poems "raw, unreworked," and in need of revision, she arranged to publish them almost totally as they were.

The Death Notebooks, completed first, is deeply flawed. The weaknesses are the familiar ones but sometimes even more exaggerated. For instance, the child's voice in "Hurry up Please It's Time" asks:

Why shouldn't I pull down my pants
and moon at the executioner
as well as paste raisins on my breasts?
Why shouldn't I pull down my pants
and show my little cunny to Tom
and Albert? They wee-wee funny.
I wee-wee like a squaw.
I have ink but no pen, still
I dream that I can piss in God's eye.
I dream I'm a boy with a zipper.

There is also a new preachiness to some of the poems, as in the sophomoric lines in "The Fury of Flowers and Worms":

If all the world picked daisies
wars would end, the common cold would stop,
unemployment would end, the monetary
    market
would hold steady and no money would float.

The best that can be said about this book is that it reveals Sexton's continued interest, however badly realized, in working with new poetic forms. For instance, the sequence of psalms is modeled after the *Jubilate Agno* of the eighteenth-century poet Christopher Smart. "Hurry up Please It's Time" (the phrase is taken from *The Waste Land*) seems to be an effort by Sexton to present a world that is sterile and without redeeming values in different voices, as T. S. Eliot had.

Although she still shows the desire to live in some poems, there is a new note of self-deprecation here as well. She is not always as in control as she is at the conclusion of "The Fury of Rain Storms," where she decides almost matter-of-factly:

> Depression is boring, I think,
> and I would do better to make
> some soup and light up the cave.

Rather, she begins to write about the ways in which she is being exploited because of her death wishes. In "Making a Living" she compares the biblical Jonah first to Christ and then to herself:

> Then he told the news media
> the strange details of his death
> and they hammered him up in the
>   marketplace
> and sold him and sold him and sold him.
> My death the same.

When the title of the poem is juxtaposed with the collection's epigraph, "Look, you con man, make a living out of your death," it becomes clear that Sexton also feared that she was a party to this process of selling her personal suffering. "Hurry up Please It's Time" reveals her disdain for her sense that she must confess all to please her audiences:

> Who's that at the podium
> in black and white,
> blurting into the mike?
> Ms. Dog.
> Is she spilling her guts?
> You bet.
> Otherwise they cough. . . .

Still, there are moments when she seems to welcome the voyeurism of others. In "For Mr. Death Who Stands with His Door Open," she asks that her own dying be "slow":

> Let it be pantomime, this last peep show,
> so that I may squat at the edge trying on
> my black necessary trousseau.

Sexton became almost obsessed with her relationship to her audience. In "Talking to Sheep," which was published posthumously in *45 Mercy Street*, she admitted shame at her compulsion to keep "confessing, confessing" in the face of her readers' avariciousness. In 1973, in the essay "The Freak Show," which she wrote for the *American Poetry Review*, she was similarly critical of what she saw as her pandering to predatory audiences.

Sexton had reason to worry. She had become obsessed with giving readings and with promoting herself for financial gain. For instance, when she was unhappy with the advance publicity for a scheduled reading at Sanders Theater at Harvard, she conducted and paid for her own publicity campaign. She had posters made up, took out full-page newspaper ads complete with a photo of herself, and ran radio spots. Her advertising was successful and she read to a standing-room-only audience. She spent much time quibbling with various sponsors about fees for readings and insisting on more money and status from Boston University. Eventually she was given the rank of professor. It becomes particularly painful, then, to read Sexton's confession to Donald Hall some ten months before her suicide: "I've just been too Christly busy—either readings or my class or hospitals. Dear God, only one poem since July and that not finished. I must remember that I am a poet—at least I must remember it now and then. . . ."

On the day of her suicide, October 4, 1974, Sexton had lunch with Maxine Kumin, and, as they had for Sexton's other books, proofread the galleys for *The Awful Rowing Toward God.* Then, without having given Kumin, family, or friends any warning, Sexton went home, locked herself in the garage, turned on the ignition of her automobile, and died.

Because *The Awful Rowing Toward God* is the last volume Sexton herself prepared for publication, the poems take on special interest and poignancy. As the title suggests, the book articulates Sexton's desire to achieve a religious faith. The opening poem, "Rowing," describes the evolution of her acceptance of God. Initially "ignorant of him," she eventually realized that "God was there like an island I had not rowed to." The most powerful lines in the poem, and perhaps the entire book, describe her efforts to reach that island:

> I am rowing, I am rowing
> though the oarlocks stick and are rusty
> and the sea blinks and rolls
> like a worried eyeball,
> but I am rowing, I am rowing,
> though the wind pushes me back
> and I know that that island will not be
>   perfect,
> it will have the flaws of life,
> the absurdities of the dinner table,
> but there will be a door
> and I will open it
> and I will get rid of the rat inside of me,
> the gnawing, pestilential rat.
> God will take it with his two hands
> and embrace it.
>   . . .
> This story ends with me still rowing.

Many of the interior poems, much like "The Jesus Papers" in *The Book of Folly*, attempt to make God seem accessible, to have "the flaws of life" and "the absurdities of the dinner table." In "The Earth" Sexton fantasizes about a God who would like to have a human body, who "would like to smoke His cigar / or bite His fingernails" or even take a bath. She also desires to find God in the dailiness of her life. Thus, in "Welcome Morning" she cooks "a

chapel of eggs" and eats at "the godhead of the table." In "Snow" she believes that each snow-covered branch "wears the sock of God," and in "Small Wire" she convinces herself that even a small amount of love, a "thin wire," will be strong enough to hold faith, for

> God does not mind.
> He will enter your hands
> as easily as ten cents used to
> bring forth a coke.

Although poem after poem explores the age-old theological dilemma of how to explain the existence of evil in the world, in the end Sexton suggests that the evil within her may be her "ignorance of God." She admonishes her readers in "The Wall" to open themselves up to God:

> take off the wall
> that separates you from God.

She decides in "The Evil Seekers" that evil may be necessary for growth because

> one must see the night
> before one can realize the day.

The concluding poem, "The Rowing Endeth," is meant to be affirmative, although Sexton's final vision of God as a poker-playing male is another disconcerting example of her assuming a dependent stance. Nevertheless, she opens the poem "mooring my rowboat / at the dock of the island called God." God then invites her to play poker, and because he has a "wild card," he ends up with five aces, which beat the poet's royal flush. This is, she believes, a triumph for them both; and she and God are joined in laughter, laughter motivated by an awareness of the absurd, of the need for a leap of faith, and of the ultimate power of love:

> Then I laugh, the fishy dock laughs,
> the sea laughs. The Island laughs.
> The Absurd laughs.

Dearest Dealer,
I with my royal straight flush,
love you so for your wild card,
that untamable, eternal, gut-driven *ha-ha*
and lucky love.

In the years following Sexton's death, her daughter Linda edited and published two volumes of poetry, *45 Mercy Street* and *Words for Dr. Y.* In addition, collaborating with Lois Ames, she put out a collection of her mother's letters, *Anne Sexton: A Self-Portrait in Letters* (1977). All three books are problematic for the same reason: they have value only in terms of what they reveal about Sexton personally. The poetry is deeply flawed and offers nothing new thematically. In all fairness to Sexton, it should be stressed that she neither revised the poetry nor arranged for its publication. Still, except for the fact that they reveal an increasing deterioration in the poetry, these books are harmless enough.

The letters raise a more complicated question. On the one hand they contribute little to an understanding of Sexton's art. What they provide instead is an excess of details about her intimate life and, sadly, the portrait that emerges is of a woman even more tormented, more pathetic, and often more adolescent than the poetry reveals.

To be sure, a few letters about specific poems and some broader statements about poetry in general are illuminating and interesting, but these occur only sporadically. The editors' biographical notes are more useful, suggesting that Sexton might have been better served by a critical biography that drew on and included the important letters.

On the other hand Sexton herself made and kept carbons of her letters, apparently tens of thousands of them, a habit that suggests she would have sanctioned their publication even though many of them merely pander to the sort

of voyeurism that was making her increasingly uncomfortable toward the end of her life.

In essence the original problem that Sexton's poetry occasioned—the tendency to read it as a case history or a social document and not as art—persists. Certainly the growing body of Sexton criticism is dominated by those who praise her for her honesty and not her artistry. Indeed, an almost anti-intellectual bias emerges, with many readers either ignoring aesthetic and formal questions or insisting, sometimes fervently, that traditional standards of literary analysis should be replaced by extra-literary considerations.

Robert Boyers, who most values Sexton because her concern is "herself and her emotions," finds it particularly "remarkable that she never flinches from the task at hand, never attempts to use her art as a device for warding off final perception." J. D. McClatchy similarly praises Sexton's honesty while echoing Boyers' reservations about art itself. Emphasizing Sexton's refusal to "dodge or distort" the details of her life, McClatchy favorably contrasts Sexton's directness with what he calls the "covers" of other confessional poets: "Lowell's allusiveness, Snodgrass's lyricism, Berryman's dazzle, Plath's expressionism."

But what McClatchy denigrates as "covers" generally are prized as the tools of poetry. It is not surprising that it is Sexton's "courage in coming true," and not her artistry, that McClatchy cites as the reason why she should be considered "one of the most distinctive voices in this generation's literature, and a figure of permanent importance to the development of American poetry."

Some feminists also reject as obsolete the conventional critical standards by which Sexton might be judged negatively. They argue that because new forms are necessary to express feminine sensibilities, new criteria by which to evaluate those forms are necessary as well.

They urge that the New Critical concern with form be replaced with such criteria as the authenticity of the presentation of female experience by a work and the ability of that work to raise the consciousness of its readers.

From this vantage point, feminists such as Erica Jong and Suzanne Juhasz define as virtues the aspects of Sexton's poetry that a New Critic might perceive as flaws. Jong, in her tribute to Sexton (thinly disguised as the fictional Jeannie Morton) in *How to Save Your Own Life* (1977), asserts that those who criticize Sexton do so because "She was a woman—and her images (even of God) were kitchen images. . . . She was easy to mock." Jong, in her turn, admires Sexton because "She wrote about all the things we had been told in college were unfit subjects for poetry—blood, madness, excrement, the transmigration of the soul."

Juhasz, in *Naked and Fiery Forms* (1976), rejoices in Sexton's devotion to the particulars of her life precisely because Juhasz rejects the effort to universalize as a masculine (and therefore undesirable) trait. She takes pleasure in the fact that

. . . unlike the confessionalism of so many male poets (Robert Lowell's, for example, in *Life Studies*), Sexton's poetry does not plug into a larger tradition—that of being a poet whose life and consciousness is in some sense meant to typify the consciousness of his age.

Juhasz offers a feminist variation on Alvarez's linking of the artistic temperament with death wishes, arguing that for both Plath and Sexton "madness and ultimately suicide seem integrally linked to the conflict and strain experienced in trying to be both woman and artist." Because Juhasz sees poetry as having traditionally been a male domain, she argues that Sexton, like Plath, "finds the double bind" of trying to be both a woman and a poet "to be too

powerful and kills herself." (Such theorizing of course ignores the crucial fact that in Sexton's case, at least, the suicidal impulses preceded the poetic ones. It also ignores Maxine Kumin's belief that writing poetry kept Sexton alive longer than might otherwise have been the case.)

The tragedy of such approaches to Sexton's poetry is that they negate her commitment to art and emphasize her psychological demons instead. She wrote to an admirer, "Madness is a waste of time. It creates nothing." She similarly insisted to Patricia Marx, "I do not think genius and insanity grow in the same bed." She also affirmed herself as a poet and as a woman, saying that the two roles were compatible because "It's within a woman to create, to make order, to be an emotional, full human being." But most of all Sexton valued art above death. As she wrote after Plath had killed herself, "Suicide is, after all, the opposite of the poem."

Denise Levertov, in her remarkable essay "Light up the Cave," has attempted to direct attention back to Sexton's artistry and away from her death. Noting that Sexton's death was followed by a surge of articles and essays equating the poetic sensibility with emotional instability, Levertov rails against what she sees as a dangerous tendency to romanticize alienation. Specifically, she suggests that Sexton's "private anguish" was exploited "by a greedy public" and that Sexton, like so many others, "internalize[d] the exploitive, unwittingly becoming self-exploitive."

In her introductory notes to *Words for Dr. Y*, Linda Sexton promises that an edition of her mother's collected works will be forthcoming. Levertov's ultimate tribute to Sexton would be both a fitting and a welcome epigraph to such a book and to future readings of Sexton as well:

To recognize that for a few years of her life Anne Sexton was an artist *even though* she had so hard a struggle against her desire of death is to fittingly honor her memory. To identify her love of death with her love of poetry is to insult that struggle.

Selected Bibliography

WORKS OF ANNE SEXTON

POEMS

To Bedlam and Part Way Back. Boston: Houghton Mifflin, 1960.
All My Pretty Ones. Boston: Houghton Mifflin, 1962.
Selected Poems. London: Oxford University Press, 1964.
Live or Die. Boston: Houghton Mifflin, 1966; London: Oxford University Press, 1967.
Poems. London: Oxford University Press, 1968. With Thomas Kinsella and Douglas Livingstone.
Love Poems. Boston: Houghton Mifflin, 1969; London: Oxford University Press, 1969.
Transformations. Boston: Houghton Mifflin, 1971; London: Oxford University Press, 1972.
The Book of Folly. Boston: Houghton Mifflin, 1972; London: Chatto and Windus, 1974.
The Death Notebooks. Boston: Houghton Mifflin, 1974; London: Chatto and Windus, 1975.
The Awful Rowing Toward God. Boston: Houghton Mifflin, 1975; London: Chatto and Windus, 1977.
45 Mercy Street, edited by Linda Gray Sexton. Boston: Houghton Mifflin, 1976; London: Martin Secker and Warburg, 1977.
Words for Dr. Y, edited by Linda Gray Sexton. Boston: Houghton Mifflin, 1978.

CHILDREN'S BOOKS (with Maxine Kumin)
Eggs of Things. New York: Putnam, 1963.
More Eggs of Things. New York: Putnam, 1964.
Joey and the Birthday Present. New York: McGraw-Hill, 1971.
The Wizard's Tears. New York: McGraw-Hill, 1975.

PROSE
"The Barfly Ought to Sing." *Tri Quarterly*, 7:89–94 (Fall 1966). Reprinted in *The Art of Sylvia Plath*, edited by Charles Newman. Bloomington: Indiana University Press, 1970. Pp. 174–81.
"The Freak Show." *American Poetry Review*, 2, no. 3:38, 40 (May/June 1973).

LETTERS
Anne Sexton: A Self-Portrait in Letters, edited by Linda Gray Sexton and Lois Ames. Boston: Houghton Mifflin, 1977.

BIBLIOGRAPHY

Northouse, Cameron, and Thomas P. Walsh. *Sylvia Plath and Anne Sexton: A Reference Guide*. Boston: G. K. Hall and Co., 1974.

CRITICISM AND REVIEWS

Alvarez, A. *Beyond All This Fiddle: Essays, 1955–57*. New York: Random House, 1969.
Boyers, Robert. "*Live or Die*: The Achievement of Anne Sexton." *Salmagundi*, 2, no. 1:41–71 (Spring 1967). Reprinted in *Anne Sexton, The Artist and Her Critics*, edited by J. D. McClatchy. Bloomington and London: Indiana University Press, 1978 (hereafter referred to as McClatchy).
Dickey, James. "Five First Books." *Poetry*, 97, no. 5:318–19 (February 1961). Reprinted in his *Babel to Byzantium*. New York: Farrar, Straus and Giroux, 1968. Also in McClatchy.
Fields, Beverly. "The Poetry of Anne Sexton." In *Poets in Progress*, edited by Edward Hungerford. Evanston, Ill.: Northwestern University Press, 1967. Pp. 251–85.
Gullans, Charles. "Poetry and Subject Matter: From Hart Crane to Turner Cassidy." *The Southern Review*, 7, no. 2:497–98 (Spring 1970). Reprinted in McClatchy.
Howard, Richard. "Anne Sexton: 'Some Tribal Female Who Is Known but Forbidden.'" In his *Alone with America: Essays on the Art of Poetry in the United States Since 1950*. New York: Atheneum, 1971. Pp. 442–50.

Juhasz, Suzanne. *Naked and Fiery Forms: Modern American Poetry by Women, A New Tradition.* New York: Harper Colophon, 1976.

Kumin, Maxine. "A Friendship Remembered." In McClatchy. Pp. 103–10.

Lehmann-Haupt, Christopher. "Grimms' Fairy Tales Retold." *New York Times*, September 27, 1971, p. 37. Reprinted in McClatchy.

Levertov, Denise. "Light up the Cave." *Ramparts*, 13, no. 5:61–63 (December 1974–January 1975). Reprinted in McClatchy.

McClatchy, J. D. "Anne Sexton: Somehow to Endure." In McClatchy. Pp. 244–90.

Mills, Ralph J., Jr. *Contemporary American Poetry.* New York: Random House, 1965.

Phillips, Robert. *The Confessional Poets.* Carbondale: Southern Illinois University Press, 1973.

Rosenthal, M. L. *The New Poets: American and British Poetry Since World War II.* New York: Oxford University Press, 1967.

Spacks, Patricia Meyer. "*45 Mercy Street.*" *New York Times Book Review*, May 30, 1976, pp. 3–4. Reprinted in McClatchy.

Additional reviews are reprinted in McClatchy, pp. 115–90.

INTERVIEWS

Heyen, William. "From 1928 to Whenever: A Conversation with Anne Sexton." In *American Poets in 1976*, edited by William Heyen. Indianapolis: Bobbs-Merrill, 1976. Pp. 304–28.

Kevles, Barbara. "The Art of Poetry XV: Anne Sexton." *Paris Review*, 52:159–91 (Summer 1971). Reprinted in *Writers at Work: The Paris Review Interviews, Fourth Series*, edited by George Plimpton. New York: Viking Press, 1976. Also in McClatchy.

Madden, Charles. "Anne Sexton." In *Talks with Authors*, edited by Madden. Carbondale: Southern Illinois University Press, 1968. Pp. 151–79.

Marx, Patricia. "Interview with Anne Sexton." *Hudson Review*, 18, no. 4:560–70 (Winter 1965–66). Reprinted in McClatchy.

Showalter, Elaine, and Carol Smith. "A Nurturing Relationship: A Conversation with Anne Sexton and Maxine Kumin, April 15, 1974." *Women's Studies*, 4, 1:115–36 (1976).

—SUSAN RESNECK PARR

Karl Shapiro

1913–

"*I* am an atheist who says his prayers," Karl Shapiro wrote in *The Bourgeois Poet* (1964). "I am an anarchist, and a full professor at that." A versatile poet and a serious, if light-hearted, critic, he is at the same time a bundle of contradictions; and any generalization about his poetry, his criticism, or his life calls for immediate qualification, as one accounts for conflicting evidence.

Shapiro is a lyrical satirist and a pedantic antiformalist, a neomodernist and a "true contemporary." These contradictions are evident in his earliest poems, in his later criticism and fiction, and in his public life as editor and teacher, as enfant terrible and defender of the status quo.

Without these conflicts, Shapiro would not have been the kind of poet who speaks to a large audience, in an age when poetry remains distressingly unread. He is a poet both closely attended to, with several early books still in print, and surprisingly neglected by literary historians and influential critics—a member of a select group of distinguished artists, yet a renegade well outside the centers of power. If he were asked to speak at the White House, he would probably arrive dressed in a Hawaiian shirt, orange trousers, and sneakers; at a rock concert he would be the one in white tie and tails. "If I don't take the wrong side, who will?" he asks in one poem. For most people, such contrary be-

havior would be viewed, justifiably, as posing; for Shapiro, it is natural. He is the man, like the one in Mark Strand's poem "Keeping Things Whole," who does what no one else is doing; "In a field" he is "the absence / of field."

These conflicts are the source of Shapiro's power and originality, as well as the cause of his periodic estrangement from the artistic and political establishment. They may be understood with reference to the ages in which he has lived, his background, and his places of residence. They are also the result of a series of choices he has made that keep him at the edge of things. Attending to these facts of biography does not explain his particular genius as poet and critic, but it does call attention to his way of being in the world, as man and writer. More important, it helps one appreciate his achievement and his dedication to certain principles concerning the relationship of poet and audience, of the writer and his craft, and of the responsibilities of the artist and the needs of American society.

Shapiro has written directly and indirectly about his own life on numerous occasions and twice at some length: in the poem "Recapitulations" (1946), which gives biographical details up through World War II, and in the essay "American Poet?" (1964), which discusses why and how he became a writer.

Born in Baltimore, Maryland, on November

10, 1913, "under the [hospital] roof where Poe expired," Karl Jay Shapiro is the grandson of Russian-Jewish immigrants who settled in America in the 1880's, and the younger son of Joseph and Sarah (Omansky) Shapiro, who were both natives of Baltimore. His father, a traveling salesman who kept a book of Oscar Wilde's poetry on a living room table, taught him "to be superior, as befits / A nation of individual priests." He attended private and public schools in Norfolk, Virginia; Chicago; and Baltimore; and the University of Virginia (1932–1933) and Johns Hopkins University (1937–1939), but never took a degree.

Shapiro began writing in high school, somewhat in imitation of his older brother, who had already won a literary reputation locally. Afterward he had what he called "a long and lonely apprenticeship during the Depression," although the record of those years suggests differently. At the age of twenty-one, with the help of his uncle and a medical publishing company, he published a book of poems, "imitations of William Carlos Williams and William Shakespeare." In "Recapitulations" he describes the circumstances surrounding that event:

My first small book was nourished in the
  dark,
Secretly written, published, and inscribed.
Bound in wine-red, it made no brilliant mark.
Rather impossible relatives subscribed.

The best review was one I wrote myself
Under the name of a then-dearest friend.

In the mid-1930's, working for an oil company, "listening to the Communists," and studying at Johns Hopkins and the Pratt Library School in Baltimore, he discovered the works of Stephen Spender and, later, W. H. Auden, who helped him find the direction he needed as a poet. Shapiro was drafted into the army prior to the bombing of Pearl Harbor; soon afterward he received two literary prizes

from *Poetry* magazine. While with the Fifth Medical Training Battalion at Fort Lee, Virginia, and shortly before being shipped to the South Pacific, he published his first substantial group of poems in *Five Young American Poets* (1941). His first major collection, *Person, Place and Thing,* appeared in November 1942, as he was on his way to war. A collection of very different writings, prose poems and Whitmanesque verse, *The Place of Love,* was published in Australia the same year. In writing the latter book, Shapiro found himself "with Lenin in one hand and the Old Testament in the other, although with little sense of desperation or loss of joy in the adventure." Later, he suspected that these poems were written with "hidden panic" and from the perspective that this might be "the last personal moment."

In *V-Letter and Other Poems* (1944), Shapiro proved that he was better prepared than most writers of his generation to make poetry out of the experience of World War II. The book brought him a Pulitzer Prize, a grant from the National Institute of Arts and Letters, and "some very heady praise from the critics." Earlier, in a sharply worded review of two World War I poets, Edmund Blunden and Siegfried Sassoon, Shapiro had said that they gave very tame promise of being useful to later poets; and in the introduction to *V-Letter and Other Poems,* he declared his independence of them: "Since the war began," he wrote, "I have tried to guard against becoming a 'war poet'"—that is, a writer totally defined by that subject, and the volume indicated that he had successfully escaped that fate.

After returning from the South Pacific in 1945, Shapiro spent the last months of his army duty with the Office of Strategic Services, in Washington, D. C. The publication of *Essay on Rime* (1945), written while he was still on duty in New Guinea, helped to confirm his reputation as a knowledgeable prosodist, as well as a poet. A 2,070-line poem in iambic pentameter, it discusses three "confusions"—in prosody, language, and belief—that allegedly characterized much contemporary verse. Francis Matthiessen, among others, praised the book rather extravagantly. That same year, Shapiro married Evalyn Katz, who had acted as his editor and agent during his years overseas. They had three children—*Poems 1940–1953* (1953) is dedicated to them—and were divorced in 1967. His second marriage was to Teri Kovach in 1969.

After a year as a fellow of the Library of Congress and another as consultant in poetry, Shapiro began his career as a teacher at Johns Hopkins University (1947–1950) and the University of Nebraska (1956–1966), and in 1968 moved to the University of California at Davis—with shorter terms as visiting professor at other universities in the United States, Austria, India, and Japan. He also served as editor of *Poetry* (1950–1956), the *Newberry Library Bulletin* (1953–1955), and *Prairie Schooner* (1956–1966).

Although a nonconformist and an "anti-critic," Shapiro has been honored principally by traditionalists. He was twice a fellow of the Kenyon School of Letters (1956, 1957), was elected to the American Academy of Arts and Sciences and the National Institute of Arts and Letters (1959), and was awarded the Bollingen Prize for Poetry (1969). Since the publication of *In Defense of Ignorance* (1960), an attack on the influence of T. S. Eliot, Ezra Pound, and the New Criticism, he has been widely read and even influential as a critic. Regarded as eclectic and unpredictable, even idiosyncratic, he is always intelligent and readable, and expresses opinions boldly and often with wit. A discussion of American culture in *To Abolish Children and Other Essays* begins with a characteristic flourish: "This is going to sound far-fetched, but here goes."

Early on, Shapiro established a reputation as a poet fond of regular, if sometimes untraditional, verse forms—"telling poems in iambic pentameter," he once wrote disparagingly of them, "with a masculine inversion in the second foot." But, like his contemporaries Robert Lowell and Stanley Kunitz, he altered his approach in the early 1960's. The result was *The Bourgeois Poet,* the collection of prose poems that appeared in 1964. Four years later, in *White-Haired Lover,* he turned sharply to the sonnet and variations on similar verse patterns. Subsequent books include, most notably, *Selected Poems* (1968); the novel *Edsel* (1971); selected essays in *The Poetry Wreck* (1975); and *Collected Poems: 1940–1978* (1978); as well as a film, *Karl Shapiro's America* (1976).

Although he has written significant works in prose and possesses a particular genius as polemicist and pamphleteer, Shapiro is first and foremost a poet, and any discussion of his writing must focus on this aspect of his life. Shapiro's criticism and, in a lesser sense, his novel, contribute, nonetheless, to our understanding and appreciation of him as an artist. In them he works out a poetics for "the bourgeois poet" and "the American poet," as he understands these terms.

Shapiro's career is usually discussed in relation to writings before and after 1958. But if one looks closely at the interrelationships between the poetry and the criticism, and the way in which that interplay has affected his various styles, his career falls more precisely and naturally into four clearly defined periods. For reasons explored later, one can usefully approach his writings with reference to particular emphases, changes, and developments during (1) the period of apprenticeship, from the beginnings to 1944, the year of publication of *V-Letter and Other Poems;* (2) the period of the "anti-critic," 1944–1958, including *Essay on Rime, Beyond Criticism,* and *Poems of a Jew;*

(3) the period of "the true contemporary," 1958–1968, including *In Defense of Ignorance, The Bourgeois Poet,* and *Selected Poems;* and (4) the period of "the American poet," beginning in 1968, including *Edsel,* the later essays in *The Poetry Wreck,* and the new work in *Collected Poems: 1940–1978.*

The changes in style and in preoccupations that these designations suggest are usually matters of emphasis rather than of radical transformation, calling attention to the forces that struggle for dominance in Shapiro's work at various times. If the conflicts had ever been totally resolved, one might expect him to turn to other work. As things stand, they create a tension between what he once called "the lyrical ego" and the critical conscience, making his poetry vigorous in feeling and intelligence.

To the first period, the long apprenticeship, belong the privately printed *Poems* (1935); his initial appearance in magazines, especially *Partisan Review* and *Poetry,* as well as *Five Young American Poets;* the books edited by Evalyn Katz during his years in the South Pacific; and the important prizes and serious critical attention that established Shapiro as a national literary figure while he was still in his early thirties.

In form, the early poems are usually metrically regular with a fixed, though untraditional, stanza form, employing enjambment and regular rhyme. The language is tough, flat, and prosaic, like the hard outlines of an Edward Hopper painting; but the overall effect can be celebratory or ceremonial. Although attentive to the integrity of the person, place, or convention they describe, these poems border on or occasionally plunge headlong into satire.

Poems (1935) is written in a conventional poetic language, with obvious echoes of Shapiro's early enthusiasms, especially Shakespeare and William Carlos Williams. Shapiro's own judgment that his imitations of Williams were better than those of Shakespeare is confirmed in a short poem reminiscent of Williams in form and imagery: "First / I look / (O wondrous / apple with / the window in your cheek) / then bite—." It also acknowledges the fact that his ear for American speech was, even then, superior to his ear for English cadence.

Although less overtly political than several of his contemporaries, especially Muriel Rukeyser, Shapiro in his first verses does write about the turmoil and struggle during the Great Depression. The long poem "Irenicon," which explores the poet's relation to society, includes a "Marxian invocation." And "Shenandoah," beginning "This poem is for eleven / on the hill / who came to my door / in the dark," ends with the line, "This poem is not for Poe," suggesting a natural dichotomy between "pure" poetry and poetry with a message. This division of interests and conflict of impulses is observable in Shapiro's poetry and criticism from then on.

A more characteristic early poem, "University," indicates a sophisticated sense of cultural and political history and a preference, formally, for the modernist tradition of Eliot and Auden, rather than the contemporary style of Williams. Based on Shapiro's experience at the University of Virginia, this satiric lyric begins with these justly famous lines, "To hurt the Negro and avoid the Jew / Is the curriculum," and then enumerates the prejudices, pretensions, and stupidities of an institution gone wrong. The first three of the five stanzas describe the injustices sanctioned by students, faculty, and administration:

The Deans, dry spinsters over family plate, . . .
  Humor the snob and lure the lout.
  Within the precincts of this world
    Poise is a club.

Although he is never named in the poem, Thomas Jefferson hovers nearby, as the prototype of the founder, "the true nobleman, once a democrat, / [who] Sleeps on his private mountain."

"University" conveys a feeling, a sense of injustice, that characterizes many poems of the Great Depression; though one associates its technique with the Augustan satirists of the eighteenth century. Shapiro not only exposes the dunces, in the manner of Alexander Pope; he also chastises them, in the manner of Samuel Johnson and other Juvenalian satirists. Yet, as Allen Tate once said of Pope, Shapiro transforms his rage into art. In "University" one understands and shares his disappointment in seeing an institution perpetuate what it pretends to resist. A central theme is the conflict between the ideal and the real, between what Thomas Jefferson—or any person with a dream of a just society—imagines and what the institution that he founded later becomes. "University" is the angriest of the angry poems in Shapiro's first commercially published collection, *Person, Place and Thing*. It is also one of his best poems, building successfully on a young man's disappointment, even disgust, at seeing an ideal corrupted and an evil, slavery, perpetuated.

The need to expose and purge is at the heart of several poems from Shapiro's first period; it was, in fact, one of the strongest and most remarkable qualities of his early achievement. This discontent informs much of the literature of the 1930's—the early poems of Spender and Auden, the novels of James T. Farrell, John Steinbeck, and Nathanael West—and, in Shapiro, that anger is particularized, delineated, and clearly focused on various aspects of American life. Usually he tempers his fury with appreciation or sympathy, recognizing that hate and love are not necessarily mutually exclusive but move, like wind and water, in several directions at once.

These conflicting emotions are successfully rendered in "The Fly," which begins on a note of exasperation: "O hideous little bat, the size of snot." But by the end of the sixth stanza, which includes precise descriptions of the insect's seedier habitations and habits, the speaker regains his composure and proper aesthetic distance. Finally victorious in his battle against the fly, he feels some pity for the poor creature, that falls

And stunned, stone blind, and deaf
   Buzzes its frightful F
And dies between three cannibals.

The satire that is so strong in *Person, Place and Thing* is muted at times by the arrangement of the poems, as well as in individual works like "The Fly," in which a slight twist or shift in mood softens the negative tone. Read together, "University," "The Fly," "The Snob" ("Nothing but death will smash this ugly cast"), and "The Glutton" ("The jowls of his belly crawl and swell like the sea") give the impression that "the tooth of satire," as Pound called it, dominates Shapiro's first book. Yet these poems represent less than half of the total collection. As in his later critical essays, Shapiro, the true polemicist, infuriates and charms at the same time.

The other group of poems that, like the satires, constitute a significant part of *Person, Place and Thing* are the "still photographs" of American life, scenes that Norman Rockwell sentimentalized, but that Shapiro views with an occasionally jaundiced but always attentive eye: "Drug Store," "Buick," "Emporium," "Honkytonk," "Midnight Show," and "Conscription Camp." The titles alone suggest a kind of encyclopedia of slang for this period in American history; and Shapiro, with what Delmore Schwartz called a "limitless capacity for detail," captured the times.

Some of these poems risk being circumscribed by the period in which they were written, during the later years of the Great Depression and the early 1940's. Yet, like the plays of Anton Chekhov, their timeliness is also their strength, capturing a style or a mood confined to a physical place, just as it is on the verge of extinction. They seem peculiarly American and quite untranslatable; like the "Drug Store," they baffle "the foreigner like an idiom." But these ordinary subjects are presented with energy and humor, a mixture of positive and negative feeling that characterizes Shapiro's style throughout much of his career.

The reason for Shapiro's ambivalence toward his world is perhaps best suggested by the most philosophical of the early poems, "Auto Wreck," more frequently anthologized, perhaps, than any other American poem of the period. It is a powerful, naturalistic portrait of what Ernest Hemingway called the commonest occurrence in modern life: violent death.

The poem focuses not on the victims of an automobile crash but on the emotional reactions of the witnesses. It describes the incident, from the ambulance's arrival, as it "Wings in a heavy curve, dips down, / And brakes speed, entering the crowd," until its departure, "with its terrible cargo / . . . As the doors, an afterthought, are closed."

Through the four stanzas of the poem, observers reflect upon the wreck, in a language and mood resembling those of a Greek chorus, trying to place the event in context and to understand its implications in relation to their own lives. They proceed, like the citizens of Thebes, by question and answer, through strophe and antistrophe:

We are deranged, . . .
The traffic moves around with care,
But we remain, touching a wound
That opens to our richest horror.
Already old, the question Who shall die?
Becomes unspoken Who is innocent?

Their response to the casual cruelty of the accident is fatalistic and primitive in its implications:

For death in war is done by hands;
Suicide has cause and stillbirth, logic;

An auto wreck, though, makes no sense and invites, rather, "the occult mind, / Cancels our physics with a sneer, / And spatters all we know of denouement"—that is, of meaningful resolution—"Across the expedient and wicked stones."

The answers to the questions provide not only a fitting resolution to the observers' dilemma, in the face of a senseless death, but also an insight into Shapiro's own way of looking at the world during this period of his life as a poet. It is a philosophy that sustained him through a long apprenticeship and the early years of World War II.

Such naturalism was as appropriate for wartime, in other words, as it was for the Great Depression, and it gives a point of view and depth to the poems Shapiro wrote while in the medical corps in Australia and New Guinea. "We . . . fought the Second World War before it happened and then again when it did happen," Shapiro said, regarding the poets of his generation. Being shipped to the South Pacific, just after the appearance of his first poems, left him "almost insane with fury." But it was to be a time and place of great productivity, bringing his apprenticeship to an end and giving a new direction to his career as a writer.

In addition to the poems that appeared in *The Place of Love,* erotic lyrics, personal prose poems, and excerpts from letters in the contemporary style of Williams rather than in the neomodernist style of Auden, he wrote most of the poems that appear in *V-Letter and Other Poems* and a long verse essay on poetry. In a cautionary note to the war poems he said: "I have not written these poems in accord with any doctrine or system of thought or even a theory of composition. I have nothing to offer in the way of beliefs or challenges or prosody. I try to write freely, one day as a Christian, the next as a Jew, the next as a soldier who sees the gigantic slapstick of modern war. I hope I do not impersonate other poets." He didn't.

Although the principal subject of *V-Letter and Other Poems* (the title refers to the serviceman's small photostat of a letter) is clearly the war, *V-Letter* contains a number of poems that might easily have appeared in *Person, Place and Thing.* "Fireworks," "Movie," "Christmas Tree," "Public Library," and "The Communist" discuss topics and express attitudes and sentiments that belong to Shapiro's Americana of the 1930's, giving the book a markedly different tone from that of previous poetry collections dealing with battlefield experience.

Since accounts of total war in 1918 had been a part of literature for over twenty years, in the novels of Hemingway and John Dos Passos as well as in the poetry of Wilfred Owen and Sassoon, it would not have been appropriate for a soldier in 1943 to have been "surprised" by the horror; and Shapiro surveyed the destruction not unfeelingly but with a casualness implying that he had traveled this way before. "Troop Train," for example, speaks of men moving

. . . on through continents and days,
Deliberate, grimy, slightly drunk we
    crawl,
The good-bad boys of conscience and
    chance, . . .
Trains lead to ships and ships to death or
    trains,
And trains to death or trucks, and trucks
    to death,
Or trucks lead to the march, the march
    to death, . . .

The horror of war, or what Owen in 1918 had called "the pity of war," has become "the monotony of war." As in similar poems by his contemporaries Richard Eberhart, Randall Jarrell, and Rukeyser, Shapiro speaks not melodramatically but matter of factly about the event. His heroes, like the men in Joseph Heller's *Catch 22* (1961), are often antiheroes. Such soldiers do not expect to be praised for their courage under fire but, like Jarrell's ball turret gunner, to be "washed out of the turret with a hose."

In this last book of Shapiro's learning period, the one that brought him a large audience and a Pulitzer Prize, the soldier-narrator also speaks about the irony that arises because of the contrast between the romantic setting and the ominous fate of men at war. "These nights we fear the aspects of the moon," the beautiful lyric "Full Moon: New Guinea" begins; the soldiers

Sleep lightly in the radiance falling clear
On palms and ferns and hills and us; for soon
The small burr of the bombers in our ear
Tickles our rest; . . . These nights
We fear Orion and the Cross. . . .

And in "V-Letter," a young man writes from the battlefield about what his lover teaches, by her absence, about survival:

    I love you first because your years
Lead to my matter-of-fact and simple death
        Or to our open marriage,
And I pray nothing for my safety back,
Not even luck, because our love is whole
        Whether I live or fail.

In these poems, the war seems almost distant, an event described with awkward acceptance and complacency. It was only later, in poems written during his last days in the South Pacific or after returning home, that Shapiro began to explore the deeper psychological effects of his experience, to combine precise outward description with inwardness. By 1944 his work was beginning to take a slightly different direction, still intelligent, emotional, and humorous but with a deeper personal investment in the consequences of his satiric comments. For the next fourteen years he wrote not as an apprentice but as a critical iconoclast.

This second period, 1944–1958, that of the "anti-critic," marks the beginning of Shapiro's influence as a commentator on the work of other writers and his growing sophistication and ambition as a poet. In *Essay on Rime* (1945), one hears the voice of a man very aware of his audience and somewhat self-conscious about his responsibilities as a man of letters. He speaks with an assurance and subtlety that are only fleetingly apparent in the early works. To this period belong his early writings on prosody, as well as several long poems in a style similar to that of the first period, but polished, even perfected. In the long poems "Recapitulations" and "Adam and Eve," he is able to sustain a narrative and a mood through several pages of discourse. In the criticism, he thinks through his preoccupations as a writer, being explicit about his similarities to and differences from his predecessors. A writer's sensibility and ultimately his life are forged upon the dichotomy between "what is without and what is within, the models he is given and his reaction to them," Shapiro wrote in "A *Malebolge* of Fourteen Hundred Books" (1964). And during this period he began to shape his own aesthetic, to write criticism "in the first person singular."

The contrast between the first two periods of Shapiro's career are evident in the works written before his return from the South Pacific. On the basis of his success, even before receiving the Pulitzer Prize, he apparently became confident of his ability to "take on" poets past and present, including those from whom he had learned his craft: William Blake, John Keats, Edgar Allan Poe, Charles Baudelaire, Walt Whitman, T. S. Eliot, Rainer Maria Rilke, William Carlos Williams, D. H. Lawrence, Stephen Spender, and W. H. Auden. In doing so, he resembles the poets of an earlier generation who performed a similar task after World War I. Much as he would dislike the comparison, Shapiro in *Essay on Rime* sounds much like Eliot, who in *The Sacred Wood* rearranged the monuments of Western literature, enthroning those who most resembled him (John Donne and George Herbert) and devaluing those who did not (John Milton and Percy Bysshe Shelley).

The conditions under which *Essay on Rime* was written, from Shapiro's own account, are pertinent. He was living in New Guinea as a soldier, resting for ninety days before moving further inland with his medical unit. As a company clerk with a typewriter, he decided to write the poem, blocked out the sections with titles, and "even figured out how many lines a day I'd be able to write." William Van O'Connor, a fellow soldier and later a colleague at the University of California at Davis, loaned Shapiro a copy of William Butler Yeats's *Oxford Book of Modern Verse*. That and his own copy of Baudelaire "was about the extent of my library at that time."

Although something of an anomaly, comparable to James Russell Lowell's *A Fable for Critics* (1848) or Amy Lowell's *A Critical Fable* (1922)—both poetic evaluations of their contemporaries—*Essay on Rime* is of particular interest, directly related to Shapiro's growth and change as a poet and indicative of the direction of American poetry ten years after the appearance of his first book. The words "essay" and "rime" in the title are used in their original senses: "essay" meaning "an attempt at understanding" and "rime" understood as "the art of poetry," rather than just as "a strict science of metrics and versification."

This long poem in blank verse, composed in

three sections on confusions in prosody, language, and belief, is a knowledgeable if highly personal view of modern poetry and the direct statement of what a young poet had absorbed, as Matthiessen said, "from thirty years of living and ten of learning his craft." Its principal argument, to which Shapiro often returned over the next twenty-five years, is "that criticism / Has charted poetry into dangerous narrows / And dashed its own brains out upon the rocks / Of absolute meaning." Each of the three sections substantiates this charge by enumerating the confusions, with particular references to poets and critics.

In naming and describing the confusions that weaken neomodernist poetry, in a concluding section on "The Dead Hand and Exhaustion of Our Rime," Shapiro is obviously thinking seriously about his own future as a poet, as well as the future of American poetry. The conditions under which he wrote, as a participant in World War II, give him little cause for hope:

The rime produced by soldiers of our war
Is the most sterile of our century.

In this poem, as in his later criticism, Shapiro is clearly trying to plot a course between the formalists, represented by Yeats, Eliot, and Tate, and the so-called antiformalists, represented by Williams, Lawrence, and Hart Crane. It is a defense of poetry expressed in language similar to William Wordsworth's in the preface to the *Lyrical Ballads* (1798) and to other statements acknowledging the common speech as the source of poetic language in a new age:

The measure of prosody is the current speech,
The cadences inherent in the voice
Of one particular generation. Each
Has its own standard, and no choice exists
Between the past and present. . . .

As a prosodist, Shapiro is haunted by the specter of the past, which he associates primarily with English formalists and the early modernists. Like most original poets responsive to their own time and attentive to a contemporary audience, he wants to find a tradition other than the one immediately available to him, without the proscriptions that prevent him from speaking about the pressures of the moment. Much of *Essay on Rime* concerns itself, therefore, with elementary questions about nature, love, beauty, and "the plain statement of feeling":

At what point in the history of art
Has such a cleavage between audience
And poet existed? When before has rime
Relied so heavily on the interpreter,
The analyst and the critic? . . .

Never, Shapiro answers, and then ends the poem, having given only a few hints of a positive alternative to the dead-end situation he decries.

The way out is there, nonetheless, to be plotted; and after returning to the United States, Shapiro begins to do so, not in poetry so much as in criticism. Of the four people mentioned in *Essay on Rime* as possible guides for the future—James Joyce, Lawrence, Williams, and Auden—the middle two become increasingly important over the next twenty years. In the early poems, as mentioned above, and in *The Place of Love*, with thirteen of its thirty-one poems in prose, he had followed Lawrence's and Williams' lead in writing about personal feelings more intimately and less formally than in any of his books published commercially before 1964. In the preface to *The Place of Love*, Shapiro complains about being "brought up to shun the lyrical ego, to look at ourselves from without, to make a science of our acts." Thinking obviously of the modernist criticism of "personality" in poetry, he laments that "the poet in particular has reacted to a revolution in knowledge by developing the most advanced self-consciousness possible, an intolerance for his own personality that is just short of madness." Shapiro here anticipates by more than a decade a complaint repeated by the poets of open form and the beat generation.

Pressures to conform to the early modernist attitude kept Shapiro at war with himself for a long time, venting his anger as an "anti-critic" but adhering for the most part to the standard and writing style inherited from Eliot and Auden. For twenty years he worked to justify intellectually the kind of poetry that he had yet to master, while writing the kind of poetry for which he was known and admired. Returning to the United States, he enjoyed the personal success that *Person, Place and Thing* and *V-Letter and Other Poems* had won for him: national awards, fellowships, lectureships in this country and abroad; and in 1950 he was appointed editor of *Poetry* magazine, "as formidable a literary institution as any in the country," he said later. In lectures, eventually published in periodicals, small editions, and later in several collections, he continued to explore the issues raised in *Essay on Rime,* railing against the oppressive effect of an age of criticism on poetry and politics.

Although *Essay on Rime* occupies a relatively minor place in the canon of Shapiro's poetry and does not appear in *Collected Poems, 1940–1978,* it is significant in the development of his aesthetic. From that seed would flower his later poems and essays, suggesting new life and color, in the midst of the wasteland of American poetry catering to the New Criticism. The subject of prosody also continued to occupy his attention in several academic treatises: *English Prosody and Modern Poetry* (1947), a transcript of a lecture at Johns Hopkins University; *A Bibliography of Modern Prosody* (1948), compiled during his tenure as consultant in poetry at the Library of Congress; and, much later, *A Prosody Handbook* (1965), written

with Robert Beum. "Prosody," one of the wittiest poems in *The Bourgeois Poet,* describes his fascination with this subject: "I make a muse of prosody, old hag. She's just a registered nurse, I know, I know, but I have her sashay, grind and bump, register Alcaics, Sapphics, choriambs. . . ." At that task, he adds, "I burn with an even flame, I'm cooking with gas."

In the poetry of the second period, there were discernible changes in tone, if not in form and content. Subtleties of feeling and perception informed the poems about war in particular; and *The Trial of a Poet,* published two years after he received the Pulitzer Prize, includes three poems that are among the most powerful of his career. The prose poem "The Dirty Word," which had appeared in the volume published in Australia, resembles in style the lyrics of the third period. (St.-John Perse's admiration for this poem contributed to Shapiro's further experimentations in prose.) "Recapitulations" and "The Conscientious Objector," although similar in form to the poems of the first period, are markedly different in their judgment of the war.

In "Recapitulations," Shapiro's longest poem in regular stanzaic patterns up to that time, the war "was the death he never quite forgot / Through the four years of death, and like as not / The true death of the best of all of us / Whose present life is largely posthumous." Although still somewhat detached in tone, like the earlier poetry, it is more inward and autobiographical than he risked before; one section, originally entitled "A Song of Conscience," explains his inactivity during the Spanish Civil War and his unresponsiveness during the Soviet invasion of Finland and the bombing of Britain.

Unlike Pound's *Hugh Selwyn Mauberley,* written just after World War I and with which Shapiro's post-World War II poem is often compared, "Recapitulations" uses no persona to voice the poet's frustrations and dissatisfactions with contemporary life. Originally a series of sixteen short poems, usually in quatrains, "Recapitulations" is significantly altered in later printings. In the poem, the speaker describes the ethnic, religious, and artistic influences that shaped him, underscoring the conflicts and contradictions that are evident in Shapiro's own life: his Jewish heritage and his Catholic inclinations, his bourgeois background and his radical sympathies, his individual choices and his communal feelings, his active militarism and his pacifist leanings, his public good behavior and his private confessions.

One of the best poems of its kind, it records experiences common to those born just before World War I, who grew up and came of age in the shadow of another war. If, as Virginia Woolf said, the world spun on its axis about 1910, it had made several more revolutions by 1945, and Shapiro's poem accurately renders the confusion of those times. But it ends somewhat inconclusively—suggesting Shapiro's own uncertainty about the present, as well as about his future, as man and poet.

As a statement about the causes of his confusion, "The Conscientious Objector" is a clearer poem than "Recapitulations," describing the psychological conflict that many men felt once World War II had ended. The resemblances between Shapiro's poem and the anti-war poems of Sassoon and Owen, especially the latter's "Mental Cases," are obvious; the differences, like those between the two world wars, are related to the reflections of someone confronting total war as an innocent and those of someone confronting it as a veteran. The hatred of war reflected in Shapiro's poems is mixed with a profound sympathy for brave men fighting senseless battles. And the conflict between his hatred of the warmaking state and his admiration for his comrades goes to the very heart of the poem.

"The Conscientious Objector," a blank verse poem in four eight-line stanzas, follows a war resister (probably a close friend or perhaps Robert Lowell, Shapiro's fellow poet) through his journey into resistance. The prisoner of conscience is compared to a pilgrim on a journey to a new land. His jail cell and prison become a Noah's ark or Mayflower, as he sets out "To establish new theocracies to west":

Like all men hunted from the world you made
A good community, voyaging the storm
To no safe Plymouth or green Ararat;

One of the main sources of the poem's power is the speaker's awareness of the conscientious objector's unpopularity—the public indecency of being a noncombatant—and his understanding about what it cost pacifists to maintain their moral position. As a combatant, Shapiro recognizes the integrity of those who, because of conscience, did not fight:

Well might the soldier kissing the hot beach
Erupting in his face damn all your kind.
Yet you who saved neither yourselves nor us
Are equally with those who shed the blood
The heroes of our cause. Your conscience is
What we come back to in the armistice.

In later years Shapiro the "anti-critic" fleshed out in prose the opinions expressed in *Essay on Rime,* suggesting, like the poems, a growth in sophistication and ambition. *Beyond Criticism* (1953), based on the Montgomery lectures at the University of Nebraska, was once summarized by the author in one sentence—"Stop lecturing, for God's sake." They speak to the modernist academic critics and their disciples, those who dominated the literary scene during the cold war, as well as to himself. They are negative statements about what not to do in poetry; the positive statements describing possible alternatives belong to a later period. In poetry, the concluding years of the "anti-critic" include the publication of *Poems 1940–1953,* which adds his longest work to date, "Adam and Eve," and another selection, *Poems of a Jew* (1958).

Shapiro has always been a careful, even severe, critic of his own work, continually editing out poems, in successive editions, that fail to meet his own high standard of performance, and *Poems 1940–1953* is interesting as the first large selection of previously published poems that withstood that test. Among the eighteen poems not previously published in book form, there is "Adam and Eve," a spectacular demonstration of Shapiro's versatility as a poet and an appropriate finale, in some ways, to one of the formalist phases of his career.

Using several stanza forms, regular rhyme, and a range of traditional metrical patterns and rhythms—quatrain, sonnet, couplet, versions of the seven liner—Shapiro gives in "Adam and Eve" his version of the Genesis story. With imagery drawn from the Zohar and from Wilhelm Reich, he concentrates on the early days of Adam and Eve's creation, their lovemaking, sin, and exile. God, he says, "determined" Adam to leave Eden; the poem's view that "man is for the world, not for the afterworld, is Jewish," according to Shapiro. Although the narrative is too casually developed to carry the weight of the poem, he does maintain the story line, and individual passages, especially the banishment of Adam and Eve from Paradise, are among the most beautiful in Shapiro's early work:

They turned in dark amazement and beheld
Eden ablaze with fires of red and gold.
The garden dressed for dying in cold flame,

And it was autumn, and the present world.

Although Shapiro usually describes himself as having no religion and no politics, he has been persistently preoccupied with his origins, including his southern and mid-Atlantic inheritance and early background. *Poems of a Jew*

gathered together poems exploring one aspect of his past, a consciousness "that never really goes away," Shapiro later said on the subject, especially if Jews are in trouble. In poems extracted from the previous volumes that had nothing to do with this "obsession," the book talks about being a Jew among Christians and in several poems, including "The Crucifix in the Filing Cabinet," about one Jew's "private flirtation with Catholicism."

This clear identification of his origins, in poems about people and incidents from history, mythology, and his own life, gives *Poems of a Jew* an obvious unity and structural clarity. It expands upon and deepens a theme central to modernist art, symbolized for Shapiro by Joyce's portrait of Leopold Bloom in *Ulysses,* and builds upon the modernist theme of the impersonality of history, so central to literature since World War I. Implicit in individual poems and throughout the book is the threat posed by political purges, by total war, and even by nuclear holocaust, with the question of survival and the threat of annihilation always at the edge of consciousness.

When Ezra Pound was nominated in 1949 for the Bollingen Prize for Poetry, Shapiro voted against him, saying, "I am a Jew and cannot honor anti-semites," and publicly defended his position in the literary furor that surrounded the event. In *Poems of a Jew* he again indicated the depth of his loyalty to that ethnic history. Although the book adds little to Shapiro's canon, it is significant biographically and attitudinally, allowing him to move toward a new understanding of himself as a writer, as "the true contemporary," and toward responsibilities other than those imposed by the past. Publishing *Poems of a Jew,* Shapiro wrote later, "decolonized" him, making him "as rootless as a Texas millionaire with Negro and Indian blood in his veins."

As a public manifestation of his inheritance

and of his "decolonization," the publication of *Poems of a Jew* coincides with the end of the second period of Shapiro's career. By then he had begun to surrender his old identity as a neo-modernist in style, with loyalties to Baudelaire, Yeats, Eliot, and Auden, and to ally himself, as "the true contemporary," with Whitman, Lawrence, and Williams. As a break with the past, this change resembles previous changes in sensibility in literary history, including the one by English poets in the late eighteenth century from neoclassicism to romanticism and the one by English and American poets in the early twentieth century from late Victorianism to early modernism. For Shapiro, it was a natural expansion of ideas and practices observable in his experiments in criticism in *Essay on Rime* and, in poetry, in *The Place of Love.*

During the third period, 1958–1968, Shapiro becomes less concerned with keeping up appearances than with plummeting depths. He turns away from a preoccupation with "good form" toward a peculiarly American preoccupation with discovery. In *In Defense of Ignorance* he rephrases Ralph Waldo Emerson's literary declaration of independence from Europe, in criticism; and in *The Bourgeois Poet* he repeats Whitman's celebration of the democratic people en masse, in poetry.

Shapiro forgets Poe, one might say, to remember Whitman, turning his back on "the jingle man" and the French symbolists and toward the man chanting his barbaric yawp and his contemporary disciples. He moves away from the dominant poetry of the twentieth century, which prides itself on its adherence to tradition, ritual, metaphysical wit, learned irony, and the need for discipline in art and society, and moves toward a new poetry that took pride in originality, spontaneity, immediacy, and the need for experimentation in art and society. In doing so, he not only risked working in a style, the prose poem, in which he had not excelled pre-

viously but also alienated admirers, especially formalists and academics—Tate and other New Critics—who had encouraged and praised his early work.

Shapiro's substantive change in style and subject matter during this period parallels a general movement in American poetry at this time, symbolized by the publication in 1956 of Allen Ginsberg's *Howl,* by the popularity of the beat poets, and by the sudden emergence of Williams as a major influence on writers a decade or so younger than Shapiro—John Logan, Denise Levertov, and Robert Creeley. It coincides also with the political and social upheaval associated with the civil rights movement and the early years of the movement against the Vietnam war. As a reawakening of social conscience in American society, the decade is superficially more dramatic but essentially less radical than that of the 1930's, whose politics had strongly influenced Shapiro's life and work.

How and why this shift in attitude came about, around 1960, is understandable also in light of several correspondences in Shapiro's own life. It had something to do with the clear and inevitable identification of himself as a true "outsider," as a poet and person who could not belong even if he wanted to. No matter how "establishment" his behavior or how many honors and professorships were heaped upon him, he was that most bizarre of creatures, an American poet. From the example of the beats, he seemed to derive, as well, some confidence in stepping up his own campaign against the critical citadels of the cold war aesthetic. "Each age takes down the masterpieces of its fathers," he wrote in "Romanticism Comes Home" (1957), and "stores them in the cellar where someday they will be exhumed by other judges. In San Francisco they are building the crates." And in an influential book, *In Defense of Ignorance* (1960), he repeated the arguments of his earlier criticism in a diatribe against neomodernists and the poets who made him a poet; more important, he laid down a new canon, with a different tradition, that would sustain him as a poet over the next decade.

In Defense of Ignorance is an apologia in the classic sense for turning one's back on what has been defined by the culture as the "right," the "informed" opinion. For the future of poetry, Shapiro argues, one must forget the great names of early modernism, whose legacy is an artistic wasteland, not unlike that described in Eliot's poem. In successive essays on Pound, Yeats, and Eliot, Shapiro challenges their reputations as major poets and their influence as critics, describing them as antiquarian in their interest, reactionary in their politics, and altogether questionable in their aesthetics. On the basis of his reading of Whitman, Lawrence, Williams, and Henry Miller, and of several more philosophical writers, especially Wilhelm Reich and Martin Buber, Shapiro argues for the primacy of intuition over reason as a guide to wisdom and poetic vision. Through these writers, he forges a new aesthetic that, he believes, will finally dispel the false and unnecessary dualisms imposed by modernist poetry and criticism.

Four years after the appearance of *In Defense of Ignorance,* which described Whitman as America's "most original thinker . . . the poet of the greatest achievement; . . . the most accomplished artist" and Henry Miller as America's "greatest living author," Shapiro published a collection of poems, *The Bourgeois Poet,* based upon this new poetics. In an effort to win his audience back to poetry, he speaks not only in the language of the moment but also in a style proper to the moment, that is, in the prose poem. In doing so, he makes a conscious break with a European tradition dating from the time of the Greeks to the romantics, in order to ally himself with an American tradition that began with Whitman. Turning away from his old master, Baudelaire, who advised the poet

"to shake up the middle class," Shapiro writes, instead, to celebrate it.

The title, *The Bourgeois Poet,* came inadvertently from a casual remark by Theodore Roethke, during an introduction for Shapiro, in Seattle, in the late 1950's. Said in a tone of "admiring contempt," the phrase prompted the "equivalent to a ten year psychological analysis," Shapiro wrote later. *The Bourgeois Poet,* like *In Defense of Ignorance,* is a direct assault on "cultured" behavior and a loud Rotarian hymn to middle-class sensibility and bourgeois taste, in language that is often witty, joyous, erotic, and nonsensical.

The Bourgeois Poet is a collection of lyrical ballads, in prose, by a purposefully unsophisticated artist who arranges his books, one poem says, "with a view to their appearance. Some highbrow titles are prominently displayed." He lives among businessmen, militarists, and tenured professors—all with living rooms "like beauty parlors, like night-club powder rooms, like international airport first-class lounges"; and he loves almost everything about it. His affection for the mundane and the mediocre appears boundless; so does his capacity for all remembered incidents, recorded, like jottings in a journal, as they occur.

It is a book of poems not only about the life of the bourgeoisie and material success but also about the social conditions that made them possible. It glorifies the melting-pot view of American history, the social confusion, and the lowered standard, where even the writing of poetry is made easy. Bourgeois poem #9, for example, entitled in later editions, "Lower the Standard," describes both a method for enthroning the ordinary and the reasons for adopting that system of evaluation:

Lower the standard: that's my motto. Somebody is always putting the food out of reach. We're tired of falling off ladders. Who says a child can't paint? A pro is somebody who does

KARL SHAPIRO / 715

it for money. Lower the standards. Let's all play poetry.

The key to Shapiro's "new" attitude, promoting a kind of social and cultural anarchism with its corresponding joie de vivre, is indicated in the closing lines of the poem:

The law of gravity is the law of art. You first, poetry second, the good, the beautiful, the true come last. As the lad said: We must love one another or die.

The sentiment of the last line is Auden's, taken from his "September 1, 1940," but that is the book's only resemblance to the work of Shapiro's former mentor. Its principal direction is toward a transvaluation of values, seizing the "old" values and standing them on their heads. In "Lower the Standard," as in many of the poems, the enemies of good behavior are "morals," "beliefs," "style," and "culture." It is a poetic statement in support of an underground culture, anticipating Theodore Roszak's popular *The Making of a Counter Culture* (1969) and its various imitators in prose and poetry.

Shapiro writes in *The Bourgeois Poet* in sympathy with the theme of Ginsberg's *Howl* (1956), Norman O. Brown's *Life Against Death: The Psychoanalytical Meaning of History* (1959), and Paul Goodman's *Growing Up Absurd: Problems of Youth in the Organized System* (1960), the other scriptures of the generation that came of age in the 1960's. In a society in which organization is symbolized by the bomb and by the impersonal, bureaucratized, repressive state, the absence of law is preferable. "Better mendacities, than classics in paraphrase," Pound wrote in 1919, in overthrowing the aesthetics of the late nineteenth century. "Burn the *Syntopicon* and *The Harvard Classics*," Shapiro writes in a similar vein forty-five years later: "Keelhaul the poets in the vestry chairs. . . . Get off the Culture Wagon."

In turning his back on the aestheticism and the religiosity of modernism, Shapiro associates himself quite rightly with Whitman, who praises what is, rather than with one who laments what was or might have been. *The Bourgeois Poet* celebrates himself and sings himself, but in a manner somewhat different in voice and tone from Whitman's. "Of love and death in the Garrison State I sing," the speaker says in one poem, dreading not the overthrow of nations, but the loss of a head of hair. "One by one my troops desert," he says in "Hair"; "in the bath the other day," he laments, "a pubic hair turned silver gray!" The man speaking is many-voiced but usually middle-aged, relatively comfortable with himself, attentive to a diverse world, reminiscing about his survival through adventures and misadventures, fascinated by but skeptical of belief. "When I say the Hail Mary I get an erection," he confesses to a priest. "Doesn't that prove the existence of God?"

This last line is from "The Missal," which begins "Priests and Freudians will understand." Like several other poems in the book, it returns to a subject discussed in Shapiro's early war poems and religious poems, especially those about his fascination with Catholicism. It is a poem that recognizes the common ground of human and divine love, the complex of feelings that characterize the mystical writings of St. John of the Cross and the erotic lyrics of John Wilmot, the earl of Rochester, as well as the physical passion and longing for union in the Holy Sonnets of John Donne. Both priests and Freudians, with their conflicting views on the soul, know why a soldier "In the throttling Papuan heat, . . . Deprived of love and letters and the sight of woman," needs help and possible forgiveness:

I set up mental prayer wheels and spin them with the whips of fear. Help me, Freudians and priests: when I say the proud Hail Mary, the serpent takes me in the groin.

In this poem, as in several others, a persistent theme is the thinness of the veil separating civilization and barbarism. The speaker or persona seems quite uncertain about which is which. He is thrown back and forth between civilization and barbarism, finding the latter often preferable. He moves as an aborigine in a polite society, surrounded by the furniture of Western culture ("classics, battleships, Russian ballet, national anthems"), and dismisses most of it as useless.

Shapiro's predecessors after World War I regarded their inheritance as "an old bitch gone in the teeth, a botched civilization," on the basis of the devastation brought about by war. But in their criticism and, by implication, in their poetry Yeats, Pound, and Eliot recommended an alternative structure; nothing could happen, in fact, without it. Shapiro, a survivor of World War II, speaks from experience more shattering than theirs, and is more skeptical than they of all structures. "Order became the enemy, the concentration camp, the totalitarian state," Karl Malkoff says of Shapiro. "The nothingness persisted, but now almost as an ally rather than an antagonist; meaninglessness had to serve as the source of meaning." Even Shapiro's identity as a Jew, which sustained him or at least defined his human boundaries in the earlier books, is insufficient to the post-World War II experience. His ironic view, expressed in previous poems from a single angle of vision, now shifts from poem to poem and even, as Malkoff says, from line to line.

The affirmative tone, though, is persistent, and the unity of *The Bourgeois Poet* is maintained by this factor, if by no other. The feeling is predominantly one of joy. Read as one long poem, *The Bourgeois Poet* bears obvious resemblances to *Howl* but omits, one might say, the first two sections of the Ginsberg poem, that is, the accusatory sections about the destruction of a generation by madness and the sins of the sex-

less hydrogen bomb created by the servants of Moloch. It elaborates, instead, on the two final sections of *Howl,* the litany to Carl Solomon, gone mad in Rockland State Hospital, and the ecstatic hymn in Ginsberg's "Footnote" to *Howl,* beginning "Holy, Holy, Holy, Holy, Holy." In *The Bourgeois Poet,* Shapiro sings his barbaric yawp, like Whitman; he howls the world's holiness, like Ginsberg. In comparing Shapiro to these poets, I mean to suggest not his derivativeness but a common heritage, a resemblance to an earlier and a later American Jeremiah.

Shapiro's random celebration of spontaneity, gaiety, and open form was temporary; within three years after the publication of *The Bourgeois Poet,* he turned his back on this generally absurdist view of the human condition to espouse more traditional humanistic values. After the publication in 1968 of *Selected Poems,* he returned to the attitudes that informed his early criticism and poetry.

In this period of "the American poet," Shapiro begins to reconcile the two major and conflicting directions of his life and work and to arrange a tense alliance between Poe and Whitman, between Eliot and Williams, between the modernists who returned to Europe for form and idea and the aborigines who relied upon the "precultural" American language created by natives and refugees from three continents. By 1968, Shapiro became uneasy as "the true contemporary," rebelling against the "now" aesthetics that he had espoused in criticism since 1958 and against the lyrical and meditative prose poems that characterized his poetry during the same period. The change is prompted in part by a dissatisfaction with the social scene. Rather suddenly and inconsistently, he disapproves of political dissidence and of poetic responses to political upheaval associated with student protests and the antiwar movement. "Their poetry has sunk to a low which even the most gifted enemies of the Movement could not foresee," he wrote in 1968.

This transformation is perhaps the least surprising of Shapiro's changes as a writer. It is a change in politics and aesthetics that altered the perceptions and rhetoric of many people in the 1970's and that he anticipated by a few years. Like the three previous periods of Shapiro's life, this change led him in some positive directions—to some new poetry, to some insightful criticism, and, most surprisingly, to fiction. One can trace its origins in an important tribute to the late Randall Jarrell, in an address at the Library of Congress in 1967, and to a collection of love poems, in sonnets and other structured metrical forms, in *White-Haired Lover* in 1968. The essay on Jarrell, the poet whose work he admired most after Williams', is the first in a series of essays in the fourth period defining the term "American poet." The book of love poems, undoubtedly the weakest collection in his many years as a writer, indicates his return to traditional metrical forms. Shapiro's own opinion of this book is reflected in the fact that he includes only six of these poems in *Collected Poems 1940–1978.* They are conventional poems of an overwrought lover, more attentive to the person than to his art, and are interesting primarily in relationship to subsequent criticism and fiction.

Shapiro's most direct statement about his change in attitude is an essay denouncing advocates of spontaneity and contemporaneity, entitled "To Abolish Children" (1968), a rather hysterical argument later refined and restated in a somewhat more coherent fashion for the California Library Association in 1970. The latter version, which became the title essay in *The Poetry Wreck: Selected Essays 1950–1970,* warns against the "barbarism and savagery" that threatens every aspect of contemporary life. In this essay, as in his other writings, aesthetics and politics complement one another. He is clearly disturbed by the direction of re-

cent art and thought, represented by the popular songs of rock bands, by the psychobabble of contemporary social sciences, and by the popular poetry of Rod McKuen.("His writing is not even trash.")

The solution to this chaotic or melodramatic state, outlined in "To Abolish Children," is to rid the culture once and for all of the nonstate of being called "adolescence" and to make a clearer line of demarcation between "child" and "adult." The call for reform in "The Poetry Wreck" is more directly related to his cure for our poetry ills. Briefly stated, it tells us to go back to the library and to reclaim the university's proper functions, "to train the qualified student to the height of his capacity for learning, productivity in his skills, and imaginative research." To use the university, as it is now being used, "as an intellectual testing-ground of the personality is criminal," Shapiro says. "Sensitivity training for twenty-year-olds is obscene."

The manner in which Shapiro came to these insights and judgments regarding contemporary culture is hinted at in his only novel, *Edsel* (1971), about a teacher-poet who goes through an identity crisis, or "passage" as psychologists sometimes call it, and is eventually converted from barbarism to civilization. The book, a kind of twentieth-century *Tom Jones,* is a picaresque novel about a middle-aged male whose adventures are as erotic as the eighteenth-century hero's and who is brought to heel as successfully by his lover as Tom Jones is by Sophie at the end of Henry Fielding's novel.

Edsel is not so much about the central character, Edsel Lazerow, Regent's professor of English at Milo University, as it is about Edsel's "thing," its fall and rise. It is the story of an impotent, loquacious man who has lost his capacity for lovemaking and his sense of purpose—a man who has a reputation, after separating from his first wife, for promiscuity, for being "a character," for destruction. His latest affair, with Wanda Shontz, his wife's hairdresser, symbolizes the depth of his nightmarish depression, and their lovemaking sessions indicate the extent of his depravity. "We were rolling naked on the basement carpet, ... on broken glass, bleeding and grunting and cursing, biting and punching, burnt with cigarette ends, crawling to the bathroom like wounded animals, slimy with anger and lust, lower than hogs strung up by the hocks for the kill. . . . I remember mostly that we cursed each other, . . . until we ran out of that vocabulary. It was a hate-fest and a good one," Edsel says.

Returning from a European tour, as a representative of the United States Information Service, Edsel proceeds "to degrade degradation a notch at a time" and to throw himself into other hate-fests with Wanda. Several members of the faculty, aware of his psychological state, accuse him of slumming with Wanda, but the two continue their affair, with feelings of self-loathing and foulness. "You're in real bad trouble," Wanda tells Edsel at one point, "because you can't even love yourself." Dropped from the editorship of *Tracks West,* the university's literary quarterly, Edsel returns to teaching creative writing classes made up of athletes, sorority girls, faculty wives, and a hippie—who eventually sets fire to Edsel's office.

With a little help from his friends, Edsel manages to escape being arrested at two wild parties engineered, or at least encouraged, by Milo University's leading sociologist. The first is an illegal cockfight, reminiscent of the grotesque scene in Nathanael West's *The Day of the Locust;* the second is a groupie gathering, with strobe lights, Jamaican dancers, and marijuana, which coincides with a campus visit from Akiba Mem (alias Harry Peltz), America's leading beat guru and poet. As a writer, Edsel feels compelled to dissociate himself from both Akiba Mem and Richard Wigglesworth,

another famous poet and publicity hound, who eventually comes to Milo to demonstrate against the dismissal of two faculty members and to spout vague generalities about love, freedom, and sex to sympathetic—and unthinking—students and faculty.

Akiba Mem and Richard Wigglesworth, thinly disguised portraits of Allen Ginsberg and Robert Lowell, are associated in Edsel's mind with the corruption of language and of American life by mindless people who dominate the old professions. Watching the Wigglesworth demonstration on television, after telling the university president and the governor of the state that he has nothing to do with it, Edsel describes the counterculture theology and liturgy of such gatherings as "ill-digested gobbets of Zen and the Vedas, acid highs, hepatitic needles, electric jazz." In Edsel's view, the literary scholars, poets, scientists, and public officials have teamed up to corrupt the university, to defame poetry, and maybe to blow up the world.

The novel consists of Edsel's monologues and dialogues—his lectures on poetry, his arguments with colleagues and with Wanda, and eventually his conversations with Marya Hinsdale, the woman of his dreams. In the novel's last scene, Edsel makes love to Marya, exploding "into a red, white and blue orgasm spangled with silk and iridescent stars and golden fringe." He has regained not only his potency and patriotism but also, apparently, his ability to start a new life as man and poet. It is, like Bernard Malamud's *A New Life* and similar fiction with an academic setting, a comic novel, even a romance, and the lovers presumably live happily ever after. Edsel Lazerow (Lazarus) is resurrected and ascends into heaven with Marya.

Much of the humor of the novel—and this is probably not intentional—arises from the fact that Edsel sees through the stupidities of everyone but himself, especially his compulsion to bore everyone to tears. One wonders how anyone with normal hearing can tolerate him, especially the idyllic heroine, Marya, who resembles a figure in a pre-Raphaelite painting in her beauty and serenity. Perhaps Edsel will recover his rational faculties along with his sexual faculties and cut back on the chatter, the torturous analysis of practically everything. Although he never realizes it, his intense verbalizing is like an iron screen separating him from his feelings.

Mem and Wigglesworth, the other poets, are self-centered publicity hounds; but Edsel, in spite of his insistence on his own integrity, is not any better. In an effort to avoid being seduced by the media, by public relations, and by state politics, he identifies with people in power and even panders to them. He seeks the approval of the governor rather than remain quiet or take responsibility for his earlier complicity with the innocents and barbarians, "out of boredom, out of mischief, out of personal unhappiness." At the end, he turns his back on them all, self-righteous and pretentious man that he is. His conversion to older values, presumably more humane and lasting, is not convincing, though. "Virtue Rewarded," the subtitle of Samuel Richardson's *Pamela,* another eighteenth-century novel, might serve as the subtitle of Shapiro's romance. But Edsel, like Pamela, has done it for a price.

Although Edsel Lazerow is not always credible as a person, the novel works, generally, as a readable and revealing story because of Shapiro's extraordinary ability to pile detail on detail in a convincing and intelligible manner. The major flaw is the novel's attempt to reach beyond the confines of the story, without letting the reader in on its reasons for doing so. It is a two-dimensional comedy and succeeds in that genre until the problems of the principal characters call for a three- or four-dimensional exploration or dramatization.

Edsel contributes to the reader's understanding of Shapiro's change from "true contemporary" to "American poet," but it is not, strictly speaking, a roman à clef, and the association between Shapiro and Edsel need not be overemphasized. Both are poets, editors, and teachers at large, midwestern universities, and there are other direct associations between historical fact and fictional events. But Shapiro's statement that *"Edsel* is autobiographical in the sense that it has to do with my uneasiness at being the academy" is generally accurate. It has to do also with his uneasiness with the unconventional in poetry, politics, and private and social relationships. And it indicates something about Shapiro's nervousness about identifying with or adopting "bourgeois" attitudes for any length of time. It touches, in other words, upon that conflict between traditional and new forms and values that is observable in all of Shapiro's writing.

In the fourth period, Shapiro, like Edsel, views American culture with a critical eye, with a brusqueness similar to that in early poems such as "University" and "The Dome of Sunday," the camera depicting "Row-houses and row lives," as the latter poems says. There are no more prose poems on nonsensical, obscene, or absurd subjects, as in *The Bourgeois Poet.* Although occasionally personal, erotic, and informal, the better ones tend to deal with subjects, styles, and themes from the periods of apprenticeship and the "anti-critic," rather than of "the true contemporary." He writes again about Jefferson, the model political figure, the hero; about typical American scenes, such as "Garage Sale" and "The Humanities Building"; about other writers, including Eliot and Auden; and on a theme suggested by Yeats's "Adam's Curse," "that we must labor to be beautiful."

The poetry of the fourth period is uneven, as has already been suggested, but after *White-*

Haired Lover, it improves. "The Sense of Beauty," for example, indicates a decline in Shapiro's ability to write about that subject in poetry; but "The Rape of Philomel," from *Adult Bookstore,* shows him at his best, retelling a classical myth in contemporary language of great precision and simplicity.

Shapiro chose the latter poem as a fitting conclusion to *Collected Poems 1940–1978,* emphasizing in this way a persistent theme in his work: the natural relationship but inevitable conflict between beauty and power. The subject is a traditional one, popular with poets since the time of the Greeks; and Shapiro deals with the conflict in the midst of another culture that seems, like the earlier empire, to verge on decline if not on the edge of doom. "The feathers of these birds are stained with murder," concludes "The Rape of Philomel," as Procne, Philomel's violated sister, and the lustful King Tereus, fly "down the hallways, suddenly on wings." "Will there be anyone to chant the murderous tale of this other Thrace?" Shapiro seems to ask in this poem, where the state has taken over everything, where politics and sociology have replaced or corrupted art under the pretense of making it holy.

The questions raised by this poem call attention to the fact that from apprenticeship through maturity and achievement, Shapiro's work in poetry as well as prose exhibits a continuity in purpose. In raising aesthetic questions in a context that is broadly political, he reminds the reader of his beginnings in the 1930's and of other writers who came of age in the Great Depression. Like many of them, he has retained a deep sense of the public implications of words, actions, and modes of thought. Unlike many more "personal" or confessional poets, he remains aware that speech implies an audience and that writing is addressed to a reader, two qualities that have enabled him to speak to a rather large audience while maintaining a devotion to his craft.

It is a hard task, but Shapiro has succeeded in accomplishing it, as he has moved back and forth between an inherited tradition and the psychological and political necessities of the present. In his poetry, there have been occasional excesses, with echoes of Whitman and Williams in the beginning and the obvious indebtedness to Eliot and Auden slightly later. The poems of World War II were sometimes formalist and rationalist to an extreme; and the love poems of the "beat" Shapiro erred in the opposite direction. But this effort to change and to purify his language has also produced some of the most memorable and remarkable poems of the time, including twenty or so that are among the best known and truly skillful lyrics in American literature. The most obvious among them, including several discussed above, are "Auto Wreck," "University," "The Fly," "The Conscientious Objector," and "The Dirty Word"; several from *The Bourgeois Poet,* including "Lower the Standard," "Nebraska," and "I Am the Atheist Who Says His Prayers"; as well as "The Rape of Philomel."

To these poems must be added the essential essays in *The Poetry Wreck: Selected Essays 1950–1970,* especially those from *In Defense of Ignorance.* Those on individual poets, among the most influential critical statements since the essays of T. S. Eliot, helped to confirm a revitalizing change in canons of taste around 1955. There are, in addition, the interesting commentaries on his predecessors and his contemporaries, in prose and poetry—especially those on Whitman, Baudelaire, Yeats, Eliot, Pound, Lawrence, Hart Crane, Auden, Henry Miller, Saul Bellow, and Randall Jarrell. His political loyalties are indicated by his special praise of Jefferson and by his various social commentaries on the place of the library and the university in the general culture.

Shapiro's achievement as a critic may be understood by comparing him with a contemporary, Paul Goodman, another poet and enfant terrible, with obvious differences and surprising similarities. Like Goodman, Shapiro is able as an essayist to make unlikely or even outrageous positions understandable and acceptable when the whole world seems to be marching to another rhythm. His writings have that sense of conviction, that believable voice that overwhelms, badgers, ridicules, exposes, and finally wins the reader over.

Shapiro and Goodman share other similarities: born two years apart, they grew up in large cities on the Eastern seaboard, wrote for some of the same magazines, and were both introduced to a larger public in the same volume, *Five Young American Poets* (1941). Both regarded themselves at various times as anarchists, with Shapiro writing a poem, "Death of Emma Goldman" (1940), and an essay, "To Revive Anarchism" (1960), from that perspective. Their theories of language, in *Essay on Rime* and *Speaking and Language* (1971) might both be subtitled, as Goodman's was, "defence of poetry." Both argued vigorously against the values of the neomodernist period and were sympathetic to the assault on the formalist, official culture of the cold war years. Yet both, about 1970, condemned the excesses of the counterculture that developed in opposition to it, Shapiro in *To Abolish Children and Other Essays* and Goodman in *New Reformation: Notes of a Neolithic Conservative* (1970). Both were appalled by what Shapiro called "the intellectual infantilism of the American radical." Having survived the hard ideological battles of the 1930's, they knew when the rhetoric of armchair radicals had grown thin in the 1960's. In their unhappiness and disillusionment, both critics began to sound, as they neared sixty, like disgruntled old men adopting a reactionary position that would have appalled them during their younger days.

I have called the last period of Shapiro's career the period of "the American poet" because since 1968 he has been particularly preoccupied with exploring the meaning of that designation and because it calls attention to an important aspect of his achievement. Some years ago, in response to a request from the French National Radio, he wrote a note on American poetry (explored much more extensively in "Is Poetry an American Art?" and "American Poet?") in which he said that the United States would probably never create a great poetry until our poets establish "some equilibrium between themselves and the nation." "I cannot say whether we shall ever have another Poe," he continued, "but this is what we need—a spirit to lead us not to and fro in the land but into our own special genius." In his poetry and criticism, Shapiro, like Poe, has led us "into our own genius," exhibiting both the dark and doubting side of Poe and the affirming flame of Whitman. In remarks about his contemporaries, Shapiro suggests several other bases for evaluating and understanding his contributions to American letters.

In talking about Jarrell, Shapiro described his fellow poet in terms that can be applied usefully to himself. He was a man, Shapiro said, whose literary style and life-style grew out of his soul's conflict "between his instinct for freedom and his desire for cultural asylum." The conflicts Shapiro struggles with are similar but move in the opposite direction, between a desire for freedom and an instinct for cultural asylum. By his life-style, Shapiro has freed himself from the orthodoxies that have kept several of his contemporaries from speaking in their own voices. By his literary style, Shapiro has kept close to a culture that he wears well and lightly in his best work.

His talent, including his conflicts, has given him both an appreciation and love for the tradition and a distance from it. The results are a body of work that conveys both the confusion of a world on the edge of dissolution and its expansiveness and dynamism. He captures its momentary existence and celebrates it, even as he exposes the hint of weakness, decay, or dissolution, "And shows us, rotted and endowed,/ Its senile pleasure."

His arguments with, yet admiration for, bourgeois values have enabled him to be both a highly skilled satirist and a lyricist of the commonplace, allowing him to understand the American experience and to show it fully, as it is. Among his achievements as a poet are his ability to dramatize the culture's strengths—the accomplishments of its bourgeois revolution—and its weaknesses—the failure to transform an economic and political system that threatens its very survival. This rendering of the national life is accomplished not in an epic poem, characteristic of a heroic age, but in lyric poems that convey the diversity, the random joyousness, and the ridiculousness of contemporary American culture.

"An age's poetry does not purify the dialect, or any of that nonsense which aesthetic moralists believe," Shapiro wrote in 1967, "but an age's poetry fixes the age for those who care to gaze upon it in another age." He had said something similar in discussing Auden's poems ten years earlier, emphasizing the relationship between the longevity of a work of art and the date of its birth.

The goal, fixing the age "for those who care to gaze upon it," says a lot about Shapiro's vision of what and whom art is for, now and in the future. Although less influential among younger poets than several of his contemporaries and less frequently discussed by literary critics in his later years, Shapiro continues to enjoy that happy condition of being read for pleasure rather than merely being studied. Long known for his biting wit and occasional temper, he may simply have scared away commentators for whom poetry is only academic. With many of his books still in print decades after their initial publication, he has already survived several decades of sifting and selecting among American readers. For this reason, among others,

some readers are confident that his work will survive many more. One often regards him as he regarded Jarrell: "I rush to read you, whatever you print. That's news."

Selected Bibliography

WORKS OF KARL SHAPIRO

POETRY

Poems. Baltimore: Waverly Press, 1935.

Five Young American Poets, 2nd series, with Paul Goodman, Jeanne McGahey, Clark Mills, and David Schubert. Norfolk, Conn.: New Directions, 1941.

The Place of Love. Malvern, Australia: Bradley Printers, 1942.

Person, Place and Thing. New York: Reynal & Hitchcock, 1942.

V-Letter and Other Poems. New York: Reynal & Hitchcock, 1944.

Essay on Rime. New York: Reynal & Hitchcock, 1945.

Trial of a Poet and Other Poems. New York: Reynal & Hitchcock, 1947.

Poems 1940–1953. New York: Random House, 1953.

Poems of a Jew. New York: Random House, 1958.

The Bourgeois Poet. New York: Random House, 1964.

Selected Poems. New York: Random House, 1968.

White-Haired Lover. New York: Random House, 1968.

Adult Bookstore. New York: Random House, 1976.

Collected Poems 1940–1978. New York: Random House, 1978.

NOVEL

Edsel. New York: Bernard Geis, 1971.

CRITICISM

English Prosody and Modern Poetry. Baltimore: Johns Hopkins Press, 1947.

A Bibliography of Modern Prosody. Baltimore: Johns Hopkins Press, 1948.

Beyond Criticism. Lincoln: University of Nebraska Press, 1953.

Start With the Sun: Studies in Cosmic Poetry, with James E. Miller, Jr., and Bernice Slote. Lincoln: University of Nebraska Press, 1960.

In Defense of Ignorance. New York: Random House, 1960.

A Prosody Handbook, with Robert Beum. New York: Harper and Row, 1965.

To Abolish Children and Other Essays. Chicago: Quadrangle Books, 1968.

The Poetry Wreck: Selected Essays 1950–1970. New York: Random House, 1975.

LIBRETTOS, ANTHOLOGIES, ARTICLES, PLAYS, AND TRANSLATIONS

"The Question of the Pound Award." *Partisan Review,* 16:512–22 (May 1949).

Modern American and Modern British Poetry, revised and abridged edition by Karl Shapiro, Louis Untermeyer, and Richard Wilbur. New York: Harcourt, Brace, World, 1955.

The Tenor. Opera by Hugo Weisgal, with libretto by Karl Shapiro and Ernst Lert. Bryn Mawr, Penn.: Merion Music, 1957.

A Telescope for the Emperor (in Japanese). Play. *Eibungaku Fukei,* 1:9–35 (Winter 1958).

American Poetry, edited by Karl Shapiro. New York: Thomas Y. Crowell, 1960.

Prose Keys to Modern Poetry, edited by Karl Shapiro. New York: Harper and Row, 1962.

The Soldier's Tale. Music by Igor Stravinsky, with libretto by C. F. Ramuz, translated by Karl Shapiro. Chicago: University of Chicago Music Department, 1968.

BIBLIOGRAPHIES

Lee Bartlett. *Karl Shapiro: A Descriptive Bibliography, 1933–1977.* Foreword by James Woodress and checklist of criticism and reviews by David Huwiler. New York: Garland Publishing, 1979.

William White. *Karl Shapiro: A Bibliography.* Detroit: Wayne State University Press, 1960.

BIOGRAPHICAL AND CRITICAL STUDIES

Aiken, Conrad. *A Reviewer's ABC.* New York: Meridian Books, 1958.

Berryman, John. "From the Middle and Senior Generations." *American Scholar,* 28:384–90 (Summer 1959).

Bogan, Louise. *A Poet's Alphabet: Reflections on the Literary Art and Vocation,* edited by Robert Phelps and Ruth Limmer. New York: McGraw-Hill, 1970.

Childress, William. "Karl Shapiro." *Poetry Now,* 2, no. 5:1–3 (September 1975).

Ciardi, John, ed. *Mid-Century American Poets.* New York: Twayne Publishers, 1950.

Coleman, Alice. "'Doors Leap Open.'" *English Journal,* 53:631–33 (November 1964).

Cowley, Malcolm. "A Lively and Deadly Wit." *Poetry,* 61:620–22 (February 1943).

Daiches, David. "The Poetry of Karl Shapiro." *Poetry,* 66:266–73 (August 1945).

Deutsch, Babette. *Poetry in Our Time: A Critical Survey of Poetry in the English-speaking World 1900 to 1960,* 2nd ed. rev. and enl. Garden City, N. Y.: Doubleday, 1963.

Donoghue, Denis. "Life Sentence." *New York Review of Books,* 17:28–30 (December 2, 1971).

Eckman, Frederick. "Karl Shapiro's *Adam and Eve.*" *University of Texas Studies in English,* 35:1–10 (1956).

Engle, Paul, and Joseph Langland. *Poet's Choice.* New York: Dial Press, 1962.

Fiedler, Leslie. *Waiting for the End.* New York: Stein and Day, 1964.

Flint, F. Cudworth. "Poets on the Way from Tarawa to Aldebaron." *New York Times Book Review,* 49, September 3, 1944, pp. 4, 13.

Fussell, Edwin. "Karl Shapiro: The Paradox of Prose and Poetry." *Western Review,* 15:225–44 (Spring 1954).

Glassberg, Rose. "Karl Shapiro: Poet Versus Critic." Ph.D. dissertation, Temple University, Philadelphia, 1972.

Gunn, Thom. "Poetry as Written." *Yale Review,* 48:297–305 (December 1958).

Jarrell, Randall. *The Third Book of Criticism.* New York: Farrar, Straus and Giroux, 1969.

Kazin, Alfred. *Contemporaries.* Boston: Little, Brown, 1962.

Keltner, Jeanie Ellen. "Karl Shapiro: The Bourgeois Poet." Ph.D. dissertation, University of California, Los Angeles, 1973.

Kunitz, Stanley. "Shapiro, Karl Jay." In *Twentieth Century Authors.* First Supplement. New York: H. W. Wilson, 1955.

Lieberman, Laurence. *Unassigned Frequencies: American Poetry in Review 1964–77.* Urbana, Ill.: University of Illinois Press, 1977.

Logan, John. "Broadside Attack on the Patriarchs of Modern Poetry." *Commonweal,* 73:438–40 (January 20, 1961).

Malin, Irving. *Jews and Americans.* Carbondale, Ill.: Southern Illinois University Press, 1965.

Malkoff, Karl. "Karl Shapiro," *Crowell's Handbook of Contemporary American Poetry.* New York: Thomas Y. Crowell, 1973.

———. "The Self in the Modern World: Karl Shapiro's Jewish Poems." In *Contemporary American-Jewish Literature,* edited by Irving Malin. Bloomington, Ind.: Indiana University Press, 1973.

Matthiessen, Francis O. *The Responsibilities of the Critic: Essays and Reviews.* New York: Oxford University Press, 1952.

Mills, Ralph J., Jr. "Karl Shapiro." In *Contemporary American Poetry.* New York: Random House, 1965.

Nemerov, Howard. *Poetry and Fiction: Essays.* New Brunswick, N. J.: Rutgers University Press, 1963.

O'Connor, William Van. "Karl Shapiro: The Development of a Talent." *College English,* 10:71–77 (November 1948).

Reid, Alfred S. "The Southern Exposure of Karl Shapiro." *Southern Humanities Review,* 6:35–44 (1972).

Rich, Adrienne, "On Karl Shapiro's *The Bourgeois Poet.*" In *The Contemporary Poet as Artist and Critic,* edited by Anthony Ostroff. Boston: Little, Brown, 1964.

Rosenthal, Macha L. *The Modern Poets: A Critical Introduction.* New York: Oxford University Press, 1960.

———. *The New Poets: American and British Poetry Since World War II.* New York: Oxford University Press, 1967.

Rubin, Louis D., Jr. "The Search for Lost Innocence: Karl Shapiro's *The Bourgeois Poet.*" *Hollins Critic,* 1:1–16 (December 1964).

Schwartz, Delmore. "The Poet's Progress." *Nation,* 156:63–64 (January 9, 1943).

"Shapiro, Karl (Jay)." In *Contemporary Authors,* edited by James M. Ethridge and Barbara Kopala. Vols. 1–4, 1st rev. Detroit: Gale Research, 1967. Pp. 854–55.

"Shapiro, Karl Jay." In *Contemporary Poets,* 2nd ed., edited by James Vinson. London: St. James Press, 1975.

"Shapiro, Karl (Jay)." In *Current Biography: Who's News and Why, 1944,* edited by Anna Rothe. New York: H. W. Wilson, 1945. Pp. 611–13.

Slotkin, Richard. "The Contextual Symbol: Karl Shapiro's Image of 'The Jew.'" *American Quarterly,* 18:220–26 (Summer 1966).

Solotaroff, Theodore. "The Irrational Karl Shapiro." *Commentary,* 30:445–48 (November 1960).

Southworth, James G. "The Poetry of Karl Shapiro." *English Journal,* 51:159–66 (March 1962).

Spender, Stephen. "The Power and the Hazard." *Poetry,* 71:314–18 (March 1948).

Stauffer, Donald Barlow. *A Short History of American Poetry.* New York: E. P. Dutton, 1974.

Stepanchev, Stephen. *American Poetry Since 1945.* New York: Harper and Row, 1965.

True, Michael. "Alive with Necessary Poems." *Commonweal,* 105:725 (November 10, 1978).

Waggoner, Hyatt H. *American Poets from the Puritans to the Present.* Boston: Houghton, Mifflin, 1968.

Williams, William Carlos. *Selected Essays.* New York: Random House, 1954.

FILMS

Karl Shapiro's America. Produced and directed by Arthur Hoyle, 1976.

—*MICHAEL TRUE*

Carl Van Vechten

1880–1964

CARL VAN VECHTEN had three more or less chronologically sequential careers—as critic, novelist, and photographer—and a fourth one spanning the other three, as discoverer and promoter of the work of others. Throughout his eighty-four years, he contradicted any pejorative suggestion in that outworn epithet, "dilettante," and returned it to its initial definition: a lover of the arts, a connoisseur. If, in the view of some critics, he was a dabbler, he dabbled productively, and the full landscape of the arts and letters of the first half of this century owes some of its order to him. Few figures in American literature demonstrated his range or possessed his vision, and any serious attention to his full achievement will support this claim. In none of his careers was he an artist of the first order, but the collective performance is invaluable and demands assessment.

As a music critic, he introduced the work of Igor Stravinsky and Erik Satie to America, and he was among the first to write seriously of the music dramas of Richard Strauss; he evaluated and analyzed jazz and ragtime far in advance of anyone else; he rightly predicted that serious composers would write musical scores designed specifically to accompany motion pictures; he may have originated the personality interview through his newspaper articles on opera luminaries; and he was the first serious writer to pay attention to ballet and modern dance in this country. Furthermore, he wrote the first book in America about Spanish music, and the first extensive essays about Negro spirituals and blues, fostering in the process the careers of Paul Robeson, Ethel Waters, and others.

As a literary critic, he gave undiscovered writers like Gertrude Stein, Arthur Machen, and Ronald Firbank their initial attention in America, and he was partly responsible for Herman Melville's resurrection during the 1920's; his efforts on behalf of black artists and writers never ceased; and the first books of poets as diverse as Wallace Stevens and Langston Hughes reached print because Van Vechten brought them to the attention of his own publisher, Alfred A. Knopf.

As a novelist, Van Vechten documented what he called the "splendid drunken twenties" in a loosely connected trilogy about New York and in two adjacent books, one about Hollywood, the other about Harlem. One of his other novels was characterized by W. Somerset Maugham in a letter to Van Vechten that might apply to all seven of the novels: "Most writers think that a light book is a frivolous one, and do not realize that it requires really much more thought, knowledge and culture and experience than a book dealing with the elemental emotions."

At fifty-two, Van Vechten gave up writing,

turned to photography, and spent his remaining thirty-two years in cataloging the celebrated artists and writers of the century, often in connection with collections he established. These include the James Weldon Johnson Memorial Collection of Negro Arts and Letters at Yale University and the George Gershwin Memorial Collection of Music and Musical Literature at Fisk University. He established additional archives in theater and dance at the New York Public Library, the Museum of the City of New York, and the Museum of Modern Art. In drama, his subjects began with Eugene O'Neill and ended with Edward Albee; in opera, with Mary Garden and with Beverly Sills; in art, with Henri Matisse and with Alexander Calder; in fiction, with Thomas Mann and with William Faulkner; in poetry, with W. H. Auden and with Amiri Baraka (LeRoi Jones). Moreover, he photographed nearly every celebrated black person in America, from W. E. B. Du Bois to Sammy Davis, Jr., and from Leontyne Price to Ralph Bunche. The catalog encourages namedropping.

Van Vechten's legacy includes nineteen published books; twenty-six books with introductions or prefaces, for several of which he acted as editor; fourteen years of newspaper criticism; dozens of book reviews and periodical essays in praise of his enthusiasms; and fifteen thousand photographs. As a critic, admittedly, he lacked the objective perceptions of many of his contemporaries, H. L. Mencken and Edmund Wilson, for example; and as a novelist he failed more often than he succeeded in finding a comfortable middle ground between farce and melodrama where his wit and erudition could coexist. His photography sometimes suggests the work of an Instamatic sycophant rather than that of a Leica amateur, despite many truly superb portraits. On the other hand, he rarely miscalculated in assessing talent in others. Taken as a whole, the quality of his various careers is as enviable as the quantity; a few wrong notes cannot undermine the success of a performance.

Born on June 17, 1880, the late, and youngest, child of indulgent parents of comfortable means, Van Vechten grew up in Cedar Rapids, Iowa. The late nineteenth-century midwestern bucolic scene has often served as a friendly background in fiction; the stifling atmosphere of an urban setting has led more often to bitter indictments. Van Vechten documented that era and its milieu in his third novel, *The Tattooed Countess,* but by the time he wrote it, in 1924, his adolescent scorn for the emotional as well as the geographical landscape had tempered, lacing his contempt with nostalgia and decorating his memory with a finely honed irony.

The Tattooed Countess draws upon Van Vechten's own upbringing and influences, the wide range of theatrical experiences to which he had been exposed at an early age, and the reading and musical training that formulated much of his taste as a critic. Cedar Rapids served as a convenient stopover for one-night stands as traveling theater troupes moved west from Chicago. By the time he left home for college, Van Vechten had already seen many of the well-known actors and singers of the period. Richard Mansfield and Otis Skinner played in Shakespeare, and the Emma Abbott Opera Company toured regularly; in his youth, Van Vechten had also seen not only Ellen Terry and Eddie Foy and Loie Fuller and Little Egypt, but also Sissieretta Jones. This remarkable soprano, billed as "the Black Patti" after the opera star Adelina Patti, sparked Van Vechten's initial enthusiasm for black entertainment and led to his later commitment to black arts and letters in America.

The Tattooed Countess recounts more directly the lap suppers, tea parties, local musical recitals, and other social endeavors of fin de siècle ("fin de seekle" in the novel) America. The slender plot seems almost incidental to the delineation of fashion, decor, and gossip against which it transpires. In 1897, Ella Nattatorrini (née Poore), widow of an Italian count and subsequent mistress of many handsome young gigolos, returns to her hometown in Iowa, promptly falls in love with Gareth Johns, a local seventeen-year-old, and takes him back to Paris. Before the escape, Gareth breaks the heart of his repressed spinster schoolteacher, and the countess shocks the town by smoking cigarettes, wearing makeup, and flaunting her tattoo: *"Que sais-je?"* "But on the wrist, where it *shows!*" her sister cries in dismay. "It wouldn't have been so bad if it had been on the back of the . . . thigh, where it could be covered."

The book is subtitled "A romantic novel with a happy ending," but with equal qualification it is an autobiography as well—at least to age seventeen:

I want to know everything, *everything* . . . and . . . I'm going to. . . . I want to get away from this town. . . . I want to visit the theatre and the opera and the art galleries. I want to meet people. I want to learn. Somewhere there must be people like me. . . .

Both the town and its inhabitants come perilously close to caricature, but even a cursory examination of the Cedar Rapids newspapers of the period indicates Van Vechten's deadly accuracy. Gareth escapes; Van Vechten never entirely did, in spite of his resolute sophistication. A strong sense of the past, firmly grounded in nostalgia, never deserted him. Late Victorian bell jars, portieres, and other artifacts of the 1890's gave way in the 1920's to taffeta walls and lapis lazuli bathtubs: Van Vechten's preoccupation with setting and decoration was always significant in his novels and, later, in the background and composition of his photographs.

Gareth Johns, who turns up in other novels as a celebrated writer, is a fairly consistent portrait of Van Vechten as he may be pieced together from random autobiographical fragments. Despite his disdain for Cedar Rapids and its preoccupation with gossip and fashion, it supplied a not unfruitful landscape from which to develop; and much of his interest in decor, his clear eye for detail, and his involvement with music and theater came about because of what was available to him and not in contradiction to it. Van Vechten escaped as soon as he could, not in the arms of a middle-aged demimondaine, but to the University of Chicago.

He studied under William Vaughn Moody and Robert Morss Lovett but wrote nothing of value. His strongest influence came from his studies in Restoration and eighteenth-century drama rather than from these professional writers. When Van Vechten turned to writing novels during the 1920's, the comedy of manners gave him a frame of reference on which to draw, in a pattern extending forward from William Wycherley and William Congreve to Oscar Wilde and Ronald Firbank. Several Lady Bracknells populate the background in *The Tattooed Countess;* and however provincial it may be, the novel's school for scandal is just as malicious and amusing as Richard Brinsley Sheridan's. Speakeasies in other novels replace the chocolate houses of an earlier age, but husbands still visit their spouses to recuperate from casual affairs, and women, like Millimant, "may by degrees dwindle into a wife" but only on their own emancipated terms.

At least five of Van Vechten's novels are clearly comedies of manners, brittle and artificial, and therefore serve as incisive examinations of the societies they reflect. Indeed, they may be as accurate evaluations as the endeavors of cynical novelists like Sinclair Lewis, serious ones like Theodore Dreiser, popular ones like

Joseph Hergesheimer, or young ones like F. Scott Fitzgerald. *The Tattooed Countess* is set twenty-five years before the 1920's began to roar, and as an escape-from-the-village novel its rebellion is still an offstage rumble. But the signs are unmistakable. The countess, after all, is "at that dangerous age just before decay sets in," a "sex-beset moron," as Van Vechten described her to a friend, seduced by a ruthless youth whose imagination transcends all of poor Ella Nattatorrini's experience. Gareth is simply indifferent, although a more than willing participant in a love affair that will get him out of town. He is emotionally asexual, not an unfamiliar attitude in Van Vechten's fiction, especially so for the characters whose points of view would seem to reflect his own. Gareth's "hour has come," and the countess has anticipated its arrival early in the novel when the town's provincial attitudes lead her to cry, "You'd better look out! You don't know what you're doing to the next generation. They won't stand it, no one with any brains would stand it! They'll revolt! They'll break loose!"

Gareth escapes at seventeen; Van Vechten lingered on two years longer before leaving for the University of Chicago. In 1903, after graduating with an undistinguished scholastic record and a bachelor of philosophy degree, he became a reporter for William Randolph Hearst's *Chicago American* and, as "The Chaperone," detailed the "Gossip of the Chicago Smart Set." His material, however superficial, and his style, however sophomoric, give a fair indication of his later manner. If he was star struck by the glamour of the social queens of the period, he laced his precious prose with a healthy disdain: "One of my contemporaries has it that 'Mrs. Potter Palmer continues to be feted in London in spite of the warm weather.' This shows a woeful lack of knowledge about Mrs. Palmer, who is feted in cold weather and in warm weather, in Summer, Winter, Autumn, and Spring; in Paris, Berlin, St. Petersburg, London, or Chicago. She is always being feted. It is her fate."

In 1906, after poking fun in his column at some overdressed matrons as "clothes horses" at the annual horse show in Chicago, Van Vechten was taken off the society page. He interpreted that to mean that he had been "fired for lowering the tone of the Hearst newspapers." Six months later, he went to work as a reporter for the *New York Times.* When he published a long article about Richard Strauss's *Salome* and its impending Metropolitan Opera premiere, in Theodore Dreiser's *Broadway Magazine,* the *Times* appointed him assistant to Richard Aldrich, the music critic.

For the next six years, Van Vechten's work was largely devoted to documenting the private lives and public performances of opera stars. Usually based on extensive interviews, his work quickly established him as a sympathetic listener. His friendship with Olive Fremstad, the soprano scheduled to sing *Salome,* led to a direct involvement with several other singers as well, notably Luisa Tetrazzini, whose memoirs Van Vechten ghostwrote for *Cosmopolitan* magazine, Feodor Chaliapin, Mary Garden, and dozens of others. He also covered the first appearances in America of Sergei Rachmaninoff, Camille Saint-Saëns, and Gustav Mahler, and he wrote the first interviews with Pietro Mascagni, Ermanno Wolf-Ferrari, and Giacomo Puccini, since Richard Aldrich did not share his enthusiasm for contemporary music.

Van Vechten broadened his experience through European opera and concerts, first on a trip in 1907 during which he married Anna Snyder, a high school friend. In 1908, he returned as Paris correspondent for the *New York Times* for a year. He accounted for the period, drawing on both trips, in *Peter Whiffle: His Life* and Works, written in 1921 and published the following year. Few books reflect the excitement and enchantment of a young man's initial response to Paris so well, although long afterward Van Vechten said he had written *Peter Whiffle* when he was no longer enthusiastic about Paris. That attitude is remarkably well hidden, for his description of the city and its prewar atmosphere is superbly rendered (preferably in the version Van Vechten revised for an illustrated edition of the book in 1927).

On his return to New York, Van Vechten instituted a series of Monday interviews for the *Times* that may be the foundation for the kinds of personality interviews that now appear in many weekly journals and newspapers. They consist largely of quotations of answers that reveal his ability to anticipate, rather than judge, the right questions for the right person. One remarkable feature of Van Vechten's method lay in his ability to capture the voice of the singer he was quoting. Interviews with Mary Garden, his most frequent subject, Geraldine Farrar, or Emmy Destinn, for example, reflect entirely different personalities, not so much on the basis of what they say as how they express themselves. All this activity occurred long before the days of cassette recorders, of course; moreover, Van Vechten took no shorthand. *Interpreters,* first published in 1920 and reissued in 1977, is a volume of essays growing out of these interviews, and it gives a permanent record of Van Vechten's success in recreating people on paper.

During the years of his Monday interviews, Van Vechten covered three significant premieres as well, through a series of articles on each: Christoph Gluck's *Armide,* with Enrico Caruso and Fremstad, leading to a later, extended analysis of the opera; Strauss's *Der Rosenkavalier,* a natural assignment because of his familiarity with Strauss's earlier operas; and Puccini's *La Fanciulla del West* In each case,

he was able to analyze the scores for his readers—an opportunity that did not often come his way—because of his musical training. He had studied piano in Cedar Rapids, and in Chicago he gave infrequent public recitals; he also composed a good deal of music in Chicago.

Van Vechten was not an expert performer, nor was he encouraged to continue composing, but his training was broad. Theodore Thomas and the Chicago Symphony Orchestra regularly played César Franck, Strauss, Claude Debussy, Pëtr Ilich Tchaikovsky, Maurice Ravel, Gustave Charpentier, even the American composer Edward MacDowell (whose obituary Van Vechten later wrote for the *New York Times*), often in advance of performances in New York. Furthermore, Van Vechten was well acquainted with a vast number of operas, for in both Chicago and New York he had joined the casts onstage and "suped," donning a robe or carrying a spear as a member of the nonsinging chorus. Because of his early, warm association with Oscar Hammerstein and the Manhattan Opera Company, he was thoroughly familiar with scores of operas—Strauss's *Elektra,* for example—long before the premieres, so his analyses of the music and of the singers' interpretations were, then as at present, valuable source material for musicians as well as for opera buffs.

By way of an art that utilized music, rather than through music itself, Van Vechten made his most important contribution in his career as a critic. In 1910, Richard Aldrich demurring again, Van Vechten began to review dance performances, first those of Isadora Duncan and shortly thereafter those of Anna Pavlova. By 1916, when Waslaw Nijinsky and the Diaghilev Ballets offered further subject matter for Van Vechten's dance writings, he had become, by default, America's first ballet critic. Time has proven his vision true. His collected dance writings, edited by Paul Padgette in 1975, give an excellent account of his range and facility. Others have already pointed out his importance, including Arlene Croce, Lincoln Kirstein, and John Martin, the last of whom assessed Van Vechten's work as the product of "a remarkably sensitive and forward-looking mind" in reviews that were "the quick and accurate judgments of an artist who happened also to be an excellent newspaper man. . . ."

Van Vechten had no particular understanding of the technique of ballet, but that may have worked in his favor. He described what he saw in his own prose, unhampered by terminology. A critic interpreting a visual art must use words more familiar than the French names of ballet steps; he must see like a photographer and hear like a musician, but with only his own vocabulary as the medium. In the spell of Van Vechten's own excitement, the reader understands clearly what minor miracle occurred, in 1910, when Pavlova "twirled on her toes." Van Vechten later reworked some of these reviews into extended essays about the Russian ballet, Duncan, Nijinsky, and, still later, about Spanish and black dancing. They may well contain some of the most lyric writing in the whole field of criticism:

The ennobling effect of all great and perfect art, after the primary emotion, seems to be to set our minds wandering in a thousand channels, to suggest new outlets. . . . No writer, no musician, no painter, can feel deep emotion before a work of art without expressing it in some way, although the expression may be a thousand leagues removed from the inspiration. And how few of us can view the art of Nijinsky without emotion! To the painter he gives a new sense of proportion, to the musician a new sense of rhythm, while to the writer he must perforce immediately suggest new words; better still, new meanings for old words. . . . We look enraptured, we go away enthralled, and perhaps even unconsciously a new quality creeps into our own work.

Fortunately, Van Vechten's work on the *New York Times* occurred at the time of America's balletic coming of age. He attended the performances not only of Pavlova and Duncan, but also of Ekaterina Gelzer, Maude Allan, Loie Fuller, and La Argentinita. He traced the whole development of Isadora Duncan's dancing, from her early experiments, which he had seen in Munich in 1907, to her interpretation of the *Marseillaise* at the outbreak of World War I, and credited her with having freed from tradition the later Russian ballet. His account of the first performance, in Paris, of Igor Stravinsky's *Le Sacre du Printemps* is well known, a vivid example of his best reporting. As a working reviewer, Van Vechten was able to use the influence of his paper to encourage popular interest, and his ability to fix the dancer on paper with analogies from his other concerns gives his dance criticism its enduring vitality.

In 1913, Van Vechten left the *New York Times* to become drama critic for the *New York Press,* writing nearly daily reports of theatrical performances and weekly editorials about current productions, including the premiere of George Bernard Shaw's *Pygmalion* (first performed in America in German), many of William Shakespeare's plays, and the first performances of two perennial favorites, Victor Herbert's *Naughty Marietta* and *Sweethearts.* In writing about *The Darktown Follies* and Ridgely Torrence's *Granny Maumee,* he became the first writer of significance to give serious attention to black entertainments and to black subject matter, discovering in them the roots of what would become a major preoccupation as well as occupation in later years, and urging the formation of a "Negro Theatre" to which black artists and writers could contribute their talents.

During that same period, Van Vechten had become involved with Mabel Dodge (later Mabel Dodge Luhan) and her salon at 23 Fifth Avenue, where art and politics mingled reciprocally. A kind of mutual affection developed almost immediately, or "a mutual stimulation with none of the usual elements of sex," as Mabel Dodge described it in her 1936 memoir, *Movers and Shakers.* Van Vechten's wife had divorced him in 1912 and although "occasionally his Dutch warmth went out in warm friendships for other men," he and the Russian actress Fania Marinoff were lovers for two years before they married in 1914. It was "a strange conjunction," Mabel Dodge rightly observed, "rooted in eternity, odd and everlasting." They celebrated their fiftieth wedding anniversary shortly before his death in 1964.

His friendship with Mabel Dodge continued through the excitement of the International Exhibition of Modern Art, popularly referred to as the Sixty-Ninth Regiment Armory Show, in 1913, which introduced postimpressionist painting to America; through two engaging visits, as one of her "jeunes gens assortis," at her Villa Curonia in Florence; through his acquaintance with George Moore in England, the futurists in Italy, and Gertrude Stein in France, all of whom strongly influenced his later work; and through his escape from Europe at the outbreak of World War I. Van Vechten included many of these events and associations in *Peter Whiffle* with enough accuracy to give that book a degree of historical significance, although this seemingly autobiographical work—the narrator's name is Carl Van Vechten—makes no mention of his first marriage, and Fania Marinoff is referred to only once in passing. The period between his marriages is simply ignored. Perhaps the deletions from Van Vechten's own life in *Peter Whiffle* are as significant as the inclusions.

Peter Whiffle is an invented character in a roman à clef, although Van Vechten later claimed he had not been aware he was writing a novel during the time of its composition. Van Vechten's first biographer, Edward Lueders, was probably the first to suggest that Peter Whiffle was his author's doppelgänger, although, when the book first appeared in 1922, an unknown admirer wrote that she "could not help wondering politely how much of Peter was simply what Carl Van Vechten would be." Certainly, Peter speaks often enough in Van Vechten's voice, notably during a long conversation at the Florentine Villa Allegra of Edith Dale (obviously Mabel Dodge's Villa Curonia): "Good critics, I should like to believe," says Peter, "are always loose writers; they perpetually contradict themselves; their work is invariably palinodial. How, otherwise, can they strive for vision, and how can they inspire vision in the reader without striving for vision themselves? Good critics ... should constantly contradict their own definitions. ... Criticism should open channels of thought and not close them; it should stimulate the soul and not revolt it. And criticism can only be wholesome and sane and spiritually stimulating when it is contradictory. ... It is better to turn the leaf and begin afresh on a new page. Artists are never consistent. ... Any critic who is an artist will be equally inconsistent."

Van Vechten gave up newspaper criticism in 1914. Briefly, he was identified with a group of writers he called the Post-Decadents, and for a time he was regularly in the company of Wallace Stevens, William Carlos Williams, Walter Arensberg, Allen and Louise Norton, and Donald Evans, many of whom were influenced in greater or lesser degrees by Gertrude Stein's *Portrait of Mabel Dodge at the Villa Curonia* and *Tender Buttons.* These writers seem to have been less than congenial, although Van Vechten was largely responsible for getting some of their work in print in *Trend,* a magazine he edited for three months in the fall of 1914. The attempted movement died as these disparate writers went their various ways; Van Vechten's way led to a series of essays. They were published in annual volumes, the first in 1915, entitled *Music After the Great War.*

The music would be Russian, Van Vechten contended, basing his belief almost exclusively on the memorable performances in Paris by the Diaghilev company. Every age had had to come to terms with its own innovators, he observed; Ludwig van Beethoven and Richard Wagner, like Strauss and Debussy, had suffered under the charge that they could not write melody. About Stravinsky, whose work occupied three of the seven essays in *Music After the Great War,* Van Vechten explained the necessity of discovering new methods of harmony, actually "a school of disharmony," not unlike an earlier observation he had made about Gertrude Stein, who had "deliberately forgotten how to write." Disposing of most other new music with the exception of that of Arnold Schönberg ("a stone in the architecture of music—and not an accidental decoration") in "Music for Museums?" he contended that repetition did not lead to discovery but to "fossilization."

If Van Vechten's generalizations swept too neatly, the result was at least clean: "It is alone the critic's point of view, well-defined, which makes him comprehensible when he disdains to be more scientific in his criticism." To too many critics, discordant simply meant different, but to Van Vechten the word suggested the kind of freedom that music required to survive. In other pieces, his championing of Russian music took more specific direction. "The Secret of the Russian Ballet" lay in the choreographer's use of dancers, not as a corps but as choirs with independent responsibilities, coordinated with the polyphony of the music, synchronized in movement rather than serving only as decoration for the principals. Forty years later he came to believe that the method explained George Balanchine's unique success with the New York City Ballet, for it insisted that all dancers dance more or less continuously and in close collaboration with the music until the two were inseparable. In Russian ballet, one might, indeed, hear the music by watching the dancers in silence. Much of the success, Van Vechten admitted, lay in the music of Stravinsky and in the roots of serial music, achieved through "terseness rather than formal 'working out'" and "dissonance through inversion."

Elsewhere in *Music After the Great War,* Van Vechten directed his attention to stage decoration, noting that a degree of Nijinsky's success, at least, might be explained through the decor of Léon Bakst; that the practical value in engaging artists for such work—Gordon Craig, for example—gave the "charm of suggestion" more appropriate to theatrical entertainments than cumbersome attempts at realism. Stage decoration, he insisted, was a "fine art," basing that essay, like others, on earlier newspaper editorials.

Van Vechten's second book, "Pastiches et Pistaches," was never published in its original form, but the contents are of some interest because they demonstrate the faults that have led more than one critic to dismiss him as an inconsequential writer. Composed of thirteen "semifictional" essays in the style, Van Vechten believed, of George Moore, "Pastiches et Pistaches" eventually found its way into print in various fugitive magazines, and beginning in 1922 Van Vechten used the title and even some of the material for a series of six contributions to the *Reviewer,* the Richmond, Virginia, literary quarterly to which many celebrated writers contributed without pay in the spirit of literary camaraderie. Van Vechten's material is often embarrassingly precious. After several other publishers turned it down in 1916, Alfred A. Knopf suggested a second volume of musical essays instead. Van Vechten responded with *Music and Bad Manners,* the first of seventeen books published by Knopf during their long and fruitful association.

The title essay was an outgrowth of Van Vechten's Monday interviews for the *New York Times,* an engaging collection of incidents illustrating the rudeness of musicians, blending amusing anecdotes about flamboyant opera singers—Fremstad, for instance, who threw the roast on the floor at a preperformance dinner, sneering, "Pork before *Parsifal!*"—with musical history of some interest. The value of the work lies not in its gossip, but in essays such as "Music for the Movies," in which Van Vechten rightly predicted "that the time is not far distant when moving picture scores will take their places on the musicians' bookshelves. . . ." The technique of the film would undermine conventional resolution in musical but not in thematic terms, he claimed, and the future might workably employ accompaniments by Stravinsky and Strauss: "The swift flash from scene to scene, the 'cut-back,' the necessary rapidity of the action, all are adapted to inspire the futurist composer to brilliant effort; a tickle of this and a smash of that, without 'working out' or development; illustration, comment, piquant or serious, that's what the new film music should be."

Elsewhere in the collection he returned to stage decoration in an essay about Wagnerian productions and the dangers in "slavish adherence" to Bayreuth tradition, urging the unit sets of Adolphe Appia and Gordon Craig again, and of the Russians, Bakst and Aleksandr Benois, and the directorial appproaches of Max Reinhardt and Konstantin Stanislavski. Finally, in "The Bridge Burners," Van Vechten took to task all academic music critics, urging them to pay attention to the Russians and defending Stravinsky against Richard Aldrich's complaint that his music required explanation. Far in advance of electronic and computer music, Van

Vechten wrote: "Machinery has changed the world. We are living in a dynasty of dynamics. A certain number of futurists even give concerts of noise machines in which a definite attempt is made to imitate the sounds of automobiles, aeroplanes, etc." He asked the critics simply to listen: "Your ears will make progress in spite of you and I shouldn't wonder at all if five years more would make Schönberg and Stravinsky and Ornstein a trifle old fashioned. . . . The Austrian already has a little of the academy dust upon him."

Van Vechten rarely wrote negatively or took individuals specifically to task, although here he attacked the entire musical hierarchy for conservatism. Nothing, he later observed, was gained by negative criticism; it was only an excuse for the critic to show off. Van Vechten showed off regularly, but the thrust was nearly always constructive and his erudition always practical, however intimidating it might be because of his own strong sense of prose, coupled with too arch a turn of phrase.

His third book, *Interpreters and Interpretations,* was also made up of a series of essays based on his Monday interviews with opera stars and others, all intensely personal, giving the clearest idea of the artists' methods, appearances, and personalities short of photographs or recordings. The second half, "Interpretations," includes a strong paper about American music, advancing the belief that in ragtime lay the whole of the foundation for the future, Irving Berlin, Louis A. Hirsch, and Lewis F. Muir being the "true grandfathers of the Great American Composer in the year 2001."

At that time, Van Vechten's exposure to black music had been limited to turn-of-the-century entertainments in Chicago by Bert Williams and his partner George Walker, to an early appreciation of the popular singer Carita Day, and to the 1913 Darktown Follies production of J. Leubrie Hill's *My Friend from Kentucky,* about which he had written extensively for the *New York Press.* Scott Joplin had died (in 1917), apparently unknown to Van Vechten; there is no mention of him anywhere in Van Vechten's work, even during the 1920's when he devoted so much of his energy to promoting black music. Nobody seems to have paid much attention to Joplin at the time, and in *Interpreters and Interpretations* Van Vechten wrote: "Curiously enough the best ragtime has not been written by Negroes, although *Under the Bamboo Tree* and the extraordinary *At the Ball* are the work of black men."

Van Vechten was unaware that ragtime had more or less evolved in the 1890's; instead, he likened it to other music through its syncopation: "Nearly the whole of Beethoven's Seventh Symphony is based on it. . . . But ragtime syncopation is different, its melody and harmony being separately syncopated." Van Vechten was insecure here, as he realized, pointing out that the prelude to *Parsifal* required the conductor to beat 6/4 with one hand and 4/4 with the other, that in Spanish music the singer, dancer, and guitarist would "vie with one another to produce a complexity of rhythm," and that *Le Sacre du Printemps* was built on syncopation. It was not likely, Van Vechten admitted, that one would find much resemblance between "Everybody's Doin' It" and *Parsifal;* ragtime was a hybrid, dependent on black and Spanish rhythms, of which both serious and popular composers might make profitable use.

In another essay, on "electrical picture concerts," Van Vechten urged the orchestras accompanying the movies to play good rather than inferior music, new music rather than old; in that way, young people in need of musical education could "pick up the routine of the concert and opera world in a ten weeks' course at the Rialto or the Strand." The suggestion is not

so frivolous as it might at first appear; the age of television has proven the influence of audiovisual media, for good or ill.

In the concluding essay in *Interpreters and Interpretations,* Van Vechten divided musical criticism into two classes, the first represented by critics who try to render their feelings by quoting other writers, Beethoven's Seventh Symphony inspiring passages from Percy Bysshe Shelley's "Ode to a Skylark," and the second by critics who "bristle . . . with semitechnical conjurations, abjurations, and apostrophes," avoiding all metaphor in favor of a manner "formidable, exegetical, eupeptic, adynamic . . . asthenic." Both types cause indifference, Van Vechten claimed. A unique alternative, on the other hand, might represent Van Vechten himself: "He is accurate without being pedantic; he paints the human side of art. He draws us nearer to compositions by talking about the composers. When he writes of a singer it is not as if he were describing a vocal machine emitting nearly perfect notes; he pictures a human being applying herself to her art; his account is vivid, often humorous. He enlivens us and he awakens our interest. This is not altogether a matter of style: it is a matter of feeling. The style is perhaps the man!" Above all else, Van Vechten concluded, "criticism should be an expression of personal feeling. Otherwise he [the critic] has no value."

In *The Music of Spain* and *The Merry-Go-Round,* published within six weeks of each other in 1918, Van Vechten offered further musical essays. The former was the first book on the subject in America, and it remains an important reference work. The latter broadened Van Vechten's perspective through various literary subjects: Edgar Saltus; George Moore; modern playwrights Avery Hopwood and Philip Moeller; and several views of contemporary theater. Two essays that looked back nostalgically to personal experience are of greater significance in his own development toward fiction. In each, Van Vechten's sexual attitudes are given some play, however elliptically.

In "An Interrupted Conversation," ostensibly about George Moore, Van Vechten and a friend visit a Paris brothel. When the proprietor offers girls to both of them, Van Vechten cries out, "Je suis puceau!" as his excuse for demurring. In "Au Bal Musette," he and an unnamed Fania Marinoff visit cafés and bars reflecting the world of Simone Signoret in *Casque d'Or,* which he so much admired in later years, but his companion's attitude is unaccounted for and his own is curiously aloof from the menacing eroticism for which he accounts. The essays are both unsatisfactory because his intentions are only tentative, although he chose to preserve them in his later collection of autobiographical essays, *Sacred and Profane Memories,* which followed his novels. The use of personal incident begins in *The Merry-Go-Round,* pointing the way toward his fiction, and on the manuscript of *The Music of Spain,* completed about the same time, Van Vechten noted as a possible title "The Life and Works of Peter Whiffle." *Peter Whiffle: His Life and Works* had begun to take shape a year earlier.

In 1917, Van Vechten wrote three drafts of a piece of fiction called "Undecided Sasha," a series of incidents loosely based on the behavior and personalities of the poet Donald Evans and the playwright Avery Hopwood (whose nickname was Sasha), both intimate friends. Two years later, in an essay called "La Tigresse," Peter Whiffle first turns up as a companion. At what point the character took shape in Van Vechten's mind is difficult to determine; he later said he conceived of "a sort of loose biographical form, a free fantasia in the manner of a Liszt Rhapsody," presumably after September 1920. It is more likely that the personage, the

doppelgänger—named Peter Whiffle or not— had been with him from his youth. There was often a companion, named or unnamed, with him in his essays.

As early as 1905, in writing his Chicago gossip columns, Van Vechten was frequently accompanied by "The Angel Child," an audacious and impertinent friend who expressed naughty opinions, like some ventriloquist's wise dummy. In Van Vechten's case, then and later, the dummy was invariably glamorous, invariably male. If the relationship in *Peter Whiffle* is never sexual, it is at least sexually ambivalent, and in the novels that follow *Peter Whiffle* the characters who seem to speak most often for Van Vechten—female as well as male—are always sexually aloof. Both Sasha and Peter derive from "The Angel Child," but after *Peter Whiffle* was completed, Van Vechten withdrew from direct participation entirely, hiding behind the disguises of various fictional characters. Peter Whiffle himself is only tentatively fictional, and *Peter Whiffle: His Life and Works* may not be a novel after all.

Peter Whiffle first appears in print in *In the Garret,* Van Vechten's last collection of essays, except for two volumes of reprints during the 1920's. *In the Garret* is more personal than any of the earlier books, and only two or three of the papers are devoted exclusively to music. An autobiographical account of an encounter with a religious cult in the Bahamas, "The Holy Jumpers," is of interest, and an evocative portrait of Oscar Hammerstein, redoubtable impresario of opera and inventor of cigarmaking machines, is one of Van Vechten's most successful essays. His seminal essay on "The Negro Theatre" gives the collection its permanent value. "La Tigresse," in which Peter Whiffle is first named, employs a method of digression that never entirely disappeared from Van Vechten's work, introducing materials not directly relevant, even in his novels. Lengthy, discursive passages of various interests simply interrupt the flow of the narrative, and lists of words, titles, catalogs, and examples become self-indulgences.

Van Vechten inserted a two-page essay on book dummies—those mock-up volumes designed to reflect the eventual appearance of a binding—in *Peter Whiffle* merely because it amused him. At another point in this book, when Carl and Peter are having a rambling discussion about criticism and attendant arts, Edith Dale is made to say, at considerable length, the entire contents of a letter that Mabel Dodge had written to Van Vechten following publication of his book about cats, *The Tiger in the House.*

Van Vechten compiled his huge treatise on cats in 1920, before turning to fiction. It remains without much dispute the best book ever written about cats, but "compiled" is the appropriate verb to describe Van Vechten's method. It demonstrates the essential approach in many of his essays: to collect dozens, even hundreds, of examples from his reading on a particular subject, and then to stitch them together in his own unique prose. Divided into a number of chapters, *The Tiger in the House* treats the history of cats in law, music, art, and poetry. It has a series of stories about literary figures who admired cats, a chapter on traits, a chapter on cat-haters—all, as he wrote to Alfred Knopf, with the history "subtly inserted like castor oil in a sweet drink." Elsewhere, he compiled a book of thirteen cat stories, *Lords of the Housetops,* and wrote a brief biography of one of his own cats, Feathers, for the Random House Prose Quartos. Ironically, *Feathers,* his most often reprinted work, is uncharacteristically sentimental, free of all his customary mannerisms, and even moving.

His work in nonfiction did not cease with *The Tiger in the House,* but after completing it he turned his attention primarily to fiction. A critic's arteries began to harden after the age of forty, he half-seriously believed, and "prejudices were formed which precluded the possibility of the welcoming of novelty." As a critic, Van Vechten lacked the degree of academic insight that usually marks American critical writing. He was more European, which is to suggest more personal, in writing about matters of deep concern to him, and frequently more amusing.

One inevitably feels that Van Vechten genuinely enjoyed what he wrote about. There is rarely any devotion to subjects not of importance to him, and never any anger. To a friend, he once wrote, "Do not dislike people, it is a waste of time, energy, and personality. Cultivate indifference. You cannot possibly consider disliking anyone you haven't loved. It is the reverse of the shield." When he took up Arthur Machen and Ronald Firbank, for quite different reasons, his response to them was genuine and his efforts in gaining popular audiences for them in America were tireless. His unpaid press-agentry for Gertrude Stein began in 1914, with an article in *Trend,* "How to Read Gertrude Stein," as cogent as anything written about her during her long career; and his devotion to her continued long after her death. He interested editors and publishers in her work; he encouraged her American lecture tour; he convinced Random House to become her exclusive American publisher; he edited a volume of her selected writings and another of her unpublished plays; acting as literary executor, in collaboration with Yale University, he edited eight posthumous volumes of her unpublished writings. Time has vindicated his constancy on her behalf, now that the academies have admitted her.

Van Vechten was equally capable of bringing

some degree of such devotion to less controversial figures. Before the 1920's, for example, Herman Melville's *Moby Dick* was largely ignored, but at the outset of its revival Van Vechten wrote:

Not only is *Moby Dick* the greatest book that has yet been written by an American but it is also one of the greatest books that has ever been written by anybody. It is epic in its grandeur, and its style is the style of masterpieces. . . . Of only one other book produced in America can anything like as much be said and that is Mark Twain's *Huckleberry Finn*. . . . *Moby Dick* is an allegory of man's struggle with the supernal forces of the infinite, and his final complete routing, for man is always worsted in this inequal battle. . . . *Moby Dick* is certainly America's masterpiece and it will still be read in a century or so when all but the student will believe that Nathaniel Hawthorne is the name of a general in the Confederate Army. . . .

These observations appeared in an essay dated August 1921, only in Yiddish translation, in *Die Zeit*. Two months later, Van Vechten wrote in praise of Melville's later novels as well, notably *Pierre,* which other reputable writers at the time had accused of "raving over moral ambiguities." Van Vechten read it with two earlier novels as "a kind of tragic triptych: *Mardi* is a tragedy of the intellect, *Moby Dick* a tragedy of the spirit, and *Pierre* a tragedy of the flesh; *Mardi* is a tragedy of heaven, *Moby Dick* a tragedy of hell, and *Pierre* a tragedy of the world we live in." *The Confidence Man,* dismissed by others as "middle-western sketches," Van Vechten contended was Ralph Waldo Emerson in a "great transcendental satire." These assertions appeared in an essay in *Double Dealer* in January 1922, a date Melville enthusiasts might well follow with an exclamation mark rather than a period.

The sexual ambiguity in Melville's novels may explain part of Van Vechten's attraction, for disparate writers in whom he took interest share that particular quality in their work. Ronald Firbank's perverse fiction, of which Van Vechten made a fairly obvious imitation in his novel *The Blind Bow-Boy,* was frequently though not always with justification linked to his own. Henry Blake Fuller is a more telling case in point. Nearly forgotten after a brief popularity during the 1890's—both Gareth Johns and Peter Whiffle admired his *Chevalier of Pensieri-Vani* extravagantly—Fuller wrote several books about Italy and about Chicago that met with increasing indifference from the public. He drifted into a decade of silence after 1919, when he published *Bertram Cope's Year,* a novel with homosexual characters. His friends seem to have been embarrassed by it, and his readers seem not to have understood it. Critics simply ignored it.

As Van Vechten realized, Fuller had chosen a subject "generally taboo in English literature," nor did "the love that dare not speak its name" get named in 1922. Van Vechten called *Bertram Cope's Year* an "ironic comedy" and suggested that Thomas Mann's *Death in Venice* was "a tragic version of the same subject." Bertram Cope is an androgynous beau ideal whose catastrophic effect on a variety of people—most profoundly on a middle-aged bachelor—is emotional rather than physical, spun in Fuller's "studiedly restrained manner." Van Vechten could name no other American writer "who could have surveyed the ambiguous depths of the problem presented so thoroughly, and at the same time so discreetly."

Sex is never a "problem" in Van Vechten's own novels, but it is never exploited either; they are much involved with sex, as Edward Lueders once suggested, but they are rarely sexy. Sex is always present but always curiously neutral.

Once Van Vechten wrote to Mabel Dodge Luhan that his intention in fiction was to "awaken unconscious echoes of the past, to render to shadows their real importance." At midcareer, several successful novels behind him, he claimed that he never thought at all about sex: "It plays around here and there, but that's not what my books are about. They seem to me to be books about a man who is alone in the world and is very sad."

Whether or not Van Vechten was entirely truthful with himself, he later claimed he had to be told that *Peter Whiffle* was a novel. Certainly, great chunks of it read like his essays, a thread of narrative tying together accounts of his various enthusiasms and interests. As mentioned earlier, Carl Van Vechten is the narrator of a biography of a friend named Peter Whiffle, whom he meets for the first time in Paris in May 1907—the occasion of Van Vechten's first trip abroad—and not again until the winter of 1912–1913 in New York. Together they travel back to Europe for a holiday at Edith Dale's Villa Allegra in Florence. They meet again in New York, just before the outbreak of the war in Europe, and for the last time in 1919, when Peter dies, or when Van Vechten kills him off. The hiatuses, and Van Vechten's own activities during them, are worth remarking. At the beginning of their association, Peter plans to write a book that from his avowed intentions will be studied and precious, but later he opts to write the great proletarian novel. He dies having written nothing, following the period during which Van Vechten's collections of essays were published.

The use of the double is not unique. In *Peter Whiffle,* Carl and Peter serve as each other's alter ego, and fairly conventionally so. One senses, even within the contrivance of their friendship, that they are "something of a necessity" for each other, although Van Vechten calls Carl "something of a necessity" for Peter. As doppelgänger, Peter fulfills a number of desires and pastimes, beginning with casual affairs in Paris, surpassing good looks, and a resolute freedom from convention.

The autobiographical parallels work ironically: Van Vechten's first trip to Europe was to expand his musical knowledge and to marry his first wife; Carl's first trip is given over entirely to his involvement with Peter, whose flamboyance and literary intentions perplex him. Peter's background is Van Vechten's own, transplanted from Iowa to Ohio, and anyone at all familiar with *The Tattooed Countess* will have no trouble identifying it, despite the change in geography. By the time they meet again in New York, the "necessity" Carl has become as "the proper outlet for his artistic explosions" leads to Peter's "necessity" for Van Vechten as well: "Alas, both for my career as a private citizen and my career as a writer I find it impossible to limit myself," he had written two years before in "La Tigresse." "I cannot get along without knowing Peter Whiffle. . . ." At the early death Van Vechten arranges for him in the book, Peter hopes he has communicated something of "sympathy and enthusiasm" and wonders what he might have accomplished had he found a new "formula," a "white magic" to communicate what he has loved. Perhaps it was necessary to lay his "Peter Whiffle" to rest before Van Vechten could move on to the more conventional novels that followed.

Interestingly, Peter never knows any of Carl's friends intimately, except Edith Dale who is Mabel Dodge; nor does he ever meet any of Carl's friends at all after 1914, when Van Vechten married Fania Marinoff and began writing books. In the preface to *Peter Whiffle,* Carl observes that Edith Dale's "interest, in a sense, was as special as my own. Her loss was not so personal, however, nor her grief so deep."

Elsewhere, Van Vechten wrote that Mabel Dodge had "done more to encourage a point of view, if it was only by way of argument, than any one else I have known," paying tribute to her "original and extraordinary" taste, and her influence on his own taste. If Carl was "present, indeed, at the bombing of more than one discarded theory" of Peter's, so was Mabel Dodge present as Van Vechten matured. When Carl first meets Peter, he exclaims, "You must tell me who you are." They have met through Martha Baker, a Chicago portrait painter who is having trouble getting past Carl's mask; when Peter arrives, Carl suddenly has "the right expression." Several days later, following a long conversation with two new acquaintances about inspiration and art and the difference between public and critical response to art, Peter arrives. "I am glad to see you," he cries to Carl, and he is "burning for adventures." Peter then engages in a series of outrageous and amusing stunts: "all gay, irresponsible and meaningless, perhaps, but *gay*," Carl calls them, but they sink Peter into misery and despair.

The period of Van Vechten's own unhappy first marriage is referred to, in Peter's life, as "phantom years," and in reply to Carl's later query about them, he answers, "I lived." When they renew acquaintance for the last time, Peter has aged a great deal, having rid himself of "many excrescences and extraneities, the purely adscititious qualities, charming though they might be, which masked his personality. He had, indeed, discovered himself. . . ." during the period that Van Vechten wrote six books of essays. Of the most recent, *In the Garret,* Peter says, "You are becoming freer. . . . You are loosening your tongue; your heart is beating faster. In time you may liberate those subconscious ideas which are entangled in your very being. It is only your conscious self that prevents you from becoming a really interesting

writer. . . . You must search the heart; the mind is negligible in literature as in all other forms of art. . . . That is the lesson . . . that the creative or critical artist can learn from the interpreter, the lesson of the uses of personality."

Peter then simply languishes toward death, at the end feeling he has accomplished nothing but at the same time believing that his life has not been a failure. He has communicated something of his love for "ideas and objects and people"; next to creation, he believes, affection perhaps "is everything." *Peter Whiffle* is not, then, a novel; it is a necessary, personal exorcism. Van Vechten never again wrote anything so intriguing, but two of his subsequent novels are of considerable historical significance: *Nigger Heaven* for its role in the Harlem Renaissance, *Parties* as an epitaph for the decade of the 1920's. The others are of some interest as well.

Three of the novels might be collected as a trilogy called *The Splendid Drunken Twenties,* a phrase Van Vechten used in describing a narrow world "easily encompassed without the aid of a bicycle; glamorous with literary teas, encounters with the great, in speakeasies as conspicuously popular as the coffeehouses of Addison's day, and bathtubs so full of synthetic gin that ablutions had to be performed extramural."

Van Vechten came to fiction when he was past forty, with none of the usual angst that can riddle young novelists. Few writers more clearly indicate the intellectual climate—or lack of it—during the 1920's. It was a period when presumably sophisticated readers could proclaim Joseph Hergesheimer America's foremost novelist, and critics like Carl Van Doren and H. L. Mencken could proclaim James Branch Cabell a "great" writer, the same adjective they used in describing Melville and Joseph Conrad.

The frequently repeated story about Van Vechten's torchlight parade through the streets of Manhattan in honor of Elinor Wylie's arch novel, *Jennifer Lorn,* has proven apocryphal, but its evolution is symptomatic of a fashionable intelligentsia eager for "fine writing." Alfred Kazin dismissed this particular quartet because it represented the "ambitious baroque luxury of a period that had finally attained a self-conscious splendor of its own." Cabell, Hergesheimer, Van Vechten, and Wylie were, in Kazin's damning title for them, "The Exquisites."

All four fell into a common age group, far removed from the flaming youth that gave rise to F. Scott Fitzgerald. Cabell had been a practicing novelist for twenty years with a small audience; Hergesheimer had been a painter, then a writer, for an equal length of time, quietly turning out historical fiction in relative obscurity; Wylie had been writing poetry since 1912. By the time these three came into their momentary fashion they were, like Van Vechten, seasoned writers in their forties, ten or fifteen years past the age Fitzgerald equated with senility—when, as he was wont to say, everything would be over.

Beginning with *The Blind Bow-Boy* (1923), the cheerfully perverse novel Van Vechten said he wrote "with the greatest of ease" immediately after *Peter Whiffle,* to the series of vignettes in *Firecrackers* (1925), to the humorless drinking and carnality of *Parties* (1930), Van Vechten's trilogy documents the rise and fall in New York of the decade that took its sex and liquor rather more seriously than it pretended to. Despite his own involvement, he maintained a fairly steady objectivity, even though the air of self-parody in the novels is not sufficiently paramount to suggest that Van Vechten was always aware of the essential emptiness of his material. Still, his detachment is unusually clear; in part, perhaps, because of his earlier experience as a professional writer and because of

his age. Each of the novels in its own way reflects the rebellion of the 1920's against the mores of the previous generation, but Van Vechten's critical judgment does not always seem at ease with his inventiveness.

Of *Firecrackers,* the second of these novels, Mencken wrote: "Human life is here depicted as gay, senseless, and orgiastic. Is this realism too? Is it, in fact, a more penetrating and accurate realism than that of the orthodox realists?" If, as Alfred Kazin contended, Van Vechten was "giggling steadily at his own pretensions," the juxtaposition of content and comment is sometimes jarring. Two years earlier, in *The Blind Bow-Boy,* Van Vechten's worldly Campaspe established an attitude for nearly all of the novels: "a book . . . should have the swiftness of melodrama, the lightness of farce, to be a real contribution to thought. . . . How could anything serious be hidden more successfully than in a book which pretended to be light and gay?"

The Blind Bow-Boy tries hard to live up to Campaspe's description, but Van Vechten's analytical mind gets in the way of his Firbankian revelry, and the seams often show. The lengthy philosophical digressions that seem inevitably right in *Peter Whiffle,* the outré catalogs, obscure quotations, and other digressions emerge from the action less naturally. Readers must find themselves impatient to return to Van Vechten's cheerful bildungsroman: Harold Prewett, a conservative innocent fresh from college, is deposited by his father in the midst of a sophisticated, uninhibited court of the kind Van Vechten described in his essay about the novels of Edgar Saltus, in which "there is no poverty. . . . His creatures do not toil. Usually, they cut coupons off bonds. Sometimes they write or paint, but for the most part they are free to devote themselves exclusively to the pursuit of emotional experience, eating, drinking, reading, and travelling the while." The elder Prewett has advertised for a tutor, a "young man of good character but no moral sense." Paul Moody, an effete young man who looks like Rupert Brooke, takes on the job of educating Harold, who has reached the age of twenty-two with "a slender philosophy" that there are unknowns in the world and a sense of shame that his father must be in business. "We try to keep that sort of thing in the background," Van Vechten's worldly Campaspe declares. "We try not to be aware of it. It is the smart thing to do nothing."

In addition to Paul, the cast of amiable characters designed to instruct Harold include Bunny Hugg, who writes "music of the future," compositions of two or three measures' length; a Coney Island snake charmer named Zimbule O'Grady; Ronald, Duke of Middlebottom, who dresses up like a sailor but carries an umbrella and has his stationery engraved with the pronouncement "A thing of beauty is a boy forever"; and the inscrutable Campaspe Lorillard, who wears geraniums at her waist, has "a good artificial colour," and talks just like Carl Van Vechten.

Harold's father has exposed his son to this essentially friendly decadence to turn him against it. Harold embraces the life he was expected to renounce, shifts from his wife of two weeks to a brief but steamy affair with the snake charmer, and, after a momentary pause over Campaspe's impassive attractions, sails for Europe with the infamous Duke of Middlebottom. The determined frivolity of the plot does not mask Van Vechten's fascination with the waywardness of love, or with what masquerades for love. When Campaspe's husband, frustrated by her remoteness—indeed, she seems uninterested in any kind of sexual alliance—turns to the snake charmer for solace, Campaspe asks rhetorically, "Cupid, why will you always be so

romantic? Will you never believe me when I tell you that I don't care in the least what you do? I should never have married you if I had planned to worry about you." For Campaspe, "Indifference is the purer method."

Early in the novel, musing over a book that has bored her, Campaspe reflects: "How is it possible to read an author who never laughed? For it was only behind laughter that true tragedy could lie concealed, only the ironic author who could awaken the deeper emotions. The tragedies of life . . . were either ridiculous or sordid. The only way to get the sense of this absurd, contradictory, and perverse existence into a book was to withdraw from the reality." Following this, Van Vechten supplied a catalog of books Campaspe knows that illustrate the point, reinforced with quotations to prove it. Campaspe goes through four cigarettes during this particular internal monologue, which is not the only one in the novel.

Van Vechten tried hard to be Campaspe's "ironic author," but after *Peter Whiffle, The Blind Bow-Boy* is a disappointment because the elements will not fuse, perhaps because they are too disparate. At one extreme, Campaspe's reflections, for all their interest, simply hold up the novel's progress; at the other extreme, Van Vechten's perversity runs away with him and yearns for shock: "I don't know what reminds me," Paul says, "but have you heard about Bunny? He's had Zimbule's name tattooed on his person so cunningly that it can only be deciphered under certain conditions." After the quick laugh, readers might wonder, too, what reminded him. If *The Blind Bow-Boy* was trying to be light and gay, Van Vechten did not entirely succeed in disguising its urge to instruct, even though he had "sworn before a notary public," according to the dust jacket, that no ideas were concealed beneath the surface.

The voices of critic and novelist merged fully,

however, in *The Tattooed Countess,* Van Vechten's third novel and his own favorite, written in 1924. As social criticism, it shows rather than tells; its milieu is accurate without exaggerating anything, although the temptation toward parody must have been strong; compared to the marionettes of *The Blind Bow-Boy,* its people are often painfully real. The thinly veiled self-portrait in Gareth Johns reflects Van Vechten's own frustrations as a boy of seventeen. Ella Nattatorrini, despite her lusting after teenagers and her tattoo, is so vulnerably human that she arouses compassion far more readily than the world-weary, inscrutable Campaspe ever can. Most tellingly, Gareth's frustrated, lonely schoolteacher, Lennie Colman, demands the heart's attention. Gareth and the countess will somehow escape the town, but Lennie is rooted there, not only by "the treadmill she would be forced to walk until the end of her days," teaching school to support her parents, but by her own repression. When she finally expresses her love for Gareth, it is too late; the countess' glamour has intervened, and Gareth can see Lennie Colman only as "a sentimental old maid." The lightness of Van Vechten's touch—what Sinclair Lewis called his "insouciant flippancy"—is cruelly successful in making the realism of this "romantic novel with a happy ending" all the more bitter.

Van Vechten actually subtitled *Firecrackers,* which followed in 1925, "a realistic novel," although it returned in manner and for some of its characters to *The Blind Bow-Boy.* Into the lives of Campaspe Lorillard and Paul Moody, the latter now married to an elephantine, rich widow, comes Gunnar O'Grady. Like Billy Budd or Bertram Cope or perhaps Peter Whiffle, he is a beau ideal whose mysterious appeal even leads others to believe that at times he is crowned with a halo. Everyone loves him; no one understands him, although Paul, who is

first attracted, tries hard. Gunnar reads the Persian poets in search of the perception of truth, longs to have sparred in Hell's Kitchen, and tells Paul about "a hive of thrifty English bees" that, transported to the West Indies, stopped saving their honey because there were too many flowers, and debauched themselves by stinging the natives. "Everything," Gunnar contends, "is everybody's business, . . . only you've got to make it *your* business and not mere vulgar curiosity in someone else's."

Paul is desperate for an explanation of this "philosophy of life or a mode of living that makes you happy, or healthy, or at least amuses you. . . ." Van Vechten's casting of Gunnar's response points up where *Firecrackers* is leading: "What do you want me to do? O'Grady questioned him sadly, peering at the same time out into the steel-blue atmosphere, splashed with the warm glow of the street-lamps. A feeble voice in the distance could be heard calling, Sex Weekly! Sex Weekly!"

Gunnar is apparently disinterested in sex—at least he thinks he is—but eventually he loses his halo, as it were, to Paul's mistress, a conniving flapper named Wintergreen Waterbury, proving himself a prey to the same human limitations as everyone else, except, of course, for Campaspe.

Gunnar's adventures unite several of the vignettes in *Firecrackers,* a title Gareth Johns explains as representing "the incoherence of life," like "a packet of firecrackers," the first one firing the next, until they have all exploded. Contrarily, he observes, if the first is not fired, the packet is only "a collection of separate entities, . . . but if you avoid the explosions you perdurably avoid intercourse."

Johns, now a celebrated novelist, speaks for his own creator, extending earlier reflections of Campaspe's about fiction: "It doesn't seem to occur to the crowd that it is possible for an au-

thor to believe that life is largely without excuse, that if there is a God he conducts the show
aimlessly, if not, indeed, maliciously, that men
and women run around automatically seeking
escapes from their troubles and outlets for their
lusts. The crowd is still more incensed when an
author who believes these things refuses to write
about them seriously." *Firecrackers* contains
some memorable set pieces, and they seem,
after the fact, much a part of the same packet,
although in a first reading the novel seems dis-
jointed. What Gunnar represents, rather than
Gunnar himself, draws them together.

At an elaborate party, the wealthy host offers
some of his guests an 1804 Napoleon brandy.
At first it is pronounced "marvelous," "deli-
cious," "exquise"; then the host is not certain:
"There were two carafes on the shelf. One of
them certainly contains 1804 brandy. The other
holds some whiskey left over from our bootlegger's latest call." The guests begin to sample
both, arguing which is brandy, which is whiskey. One person insists that the brandy is
scotch; another, blindfolded for the test, contra-
dicts his own judgment; while Paul executes a
few steps of the Charleston, Campaspe pronounces the contents of both bottles identical.
Finally, they decide to ask the bartenders: "The
servants readily agreed to decide the matter,
but when George handed them the carafes it
was discovered that both were empty."

Elsewhere, other fads of the 1920's are given
free rein: Pinchon's Prophylactic Plan, a spoof
on private schools for the children of wealthy
parents, is predicated on "Deep breathing while
standing on the head during the simultaneous
consideration of the ultimate oneness of God
with humankind, . . . and identity of the som-
ersault with the freedom of the will. . . ." Van
Vechten also supplied a problem child to inspire
it. Her name is Consuelo, and she speaks
French, wears orchids and sables, and has an
intimidating IQ and a crush on Gunnar
O'Grady.

Firecrackers takes a jaundiced view of big
business on Wall Street as well, when Paul goes
to work out of boredom and quickly acquires
plenty of money and a mistress in "an adventure replete with thrills, false trails, happy discoveries, comic coincidences. There was so
much, indeed, of sportsman's luck in everything
that went on there that Wall Street was prone
to impress him as a kind of glorified Monte
Carlo. . . ."

At the other extreme in *Firecrackers* is an
account of the death of Ella Nattatorrini, the
tattooed countess. Aging, and abandoned by a
final young lover, she has returned to New York
and, knowing death is near, summons a priest
to give her final absolution. Then, after recounting to Campaspe her long series of opportunistic
gigolos—Gareth Johns included—and what
she calls her wickedness, "weary lassitude"
gives way to a "grisly leer," for she is convinced
that in His mercy, God is going to send her "a
young, beautiful priest!" The countess cries out
for her teeth, her comb, her lipstick, and she
urges Campaspe to strew the bed with the
tuberoses and white violets that decorate her
room. "Gruesome in this ghastly makeup, horrible in its wild expression of forlorn and un-
gratified lust," she awaits the holy father. But
even in death she is "doomed to disappointment. The priest was an old man."

The scene gains its strength in part because
Campaspe later finds it "inextricably complicated and confused in her mind with the
thought of her own great desire" for Gunnar.
The attraction is mutual but both fear "the ar-
duous rigors of sex." Gunnar would stamp it
out; Campaspe now knows "no life is possible
which excludes sex."

At the beginning of the novel, Gunnar has
started to tell Paul about the philosophy of Hip-

pias, then changes his mind in favor of Darwin's profligate bees who feed on their own reserves; now he tells Campaspe of Hippias, who contended "that one should cultivate everything inside oneself." Rather than risking his free will through his "awful agony of love" for Campaspe—there is no doubt about her own self-possession—Gunnar runs away again, as he has several times earlier in the novel. Campaspe observes that his halo seems to have begun to flicker uncertainly, and even in the face of love Campaspe's preoccupation with her own implacable superiority triumphs. Van Vechten's clever vignettes and extravagant wit only partially mask an essentially selfish philosophy. The brittle ironies of *Firecrackers* clearly anticipate those of *Parties,* his final novel, but two intervening fictional excursions—one to Harlem, one to Hollywood—interrupted the trilogy.

Nigger Heaven concluded one phase of Van Vechten's involvement with black arts and letters. During the early 1920's, when he had become acquainted with several black writers and the coming Harlem Renaissance, he published a number of articles and essays on spirituals and the blues, on singers as disparate as Bessie Smith, Paul Robeson, and Ethel Waters, and on black subject matter in the theater and in fiction. He also arranged for his publisher to take on Langston Hughes's first book of poems and for Countee Cullen's poetry to be published in *Vanity Fair,* the popular and influential magazine in which many of his own essays had appeared. All of this material as well as his subsequent writings about black artists and many of his photographs of them were collected in 1979 in *"Keep A-Inchin' Along,"* demonstrating how far ahead of his times he really was.

When his friend James Weldon Johnson, the black humanitarian and writer, urged Van Vechten to turn his experience and enthusiasm into fiction, *Nigger Heaven* resulted, part sociological tract, part aesthetic anthropology, and certainly part delineation of Harlem's erotic underworld. The novel's success with most white critics and its failure with most black ones may stem from the fascinating accounts of a glamorous milieu for sensual pleasures, although only about a third of *Nigger Heaven* occurs in Harlem's cabarets and bedchambers. It may have been difficult to take Van Vechten seriously, for he was well known not only as a writer of light, popular novels, but also as a dilettante, flamboyant in his dress and behavior, and a frequent patron in black nightclubs.

Many familiar Van Vechten types turn up in *Nigger Heaven,* and at a time when black intellectuals strove to gain respect for the race and its achievements, the novel was easy to misread, reinforcing stereotypes for white readers, embarrassing black ones. Actually, Van Vechten was more successful with those characters who reminded his readers of earlier extravagant personalities. The black social queen, Adora Boniface, for example; Lasca Sartoris, the steamy courtesan; and Randolph Pettijohn, the paunchy bolita king, like the elegant whores and Harlem dandies, are vastly more engaging than his protagonists.

Van Vechten's pathetic librarian, Mary, and Byron, an angry boy who atones for his lack of talent by blaming the white world for his failure to write anything of value, hardly inspire much empathy. Most of the novel is devoted to their antiseptic love affair and to literary and sociological discussions among the black intelligentsia, reinforced by Van Vechten's familiar strings of quotations and catalogs. But some readers never got past the title to discover any of this, nor so far as the footnote that explained the race's fierce resentment of the word "nigger."

Early in the novel, at the conclusion of a deliberately sleazy prologue, a young prostitute "rapturously" calls Harlem "Nigger Heaven": "I jes' nacherly think dis heah is Nigger

Heaven!" Later, the irony is underlined when Byron reacts to the epithet:

"Nigger Heaven! . . . That's what Harlem is. We sit in our places in the gallery of this New York theatre and watch the white world sitting down below in the good seats in the orchestra. Occasionally they turn their faces up towards us, their hard, cruel faces, to laugh or sneer, but they never beckon. It never seems to occur to them that Nigger Heaven is crowded, that there isn't another seat, that something has to be done. . . . Harlem! The Mecca of the New Negro! My God!"

Van Vechten applauds without apology and criticizes without condemning nearly every facet of black Manhattan. All his recognizable mannerisms are present, although rather more resolutely under control. Too frequently, the writing lacks his usual elegance and becomes pedantic in its zeal to justify the black intellectual. Similarly, his familiar, mannered dialogue seems stilted.

The reader's eye and ear may be at fault, of course, preoccupied with the characters as blacks rather than with blacks as the characters, especially when they speak about themselves. Often enough, though, the writing carries sufficient strength, and many of its disclosures must have come as revelations:

"Try Harlem, will you? Dick's lip curled cynically. I guess you won't find that much easier. Howard here is a lawyer, but the race doesn't want coloured lawyers. If they're in trouble they go to white lawyers, and they go to white banks and white insurance companies. They shop on white One hundred and twenty-fifth Street. Most of 'em, he added fiercely, pray to a white God. You won't get much help from the race."

Such passages led more than one black friend to suggest that Van Vechten's honest observa-tions would be regarded as betraying "family secrets."

Against this background, Mary and Byron struggle to survive; but he is too easily enraged by iniquitous discrimination, and she is not strong enough to give him stability. Byron succumbs to Lasca Sartoris, surely Van Vechten's most sublimely erotic figure, only to be jilted by her for Pettijohn. The melodramatic conclusion, in which Byron senselessly shoots Pettijohn, who has already been wounded by a Harlem pimp, is too theatrically tidy for Van Vechten's more serious intentions in *Nigger Heaven*.

The novel is the most thorough piece of writing Van Vechten ever achieved, and its successive drafts show the extreme care he took in its preparation. If it is not his best novel or his most satisfying one, it is sufficiently significant for its influence. Novels by Claude McKay, Wallace Thurman, Rudolph Fisher, and Arna Bontemps derive from it in a variety of ways, and a larger, white audience was created for such novels by it.

Since its publication, various critics have accused *Nigger Heaven* of capitalizing on the lurid aspects of Harlem in the 1920's and Van Vechten on the work of young black writers. Langston Hughes dismissed such charges as "sheer poppycock," contending that "bad Negro writers were bad long before *Nigger Heaven* appeared on the scene, and would have been bad anyway, had Mr. Van Vechten never been born." Bad before *Nigger Heaven*, as Hughes claimed in his autobiography, *The Big Sea*, they may have been, but publicized they were not. Certainly on occasion Van Vechten was attracted to black writing, performing, or painting simply because it was black and not because it was exceptional.

The residual effect of such zeal may explain some negative attitudes toward *Nigger Heaven*. Nevertheless, the novel went through a dozen printings in America and in England, and it was translated into ten languages, doubtless partly because of its notoriety. Perhaps the speed with which Van Vechten had discovered and documented black life offended many people. Perhaps, too, an age that thrived on fads is itself open to suspicion. On the other hand, his passionate commitment to black arts and letters did not cease with the end of the Harlem Renaissance. Until his death, he continued to amass material for the truly remarkable James Weldon Johnson Memorial Collection of Negro Arts and Letters, which he founded at Yale University in 1941.

In 1927, the year after the publication of *Nigger Heaven,* Van Vechten went to Hollywood out of curiosity over the peculiar film version of *The Tattooed Countess,* starring Pola Negri, and called *A Woman of the World.* It bore little resemblance to the novel, and Hollywood proved to bear little resemblance to reality, according to a quartet of amusing essays Van Vechten wrote for *Vanity Fair.* Not surprisingly, his next novel, called *Spider Boy,* was "a scenario for a moving picture" in which a celebrated writer, fleeing New York to avoid the publicity following a Broadway success, gets sidetracked on his way to Santa Fe by an exotic movie queen who spirits him off to Hollywood to write a film for her.

Van Vechten's style had grown more assured over the decade, but in *Spider Boy* it came dangerously close to self-parody, and despite the calculated subject matter there were lamentable lapses into Mack Sennett slapstick. It is insufficient, for example, for Van Vechten's hero, Ambrose Deacon, to balance precariously on the mudguard of a milk truck in which he is trying to escape the clutches of Imperia Starling, the movie vamp. He is required to fall "flat on his belly in the street" afterward. Similarly, he is slammed by a reflector in one of the studios and knocked to the floor. He upsets finger

bowls, stumbles over his own feet, and much of the time behaves like a silent screen comedian. The sight gags in one direction are too extravagant, and the satire in the other direction is not sharp enough to be incisive.

Van Vechten does manage a clear enough picture of Hollywood, if actual films produced at that time are any gauge for measuring its excesses, and several thinly disguised film stars—Pola Negri, Aileen Pringle, Lois Moran, Emil Jannings—participate in the plot and lend a sense of authenticity. Van Vechten's determinedly precious stylistic tricks even seem at home in such a preposterous atmosphere. His big words, dislocated syntaxes, theatrical dialogue, and exaggerated lists are most comfortable in Hollywood. As an indiscreet actress confides:

You see, . . . most of the houses out here are made of stucco. You can kick your foot right through them. You can kick your foot through everything else here too. Nothing is real, except the police dogs and the automobiles, and usually those aren't paid for. To be concrete, there are no stenographers at the studios: they're all secretaries.

Eventually, Ambrose is persuaded to write a screenplay, not without assistance: "When you write a story for the pictures," advises the producer, "always keep in mind . . . the wages of sin is death, but if the motive is moral you can get in quite a bit o' necking." Indeed, someone else will write it for him and use his name: "Where do you think you are?" asks his ghostwriter. "This is Hollywood, HOLLYWOOD, not the Louvre. Of course I know your name isn't worth a damn in pictures. . . . Everybody out here knows it. The point is they want to *think* it is. Why else do you suppose you're hauling in the dough?" The film itself, originally called *Spider Boy,* about a bareback rider in love with a ceiling walker in a circus, turns out to be *Love and Danger,* the same plot but about a Russian spy in drag.

Ambrose marries a pretty starlet in a wedding staged like Paolo Veronese's *The Marriage at Cana,* embellished with a ceiling covered in orchids, a jazz band, fireworks, a parade of peacocks and baboons, turquoise fans and platinum cigarette cases as favors, and among other wedding gifts a solid gold tea service and an embossed silver refrigerator. If Hollywood is different from the rest of the world, the bride explains, blame it on the climate.

Nigger Heaven may have had a negative effect on Van Vechten's customary light touch. As if to recover some of his former equilibrium, he indulged in *Spider Boy* in the kind of farce dead since *The Blind Bow-Boy.* Two years later, with *Parties,* his fiction achieved a new authority, combining all the best elements of his usual insouciance with the sober realities of *Nigger Heaven.* It is a strange and unsettling book, uniquely his own, and in the view of more than one critic his most significant contribution to American letters. In November 1929, two weeks after the stock market crash, Van Vechten began this final part of the trilogy. *The Blind Bow-Boy* and *Firecrackers* smiled at "the splendid drunken twenties," but *Parties* frowned at them; perhaps it wept. Reviewers labeled it "unsavory," "sniggering," "specious," and "cheap"; only George Dangerfield, writing in *Bookman,* recognized it as "a tragedy of manners," damned by the "same fate . . . which overtook an earlier comedy of manners," driven by its own excesses "from the unmoral to the moral."

The manipulation of various plots, which Van Vechten had attempted in *Firecrackers,* worked more successfully in *Parties.* Its vignettes actually supply the only cohesiveness because they echo each other in stultifying repetition. All the familiar devices are at hand: recognizable personalities, thinly disguised, like Scott and Zelda Fitzgerald, Muriel Draper, Louise Hellström, Max Ewing, Aileen Pringle, Van Vechten himself; speakeasies and drawing rooms, sleazy or glamorous; scabrous jokes; exaggerated satire.

Readers sobered by the stock market crash did not welcome a morality play in which nearly all seven of the deadly sins wander aimlessly from drink to drink, avoiding pause for fear of what sobriety might bring. Van Vechten chose familiar types in which to masquerade them, but people who might have grown to imitate the Pauls and Campaspes and Lascas and Peters from earlier books resented discovering themselves. Simone Fly, for instance, resembles "a gay Death." Noma Ridge does not smoke or drink and therefore "atoned for the lack of these semi-precious vices by describing in an endless monotone the various forms of her amorous transports and the characteristics of the persons with whom she enjoyed them." Donald Bliss, New York's best-looking bootlegger, gives the ladies no cause to complain if they are "clever enough to remember the old proverb, Handsome is as handsome does." King Swan stows cigarette ashes in his trouser cuffs, which is "Swan's way." Midnight Blue, an actress parodying the popular Tallulah Bankhead, "takes off her drawers mentally when she talks" and "takes them off literally when she doesn't talk." An aged German Gräfin discovers all of the Old World pleasures denied her in her youth when she discovers the decadent New World of the speakeasy. David and Rilda Westlake share a "damned faithfulness" to each other by deliberately engaging in extramarital affairs. Roy Fern is a haunted, homosexual drug addict. Rosalie Keith gives the worst parties in town, to which everybody goes.

Finally, Hamish Wilding, a descendant of

earlier Van Vechten protagonists, is the Carl Van Vechten of *Peter Whiffle,* but several years older, sadder, wiser. Apparent from the first chapter, he hovers on nearly every page; sardonic and sentimental, he touches the reader only subtly because of the more flamboyant David, whom he loves. Hamish is clearly Van Vechten's "man who is alone," trapped on a treadmill that can lead only to moral suicide. Not surprisingly, David, rather than Hamish, has been involved somehow with Roy Fern. He appears to be bisexual while Hamish, as might be anticipated, seems sexless or at least asexual.

Late in the novel, during an encounter with a black seeress (based on an actual encounter of Van Vechten's at Fannie Hurst's apartment), Hamish learns what Van Vechten may have come to realize through his fiction: "You do not know yourself. . . . You don't know where you are, or who you are, or what you are, or what you want. You are not unhappy, you are miserable. . . ." Hamish must "occasionally do something, out of the way, to behave in a manner that would be considered almost bad form by some of his friends." But the attempt is futile; he cannot break away. David is the active partner here, suffering Hamish's malady, but Hamish is infinitely more tragic, unable to function independently.

Despite the perversions and immorality that both dull and sharpen every situation, the novel's conclusion leaves no doubt about Van Vechten's intentions. Most of the characters gather for a final party, at the Westlake apartment, with the stock market in the process of its crash. "It's just like the opening chorus of an opéra-bouffe," Simone Fly remarks, "all of us here clinking glasses like villagers on the village green." The Gräfin corrects her: "Somehow, it's more like the closing chorus. . . . I think we're all a little tired." The singing stops only with David's hopeless coda. He is not bitter about "the life of our times" and he accepts it "as the best we can do. . . . We're here because we're here, and we should be extremely silly not to make the worst of it."

Those who had been making the worst of it for ten years needed no reminders. On the surface of *Parties,* Van Vechten's world-weary buffoonery, glittering alcoholism, and cheerful carnality hold their usual court, but his omniscience holds everything in severe check. From the first-person narrator in *Peter Whiffle,* through central characters in the intervening novels, Van Vechten took measured steps toward *Parties.* Because Campaspe in *The Blind Bow-Boy* and Gareth—not surprisingly a novelist—in *Firecrackers* are actors, their function as commentators is necessarily constricted by the demands of plot.

In *Parties,* although the responsibility is momentarily shifted from one character to another, none is ever given to extended speculation or internal monologue; the enigmatic narrator takes that responsibility. Some chapters even open with several pages of casual exposition—about the New York season, the weather, or the lindy hop, for example—that are among Van Vechten's happiest catalogs and small essays, but they did not save *Parties* from failure in 1930, despite their ballast.

Parties made an almost wistful condemnation of all the pleasure seekers in all of Van Vechten's novels and of himself as well. The material had run out, of course, but it is also probable that Van Vechten lacked the temperament and the artistic equilibrium to develop much further. Perhaps the artificial comedy of any period is doomed immediately after its own time, just as the Jeremy Colliers are always prepared to grind out a *Short View of Immorality and Profaneness* after the fact. On the other hand, if William Wycherley and William Congreve are capable after more than two centuries of delineating their own times, so is Carl Van Vechten. In the descriptive dialogue that prefaces *Parties,* a character says of himself: "I have got a good deal out of life, perhaps more than was in it." It is an observation Van Vechten might have made of himself when the 1920's finally died.

In the preface to *Peter Whiffle,* Van Vechten quotes a letter, supposedly written to Carl by Peter, explaining how difficult it is to recover moments of vision: "To recapture them I should have been compelled to invent a new style, a style capricious and vibratory as the moments themselves. In this, however, as you know, I have failed, while you have succeeded." Van Vechten's vanity seems pardonable now, although he could hardly have made the claim so securely at the outset of his career as a novelist. His special style, always elegant, always slightly arch, evolved over the decade, but its roots stretched back to the beginning of the century. It was as recognizably his own as the buckteeth that disfigured his otherwise handsome features. "Really, those teeth," Mabel Dodge had thought on first seeing them in 1913. "They seem to have a life of their own apart from the rest of him. They are always trying to get on to the outside of his face." It might be said of his style, which he described best himself, on the dust jacket for *Firecrackers:*

Another of Carl Van Vechten's unimportant, light novels, disfigured by all of this author's customary mannerisms: choice of a meaningless title, rejection of quotation marks, adoption of obsolete or unfamiliar words, an obstinate penchant for cataloguing, and an apparent refusal to assume a reverent attitude towards the ideals of life which are generally held most precious.

Five years later, Van Vechten had completed his last novel, and two years after that, in 1932, he concluded his career as a writer with a group of quasi-autobiographical essays that he revised from earlier versions, in *Sacred and Profane Memories*. It blends all his best qualities and avoids much of the studied archness that frequently weakens the novels. Many of these essays deal with his own past, and his fine sense of nostalgia decorates them handsomely.

In addition to a "long autobiographical rhapsody on American themes," recounting his boyhood in Iowa, *Sacred and Profane Memories* includes accounts of his escape from Europe at the outbreak of World War I, originally intended as part of *Peter Whiffle* and then deleted; his frequently reprinted cat biography, *Feathers;* and amusing essays on breakfasts, the courtship of nightingales, and George Moore; finally, "Notes for an Autobiography," beginning, "I cannot remember the time when I was not trying to write, often with no reasonable amount of skill," and later remembering a question posed to him by the poet-anarchist John Reed: "Why don't you try to write the way you talk?"

With the exception of a collection of his essays about his friends—Theodore Dreiser, Mencken, Cabell, Hergesheimer, Ellen Glasgow, Stein, and others—written for the *Yale University Library Gazette* (1948–1952) at the time he donated their books and letters to the Collection of American Literature at Yale, he wrote little more, although his prodigious correspondence, when published, will eventually illustrate yet another facet of his protean activity. He continued to write book reviews and introductions or prefaces to account for his various enthusiasms, but during the remaining thirty-two years of his life he devoted most of his attention to photography and to the collections he established. Posthumous collections of his writings about the dance and about black arts and letters offer incontrovertible evidence of his significance in these two fields, and some readers will continue to find his essays and novels not only entertaining but enlightening.

Dorothy Parker once complained that "Carl Van Vechten writes with his tongue in someone else's cheek." He took that as a compliment, and long afterward observed that she had delivered her epigram "probably not without envy."

Selected Bibliography

WORKS OF CARL VAN VECHTEN

Music After the Great War. New York: G. Schirmer, 1915.

Music and Bad Manners. New York: Alfred A. Knopf, 1916.

Interpreters and Interpretations, New York: Alfred A. Knopf, 1917.

The Merry-Go-Round. New York: Alfred A. Knopf, 1918.

The Music of Spain. New York: Alfred A. Knopf, 1918.

In the Garret. New York: Alfred A. Knopf, 1919.

Interpreters. New York: Alfred A. Knopf, 1920.

The Tiger in the House. New York: Alfred A. Knopf, 1920.

Peter Whiffle: His Life and Works. New York: Alfred A. Knopf, 1922; revised 1927.

The Blind Bow-Boy. New York: Alfred A. Knopf, 1923.

The Tattooed Countess. New York: Alfred A. Knopf, 1924.

Red. New York: Alfred A. Knopf, 1925.

Firecrackers. New York: Alfred A. Knopf, 1925.

Excavations. New York: Alfred A. Knopf, 1926.

Nigger Heaven. New York: Alfred A. Knopf, 1926.

Spider Boy. New York: Alfred A. Knopf, 1928.

Parties. New York: Alfred A. Knopf, 1930.

Sacred and Profane Memories. New York: Alfred A. Knopf, 1932.

Fragments from an unwritten autobiography. New Haven: Yale University Library, 1955.

The Dance Writings of Carl Van Vechten, edited by Paul Padgette. Brooklyn: Dance Horizons, 1975.

Portraits, The Photography of Carl Van Vechten. Indianapolis: Bobbs-Merrill Company, 1978.

"Keep A-Inchin' Along": Selected Writings of Carl Van Vechten About Black Arts and Letters, edited by Bruce Kellner. Westport, Conn.: Greenwood Press, 1979.

WORKS EDITED BY CARL VAN VECHTEN

Lords of the Housetops: Thirteen Cat Tales. New York: Alfred A. Knopf, 1921.

Rimsky-Korsakov, Nikolai, *My Musical Life.* New York: Alfred A. Knopf, 1923; revised 1942.

Selected Writings of Gertrude Stein. New York: Random House, 1946.

Stein, Gertrude, *Last Operas and Plays.* New York: Rinehart, 1949.

The Yale Edition of the Unpublished Writings of Gertrude Stein. New Haven: Yale University Press, 1951–1958. Eight volumes published under the general editorship of Van Vechten, with an advisory committee of Donald Gallup, Donald Sutherland, and Thornton Wilder.

BIBLIOGRAPHY

Cunningham, Scott. *A Bibliography of the Writings of Carl Van Vechten.* Philadelphia: The Centaur Bookshop, 1924.

Jonas, Klaus W. *Carl Van Vechten: A Bibliography.* New York: Alfred A. Knopf, 1955.

Kellner, Bruce. *A Bibliography of the Work of Carl Van Vechten.* Westport, Conn.: Greenwood Press, 1980.

BIOGRAPHICAL AND CRITICAL STUDIES

Andrews, Clarence. "Le Comte de Cedar Rapids." *The Iowan,* 19:12–14, 48–50 (March 1972).

Beach, Joseph Warren. *The Outlook for American Prose.* Chicago: University of Chicago Press, 1926.

Clark, Emily. *Innocence Abroad.* New York: Alfred A. Knopf, 1931.

Coleman, Leon D. "Carl Van Vechten Presents the New Negro." *Studies in the Literary Imagination,* 7:85–104 (Fall 1974).

Gloster, Hugh M. "The Van Vechten Vogue." *Phylon: The Atlanta University Review of Race and Culture,* 6:310–14 (Fourth Quarter, 1945).

Gordan, John D. "Carl Van Vechten: Notes for an Exhibition in Honor of his Seventy-Fifth Birthday." *Bulletin of the New York Public Library,* 59:331–66 (July 1955).

Helbling, Mark. "Carl Van Vechten and the Harlem Renaissance." *Negro American Literature Forum,* 6:39–47 (July 1976).

Huggins, Nathan Irvin. *Harlem Renaissance.* New York: Oxford University Press, 1971.

Hughes, Langston. *The Big Sea.* New York: Alfred A. Knopf, 1940.

Jablonski, Edward. "Carlo Patriarch." James Lyon. "Evviva Carlo." *American Record Guide,* 26:776–805 (June 1960).

Kazin, Alfred. *On Native Grounds.* New York: Reynal & Hitchcock, 1942.

Kellner, Bruce. *Carl Van Vechten and the Irreverent Decades.* Norman: University of Oklahoma Press, 1968.

———. "Alfred Kazin's Exquisites: An Excavation." *Illinois Quarterly,* 38:45–62 (Fall 1975).

———. "Baby Woojums in Iowa." *Books at Iowa,* 26:3–18 (April 1977).

———. *Friends and Mentors: Richmond's Carl Van Vechten and Mark Lutz.* Richmond, Va.: Boatwright Memorial Library, University of Richmond, 1980.

Kirstein, Lincoln. "Carl Van Vechten, 1880–1964." *Yale University Library Gazette,* 39:157–62 (April 1965).

Lueders, Edward. *Carl Van Vechten and the Twenties.* Albuquerque: University of New Mexico Press, 1955.

———. *Carl Van Vechten.* New York: Twayne Publishers, 1965.

Luhan, Mabel Dodge. *Movers and Shakers.* New York: Harcourt, Brace, 1936.

Schneider, John. "A World of Whiffles." *Wagner Literary Magazine,* 3:26–42 (Fall 1962).

Schuyler, George. "The Van Vechten Revolution." *Phylon,* 11:362–68 (Fourth Quarter, 1950).

Stein, Gertrude. *The Autobiography of Alice B. Toklas.* New York: Harcourt, Brace, 1933.

—*BRUCE KELLNER*

Kurt Vonnegut

1922—

In *Between Time and Timbuktu* Kurt Vonnegut writes: "I have always rigged my stories so as to include myself, and I can't stop now. And I do this so slyly, as do most novelists, that the author *can't* be put on film."

And he does indeed include himself in all his novels, perhaps not always "slyly," but often indirectly and sometimes in the most complex fashion, where the intrusion may not seem obvious. In his fiction—and one senses the same is true in his life—he is an interesting mixture of extrovert and retiring private person. Those contrary impulses add to the complexity, and to the interest, of Vonnegut's presentation of self in his writing, as he successively (and sometimes concurrently) explores and celebrates self, seeks cathartic release, declares personal doubt, deeply held belief, and passing whim, yet also hides and evades, shielding a private self behind irony, persona, and all the other tricks of narration. But whatever their variations in expression, the autobiographical elements in Vonnegut's writing remain so important a source of plot, character, theme, and even technique that they are worth exploring at some length before proceeding to their manifestations in the works themselves.

Vonnegut's forebears came to the United States during the extremely heavy wave of German immigration of the mid-nineteenth century. Both his great-grandfathers, Clemens Vonnegut, Sr., and Peter Lieber, arrived in 1848, and both eventually found their way to Indianapolis, Indiana. Both the Liebers and the Vonneguts prospered and became prominent in a flourishing German-American society.

Peter Lieber bought into a brewery in the 1860's, and with a combination of business acumen and political awareness made his fortune. By the end of the century he retired in style to Germany, leaving his son Albert to run the brewery and to indulge his rather extravagant tastes. Meanwhile, Clemens Vonnegut's son Bernard had become an architect, as did in turn his son Kurt. They were cultured men who revered the arts, especially poetry and music.

Both families, then, became well established professionally and socially, and when, on November 22, 1913, the two were joined by the marriage of Kurt Vonnegut and Albert Lieber's daughter, Edith Sophia Lieber, it was a gala occasion. From this marriage came three children: Bernard, born in 1914; Alice, born in 1917; and Kurt, Jr., born on November 11, 1922. As Vonnegut notes in the reflections on his family in the introduction to *Slapstick*, the children were born into a large, prospering family that offered the support of many close relatives and the security of a preserved cultural heritage.

The security of family and shared culture is something for which Vonnegut was later to yearn nostalgically, because it was already fading when he was born—perhaps even before. Less than a year after his parents' marriage came World War I and, in its wake, the anti-German feelings that swept the United States. One consequence of this sentiment was the prohibition of courses in the German language in many schools.

This wave of prejudice was to have marked economic and social consequences, although Vonnegut himself dwells most on the psychological damage to his family's self-esteem and its heritage of language and culture. The postwar anti-German sentiment gave added impetus and bite to a more universal process implicit in the period that Vonnegut also laments: the general erosion of distinctions of place and heritage in an increasingly mobile, homogenized America.

Other blows were to follow. Prohibition ended the Lieber income from brewing and the Great Depression brought a halt to building and hence unemployment to Vonnegut's architect father. Looking back on those years, Vonnegut has said that the time of the Great Depression was not particularly hard for him. His family never went hungry, and although they moved to a new, somewhat smaller house (designed by his father) their life-style was not crimped.

Yet there were consequences. His father was unemployed, Vonnegut says, for ten years, and during that period he apparently became more and more withdrawn and tentative in his manner. It was something Vonnegut seems never to have forgotten, and his fiction abounds with characters who fall into self-doubt when they lose productive social roles. The strains on Edith Vonnegut were considerable, too, and she perhaps felt the family's financial decline most acutely, having known the style of her flamboy-

ant father before the war. In an attempt to bring in money, Edith began writing stories for magazines, taking writing courses, studying the accepted styles, and sending her work off. None of her stories was published, but her attempt seems to have made an impression on her younger son.

Again, Vonnegut speaks of the Great Depression as not imposing any real hardships on him, and the childhood memories he most often recalls are happy. In interviews he speaks of growing up with his brother and sister, noting particularly that Alice shared his sense of humor. There seems to have been a lot of laughter; he recollects how, as the youngest of the family, he found the surest way to get attention was to be funny. Family movies show him as a toddler always playing the clown. He also speaks, especially in the introduction to *Slapstick*, of enjoying the comedians of the day on radio and in film, and of the lasting impression made on him by Jack Benny and the team of Stan Laurel and Oliver Hardy.

A somewhat different effect of the Great Depression shows up in Vonnegut's education, and this, too, proved to be lasting. Whereas Bernard and Alice had governesses and then went to private schools, Kurt went to public schools, graduating from Shortridge High School. Shortridge was the first high school in America to have a daily newspaper, the *Echo*, and Vonnegut became one of its correspondents.

The connection with news writing was to continue. When Vonnegut went to Cornell University, he wrote for the *Cornell Sun*, and in 1946 he worked as a police reporter for the Chicago City News Bureau. The circumstances that steered him to Shortridge and its daily paper, then, led Vonnegut into the practice of writing working prose regularly and for the critical eyes of his peers. His style as a fiction writer owes much to this apprenticeship.

After Shortridge, Vonnegut went to Cornell in 1941, majoring in biochemistry more because his scientifically minded family expected it of him, he says, than out of any great interest. In any case, Pearl Harbor was to resolve his various uncertainties about both his own future and the European war, and by March 1943 he was in the army.

Vonnegut's enlistment came as a final blow to his mother, who had already become increasingly prone to depression. He sought a special leave to return home for Mother's Day the following year, but the night before he arrived she died of an overdose of sleeping pills. Vonnegut's most direct references to this occurrence come in *Breakfast of Champions*, but there are other indications of its impact in his recurrent references to the mental health of his characters and himself, and conceivably in his portrayals of women and of conjugal relationships.

The trauma of even this loss seems to have been overshadowed by another episode that was to have a major influence on his later literary career. Like other writers he was to draw on experiences of army life, the war, and even of being taken prisoner, but the unique one was to come at Dresden. In December 1944, he was captured by the Germans during the Battle of the Bulge and was subsequently held prisoner in Dresden. There, on the night of February 13, 1945, he was sheltered in an underground meat locker while the Allies unleashed one of the most relentless air raids of the war. A firestorm was created that essentially annihilated the historic half-timbered city and left some 35,000 people dead. After the raid, the prisoners emerged to the blasted landscape that Vonnegut describes so vividly in *Slaughterhouse-Five* (1969).

One would expect this rapid and dramatic series of events to have a profound effect: the shock of battle, of being lost and taken prisoner;

the anxiety and privation of being a prisoner of war (his weight fell from 175 to 134 pounds); the Dresden raid and its aftermath, the horrors intensified when the prisoners were employed to dig through the rubble for corpses. The carnage of that raid must have had a multiple impact on Vonnegut. In the first place he experienced the receiving end of what his own side in the war could do. Was this the work of the "good guys"? Then again the victims were Germans like his own relations on both sides of the Atlantic. Perhaps such thoughts would not come until later, after the more general revulsion at the horror inflicted on the innocent had subsided.

It would be natural, then, for Dresden to seem the quintessence of the absurd and the meaningless in life. It provides a symbol for all that human compassion and reason cry out against, all that they struggle against accepting. For Vonnegut, the experience seems to have been all these things and to have become the subject about which he felt compelled to write and yet with which he still found it hard to come to terms. Wars, fires, and final catastrophes of various kinds appear in his fiction as Vonnegut nudges closer to what he finally confronts in *Slaughterhouse-Five*.

Later, Vonnegut sought to put the Dresden experience into perspective, claiming that it had less influence on his life than *Slaughterhouse-Five* would suggest. Perhaps it was easier for him to make such a disclaimer after whatever therapeutic benefits accrued from writing about Dresden. Perhaps, too, characteristic modesty urged him to back away from something he might have felt was already being sensationalized. Nevertheless, the importance of the event to his fiction, if not to his life, seems undeniable, as apocryphal disasters, visions that embody the symbolism of Dresden, haunt novel after novel. Vonnegut's resistance to exaggerating the importance of a "short-term event" does reinforce the point, though, that earlier, less dramatic experiences influence his fiction quite as significantly.

By September 1945 Vonnegut had returned to civilian life. He married Jane Marie Cox on September 1, and enrolled as an anthropology student at the University of Chicago. As noted earlier, he worked as a police reporter for the Chicago City News Bureau during this period. He left Chicago without a degree when his M.A. thesis, "Fluctuations Between Good and Evil in Simple Tales," was rejected. By this time he had attended four colleges without earning a degree from any of them.

In 1947 Vonnegut moved to Schenectady, New York, to work as a public relations writer for the General Electric Company. The job, the plant, the town, and the personnel that he encountered here were to provide much material for his fiction in later years. Initially, though, it provided well-paid employment that enabled him to draw on both his journalistic experience and the scientific emphasis of his education. These elements seem to have combined when he began writing fiction. Dresden was the subject he felt compelled to write about, but finding the form through which to approach it proved difficult.

In the meantime Vonnegut began more modestly with short fiction and with the closer-to-home novel *Player Piano*, which drew heavily on his Schenectady environment. His first story, "Report on the Barnhouse Effect," was accepted by *Collier's* in 1949 (it appeared in February 1950). As even its title suggests, the story combines the reportorial and the scientific, as does much of the fiction that followed. The combination led to his being categorized as a science fiction writer, an appellation that he rues, but that most consistently manifests itself in his use of distanced, objectified narrative perspectives and his recognition of the social, cultural, and psychological implications of technological innovation.

Years later Vonnegut spoke disparagingly of being a public relations man, enjoying the salary but not the frequent need to camouflage truth and mislead newspaper reporters with whom he readily identified. (In novels, public relations writing is presented as the artist's ultimate prostitution of his talent and as the philistine's vision of a writer's highest achievement.) Such reservations, along with his success in placing short stories, led to his deciding to leave General Electric to devote himself full time to writing.

In 1951 Vonnegut moved to Cape Cod, where he lived for some twenty years. His stories, meantime, were being accepted by *Collier's*, *Cosmopolitan*, *Esquire*, *Ladies' Home Journal*, and the *Saturday Evening Post*. He later called them "work I sold in order to finance the writing of the novels." While they hardly deserve such easy dismissal, the short pieces have attracted little critical attention and remain less important artistically than the novels. But their place in Vonnegut's literary career should not be overlooked. They were his primary works through the 1950's; at as much as $2,700 a story, they provided most of his income; and they brought him into contact with figures in the publishing world, such as *Collier's* editor Knox Burger and literary agent Kenneth Littauer, who aided and influenced him. Littauer encouraged Vonnegut in the direction of telling stories, shaped narratives with a beginning, middle, and end. The beginning point for this kind of writing still suggests the earlier journalism; Vonnegut speaks of seeking out subjects for stories in the way that a cartoonist might—or, one must think, as a reporter might search out "the story."

The range of subjects used for Vonnegut's

short stories is remarkably varied. Some deal with the fantastic and futuristic—an astronaut who enters the "Thanasphere," where the dead converse with him—others with the homespun—the unreachably beautiful young woman who turns out to be "plain folks"; yet some characteristics remain constant. They are thematically consistent in espousing traditional middle-class values, the kind of ethics that would "play in Peoria." The future and the fantastic invariably serve to vindicate these values, while the struggler's dreams of an exotic, charmed life always fade to reassert the solid worth of the mundane one.

Perhaps inevitably, such stories are frequently tinged with sentimentality and nostalgia, traits that reappear in the novels, where they are rather more closely controlled. These traits continue to have an important function in Vonnegut's writing, contributing to the humor, to feeling, and to human warmth, frequently by countering the coldness of an alien world. They bring to the stories an implicit revelation of self and a declaration of theme that later become more explicit in the novels. Their quality may be uneven, but the stories are rich in variety as well as in entertainment. Vonnegut learns fiction writing in them, and they are unified in a way the longer narratives sometimes are not. Yet one reason the novels surpass them is that, as Vonnegut's career progresses, it becomes increasingly apparent that he flourishes in the looser, more comfortably digressive, and more easily intruded upon narration of the novel.

Player Piano (1952), Vonnegut's first published novel, enjoyed at best a mixed success. Certainly it was not the money-maker the short stories were, although the original Scribner edition was followed by two others within two years: the Doubleday Science Fiction Book Club edition in 1953, and a Bantam paperback with the new title *Utopia 14* in 1954. The latter

two editions brought mixed blessings. They increased sales, but they further categorized the author as a science fiction writer, something that threatened to exclude him forever from consideration as a mainstream American novelist.

Vonnegut worked on another novel during this period, the unfinished *Upstairs and Downstairs*, but seven years passed before a second was published—*The Sirens of Titan* in 1959. The popular story of the book's genesis—that at a cocktail party Knox Burger asked Vonnegut why he didn't write another novel, and he responded that he was and proceeded extemporaneously to spin off the plot of *Sirens*—is scarcely more interesting than the actual background of it.

By the mid-1950's Vonnegut was placing short stories frequently in the better-paying magazines. His career seemed to be developing successfully, although not in the medium of the novel. As the decade advanced, there were some ominous setbacks. The failure of *Collier's* in 1957 presaged a decline in the market for short fiction that the weekly family magazines had provided.

There were sharp personal setbacks, too. In October 1957 Vonnegut's father died. For a year, he found it impossible to write. Then in 1958 the double tragedy that he discusses in the prologue to *Slapstick*—the almost simultaneous deaths of his sister Alice and her husband—occurred. Vonnegut adopted three of the orphaned sons, doubling the size of his family. He found himself faced with greater responsibilities at the very time when his market was declining.

One response was to shift more attention to the science fiction magazines. Another was to return to the novel, this time writing specifically for the paperback market. Here he was aided by Knox Burger, who had also moved to paperback publishing. *The Sirens of Titan* and *Mother Night* (1962) were both written to paperback contracts. Another paperback publication of this era, written like *Mother Night* to a Fawcett contract, was the short story collection *Canary in a Cat House* (1961). The twelve stories had all been published previously, and all but one were later reassembled in *Welcome to the Monkey House* (1969).

Although these paperbacks helped ease Vonnegut's financial plight, they did little at the time to advance his career. They went unreviewed, and whatever notice they received served only to entrench his reputation as a science fiction writer. *The Sirens of Titan* was reissued as a hardcover in 1961, but went largely unnoticed, except by a small college underground.

The next novel, *Cat's Cradle* (1963), although begun with the paperback market in mind, appeared first in hardcover. Samuel Stewart, who had been with the Western Printing Company when it printed *The Sirens of Titan*, was now with Holt, Rinehart and Winston and helped arrange for them to publish the new book. So Vonnegut was at last launching novels in hardcover again, but once more the book could be labeled science fiction. Sales were very small, as they were for the next book, *God Bless You, Mr. Rosewater* (1965), another Holt, Rinehart and Winston hardcover. Vonnegut's feelings about his dilemma as a writer who seemed doomed not to be taken seriously find their way into both these novels in the portraits of writers and the preoccupation with financial inequality. These two motifs come together most strikingly—and poignantly—in the figure of Kilgore Trout, the science fiction writer whose struggles in obscurity reflect, with comic distortion, those of the author. First encountered in *God Bless You, Mr. Rosewater*, Trout reappears in later novels.

Once again Vonnegut moved toward new activities. He began writing nonfiction, including book reviews, travel pieces, and other essays, a number of which were subsequently collected in *Wampeters, Foma, & Granfalloons* (1974). These are of interest not only because they would appear in some respects to reach back toward Vonnegut's earlier journalism but because they relate to the evolution of his technique in fiction writing. On the one hand is the fact that Vonnegut's later fiction has tended to incorporate increasing amounts of reportage, of factual material drawn from contemporary events, into its fictional world. The other interesting aspect of these pieces is that though nonfictional they characterize their narrator (or author). In fact, a great deal of their interest lies in this revelation of authorial perspective and personality. It is at about this time that the autobiographical content of the novels becomes overt, to the point that Vonnegut introduces himself directly as a character in his next novel, *Slaughterhouse-Five*.

These two latter changes, the personal prefaces and the introduction of self as character, are coincident with another new direction that Vonnegut took. In 1965 he accepted a two-year appointment to the Writers Workshop at the University of Iowa. Vonnegut claims that one of the things he learned there was that it was not, as editors had told him, wrong to speak directly of himself in his fiction. He now wrote personal reminiscence into a preface for a hardcover reissue of *Mother Night*, and was to use that device for all his subsequent fiction.

Vonnegut's stay at Iowa brought him into contact with teachers and students, some of whom were active fiction writers themselves, like novelists Verlin Cassill, Richard Yates, William Murray, and Vance Bourjaily. Even among the academic critics there were genuine admirers like Robert Scholes. Vonnegut seems to have hoped the appointment would lead to a permanent position, and certainly he could have used such financial security.

No such appointment was forthcoming, but

a Guggenheim fellowship in 1967 made possible a return to Dresden, so that somehow out of the total experience of 1965–1968 the way was cleared at last for Vonnegut to get at his original motivating subject of Dresden. At the same time Dell and Avon reissued paperback editions of his novels. By the time *Slaughterhouse-Five* was released in 1969 Vonnegut was already rising rapidly in popularity. The sales of that novel, and the motion picture based on it, were to confirm his popularity and to assure the recognition that had eluded him for almost twenty years.

In particular, that recognition came from the academic world, where it may well have originated in the students' ranks and worked its way up. Invitations and honors came rapidly to Vonnegut. He spoke at a symposium on the novel at Brown University in 1969, to the graduating class at Bennington in 1970, and, in the same year, was invited to teach creative writing at Harvard (and three years later at the City College of the City University of New York). He was the subject of many published interviews, was at last granted an M.A. in anthropology by the University of Chicago (when *Cat's Cradle* was accepted as his thesis), and received honorary degrees, including an L.H.D. from Indiana University in 1973. He also received the Literature Award for 1969 from the National Institute of Arts and Letters, and in 1975 served as vice-president of the association.

Simultaneous with this public recognition came disruption in Vonnegut's personal and literary lives. His six children were old enough to leave home. The big Cape Cod house seemed emptied, and perhaps his melancholy at the scattering of the family cohered with a certain postnatal depression accompanying the completion of *Slaughterhouse-Five*, his "Dresden" book. He spoke of being "through with novels," with "spooks in a novel" rather than flesh-and-blood characters: "It's plays from now on." And

in the prologue to *Happy Birthday, Wanda June* (1970) he tells of his effort to write himself a new family in a company of actors. The play (which ran for five months off-Broadway) represented a new direction for Vonnegut, although the script itself owed much to one written (but never published) fifteen years earlier under the title "Penelope."

By 1971 Vonnegut had separated from his wife and moved to New York. The next year brought another personal trauma when his son Mark suffered a schizophrenic breakdown while living on a commune in British Columbia. In 1975 Mark published his account of this episode in *The Eden Express.*

Vonnegut, meanwhile, seemed to be uncertain about what direction to steer his work. In 1972 a screenplay based on his fiction, *Between Time and Timbuktu*, was produced by National Educational Television and was published by Delacorte. Despite his earlier proclamation, a new novel, *Breakfast of Champions*, was published the following year. As if this title were not enough to signal the dawn of happier days, Vonnegut added the subtitle *Goodbye Blue Monday.* In part Vonnegut treated this seemingly whimsical book as a self-indulgent birthday present to himself, and in part he intended it as a clearing out of old ideas, obsessions, and characters. It did look like an attempt at a new start, but although it enjoyed better sales than any of his previous books it drew generally weak reviews.

The next year *Wampeters, Foma, & Granfalloons*, a collection of speeches, reviews, essays, and interviews that the author categorizes as "opinions," was published. In it Vonnegut addresses the issue of finding himself very much in demand for public statements and of having his opinions on many issues, including politics, sought. Because he speaks so directly on many topical subjects in his fiction, and because of the nature and popularity of the novels, Vonnegut was finding himself increasingly in demand as a speaker and more and more perceived as a "guru" figure by the younger generations. It was a role in which he was not particularly comfortable, and he reduced his public appearances. *Wampeters* responds to this continuing interest in the man behind the novels, the author who speaks in the prologues or who intrudes with increasing frequency in the fiction.

The presence of *Wampeters* between *Breakfast of Champions* and the next novel, *Slapstick* (1976), seems appropriate in that it underlines the character of these two novels. *Wampeters* contains both the autobiographical and what might be called the documentary, the kind of factual (or editorialized) reportage found in "Biafra: A People Betrayed" or "Brief Encounters on the Inland Waterway." The two novels, even more than *Slaughterhouse-Five* before them, emphasize these two elements of autobiography and documentary.

In truth the earlier novels did so, too, but in a markedly different way. There the autobiographical elements were not explicit and the documentary element was, in effect, blended rather than spliced into the fiction. That is, in a novel like *Player Piano* the fiction, if not always rendered in the traditional terms of realism, has a strong factual base. The Ilium Works, for example, draw heavily on the General Electric plant in Schenectady in which Vonnegut had worked.

In the later works much of the realism is distilled, as it were, into direct reportage. Spliced into the fictional narrative are elements from the surrounding factual context—the author saying "that was me" in the midst of the action of *Slaughterhouse-Five* or giving lectures on strip mining in West Virginia in *Breakfast*. At the same time, elements of the fictional are heightened and separated, rather than blended and given the marks of plausibility. The seven-foot-six neanderthaloids, variable gravity, and miniaturized Chinese of *Slapstick*, for example, are frankly declared fantasies presented as givens in a setting that is presented as plausible and that is equally studded with references to historical events and persons.

In some respects the technique might be seen as related to what happens in *Slaughterhouse-Five* when Billy Pilgrim watches a war movie on television. Because of his ability to travel in time, he is able to watch the film forward and backward. Forward it seems to be straight documentary coverage of an air raid. Backward the same factual material is transformed into a comic fantasy (of aircraft magically resurrecting shattered cities, sucking up metal fragments to be returned as ore to the earth) that nevertheless retains thematic relevance. Both the documentary and the fantastic in these novels often appear in the form of inclusions from other sources—an imaginary story by Kilgore Trout or an actual book on a factual subject.

The documentary fantasy form is at its best in *Slaughterhouse-Five* and at its most misunderstood in *Slapstick*. The negative reviews of the latter, many of which might have been measuring it by the wrong standard, understandably disappointed Vonnegut and might have contributed to the delay in the publication of the next novel, *Jailbird* (1979). This book is technically akin to the previous three works but thematically closer to earlier novels, which it also resembles in tone and narrative style.

By the end of the 1970's Vonnegut had been publishing for thirty years. In that time he had to his credit nine novels, two collections of short stories, a play, the teleplay *Between Time and Timbuktu*, the work gathered in *Wampeters, Foma, & Granfalloons*, and numerous other short stories, essays, reviews, introductions, and addresses. In October 1979 a highly effective musical adaptation of *God Bless You, Mr. Rosewater* opened at the Entermedia Theater in

New York, produced by Vonnegut's daughter Edith.

Another work that almost claimed Vonnegut's authorship was *Venus on the Half-Shell;* the title is Vonnegut's, invented for a novel by Kilgore Trout. When a book with the same title and opening line appeared, claiming authorship by Kilgore Trout, many assumed that it was the work of Vonnegut. In fact it was written by Philip Jose Farmer. Perhaps this episode underscores the separation of Vonnegut from Kilgore Trout and proves that his career has indeed taken him beyond the kind of self-doubt and public failure as writer projected into that bumbling but lovable figure.

When Vonnegut wrote *Player Piano* those fears were evident, although the figure of Kilgore Trout was not. Rather, any doubt about his resignation from General Electric to embark on a literary career is divided between the protagonist Paul Proteus and a writer who remains a minor character. The latter we know simply as "Ed," the husband of the brunette who has turned to prostitution rather than have him compromise his artistic integrity by writing a book that will sell. His first novel has been rejected for being twenty-seven pages too long, being too intellectual, and having an anti-machine theme. Moreover, he has refused psychiatry:

" . . . And my husband says somebody's just *got* to be maladjusted; that somebody's got to be uncomfortable enough to wonder where people are, where they're going, and why they're going there. That was the trouble with his book. It raised those questions, and was rejected. . . ."

Finally, Ed has refused to report to work as a public relations writer (which actually has a higher rating in his society than novelist). By a kind of comic inversion, this episode says a lot about Vonnegut's own situation. Ed writes "beautifully"; Vonnegut is soon to begin self-deprecating jokes about his style. Ed writes antimachinery novels; Vonnegut is already beginning to encounter the disfavor of his society by writing about technology. The description of why Ed wants to remain "maladjusted" is not the inverse of Vonnegut's position; rather, he frequently seems to share that stance as the proper one from which to view society's upsidedown values.

Obviously, Vonnegut had made some of the compromises that Ed is refusing: he had written public relations material, he was now aiming short stories at a commercial market, and at times things must have been precarious enough to raise questions about the integrity that led him from General Electric to full-time fiction writing. In Ed, then, we find the forerunner of Kilgore Trout, Philboyd Studge, and the other personae that Vonnegut uses to tease his own role.

Yet it is in the figure of protagonist Paul Proteus that Vonnegut may actually reflect upon his own situation most searchingly. Proteus becomes more than the minimum character necessary to serve Vonnegut's theses, even in a book in which ideas clearly dominate over characterization. There is psychological realism to Paul's uncertainty about his career, about the sources and nature of the changes stirring in him. Doubts about the job mix with questions about his general values and even about his marriage, until he reflects "perhaps that suspicion was part of what he was beginning to think of as his sickness." Vonnegut makes it hard to separate the external choices facing Paul from the inner, psychological ones. Other characters, as well as Paul himself, suspect that he may be going through a personal reorientation, not to be taken seriously as a reevaluation of his social and professional environment.

Doubts such as these possibly worked at some level, conscious or unconscious, in Vonnegut while the novel was being written. He had, after all, made an abrupt change in life-style that proved economically risky and that in its own way involved turning away from his involvement in a technological society. Just as Paul Proteus does, perhaps he recoiled, half-seriously, half-laughingly, from becoming like Ed Finnerty and breaking with former friends and their world to become the iconoclastic outsider. And perhaps he retains, like Paul and Finnerty, an affection for what he has turned away from; as they remain emotionally tied to their machine-designing heydays, Vonnegut never abandons his interest in the scientific and the technological and in their impact on society. There is even the suggestion that Paul's social rebellion is in fact the expression of a wish to destroy his father. Father-son relationships develop into a continuing motif in Vonnegut's work, to be addressed in direct autobiographical terms in the later fiction and involving Vonnegut as both father and son. It might be noted here that just as Paul turns away from emulating his engineer-manager father, Vonnegut has departed from the scientific educations and professions of the males in his family.

Paul Proteus—"protean" in fulfilling several roles in the novel—may be seen as expressing not only his creator's social criticism but, indirectly, his psychological searchings as well. This kind of autobiographical exploration is not as clear or direct as it becomes in later prefaces or novels; nor is it embodied in one or even two characterizations. As noted, both the writer Ed and Paul Proteus can be seen as having some autobiographical basis. And so, perhaps, may Ed Finnerty. His breezy irreverence reflects a side of Vonnegut expressed most fully twenty years later in *Breakfast of Champions*. Kilgore Trout, when he arrives, may take as much parentage from this unkempt Irish outsider as from the writer Ed.

Not only character, but also the relationship of character, the very structure of the novels,

often serves the autobiographical bent. As Vonnegut acknowledged later, many of his stories involve a two-men-and-one-woman triangle, just as *Player Piano* does. In this first novel the triangle takes on a curious blurring. Paul and Anita are the two obvious corners; the third would appear to be Dr. Lawson Shepherd, since he is the boy who eventually gets the girl and who, as the exemplary company man, personifies the attitudes and aspirations Paul comes to reject. Finnerty, the opposite of Shepherd in everything from personal hygiene to ethics, represents Paul's other choice and so might also be viewed as, or as a part of, the third corner. And Paul's father might also be lurking somewhere in that corner, as the role others would have Paul emulate and whom Paul himself feels he does come to emulate in his moment of rebellion.

Curiously, Anita is fascinated with the figure of Paul's father, identifying him with Paul in their earlier years but then coming to see him as resembling Shepherd when her faith in Paul wanes. So perhaps the third person remains, like the autobiographical personification, splintered in this book. The basis for the pattern, Vonnegut reminds us, is in his childhood family: older brother Bernard, the scientist; sister Alice; and himself the youngest.

A related device that becomes characteristic of Vonnegut is the use of an outside observer as a commentator who provides a fresh, unconventional, but revealing perspective on society. Obviously, the device is not original with Vonnegut, but it is one in which he delights and that relates to the matter of his intruding himself into his novels. These observers do not necessarily reflect aspects of Vonnegut personally, but they frequently are spokesmen for his point of view. Often they come from another time or country or planet; invariably their viewpoint will be somewhat zany if not, at least in the eyes of conventional society, downright crazy. Sometimes several characters will share in this observer role to a degree, but one person, distinguishable in his detachment, will remain the principal.

In *Player Piano*, Paul is one such observer whose sanity is viewed as suspect, particularly when his judgments are arrived at by detaching himself and nostalgically going back in time. Revealingly, those judgments are the ones obviously approved of within the moral framework of the book. Ed Finnerty, of course, is considered suspect as a drunk, and the collective evaluation of the other Ed, the writer, is summed up by the shah of Bratpuhr's saying that "some of the greatest prophets were crazy as bed bugs." Ironically, the shah is the outsider in this novel and the one viewed by the other characters as totally out of touch. Yet repeatedly Vonnegut uses him to deliver the devastating final assessment of various episodes illustrating technological Western life.

The pattern is suggestive in a number of ways. When the sanity of Vonnegut's commentators on society is persistently made uncertain throughout his novels it may suggest that their judgments are being undercut. That, indeed, typifies Vonnegut's manner in his refusal to be dogmatic, his almost frustrating insistence on considering both sides, and his propensity to deflate any pretense comically. But the apparent craziness of all these commentators suggests that the social norm is insane, or that where craziness is bliss 'tis folly to be sane.

At the same time, some of the observers—those we might call "partially detached," like Finnerty, Ed, and Proteus—are the very characters seen to embody autobiographical elements. Their craziness, therefore, comes to reflect on the author himself, partly by design as a zany eccentricity adopted as a narrative stance and partly, perhaps, showing a more serious concern about his own emotional stability. The latter emerges subsequently in prefatory ruminations about depression, his mother's suicide, and schizophrenia. Ed in *Player Piano*, as already noted, maintains that the socially critical writer needs to be "maladjusted," and crazily perceptive artists appear regularly in the novels. Varying degrees of "maladjustment" or insanity are widespread in Vonnegut's worlds, again demonstrating the questionable sanity of the "normal" and the emotional cost of life in contemporary society.

At this beginning point in his career as a novelist, Vonnegut is most concerned with the kind of structure and characterization that best serves his social criticism. Yet besides the broader social view, the need remains for the kind of personal expression that apparently finds an outlet in the ways considered here. Despite the autobiographical elements in the character of Paul Proteus, this is not the kind of first novel in which the whole focus is on a distinctly autobiographical protagonist. Such novels tend to be long on "life," on immediacy and verisimilitude, but short on generalization and conclusion on the larger patterns in life.

Vonnegut searches for a form that will combine both dimensions. Such a form needs to be inclusive, and one of the comments most often made about Vonnegut's style is that it is tight in its clipped phrases and curt sentences but looser in its larger structure, sometimes rambling and digressing. The latter observation often ignores the thematic unity between parts, but points up Vonnegut's problems in organizing the kind of novel he needs.

In *Player Piano* the organization seems ingenious if perhaps extravagant in execution. In order to encompass the full range of social commentary he desires, Vonnegut creates a series of parallel subplots, each of which needs human scale. That is, the consequences to the individual human being of the way each segment of society operates need to be registered on a particular person. Even a protagonist as protean as

Paul cannot stretch to all these situations, so Vonnegut places a barometric figure in each subplot. All have names beginning with H: Haycox, Hacketts, Hagstrohm, and Halyard. The initials reflect the structure; *Paul Proteus* at the center of *Player Piano*, with the H plots clustered around. Some form of "clustering" will continue to fascinate Vonnegut until he is able to perfect it in *Slaughterhouse-Five*. In the first novel it seems useful if at times diversionary and slow; in the next novel, *The Sirens of Titan*, he achieves a remarkable fluency by turning to a purely linear structure in which the protagonist, like that of the traditional picaresque novel, enters a succession of different worlds in turn.

One other significant pattern in the structuring of *Player Piano* deserves mention as a characteristic to be traced in the subsequent novels. It involves the classical mythic pattern of the hero's descent into a netherworld to be resurrected as a rejuvenated being and hailed (often ironically) as a messiah figure. Paul's journeys across the river to Homestead are viewed as a social descent but, more important, lead him into the underground Ghost Shirt Society and its subterranean hideout. He emerges with new purpose and identity, becoming at least the titular leader of the rebels. In the public role he fails; but privately, in coming to terms with himself and arriving at values that permit him self-respect despite society's rejection, he succeeds. Variations of the pattern recur, frequently having in common the fact that the protagonist, like William Shakespeare's King Lear, comes to feel through this progression more compassion for the "poor naked wretches" of society.

Vonnegut's social consciousness is, naturally enough, discernibly shaped by autobiographical experience. Childhood memories of the Great Depression and particularly of seeing his father

unemployed and directionless contribute to the populating of his novels with unfortunates who ask, "What are people for?" Paul's attempt to answer that question leads him to social rebellion and steers Vonnegut's other messiahs to their own socially unconventional stances.

For all that, there is plenty of orthodoxy to *Player Piano*. Even as an antiutopian novel it owes much to a widely popular forebear, Aldous Huxley's *Brave New World* (1932). In their rejection of a utopian future, the novel and its protagonist both show much nostalgia for earlier, simpler times. Some of that nostalgia is undercut as delusory and sentimental; but, as observed earlier, sentiment in Vonnegut is often the symptom of human feeling, and the nostalgia reveals his commitment to fundamentally middle-class, traditional values.

Vonnegut's complaint, here and subsequently, is that middle-class Americans now so often betray those values. The importance of family is argued by the failure of the families portrayed—Paul and Anita, the Hagstrohms—and by the artificiality of the substitutions—the paternalism of Kroner and his wife's insistence that everyone call her "Mom." Friendship and loyalty are praised by their inversion in the cannibalistic treachery of "Dog-Eat-Dog" Lawson Shepherd, but above all in Paul's refusal to betray his friend Ed Finnerty. There is also approval of pride in work, of ingenuity and initiative and tinkering, and of the job as a source of fulfillment and identity.

Above all, we see here the beginnings of Vonnegut's absorption with treating people who lack such fulfillment and identity with understanding and dignity, according them value as human beings. Vonnegut eschews the word "love"; certainly romantic or conjugal love repeatedly fails in his fiction, just as it does here with Paul and Anita. But in Paul's loyalty to Finnerty, or by bad example in Shepherd's exploitation of a colleague, Vonnegut's advocacy of compassionate respect, or of what he himself later calls "common human decency," emerges.

Player Piano hardly sets the pattern for the rest of Vonnegut's novels, but it does contain many recurring threads of theme, characterization, imagery, and autobiographical content that deserve attention here. In certain respects it remains his most conventional novel, the least likely to surprise a reader new to Vonnegut. Its impact derives from its content, from the force of its message, not from its form, which seems to echo antiutopian novels and even other social criticism of the *Babbitt* or *Main Street* tradition of Sinclair Lewis.

With its plot and subplots, its lively humor and moral earnestness, its nucleus in the growth of its protagonist but its range extended over its widely inclusive social commentary, *Player Piano* seems to be pulled in many directions, to remain somehow unsettled, unresolved in its attempt to encompass all that it might be. For all that, it rewards rereading with the pleasant realization that it is, after all, better than one had remembered. Despite its limitations, the characterization invites involvement, the social commentary seems refreshingly free of cynicism, and the very inclusivity of topic and mood provides substance.

The Sirens of Titan is separated from *Player Piano* by seven years and by a considerable garnering of writing experiences, as recounted earlier. The second book makes its differences apparent at once. Its narration has a natural fluidity beyond that achieved in *Player Piano*, and at times it is positively lyrical, as in the description in chapter eight of the planet Mercury:

The planet Mercury sings like a crystal goblet.
It sings all the time.
One side of Mercury faces the Sun. That side

has always faced the Sun. That side is a sea of white-hot dust.

The other side faces the nothingness of space eternal. That side has always faced the nothingness of space eternal. That side is a forest of giant blue-white crystals, aching cold.

It is the tension between the hot hemisphere of day-without-end and the cold hemisphere of night-without-end that makes Mercury sing.

Mercury has no atmosphere, so the song it sings is for the sense of touch.

The song is a slow one. Mercury will hold a single note in the song for as long as an Earthling millennium. There are those who think that the song was quick, wild, and brilliant once—excruciatingly various. Possibly so.

The dialogue sounds noticeably more natural. The space opera, the form on which Vonnegut draws, is episodic and lends itself well to honest storytelling in its straightforward, linear unfolding of plot.

The form gives Vonnegut's imagination free rein; its world seems less doggedly tied to reality than that in the antiutopian novel, and less didactic. In terms of the balancing elements observed in his later fiction, described as "documentary fantasy," this novel could be seen as essentially fantasy. (*Player Piano* is more nearly documentary in its presentation of social commentary.)

The Sirens of Titan makes its comments metaphorically, in effect, through the use of the science fictional. Tralfamadorian robots in control, for instance, show a mechanistic universe. In consequence, *Sirens* seems the more profound novel, probing philosophically rather than sociologically, and to a greater psychological depth. Yet the fantastic world of *Sirens* instructs easily, like Lewis Carroll's *Alice in Wonderland*—which it resembles from the time Malachi Constant steps through the tiny door in the wall of the Rumfoord estate until the last smile of Winston Niles Rumfoord fades, like that of a Cheshire cat, into the chrono-synclastic infundibulum.

Of the characteristic patterns noted in *Player Piano*, the one that most obviously undergoes development is the mythic descent and return, which is no longer implicit but is presented directly and literally. Malachi is tested on Mars and descends into the caves of Mercury, from which he returns as the messiah of the Church of God the Utterly Indifferent, only to be condemned and made its scapegoat.

As an attempt to universalize Constant as prototypical individual in the contemporary, existential world, *Sirens* far exceeds the mythicizing of Paul Proteus. The father-son relationship also reemerges, with the protagonist again seen in both roles. Most of the emphasis falls on the relationship between Malachi and Chrono, who find it hard to show—or feel—any love for each other. The father's eventual effort to reach out toward a son who has gone off with the Titanic bluebirds is poignantly rendered—and Malachi fares better than most fathers do in Vonnegut's early novels. The autobiographically based triangle reappears with Rumfoord, Malachi, and Beatrice. Again the father seems to intrude into this relationship; Rumfoord is paternally manipulative of Malachi, and their "contest" over Beatrice partakes of the Oedipal.

Once again the conjugal relationship appears blighted. In neither the Beatrice-Rumfoord nor the Beatrice-Constant "marriage" is there any romantic love, yet the kind of love that ultimately exists between Constant and Beatrice is quite moving. It grows painfully and slowly between two people who have suffered much and have little reason to trust or admire each other. But their love, again what Vonnegut might call "common human decency," affords the model of how human beings in an indifferent, incomprehensible, and frequently painful universe can extend themselves in each other's service and treat each other with compassion, respect, and dignity.

"You finally fell in love, I see," said Salo.

"Only an Earthling year ago," said Constant. "It took us that long to realize that a purpose of human life, no matter who is controlling it, is to love whoever is around to be loved."

The emotional restraint evident in the depiction of male-female relationships recedes considerably once again in the portrayal of male companionship. The relationship between Stony and Unk seems to go on where Finnerty-Proteus left off. Like the friendship between Salo and Rumfoord it involves betrayal. Even so, that kind of friendship, that kind of "human" bond—though obviously touched with irony because Salo is a robot—provides some of the warmest, most satisfying moments in this novel, the more so because they are poised against a background of cold space and inhuman actions.

Even Salo's being a robot serves to distinguish and intensify the human qualities of the kind of behavior affirmed by the close of this novel. The use of an outside observer to comment on social behavior occurs again; that observer is, of course, Salo. Although a robot from a remote, futuristic society, Salo provides anything but a frigidly aloof perspective, even though he can see the shortcomings of much that he observes. By giving his observer "human" fallibility and emotions, Vonnegut removes the cynicism usually implicit in this technique—a welcome reversal in this novel where the people are all too often coldly cynical and unfeeling.

Other motifs in this novel will reappear: Tralfamadorians, Rumfoords, a dog with a bark sounding like a brass gong, physical handicaps to create equality, and, above all, religion. Rumfoord's Church of God the Utterly Indifferent is the first of Vonnegut's experiments in the creation of a religion that will reconcile people to an indifferent universe and lead them toward mutual help rather than performing as if for some ever-watching eye in the sky. The religion is lampooned, but Vonnegut has a serious point behind his satire, as he does when he amplifies the subject of religion in *Cat's Cradle*. "Gimcrack religion" is not the only appealing escape examined; regression into a personal or social past again offers itself.

In *Player Piano* revulsion with the present and with what trends suggest of the future leads to nostalgia for the past—for Homesteaders the old-style Victorian bar, for example, and for Paul the Gottwald farm. In *Sirens* the caves of Mercury offer Boaz a secure womb in which he can tell himself "you a good boy" and go to sleep. In both novels, and subsequently, Vonnegut makes clear that he feels sympathy toward the impulse but also recognizes its dangers.

Time becomes important in other ways in this novel. The structuring of narrative time is carefully done, using three tenses. First there is the assumed literal present, the time in which the reader lives—call it *T*. The narrator speaks from a future time—*T*2. He looks back on an intermediate time, a future closer to *T* than to *T*2—call it *T*1. Understanding *T*1 explains how people came to think as they do in *T*2. In effect, then, the narrator is explaining *T*2 to *T*.

The narrative technique relates to theme and to the perception of time as relative. Or, as the Tralfamadorians put it, "everything that ever was always will be, and everything that ever will be always was." This idea recurs in *Slaughterhouse-Five*, where it affects structure' more dramatically and where its implications of inevitability contribute, as here, to the portrayal of a universe in which compassionate human behavior is imperative.

The first two novels both use omniscient third-person narrations. In the novels that fol-

low, Vonnegut moves closer to including himself directly with the introduction of first-person narration. He makes an interesting intermediate step in *Sirens* in his use of Rumfoord. As the one who knows what is going on and who informs the other characters, he becomes a secondary narrator within the book (and, at times, in his manipulations of character and situation, almost a surrogate author figure). And, as the voice of its more pessimistic and cynical elements, he preserves the neutrality of the basic narrative voice and hence the tone of the novel.

In *Mother Night*, something of this technique is repeated through the ambiguity of the first-person narrator, the Howard Campbell that was and the one that is, the playwright and the spy, or the two sides of a schizophrenic personality. *Cat's Cradle* extends the technique through Bokonon, who as character continues Rumfoord's role as inventor of religions, prophet, historian, and social manipulator, and who as secondary narrator assumes an even bigger role as author of the books that are at the heart of the novel and its philosophy. Bokonon voices some of the novel's most important yet most cynical ideas, allowing both narrator Newt Hoenikker and author Vonnegut to remain at some distance from that cynicism and preserve the book's comic tone.

In the next three novels Vonnegut seems to settle into a style of his own, somewhere between the antiutopian mold of *Player Piano* and the science-fiction cast of *The Sirens of Titan*. For all their differences in tone and setting, *Mother Night* (1962), *Cat's Cradle* (1963), and *God Bless You, Mr. Rosewater* (1965) share much in content and form. Where *Player Piano* with its multiple plots tries to examine the plight of contemporary human beings in numerous social settings, *The Sirens of Titan* backs away to a cosmic view of the human being's existential situation.

Mother Night returns to close-up reality, portraying firsthand (and first person) the dilemma of a single human being caught up in a historical situation illustrative of the general condition rendered metaphorically in *Sirens*. Ultimately, the protagonist Howard Campbell cannot survive in that world. *Cat's Cradle*, shifting to a much brighter tone, looks at what it might take to keep going. In their attempts to survive, however, Campbell and Bokonon both compromise their morality.

God Bless You, Mr. Rosewater tests moral survival. It asks whether, even if "love" is too much to ask for, the more modest "common human decency" is possible. In *Sirens*, Boaz wants to "do good without doing any harm" while unwittingly killing thousands of harmoniums, and the road to the Ilium Works seems to have been paved with similar good intentions. These three books (*Mother Night, Cat's Cradle,* and *God Bless You, Mr. Rosewater*) examine the intentions and accomplishments of a series of "saints" and "villains."

Classifying these characters as either saints or villains proves difficult, above all to the characters themselves, and often seems to depend on where the viewer is standing. (There is the story of Vonnegut's agreeing with his father that there are no villains in his fiction.) Campbell, Bokonon, and a number of lesser characters stand convinced of the imperative of evading reality (if indeed that can be registered accurately) through some kind of make-believe. Bokonon's religion rests on "foma," harmless lies that make life more tolerable and that afford a basis for community and caring.

Most of Vonnegut's "solutions" involve some degree of deception, from tacit endorsements of Christianity (in which he does not believe) to the artificially extended families proposed in *Slapstick*. The problem rests in the distinction between harmless lies and cruel hoaxes. Is Bokonon benefactor or tyrant? With cheerful cynicism he leads his flock to suicide. Where are the dividing lines between him and a fanatical religious cult leader or even a national tyrant whose comforting lies may lead their communities to self-destruction?

Equally fundamental is the question of how harmless such lies can remain to the self. As Vonnegut moralizes in his introduction, "We are what we pretend to be, so we must be careful about what we pretend to be." Campbell argues that he survived Nazi Germany through "that simple and widespread boon to modern mankind—schizophrenia." And certainly schizophrenia (or other mental illness) pervades these novels, often, as with Sylvia Rosewater's "samaratrophia," as the ultimate self-deception of a mind no longer able to face the terrors of contemporary life. The theme of inverted values continues, though, so that the society's judgments of what is sane or moral in the protagonist often reflect back on itself. Nowhere is this truer than with the eccentrically altruistic Eliot Rosewater.

Inevitably the theme of harmless deceptions also leads to writers and other artists. The topic—the artist as con artist, as confidence man, as magus—is not new. When Rosewater becomes patron to Arthur Garvey Ulm he tells him to write "the truth." Ulm eventually overcomes his writer's block only to write pornography. The "Editor" in *Mother Night* tells us that Campbell's being a writer meant that

the demands of art alone were enough to make him lie, and to lie without seeing any harm in it. To say that he was a playwright is to offer an even harsher warning to the reader, for no one is a better liar than a man who has warped lives and passions onto something as grotesquely artificial as a stage.

In *Cat's Cradle* not just *The Books of Bokonon* but other literature is several times presented as "foma." Even poor Kilgore Trout is seen as a kind of harmless liar, at least by Senator Lister Rosewater, who hires him as a public relations man to rationalize Eliot's behavior. Yet writers are also viewed positively as these books progress. In *Cat's Cradle* they provide healing laughter:

"I just can't help thinking what a real shaking up it would give people if, all of a sudden, there were no new books, new plays, new histories, new poems . . . " [says Philip Castle].

"And how proud would you be when people started dying like flies?" I demanded.

"They'd die more like mad dogs, I think—snarling and snapping at each other and biting their own tails."

I turned to Castle the elder. "Sir, how does a man die when he's deprived of the consolations of literature?"

"In one of two ways," he said, "petrescence of the heart or atrophy of the nervous system."

"Neither one very pleasant, I expect," I suggested.

"No," said Castle the elder. "For the love of God, *both* of you, *please* keep writing!"

In *God Bless You, Mr. Rosewater,* science fiction writers are Eliot Rosewater's visionaries, who alone understand not just the future but, more important, the present.

The increased interest in writers in these books coincides with that period in Vonnegut's career when he might understandably have been preoccupied with his own role as a writer. His short-story market had begun to fail, and he turned to writing paperbacks. He may have experienced some doubts about the direction of his career and indeed felt himself faced again with the kind of ethical self-examination most writers confront, given the commercial necessity of compromise.

Vonnegut also probes the artistic morality of the author. In one filmed interview he laughed at the notion of some "damn fool" moved to tears over a fiction on a sheet of paper. But although he sees the funny side of this situation—perhaps because he does—he obviously feels the moral responsibility that must go with this extraordinary power. Later, when more famous, he showed some discomfort at having such power over his young followers.

Equally, Vonnegut reveals a strong interest in the author's relationship to the created characters and the moral implications of that relationship. That theme initially receives attention through surrogate author figures. There is Rumfoord, who manipulates characters to his own plots; then Campbell, who makes characters of the real people he meets, including, finally, not just his beloved Helga but himself; and Bokonon, though to a lesser degree. All, like Boaz in *Sirens,* have good intentions but end up hurting people. In *Breakfast of Champions* Vonnegut proposes why people mistreat each other:

As I approached my fiftieth birthday, I had become more and more enraged and mystified by the idiot decisions made by my countrymen. And then I had come suddenly to pity them, for I understood how innocent and natural it was for them to behave so abominably, and with such abominable results: They were doing their best to live like people invented in story books. This was the reason Americans shot each other so often: It was a convenient literary device for ending short stories and books.

In all of this, Vonnegut explores not just his personal role as artist, but the role of all artists—the role of all of us as artists shaping our own and others' lives—and, perhaps, by projection, the role of the ultimate artist, God. For Vonnegut, an atheist, the last stage remains metaphor, another avenue to the "What are people for?" motif, a means of describing a world in which if there were a God he could surely be only a whimsical, cynical, detached figure in the mold of Bokonon.

Eliot Rosewater is not an artist. In fact, he even cautions his heirs on the futility of investing in the arts as a way of helping the less fortunate. But he does play a deific role in Rosewater County and loves science fiction writers. His identification of himself with Shakespeare's Hamlet is telling. Obviously the question of whether he is really mad hovers over each of these figures, and each drives the woman he loves crazy. Like Hamlet, Eliot wants to be sure he is doing the moral thing rather than simply following the dictates of his father, and ends up hurting innocent people out of the very desire not to. And each finds himself confronted with a time that is "out of joint" and tries "to set it right." In this way there is a transition from the surrogate author figure to, as it were, the other side of the coin, the author as character. Eliot tries to control some aspects of life within a limited sphere but finds, like Hamlet, that "There's a divinity that shapes our ends, / Rough-hew them how we will."

The author-as-character line continues into *Slaughterhouse-Five,* where Vonnegut interjects himself as a character—"That was me"—and also has, in Billy Pilgrim, a protagonist who is partly autobiographical and even more allusive. In *Breakfast of Champions* Vonnegut gives the theme its most overt treatment not only by speaking of giving his characters their freedom (after a graphic demonstration of his ability to manipulate them), but also by making himself an author who appears within the book as a character. This "Chinese boxes" treatment of a theme that begins in *Sirens* emphasizes a vision of a life that imitates art, in which the artist is in turn the character, and in which no ultimate, verifying reality appears.

The previously established patterns of autobiographical influence take on interesting forms in these three novels. The two-men-and-one-woman triangle, for example, becomes ambiguous in *Mother Night* partly because everyone has a dual identity. Even the "nation of two" that Campbell and Helga create grows in population as they assume the roles recorded in his *Memoirs of a Monogamous Casanova.* The Helga resurrected after the war turns out to be her sister Resi, so that there may even be a two-women-and-one-man triangle here, as well as one formed by two Campbells (public and private) and Helga/Resi. The other candidates for third man—Major Frank Wirtanen and George Kraft—also have double identities.

In *Cat's Cradle* the pattern appears straightforwardly autobiographical: older brother Frank, middle sister Angela, baby brother Newt, even to having the older brother a scientist and the younger one a writer. (Vonnegut's making Newt a midget looks forward to *Slapstick,* where he makes the twins, whom he identifies with his sister and himself, giants.) By *Rosewater* the triangle has again weakened: Norman Mushari is Eliot's natural antagonist and also lusts after Sylvia, but the dominant third person remains the father, Lister.

This accords with the steady growth of another previously noted motif in the three novels—that involving the father figure. In *Mother Night,* Kraft and Wirtanen both relate paternally to Campbell. Felix Hoenikker in *Cat's Cradle* may parody Vonnegut's father in some respects, although Vonnegut has claimed the late Dr. Irving Langmuir of General Electric as a source for this characterization. Senator Rosewater is compelling, at once an embodiment of all that the son rebels against and a figure for affection. In some respects, including his desire to see Eliot's marriage succeed, he departs from the usual blocking role of the *senex* in comedy—as do several second men of these triangles.

Some ambiguity exists, then, about this second male figure, including whether it is based more closely on the father or on the older brother. Such blurring has a general psychological validity; it also accords with what Vonnegut cheerfully reveals in the preface of *Slapstick* when describing how Bernard, as older brother, makes all the arrangements when they travel together. A rigid correspondence between these real and fictional relationships remains improbable, but informing glimpses of connections do occur.

Mother Night becomes the first of Vonnegut's novels to be written in the first person. Its "Editor's Note," signed Kurt Vonnegut, Jr., although that is obviously a persona, moves the novel another step closer to direct personal expression. Having been told by colleagues at the University of Iowa that there was nothing wrong with introducing himself directly into his fiction, he added an introduction to the novel in 1966 that takes the last step beyond that of his two personae. The first of the prefaces that are to become integral to his novels, it speaks about family, his German ancestry, being a prisoner of war, and Dresden. It reveals aspects of Vonnegut's life that add autobiographical significance to the novel, but even more important, it points up how the novels will progress inevitably toward direct address of those motivating subjects.

Cat's Cradle also uses a first-person narrator, one who mimics the narrator of *Moby Dick* as a way of signaling the fictiveness of his story and, indeed, of himself. Within his narrative is another, *The Books of Bokonon,* vital to the message of *Cat's Cradle,* so that once again Vonnegut uses the veils of double personae while moving closer to being philosophically declarative.

God Bless You, Mr. Rosewater moves away from direct authorial expression in form, but the content compensates. There is much of Kurt Vonnegut in Eliot Rosewater, one feels—in his wide-ranging observations on American society and the lives of individuals within it, in the almost childlike freshness of his way of looking at

things, and even, perhaps, in the mixture of compassion and frustration expressed in Eliot's characteristic, "Goddamn it, you've got to be kind."

Another Vonnegut surrogate, Kilgore Trout, has a major and largely serious role in the ending of this book and provides Vonnegut with additional access, especially where Trout explains the sanity of Eliot's actions within the context of a society pervaded by mental and physical malaise.

In content, these novels move progressively closer to the author's traumatic Dresden experience. Much of *Mother Night* is set in wartime Germany, and perhaps some of the ambiguities that divide Campbell reflect feelings of an author who, being of German descent, wonders how he might have acted had he been on the other side. "If I'd been born in Germany," he reflects in the introduction, "I suppose I would have *been* a Nazi, bopping Jews. . . ."

Vonnegut was not born in Germany, and instead of participating in one kind of holocaust got caught in another, the firebombing of Dresden by the Allies. There he witnessed apocalypse; his own world almost literally ended (significantly, when Bokononists commit suicide they say, "Now I destroy the whole world").

The Dresden to which Vonnegut surfaced was destroyed, and in that act, in the technical and moral ability of human beings to commit such an act, he saw implicit ultimate destruction. Those are things he talks about in *Cat's Cradle,* in which Newt Hoenikker sets out to write a book on Hiroshima called *The Day the World Ended* and ends up witnessing doom wrought by ice-nine.

In *Rosewater* the theme of apocalypse, particularly that aspect of it which connects social, physical cataclysm with individual, psychological collapse, reappears in Eliot's vision of the destruction of Indianapolis by firestorm at the moment of his breakdown. The theme is enlarged in the novel by the crucial episode in which Eliot kills German auxiliary firemen in a burning building and by Kilgore Trout's story of the destruction of the Milky Way.

Both stories contribute to the nature of Eliot's breakdown; he feels guilt over killing the firemen and had been reading Trout immediately before his vision. Each story points in an opposite direction from Indianapolis-become-Dresden: the killing of the firemen to the poignant, personal level, the science fiction tale to the dumbfounding prospect of total annihilation.

All three novels reveal autobiographically based content in ways other than allusion to World War II. *Cat's Cradle,* for instance, might be seen as an expression—albeit a comic one—of the Vonnegut family's tradition of atheism, something he refers to several times. Yet surely that remains less important than the effort to characterize an absurd universe in which individuals need help—psychological, economic, and social—to make life endurable and to give it purpose.

Similarly, *God Bless You, Mr. Rosewater* addresses economic issues and their effect on the psychologies of people, reminding us of the financial erosion of the Vonnegut family, his mother's struggle through the Great Depression, and the withdrawal of his unemployed father. These topics inherit an emotional force by drawing on personal experience, but are objectified and broadened to assume a general significance. Vonnegut's adaptation of autobiographical material and his development of a style permitting him to be more confident in establishing an authorial presence in the novels move him closer to the long-sought confrontation with Dresden in *Slaughterhouse-Five.*

In the first chapter of *Slaughterhouse-Five,* Vonnegut likens himself to Lot's wife, who looked back on the destroyed Sodom and Gomorrah:

And Lot's wife, of course, was told not to look back where all those people and their homes had been. But she *did* look back, and I love her for that, because it was so human.

So she was turned to a pillar of salt. So it goes.

People aren't supposed to look back. I'm certainly not going to do it anymore.

He suggests that one should not look back, that past feelings are hard to recapture, and that the novel fails to close with its subject. Yet the book actually succeeds remarkably well in encompassing his Dresden experience, giving its personal trauma expression but emphasizing its universal human significance. That demands Vonnegut's most daring artistic innovation. Out of the evolving form of the previous three novels he derives the structure that at last can bear his originally motivating subject.

Nowhere is this evolution more apparent than in the establishment of a narrative perspective. The novel is, in fact, a first-person narration, although glancing at any page in the middle chapters may make it seem to be both third-person and omniscient. The integration of authorial presence is more complete than that achieved through the combined effects of the "Editor's Note" and 1966 introduction to *Mother Night.*

Vonnegut speaks about himself, his experiences, and the writing of *Slaughterhouse-Five* not in a separate preface or introduction but in the first chapter. He returns again in the tenth and final chapter. In between he declares himself periodically as someone present in the action of the novel, as by saying "that was me" or "I said that."

This narrative presence makes a crucial impact on the novel's tone. The reminiscences, the discussion with the O'Hares, the openness in declaring his difficulties with the subject all authenticate Vonnegut as narrator. His authenticity is vital to the telling of this extraordinary story, to making compelling a tale from which the rational mind recoils.

The narrative presence is also established as an involved and compassionate one—the voice recounts this story not simply with objectified detachment or stern moralizing, but with something like an understanding yet urgent resignation. Paradoxical, yes, but evident in the injunctions like "Listen," which reveal the narrator's compulsion—like Billy Pilgrim's—to tell his story, and in the apparent acceptance of the inevitable and the repetitive in the weary, but not unfeeling, "So it goes."

The first person, then, affords Vonnegut the kind of direct expression necessary to authenticate the novel and, no doubt, to satisfy his need for catharsis. To have continued throughout with a first-person narrator-protagonist, though, would almost certainly have restricted the novel's scope and meaning, limiting it much more closely to a personal recollection.

Clearly, Vonnegut wants the emphasis to fall not simply on himself, on his experience, or even on Dresden alone, but on the symbolic meaning of Dresden to all human beings. An omniscient, third-person narration might serve well the description and analysis of social events or the human condition, as it does in *Player Piano.* But that perspective remains too distant, too detached for achieving the combination of the personal and the symbolic relevance of the event that he now wishes to portray. In *Slaughterhouse-Five* Vonnegut creates the best of both worlds for himself: a first-person frame, one to which he can allude throughout and that builds a narrative presence into the novel, and the use by that narrator of a seemingly omniscient, third-person voice throughout most of the story.

The narrative stance just described and a protagonist like Billy Pilgrim—a figure omnisciently described and apart from the narrator—give Vonnegut the two dimensions his novel needs. Linking Dresden to other holocausts like Sodom and Gomorrah or Hiroshima and Nagasaki—and even to single deaths—universalizes it, as do the other connections, such as comparing himself to Lot's wife or the young American troops to the Children's Crusade. The narrative stance, then, furthers Vonnegut's effort to integrate the personal, the autobiographical, or the factual with the objectified, the universal, or the mythical.

The same kind of evolution is evident in the novel's central character, Billy Pilgrim. Looking back to *Player Piano,* one sees Paul Proteus as the first of those changing, multiroled protagonists, the "protean everymen" of whom Pilgrim is the ultimate. But his role has been extended in two directions: he is both more directly autobiographical and more profoundly universal.

Most of what Billy Pilgrim goes through as a soldier and a prisoner in Germany resembles closely what Vonnegut himself experienced. His is the presence through which we share the Dresden experience, the "eyes" through which we see it (appropriately, he later becomes an optometrist). The innocent receptivity of his childlike vision makes him the perfect vehicle for the author, and it often accords with Vonnegut's own habit of reexamining what convention has accepted by looking at it in the simplest possible way. Finally, the "I was there" reminders connect author and protagonist in circumstance and sympathy. In all, Pilgrim becomes the most autobiographical of Vonnegut's protagonists to this point without being "like him" and while retaining fully the capacity of his predecessors to be representative.

Perhaps the name Billy Pilgrim itself implies that he represents an Everyman in a contemporary *Pilgrim's Progress.* Like his predecessors he is protean, assuming many roles in the course of a novel that affords glimpses of him at every stage of his life. As beguiled man-child he is likened to those swept up in the Children's Crusade. In innocence, vulnerability, and eagerness to please he is likened to Adam and Eve. Several times Billy's description appears in terms of allusions to Jesus Christ, particularly as silently suffering victim.

Christ is also introduced into the book by Vonnegut's old technique of the outside observer—who in turn uses another favorite technique, the story within the story. In the hospital Billy talks to Eliot Rosewater, who is reading a Kilgore Trout novel named *The Gospel from Outer Space* in which an extraterrestrial visitor offers fresh interpretations of how Christianity does and should work on earth. The method enlarges, by including this supposed cosmic view, and there is also a kind of literal universalizing (as with Malachi Constant, the space wanderer) in making Billy a traveler in time and space.

If Billy Pilgrim seems at once personalized in his closeness to his creator and objectified as a universally representative figure, that duality appears again in the content of the novel. In some ways, *Slaughterhouse-Five* remains intensely personal, not only in its focus on events experienced by the author but also in its constant recapitulation of material drawn from the previous novels. Characters (as noted above), phrases, and images recur in number, making this work self-consciously "Vonnegutian" in nature. At the same time, the central event of the novel—the bombing of Dresden—is historical and therefore public and accessible.

The same is true of the many other historical allusions. In using them Vonnegut invites connection to amplify the notion of recurrent pattern in the human situation. His reuse of his own materials has a somewhat similar effect. It is as if the previous works cohere in this one to suggest that what they have all pointed toward and what they all mean, ultimately, achieve fruition here.

Recapitulation also becomes an important part of the structure of *Slaughterhouse-Five*, which is one of its most fascinating aspects. Vonnegut invites us to see it, as he says on the title page, as "a novel somewhat in the telegraphic schizophrenic manner of tales of the planet Tralfamadore." The tales of Tralfamadore are recounted in short books made up of clumps of symbols:

" . . . each clump of symbols is a brief, urgent message—describing a situation, a scene. We Tralfamadorians read them all at once, not one after the other. There isn't any particular relationship between all the messages, except that the author has chosen them carefully, so that, when seen all at once, they produce an image of life that is beautiful and surprising and deep. There is no beginning, no middle, no end, no suspense, no moral, no causes, no effects. What we love in our books are the depths of many marvelous moments seen all at one time."

As with much else in the novel, there is an element of comic parody here, but equally much that seems apt.

Vonnegut's novel, with its short chapters and paragraphs, its short sets of sentences or paragraphs with space between them, has a physical resemblance to the Tralfamadorian model. Many of these juxtaposed segments do not relate directly (sequentially or thematically) but do, taken together, build a total meaning, perhaps not quite like the Tralfamadorian novel but certainly going beyond mere montage. Although Vonnegut cannot arrange for us to read all of the novel's segments simultaneously, the effect that he achieves comes remarkably close.

Events from two basic time spans (1944–1945 and 1968) and from other points in Pilgrim's life are intermixed. His life is not revealed chronologically, by beginning in medias res, or by flashback; rather, we know its end from the start and the parts are filled in, from all segments of his life, as the novel progresses.

The portrait of Billy Pilgrim is completed on the basis of coincidence of time and event rather than of sequence and causality. Thus the form relates to the Tralfamadorian conception that everything that happens always was and always will be. At one point an American prisoner of war asks an offending guard, "Why me?" "Vy you? Vy anybody?" the guard responds. (The Tralfamadorians would say, "Because that is the way the moment is structured.") This vignette captures not only Vonnegut's perception of an essentially existential universe but also his challenge to the traditional realistic novel, which would show its audience, if not the character, exactly why.

Vonnegut cannot use the traditional form of the novel in the presentation of life viewed in contemporary terms because it conforms to assumptions of cause and effect and rigidities of time and substance that he questions. In particular, he needs a form that recognizes duration as a fourth dimension. This is a view of reality that he has sought to incorporate into his fiction from the start. It means that object or character *is* its history, not something that exists and has a history. In contrast with the portrayals of Proteus and Constant, the nonlinear characterization of Pilgrim emphasizes that he is not simply an established identity who undergoes a series of changes, but all the different things he is at different times.

The same principles that govern character govern event as well. Dresden is "led up to," as it were, by events that precede and follow it. It is surrounded by allusions to other catastrophes and to other events with comparable victims. Its being is its history, so that it ceases to be a single event with a single explanation or meaning. It is as Kurt Vonnegut and Billy Pilgrim see it, as those stunned German guards see it, as the weeping civilian couple sees it, in all the am-

biguity that this implies. The relationship between parts in the novel resembles the relationships in life—relative, ambiguous, and frequently subjective.

Part of Vonnegut's artistry shows in his giving his peculiar brand of realism a strong pattern in its apparent randomness. A subtitle describes the novel as *A Duty Dance with Death,* and it seems appropriate, since there is a kind of sweeping circularity in its movement. Dresden, death, is always at the center; it begins where it ends, with the author speaking; throughout, characters appear and reappear; and the historical allusions suggest cyclic repetition.

War and catastrophe recur in Vonnegut's novels. If war serves as his metaphor for the larger human condition, and holocaust functions as its ultimate consequence, it is in Dresden that Vonnegut finds the quintessential embodiment of those perceptions. It becomes the keystone of all that he has to say about human behavior or the nature of human existence. Although it remains the trauma that could shock Vonnegut personally into a unique awareness, in its public, historical perspective it must stand as the symbol of all that most revolts, bewilders, and terrifies us. This combination of personal involvement, historical authenticity, and symbolic meaning invests the Dresden of *Slaughterhouse-Five* with an impact more profound than that in Vonnegut's previous world-ending catastrophes.

In all respects *Slaughterhouse-Five* remains an integrative novel. It relates author-narrator and protagonist closely, draws all the historical and fictional events of its plot into a web around Dresden, and connects all its ideas to that central symbol. In recapitulating themes, characters, episodes, and phrases from previous works, this novel retrospectively confirms their direction. It fulfills their aspiration.

Slaughterhouse-Five integrates the personal

and the public to achieve a unique richness; it remains its author's most intensely cathartic novel but also carries perhaps his most compelling social message. To do so it combines personal reminiscence and public history, the plausibly fictional and the wildly fantastic.

One might well ask how, in a novel with historical basis and serious purpose, there is a place for flying saucers and time travel and Tralfamadorians. But it is precisely through this combination of fact and fantasy that Vonnegut can render the nature of the reality he perceives. The "documentary," as confirmed by David Irving's *The Destruction of Dresden* and the historical account of the Children's Crusade, seems no less farfetched than the "fantasy" of Kilgore Trout's *The Gospel from Outer Space* or the Tralfamadorian version of how the world ends.

Thus in the documentary-fantasy technique the two elements measure each other's dimensions, characterizing reality, in fact, by its unreality. It becomes a form for dealing with reality in which fact seems as bizarre as fantasy. It also seems worth noting that the fantastic elements contribute to the novel's humor, and that another way in which this book may be seen as integrative is that while it remains deeply moving it is frequently funny.

That completing the long-sought book on Dresden would leave Vonnegut fulfilled yet drained seems predictable. "I felt after I finished *Slaughterhouse-Five* that I didn't have to write at all anymore if I didn't want to," he says in *Wampeters, Foma, & Granfalloons.* "It was the end of some sort of career." Later, he speaks rather differently:

The importance of Dresden in my life has been considerably exaggerated because my book about it became a best seller. If the book hadn't been a best seller, it would seem like a very minor experience in my life. And I don't think people's lives are changed by short-term events like that. Dresden was astonishing, but experiences can be astonishing without changing you.

It is not the sudden but dramatic incidents that shape one's life, he maintains, so much as the longer-lasting events. He points to the Great Depression and his family as having supplied such influences.

Vonnegut's denial of Dresden as a major influence seems understandable, especially after the doubtless therapeutic benefits of having at last confronted it artistically. But although there seems little question of its overwhelming importance to his artistic motivation, there is little doubt that the influences on his earlier life had supplied much of the material and motivation for his previous work and became increasingly important afterward. Meanwhile, as noted earlier, Vonnegut said he would write no more novels and suggested, "The play's the thing. . . ."

The play was *Happy Birthday, Wanda June* (1971), a rehash of one written fifteen years earlier with the title "Penelope." One of its most interesting aspects is its almost feminist theme—this from a writer who by his own admission has few important or fully delineated female characters and even fewer satisfactory conjugal relationships. The play enjoyed a successful run off-Broadway, and has been performed elsewhere. Its ending, which underwent several revisions, remains its most troubling feature. If it attempts to show a new hero vanquishing the old hero, it fails. Harold Ryan, in spite of representing a lot of things we do not like, has a force and a vivacity that make him a compelling presence, while Dr. Norbert Woodly lacks these qualities and needs to have been given more substance earlier in this play. Penelope, on the other hand, has that substance and succeeds dramatically in her opposition to Ryan. But she is gone at the end and is not part of the final confrontation. So the dynamics of opposition and conflict in the play remain unbalanced.

Perhaps the imbalance is meant to show that the new age has no heroes, although the play seems to argue for a new type of unaggressive hero. More than that, in Penelope the play goes far toward offering the new woman who might be the counterpoise to Ryan, but at the end its own logic gets shaky and seems to falter.

The structural imbalance in the play, if viewed in the light of his novels, might be explained by the very thing that Vonnegut says led him back to novels. Part of his statement forms the opening of this essay, and in it he says that he has always included himself in his novels and must continue. He cannot do so on film or in drama. Perhaps at heart his play lacks balance because it lacks Vonnegut's presence, because it lacks one of those protagonists in whom he invests so much of himself. The lack of a psychological investment of this kind, which evidently made the play unsatisfying to its author, is the very thing that gives it its structural shortcoming. The lesson is how important to form as well as content are the autobiographical elements of Vonnegut's fiction.

Vonnegut's return to the novel with *Breakfast of Champions* (1973) shows the infusion of self made overt. In fact, authorial indulgence becomes one of the novel's themes. Vonnegut describes the book as a fiftieth birthday present to himself, a great "clearing out" of his mind that will dispense once and for all with the repeated ideas and characters and catch phrases. One character "liberated" by the end of the novel is Kilgore Trout, who now shares the dilemma of his creator, being suddenly both "fabulously well to do" and famous. Like Vonnegut, Trout often views things afresh by reducing them to their simplest terms, and they often share the technique of taking one of these simplified perceptions to an extreme. Vonnegut

calls this technique "solipsistic whimsy." One consequence of Trout's indulging it is that another character in the novel, Dwayne Hoover, buys the notion that everyone but him is a robot that he can attack at will. Obviously, all of this relates to Vonnegut's uncertainties about being taken as a "guru" and his concerns with the moral responsibilities of writers, of being (like Trout) taken seriously when he is trying to be funny and vice versa.

Breakfast of Champions appears heavily autobiographical, as if *Slaughterhouse-Five* had burst a dam for Vonnegut. It contains some forthright ruminating over his own frame of mind and his anxieties about depression and suicide. He speaks of his mother, mentally disturbed and a suicide and therefore still a rather frightening figure to him: "'You're afraid you'll kill yourself the way your mother did,' I said. 'I know,' I said." There are affectionate allusions to his father (some of his characteristics are transferred to Kilgore Trout) and even to his grandfather. And the novel ends with Trout's calling—perhaps echoing Vonnegut's own wish—"Make me young!"

Besides these inclusions of self, there is the most obvious one of all, his appearance as a character, so that he exists both outside and within the fiction as he sits in a Midland City bar watching his own characters and debating what to do with them.

I had made him up, of course—and his pilot, too. I put Colonel Looseleaf Harper, the man who had dropped an atomic bomb on Nagasaki, Japan, at the controls.

I made Rosewater an alcoholic in another book. I now had him reasonably well sobered up, with the help of Alcoholics Anonymous. I had him use his new-found sobriety, to explore, among other things, the supposed spiritual and physical benefits of sexual orgies with strangers in New York City. He was only confused so far.

I could have killed him, and his pilot, too, but I let them live on. So their plane touched down uneventfully.

More solipsistic whimsy, perhaps, but a comment on the roles of writer and fiction in the contemporary artistic world (an arts festival comprises the novel's central public event) and particularly on his own changed role. Again, Trout reflects that change, and so remains an autobiographical character in part.

Dwayne Hoover perhaps represents those solid middle-class origins with which Vonnegut never loses touch, and he may also reflect some of the author's anxieties about mental stability, sharing with him the disturbing suicide of a close female relative. Even the fraudulent artist Rabo Karabekian becomes at least a mouthpiece for Vonnegut. He expresses the ideal of recognizing individual worth that counters the novel's pervasive solipsism. That solipsism, which leads to seeing others as mere robots or as characters in fiction to be conveniently dismissed, constitutes the personal and social malaise that this novel attacks.

The drawings in *Breakfast* are more "solipsistic whimsy," included to demonstrate theme but also to indulge that very impulse. They contribute to an apparent breeziness that characterizes much of the novel but that also has been misunderstood, since it overlies a serious and carefully constructed moral framework.

The documentary-fantasy aspects of this book and of the next, *Slapstick,* have also elicited negative responses. In *Breakfast* the fantasy is supplied (not for the first time) by Trout: that all other human beings are robots. This fantasy projects to an extreme a prevalent social attitude documented frequently in the treatment of slaves, blacks, women, and prisoners, and less conspicuously but nevertheless insistently in the treatment of many other people. In

Slapstick the two central characters are hideous neanderthaloids, fantastic creatures about whom everything is exaggerated—age, height, numbers of nipples and fingers. Their treatment is used as a measure against which to judge normalcy in the treatment of relatives and others, especially in the ability to love and to accept differentness.

Slapstick has an intensely autobiographical introduction, recounting much from Vonnegut's past and present life and underlining his return to topics that predate Dresden in his experience. Family, the Great Depression, the question of what people need to make life more tolerable are the issues that this novel addresses in its hyperbolic fashion. The topics relate to Vonnegut's earliest ones, and in tone this novel reaches back toward them, partly because of its authorial stance. An autobiographical prologue precedes a first-person narration by the central character, which in turn ends with omniscient third-person narration. Partly because Vonnegut describes this as "the closest I will ever come to writing an autobiography," so that we look for him in Wilbur Swain, the impression of the author's presence is sustained in the narration. The intrusion of self remains implied, particularly in the last section, much more in the manner of the earlier novels.

The declaration of *Slapstick*'s autobiographical nature may be misleading. At the least, one needs to note Vonnegut's qualifier that it describes "what life *feels* like to me." The casting of himself and the sister whom he acknowledges as an influence, and an audience in the form of neanderthaloids, may underline the kind of closeness in separation from the rest of the world that young siblings can achieve. Other things—sharing the same jokes and discoveries, feeling brighter as a pair than alone, the inevitable separation, the sense of loss in the other's death, even perhaps the distance from parents who have trouble communicating love—may all reasonably have an autobiographical basis.

But the depiction of "how life feels" remains primary, the sense of being constantly confronted, like Laurel and Hardy, with tests of one's agility and inventiveness, "bargaining in good faith with destiny." It is a painful world, one characterized by his dying sister's saying, on hearing of the death of her husband, "Slapstick." And it is a lonely world, against which he poses a solution drawn from his childhood and his experiences visiting Biafra—the extended family. Proclaimed on campaign buttons, "Lonesome No More" becomes the motto of Swain's presidency, to be enacted through a system that Vonnegut had proposed to Sargent Shriver in 1972 and recollected in an essay published in *Wampeters, Foma, & Granfalloons:*

I wanted Sarge Shriver to say, "You're not happy, are you? Nobody in this country is happy but the rich people. Something is wrong. I'll tell you what's wrong: We're lonesome! We're being kept apart from our neighbors. Why? Because the rich people can go on taking our money away if we don't hang together. They can go on taking our power away. They *want* us lonesome; they want us huddled in our houses with just our wives and kids, watching television, because they can manipulate us then. ... We're going to vote in George McGovern, and then we're going to get this country on the road again. We are going to band together with our neighbors to clean up our neighborhoods, to get the crooks out of the unions, to get the prices down in the meat markets. Here's a war cry for the American people: 'Lonesome no more!'" That's the kind of demagoguery I approve of.

The tone of loneliness that pervades *Slapstick* continues implicitly in *Jailbird* (1979), in which the protagonist, typically, has lost his wife and is scorned by his son. Loneliness re-

mains the dominant condition of the individual, particularly the elderly, in Vonnegut's description of contemporary society.

These three novels focus on related aspects of contemporary American life. *Breakfast* reflects the spirit preceding the nation's two-hundredth birthday in pondering what America was and had been. In characteristic style it reexamines with childlike simplicity national emblems, symbols, songs, and mottoes, creating hyperbolic distinctions between pretense and reality, intention and achievement. *Slapstick* examines the social malaise in broad terms, using a futuristic setting. *Jailbird* repeats the theme but again narrows the focus, observing a particular—and real—presidency and the effects of the American system on two elderly people. It is a world of conglomerates and mergers, of thirst for power and acquisition, yet at the same time a world of the lonely and dispossessed.

Thematically, *Jailbird* shows its kinship to *God Bless You, Mr. Rosewater.* The RAMJAC Corporation is its Rosewater Foundation and Mary Kathleen its Eliot, but much of its emphasis falls on the other side of the coin—or fortune. Nicola Sacco and Bartolomeo Vanzetti serve *Jailbird* as *Slapstick* uses Laurel and Hardy, there are glimpses of American union history, and various episodes debate the achievement of socioeconomic equality.

The prologue makes clear that just as Laurel and Hardy came out of his personal past, out of Vonnegut's memory of childhood in the Great Depression, so do Sacco and Vanzetti. They are arrived at through more recollections of his father and his uncle Alex, and of their acquaintance, Powers Hapgood. So the economic circumstances that colored his childhood less by deprivation than by their psychological impact on his parents reappear. It is in this respect that *Jailbird* has autobiographical content.

In the first chapter, the narrator-protagonist says that years as well as people are characters in the book, "which is the story of my life," and goes on to elaborate dates—like 1929—that shape his story. Hence *Jailbird* may be seen as another autobiography in treating the mileposts of recent history that provide the context for Vonnegut's, and many another American's, life.

The prologue, however, remains the only overtly autobiographical part of *Jailbird,* continuing the serialized self-portrait contained in the prefatory chapters to the later novels. Again this technique helps establish a narrative tone for the novel. This prologue differs in that while the first half is autobiographical, in part devoted to explaining the wellsprings of the novel's theme, the second half is fictional, providing an invented background for events in the novel.

The body of the novel, too, mixes fact and fiction; Roy Cohn, Richard Nixon, Charles Colson, and others join with fictional characters; and events and places undergo a similar mixture. Finally, an index lists the real and the invented with like authenticity. No longer does the real frame the fictive—the mix of the two has become more pronounced and complete. We sense the same thing in individual episodes; Mary Kathleen as bag lady seems "realistic" until it comes to her huge tennis shoes and all their contents, which lead to her reclusive existence.

Such mixes of the reportorial and the fantastic keep recurring; real places, people, and events combine with nonexistent bird species, space travelers from Vicuna, and so forth. Yet these incongruities, like the flourishing restaurant in the derelict Arapahoe Hotel, draw attention to the economic disparities in society that are the novel's theme.

The reception of these last three novels, spaced over the ten years after publication of *Slaughterhouse-Five,* has been mixed. All have enjoyed good sales but have received mixed reviews. Two consistent complaints have been that the style of these books is extreme, approaching self-parody, and that they seem thin, lacking the substance or the urgency of the earlier work. Certainly in *Breakfast of Champions* the prose is curt and clipped, and the repetitions and catch phrases conspicuous, but that is in character with the novel's purpose and has been less true of the subsequent books.

One does sense a lessening of intensity, as if the motivation for the first six novels were diminished. Of course, by this point the spur of fame must have dulled, and Vonnegut had worked for thirty years as a publishing author. At the same time, one wonders to what extent circumstances contribute to an author's catching an audience's ear. There seems little doubt that the late 1960's provided the ideal setting for the antiwar, antiestablishment themes and the tireless questioning in Vonnegut. The climate a decade later was less receptive, not necessarily to the themes or questions, one senses, but to the experimentation in form that accompanied them. Perhaps Vonnegut is still haunted by some variant of the old reluctance to take seriously a writer who writes anything resembling science fiction.

Ironically, Vonnegut can be seen as standing firmly within American literary tradition. As early as 1970, Leslie Fiedler argued that Vonnegut was in the mainstream of fiction, that confluence of myth and entertainment from which the more esoteric High Art novel of the first half of the century had wandered.

A case can also be made for finding in Vonnegut's novels those characteristics that have been used to distinguish the European (especially British) novel from the American novel—"romance novel" or simply "romance." *The American Novel and Its Tradition* (1957) by Richard Chase remains a landmark work that conveniently spells out some of these characteristics in its introduction. In contrast to the novel, Chase argues, the romance "feels free to render reality in less volume and detail."

It tends to prefer action to character, and action will be freer in a romance than in a novel, encountering, as it were, less resistance from reality. . . . The characters, probably rather two-dimensional types, will not be complexly related to each other or to society or to the past. . . . Character itself becomes, then, somewhat abstract and ideal, so much so in some romances that it seems to be merely a function of plot. The plot we may expect to be highly colored. Astonishing events may occur, and these are likely to have a symbolic or ideological, rather than a realistic, plausibility. Being less committed to the immediate rendition of reality than the novel, the romance will more freely veer toward mythic, allegorical, and symbolistic forms.

Examples of such characteristics suggest themselves readily; there is hardly need for a reiterative demonstration. Recognizing this traditional context for Vonnegut's work seems every bit as important as observing the influence of more contemporary arts—films, cartoons, television—on his technique. Similarly, the content and attitudes in his work are as firmly grounded in that tradition as they are reflective of modern technology and scientifically educated thinking. Yet Vonnegut has rarely been seen in these terms.

Considering Vonnegut's fiction in light of the characteristics traditionally ascribed to the romance can be helpful. For instance, in the matter of characterization, it helps to explain some of the problematical aspects of those protean protagonists. Assessed by the criteria typically used in evaluating characters in a novel, these people often seem burdened with too many roles and change too much without a very deep psychological accounting for the changes. The lat-

ter seems particularly troublesome in view of the moral consequences of the changes.

Viewed in terms of the romance, with its ancestry in allegory, the moral dimensions of these characterizations may be seen somewhat differently. Here the characters may act as embodiments of qualities (or the vehicles whereby they are tested) rather than as full-depth characters in whom those qualities are explored. That is, they are characters who might embody, or become a means to exploring, pride and prejudice, rather than characters in whom we find a psychologically profound portrayal of individual confrontation with pride and prejudice, as we do in Jane Austen's novel. Thus the moral ambiguities in the consciousness of *Mother Night*'s Howard Campbell may be less important to Vonnegut's design than what the character enables Vonnegut to say on the moral issues the book raises. Vonnegut is able in this example to proclaim a simple moral in a book containing perhaps his most complex characterization.

In the same way, the documentary-fantasy techniques may irritate at both extremes when the reader expects a traditional novel. The documentary seems too literal, violating fictitiousness, while the fantasy appears too farfetched, shattering plausibility. Yet these extremes are not atypical of the "astonishing events" that in the romance may have "a symbolic or ideological, rather than a realistic, plausibility."

The romance has been viewed as a natural product of the American Puritan heritage, with its emphasis on allegory and symbol. Vonnegut himself has evinced some pride in his family heritage of atheistic humanism and shows some distaste for anything resembling Puritanism. Nevertheless, the basic middle-class values that his fiction inevitably endorses have some Puritan origins, and his method involves a Protestant sense of personal revelation.

The latter is evident in the fact that, as we have seen, the fiction draws heavily on autobiographical material and shows the continuing urge toward direct authorial expression. The idea at the core of a book often draws on first-hand experience, the personal repeatedly enters directly through characterization and narration, and the sustaining motivation in the first six novels appears to be the strong desire to express himself on his experience in Dresden.

Sometimes an almost evangelical urge to make a point emerges—declared in such repeated injunctions as "Listen." The commentary in *Player Piano* on the uses of automation and the decrying of strip mining in *Breakfast of Champions* are two examples. Vonnegut obviously recognizes this aspect of his work, not only in his later uncomfortable rejections of the "guru" role but from the start within the fiction itself.

From *Player Piano* onward there are references to preachers, propagandists, and public relations men, all of whom have roles approaching or intersecting with those of the writer. The dangers of proclaiming personal revelation are repeated in portrayals of preachers and churches from the tyrannical to the harmlessly farcical, and in writers from the uncompromising Ed in *Player Piano* to the solipsistically whimsical Kilgore Trout in *Breakfast of Champions*. Yet Vonnegut's need to include himself in his fiction has remained and seems, in fact, to have motivated some of his best work.

The real strength of Vonnegut's work comes from the subordination of the personal to the public. One senses the author's need for an outward channeling of his emotional responses, for a coming to grips with personal trauma and casting it in terms comprehensible to himself by making it comprehensible to others. Thus the need to symbolize, to universalize, overtakes the private, cathartic impulse.

Yet in Vonnegut one need does not simply yield to the other; the autobiographical origins and authorial presence remain to intensify and personalize what has been generalized. Perhaps some of Vonnegut's experience can be seen as archetypal for the twentieth century, but he has in any case a breadth of experience and knowledge that contributes to his keen insight into the nature of our times, and he has found the appropriate public symbols.

Vonnegut has created those symbols out of his own experience, drawing from the same source the ability to speak feelingly on some generally shared aspects of the human experience in this age. His characteristic frankness and simplicity cut through the conventionalizing of that experience. The best of his work may rest largely on this ability to explore honestly the conditions general to our time and simultaneously, through investment of himself in his work, to achieve a sympathetic bond with his reader.

Selected Bibliography

WORKS OF KURT VONNEGUT

NOVELS
Player Piano. New York: Scribner, 1952.
The Sirens of Titan. New York: Dell, 1959.
Mother Night. Greenwich, Conn.: Fawcett, 1962.
Cat's Cradle. New York: Holt, Rinehart & Winston, 1963.
God Bless You, Mr. Rosewater. New York: Holt, Rinehart & Winston, 1965.
Slaughterhouse-Five. New York: Delacorte/Seymour Lawrence, 1969.
Breakfast of Champions. New York: Delacorte/Seymour Lawrence, 1973.

Slapstick or Lonesome No More. New York: Delacorte/Seymour Lawrence, 1976.

Jailbird. New York: Delacorte/Seymour Lawrence, 1979.

COLLECTIONS OF SHORT STORIES AND ESSAYS

Canary in a Cat House. Greenwich, Conn.: Fawcett, 1961.

Welcome to the Monkey House. New York: Delacorte/Seymour Lawrence, 1968.

Wampeters, Foma, & Granfalloons: Opinions. New York: Delacorte/Seymour Lawrence, 1974.

PLAYS

Happy Birthday, Wanda June. New York: Delacorte/Seymour Lawrence, 1971.

Between Time and Timbuktu. New York: Delacorte/Seymour Lawrence, 1972.

BIBLIOGRAPHIES

Klinkowitz, Jerome. "The Vonnegut Bibliography." In *Vonnegut in America,* edited by Jerome Klinkowitz and Donald L. Lawler. New York: Delacorte/Seymour Lawrence, 1977. Pp. 217–52.

Klinkowitz, Jerome, and Stanley Schatt. "A Kurt Vonnegut Checklist." *Critique,* 12, no. 3:70–76 (1971).

———. "The Vonnegut Bibliography." In *The Vonnegut Statement,* edited by Jerome Klinkowitz and John Somer. New York: Delacorte/Seymour Lawrence, 1973. Pp. 255–77.

BIOGRAPHICAL AND CRITICAL STUDIES

"An Account of the Ancestry of Kurt Vonnegut, Jr., by an Ancient Friend of His Family." *Summary,* 1, no. 2:76–118 (1971).

Burhans, Clinton S., Jr. "Hemingway and Vonnegut: Diminishing Vision in a Dying Age." *Modern Fiction Studies,* 21:173–91 (Summer 1975).

Fiedler, Leslie A. "The Divine Stupidity of Kurt Vonnegut, Jr." *Esquire,* 74:195–97, 199–200, 202–04 (September 1970).

Giannone, Richard. *Vonnegut: A Preface to His Novels.* Port Washington, N.Y.: Kennikat, 1977.

Goldsmith, David H. *Kurt Vonnegut: Fantasist of Fire and Ice.* Bowling Green, Ohio: Bowling Green University Popular Press, 1972.

Greiner, Donald J. "Vonnegut's *Slaughterhouse-Five* and the Fiction of Atrocity." *Critique,* 14, no. 3:38–51 (1973).

Hansen, Arlen J. "The Celebration of Solipsism: A New Trend in American Fiction." *Modern Fiction Studies,* 19:5–15 (Spring 1973).

Harris, Charles B. *Contemporary American Novelists of the Absurd.* New Haven, Conn.: College and University Press, 1971. Pp. 51–75.

Irving, John. "Kurt Vonnegut and His Critics." *New Republic,* 181:41–49 (September 22, 1979).

Klinkowitz, Jerome. "Kurt Vonnegut, Jr." In *Literary Disruptions: The Making of a Post-Contemporary American Fiction.* Urbana: University of Illinois Press, 1975. Pp. 33–61.

———. "The Literary Career of Kurt Vonnegut, Jr." *Modern Fiction Studies,* 19, no. 1:57–67 (Spring 1973).

Klinkowitz, Jerome, and Donald L. Lawler, eds. *Vonnegut in America.* New York: Delacorte/Seymour Lawrence, 1977.

Klinkowitz, Jerome, and John Somer, eds. *The Vonnegut Statement.* New York: Delacorte/Seymour Lawrence, 1973.

Lundquist, James. *Kurt Vonnegut.* New York: Frederick Ungar, 1977.

May, John R. "Vonnegut's Humor and the Limits of Hope." *Twentieth Century Literature,* 18:25–36 (January 1972).

Mayo, Clark. *Kurt Vonnegut: The Gospel from Outer Space. . . .* San Bernardino, Calif.: The Borgo Press, 1977.

Olderman, Raymond M. "Out of the Waste Land and into the Fire: Cataclysm or the Cosmic Cool." In *Beyond the Waste Land: The American Novel in the Nineteen-Sixties.* New Haven, Conn.: Yale University Press, 1972. Pp. 189–219.

Reed, Peter J. "Kurt Vonnegut, Jr." In *Dictionary of Literary Biography,* vol. 2. Detroit: Gale Research, 1978. Pp. 493–508.

———. *Kurt Vonnegut, Jr.* New York: Warner Paperback Library, 1972. Reissued New York: Thomas Y. Crowell, 1976.

Schatt, Stanley. *Kurt Vonnegut, Jr.* Boston: Twayne, 1977.

Tanner, Tony. "The Uncertain Messenger: A Study of the Novels of Kurt Vonnegut, Jr." *Critical*

Quarterly, 11:297–315 (Winter 1969). Reprinted in *City of Words*. New York: Harper and Row, 1971. Pp. 181–201.

"Vonnegut." *Critique,* 12, no. 3 (1971); special number.

Vonnegut, Mark. *The Eden Express*. New York: Praeger, 1975.

INTERVIEWS

[Hayman, David, David Michaelis, George Plimpton, and Richard L. Rhodes.] "Interview: Kurt Vonnegut." *Paris Review*, 18, no. 69:56–103 (Spring 1977).

Klinkowitz, Jerome. "The Vonnegut Bibliography." In *Vonnegut in America*, edited by Jerome Klinkowitz and Donald L. Lawler. New York: Delacorte/Seymour Lawrence, 1977. Pp. 228–31. (The designated pages contain a listing of interviews.)

"Playboy Interview." In *Wampeters, Foma, & Granfalloons: Opinions*. Pp. 237–85.

Scholes, Robert. "A Talk with Kurt Vonnegut, Jr." In *The Vonnegut Statement*, edited by Jerome Klinkowitz and John Somer. New York: Delacorte/Seymour Lawrence, 1973. Pp. 90–118.

—PETER J. REED

Yvor Winters
1900—1968

YVOR WINTERS is commonly thought of as a stingy critic, and rarely thought of as a poet. He yielded little. He was convinced that T. Sturge Moore and Robert Bridges were greater poets than William Butler Yeats, that Frederick Goddard Tuckerman and Jones Very deserve more credit than Ralph Waldo Emerson, that Fulke Greville wrote greater poems than John Donne did. This cantankerous fellow would give little ground. Perhaps most damaging of all, in the eyes of modern readers, he routinely dismissed his antagonists as fools—which made his readers think, quite wrongly, that he also held in contempt the poets he criticized. He did not hold to the liberal notion that different claims are seldom mutually exclusive, when viewed from the proper perspective. He was an avowed absolutist who came to disapprove of free verse and of the presentational mode of modern poetry. These positions made it almost inevitable that his contemporary readers would mistakenly think of him as a reactionary. He is one of the great poet-critics of America, and his virtues as well as his obvious limitations are thoroughly misunderstood.

Before Winters was a critic he was a poet, an important one. Like Matthew Arnold, T. S. Eliot, and Ezra Pound, he wanted to spend his best efforts in poetry. When he was nineteen years old, he wrote knowingly to Harriet Monroe about how the spectacle of poor poetry and worse criticism made him lose his patience; writing criticism was not good for his spirit. This infamously ill-tempered critic was not beyond self-awareness; he often joked, in both poems and essays, at his own expense. Although he declared himself an absolutist in intellectual matters, his politics were never reactionary, and his critical arguments are in fact usually pragmatic. Unlike Yeats or Eliot or Allen Tate, in literary matters he was wholeheartedly and enthusiastically of his times.

Winters was born in 1900 in Chicago. His father, an independent businessman, achieved moderate financial success through real estate transactions, commodities exchange, and other activities. In several poems Winters speaks with fondness of him, though "A Vision" (1930) suggests that his feelings for his mother were quite different. (His mother took him to seances when he was a boy; and he seems to have often associated her with demonic power. He twice published a poem [in 1934 and 1940] spoken by a werewolf to the "wolf-bitch who suckled me." In both printings this hateful poem is followed by "A Petition," in which he apologizes for the first poem: "It was not I that spoke: / The wild fiend moved my tongue.")

Before Winters began his schooling, his family moved to Los Angeles and remained there for nearly a decade. In 1913 they returned to Chicago, where Winters attended high school and then spent a year at the University of Chicago. At the university's poetry club he met the novelist Janet Lewis, whom he married in 1926, and his longtime friend Glenway Wescott. He had become a serious reader of poetry and the little magazines in 1914 in Chicago, where *Poetry*, the best magazine on the subject, was then published. But illness forced him to leave the university for the Southwest. After a long convalescence, he taught elementary and high school students in a couple of coal-mining towns in New Mexico, and then resumed his studies, at the University of Colorado. In 1925, he received his M.A. in Romance Languages and began teaching again, this time French and Spanish at the University of Idaho. Two years later he entered the Ph.D. program in English at Stanford; and a year later he was appointed instructor in that department, where he remained throughout the rest of his career. As he liked to remark, in the lively 1920's he "was not in Paris, nor even at Harvard."

Winters' first and best book of literary criticism, *Primitivism and Decadence,* appeared in 1937, long after he was recognized as a poet; by then six collections of his verse had been published—*The Immobile Wind* (1921), *The Magpie's Shadow* (1922), *The Bare Hills* (1927), *The Proof* (1930), *The Journey* (1931), and *Before Disaster* (1934). He knew himself to be a poet long before he became a critic, and poets he thought of romantically, as was then the fashion.

The Priesthood

We stand apart
That men may see
The lines about our eyes.

We perish, we
Who die in art,
With that surprise

Of one who speaks
To us and knows
Wherein he lies.

In 1920, when this poem came out in *Poetry,* Winters was thinking his way through received terms of what it was going to mean to be a poet. This young man from Chicago considered the subject a good deal while he lay quite alone for more than two years in a New Mexico sanitarium trying to recover from that poet's disease, tuberculosis. Poets of "The Priesthood" are bound to each other by the religion of art, and they are isolated from others by the authenticity of art. The poet is a standing reproach to those who deny the suffering displayed about the poet's eyes. By 1924 Winters argued strenuously in prose for the poet's right to sanctify his art: "The artist whose deity is art, has a religion as valid and as capable of producing great art as any religion of the past or as the recently defined religion of money. As a conscious and intelligent being, no other religion will be possible for him, and he cannot, because of his religion, be called a decadent, a heretic." Winters was adapting a conventional *fin de siècle* notion to his own purposes; from the beginning to the end of his career he thought of poetry as "the richest and most perfect technique of contemplation." This was always his reason for taking poems and criticism seriously.

Nearly all the poems in his first two collections were written during these years of convalescence in New Mexico. Solitude, inaction, and what he once called (in regard to Marianne Moore) "the hypersensitivity of convalescence" are the major themes, though the treatment was not obviously personal. The first line of "Alone" (one of the two best poems in the first book) hints at Winters' uneasiness about the personal subject matter of these poems:

> I, one who never speaks,
> Listened days in summer trees,
> Each day a rustling leaf.
>
> Then, in time, my unbelief
> Grew like my running—
> My own eyes did not exist,
> When I struck I never missed.
>
> Noon, felt and far away—
> My brain is a thousand bees.

The movement from "I" to "one" shows an inclination to turn private experience toward a general significance; in the appositional clause, the "I" is being generically categorized from an external perspective. This displaced perspective holds the first two stanzas firmly in place: the poem reflects upon past experience. The appositional clause of the first line indicates that the speaker continues to be silent, but the remainder of the first two stanzas prepares the way for a disengagement of the solipsistic past; it would have been easy to judge the past critically in the last two lines. Yet the poem closes, with a metaphorical leap, in a terrifying present, for there has been no escape from solitude, and the speaker's mind is left a scramble—though not so scrambled that the poem is left in disarray.

This is one of the most carefully structured of Winters' early free-verse poems. A ghostly rhyme scheme flits through the lines: trees / bees, leaf / unbelief, exist / missed. And in the last line of each stanza is a shadow, too, of the iambic line. More importantly, Winters brings each stanza to a powerful close, with a plainly memorable line. The movement from one stanza to the next in both cases takes the poem forward in time; the third and seventh lines solidify the first two stanzas and chisel out the temporal contours of the poem. Even such a

specific matter as the placement of the caesura is handled so as to stress the orderliness of the poem. With one clever exception, the only caesuras occur after the first syllable of the first line of each stanza, breaking off the most elementary poetic unit—the initial syllable, the "I." The exception is the pause after "in time": that one extra pulsation nicely approximates the stretching out of time in this process of self-absorption.

These details are worth noticing. This is a poem about the hazards of solitude. The first two lines distinguish between speaking and listening: the speaker of the poem is (paradoxically, of course) a passive listener for whom one day, like one leaf, is indistinguishable from another. The poem is thematically surprising in its claim that absorption in sensual experience doubles back upon itself until one doubts the very existence of the sensual world. The speaker cannot miss because the target ceases to exist for him; nor can he measure a miss because his eyes do not exist. In writing about this subject, Winters implicitly stresses certain paradoxes. In the first line the speaker claims that he is always silent, and in the last he says that his brain is a scramble, even though his utterance is markedly well structured. Many years after writing this poem, Winters defined the imitative fallacy as a mistaken notion that poems about experiences of disorder ought to be disordered. In this early poem, it is plain that Winters would go only so far with the notion that form ought to imitate content. The placement of the caesuras does imitate the sense of the poem, but the overall structure of the poem resists and qualifies the poem's subject. The structure of the poem is an achievement that stands against the experience of buzzing disarray. Very far from seeming insincere, the poem could only have been written, Eliot would argue along with Winters, by someone who needed to put this terrifying experience into a controlling shape; the technique, as Pound said, proves the sincerity.

The very best poem in Winters' first book is "The Immobile Wind," which first appeared in 1920.

> Blue waves within the stone
> Turn like deft wrists interweaving.
>
> Emotion, undulant, alone.
> Curled wings flow beyond perceiving.
>
> Swift points of sight,
>   mystic and amorous little hands,
> The wind has drunk
>   as water swallows sifting sands.
>
> The wings of a butterfly
> Feel of the wind
> Tentatively, as men die
> In thought, that have not sinned.

Rather few of Winters' poems reflect the process of elaborating the poem, but this is an exception. He seems to be meditating on a section of rock with blue specks in it. He imagines the specks as waves, wrists, emotion, wings, points of sight, hands, sands, and again as wings. These interpretations are cast at the stone, one after the other, but one (in line 4) stands out: he sees his own emotions departing from him, like wings on the wind. The heart of this sanitarium poem lies in the last stanza, in that one word, "Tentatively," derived from *tentare,* to try or test. The poem tries various equations: specks = waves = wrists, and so on. Winters tries various figures, committing himself to none. There is no risk of sinning, none even of error, for no choices are made: all options remain open. In "Alone," Winters examined the hazards of purely sensual experience; in "The Immobile Wind," he moved to the opposite danger, the risks of indiscriminate thought. Both sorts of promiscuity, mental and sensual, lead to the same dead end.

Throughout his career, Winters felt the pull in both these directions—sensuality and mentality, body and mind. The adjustment to these rival forces was his lifelong major theme; by any measure this is a large, intellectual subject. After the short book of six-syllable poems based on Amerindian models, *The Magpie's Shadow* (1922), he returned to this theme in the strongest poems of *The Bare Hills* (1927). The poems in this book were written while he was living in Madrid, New Mexico; Boulder, Colorado; and Moscow, Idaho; they all focus on the western landscape.

April

> The little goat
> crops
> new grass lying down
> leaps up eight inches
> into air and
> lands on four feet.
> Not a tremor—
> solid in the
> spring and serious
> he walks away.

In this humble poem, the modifiers are simple and direct—"little," "new," "eight," "four," "solid," "serious "—as though the subject required nothing in the way of poetic treatment to make it worthy of attention. As a descriptive poet, Winters aspired to "a speech without idiom and a style without mannerism, that the clarity of . . . perception may not be clouded by inessentials." In fact, this poem resides largely in one word; that last adjective, "serious," nudges the poem beyond anecdote and description. Winters attributes to the goat a motive that is meant to cover too the coming of spring and the natural process in general; one word makes that attribution convincing. Winters customarily managed syntax and rhythm confidently in descriptive poetry: the goat comes to steady rest in that secure fifth line—with its four syllables. The words are perfectly paced through these short free-verse lines. The poem is a small but deft achievement.

Late in 1922, Winters submitted to *Poetry* the poem he then considered his best, but Harriet Monroe rejected it.

José's Country

A pale horse,
Mane of flowery dust,
Runs too far
For a sound
To cross the river.

Afternoon,
Swept by far hooves
That gleam
Like slow fruit
Falling
In the haze
Of pondered vision.

It is nothing.
Afternoon
Beyond a child's thought,
Where a falling stone
Would raise pale earth,
A fern ascending.

This poem sets limits to the sort of poetry Winters had learned to write well, which is one explanation of its importance. Early in his career Winters thought of himself as an imagist. He reprinted the first poem of his first book, later entitled "A Song of Advent" (1920), as the opening to four omnibus collections of his poetry.

On the desert, between pale mountains, our cries—
Far whispers creeping through an ancient shell.

This is surely modelled after the most famous and programmatic imagist poem, Pound's "In a Station of the Metro" (1913). The trick is a total and unabashed investment in a single poetic resource, metaphor. Pound sees the faces of the metro crowd as petals on a bough; Winters sees the mountain hollow as a seashell, throwing back on us the illusory echo of our own blood. In 1924 he described this technique as especially privileged: " . . . two perceptions, coming together with an almost infinite speed across the mental distances that naturally lie between two separate observations . . . cause a kind of mental vibration that is known as aesthetic emotion." The first two lines of "José's Country" start out with the imagist strategy: the horse's flying mane becomes dust, which really flowers in the second strophe, when the horse's hooves are seen as fruit.

These twelve lines are excellent descriptive verse. Winters singles out details from what seems considerable distance, and this gives the impression of strenuous and exact effort on his part; and he manages to locate himself firmly in relation to what he sees. Most important (and he would do this again in later, greater poems) he indirectly conveys the oppressive silence of haze, the blankness of this dry landscape. The figures—the flowers, the sound, the fruit—all tell what this landscape lacks. The phrases and clauses sit comfortably in these short lines: no line break interrupts a phrase or clause, yet no single line is syntactically complete. But the thirteenth line breaks that rhythm with a single sentence of categorical judgment. (Winters later used this breaking trope in two of his most important poems: "That is illusion. . . . That was the ocean" ["The Slow Pacific Swell"]; "This was hallucination" ["Moonlight Alert"].) He tries to dismiss the first two strophes because they are without meaning. Afternoon is simple beyond a child's thought. If seeing the mane as flowery dust was once impressive, by the poem's close he remembers that an inert stone, falling senselessly, could make the dust seem to flower. The title poem of this volume, "The Bare Hills," pushes this perspective all the way. The man who is closest to this austere landscape is dully brutish, uncivil:

> . . . he sat down
> and ate the bread
> as if he ate rock,
> while he ground
> his buttocks.
> He got up and smiled
> and went upstairs
> to meet the monstrous
> nakedness of
> his own face
> with unchanged step.

This earthen man communicates through only the blandest gestures ("and smiled"), for he is locked in the reflection of his own face. Pure sensuality holds one away from language and thought. But the judgment of the thirteenth line of "José's Country" does not stand unqualified—which is part of what makes this a fine poem. The last line starts the metaphorical process going again, with a fresh revision of the second line. And the fragmentary syntax of the last five lines rather perforates the tight, declarative syntax of that bleak thirteenth line. In the end, Winters will not quite surrender what he fretfully sensed was an intellectually limited method of writing. In fact, for the next few years Winters forcefully denied the lesson he feared he was learning—that certain methods, and especially the imagist method, have inherent limits: "It is infantile to say that [a poet] can do this or that only with this or that technique" (1924); "I believe that Mr. Tate goes too far in intimating that the imagistic method is of necessity limited in its possibilities: the possibilities of any method depend not on itself but on the poet who happens to find himself adapted to it . . ." (1927).

The poems of *The Bare Hills* reveal, however, an awareness that he was pressing against technical as well as intellectual limitations. Two poems from this book, "The Cold" (1925) and "The Rows of Cold Trees" (1924), both of which he reprinted in his four omnibus collections, suggest that he was fitfully trying to move beyond descriptive poetry. His uncertainty about this move can be heard in the rhythms. "The Cold" is by far the better of the two poems:

> Frigidity the hesitant
> uncurls its tentacles
> into a furry sun.
> The ice expands
> into an insecurity
> that should appal
> yet I remain, a son
> of stone and of a
> commentary, I, an epitaph,
> astray in this
> oblivion, this
> inert labyrinth
> of sentences that
> dare not end. It
> is high noon and
> all is the more quiet
> where I trace
> the courses of the Crab
> and Scorpion, the Bull,
> the Hunter, and the Bear—
> with front of steel
> they cut an aperture
> so clear across the
> cold that it cannot

be seen: there is no
smoky breath, no
breath at all.

Winters felt stretched across an old dichotomy: the chilly vacancy of the senses and the abstract exercises of the mind—stone and commentary. The descriptive poet is paradoxically left trying to chart what cannot be seen, the constellations, hypothetical fauna, at noon, because with winter the sensible world is running its natural but inhuman course toward vacancy. In these early poems he felt no middle ground; a poet could only oscillate between these two modes of writing, description or commentary. The sentences dare not end, because only emptiness remains when writing is done. The fascinating thing here is that the lines of these two poems are in fact ending and noticeably facing vacancy. Despite Winters' ability to handle free-verse rhythms unusually well, this poem is poorly, desperately enjambed: lines eight through fifteen are rhythmically inert, which is clear as soon as any one line is heard, even momentarily, as a single unit.

The worst deficiencies of "The Rows of Cold Trees," which Hart Crane admired, are rhetorical: "I have walked upon / the streets . . ."; "I have / walked among the tombs. . . ." The last strophe of this poem shows, though, as "The Cold" does too, the direction in which Winters was pushing.

It was the dumb decision of the
madness of my youth that left me with
this cold eye for the fact; that keeps me
quiet, walking toward a
stinging end: I am alone,
and, like the alligator cleaving timeless mud,
among the blessèd who have latin names.

The lines of this poem are even more uncertain than those of "The Cold," but in both poems one can hear Winters calling for a larger form, a line that would encompass the sort of commentary of this last strophe. He is having problems of enjambment; the line endings waver because he does not yet know what sort of line he needs to write, though he had an inkling, even as early as 1924. The last strophe of "The Rows of Cold Trees" and the first five lines as well (that is, the most powerful and discursive sections of the poem) and most of the lines of "The Cold" move (over the line endings) to an iambic beat. As early as 1924, Winters seems to have sensed that, in order to develop the side of his writing that he spoke of as "commentary," he would turn toward traditional metrical forms. But before he made that difficult and unfashionable move, he took one last try at developing his free verse into larger units.

Thomas Parkinson points out that the "Fire Sequence" (1927) is the turning point in Winters' writing. Winters was writing this lyric sequence while he was corresponding with Hart Crane, who was then at work on *The Bridge.* They exchanged manuscripts and suggestions. When the correspondence was over, Winters had severely criticized Crane's poem and had failed after two years' effort to shape a book of his own around the "Fire Sequence." Only four of the poems shown to Crane, it seems— "Bison," "November," "The Bitter Moon," and "The Deep"—appeared in Winters' next book of poems, *The Proof* (1930), and none of these was included by Winters in his *Collected Poems* (1952). For Winters, the sequence was a profound disappointment. Parkinson observes that Crane, however, never noticed that he and Winters were working on similar projects—though Winters certainly did. The first three poems of Winters' sequence attempt to collapse distinctions between continental ("Coal: Beginning and End"), personal ("Liberation"), and social activity ("Return of Spring"); the story of one is the story of them all. This is the major thematic connection between Winters' and Crane's sequences, though there are more particular ones: Winters' attention to "the shrieking/ steel amid the wilderness of spring" registers an antipathy to the history of industrialism similar to that of Crane's phrase, "the iron-dealt cleavage"; Winters' focus on "the Slav" and Crane's sense of the Genoese washerwoman indicate both poets' understanding that American history is a story of immigration and racism; and both of them (Crane in "Cutty Sark" and Winters in "Bill") tried to bring into verse the drunken idioms of the individual who takes on his own shoulders the failure of collective goals. Winters was not imitating Crane, and Crane was deliberately imitating Eliot. But to Winters' eye, his own failure and Crane's were not wholly distinguishable. His most severe critical essay, "The Significance of *The Bridge* by Hart Crane: or What Are We to Think of Professor X" (1947), was written in recognition of the fact that his own writing turned away from Crane's example only after obvious failure. Winters burned his letters to his wife, Janet Lewis, but he preserved Crane's letters. He knew that he learned from Crane's mistakes and that that should be part of the record.

Winters' father had hoped that his son would become a doctor, or at least take over his business. But he accepted his son's decision to study literature at Stanford, and his munificence gave Winters one year free to devote entirely to his studies and his writing; then Winters became a full-time instructor, with as many as 150 freshman themes to grade weekly. His first few years at Stanford were crucial, and his book *The Proof* (1930) gives a graphic account of the changes he went through in those years. The book, dedicated to his father, is divided into three sections: the first consists of nineteen free-verse poems, most of them descriptive; the second has ten sonnets; and the last comprises eleven metrical poems, most of them in qua-

trains or other short stanzaic forms. The very best poem, "The Empty Hills," opens the third section auspiciously, but it should be approached through "The Fable," the last sonnet of the second section.

Beyond the steady rock the steady sea,

In movement more immovable than stasis,
Gathers and washes and is gone. It comes,
A slow, obscure metonymy of motion,
Crumbling the inner barriers of the brain.
But the crossed rock braces the hills and
     makes
A steady quiet of the steady music,
Massive with peace.

                    And listen, now,
The foam receding down the sand silvers
Between the grains, thin, pure as virgin words,
Lending a sheen to Nothing, whispering,
Flower-surface sucked away, discriminate.
I found a fable here, but it is gone.
The mind alone is mind, and it must wait.

Winters developed some misgivings about this poem. The first line of the first sonnet in this section suggested that the use of metrical form was going to allow a direct approach to serious subjects: "Death. Nothing is simpler. One is dead." Grimly blunt perhaps, but this poem shows Winters in perfect control of his statement; the many metrical variations indicate great assurance. "The Fable" is different. The sonnet section of the book draws to a close with a convincing dissolution of the sonnet form: this poem is in blank verse; and the eighth line, the *volta,* is not only split in two but is also one foot short. The first twelve lines of the poem suggest that the fable concerns Winters' familiar theme: the tension between matter and mind. The ocean erodes mental structures and is best resisted. But as the waves recede, so does Winters' confidence; in the last two lines, he admits that the mind cannot function on its own. The last quality attributed to the ocean, "discriminate," complicates the dichotomy. The word is used adjectivally in its etymological sense of separate, but as a verb it customarily refers to the essential operation of the brain. The ocean retreats, then, taking with it the ability of the brain to perform its normal function. The sheen of matter, at the least, allows the mind to elaborate meanings, fables; when the wave ebbs, the fable is gone. The poem is cast in this partly dissolute sonnet form in order to suggest just how enamored Winters really was of the "Flower-surface" of the material world. When he reprinted the poem in his *Poems* (1940), he nearly destroyed it by leaving off the last three lines; having committed himself to a more balanced, less plaintive version of this "fable" in "The Slow Pacific Swell" (1931), he seems unwilling to let the ocean heave its potent sway over the mind. Unfortunately, only the truncated version of this poem is known to most of Winters' readers.

The next poem in both *The Proof* and the *Collected Poems,* "The Empty Hills" (1929), describes the area around his father's home in Flintridge, Pasadena; it is the first of two remarkable poems about the very distinctive southern California landscape.

> The grandeur of deep afternoons,
> The pomp of haze on marble hills,
> Where every whitewalled villa swoons
> Through violence that heat fulfills,
>
> Pass tirelessly and more alone
> Than kings that time has laid aside.
> Safe on their massive sea of stone
> The empty tufted gardens ride.
>
> Here is no music, where the air
> Drives slowly through the airy leaves.
> Meaning is aimless motion where
> The sinking hummingbird conceives.

> No book nor picture has inlaid
> This life with darkened gold, but here
> Men passionless and dumb invade
> A quiet that entrances fear.

A number of themes from other poems in *The Proof* are drawn together here. Most obviously, the poem develops three key terms—music, meaning, and motion—from "The Fable." In this landscape, meaning and motion are not alternatives vying with each other—motion is the only meaning here; conception is left to the hummingbird, which spends all of its energy in motion. The poems in both of the other sections ("The Red Month," "The Vigil," and "Apollo and Daphne" are examples) depict natural processes as physically violent; Parkinson observes that Winters had been especially affected by the mechanistic physics of Jacques Loeb. When Winters refers to the air driving through the leaves, he is speaking literally: throughout this book, he examines the natural process on the molecular level; on that level, heat is violent. Conversely, from the bird's-eye view, the Pasadena hills are riding on a sea of stone. Part of his accomplishment in this poem is maintaining both these analytical perspectives—molecular and geological—at once, though the main force of Winters' technical power is felt elsewhere: in the way the syntax is varied and stretched over the metrical grid of these stanzas.

When he began to write metrical verse, Winters was a sufficiently mature and sophisticated poet to realize that metrical norms are not simply to be fulfilled. In both "The Fable" and "The Empty Hills" he plays his wiry syntax against the backdrop of stanzaic patterns whose demands are simple and routine—the sonnet, the quatrain. The particular achievement of "The Empty Hills," however, is Winters' analysis of the quality of suburban life in southern California. The dominant quality is emptiness, and the diction ("pomp," "swoons") and imagery ("kings," "music") quietly associate this emptiness with pretension and theatricality. "Grandeur" and "pomp" are qualities of human culture; they depart from southern California without notice—for this is a community, the last quatrain claims, without culture. The mute landscape possesses a dignity that the people abjure. The last two lines claim, with very tight phrasing, that men are attracted to this powerfully silent and vacant landscape by their fear of all that culture comprises: social distinction ("grandeur" and "pomp"), music, meaning, books, and painting. This landscape has the power to drug the fears of those who are without passion, without language.

Just one year after *The Proof* appeared, Winters published *The Journey and Other Poems,* his greatest single collection of poems. He developed amazingly in what seems to have been a single year; in 1931 he was a new poet. One small sign of the change is that he had the confidence to begin and end the book with poems that display an aspect of himself that had not appeared earlier in his verse: both of these poems were written by a critic. The first, "The Critiad," is "A Poetical Survey of Recent Criticism"; Winters has his fun with nearly everyone. Speaking of Morton Dauwen Zabel and Edmund Wilson, then editors of two journals that routinely published Winters, *Poetry* and the *New Republic,* he says:

Men with less mind than Blackmur or than
    Burke,
And so just able to find steady work,
Meticulous with influence and date,
They hesitate, suggest, and hesitate,
Not seldom right, always a trifle late.

His point of course is serious. He was convinced that he lived in a great era of verse writing. Critics then had the opportunity and responsibility to help direct contemporary poetry; to leave the job of judging to posterity was, for Winters, a lack of nerve—and that would surely damage those talents that could profit from instruction. And without sound criticism, the great poets, the best models, may not even be read:

And meanwhile Hardy, that heroic oak,
Is still found dull, Williams a standing joke,
And Bridges simple; Sturge Moore goes
    unread;
Miss Crapsey and Miss Moore alike are dead.
On any bargain counter you can buy
Old Stevens for a quarter: let him lie.
Now Mina Loy's hard rhetoric is nought,
Waits naked in a night of print, unsought.
Malice, suspicion, calculating hate
Are meted justly out to Allen Tate.
Each metaphysic foetus judges best.
Great poets all! God give them all good rest!

Winters had resisted thinking of himself as a professional critic until 1931, but with the publication of *The Journey* he had achieved his poetic style and could then afford to identify himself as a teacher and critic. In the last poem, "December Eclogue," he gives a candid, compelling account of his own daily activity as a heavily burdened instructor of English and a wearied polemicist:

Nights that I've spent alone with pen and
    page,
Mastering shadows of our daemonic age,
For innocence to fumble, fill the mind.
And I am sunk in stupor, gone half-blind.
Such are my country nights! By the full moon
I cool the blood that coffee heats too soon,
Coffee and critics, and the mouldering fire.
For academic rites outlive desire,
And Controversy's very self is dead—
Bred in the heart, she perished in the head.

This is not the sort of personal experience that poets of Winters' generation and later have felt comfortable describing in their poems; to admit in a poem to an academic career entails considerable risk. Suicide, cruelty, alcoholism, or promiscuity—these are now the more common, conventional admissions. The still powerful common taste is for picturesque poets. Winters knew that to capitulate to such base taste often involves a dishonest and cowardly betrayal of one's own class. He was never ashamed or even timid about being an intellectual and an academic poet, and before 1931 he had learned to take pride in his activity as a critic.

At the same time, he showed another kind of candor, one that should be easy to admire:

What has he found there? Life, it seems, is
    this:
To learn to shorten what has moved amiss;
To temper motion till a mean is hit,
Though the wild meaning would unbalance it;
To stand, precarious, near the utter end;
Betrayed, deserted, and alone descend,
Blackness before, and on the road above
The crowded terror that is human love;
To still the spirit till the flesh may lock
Its final cession in eternal rock.

This is the middle stanza of "The Grave," a poem written after his father's death, and the writing is very powerful. The courage to speak plainly about the meaning of life was extremely rare among Winters' contemporaries; it rests upon a conviction that poetry engages the grand, perennial, urgent human issues. Winters speaks his mind—and the sense of a speaking voice in 1931 is convincing—without coyness, without irony or evasive figures, about what every person wants to know, what life is, or seems to be. This stoical, dignified, and measured statement will bear comparison to the writing of the greatest poet-critic in English, Samuel Johnson. And the earnestness that enabled Winters to write so directly is exactly what warrants such lofty comparison.

Between the opening and closing poems of *The Journey* are six extraordinary poems—

"The Slow Pacific Swell," "The Marriage," "On a View of Pasadena from the Hills," "The Grave," "The Journey," and "A Vision"—that assure Winters a permanent place in American literary history; two of these are the best poems of his career. This is the first strophe of "The Slow Pacific Swell," the second poem in *The Journey*:

Far out of sight, forever stands the sea,
Bounding the land with pale tranquillity.
When a small child, I watched it from a hill
At thirty miles or more. The vision still
Lies in the eye, soft blue and far away:
The rain has washed the dust from April day;
Paint-brush and lupine lie against the ground;
The wind above the hill-top has the sound
Of distant water in unbroken sky;
Dark and precise, the little steamers ply—
Firm in direction, they seem not to stir.
That is illusion. The artificer
Of quiet, Distance, holds me in a vise
And holds the ocean steady to my eyes.

None of Winters' earlier poems is quite like this; in 1931 he was writing with his full powers. The play of syntax, lineation, and rhyme holds these lines together in a unit coherent enough to be spoken of as a paragraph. Winters was concerned that the poem have just this sort of structural unity, which must be why he composed the poem in three fourteen-line stanzas, although this suggestion of stanzaic structure is superfluous. The very first lines of the poem lay claim to a full, unrestricted diction: words such as "forever," "pale," "small," "soft," and "distant" were debased coinage in 1931; Winters redeemed these words from stale poetic diction by employing them in this context of exact, fresh description (lines 6 and 7) and tough concision.

This commanding poetic style is used in the first stanza, as Winters says, to recreate an illusion, a child's perception. The exact description and the present-tense verbs following the colon convey that childish vision. When the third-from-last line pulls the stanza up short, the sense of illusion applies not only to the ships that seem to stand still but also to the entire vision of a peaceful sea. Only distance can make the material world seem peaceful; examined closely (as it was in the "Fire Sequence"), matter is thoroughly violent with entropy. In the second stanza Winters recalls a time when he overcame that distance and nearly drowned:

> . . .The skull
> Felt the retreating wash of dreaming hair.
> Half drenched in dissolution, I lay bare.
> I scarcely pulled myself erect; I came
> Back slowly, slowly knew myself the same.
> That was the ocean. . . .

There is no illusion of presence here; the experience was sufficiently terrifying that Winters does not try to bring it back to immediacy with present-tense verbs. The experience stays in the past as a reminder of a lesson: to know himself means knowing the difference between himself and the ocean; to confuse the two (which confusion the romantic iconography—"dreaming hair," "Half drenched in dissolution"—represents as a cultural and not just personal error) can be fatal. Human beings are not just matter, like the ocean; nor are they merely mammals, like the whale, which is described gorgeously at the close of the second strophe.

Seeing the whale rise majestically and sink mysteriously convinces Winters that he himself is no Ishmael: "A landsman, I. . . ." Yet the next three lines of this last stanza express a desire for cautious proximity to the sea.

> I would be near it on a sandy mound,
> And hear the steady rushing of the deep
> While I lay stinging in the sand with sleep.

From thirty miles away, the imagination can romanticize the sea; Winters wants to stay at the shore's edge, where he can know the sea for what it is without being overwhelmed by its power. As a child, he could only imagine the sound of the water (lines 8 and 9); now he wants to live with its sound. Sleeping on the sand is Winters' way of repeating the experience of immersion (in stanza 2), when the water "like sand" pressed his "dreaming hair" to the deck. Once this measured relation to the sea has been expressed, Winters begins to unveil the allegory of the poem. The land represents the unfeeling ("numb") but precise security of a life led by the mind; the sea, of course, represents all the dark, unconscious ("Sleeping"), blind, chaotic power that the mind cannot master. The poem is written in praise of having it, after some discriminating adjustments, both ways.

"On a View of Pasadena from the Hills" is Winters' greatest achievement and a wonderful poem in absolute terms. "The Empty Hills," published just a year earlier, was the first attempt to write this extraordinary landscape poem, as "The Fable" was an early attempt at "The Slow Pacific Swell." The death of Winters' father that year seems to have been the impetus for three of the eight poems of *The Journey*—"On a View," "The Grave," and "A Vision." One of the effects of this loss was the opening up of new subject matter for Winters, whose tendency, like Wallace Stevens', was to return repeatedly to the ideas that mattered most to him. With impressive honesty, "On a View" examines urban, technological progress. Before 1931, Winters had considerable success with descriptive poetry and with intellectual–historical and philosophical themes; some of the best of his later poems, like "On a View," deal with cultural–historical subjects.

The poem opens in the less than half-light before the early dawn. Winters describes with great exactness the way the light varies across the hilly landscape. Nowhere is it plainer that he is a western, nonurban poet:

That summer crater smoked like slaking lime,
The hills so dry, so dense the underbrush,
That where I pushed my way the giant hush
Was changed to soft explosion as the sage
Broke down to powdered ash, the sift of age,
And fell along my path, a shadowy rift.

These excellent lines come from familiarity with a strange locale; Winters spent most of his boyhood in southern California. But they come too, of course, from William Wordsworth, who presides rather grandly over much of this poem. (The occasion of the poem—a return to a landscape known physically as a child—is almost Wordsworth's special property; and several thematic and verbal echoes of Wordsworth here are too obvious to deserve remark. The last two lines quoted, though, are Wordsworthian in another sense: they place the caesura just after the third foot and before an appositional phrase beginning with an article, which is a Wordsworthian metrical signature—"We have given our hearts away, a sordid boon!") Winters renders the particular strangeness of this landscape partly by showing how it is at times and in particular areas lush, at other times or just over a hill, powdery dry. This aspect of the Los Angeles landscape comes, in the course of the poem, to be overlaid by the competition of trees, deer, and concrete. One of the most striking things about Winters' descriptive language, and about his mature poetry in general, is that he makes traditional poetic diction render his unusual perception with extreme accuracy:

Below the windows, the lawn matted deep,
Under its close-cropped tips, with dewy
    sleep,
Gives off a faint hush, all its plushy swarm
Alive with coolness reaching to be warm.

This is an act of poetic renovation, but also of muscle-flexing. No conventions of poetic diction could be more obvious to Winters' readers than the once Miltonic and later eighteenth-century habit of converting a noun into an adjective by adding a "-y" and pairing that manufactured modifier with another noun. Winters invokes this formula twice here in a passage based on close observation and intimate knowledge of the coming of light to this landscape, where the dews are in fact quite heavy. There are other seventeenth-century techniques worth noting here: the prosodic elisions of "towers," "shadowy," "tremulous"; and the rhyming of primary- and secondary-stressed syllables ("perplexedly" / "living tree"). These techniques of diction and prosody situate Winters' effort in a complicated relation to literary history: his readers should understand that this poem derives from a tradition of landscape poetry, in particular the prospect poem that throve in the seventeenth (most notably in John Denham's "Cooper's Hill"), eighteenth (Alexander Pope's "Windsor Forest," Thomas Gray's "Ode on a Distant Prospect of Eton College"), and nineteenth centuries (Percy Bysshe Shelley's "Lines Written Among the Euganean Hills," John Keats's "I Stood Tiptoe Upon a Little Hill"). Winters goes out of his way to remind his reader of the importance of Wordsworth as a model here, partly because Wordsworth worked so hard to isolate himself from the very conventions of poetic diction that Winters exploits. Winters had no sympathy with the argument of the preface to Wordsworth's *Lyrical Ballads* (in fact, he ignores this crucial document of literary history). All corners of the language, Winters thought, could be occupied by a contemporary poet. (Pound and Eliot held this position too.) Conventions rule out no word, but they do load some with the weight of history. Winters prides himself here on being able to heft a heavy load of poetic conventions into his greatest poem; "On a View" cries out for elevation above a number of the famous poets Winters thought overrated—Pope, Gray, Wordsworth, Shelley,

Keats. There is a sense, in "On a View," of beating the opposition at its own game.

This particular landscape is especially marked by cultural aspirations. Winters does not explore the ways in which the Spanish displaced and subjugated the native population, nor the ways in which Anglo-Americans have more recently displaced the Latin-American culture; these themes would wait until "The California Oaks" (1936). He is more struck by the fact that the recently imported palm trees have yet more recently been eliminated, though the nonnative acacia and eucalyptus trees now obscure the hills from view. These matters are telling, because they reflect the southern California tradition of supplanting the native. Winters' father's garden is still young, terraced against the sloping, eroding hill, and the glass house has no more convincing claim to native authenticity than does William Randolph Hearst's San Simeon. Still, Winters frankly expresses his sympathy for his father and his father's friends:

Too firmly gentle to displace the great,
He crystallized this vision somewhat late;
Forbidden now to climb the garden stair,
He views the terrace from a window-chair.
His friends, hard-shaken by some twenty
        years,
Tremble with palsy and with senile fears,
In their late middle age gone cold and gray.
Fine men, now broken. That the vision stay,
They spend astutely their depleted breath,
With tired ironic visage wait for death.

The judgments expressed in this poem are, above all, poised. The first line of this particular passage might almost have come from Johnson's poem "On the Death of Dr. Richard Levet," so discriminating is the epithet "firmly gentle," so understanding is Winters of his father's social humility, even after the archness of the next line has been taken into account. His father's friends have suffered mainly time and suburbanization, and not all that much of time, though they are thoroughly broken now. The last line of this passage turns back against the confidence that allowed Winters himself the irony of the line about his father's late-crystallized vision; these men wear an irony more easily justified, probably more knowing than Winters' own. These are some of the people who have imposed their fantasies on the landscape, for a little while, and now they are passing, like the palms, like the deer.

Here is the last strophe of this great poem:

Cement roads mark the hills, wide, bending
        free
Of cliff and headland. Dropping toward the
        sea,
Through suburb after suburb, vast ravines
Swell to the summer drone of fine machines.
The driver, melting down the distance here,
May cast in flight the faint hoof of a deer
Or pass the faint head set perplexedly.
And man-made stone outgrows the living tree,
And at its rising, air is shaken, men
Are shattered, and the tremor swells again,
Extending to the naked salty shore,
Rank with the sea, which crumbles evermore.

Winters saw the home of his father's imagining sit hardly lived in, like a newly manufactured museum piece, and saw too his father's friends gone prematurely feeble, "shaken" by the growth of Los Angeles concrete; he knew too that the brush and trees described so well in the second, third, and fourth strophes were being edged out by the new freeways. Yet the automobiles are genuinely "fine"; they drone like the bees hiving in these suburban villas. The omnidirectional sprawl of Los Angeles is part of a long-continuing process, like erosion, that must run its course. Judgments cannot be final; no one's hands are clean. The poem ends with a sense of the inevitability of the historical process, and this was to be Winters' great theme in many of the best of his remaining poems, especially those about World War II.

Winters was able to write "The Slow Pacific Swell" and "On a View of Pasadena from the Hills," his two best poems, only because he found a new form. All of the poems in *The Journey* are written in heavily enjambed iambic pentameter couplets. The first poem in the book, "The Critiad," might make one think that Dryden and Pope were the models for this use of the couplet, but that was not the case. Neither of them used enjambment in a way comparable to that of Winters. One critic claims that Winters pretty much invented this style in which enjambed couplets accrete into verse paragraphs, but that is not quite right either. Winters often spoke of his deep admiration for Ben Jonson's use of the couplet, and in his early years at Stanford he studied Jonson with his mentor William Dinsmore Briggs. These are the last ten lines of Jonson's "To Heaven":

I know my state, both full of shame, and
    scorn,
Conceived in sin, and unto labor born,
Standing with fear, and must with horror fall,
And destined unto judgment, after all.
I feel my griefs too, and there scarce is
    ground,
Upon my flesh t'inflict another wound.
Yet dare I not complain, or wish for death
With holy Paul, lest it be thought the breath
Of discontent; or that these prayers be
For weariness of life, not love of Thee.

Winters admired this poem immensely ("The poem has no faults that I can discover..."), largely for technical reasons. He said in 1967:

The heroic couplet is used in these respects with a skill that one can seldom find equalled within similar limits by Dryden or Pope. The relationship of sentence-structure to linear and stanzaic

structure is similarly brilliant.... Within these sentences there is considerable variety of structure regardless of length, this variety affecting not merely the sentence but the rhythm of the line and of the group of lines.

Winters was perfectly right about "To Heaven," and the same observations must be brought to bear on the verse of "The Slow Pacific Swell" and "On a View," if those poems are to be fully appreciated; Winters' own departure from the confines of this small stanzaic form are even more frequent and marked than Jonson's. His sense in 1931 of how far the heroic couplet had been stretched by didactic poets using the syntax of explanation certainly derived in part also from Henry Vaughan's "The Lamp":

'Tis dead night round about: Horrour doth
    creepe
And move on with the shades; stars nod and
    sleepe,
And through the dark aire spin a firie thread
Such as doth gild the lazie glow-worms bed.
    Yet, burn'st thou here, a full day; while I
    spend
My rest in Cares, and to the dark world lend
These flames, as thou dost thine to me; I
    watch
That houre, which must thy life, and mine
    dispatch;
But still thou doest out-goe me, I can see
Met in thy flames, all acts of piety;
Thy light, is *Charity;* thy heat, is *Zeale:*
And thy aspiring, active fires reveale
Devotion still on wing; Then, thou dost weepe
Still as thou burn'st, and the warme droppings
    creepe
To measure out thy length, as if thou'dst
    know
What stock, and how much time were left
    thee now. . . .

Although Winters did not comment upon the play of syntax across the couplets here, Vaughan was probably an even more adventurous model in this regard than Jonson. And by 1929 Winters' need for such a form was apparent. As early as 1924, when "The Rows of Cold Trees" appeared, his poems show a desire to write longer poems that could be successfully descriptive and discursive, poems that could sustain a line of statement over many lines. "The Rows of Cold Trees" was not successful, and neither was his subsequent attempt to elaborate a larger form, the "Fire Sequence" (1927). Vaughan and Jonson seem to have shown Winters a way of accomplishing what he and Crane had failed to achieve. In Winters' hands this form was so effective that he could write satiric verse, like that in "The Critiad"; meditative poems, like "The Slow Pacific Swell" and "On a View"; and psychological-visionary poetry, like that of "A Vision." It was an all-purpose form for a short while, and the result was great poetry.

In 1934 Winters published a pamphlet of mostly short poems, *Before Disaster;* and he was sure enough of his intent to set out a thematic and stylistic apology for the poetry in a foreword. Winters was proud of the fact that he was both poet and critic. The poems in this collection were not so ambitious as those of *The Journey,* but there are a few excellent ones here and significant reasons too for Winters' modesty. In 1934, he knew that war was coming. Just how intellectuals and poets ought to comprehend and represent the historical events leading to war and the cultural effects of those events was a more difficult matter for him than for many of his contemporaries—consequently, he managed to write fine poems on this theme.

By the Road to the Air-Base

The calloused grass lies hard
Against the cracking plain:

Life is a grayish stain;
The salt-marsh hems my yard.

Dry dikes rise hill on hill:
In sloughs of tidal slime
Shell-fish deposit lime,
Wild sea-fowl creep at will.

The highway, like a beach,
Turns whiter, shadowy, dry:
Loud, pale against the sky,
The bombing planes hold speech.

Yet fruit grows on the trees;
Here scholars pause to speak;
Through gardens bare and Greek,
I hear my neighbor's bees.

This is a deliberate revision of a famous poem by William Carlos Williams that Winters admired, "By the Road to the Contagious Hospital." Williams' poem concerns the coming of spring; Winters' the coming of war. The first three quatrains suggest, through the imagistic techniques that Winters had long mastered, that the planes taking off on maneuvers from the air base near his home will render the landscape below as barren as the one from which the bay waters have retreated. However, even before the adversative last quatrain, he suggests an ambiguous doubt in the last line of the third quatrain: the planes seem to "hold speech" in the sense that their noise prevents one from speaking; but there is also the suggestion that what the bomber planes "hold," that is, carry, can be understood as a form of statement (presumably about American willingness to curb militarily the growth of fascism). In the last quatrain, Winters' doubt is plain and unresolved. He juxtaposes (though with that non-modernist signpost "yet") apparently opposed aspects of life in the Palo Alto area: the military, domestic, and academic lives in fact all proceed in close proximity, and may even be systematically interdependent. Yet just how one aspect may depend upon another, Winters does not presume to explain; to express that humility in the face of so difficult and momentous a situation, the modernist methods of juxtaposition and verbal or imagistic echo ("Shell-fish deposit lime" / "bombing planes"; "planes hold speech" / "scholars pause to speak"; "bombing planes" / "neighbor's bees") were exactly right. Winters was sufficiently impressed by the complexity of political events in 1934 to see the need to refrain from judgment.

After going through the most important changes of his poetic career between 1928 and 1931, and writing the great poems of *The Journey,* Winters continued to develop in still another direction in the early 1930's. After 1931 he seems to have written only five other poems in his major form, the enjambed heroic couplet: "Alcmena" (1935), "Time and the Garden" (1940), "A Dedication in Postscript" (1940), "To Edwin V. McKenzie" (1941), and "Moonlight Alert" (1943). He wrote many poems in shorter lines and many in quatrains of various line lengths. The most unusual form he developed in these decades was based on the prosody of Emily Dickinson ("There's a certain slant of light") and Fulke Greville ("Sonnet LVI"), although William Blake ("The Tyger") may have been in his memory too. "Midas" (1932), "Chiron" (1932), "Orpheus" (1934), "Dedication for a Book of Criticism" (1934), "To David Lamson" (1940), and "Two Old-Fashioned Songs" (1957) are all written in an oddly truncated trochaic tetrameter. The very best poem in this meter is "Before Disaster," originally published in September 1933 in the *New Republic.*

> Evening traffic homeward burns,
> Swift and even on the turns,
> Drifting weight in triple rows,
> Fixed relation and repose.
> This one edges out and by,

> Inch by inch with steady eye.
> But should error be increased,
> Mass and moment are released;
> Matter loosens, flooding blind,
> Levels driver to its kind.
> Ranks of nations thus descend,
> Watchful, to a stormy end.
> By a moment's calm beguiled,
> I have got a wife and child.
> Fool and scoundrel guide the State.
> Peace is whore to Greed and Hate.
> Nowhere may I turn to flee:
> Action is security.
> Treading change with savage heel,
> We must live or die by steel.

This poem includes, just below the title, the date "Winter, 1932–3," a season of changes. Roosevelt had won the election of 1932 and was waiting to take over the presidency from Herbert Hoover, Stanford University's most famous alumnus—evidently a fool in Winters' eyes. A year earlier, Japan had established a puppet state in Manchuria, after betraying its own pledge to the League of Nations to withdraw its army from there. In Europe, Hitler assumed the chancellorship of Germany in January 1933; in February the Reichstag burned; in March he was given dictatorial powers. The disaster Winters foresaw, of course, arrived in time. And the poem suggests that there was no way for Europeans, Asians, or Americans to rise above or anyway escape the calamitous course of history. Hope lay only in skillful, astute maneuvering within a situation governed largely by necessity; the conspicuous rhythm of the poem makes just this point by pulsing emphatically along, four beats and seven syllables to a line—without a single substitution: "Nowhere may I turn to flee."

Within the historical process, the range of practical moral activity is not great, although this was never a cause of despair or even chagrin for Winters, who is a bit wrongly thought of as a moralist. In 1922 he told Harriet Monroe that he was interested in art and intellectual activity and not in morality. He was a pragmatic man who measured one poem against another, who had no trouble understanding the need, in some circumstances, for Machiavellian strategies:

The Prince

The prince or statesman who would rise to
    power
Must rise through shallow trickery, and speak
The tongue of knavery, deceive the hour,
Use the corrupt, and still corrupt the weak.

And he, who, having power, would serve the
    State,
Must now deceive corruption unto good,
By indirection strengthen love with hate,
Must love mankind with craft and hardihood:

Betray the witless unto wisdom, trick
Disaster to good luck, escape the gaze
Of all the pure at heart, each lunatic
Of innocence, who draws you to his daze:

And, this frail balance to immortalize,
Stare publicly from death through marble
    eyes.

Winters finally had great admiration for those individuals who, after disciplining their feelings, were able to compel corrupt systems to serve noble ends, but they always were, for both Winters and Machiavelli, lone individuals.

In March 1933, one of these individuals died, and Winters was moved to write "On the Death of Senator Thomas J. Walsh," an elegy that appeared in the *New Republic:*

An old man more is gathered to the great.
    Singly, for conscience's sake, he bent his
    brow:

He served that mathematic thing, the State,
    And with the great will be forgotten now.
The State is voiceless: only, we may write
    Singly our thanks for service past, and
      praise
The man whose purpose and remorseless sight
    Pursued corruption for its evil ways.

How sleep the great, the gentle, and the wise!
    Agëd and calm, they couch the wrinkled head.
Done with the wisdom labor could devise,
    Humbly they render back the volume
      read—
Dwellers amid a peace that few surmise,
    Matters of quiet among all the dead.

Thomas J. Walsh was a senator from Montana from 1913 to 1933, when he died on his way to Washington to assume his duties as Roosevelt's newly appointed attorney general. He was a liberal Democrat who advocated woman suffrage and child labor amendments; he tried, against serious opposition, to uphold the exemption, under the Clayton Act, of unions from antitrust prosecution. Most important, for this poem, he investigated the leasing of oil rights in California and Montana and uncovered the Teapot Dome and Elk Hills scandals. The one modifier that is significantly repeated in the poem is "Singly," which takes pride of place in two lines. Winters, like Charles Olson and Robert Lowell, held to the New Deal notion that leadership counts; one resistant individual can make all the difference. In fact, the state is almost a fiction, a "mathematic thing." In political contexts, Winters was a loyal and active member of various groups, such as the American Civil Liberties Union and the National Association for the Advancement of Colored People, but of course in literary battles he saw himself as that one individual, and he was in the habit of referring to himself as "the Old Man."

In 1937, after publishing six collections of

verse and many essays and reviews, Winters' first critical book, *Primitivism and Decadence,* appeared. The opening sentences of this classic of modern criticism give an indication of why he deserves a distinguished place in the history of criticism:

Before attempting to elucidate or to criticize a poetry so difficult and evasive as that of the best moderns, it would appear wise to summarize as clearly as possible those qualities for which one looks in a poem. We may say that a poem in the first place should offer us new perceptions, not only of the exterior universe, but of human experience as well; it should add, in other words, to what we have already seen. This is the elementary function for the reader. The corresponding function for the poet is a sharpening and training of his sensibilities; the very exigencies of the medium as he employs it in the act of perception should force him to the discovery of values which he never would have found without the convening of all the conditions of that particular act, conditions one or more of which will be the necessity of solving some particular difficulty such as the location of a rhyme or the perfection of a cadence without disturbance to the remainder of the poem.

Winters was a direct and explicit critic, at a time when others were not beyond coyness. His ability to state so forthrightly what is to be expected from poetry, for both readers and writers, puts him well beyond the conventions of academic criticism: poet-critics, not professor-critics, say at the outset why poems count. And they count, for Winters, because they add to human knowledge, not because they teach old truths. Like other New Dealers, Winters believed in progress, even in literature, where it has always been rare to imagine overall improvement. The poet makes progress not so much by examining unheard-of subjects as by

exploring language along new paths; like Pound and Eliot, Winters conceived of language as the richest repository of human experience, the wisest, most learned teacher. Finding a rhyme, one may discover an unrecognized truth, hearing one may chart a proper action, for a poem renders "greater the possibility of intelligence in the course of future action; and it should offer likewise a means of inducing certain more or less constant habits of feeling, which should render greater the possibility of one's acting, in a future situation, in accordance with the findings of one's improved intelligence." Poems are instruments of contemplation, but contemplation for this 1930's critic was the proper preparation for action.

Not without reason, Winters is generally considered a severe critic. Even in his first book his edge is clear. He would not suffer Robinson Jeffers, another West Coaster, quietly: "his writing, line by line, is pretentious trash." Whether or not he was right is usually not the first question that arises. Winters was impolite. There is a story, one among many like it, that is still told at Stanford English department luncheons: one of his colleagues once complained to Winters that at departmental social affairs the Old Man would talk about Airedales and fruit trees but seldom about literature. "That's because none of you know anything about literature," Winters is said to have replied. After quoting his friend Allen Tate's assessment of his late friend Hart Crane, Winters said simply, "This seems to me sheer nonsense." And about another poet from whom he learned a great deal Winters wrote: "Mr. Pound resembles a village loafer who sees much and understands little." These breaches of decorum unsettle academics but not poets. Ezra Pound was equally outrageous and never lost a friend on that account. Poets are expected to speak their minds, as professors are not; they dance to different pipers. But to think of Winters as simply arrogant is a little (though not entirely) misleading. He was arrogant. But part of the story is that in print he was sometimes more importantly modest than his academic contemporaries. He did not claim originality as a critic; Sir Philip Sidney, Matthew Arnold, and Cardinal Newman were his avowed predecessors. More important, he was modest about the capacity of critical language to account for the literary process:

It should be remembered in connection with this and other definitions that a critical term ordinarily indicates a quality, and not an objectively demonstrable entity, yet that every term in criticism is an abstraction, that is, in a sense, is statistical or quantitative in its own nature. This means that no critical term can possibly be more than a very general indication of the nature of a perception.

Although Winters is known for having rushed into the area of evaluation, where others have tread more quietly, in this early volume he was not at all naive about the mysteriousness and "logical" status of the evaluative process. The definition of canons of judgment, he said, rests upon "certain feelings of rightness and completeness."

[They] can never be exact beyond misconstruction, but by dint of careful description and the use of good examples, one may succeed in communicating standards with reasonable accuracy—to those, at least, to whom it is important that communication should be made. For if values cannot be measured, they can be judged; and the bare existence of both art and criticism shows the persistence of the conviction that accuracy of judgment is at least ideally possible, and that the best critics, despite the inevitable duller moments, approximate accuracy fairly closely: by that, I mean that great men tend to

agree with each other, and the fact is worth taking seriously.

For all his statements of principle, Winters was a pragmatist: one poem must be measured more against another than against an eternal standard, and principles command only as much authority as the instances they cover.

Winters is one of the greatest critics to have written in detail about matters of poetic style, but subject matter was more important for him than for almost any of his contemporaries. He wrote with a hierarchy of subjects in mind, and in doing so he spoke with the voice of tradition:

If a poem, in so far as it is good, represents the comprehension on a moral plane of a given experience, it is only fair to add that some experiences offer very slight difficulties and some very great, and that the poem will be the most valuable, which, granted it achieves formal perfection, represents the most difficult victory.

Modern critics often try to be democratic and in doing so pass by opportunities to make important distinctions regarding matter and manner as well. Poems that represent revery and conversation, Winters claimed, "tend to great similarity notwithstanding the subject matter, and they simply are not the most vigorous or important feelings of which the human being is capable." Some matters are more important than others, and paraphrase makes this distinction clearest. Certain poems are more or less betrayed by paraphrase than others, according to their investment in formal uniqueness. It is easy enough to say that paraphrase encompasses what is least important to poetry, but Winters claimed, against fashion, that "many poems cannot be paraphrased and are therefore defective." He was clear about poetry's obligation to its subject, as very few of his contemporaries were. When poets took for granted the connection between the sign and its referent, Winters became edgy:

[when] the denotative power of language is impaired, the connotative becomes proportionately parasitic upon denotations in previous contexts, for words cannot have associations without meanings; and if the denotative power of language could be wholly eliminated, the connotative would be eliminated at the same stroke, for it is the nature of associations that they are associated with something. This means that non-rational writing, far from requiring greater literary independence than the traditional modes, encourages a quality of writing that is relatively derivative and insecure.

Critics who claim that poetry is autotelic, as many of his influential contemporaries did, in Winters' view were, perhaps unwittingly, trying to make poetry trivial. On the connection between the sign and its referent, everything depends.

Winters is rightly thought of as a formalist; the great virtue of his first critical book is the close, logical, and explicit connections drawn between moral values and literary techniques. The analytical categories he defined (pseudo-reference, imitative fallacy, "convention") and refined (romantic irony, free verse) rest upon an analysis of larger values. "One feels, whether rightly or wrongly, a correlation between the control evinced within a poem and the control within the poem behind it." In Winters' criticism there is no question why certain faults of expression are commonly spoken of as corruptions of style. Developing the terminology of Friedrich Schlegel and Irving Babbitt, Winters said:

The essence of romantic irony . . . is this: that the poet ridicules himself for a kind or degree of feeling which he can neither approve nor control; so that the irony is simply the act of confessing a state of moral insecurity which the poet sees no way to improve.

No one has written with greater specificity about this difficult and widely used rhetorical term. And there, in the details (his analysis of Hart Crane's diction or of the heroic couplet), Winters is most useful as a critic. He was an innovative and acute analyst of prosody: he sometimes focused on the subtle relationship between the scansion of a metrical foot and of a word (a trochaic word, for example, stretched over the boundary between two iambic metrical feet); he devised a system of scanning free verse (in the nearly half-century since he proposed this system, almost no headway has been made in the prosodic analysis of free verse); he argued provocatively (though unconvincingly, to my mind) that free verse has a special capacity for a rhythm that runs on rapidly from line to line, conveying meaning in a fast and loose fashion and tending toward a "breathless rush" in which only the most intense feelings are expressed. He was able to show repeatedly that the most exact analysis of poetic technique always offers ways of understanding the meaning of poems.

Coming when it did in his career, this first critical book not surprisingly addresses often directly the issues that determined his development as a poet. The argument for metrical poetry, for instance, is that of a recent convert, though in this book he shows himself the closest analyst of free verse of his time. But the most interesting connection between the poetry and prose concerns his very special sense of poetic convention. He defines convention as "the initial assumption of feeling, or value, to which the poem is laying claim." In order to establish a convention, in Winters' sense, generally accepted literary devices may be employed, but they themselves do not constitute the convention.

Conventional language, then, is not in itself stereotyped language, though a strongly defined convention may safely carry a little stereotyped language: in fact stereotyped language may often be used deliberately to establish a convention. . . . In so far as any passage is purely conventional, that is, conventional as distinct from perceptual, it does not represent a perception of its own content, the feeling it assumes is not justified within the passage in question.

This is a curious use of the words "convention" and "conventional." Conventions, by this account, are not the inherited weight of literary tradition; they are newly established by individual poets for the purposes of a particular poem. It makes sense that an enthusiastic New Dealer would propose that a term formerly used to designate the limits and rules established by literary history should now be used to indicate the particular program that an individual poet considers relevant to the particular poetic problems before him. Winters' use of the word gives the poet a great deal of freedom, but the retention of this particular term ought to remind one that in the past poets could assume as generally accepted norms of feeling with regard to particular subjects. The modern poet is more on his own in this regard and must improvise.

This difficult explanation of convention has a direct bearing on Winters' own poetry, which is most striking in terms of diction. In his early poems, and probably because of the isolation of convalescence, he evolved a stable of words that sometimes seem to constitute the rudiments of a personal code—"cold," "stone," "silent," "alone," "bees." (Several of these words actually came—through the influence of Robert Bly and W. S. Merwin, not Winters—to constitute a generation's poetic diction forty years later.) And the best of his later poems often in-

corporate antique and stereotyped words and phrases; he is a consciously anachronistic poet. Freshness of phrasing generally counts for less with him than accuracy of tone. To establish tone, to express his attitude toward his subject with exactness and brevity, he employs his own code words (in the later poems, "pure," "perfect," "the mind," "the brain," "dust," "wisdom," "justice") and the traditional language and patterns of phrasing that are recognized as having once been "poetic." This very deliberate, even willful, use of words permits him to situate his own utterances in implicit relation to the utterances of older poets or earlier poems of his own. His repetition (three times) of the phrase "the great" in "On the Death of Senator Thomas J. Walsh," for example, may seem artless, but it establishes a dignified, stoical norm of feeling derived from the elegiac and panegyrical traditions. This is accomplished without Winters' having to attempt what could not be managed here: the discursive definition of greatness and identification of "the great." Few poets of Winters' time would have attempted to write a political elegy invoking such feelings. Winters could do so because he had thought his way through the relationship of particular feelings to particular subjects—and because he was an artful poet.

The importance of *Primitivism and Decadence* does not depend, however, on interest in Winters' poetry. After almost a half-century and any number of studies of modernist poetry, it is still one of the two or three most instructive books on the subject. In 1937 it was a stunningly radical and independent book advocating unfashionable causes (to take one little-noticed example: exposition in poetry). Two years earlier a version of the book had served as Winters' doctoral dissertation at Stanford. The initial readers criticized it seriously enough that the chairman of the English department relieved them of responsibility for the project and "directed" the dissertation. Winters was the last person to have to defend his dissertation in a special, second oral examination. He paid a high price for intellectual independence and for working as both a professor and a poet. His superiors at Stanford once attempted unsuccessfully to fire him, but they succeeded in firing his untenured friend and student, James Vincent Cunningham. Winters was a member of the Stanford faculty for twenty-one years before he was made professor at the age of forty-nine. The director of his dissertation, William Dinsmore Briggs, commanded his respect, and Winters listened when Briggs urged him to study American literature.

Maule's Curse: Seven Studies in the History of American Obscurantism (1938) was intended as a sequel to *Primitivism and Decadence;* Winters wanted to examine the "relationship of the history of ideas to the history of literary forms," which meant that this book would focus more on subject matter than its predecessor did. In fact, much of the book is a meditation on the proper importance of subject matter in poetry. The essay on Poe is Winters' only fully negative critical essay; for all the other writers he ever criticized extensively, Winters felt some significant measure of admiration. Poe is criticized most strenuously for believing that subject matter was of little consequence to poetry:

If, indeed, certain human experiences are admitted [by Poe] as legitimate subjects, they are admitted, as we shall see, because the poet cannot write without writing about something— even the most irresponsible use of language involves an inescapable minimum of statement, however incomplete or dismembered; and those experiences are admitted which seem to involve the minimum of complexity.

Poe, Winters claims, displayed a comprehensive ignorance of the history of ideas, and this limitation left him "thoroughly at the mercy of

contemporaneity." Although Winters stresses the importance of the history of ideas in this book, and later in others, he was careful to say that "to explain a man's place in history is not the same thing as to judge his value"; understanding and evaluation are finally separate processes. This book is directed chiefly to understanding.

The proper place of subject matter in the evaluation of poetry is, as Winters saw it, complicated: "truth is not poetry; poetry is truth and something more." Emerson, for instance, fares poorly by this measure, because his poetry is "gnomic or didactic" and based upon ideas that "will not stand inspection"; consequently, the poetry is "poor in spite of a good deal of vigorous phrasing." This is not to say, however, that there are subjects upon which Winters could not imagine good poems; he claimed that Arthur Rimbaud's "Larme," "an excursion into the incoherencies of dream-consciousness," surpassed, by virtue of style, Poe's attempts to deal with the same subject. And Winters championed the poetry of Jones Very, of whose ideas he explicitly disapproved. Rimbaud and Very, unlike Emerson, render the truth of certain experiences, even though the ideas they derive from those experiences seem unsound to Winters; Emerson, as a didactic poet, stayed with the ideas, and insofar as they were poor ideas his poems suffer. A genuinely original poem, Winters says, presents not a new idea but "personal intelligence" brought to bear upon an experience, and that intelligence shows in "the minutiae of style."

Intelligence, he thought, rests upon the assumption that judgment can be more or less sound and that the human will is a consequential faculty. In American thought, Unitarianism and Puritanism (Emerson and Very) collaborated to discount the importance of the will. The alternative intellectual position, which Winters espoused, derived from Aristotle's *Ni-*

chomachean Ethics and survived through the work of the church fathers and the institution of the Catholic church. But Winters held this position on strictly intellectual grounds; as late as 1950 he said with some disappointment and trepidation, "I cannot find my way to Nazareth."

Maule's Curse was an important book in the development of Winters' thought; he could not have written it a decade earlier, when he planned a doctoral dissertation that would defend, surprisingly, the intellectual and artistic tradition represented by Emerson, Dickinson, Williams, and Crane. But as a study in the history of ideas, the book will not bear comparison, in terms of the depth of its learning, the refinement of its analytical categories, and its representation of the transmission of ideas, with the best studies of its kind. As a study of literary ideas, it is useful and provocative, even though as literary criticism it does not show Winters at his best; in discussing fiction, always a secondary genre for Winters, he is often impressionistic (as when he describes the stylistic qualities of James Fenimore Cooper and Henry James) and sometimes even a bit laborious (as in the plot summary of *Moby Dick*). He was a better critic of poetry than of prose, a better analyst of poetic form and literary ideology than a historian of ideas, though unfortunately the history of ideas became increasingly important to his critical work in later years.

With these two critical books out in the world, Winters felt that the time was right for a large collection of his poems. He had hoped, in 1938, that James Laughlin of New Directions would publish *The Moralists: Poems 1928-1938*. Instead, in 1939 and 1940 Winters, a little bitterly, printed by hand on his own press the paperback collection *Poems*, which spanned his entire career:

The kind of political maneuvering which appears to be a prerequisite at present to the publication of a book of poems is impossible from Los Altos, even if one possesses, as I do not, the taste or the talent for it. . . . No copies of this book will be sent to magazines for review.

The three best new poems in this collection all deal with the theme of time; the two earliest of these are retrospective. In the last five lines of "On Rereading a Passage from John Muir" (1937), Winters reflects on a road not taken:

I might have been this man: a knowing eye
Moving on leaf and bark, a quiet gauge
Of growing timber and of climbing fly,
A quiet hand to fix them on the page—
A gentle figure from a simpler age.

Muir wanted to know the landscape firsthand, through his senses, which is why he had himself bound to a tree in a storm. In 1937 Winters knew that in his poetry and his criticism he had taken on the burden of ideas rather than sensual experience and, knowing that he could have remained a descriptive poet, as committed to the life of the senses as the naturalist, or that he could have become the protozoologist he once planned to be, he was not without a sense of what had been given up, although he expressed no real regret about his choices. In 1938 a more powerful poem on this subject appeared—"A Summer Commentary":

When I was young, with sharper sense,
The farthest insect cry I heard
Could stay me; through the trees, intense,
I watched the hunter and the bird.

Where is the meaning that I found?
Or was it but a state of mind,
Some old penumbra of the ground,
In which to be but not to find?

Now summer grasses, brown with heat,
Have crowded sweetness through the air;
The very roadside dust is sweet;
Even the unshadowed earth is fair.

The soft voice of the nesting dove,
And the dove in soft erratic flight
Like a rapid hand within a glove,
Caress the silence and the light.

Amid the rubble, the fallen fruit,
Fermenting in its rich decay,
Smears brandy on the trampling boot
And sends it sweeter on its way.

By 1938 it was clear that Winters was—to put it mildly—a master of the tetrameter quatrain. The theme here is Wordsworthian, as the first line of the second quatrain makes obvious, though the treatment is not. What have been lost are the delicate acuteness of the senses and a conviction of the meaningfulness of the natural process. The recompense? Not a philosophic mind, but a greater appetite. And the answer comes only in images, not in what Winters had, since "The Cold" (1925), spoken of as "commentary." In 1938 Winters moved through the landscape with the intensity of a booted hunter, catching sensations at their fullest, enjoying the crushing, not the watching, of the natural process. The last three stanzas combine the senses of sight and smell, taste and touch, to leave a convincing account of the richness of decay—his own, as well as the season's.

This appetite for intensity, immediacy, and condensation is examined and restrained in the best new poem in *Poems* (1940):

Time and the Garden

The spring has darkened with activity.
The future gathers in vine, bush, and tree:
Persimmon, walnut, loquat, fig, and grape,
Degrees and kinds of color, taste, and shape.
These will advance in their due series, space
The season like a tranquil dwelling-place.
And yet excitement swells me, vein by vein:
I long to crowd the little garden, gain
Its sweetness in my hand and crush it small
And taste it in a moment, time and all!

These trees, whose slow growth measures off
    my years,
I would expand to greatness. No one hears,
And I am still retarded in duress!
And this is like that other restlessness
To seize the greatness not yet fairly earned,
One which the tougher poets have
    discerned—
Gascoigne, Ben Jonson, Greville, Raleigh,
    Donne,
Poets who wrote great poems, one by one,
And spaced by many years, each line an act
Through which few labor, which no men
    retract.
This passion is the scholar's heritage,
The imposition of a busy age,
The passion to condense from book to book
Unbroken wisdom in a single look,
Though we know well that when this fix the
    head,
The mind's immortal, but the man is dead.

Winters considered this one of his three or four best poems. The norm of feeling, the convention, this poem assumes can be stated plainly: the ravenous, dark underside of the *carpe diem* topos, expressed most forcefully in the close of Marvell's "To His Coy Mistress":

Now let us sport us while we may;
And now, like amorous birds of prey,
Rather at once our time devour,
Than languish in his slow-chapt power.
Let us roll all our strength, and all
Our sweetness, up into one ball:
And tear our pleasures with rough strife,
Through the iron gates of life.
Thus, though we cannot make our sun
Stand still, yet we will make him run.

Winters wrote his poem to control the Marvell in him; John Muir and any descriptive poet know how much depends upon the "Degrees and kinds of color, taste, and shape" that would be prematurely sacrificed to the reckless gluttony Winters felt in himself. What Winters felt, he said, was the pressure of his time, those years when the United States and the Soviet Union were arming feverishly for the inevitable war with Germany. In *Poems* (1940), *The Giant Weapon* (1943), and his *Collected Poems* (1952, 1960), "Time and the Garden" was placed just after "An Elegy, for the U.S.N. Dirigible, Macon," which closes with these quatrains:

Who will believe this thing in time to come?
I was a witness. I beheld the age
That seized upon a planet's heritage
Of steel and oil, the mind's viaticum:

Crowded the world with strong ingenious
    things,
Used the provision it could not replace,
To leave but Cretan myths, a sandy trace
Through the last stone age, for the pastoral
    kings.

The dirigible *Macon,* based in Sunnyvale, very near to Winters' home, was used to protect the Pacific fleet. Early in 1935, it ran into severe winds off the coast of Point Sur, and the captain was forced to make an emergency landing on the water, destroying the ship but preserving nearly all of the crew. Winters was no critic of the war effort, least of all on the West Coast, where much of his energy was absorbed by a commitment to the civilian defense. Yet he saw in himself, and in his culture, its technology and history (see the fine poem, "John Sutter" [1935], on the history of American rapacity), a greedy, imprudent hunger for purity that might end disappointingly. What launched the *Macon* was a brainy need for perfection that, in the inevitable struggle with adverse circumstance, would leave behind only "a sandy trace."

In 1943 Winters put together five new poems

and twenty-eight poems from earlier collections to form a new edition of his poems; after *The Giant Weapon* he published only a broadside, *To the Holy Spirit* (1947); a pamphlet of three poems; and three editions of his collected poems (1952, 1960, 1966). His writing of poetry had slowed down, though he still had a few excellent poems to write.

The poem that gave *The Giant Weapon* its title is placed at the exact center of the volume. Here is the concluding strophe of "To a Military Rifle":

I cannot write your praise
When young men go to die;
Nor yet regret the ways
That ended with this hour.
The hour has come. And I,
Who alter nothing, pray
That men, surviving you,
May learn to do and say
The difficult and true,
True shape of death and power.

The preceding twenty-one lines of the poem describe the new M-1 rifle as a perfect weapon of destruction whose time has come. Winters was able to write deeply moving poems about World War II because he was candid enough to admit into his poetry a good deal of the complexity of the time. The M-1 was a thing to be grateful for in 1942, when the U.S. Army stepped up its adoption of the weapon: it helped win the war against fascism, and Winters held by that objective. Yet warfare technology rests upon an immoral assumption that "life is general," " . . . individual men / Are counted not at all." To maintain this assumption even during a war, he knew, entails cultural loss. The discriminations that poets, philosophers, and historians learn, in time and after sustained effort, to articulate and try to teach to the next generation—these count for rather little before the M-1. In the stately, measured speech of this last strophe, Winters faces the mix of his own feelings: he supported American entry into the war, even though his life's work was devoted to refining distinctions that are eliminated from the cultural consciousness by war. The poem derives from the tension between his political understanding of the world in 1942 and his life-long commitment to values that go beyond the historical moment. This is a great political lyric.

In 1943 Winters wrote another first-rate poem about World War II, "Moonlight Alert," which appeared in 1944. Whereas "To a Military Rifle" consists of dignified, meditative speech about the relationship of various ideas and values to an object, "Moonlight Alert" renders an experience in largely descriptive language; in Winters' terms, the first is mainly "conventional," and the later poem represents perception.

The sirens, rising, woke me; and the night
Lay cold and windless; and the moon was
    bright,
Moonlight from sky to earth, untaught,
    unclaimed,
An icy nightmare of the brute unnamed.
This was hallucination. Scarlet flower
And yellow fruit hung colorless. That hour
No scent lay on the air. The siren scream
Took on the fixity of shallow dream.
In the dread sweetness I could see the fall,
Like petals sifting from a quiet wall,
Of yellow soldiers through indifferent air,
Falling to die in solitude. With care
I held this vision, thinking of young men
Whom I had known and should not see again,
Fixed in reality, as I in thought.
And I stood waiting, and encountered naught.

Winters returned to his major form of more than a decade earlier, the enjambed heroic couplet, for this stunning poem. And although the subject matter—the death of young men in

World War II—was rather new for him ("Summer Noon: 1941" and "Night of Battle, *Europe: 1944, as regarded from a great distance"* also examine this subject), his treatment of the subject goes back in part to his earliest poems, such as "The Immobile Wind" (1920), "Alone" (1921), and "The Cold" (1925), on the dichotomy between sensual and mental experience. The horror of this nighttime air-raid alert for Winters is that it leaves him suspended in the vacancy of his thought. The siren invades the senses so thoroughly that the flowers and fruit lose their color and odor, and the young soldiers he imagines as falling like fruit; dead, they are mere objects, but alive he encounters naught. And he expresses his inability to comprehend this subject fully with a stylistic gesture of respect for the enemy; the tenth, eleventh, and twelfth lines quoted imagine the deaths of Japanese soldiers within the descriptive conventions of the haiku; the horrible dissonance between the beauty of the image and the muddy deaths of young men suggests how remotely displaced Winters felt, by his art and his age, from the terrible experience of his culture. There are other war poems in which Winters expresses regret of the deaths of young men like his students, sadness over the loss that the culture suffers when education is interrupted, and pain at being so removed from the struggle (he had tried unsuccessfully to enlist in Army Intelligence in 1941), but "Moonlight Alert" is exceptional. The poem presents a terrifying experience in verse that is masterfully managed (consider, as one small detail, the play of trochaic words through this iambic poem). Robert Lowell said that Winters' poems "pass Housman's test for true poetry—if I remembered them while shaving, I would cut myself." "Moonlight Alert" and "To a Military Rifle" will be read for some time to come.

Also in 1943 Winters published his third book of criticism, *The Anatomy of Nonsense,* and the provocative title is instructive. The book begins with a chapter, "Preliminary Problems," examining twelve problems in the theory of criticism, and *The Function of Criticism* (1957) similarly opens with "Problems for the Modern Critic of Literature." Probably because he had come to a coherent understanding of the canons of contemporary taste that interfered with the appreciation of his own poems, but perhaps too because in the 1940's the chairman of his department was trying to have him fired, Winters seems to have decided at that time to devote most of his energy to criticism and teaching; *The Giant Weapon* was his last collection of new poems. In 1952 and 1960 he added his new poems to the old and published the *Collected Poems*. In *The Anatomy of Nonsense* and his subsequent prose books, Winters deliberately elaborated a system of critical analysis and evaluation. He speaks casually of "my theory" and claims, as Eliot and Pound had, that "a really finished critic" needs the talents of both a poet and a scholar. "Unless the critics are forthcoming, literature runs the risk of falling into the hands of the barbarians." By 1957 he knew very well that his poems were behind him; as he grew older, he struck his habitual posture of the Old Man and indulged his own dogmatism. "There comes a time in the lives of some men when the spectacle is no longer informative but the theory is packed with meaning." His last book, *Forms of Discovery* (1967), was finished while he was dying of cancer of the tongue; it was expressly meant to round out his career as a critic. The older he grew, the more important systematic criticism became to him.

The last four critical books—*The Anatomy of Nonsense, Edwin Arlington Robinson, The Function of Criticism,* and *Forms of Discovery*—actually add only a little to Winters' theoretical position; on that level, they mainly repeat principles that were clear enough in *Primitivism and Decadence* and *Maule's Curse.*

One new emphasis, however, deserves special notice: madness. The moral argument of *The Anatomy* follows from a curious first principle:

if we are able to recognize the fact of insanity —... that is, the fact of the obvious maladjustment of feeling to motive, we are forced to admit the possibility of more accurate adjustment, and, by necessary sequence, of absolutely accurate adjustment, even though we admit the likelihood that most people will attain to a final adjustment but very seldom indeed.

This assumption that insanity is an inherent evil rests not on argument but on observation—"a single look at a psychopathic ward is sufficient." Sometime in the late 1930's Winters saw one of his students institutionalized after a severe breakdown, and in 1947 he likened the treatment of tuberculosis to that of some forms of insanity; he had more than one way of imaginatively comprehending—and perhaps too a reason for fearing—madness. He was convinced that some forms of insanity "can be both induced and cured"—ideas count at both ends of this process.

In his later criticism, Winters' sense of the history of ideas is clear. Most important is his notion in *The Anatomy* that single individuals have ideas. The unity of the thirteenth-century church owed "far less to the spirit of the age than to the mind of Thomas Aquinas." If Pope had "possessed as sharp a mind as Samuel Johnson the history of the age might easily have been greatly different from what it was." The last sentence of the book reveals how enabling a sense of history this was—especially for a lonely professor of poetry who devoted a great deal of effort to his graduate students: "A handful of brilliant poets, even if congenitally minor, scattered judiciously throughout our best universities, might easily begin to turn us a little in the direction of civilization." After the spectacle of World War II, Winters was more convinced than ever that a solitary thinking individual—even a poet—could turn the world around: "The Gospels gave a new direction to half the world; *Mein Kampf* very nearly reversed that direction. The influence of Rimbaud and of Mallarmé is quite as real but has operated more slowly and with less of obvious violence." How artistic literature functions is "quite as important a fact as atomic fission"— a bold claim in 1947. On the first page of *The Function of Criticism* he argues that the critical understanding of literature in general, the theoretical understanding expressed by poets, critics, and scholars, actually determines what literature will be; theory in fact governs history. Understanding, Winters claims, offers the only way of escaping the determinism of history, but it is a perfectly effective way; he held by this rationalist article of faith throughout his career.

Winters' last book shows only too plainly the literary pitfalls of this approach to the history of ideas. The greatest poets, in Winters' view, those, such as Greville, Jonson, Herbert, and Bridges, who wrote best about the best ideas, "are trying to exhibit the truth, they are not trying to exhibit themselves, and they tend to resemble each other." Literary history counts for rather little in the presence of what Winters took to be the great ideas; greatness rises above the distinctions that literary historians labor over. *Forms of Discovery* is an objectionable book on many counts. It was completed with genuine urgency; Winters knew he was dying (the last word is "dust"). And impatience shows: it is often redundant; many of the judgments (such as that of the earl of Rochester, to take an incidental example) are unsupported by analysis; sometimes, as in the case of Samuel Johnson, Winters, who was formerly capable of identifying stunning poems with surprising acuteness, made perverse choices of individual titles; it is impressionistic (Jonathan Swift's "lightness and his wit are so laborious that I, for

one, find him somewhat dull reading") where only great care could possibly render Winters' case convincing; the analyses are often wooden, as in the allegorization of "The Idea of Order at Key West"; and rhetorically this is Winters' most high-handed and least cogent performance ("Lord Byron [1788-1824] seems to have died a natural death, and I am willing to let him rest . . ."). Yet the worst failure of this ambitious book does not follow from the urgency of the occasion: Winters dismisses most of eighteenth- and nineteenth-century poetry with few qualms because for him the history of ideas, as he understood it, had nothing to do with continuity. In 1957, when he was writing parts of this book, Winters told Malcolm Cowley that a simple knowledge of history would greatly improve contemporary criticism of poetry. But historical knowledge that is too simple can produce crude explanations. Winters owed his subject, the history of English and American poetry, fuller, more refined treatment than he provides in *Forms of Discovery;* too great a faith in the independence of ideas, it seems, allowed him to try to cheat literary history. The great pity is that so sharp a critic closed his career bluntly.

Fortunately, he brought his poetic career to a more dignified conclusion. Winters took his daughter to the San Francisco airport in 1954, and she departed for Radcliffe College. In "At the San Francisco Airport," one of his very last poems, he acknowledges that she is leaving him behind in an important sense:

But you and I in part are one:
The frightened brain, the nervous will,
The knowledge of what must be done,
The passion to acquire the skill
To face that which you dare not shun.

The rain of matter upon sense
Destroys me momently. The score:

There comes what will come. The expense
Is what one thought, and something more—
One's being and intelligence.

This is the terminal, the break.
Beyond this point, on lines of air,
 You take the way that you must take;
And I remain in light and stare—
In light, and nothing else, awake.

. . .

This is a great conclusion to a poet's work.
The first stanza quoted offers a frank and mixed
inventory of personal fears, weaknesses, and
strengths; the last two lines of the stanza give a
tight, clear, and subtle account of how passion,
deliberation, skill, courage, and fear come together. In the penultimate stanza, the syntax is
toughly assertive, but behind that the rhythm
falters once (the only substitution in this metrically regular poem), in the third foot of the
third line, implying a tissue of terror that will
not bear full exposure. This is a great poem of
acceptance. Winters knows that he must face
his own approaching death empty-handed,
without illusion of immortality. The machinery
of transcendence—the easy resort of poems on
death—is only that, machinery: an airplane
takes his young daughter, not her aging father,
away from the earth "on lines of air." Winters
reaches for none of the customary consolations;
this is an honest, modern, and forthrightly atheistic poem uttered in a tone sound enough to live
with the restraint of plain truth.

Winters' major subject as a poet was the extent to which intelligence can open itself to tur-
bulent, meaningless experience, on the one
hand, and to the vacancy of solitude, on the
other. However, his greatest poem ("On a View
of Pasadena from the Hills") turns this subject
around to show the limited extent to which the
corrosiveness of historical experience can be resisted. Both ways, this is a grand and permanent subject. Winters has said that a poet can

be termed great who has written well about a
good subject. Surely he was right that greatness
in poetry rests largely on subject matter. In his
own terms, there should be no question of his
greatness as a poet: he has written with power
and intelligence about an important, humane
subject. His particular power can be located exactly: he is a masterful strophic poet, with few
equals. He could always play syntax against or
over stanzaic forms cunningly. Only the simpler, more recognizable stanzaic patterns (the
heroic couplet, quatrain, sonnet) interested him,
never the display forms—canzonas, sestinas,
villanelles—because meter was always an order
that was meaningful only to the degree to which
it was stretched, opposed, violated. Metrical
order always highlights the tough intellectual
drive of his syntax. Winters had a distinctly intelligent way of writing about the perils of
mind.

His poetry, though, surely has its limits. Winters knew what his subject was early, and he returned to it, like Wallace Stevens, relentlessly.
His poems are chaste in the sense that they hold
to this subject, untouched by the ideas that were
in the air or by the other arts of his time. He
does not deliver a comprehensive image of his
culture, nor did he try. The last paragraph of
his last book drives home one last time a point
he registered frequently—against Whitman,
and Eliot usually: "Finally, let us beware of saying that the best poets of our time deal with the
subjects which are most important to our time."
The imitative fallacy defines the formal version
of this notion: that the form of poetry should
reflect the form or formlessness of actual experience. Winters rightly advises caution here, for
there are obvious and fatal dangers to measuring poems by their contemporaneity. Yet the
greatest poetry articulates the beliefs, aspirations, and experiences of a whole culture;
Homer, Vergil, Dante, Shakespeare are the in-
disputable measures of greatness. Pound and
Eliot (and of course Hart Crane) played for just

these stakes, which is why they were drawn to long forms. They took risks and suffered failures that Winters did not, and their accomplishments can be distinguished in kind from his.

Winters is best spoken of as a master of a great, permanent subject who wrote during a period of broad and deep cultural change. Pound and Eliot are greater poets because they represent life in a fuller historical moment than Winters imagines. In no way did he resist his time; it was they, after all, who conceived of history degeneratively. But he knew, and may even have regretted, that he did not often reach out to the historical experience of his culture. When that experience reached him, as it did when his father died in Los Angeles and he wrote "On a View," and when the bombers patrolled the Pacific coast and he wrote "Moonlight Alert," and when the U. S. Army adopted the M-1 and he wrote "To a Military Rifle"—when history was his, he wrote unforgettably.

Winters wanted to be both poet and critic. His weaknesses as a critic have been widely and vigorously expounded. He seemed notoriously insensitive—though only as a critic, not as a poet—to the poetry of the eighteenth and nineteenth centuries, to the poets who were most obviously committed to the subjects of their time. His emphasis on judgment made him distrustful of irony and, more important, of dramatic methods generally; he showed an unwillingness to have confidence in an audience's ability to make proper sense of a literary experience. This is one reason why he could not write about the major poetic forms—drama and epic. (His taste in drama was not fine: *Macbeth,* as he saw it, was Shakespeare's best tragedy.) The relationships between people were not a major subject, in his view, and this is another reason for his not appreciating dramatic and narrative poetry, not to mention prose fiction. His emphasis on the history of ideas did damage to his criticism, because he analyzed ideas schematically; the result was often a simplified history, purged

of the complicating details of transmission and misunderstanding, which, after all, render the history of ideas a rich intellectual subject. In the end, he did not understand literary history as a continuous process. The breaches in his account of English and American poetry are dizzying and often appalling. His strengths as a critic follow directly from his interests as a poet. But he did construct a refined, well-illustrated account of poetry as the fullest expression of human intelligence; he left neither doubt nor mystification about its importance. He legitimated, once again, unfashionable aspects of critical analysis: convention, prosody, subject matter. And, more than any other modern critic, he succeeded at discovering or gaining attention for unrecognized or neglected poets: Fulke Greville, Barnabe Googe, Charles Churchill, Jones Very, Frederick Goddard Tuckerman, Robert Bridges. Long before fashion caught up with him, he praised Marianne Moore, William Carlos Williams, Wallace Stevens, Hart Crane, Allen Tate, Theodore Roethke, Stanley Kunitz; long after fashion passed him by, he continued to praise Edwin Arlington Robinson. He discerned literary history in the making. Finding publishers and readers for unrecognized poets was a serious matter to which Winters brought intelligence and taste—and perseverance. By all accounts, he was a great teacher of poets. When they were young men, with unpublished manuscripts in hand, Winters showed the breadth of understanding and the discrimination to sponsor, as fellows or students, Edgar Bowers, J. V. Cunningham, Donald Hall, Donald Justice, Philip Levine, Thom Gunn, Robert Pinsky, and James McMichael. He took this job seriously and hoped to influence literary history by supporting and attempting to guide young poets. Can his success be doubted? The author of "On a View of Pasadena from the Hills," "Before Disaster," "To a Military Rifle," and "Moonlight Alert" will not be long forgotten.

Selected Bibliography

Uncollected Essays and Reviews, edited by Francis Murphy. Chicago: Swallow, 1973.

WORKS OF
YVOR WINTERS

POETRY

The Immobile Wind. Evanston, Ill.: Monroe Wheeler, 1921.

The Magpie's Shadow. Chicago: Musterbookhouse, 1922.

The Bare Hills. Boston: Four Seas, 1927.

The Proof. New York: Coward-McCann, 1930.

The Journey and Other Poems. Ithaca, N. Y.: Dragon Press, 1931.

Before Disaster. Tryon, N. C.: Tryon Pamphlets, 1934.

Poems. Los Altos, Calif.: Gyroscope Press, 1940.

The Giant Weapon. Norfolk, Conn.: New Directions, 1943.

Collected Poems. Denver: Alan Swallow, 1952. Rev. ed., 1960.

The Early Poems of Yvor Winters, 1920–28. Denve Alan Swallow, 1966.

Collected Poems. Manchester: Carcanet, 1978.

CRITICISM AND PROSE

Primitivism and Decadence. A Study of American Experimental Poetry. New York: Arrow Editions, 1937.

Maule's Curse: Seven Studies in the History of American Obscurantism. Norfolk, Conn.: New Directions, 1938.

The Anatomy of Nonsense. Norfolk, Conn.: New Directions, 1943.

Edwin Arlington Robinson. Norfolk, Conn.: New Directions, 1946; repr. 1971.

In Defense of Reason. New York: Swallow Press/ William Morrow, 1947.

The Function of Criticism: Problems and Exercises. Denver: Alan Swallow, 1957.

On Modern Poets. New York: Meridian Books, 1959.

The Poetry of W. B. Yeats. Denver: Alan Swallow, 1960.

Forms of Discovery. Critical and Historical Essays on the Forms of the Short Poem in English. Chicago: Alan Swallow, 1967.

BIBLIOGRAPHY

Lohf, Kenneth A., and Eugene P. Sheehy. *Yvor Winters: A Bibliography.* Denver: Alan Swallow, 1959.

BIOGRAPHICAL AND CRITICAL STUDIES

Davie, Donald. "Winters and Leavis: Memories and Reflections." *Sewanee Review,* 87:608–18 (Fall 1979).

Fields, Kenneth. "The Free Verse of Yvor Winters and William Carlos Williams." *Southern Review,* n.s. 3:764–75 (July 1967).

Graff, Gerald. "Yvor Winters at Stanford." *American Scholar,* 44:291–98 (Spring 1975).

Hyman, Stanley Edgar. *The Armed Vision.* Rev. ed., New York: Vintage, 1955.

Kaye, Howard. "The Post-Symbolist Poetry of Yvor Winters." *Southern Review,* n.s. 7:176–97 (January 1971).

Levin, David. "Yvor Winters at Stanford." *Virginia Quarterly Review,* 54:454–73 (Summer 1978).

Lowell, Robert. "Yvor Winters: A Tribute." *Poetry,* 98:40–43 (April 1961).

Parkinson, Thomas. *Hart Crane and Yvor Winters: Their Literary Correspondence.* Berkeley: University of California Press, 1978.

Powell, Grosvenor. *Language as Being in the Poetry of Yvor Winters.* Baton Rouge: Louisiana State University Press, 1980.

Ransom, John Crowe. *The New Criticism.* Norfolk, Conn.: New Directions, 1941.

Stephens, Alan. "The *Collected Poems* of Yvor Winters." *Twentieth Century Literature,* 9, no. 3:127–39 (October 1963).

Wellek, René. "Yvor Winters Rehearsed and Reconsidered." *Denver Quarterly,* 10, no. 3:1–27 (Autumn 1975).

—*ROBERT VON HALLBERG*

SUPPLEMENT II
Index

Index

*Arabic numbers printed in bold-face type refer
to extended treatment of a subject*